Footprint

Ecuador Handbook

Robert & Daisy Kunstaetter

*No one could imagine what it was like to fly over
the Andes like a condor, with God's own view of
the world. ...They had looked straight into
Cotopaxi volcano, or seen bears climbing its
snowy sides or condors flying above its crags.
Sometimes they dipped over the jungle and
spotted headhunters paddling canoes up the
brown waters of the Amazon.*

Johanna Angermeyer, *My Father's Island*

4th edition

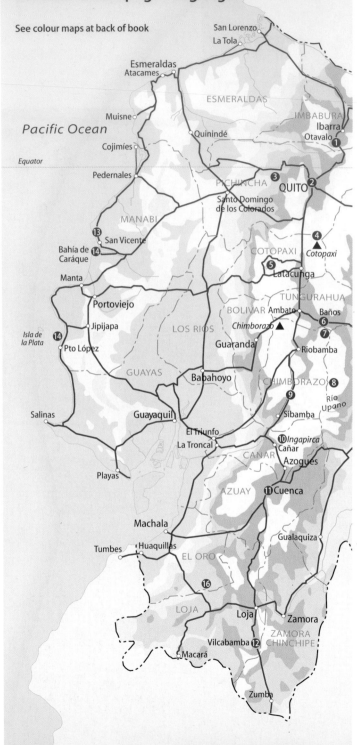

Ecuador & Galápagos Highlights

See colour maps at back of book

❶ Otavalo
Home of the largest and most colourful craft market in South America

❷ Quito
World Heritage treasure trove of colonial art and architecture

❸ Mindo
Birdwatchers' and nature-lovers' paradise

❹ Parque Nacional Cotopaxi
Where the perfect snow-capped cone of one of the world's highest volcanoes towers above herds of wild horses and llamas

❺ Quilotoa Circuit
Visit an emerald-green crater lake amid traditional native villages and markets

❻ Baños
Popular highland resort combining adventure and relaxation

❼ Tungurahua
An active volcano for the watching

❽ Parque Nacional Sangay
Trekking and climbing paradise, with three major glaciated summits

❾ Nariz del Diablo
Ride one of the Andes' most spectacular railways

❿ Ingapirca
Ecuador's best known Inca archaeological site

Pacific Ocean

Equator

San Lorenzo
La Tola
Esmeraldas
Atacames
Muisne
Quinindé
Cojimíes
Pedernales
Santo Domingo de los Colorados
ESMERALDAS
IMBABURA
Ibarra
Otavalo
PICHINCHA
QUITO
MANABI
San Vicente
Bahía de Caráque
Manta
Portoviejo
Jipijapa
Isla de la Plata
Pto López
COTOPAXI
Cotopaxi
Latacunga
TUNGURAHUA
BOLIVAR
Ambato
Baños
Chimborazo
Guaranda
Riobamba
LOS RIOS
GUAYAS
Babahoyo
CHIMBORAZO
Salinas
Guayaquil
Sibamba
El Triunfo
La Troncal
Ingapirca
Cañar
Azogues
CAÑAR
Playas
AZUAY
Cuenca
Machala
Gualaquiza
Tumbes
Huaquillas
EL ORO
LOJA
Loja
Zamora
Vilcabamba
Macará
ZAMORA CHINCHIPE
Zumba
Río Upano

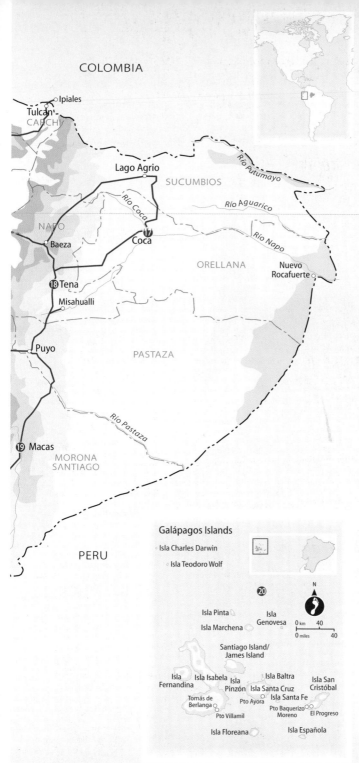

COLOMBIA

Ipiales
Tulcán
CARCHI

Lago Agrio
SUCUMBIOS
Río Putumayo

Río Coca
Río Aguarico

NAPO
Baeza
Coca ⑰
Río Napo

ORELLANA
Nuevo
Rocafuerte

⑱ Tena
Misahualli

Puyo
PASTAZA

Río Pastaza

⑲ Macas
MORONA
SANTIAGO

PERU

Galápagos Islands

Isla Charles Darwin

Isla Teodoro Wolf

⑳

Isla Pinta
Isla
Genovesa
Isla Marchena

0 km   40
0 miles   40
N

Santiago Island/
James Island

Isla
Fernandina
Isla Isabela
Isla
Pinzón
Isla Baltra
Isla Santa Cruz
Isla San
Cristóbal
Tomás de
Berlanga
Pto Ayora
Isla Santa Fe
Pto Villamil
Pto Baquerizo
Moreno
El Progreso
Isla Floreana
Isla Española

---

⑪ Cuenca
Congenial colonial city and Ecuador's cultural heartland

⑫ Vilcabamba
Fabled fountain of youth at the rainbow's end, an exceptionally scenic and tranquil resort

⑬ Canoa
Gorgeous ocean, magnificent broad beach, and a laid-back village with good facilities

⑭ Bahía de Caraquez
Ecuador's 'eco-city' resort and base for many worthwhile excursions

⑮ Parque Nacional Machalilla Whale watching in season and great visits to Isla de la Plata and Los Frailes beach year-round

⑯ Zaruma
Colonial gold mining town amid scenic uplands, an off-the-beaten-track gem

⑰ Coca
Gateway to the jungle lodges of the lower Río Napo

⑱ Tena
White-water rafting and kayaking centre with ethno-tourism opportunities

⑲ Macas
Gateway to the untouristed southern Oriente

⑳ Galápagos
One of the world's foremost wildlife sanctuaries

4

Contents

A foot in the door

Avenue of the Volcanoes (previous pages) Admire them from a distance as you travel the highway south of Quito, or climb them in search of the biggest natural high Ecuador has to offer

Galápagos Islands (top left) Home to the rarest and most exotic wildlife anywhere on Earth
Otavalo market (top right) Chickens along for the ride at Otavalo's Saturday market
Hats off (above) Cuenca market, a good place to buy Ecuador's most famous export, the 'Panama' hat
Inca ruins (right) Ingapirca, located in the southern highlands, Ecuador's prime archaeological site

Introducing Ecuador

In the vastness of South America, Ecuador can seem small and a little anonymous. Even its most famous export, the erroneously named Panama hat, suffers from an identity crisis. But though it may lack the dramatic newspaper headlines, the massive Inca ruins and gold artefacts of its heavyweight neighbours, Ecuador is every bit as beautiful, thrilling and unpredictable – and easier to explore. Glaciated summits, Amazonian rivers and Indian markets, they're all here, and so are the Galápagos islands, home to the greatest wildlife show on earth.

This small South American republic may seem like a calm oasis of peace and normality amidst the madness of Latin affairs, but first impressions can be misleading. Ecuador may be best known as the birthplace of Darwin's theory of evolution, but it's not been shy of staging the occasional revolution. The continent's first military coup of the 21st century happened here – and ended peacefully barely three hours later. The economy is equally volatile and responsible tourists who foster sustainable development are therefore among Ecuador's best friends. Running a small hotel or tour agency can be an Ecuadorean family's way out of poverty.

The country is divided geographically, politically and socially into coast and mountains. The reserved and conservative politics of Quito is a reflection of the quiet, hard-working Andean people, while the more liberal and gregarious politicans of Guayaquil represent the hot-blooded and impetuous temperament of the tropical Pacific lowlands.

The volatility of the country's political landscape is mirrored by the singular fickleness of its physical one. The beautiful Pacific coastline is periodically battered by El Niño, while up in the Andes snow-covered volcanoes erupt in spectacular bouts of chronic geological indigestion. There's no doubt that Ecuador has suffered the slings and arrows of outrageous fortune. But to see or not to see? That is the question. And there's only one answer. Ecuador should always be the natural selection.

Highlights

The phrase 'small is beautiful' could have been coined specifically with Ecuador in mind. By South American standards it is tiny (only half the size of France) and dwarfed by its neighbours Colombia and Peru. But it is this relative compactness which is one of its main attractions. If you've only got a few weeks in which to explore a place, you really don't want to spend half your time in an aircraft or on a bus. Here, you can watch dawn break over the jungle canopy, have lunch high in the Andes, then watch the sun slip into the Pacific Ocean; all in the same day.

Equatorial explorers
Ecuador also boasts great biological and cultural diversity; a fact that did not escape the attention of 18th and 19th century scientists and explorers, who came, saw and compiled large volumes extolling its many virtues. The first to put Ecuador on the map was French savant, Charles-Marie de la Condamine, who determined the precise location of the equatorial line here, hence the country's name. Today, tourists can still write home about impenetrable jungles, snow-capped volcanoes, weird and wonderful creatures and exotic peoples. Two centuries of 'progress' have not diminished the keen sense of adventure which this country inspires.

A lofty capital
The capital city, Quito, is the perfect base from which to explore the delights of the country. Although it stands a mere 23 km south of the Equator, Quito's mountain setting at 2,850m above sea level means it enjoys a pleasant, spring-like climate all year round. The city has enough to satisfy the culture vulture and hedonistic night-owl, and you don't have to be an architecture buff to appreciate its elegant and beautifully preserved colonial heart. In sharp contrast is its modern alter ego, boasting sleek contemporary buildings with shiny glass and concrete towers, making Quito one of the most attractive cities in the whole of Latin America.

Under the volcanoes
South of the capital runs the country's main traffic artery, bordered on both sides by so many snow-covered volcanoes they look like giant traffic cones deployed to section off a lane of motorway. The early 19th-century explorer Alexander Von Humboldt dubbed this the 'Avenue of the Volcanoes', a most appropriate tag which has stuck to this day. Living in the shadow of these volcanoes - many of which are still active - are the indigenous peoples of the highlands, going about their business in much the same way as they did before the Spanish arrived, still wearing traditional dress and conversing in the ancient language of the Incas. Not content with admiring the volcanoes from a distance, adventure-hungry visitors are climbing them in search of the biggest natural high this little country has to offer.

Feeling beached?
On the western side of the Andes lies Ecuador's coast, so different in atmosphere from the highlands that you could be in another country. If your idea of a good time is to lie on a beach all day soaking up rays and partying into the small hours of the morning, then Ecuador's more popular beach resorts are for you. Those who prefer their activity during daylight hours can swim, surf, snorkel, scuba dive, visit nature reserves, or watch humpback whales getting it together in the warm waters off shore.

Crafty culture
From precolonial times, Ecuadorean native artisans have excelled at their craft. Everywhere you turn there's some particularly seductive piece of artesanía on offer. This word loosely translates as 'handicrafts', but that doesn't really do them justice. The indigenous peoples make no distinction between decorative arts and functional crafts, so artesanías are valued as much for their practical use as for their beauty. The shopper can choose from a dizzying array of textiles, ceramics, carvings, and Ecuador's most famous handicraft: the 'Panama' hat.

Capital setting (below) *Few cities can match Quito's setting, wedged as it is between the slopes of Pichincha to the west and a steep canyon to the east*

Central highlands (top right) *Riding piggyback in Alausi*
Puerto Lopez (above) *This pleasant seaside town turns into Ecuador's whale-watching centre from July to September*
Colonial legacy (left) *Cuenca's blue-domed cathedral, one of the largest in all of Latin America*
High level bargaining (next page) *No visit to Ecuador would be complete without at least one full-blown Andean market experience. A truly exotic assault on the senses*

Amazon by boat (right) Explore the
Amazon at your leisure by taking a
trip through the jungle on a boat
Jungle lodge (below) Staying in a
lodge is a good way of experiencing
the jungle first hand
San Rafael Falls (bottom left) The
highest and most beautiful falls in
the country, along the gateway to
the Oriente

Jewels in the jungle (right) A million and one butterflies
make their homes in the Ecuadorean Oriente
Balsa wood parrots (next page) An eye-catching
example of Ecuador's artesanía

A wildlife paradise

The reason many people come to Ecuador is to visit a group of 19 islands lying almost 1,000 km due west. The Galápagos Islands came to the world's attention following a visit by a young Charles Darwin, whose short stay in the archipelago proved to be not insignificant for science and the study of evolution. The islands, which get their name from the giant tortoises that live there, are home to numerous endemic species of birds and reptiles. Now, this wildlife paradise has become a national park dedicated to the conservation of its many unique species. Everyone returns from this 'showcase of evolution' with a sense of wonder and a feeling of being privileged. The movement of tourists in Galápagos is carefully co-ordinated and everyone pays a park fee on arrival. It's a small price to pay for the greatest natural show on Earth. See also the colour wildlife section in the Galápagos chapter.

The greatest natural show on earth

But it is not just the scientific importance of this place that makes it so special. The animals here are so tame you could walk up and shake their hand (or flipper, wing or claw). This is nature in all its naked glory and in startling close-up. Each island also has its own particular main event; from the bizarre love dance of the blue-footed booby to the magnificent 'red balloon' courtship display of male frigate birds.

Fearless fauna

If the animals on land seem indifferent to the prying camera lenses of tourists, those beneath the waves are positively gregarious. Impossibly cute sea lion pups are always on the lookout for a new playmate, and the cheeky little Galápagos penguins dart around checking out the latest visitors. Slightly more reserved are marine turtles and graceful manta rays, while hammerhead sharks thankfully prefer to remain aloof.

Underwater magic

No visit to Ecuador would be complete without venturing into its steamy jungles. Only a few hours away from Quito by bus, the eastern slopes of the Andes give way to a vast green carpet stretching into the horizon. This is home to all manner of strange and exotic mammals, birds, fish, amphibians and reptiles. Parrots and macaws on the wing, and troops of screeching monkeys provide the noisy score for capybara (sheep-sized rodents), caiman, armadillos, tapirs, peccaries and, if you are really lucky, jaguars. There are also a million and one butterflies, some the size of your hand, and spiders as big as next door's cat. It's all part of the authentic jungle experience.

Jungle adventure

Any trip to the rainforest is an adventure in itself, but those who crave even more excitement can ride the rapids on some of Ecuador's wildest and most spectacular rivers. White water rafting here is described as some of the best in the world, with the added advantage of warm, tropical water.

Wet and wild

The tropical forests are also home to the country's few remaining lowland ethnic groups. National parks and wildlife reserves have been set up to protect the region's precious natural assets and, of course, its indigenous people. Tourist dollars are invested into local community development by the more enlightened eco-tourism projects in an attempt to preserve one of the most biologically diverse places on earth as well as the traditional way of life of its inhabitants.

Eco-ethno-tourism

There are various ways of experiencing the jungle, depending on how much you value your creature comforts. It's not everyone's idea of fun to bathe in a jungle river with piranhas and electric eels and then sleep on the floor of a native hut at the end of a hot, sweaty hike. For those who prefer to embark on their rainforest adventure from a comfortable room with private shower, there are many jungle lodges to choose from.

Creature comforts

Essentials

Planning your trip

Where to go

One of Ecuador's great attractions is its relative compactness. Travelling around is easy and unlike its larger neighbours, much of what you want to see is only a few hours by road from the capital, Quito. The exceptions are the Galápagos Islands, which are reached by air, and the jungle, which is accessible by air and road. The latter overland journey can take up to 14 hours on poor roads, especially in the rainy season; but that is still a fraction of the time required to reach the jungle overland in other countries.

Small is beautiful Ecuador is small enough to allow you to cross it in less than 24 hours, from north to south. Obviously, this won't give you much of a flavour of the place, but it does emphasize the fact that you can pack a lot into even the tightest of schedules. In fact, the biggest problem in trying to suggest various itineraries for the tourist is that there are just too many alternatives. So, instead, we'll point out some of the highlights in each region. Mix and match the options according to the time available and your own particular interests. Take a look at the section on Special interest travel (page 66) for information about climbing, trekking, rafting, kayaking, mountain biking, horse riding and other adventure sports as well as birdwatching and hot springs. We also provide information about volunteer programmes.

Quito The point of arrival for most visitors is the capital, Quito. It is actually two distinct cities: the Old City, which contains all the beautiful colonial churches and historic buildings, and the New City, with a million-and-one hotels, restaurants, bars and cafés. Quito boasts a wide range of excellent museums and it is the language course capital of South America. Just about any type of holiday or activity can be arranged here. There are many opportunities for day trips, to cultural as well as natural attractions. You could easily spend a few weeks in and around Quito without exhausting all possibilities.

North of Quito Almost everyone will make the two-hour bus journey to Otavalo, home to one of the finest craft markets in all of Latin America. It can be visited in less than a day, but many choose to extend their stay, so that they can also explore the numerous little craft villages nearby, or visit natural wonders such as Lake Cuicocha. There are also several hiking possibilities. Alternatively, you can stay in Ibarra, a bit further north, which is the starting point for the trip to San Lorenzo on the coast, or a good stop on the way north to the Colombian border. North of Ibarra is El Angel Ecological Reserve, with interesting trekking amid the area's unique *frailejón* plants.

South of Quito South of the capital is the spectacular 'Avenue of the Volcanoes' and Cotopaxi National Park, which can be visited in a day; longer if you want to climb or trek. Two hours south of Quito is Latacunga, the starting point for the beautiful Quilotoa circuit, very popular with visitors. It can be done in one day with a car, but needs longer without. Nearby is Saquisilí, with its colourful Thursday market – 2½ hours from Quito. Baños is a very popular spa town situated at the foot of Tungurahua, an imposing snow-capped volcano which has been active again since 1999. There is good day hiking and cycling nearby and it is one of the gateways to the jungle – only 3½ hours from Quito. Riobamba, four hours from Quito, is the geographic and cultural heart of the central highlands. It is a starting point for the very popular railway ride over the Devil's Nose, a good base for trekking and climbing and a convenient stop on the journey south. Towering over the city is Chimborazo, the highest mountain in the country. Ingapirca, Ecuador's most important Inca archaeological site, lies 3½ hours further south, between Riobamba and Cuenca.

Cuenca is a lovely colonial city, the heart of the southern highlands, known as El Austro, and also a great place to buy Panama hats (yes, they're made in Ecuador!). It is 10 hours from Quito by bus and 45 minutes by air. Allow a day to visit Ingaprica by bus from Cuenca, or you can find accommodation near the archaeological site. Also give yourself a couple of days to fully appreciate Cuenca's fine churches and museums and to take a trip out to nearby Cajas National Park. Four to five hours south of Cuenca is the provincial capital of Loja, another convenient stop and the jumping-off point for a trip into the wilds of Podocarpus National Park. Only one hour from Loja is lovely Vilcabamba, once a fabled fountain of youth, today the southern terminus of Ecuador's 'gringo trail' (see page 46) and another excellent trekking centre. Several new border crossings have been opened in the south. There is, for example, a beautiful and adventurous bus journey from Vilcabamba, through Zumba, to Chachapoyas, at the centre of one of Peru's finest archeological areas.

Cuenca & El Austro

Guayaquil is 45 minutes by air from Quito and eight hours by bus, 3½ hours from Cuenca, and five hours from Riobamba. It can also be reached from many foreign destinations and has the country's only international airport outside Quito. Guayaquil is Ecuador's largest city and main port, bustling with commerce and industry. It is mostly visited by business people but has undergone something of a cultural revival in recent years, and boasts a lovely *malecón* (riverfront promenade) as well as a few other tourist attractions. Guayaquil is especially well supplied with luxury hotels, restaurants and shops. Trips to the Galápagos can also be arranged from here.

Guayaquil

From Guayaquil it is 2½ hours west to the seaside resort of Salinas, Ecuador's answer to Miami Beach, on the Santa Elena peninsula. Northwards the coast has much more to offer. The town of Puerto López (about 4½ hours from Guayaquil) is a good base from

The Pacific Coast

Essentials

Essentials

which to explore Machalilla National Park. Here, you can go hiking through dry tropical forest, horse riding, scuba diving, whale watching, visit Isla de la Plata or just lie on the dazzling white sands of Los Frailes beach. Further north is Bahía de Caráquez, a resort city on the estuary of the Río Chone, with good tourist facilities and some interesting natural attractions nearby, such as Isla Corazón (where frigate birds nest). On the north side of the estuary are superb beaches, stretching for 20 km from San Vicente to the popular little village of Canoa – one of the nicest seaside spots in Ecuador. In the far north are the palm-fringed beaches of Same, Súa and Atacames, well known for their party atmosphere. Atacames is 40 minutes by road south of the city of Esmeraldas, which is only five to six hours from Quito or 30 minutes by air. From Esmeraldas you can also travel further north to San Lorenzo, a little corner of Africa in Ecuador, from which you can head up to Ibarra by road, thus completing a circuit from Quito. It is difficult to suggest the length of time you should spend on the coast since it depends how long you want to spend lazing on the beach, but a week might be enough to give a taste.

Oriente Jungle A worthwhile and enjoyable jungle trip requires a little more preparation. You can either arrange a tour in Quito (or from abroad) to one of the many jungle lodges, which should be of at least three or four nights because of the time required to travel to and from the lodge. The alternative is to travel under your own steam to one of the main jungle towns and arrange a tour from there with a local agency or freelance guide. Tours can be arranged from Puyo, Tena, Misahuallí, Coca, Lago Agrio and Baños, which is on the road from the highlands to the Oriente. The southern Oriente is less developed for tourism, but interest in the region is growing, and tours here can be arranged from Macas and Zamora. Independent travel in the Oriente takes time, especially during the rainy season, so you should allow for five to seven days if you want to go far enough to see good wildlife. River travel is possible from Coca, down the Río Napo, to Iquitos, Peru. It's still an adventurous journey, but a tourist boat might begin operating this route in 2003.

Galápagos Islands Most people arrange their tours from Quito, Guayaquil or abroad, but those with more time and less money can try flying directly from Quito or Guayaquil to Puerto Ayora on Santa Cruz island, main town of the Galápagos. If you are lucky, you can get a good last-minute deal on a sailing tour there, but you can also be stuck waiting for weeks, especially in high season. Galápagos tours range from four days up to 14 days, but seven days would be optimal if you can afford it, to fully appreciate this once-in-a-lifetime experience.

When to go

Climate
These are only broad generalizations and, simply stated, the weather in most of Ecuador is highly unpredictable

Ecuador's climate is so varied and variable that any time of the year is good for a visit. In the highlands, temperatures vary more in the course of a day, and with altitude, than they do with the seasons (which mainly reflect changes in rainfall). Every valley seems to have its own micro-climate but precipitation patterns generally depend on whether a particular area is closer to the eastern or western slopes of the Andes. To the west, June through September are dry and October through May are wet (but there is sometimes a short dry spell in December or January). To the east, October through February are dry and March through September are wet. There is also variation in annual rainfall from north to south, with the southern highlands being drier.

Along the Pacific coast, rainfall likewise drops almost linearly from north to south, so that it can rain throughout the year in northern Esmeraldas and seldom at all near the Peruvian border. The coast can also be enjoyed year-round, although it may be a bit cool from June through September, when mornings are often grey and misty. January through May is the hottest and rainiest time of the year.

In the Oriente, as in the rest of the Amazon basin, heavy rain can fall at any time, but it is usually wettest from March through September. The Galápagos are hot from January through April, when heavy but brief showers are likely. From May through December is the cooler misty season. As if all this was not sufficiently confusing, the climate in Galápagos and throughout Ecuador is also affected by the irregular 5-10 year cycle of the *El Niño* phenomenon (see page 457).

Ecuador's high international tourist season is from June to early September, which is the busiest time for trekking or climbing. There is also a shorter tourist season between December and January, when Galápagos tours may be booked well in advance. Most Ecuadoreans take long weekends around Carnival, Holy Week, and over New Year; vacations in the highlands are from July to September, on the coast January to March. While a few resort areas may become busy at these times, and prices rise accordingly, Ecuador is not overcrowded at any time of the year.

High/ low tourist seasons

Essentials

Tours and tour operators

Adventure Travel Centre, 131-135 Earls Court Road, London SW5 9RH, T020-7244 6411, www.topdecktravel.co.uk Organizes short tours as well as longer expeditions. *Condor Journeys and Adventures*, 2 Ferry Bank, Colintraive, Argyll PA22 3AR, T01700-841318, F841398, www.condorjourneys-adventures.com *Cox & Kings Travel*, Gordon House, 10 Greencoat Place, London SW1P 1PH, T020-7873 5000, F7630 6038, www.coxandkings.co.uk *Discovery Initiatives*, The Travel House, 51 Castle Street, Cirencester, Glos GL7 1QD, T01285-643333, www.discoveryinitiatives.com *Dragoman*, Camp Green, Debenham, Stowmarket, Suffolk IP14 6LA, T01728-861133,

UK & Ireland
For further information on specialist travel firms, contact the Latin American Travel Association at PO Box 1338, Long Ashton, Bristol BS41 9YA, T01275-394484

F861127, www.dragoman.co.uk Overland camping and/or hotel journeys throughout South and Central America. *Encounter*, 2002 Camp Green, Debenham, Stowmarket, Suffolk IP14 6LA, T01728-862222, F861127 www.encounter.co.uk *Exodus Travels*, 9 Weir Road, London SW12 0LT, T020-8772 3822, www.exodustravels.co.uk Experienced in adventure travel, including cultural tours and trekking and biking holidays. *Explore Worldwide*, 1 Frederick Street, Aldershot, Hants GU11 1LQ, T01252-760000, F760001, www.exploreworldwide.com Highly respected operator with offices in Eire, Australia,New Zealand, USA and Canada, who run two to five week tours in more than 90 countries worldwide, including Ecuador. *Galápagos Adventure Tours*, 79 Maltings Place, 169 Tower Bridge Road, London SE1 3LJ, T020-7407 1478, F7407 0397. Run by David Horwell who has an abundant knowledge of the Galápagos. Escorted tours to the islands as well as the Andes and rainforest. *Galápagos Classic Cruises*, 6 Keyes Road, London NW2 3XA, T020-8933 0613, F8452 5248, www.galapagoscruises.co.uk Specializes in tailor-made cruises and diving holidays. Will also organize land tours to mainland Ecuador. *Guerba Expeditions*, Wessex House, 40 Station Road, Westbury, Wilts BA13 3JN, T01373-826611, F858351, www.guerba.co.uk Specializes in adventure holidays, from canoeing safaris to wilderness camping. *Hayes & Jarvis*, 152 King Street, London W6, T020-8748 0088. Long established operator offering tailor-made itineraries as well as packages. *High Places*, The Globe Centre, Penistone Road, Sheffield S6 3AE, T0114-2757500, F2753870, www.highplaces.co.uk Trekking and climbing specialists. *International Wildlife Adventures*, PO Box 40063, RPO Nairn, Winnipeg, Canada RTL 2G2, T204-949-2050, T800-808-4IWA, F204-667-6375, www.wildlifeadventures.com Wildlife specialists with year-round Galápagos cruises and Ecuador extensions. *Journey Latin America*, 12-13 Heathfield Terrace, Chiswick, London W4 4JE, T020-8747 8315, F8742 1312, and 12 St Anne's Square, 2nd floor, Manchester M2 7HW, T0161-8321441, F8321551, www.journeylatinamerica.co.uk The world's leading tailor-made specialist for Latin America, running escorted tours throughout the region, they also offer a wide range of flight options. *Latin American Language Services*, 96 Cotterill Road, Surbiton, Surrey, KT6 7UK, T020-8286 1817, F8241 3483, www.lals.co.uk *Last Frontiers*, Fleet Marston Farm, Aylesbury, Buckinghamshire HP18 0QT, T01296-653000, F658651, www.lastfrontiers.co.uk South American specialists offering tailor-made itineraries to Ecuador including the Galápagos, as well as discounted air fares and air passes. *Naturetrek*, Cheriton Mill, Cheriton, Alresford, Hants SO24 0NG, T01962-733051, F736426, www.naturetrek.co.uk Birdwatching tours throughout the continent; also botany, natural history tours, treks and cruises. *Nomadic Thoughts*, 81 Brondesbury Road, London NW6 6BB, T020-7604 4408, F7604 4407, www.nomadicthoughts.com Specializes in tailor-made itineraries. *Quasar Nautica* (UK) Steeple Cottage, Easton, Winchester, Hants SO21 1EH, T01962-779317, F779458, pkellie@yachtors.u-net.com, www.quasarnautica.com Specializes in Galápagos cruises and diving holidays. Also offer standard country tours, as well as customized nature, cultural and adventure group tours. *Reef & Rainforest Tours*, Prospect House, 1 The Plains, Totnes, TQ9 5DR, T01803-866965, F865916, www.reefrainforest.co.uk *South American Experience*, 47 Causton Street, Pimlico, London SW1P 4AT, T020-7976 5511, F7976 6908, www.southamericanexperience.co.uk Flights, accommodation and tailor-made trips. *STA Travel*, Priory House, 6 Wrights Lane, London W8 6TA, T020-7361 6100, F7938 9570, www.statravel.co.uk *Steppes Latin America*, formerly *Destination South America*, Steppes Travel Group, The Travel House, 51 Castle Street, Cirencester, Glos GL7 1QD, T01285-885333, F885888, www.steppeslatinamerica.co.uk *Trailfinders*, 42-50 Earl's Court Road, London W8 6FT, T020-7938 3366, www.trailfinders.com *Trips Worldwide*, 9 Byron Place, Clifton, Bristol B58 1JT, T0117-3114400, wwwtripsworldwide.co.uk *Tucan Travel*, T020-8896 1600, www.tucantravel.com Offers adventure tours and overland expeditions.

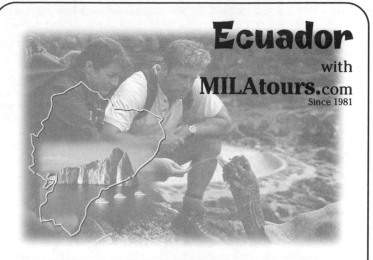

North America *eXito Latin American Travel Specialists*, 712 BancroftRoad #455, Walnut Creek, CA 94598, USA, T1800-6554053 toll free, F510-6554566, exito@wonderlink.com *ExpeditionTrips.com*, 4509 Interlake Avenue North, 179 Seattle, Washington WA 98103, T1-877-412-8527, www.ExpeditionTrips.com *Galápagos Holidays*, 14 Prince Arthur Avenue, Suite 109, Toronto ON M5R, Canada, T1800-6612512 toll free, www3.sympatico.ca/galapagos.holidays Long established company running customized itineraries to Ecuador. Daily departures to the Galápagos Islands. *Ladatco Tours*, T305-8548422, F305-2850504, www.ladatco.com Based in Miami, run 'themed' explorer tours. *MILA Tours*, 100 S Greenleaf, Gurnee IL 60031, T800-3677378, www.milatours *Quasar Nautica*, 7855 NW 12th Street, Suite 221, Miami, Florida 33126, T1305-5999008/2472925, F5927060. See entry under UK, above, for further details. *South American Fiesta*, 3774 Swallow Way, Marietta, GA30066-3031, T770-3216814/1774, F815-5505642, www.southamericanfiesta.com *TAMBO TOURS*, PO Box 60541, Houston, Texas, T2815289448, F5287378, www.2GOPERU.com *Wildland Adventures*, 3516 NE 155 Street, Seattle, WA 98155, USA, T800-3454453, F800-3650686, www.wildland.com Specializes in cultural and natural history tours to the Galápagos, Andes and Amazon.

Europe Travellers starting their journey in continental Europe may try: *Uniclam-Voyages*, 63 rue Monsieur-le-Prince, 75006 Paris, www.uniclam.com, for charters. For cheap flights in Switzerland, *Globetrotter Travel Service*, Renweg, 8001 Zürich, has been recommended. Also try *Nouvelles Frontières*, Paris, T1-41415858, or *Hajo Siewer Jet Tours*, Martinstr 39, 57462 Olpe, Germany, T02761-924120. The German magazine *Reisefieber* is useful.

Australia & New Zealand *Contours Travel*, Level 6, 310 King Street, Melbourne, Vic 3000, T3-9670 6900, F3-9670 7558, www.contourstravel.com.au Specializes in Latin American destinations.

South America *Southtrip*, Sarmiento 347, 4th floor, of 19, Buenos Aires, Argentina, T11-43287075, www.southtrip.com

Special interest tour operators **Birdwatching** Quito birding companies include: *BirdEcuador*, contact Irene Bustamante, Carrion N21-01 entre Juan Leon Mera y Reina Victoria, T02-2547403, F2228902, birdecua@hoy.net; *Neblina Forest*, contact Mercedes Rivadeneira, Centro Comercial La Galeria, local #65, Los Shyris y Gaspar de Villarroel, T02-2460189, USA toll-free T1-800-5382149, mrivaden@pi.pro.ec, www.neblinaforest.com; *Avestravel*, contact Robert Jonsson, Jorge Washington E7-23 entre 6 de Diciembre y Reina Victoria, T02-2224469, avestrav@impsat.net.ec, www.angelfire.com/biz/Avestravel.

Horse riding The following specialize in horse-trekking trips: *Shungu Huasi*, outside Cayambe, T02-2792094, shungu@hoy.net,

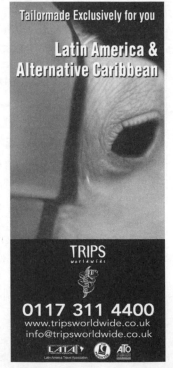

www.plentagos.com; *Green Horse Ranch*, outside Quito, contact *True Colors Travel*, Foch 831 y Amazonas, T/F02-2906409, truecolors@andinanet.net, www.horseranch.de; and *Montaruna*, in Cuenca, Hermano Miguel 4-46 y Calle Larga, T/F07-846395, www.montaruna.ch

Rafting and kayaking Quito: All agencies in Quito offer one and two day trips on the Toachi and Blanco rivers. Some of them offer additional trips which are mentioned below. *Yacu Amu*, Foch 746 y J L Mera, T02-2904054, F2904055, www.yacuamu.com 1-2 day trips on the Quijos and 5-6 day trips on the Upano Oct-Feb, customized itineraries, kayaking information, equipment rental, 4-day kayak school with qualified instructors, guiding service and all-inclusive packages for those who want to leave the organizing to someone else. Highly recommended as professional and with highest quality equipment. *ROW Expediciones*, Pablo Arturo Suarez 191 y Eloy Alfaro, T02-2239224, F2238040, row@andinanet.net 6-day trips on the Upano Nov-Feb, guides from Idaho, USA. *Sierra Nevada*, Joaquin Pinto 637 y Cordero, T02-553658, F554936, snevada@accessinter.net French-trained guides and good equipment. *Eco-Adventur*, Foch 634 y Reina Victoria, T02-2520647, F2223720, info@adventour.com *Explorandes*, Presidente Wilson 537 y Diego de Almagro, T02-222699, F556938, explora@hoy.net

Tena: *Ríos Ecuador*, 15 de Noviembre y 9 de Octubre, T06-886346, F886727, www.riosecuador.com Year-round rafting trips on the Upper Napo, and on the Misahualli Oct-Mar. Also kayaking trips, 4-day kayaking school rental and information. Good guides and high safety standards. Founded by Gynner Coronel, who is highly respected and recommended.

Baños Agencies here offer year-round trips on the Patate and Pastaza river. *Río Loco*, Ambato y Eloy Alfaro, T/F03-740929, riolocot@yahoo.com *Geotours*, Ambato y Thomas Halflants, T03-741344, geotours@hotmail.com

Finding out more

Tourist information and promotion is handled at the national level by the **Ministerio de Turismo**, Eloy Alfaro N32-300 Carlos Tobar, Quito, T02-2507559/560, F2229330, mtur1@ec-gov.net, www.vivecuador.com Details of tourism offices throughout Ecuador are given under the respective towns and cities. **Tourist Information**

The **Cámara Provincial de Turismo de Pichincha (CAPTUR)** operates information booths at Quito airport and in the Old City and New City (see the chapter on Quito). Their administrative offices are located at 6 de Diciembre 1424 y Carrión, T/F2224074, www.captur.com

Outside Ecuador, tourist information can sometimes be obtained from Ecuadorean embassies and consulates (see box on page 32).

South American Explorers (SAE) is a US based non-profit organization, which provides its members with a wide range of travel information about Ecuador and South America. It offers a resource centre, a library and a quarterly journal as well as selling guidebooks and maps. SAE can hold mail for its members. The Quito facilities are in a lovely spacious house at Jorge Washington 311 y Leonidas Plaza, T/F2225228, quitoclub@saexplorers.org Open Monday-Friday 0930-1700, Saturday 0900-1200. There are also SAE clubhouses in Lima and Cusco, Peru. USA head office: 126 Indian Creek Road, Ithaca, NY 14850, T800-2740568 or T607-2770488, F607-2776122, www.SAexplorers.org Official representatives in UK: Bradt Publications, 19 High St, Chalfont St Peter, Bucks, SL9 9QE, T/F01494-873478. SAE services are only available to members of the club. Annual membership costs US$50 single, US$80 for a couple. A visit to an SAE clubhouse is recommended, to see if this organization suits your needs. **South American Explorers (SAE)**

Essentials

Websites

See also Health, page 83, for further information about relevant health websites

In late 2002, there were almost 3,500,000 web pages related in some way to Ecuador. The websites of hotels, tour agencies, airlines, conservation and volunteer groups as well as other organizations are given throughout the book alongside their usual contact information. Since the web changes so quickly, your favourite search engine is the best place to start looking for sites about Ecuador.

The most frequently updated sites are on-line editions of Ecuador's three major daily newspapers, all in Spanish: *El Comercio* (Quito), **www.elcomercio.com**; *El Hoy* (Quito), **www.hoy.com.ec**; and *El Universo* (Guayaquil), **www.eluniverso.com**

There are many Ecuadorean government sites with administrative, economic and statistical information. A good bilingual introduction is provided by the Ecuadorean embassy in Washington at **www.ecuador.org** The sites of the Ministerio de Turismo and CAPTUR are given above. The National Geophysics Institute posts advisories of volcanic activity at **www.epn.edu.ec**

English or multilingual tourist sites for Ecuador abound. These commercial enterprises display varying amounts of background information alongside advertising. They include **www.ecuadorexplorer.com**, **www.thebestofecuador.com**, **www.ecuaworld.com**, **www.ecuadordiscover.com**, **www.ecuador-travel-guide.org**, **www.ecuadortoursonline.com** and **www.go2ecuador.com**, to name but a few. Some offer on-line booking for hotels, tours and other services.

Many, if not most, Galápagos tours are now sold on-line. English or multilingual sites specializing in tours to the Islands include **www.galapagosislands.com**, **www.galapagosdiscover.com** and **www.galapagos.ws** There are a great many others, see box Galápagos on the web (page 414). Multilingual background and scientific information about Galápagos is provided by the Charles Darwin Foundation at **www.darwinfoundation.org**

The authors maintain two multilingual sites about Ecuador, **www.ecuadorhandbook.com**, for this book, and **www.trekkinginecuador.com**, for hikers and trekkers. Footprint's site, **www.footprintbooks.com**, provides information about related titles.

Portals and search engines specializing in Ecuador (for Ecuadoreans rather than tourists, all in Spanish) include **www.explored.com.ec**, **www.bacan.com** and **www.mande.com.ec**

Language

See also page 466 for basic Spanish words and phrases

The official languages of Ecuador are Spanish and Quichua. English and a few other European languages may be spoken in some establishments catering to tourists in Quito and the most popular tourist destinations. Away from these places, knowledge of Spanish is essential. Indeed, learning some Spanish is the single most important way

Essentials

to prepare for your visit. Alternatively, you can begin your travels in Ecuador with a period of language study. Language training opportunities abound; see Spanish schools listed under Quito, Cuenca, Otavalo, Baños and other towns. With even a modest knowledge of Spanish you will be able to befriend Ecuadoreans, to interchange ideas and insights with them. Without any language skills, you will feel like someone trying to peep through the keyhole at Ecuador.

There are now very few people, even in remote highland villages, who speak only Quichua. Spanish however, may be relegated to the role of a second language in some native communities. Those who are planning to work or have extensive contact with highland Indian groups, would do well to learn some Quichua beforehand. Note, however, that dialects vary throughout the Sierra and that the Quichua spoken in Oriente is all but unintelligible to highlanders. It is therefore best to learn the language from the same group you intend to work with.

Information on travel and language schools is available from **AmeriSpan Unlimited**, one of several language school brokers in the USA, PO Box 58129, Philadelphia, PA 19102-8129, (USA and Canada), T800-8796640, worldwide T215-7511100, F7511986, www.amerispan.com An alternative specialist is **Spanish Abroad**, T888-7227623 (USA and Canada), T0800-0287706 (UK), T602-7786791, F8401545 (worldwide), www.spanishabroad.com

Disabled travellers

The website www.geocities.com/ Paris/1502 is dedicated to providing travel information for 'disabled adventurers' and includes reviews and travel tips

As with most Latin American countries, facilities for the disabled traveller are sadly lacking in Ecuador. Wheelchair ramps are a rare luxury in most of the country, but they are present in the resort town of Baños, see page 211. Getting a wheelchair into a bathroom or toilet is well nigh impossible, except for some of the more upmarket hotels (for example *Swissôtel* in Quito and the more modest *El Edén* in Baños). Pavements are often in a poor state of repair. Disabled Ecuadoreans obviously have to cope with these problems and mainly rely on the help of others to move around; fortunately most bystanders are very helpful. Quito's trolley system has wheelchair access in principle, but it is often too crowded to make this practical.

But of course only a minority of disabled people are wheelchair-bound and it is now widely acknowledged that disabilities do not stop you from enjoying a great holiday. *Nothing Ventured*, edited by Alison Walsh, gives personal accounts of worldwide journeys by disabled travellers plus advice and listings.

Gay and lesbian travellers

The 1998 constitution prohibits discrimination on the basis of sexual orientation and attitudes have gradually become more liberal in Quito and Guayaquil. Outside these two largest cities, however, values are still intensely conservative and there remains a general bias, even hostility, against gay people. As in most Latin countries, effeminate behaviour in men is condemned, and the derogatory term *maricón* is commonly used to describe such a person, irrespective of their sexual orientation. Same-sex couples travelling in Ecuador should avoid public displays of affection. A place to meet or obtain information is the *Matrioshka* bar in La Mariscal neighbourhood of Quito, Pinto 376 y Juan León Mera, T02-2552668. **Zenith Travel** in Quito, J L Mera 453 y Roca, #202, T02-2529993, www.zenithecuador.com, specializes in gay and lesbian tourism.

Student travellers

Foreign students visiting Ecuador may be eligible for some discounts, while other concessions are restricted to those who are Ecuadorean citizens. This is in a way unfair, but you should keep in mind that – no matter how tight your budget – you probably have far more resources at your disposal than the average Ecuadorean student. By all means, shop around and bargain for the best student deal you can find, but also remember to be fair, especially when dealing with individuals or small family-run operations.

Those tourist establishments in Ecuador which offer discounts to foreign students generally honour the International Student Identity Card (ISIC), but only if the card was issued in your home country. If you need to find the location of your nearest ISIC office contact: **The International Student Travel Confederation**, Herengracht 479, 1017 BS Amsterdam, The Netherlands, T31-20-4212800, F31-20-4212810, www.istc.org Student cards must carry a photograph if they are to be any use for discounts.

Senior travellers

Mainland Ecuador has long been a popular destination for the young and adventurous, while older travellers have traditionally focused their visits on Galápagos, Quito and perhaps Otavalo. There is however no good reason for more mature travellers to shun the less beaten path. Those in good health should face no special difficulties travelling independently, but it is very important to know and respect your own limits and to give yourself sufficient time to acclimatize to altitude in the highlands. If you require a special diet or medications, these must be brought from home, as they may not be available locally. Seniors' discounts in Ecuador, even more so than those for students (see above), tend to be restricted to Ecuadorean citizens, but bear in mind that a local retiree may have to make do with a pension under US$40 a month. Some discounts for foreign seniors may be available at museums and on inter-city buses. You are far more likely to benefit from the strong traditional respect for the elderly in Ecuadorean society. At the same time, you will be sure to notice that the country's demographic profile is the inverse of that in most parts of the developed world. People under 25 years of age are the majority here, so it should be no surprise that older *gringo* travellers tend to stand out.

For general information about active, adventurous travel for those 50 or better, see Travel Unlimited: Uncommon Adventures for the Mature Traveler by Alison Gardner, Avalon Travel Publishing, 2000; and www.travelwitha challenge.com

Travelling with children

Bus travel People contemplating overland travel in Ecuador with children should remember that a lot of time can be spent waiting for and riding buses. You should take reading material with you as it is difficult, and expensive, to find. Also look for the locally available comic strip *Condorito*, which is quite popular and a good way for older children to learn a bit of Spanish. Many children become nauseous, however, on the winding roads of the highlands, and reading while the bus is moving can make this worse. Always keep some plastic bags at hand.

Make sure you pack that favourite toy. Nothing beats a GameBoy, unless it's two GameBoys and a link cable

Fares On all long-distance buses you pay for each seat, and there are no half-fares if the children occupy a seat each. For shorter trips it is cheaper, if less comfortable, to seat small children on your knee. Sometimes there are spare seats which children can occupy after tickets have been collected. In city buses, small children generally do not pay a fare, but are not entitled to a seat when paying customers are standing. On domestic flights in Ecuador, children below age two pay 10% of the adult fare, between ages two and 12 they pay 50%. Make sure that any children accompanying you are fully covered by your travel insurance policy.

Food This can be a problem if the children are not adaptable. It is easier to take food with you on longer trips than to rely on meal stops where the food may not be to taste. Avocados are safe, readily available, easy to eat and nutritious; they can be fed to babies as young as six months and most older children like them. Papayas are also a good choice, but best stick to simple things like bread, bananas and tangerines while you are actually on the road. Biscuits, packaged junk food and bottled drinks abound. A small immersion heater and jug for making hot drinks is invaluable, but remember that electric current is 110v in Ecuador. In restaurants, you can normally buy a *media porción* (half portion), or divide one full-size helping between two children.

Hotels Try to negotiate family rates; if charges are per person, insist that two children will occupy one bed only, therefore counting as one tariff. You can almost always get a reduced rate at cheaper hotels. Occasionally when travelling with a child you will be refused a room in a hotel that is 'unsuitable', ie intended for short-stay couples. Travel with children can bring you into closer contact with local families and, generally, presents no special problems – in fact the path may even be smoother for family groups. Officials are sometimes more amenable where children are concerned and they are pleased if your child knows a little Spanish. For more detailed advice, see *Travel with Children* by Lonely Planet (3rd edn, 1995).

Women travellers

Generally women travellers should find visiting Ecuador an enjoyable experience. Gender stereotyping is gradually diminishing, however machismo is alive and well here. You should be prepared for this and try not to overreact. When you set out, err on the side of caution until your instincts have adjusted to the customs of a new culture.

It is easier for men to take the friendliness of locals at face value; women may be subject to unwanted attention. Minimize this by not wearing suggestive clothing and do not flirt. By wearing a wedding ring, carrying a photograph of your 'husband' and 'children', and saying that your 'husband' is close at hand, you may dissuade an aspiring suitor. If politeness fails, do not feel bad about showing offense and departing. When accepting a social invitation, make sure that someone knows the address and the time you left. Ask if you can bring a friend (even if you do not intend to do so).

If, as a single woman, you can befriend an Ecuadorean woman, you will learn much more about the country as well as finding out how best to deal with suggestive comments, whistles and hisses that might come your way. Travelling with another *gringa* may not exempt you from this attention, but at least should give you moral support.

Note that tampons may be hard to find in smaller towns; sanitary napkins are available everywhere. The largest selection of such products is found in the major cities, where you can stock up if necessary.

Before you travel

Getting in

Passports & visas
Visiting Ecuador as a tourist for a period of less than 3 months is very simple, with only a passport required for most travellers

All visitors to Ecuador must have a passport valid for at least six months and, in principle, an onward or return ticket. The latter is seldom asked for, but can be grounds for refusal of entry in some cases. Only citizens of the following countries require a consular visa to visit Ecuador as tourists: Afghanistan, Algeria, Bangladesh, China, Costa Rica, Cuba, Honduras, India, Iraq, Jordan, South Korea, Lebanon, Libya, Nigeria, Pakistan, Palestinian Authority, Sri Lanka, Sudan, Syria, Tunisia, Vietnam and Yemen. Upon entry all visitors are required to complete a brief international embarkation/disembarkation card, which is then stamped along with your passport. Keep this card in your passport, losing it can cause all manner of grief when leaving the country or at a spot check.

Spot checks
Failure to carry your passport can, in principle, result in imprisonment or deportation

You are required by Ecuadorean law to carry your passport at all times.. An ordinary photocopy of your passport is not an officially acceptable substitute and you may not be permitted to return to your hotel to fetch the original document. Some travellers nevertheless prefer to carry a photocopy and leave their passport in safekeeping at their hotel. A photocopy certified by your embassy is more likely to be acceptable, but it's a judgement call, entirely at the discretion of the individual police officer.

Spot checks for passports are most often carried out near border areas (especially in the north) and at police checkpoints on highways throughout the country, as well as in bars, discos and resorts popular with foreigners. Be cautious however when approached by someone claiming to be an immigration officer on the street. If they are in uniform, they will have a tag with their name, which you should first write down. If they are plain clothed (which is unusual) then politely ask for their ID, seek assistance from several bystanders, and insist on walking to the nearest police station before you hand over any documents. Do not get in a taxi or other vehicle with such an individual. A legitimate immigration officer should not ask to see your money at a spot check, if this is asked for then you are probably being set up to be robbed.

As long as your documents are in order, serious hassles with the immigration authorities in Ecuador are fortunately very rare. Remember however, that tourists are not permitted to work under any circumstances. Foreigners have also on occasion been detained and deported for involvement in political or other 'sensitive' activities, including environmental activism – see Prohibitions, page 43. If you should encounter serious difficulties with the immigration police, then these may be reported to your embassy or consulate. Some embassies also recommend that you register with them details of your passport and accommodation in case of emergency.

Length of visit

Tourists are entitled to visit Ecuador for up to 90 days during any 12-month period. This may, in some cases, be extended to a maximum of 180 days at the discretion of the Policía Nacional de Migración (national immigration police). Those travelling by land from Peru or Colombia are seldom granted the full 90 days on arrival, but their stay can usually be extended. When arriving at Quito or Guayaquil airport you will generally be

▶▶ Ecuadorean embassies and consulates

Australia, 11 London Circuit, 1st Floor, Canberra ACT 2601, T/F6-62625282, embecu@hotkey.net.au

Austria, Goldschmiedgasse 10/2/24, A-1010 Vienna, T1-5353208, F1-5350897, mecaustria@chello.at

Belgium, Av Louise 363, 9th Floor, 1050 Brussels, T2-6443050, F2-6442813, ecuador@wanadoo.be

Canada, 50 O'Connor St No 316, Ottawa, ON K1P 6L2, T613-5638206, F613-2355776, mecuacan@sprint.ca; 151 Bloor St West, Suite 470 Toronto, ON M5S 1S4, T416-9682077, F416-9683348; 2055 Peel St, Suite 501, Montreal, QC H3A 1V4, T514-8744071, F514-8749078.

France, 34 Ave de Messine, 75008 Paris, T1-45611021, F1-42560664, ambecuad@wanadoo.fr

Germany, Kaiser-Friedrich Strasse 90, 1 OG, 10585 Berlin, T30-2386217, mecuadoral@t-online.de

Israel, 4 Rehov Weizmann (Asia House), 4th floor, Tel Aviv 64239, T3-6958764, F3-6913604, mecuaisr@netvision.net.il

Italy, Vía Antonio Bertolini No. 8 (Paroli), 00197 Roma, T6-8076271, F6-8078209, mecuroma@flashnet.it

Japan, No 38 Kowa Building, Room 806, 12-24 Nishi-Azabu 4 Chome, Minato-Ku, Tokyo 1060031, T3-34992800, F3-34994400.

Netherlands, Koning innengracht 84, 2514 AJ The Hague, T70-3463753, F70-8658910, embecua@bart.nl

New Zealand, Ferry Bldg, 2nd Floor, Quay St, Auckland, T09-3090229, F09-3032931.

Spain, Calle Velásquez No.114-2º derecha, Madrid, T1-5625436, embajada@mecuador.es

Sweden, Engelbrektsgatan 13, S-100 41 Stockholm, T8-6796043, F8-6115593, suecia@embajada-ecuador.se

Switzerland, Ensingerstrasse 48, 3006 Berne, T031-3511755, F031-3512771, edesuiza@bluewin.ch

UK, Flat 3B, 3 Hans Crescent, Knightsbridge, London SW1X 0LS, T020-7584 1367, F7823 9701, embajada@ecuador.freeserve.co.uk

USA, 2535 15th Street NW, Washington, DC 20009, T202-2347200, F202-6673482, mecuawaa@pop.erols.com

asked how long you plan to stay in the country. Whether or not you are asked, it is best to request at least two weeks more than you think you will need, just to be on the safe side. If you have no idea how long you will stay, ask for 90 days.

Extensions   At present only a nominal fee/fine of US$0.40 is charged for extensions, but this will likely increase. Extensions for stays up to 90 days may be requested at any of the following locations: in **Quito** at the Jefatura Provincial de Migración de Pichincha, Isla Seymour 44-174 y Río Coca, T02-2247510 (note that this is not the Dirección Nacional de Migración on Av Amazonas); in **Guayaquil**, Av Río Daule, near the *terminal terrestre*, T04-2297010; in **Cuenca**, Luis Cordero 6-62 entre Presidente Córdova y Juan Jaramillo, T07-831020; in **Puerto Baquerizo Moreno** (San Cristóbal, Galápagos), Av Charles Darwin, T05-520129; in **Baños**, Halflants entre Ambato y Rocafuerte, T03-740122; and in **Ibarra**, Villamar 148 y Peñaherrera, T06-951712. Immigration offices in other cities cannot grant extensions of stay to tourists. Requests for extensions beyond 90 days can only be made in Quito, at the Jefatura Provincial de Migración de Pichincha, as above. All immigration offices are normally open Monday-Friday 0800-1230 and 1500-1830. If you are lucky, obtaining an extension can take less than an hour, but always leave yourself a few days slack as there may be delays. Also note that the above regulations are frequently subject to change, if you are unsure about current requirements, then enquire well before your time expires. Polite conduct and a neat appearance are important when dealing with the immigration authorities.

There are many options for foreigners who wish to stay in Ecuador longer than six **Visas for** months a year, but if you enter as a tourist then you cannot change your status while **longer stays** inside the country. The two classes of visas for longer stays are immigrant visas (categories 10-I to 10-VI) and non-immigrant visas (categories 12-I to 12-X). Immigrant visas are available for retirees with a guaranteed income (such as a pension or annuity), investors, professionals permanently employed in Ecuador, and spouses or other close relatives of Ecuadorean citizens or immigrants. They are granted by the Dirección Nacional de Extranjería in Quito, 10 de Agosto y Murgeón, Edificio Autorepuestos del Interior, 4th floor, T02-2231022, open Monday-Friday 0800-1300. The immigrant visa fee is US$200. Non-immigrant visas are available for students, temporary employees, missionaries, volunteers, those involved in cultural exchange programs, as well as their spouses and children. They are granted by the Cancillería in Quito, Departamento de Asuntos Migratorios (moving offices at the close of this edition, probably to 10 de Agosto y Carrión, across the street from the main building of the Cancillería), open Monday-Friday 0930-1230. Non-immigrant visa fees vary from US$30 to US$200, plus a US$30 application fee. Outside the country, applications for all visas must be filed with Ecuador's diplomatic representatives (see box on page 32). Allow several months for the application process.

After arriving in Ecuador, both immigrant and non-immigrant visa holders (but not tourists) must register first with the Dirección Nacional de Extranjería in Quito (address above) and then with the immigration police office in the province where they will live, in order to obtain their *censo* (foreign resident census card), which must be renewed annually. Those with immigrant visas must additionally get a *cédula* (national identity card) from the *Registro Civil*. Foreign men up to age 55 with immigrant visas must also obtain a *cédula militar* from the armed forces. Immigrant visa holders many not leave Ecuador for more than 90 days a year, during the first two years of their visas, nor for more than 18 consecutive months at any time; these restrictions do not apply to non-immigrant visas. All visas must periodically be renewed by the same government agencies which grant them. A request for a change of visa category must be filed at least 30 days prior to the expiration of your current visa.

All immigration procedures are complex and time-consuming, and the regulations frequently change. Many expatriates therefore choose to retain the services of a specialized lawyer, although this is not always required. Be sure to get a personal recommendation, however, before hiring such an immigration attorney, as some are unscrupulous and will severely overcharge as well as creating more problems than they resolve.

Tourists may leave Ecuador at any time with only their passport and the international **Leaving** embarkation/disembarkation card which they were issued on arrival. Other foreigners face **Ecuador** varying requirements, including a *salida* (exit permit) issued by the immigration police and *Remember to reconfirm* valid for one year; as well as the *censo*, *cédula*, and *cédula militar* mentioned above. Foreign *international flights* minors (other than tourists) travelling alone, or accompanied by only one parent, require *72 hours in advance* authorization from the *Tribunal de Menores* before they are allowed to leave Ecuador.

In addition to your passport, the following documents are useful for a visit to Ecuador. **Doccuments to** A **vaccination certificate** is seldom asked for in Ecuador but must nonetheless be **bring with you** carried by all international travellers. For details see Vaccinations, page 83.

A valid local **driving licence** from any country in the world is generally sufficient to rent a car and drive in Ecuador. An international driving licence is therefore not indispensable. See Car documents, page 55, for further details.

An **International Student Identity Card** (ISIC) may help you obtain discounts when travelling in Ecuador. See Student travellers, page 28, for further details.

Leave the following documents at home with a friend or relative whom you can easily **Documents to** contact in case of emergency: your birth certificate or citizenship certificate, a **leave at home** photocopy of your passport, copies of your airline tickets and copies (not originals) of purchase receipts for any travellers' cheques you bring with you. Do not bring any unnecessary personal documents which you cannot use in Ecuador, but which would be inconvenient to replace should they be lost or stolen. Examples include a work ID or social security card: purge your purse or wallet of these before you travel.

Insurance
Travel insurance is extremely important for all visitors to Ecuador

An adequate insurance policy should include coverage for the damage, loss, or theft of your belongings as well as health care in the event of accident or illness. You may also wish to consider coverage for repatriation by air ambulance in the event of a serious mishap. There are so many different types of policies offered worldwide that it is difficult to make specific recommendations. In all cases, however, you should read the fine print before leaving home and be sure to bring all the necessary contact information with you. Notify your insurer as soon as possible in the event of a claim. You will almost certainly have to pay all expenses out-of-pocket in Ecuador (be sure to keep detailed receipts) and request reimbursement after you return home. For this reason having some extra cash on hand is also part of your travel insurance.

Customs   **On arrival**   Customs inspection is carried out at airports after you clear immigration. When travelling by land, customs authorities may also set up checkpoints along the country's highways. Tourists seldom encounter any difficulties but if you are planning to bring any particularly voluminous, unusual, or valuable items to Ecuador (for example professional video equipment, a boat or desktop computer) then you should enquire beforehand with an Ecuadorean diplomatic representative (see box on page 32) and obtain any necessary permits, or be prepared to pay the prevailing customs duties. Reasonable amounts of climbing gear and one used laptop computer per family are generally not a problem. For details on bringing a vehicle into Ecuador see under Car documents, page 55. Never bring any firearms.

Shipping goods to Ecuador   Except for documents, customs duties must be paid on all goods shipped to Ecuador. Enforcement is strict, duties are high and procedures are slow and complicated. You are therefore advised to bring anything you think you will need with you when you travel, rather than having it sent to you once you are in the country.

On departure   Your baggage may be inspected by security personnel and will always be sniffed by dogs searching for drugs. Never transport anything you have not packed yourself, you will be held responsible for the contents. No export duties are charged on souvenirs you take home from Ecuador, but there are various items for which you require special permits. These include specimens of wild plants and animals, original archaeological artefacts, certain works of art and any objects considered part of the country's national heritage. When in doubt, enquire well in advance.

Vaccinations
& malaria pills

Check malaria prophylaxis for lowland rural areas to be visited, including the Oriente and Pacific coast. Malaria pills are not required for Galápagos. See Health, page 83, for details of recommended vaccinations,

What to take

See Health, page 85, for a medical checklist. A good general principle is to take half the clothes and twice the money you think you will need

Everybody has their own list. Obviously what you take depends on your individual travel style, your budget and what you plan to do. Listed below are a few things which are particularly useful for travelling in Ecuador. There are a million-and-one other travel accessories and gadgets on the market, all of which may well prove useful in the appropriate circumstances. At the same time, however, you should try to think light and compact. The less weight you have to carry around and the fewer your belongings which might be lost or stolen, the more carefree and enjoyable will be your travels. All but the most specialized products are available in Quito and Guayaquil, while many basic commodities are readily purchased throughout the country.

A **moneybelt** or pouch is absolutely indispensable for everyone, see Protecting money and valuables, page 46. Be sure to bring an adequate supply of any **medications** you take on a regular basis, plus two weeks spare, as these may not be available in Ecuador. Sturdy comfortable **footwear** is a must for travels anywhere, and Ecuador's uneven sidewalks, dirt roads and muddy country trails are no exception. Sun protection is very important in all regions of the country and for visitors of all complexions. This should include a **sun hat**, high quality **sun glasses** and **sun screen** for both skin and lips. Take **insect repellent** if you plan to visit the coast or jungle. Also recommended are **rubber sandals** or thongs for use on the beach, at hot springs and in hotel showers, where they protect against both athlete's foot and electric shock when instant-heating shower heads are used. If you use contact lenses, be sure also to bring a pair of **eye glasses**. A small lightweight **towel** is an asset, as is a short length of **travel clothesline**, which can be purchased or made of braided elastic, eliminating the need for pegs. A compact **torch** (flashlight), **alarm watch** and **pocket knife** may all be useful. Always carry some **toilet paper**, as this is seldom found in public washrooms unless it is sold at the entrance.

Money

There are a variety of different ways for visitors to bring their funds to Ecuador. You are strongly advised to combine two or more of these, so as not to be stuck if there are problems with any one alternative. US cash in small denominations is by far the simplest and the only universally accepted option, but clearly a serious risk for loss or theft. Travellers' cheques are safe, but can only be exchanged for cash in the larger cities and up to 5% commission may be charged (although it is usually less). Credit cards can be used to obtain a cash advance at some branches of some banks, and to pay at most upmarket establishments, but a surcharge may be applied. Internationally linked banking machines or ATMs are common in Ecuador, although their use involves certain risks (see below) and they cannot always be relied on. Funds may be rapidly wired to Ecuador by *Western Union*, but high fees and taxes apply. Although Euros are slowly gaining acceptance, it is best not to bring any currencies other than US dollars to Ecuador, neither as cash nor travellers' cheques; they are difficult to exchange and generally fetch a poor rate.

There is simply no substitute for cash-in-hand when travelling in Ecuador. Always bring some (but not all) of your funds as small US dollar bills

Currency

Since 2000, the **US dollar** is the only official currency of Ecuador. Only US dollar bills circulate, in the following denominations: $1, $2 (rare), $5, $10, $20, $50 and $100. US coins are used alongside the equivalent size and value Ecuadorean coins for $0.01, $0.05, $0.10, $0.25, $0.50 and US$1 (US-minted bronze dollar). Ecuadorean coins have no value outside the country. Many merchants are reluctant to accept bills larger than $20, both because counterfeit notes are a problem and because change may be scarce. Travellers should carefully check any bills they receive as change. Ecuador has reluctantly come to terms with its new currency, but a few old-timers, especially in small towns, may still think in terms of the country's previous monetary unit, the **sucre**, which was used for over a century. The last exchange rate for the sucre was 25,000 to US$1. Today, sucre notes and coins have no value except as souvenirs.

Travellers' cheques

US dollar travellers' cheques can be exchanged for cash in Ecuador, but usually only in Quito, Guayaquil, Cuenca, some resorts and the larger provincial capitals. *American Express* is the most widely accepted brand. The following banks exchange travellers' cheques at some but not all of their branches (commissions fluctuate with time and from branch to branch): *Banco de Guayaquil*, 1% commission; *Banco del Pacífico*, US$5 flat fee per transaction, maximum US$200 exchanged; *Banco del Pichincha*, 2% commission and the longest line-ups; *Produbanco*, 1% commission. Be prepared for long queues and paperwork at all banks. Travellers' cheques may only be exchanged during limited hours, which also fluctuate, best being Monday-Friday until 1300. A passport is required and, less frequently, the original purchase receipt for the travellers' cheques. *Casas de cambio* (exchange houses) may also change travellers' cheques, and are generally more efficient than banks, but there are not many of these establishments left after dollarization.

The more expensive hotels, restaurants and tour agencies generally accept travellers' cheques, but a surcharge may be applied and smaller establishments may not accept them at all, especially outside major centres. A good strategy therefore is to gradually convert your travellers' cheques to cash, whenever you visit a larger city. *Banco del Pichincha* in Cuenca (and only in Cuenca) charges no commission and is recommended, although terms are subject to change. *American Express* has offices in Quito and Guayaquil and they offer a very efficient service. They sell travellers' cheques against an Amex card (or a cardholder's personal cheque) and replace them if lost or stolen, but they do not give cash for travellers' cheques, nor travellers' cheques for cash. A police report is required if they are stolen.

Credit cards The most commonly accepted credit cards in Ecuador include Visa, MasterCard, Diners, and to a lesser extent American Express. Many smaller hotels, restaurants, tour agencies and shops may display credit card signs but not honour the cards 'just at the moment', or they may apply a surcharge (at least 10%) for credit card customers. Luxury or first-class establishments will usually have no difficulty honouring most credit cards. MasterCard holders can obtain cash advances at the company's offices in Quito, Guayaquil, Cuenca and Ambato as well as at some branches of *Banco de Guayaquil*, *Mutualista Pichincha* and *Produbanco*. Those with Visa cards can obtain cash advances at some branches of *Banco del Austro*, *Banco de Guayaquil* and *Banco del Pichincha*. In addition, cash advances on both Visa and Mastercard may be obtained through some ATMs (see below). Remember that you will be charged interest on cash advances; check with your home bank or credit card company before travelling to see what interest rates and regulations apply.

ATMs ATMs or banking machines are very common throughout Ecuador, and many are linked to international systems such as Plus or Cirrus. Visitors with the appropriately encoded credit cards or bank cards can therefore obtain cash from these machines. ATMs linked to Cirrus are found in most banks affiliated with MasterCard, whereas those linked to Plus are found in most banks affiliated with Visa (see above). These affiliations, however, change often in Ecuador and you have to ask around. Always check with your home bank before travelling regarding charges and conditions which apply to international ATM transactions. Also bear in mind that these electronic systems are not always reliable in Ecuador. They may be out of order or run out of cash, they may refuse to accept a valid card or even confiscate it, and the card is then very difficult to retrieve. Thieves and con-artists sometimes stake out ATMs and attempt to get hold of your card and Personal Identification Number (PIN), or simply rob you once you have withdrawn some cash.

Money transfers In addition to the above means of payment, you may need to have funds sent from your home, either on a routine basis or in an emergency. Bank transfers, wires, telexes or cables to Ecuador are not recommended for this purpose, because of potentially long delays, high taxes and service charges. *Western Union* has offices throughout Ecuador and can reliably transfer funds into or out of the country in a matter of minutes, but high taxes and charges also apply. The most efficient and economical alternative is to purchase travellers' cheques on an Amex card or with a personal cheque, as described above. Note that money orders are not accepted anywhere in Ecuador. If all else fails, you might have someone send you a small amount of US cash by regular airmail, with each bill carefully concealed in a separate envelope. This is prone to theft of course, and contravenes international postal regulations, but you may have no other choice in a pinch.

With the implementation of dollarization in 2000 the Ecuadorean economy stabilized and, at the same time, prices slowly began to rise. Ecuador nonetheless remains well within the reach of the budget traveller and even among the better deals in South America. A very basic daily travel budget is currently US$15 per person, based on two people travelling together as cheaply as possible. For US$40 a day, you can have a good deal of comfort and even a little elegance, while US$100 is getting up into the luxury range. It is impossible to predict the future, but a reasonable assumption is that the cost of living will continue slowly to increase for some time. **The prices given above and throughout this book are current at the time of publication, and the traveller should expect them to gradually rise thereafter.** Despite the US dollar economy however, it seems most unlikely that prices in Ecuador will reach or even approach international levels, and the country should remain a good travel bargain for the foreseeable future.

Cost of living
For hotel and restaurant price ranges, see inside front cover and boxes on pages 50 and 64

Essentials

Getting there

Air

International flights into Ecuador arrive either at Quito or Guayaquil. Many visitors prefer to begin their trip in Quito. This is where you will find most sources of tourist information, tour agencies, language schools and the widest selection of hotels and restaurants in the intermediate price range. If your flight only goes to Guayaquil, there are frequent shuttle flights up to the capital if you do not want to go overland. International airfares from North America and Europe to Ecuador vary with low and high season. The latter is generally July to September and December. International flights to Ecuador from other South or Central American countries, however, usually have one price year-round. The monthly guide *Transport*, available at most travel agencies, gives details of international and national flights and phone numbers of airlines in Quito and Guayaquil. Flight frequency changes regularly. You should always check current timetables.

For cheap flights, try www.fly4less.com www.flynow.com www.dialaflight.com www.what'onwhen. com

KLM offers departures from many European cities, including 16 UK airports, to Quito via Amsterdam. *Iberia* flies to Quito from Madrid. *Lufthansa* and *Air France* fly from Frankfurt and Paris, respectively, to Bogotá, where passengers are transferred to local carriers for the flight to Quito. *Continental Airlines* flies to Quito and Guayaquil from London Gatwick, Dublin, Shannon, Paris, Frankfurt, Dusseldorf, Rome, Milan, Lisbon and Madrid; all flights are via Newark or Houston. *American Airlines* flies to Quito and Guayaquil from various European cities via Miami.

From Europe
It is generally cheaper to fly from London rather than a point in Europe to Latin America

Miami's heavily congested international airport is by far the most important air transport hub linking Ecuador with all of North America. *American Airlines* has at least one flight daily from Miami to each of Quito and Guayaquil; on some days there are two flights. *Lan Chile* (whose local operations are being renamed *Lan Ecuador*) also flies from Miami to Quito and Guayaquil. Cheaper fares from Miami to Quito or Guayaquil

From North America

Essentials

▶▶ Discount flight agents

Australia and New Zealand

Flight Centres, 82 Elizabeth St, Sydney, T13-1600; 205 Queen St, Auckland, T09-309 6171. Also branches in other towns and cities.

STA Travel, T1300-360960, www.statravelaus.com.au; 702 Harris St, Ultimo, Sydney, and 256 Flinders St, Melbourne. In NZ: 10 High St, Auckland, T09-366 6673. Also in major towns and university campuses.

Travel.com.au, 80 Clarence St, Sydney, T02-929 01500, www.travel.com.au

UK and Ireland

Council Travel, 28a Poland St, London W1V 3DB, T020-74377767, www.destinations-group.com

STA Travel, 86 Old Brompton Rd, London SW7 3LH, T020-7437 6262, www.statravel.co.uk They have other branches in London, as well as in Brighton, Bristol, Cambridge, Leeds, Manchester, Newcastle-Upon-Tyne and Oxford and on many university campuses. Specialists in low-cost student/youth flights and tours, also good for student IDs and insurance.

Trailfinders, 194 Kensington High Street, London W8 7RG, T020-7938 3939.

North America

Air Brokers International, 323 Geary St, Suite 411, San Francisco, CA94102, T01-800-883 3273, www.airbrokers.com Consolidator and specialist on RTW and Circle Pacific tickets.

Council Travel, 205 E 42nd St, New York, NY 10017, T1-888-COUNCIL, www.counciltravel.com Student/budget agency with branches in many other US cities.

Discount Airfares Worldwide On-Line, www.etn.nl/discount.htm A hub of consolidator and discount agent links.

International Travel Network/Airlines of the Web, www.itn.net/airlines Online air travel information and reservations.

STA Travel, 5900 Wilshire Blvd, Suite 2110, Los Angeles, CA 90036, T1-800-777 0112, www.sta-travel.com Also branches in New York, San Francisco, Boston, Miami, Chicago, Seattle and Washington DC.

Travel CUTS, 187 College St, Toronto, ON, M5T 1P7, T1-800-667 2887, www.travelcuts.com Specialist in student discount fares, Ids and other travel services. Branches in other Canadian cities.

Travelocity, www.travelocity.com Online consolidator.

may be offered by *Copa Airlines*, which flies via Panama City, and *TACA*, which flies via San José, Costa Rica. Several South American airlines may also offer competitive fares from Miami to Quito or Guayaquil via their respective capital cities. *Continental Airlines* flies to Quito and Guayaquil from less congested Houston and Newark, with some flights routed through Panama City.

From Australia & New Zealand
See also box above

There are three options: 1) To Los Angeles (USA) with *Qantas*, *Air New Zealand* or *United*, continuing to Quito via Houston with *Continental*. 2) To Papetete (Tahiti) with *Qantas* or *Air New Zealand*, continuing to Quito via Easter Island and Santiago (Chile) with *Lan Chile*. 3) To Buenos Aires (Argentina) from Aukland with *Aerolineas Argentinas*, continuing to Quito with *Lan Chile* or another South American carrier. These are all expensive long-haul routes. The 'Circle Pacific' fares offered by some airline alliances, such as *One World* or *Star Alliance*, may be convenient alternatives.

From Latin American cities

There are direct flights to Quito and/or Guayaquil from Santiago, Lima, Bogotá, Caracas, Panama City, San José (Costa Rica) and Havana. Easy connections can be made with other South American cities. *Copa Airlines* has a hub in Panama City which offers convenient connections between Ecuador and various destinations in Central America, Mexico and the Caribbean.

Road and river

There are regular connections by bus to Quito and Guayaquil from Peru and Colombia (note public safety concerns in the latter), as well as South American countries farther afield, but no vehicle road connecting Central and South America. The most commonly used overland routes are via the Tulcán-Ipiales border crossing in the north, and the Huaquillas-Aguas Verdes border in the south, although Macará-La Tina-Sullana is an increasingly attractive crossing with Peru. There are also several new border crossings to Peru. The most frequented of these is Zumba-San Ignacio, where a vehicle bridge was under construction in 2002, but you could already cross on foot. You can also cross on foot from Lalamor, and by vehicle from Jimbura, both remote villages in the province of Loja. For details of river travel to and from Peru, see Boats in Coca (page 368). For details

on immigration procedures at these borders, see under the relevant sections of respective towns. Note that it is usually much cheaper to buy bus tickets as far as the nearest border town, cross on foot or by taxi, and then purchase tickets locally in the country you have just entered. There are some exceptions however, or times when the convenience of a direct service outweighs additional cost. For example, there are particularly convenient services from Loja and from Machala, direct to Piura, Peru. If entering Ecuador by car, details of customs procedures are given on page 53.

Touching down

Airport information

Essentials

For most visitors, the point of arrival will be **Mariscal Sucre airport** in Quito. For details of Guayaquil's **Simón Bolívar airport** see page 278.

Taxi The safest and easiest way to travel between town and the airport is to take a taxi. You can catch one from the rank right outside arrivals. The fare from the airport to the New City is about US$3-4; to the Old City or to a first-class hotel US$4-5 (more at night, but beware of overcharging). Alternatively, you can use the Trans-Rabbit van service, they have a booth at international arrivals, T227 6736, US$2-3 pp to the New City in a van with room for up to 15 passengers. This is good value if there are a few people sharing. To order a taxi by phone, see Taxis, on page 59.

Public transport to & from airport

Bus This is **not recommended** unless you have virtually no luggage or are desperately low on funds. Buses and trolley alike are usually too crowded for you to enter with even a small backpack and the chances of having something vanish on route are very high. If you really have no other choice, the bus stop is one block from the terminal to the west (towards Pichincha), in front of *Centro Comercial Aeropuerto*. For the New City take a southbound red bus marked 'Carcelén-Congreso' or 'Pinar Alto-Hotel Quito', these run along Av Amazonas and later C Juan León Mera, fare US$0.20. For the Old City and parts of the New City, take a green *alimentador* (feeder bus line) at the same bus stop, it goes to the northern terminus of the trolley, where you transfer to the trolley line; combined fare US$0.20.

There is no bus or trolley service late at night when most flights from North America arrive. Do not even think of walking into town at such times, take a cab

Quito airport is a bit cramped but functional. There are often long queues for international departures and most airlines recommend you arrive three hours before your flight. Always reconfirm international flights 72 hours in advance.

The airport is divided into four contiguous sections which are only a minute's walk from each other. From north to south are: international arrivals, international departures, national arrivals and national departures. Left luggage facilities are just outside international arrivals. There is a telephone office upstairs in international departures, plus a few debit card-operated public phones downstairs; buy the debit cards at one of the airport shops. There is a post office outside, between international departures and national arrivals. Also upstairs in international departures is a bar-restaurant which serves meals and snacks, and a fast food place in national departures; both are pricey. There are expensive souvenir shops in international departures and luxury duty-free in the international departure lounge, after you clear immigration. All the main car rental companies are located just outside international arrivals. For details of their offices in Quito, see page 133.

Airport facilities
Due to the lack of hotels near the airport, it is best to take a cab into town. See Choosing a hotel in Quito, page 104

NB Beware of self-styled porters: men or boys who will grab your luggage and offer to find you a cab in the hope of receiving a tip or stealing your bags. Legitimate porters wear ID tags and there is no shortage of taxis right at hand. Watch your gear at all times.

▶▶ Touching down

Official time *5 hrs behind GMT. The Galápagos is 6 hrs behind.*

Voltage *110 volts, 60 cycles, AC throughout Ecuador. Very low wattage bulbs are the rule in many cheaper hotel rooms, keen readers might want to carry a brighter bulb.*

Weights and measures *The metric system is generally used in foreign trade and must be used in legal documents. English measures are understood in the hardware and textile trades. Spanish measures are often used in the retail trade and in Indian markets.*

Airport departure tax A 12% tax is charged on international air tickets for flights originating in Ecuador, regardless of where bought, as well as on domestic tickets. A Quito departure tax of US$25 (US$10 in Guayaquil) is payable by all passengers leaving on international flights (except those who stay less than 24 hours in the country). Pay the departure tax when checking in with your airline, or at a booth in the international departures area. You will not be allowed to board without proof of payment.

Tourist information

For full details of the **Ecuadorean Ministry of Tourism**, **CAPTUR**, **SAE** and for on-line information, see Finding out more, page 25. The addresses of local tourist offices are given in the main travelling text.

Maps & city guides The **Instituto Geográfico Militar** in Quito (see page 139) produces a series of good topographic maps covering most of the country at the following scales: 1:250,000, 1:100,000, 1:50,000 and 1:25,000. The latter two scales are most useful for climbing and trekking. Maps of the seacoast and border areas are classified *(reservado)*, and cannot be purchased without a military permit. For further details see Maps in the Quito chapter, page 139. A recommended series of road maps and city guides by Nelson Gómez, published by *Ediguias* in Quito, includes handy pocket maps/guides of Quito, Guayaquil, Cuenca, Otavalo and Galápagos (the latter two in English). These are available in bookshops throughout the country, but most reliably in the capital.

Information for business travellers This is available from **Trade Partners UK**, a government network for British businesses overseas. Contact Pippa Lodge, T020-7215 4715, F7828 8141, pippa.lodge@ tradepartners.gov.uk The *Ecuadorean News Digest* is published by the **Ecuadorean American Association**, 150 Nassau St, New York, NY 10038. Also see Ecuadorean embassies and consulates, page 32.

Local customs and laws

Clothing Most Ecuadoreans, if they can afford it, devote great care to their clothes and appearance. It is appreciated if visitors do likewise. How you dress is mostly how people will judge you. This is particularly important when dealing with officials. Buying clothing locally can help you to look less like a tourist. In general, clothing is less formal in the lowlands, both on the coast and in Oriente, where men and women do wear shorts. In the highlands, people are far more conservative; wearing shorts is considered acceptable for sports and on hiking trails, but not at a church or cemetery. Do not go bare-chested in populated areas in the highlands. Nude bathing is unacceptable anywhere in Ecuador.

You should pack spring clothing for Quito (mornings and evenings are cold), but in Guayaquil tropical or light-weight clothes are needed. Women should pack one medium to long length skirt and men might want to consider bringing a smart sweater or jacket.

Suits and dresses are compulsory for business people. Good quality sweaters and wool shawls can be easily purchased in Ecuador and make good additions to your wardrobe.

Remember that politeness – even a little ceremoniousness – is expected and appreci- **Conduct** ated in Ecuador. In this connection professional or business cards are very useful. Men should always remove any headgear and say "con permiso" when entering offices, and be prepared to shake hands often; always say "Buenos días" (until midday), "Buenas tardes" (in the afternoon) or "Buenas Noches" (after dark) and wait for a reply before proceeding further. Remember that the traveller from abroad has enjoyed greater advantages in life than most Ecuadorean minor officials, and should be friendly and courteous in consequence. Never be impatient and do not criticize situations in public: the officials may know more English than you think and they can certainly interpret gestures and facial expressions. Politeness can be a liability, however, in some situations; most Ecuadoreans are disorderly queuers, except – interestingly enough – when lining up for the Quito trolley! In commercial transactions (buying a meal, taxis, goods in a shop etc) politeness should be accompanied by firmness; always ask the price first.

Politeness should also be extended to street vendors; saying "No, gracias" with a smile is far better than an arrogant dismissal. Whether you give money to beggars is a personal matter, but your decision should be influenced by whether a person is begging out of need or trying to cash in on the *gringo* trail. In the former case, local people giving may provide an indication. Giving money or candies to children is a separate issue, upon which most agree: don't do it. There are occasions where giving food in a restaurant may be appropriate, but first inform yourself of local practice. Instead of giving to beggars, consider donating your time or money to a community development project in Ecuador; see Volunteer programmes, page 81.

Ecuadoreans, like most Latin Americans, have a fairly relaxed attitude towards time. **Time-keeping** They will think nothing of arriving an hour or so late on social occasions. If you expect to meet someone at an exact time, you can tell them that you want to meet at such and such an hour "en punto".

In most of the better restaurants a 10% service charge is included in the bill, but you can **Tipping** give a modest extra tip if the service is especially good. The most basic restaurants do not include a tip in the bill, and tips are not expected. Taxi drivers are usually not tipped, but you can always round up the fare for particularly good service. Tipping for all other services is entirely discretionary, how much depends on the quality of service given.

Illegal drugs are the most common way for foreigners to get into serious trouble; see **Prohibitions** Drugs under Safety, page 47. Never carry **firearms**, their possession could also land you *Drugs' use or purchase* in difficulties. *is punishable by*

Ecuador is an open democratic society, but the conspicuous involvement of for- *up to 16 years'* eigners in local **politics** or other sensitive matters is seldom appreciated. The author- *imprisonment.* ities do not hesitate to arrest and swiftly deport those who are considered to have *Just don't do it!* overstepped their bounds. Such was the case in 2002 with European and North American environmentalists protesting the construction of an oil pipeline through the Mindo nature reserve. If you feel strongly about Ecuadorean matters and would like to bring your opinion to bear on them, then you will have far more success by proceeding discretely through local contacts, or by lobbying international organizations from your home country.

You are advised to avoid **litigation** under all circumstances. The Ecuadorean judicial system has many peculiarities and foreigners may be at a marked disadvantage in legal proceedings. If you find yourself unavoidably embroiled in a lawsuit, then it is safest to pursue the matter through legal counsel, without being physically present in the country. Even routine civil actions and commercial disputes have been known to lead to unexpected imprisonment.

Responsible tourism

Travel to the furthest corners of the globe is now commonplace and the mass movement of people for leisure and business is a major source of foreign income and economic development in many parts of South America. In some areas of Ecuador, such as the Galápagos Islands, it is by far the most significant economic activity. In the country as a whole, tourism is the third most important source of foreign revenue.

The benefits of international travel are self-evident for both hosts and travellers: employment, increased understanding of different cultures, business and leisure opportunities. At the same time there is clearly a downside to the industry. Where visitor pressure is high and/or poorly regulated, adverse impacts to society and the natural environment may be apparent. Paradoxically perhaps, this is as true in undeveloped and pristine areas (where culture and the natural environment are less prepared for even small numbers of visitors), as in major resort destinations.

The travel trade is growing rapidly and impacts of this supposedly 'smokeless' industry are becoming increasingly apparent worldwide. Ecuador is no exception, and may be especially vulnerable to adverse effects because of the country's small size and the high volume of tourism concentrated in certain areas. Sometimes these impacts may seem remote and unrelated to an individual trip or holiday (for example air travel is clearly implicated in global warming and damage to the ozone layer), but individual choice and awareness can make a difference in many instances (see box opposite), and collectively, travellers are having a significant effect in shaping a more responsible and sustainable industry.

In an attempt to promote awareness of and credibility for responsible tourism, organizations such as **Green Globe**, T0207-9308333, www.greenglobe21.com, and the **Centre for Environmentally Sustainable Tourism (CERT)**, T01268-795772, F795772, www.c-e-r-t.org, now offer advice on destinations and sites that have achieved certain commitments to conservation and sustainable development. Generally these are larger mainstream destinations and resorts but they are still a useful guide and increasingly aim to provide information on smaller operations.

Of course travel can also have beneficial impacts and this is something to which every traveller can contribute – many national parks are in part funded by receipts from visitors. Similarly, travellers can promote patronage and protection of important archaeological sites and heritage through their interest and contributions via entrance fees. They can also support small-scale enterprises by staying in locally run hotels and hostels, eating in local restaurants and by purchasing local goods, supplies and crafts. Such opportunities abound in Ecuador.

In fact, during the past decade there has been a phenomenal growth in tourism that promotes and supports the conservation of natural environments and is also fair and equitable to local communities. This 'eco-tourism' segment is probably the fastest growing sector of the travel industry in all of South America and especially in Ecuador. Perhaps the best known Ecuadorean example of such development on a large scale is the Kapawi lodge in southern Oriente (see under Macas, page 384). The more grassroots projects include: *Ricancie* on the upper Río Napo near Tena (see page 375), Sani lodge and Añangu on the lower Río Napo below Coca (see page 371) and Yachana lodge which is accessed from Misahuallí (see page 379). There are also many others.

While the authenticity of some eco-tourism operators' claims needs to be interpreted with care, there is clearly both a huge demand for this type of activity in Ecuador and also significant opportunities to support worthwhile conservation and social development initiatives.

Travelling responsibly

Where possible choose a destination, tour operator or hotel with a proven ethical and environmental commitment – if in doubt ask.
• Spend money on locally produced (rather than imported) goods and services and use common sense when bargaining – your few dollars saved may be a week's salary to others.
• Use water and electricity carefully – travellers may receive preferential supply while the needs of local communities are overlooked.
• Learn about local etiquette and culture – consider local norms and behaviour and dress appropriately for local cultures and situations.
• Protect wildlife and other natural resources – don't buy souvenirs or goods made from wildlife unless they are clearly sustainably produced and are not protected under CITES (the Convention on International Trade in Endangered Species).
• Don't give money or sweets to children – it encourages begging – instead give to a recognized project, charity or school.
• **Always ask before taking photographs or videos of people**, this is by far the most common indiscretion committed by most tourists in Ecuador.
• Consider staying in local accommodation rather than foreign-owned hotels – the economic benefits for host communities are far greater – and there are far greater opportunities to learn about local culture.
Mark Eckstein, Washington, DC, USA.

Organizations such as **Conservation International** (T1-202-4295660, www.ecotour.org), the **Eco-Tourism society** (T1-802-4472121, www.ecotourism.org), **Planeta** (www2.planeta.com/mader) and **Tourism Concern** (T020-7753 3330, www.tourismconcern.org.uk) have begun to develop and/or promote eco-tourism projects and destinations and their websites are an excellent source of information and details for sites and initiatives throughout South America. Additionally, organizations such as **Earthwatch** (US/Canada T1800-7760188, UK T01865-311601, www.earthwatch.org) and **Discovery International** (T020-7229 9881, www.discoveryinitiatives.com) offer opportunities to participate directly in scientific research and development projects throughout the region.

Ecuador offers unique and unforgettable experiences often based on the natural environment, cultural heritage and local society. These are the reasons many of us choose to travel here and why many more will want to do so in the future. Shouldn't we provide an opportunity for future travellers and hosts to enjoy the quality of experience and interaction that we take for granted?

Living in Ecuador

Since the early 1990s, Ecuador has attracted increasing numbers of foreign residents. They have swelled the ranks of the country's traditional expatriates (diplomats, NGO volunteers and multinational employees), with retirees of all ages, as well as those seeking a new and interesting start. Many of the latter have opened businesses in the tourist trade and their growing numbers, as well as the presence of illegal migrants, has at times prompted the authorities to tighten controls. In 2002, concern over the influx of Colombians coming to live in Ecuador (as a result of armed conflict in that neighbouring country), gave rise to calls for a clamp-down on all immigration.

Also see Visas for longer stays, page 33

Ecuadoreans have traditionally welcomed outsiders warmly, although a certain cultural barrier was always noticeable, especially in the highlands and even more so among indigenous inhabitants. Growing numbers of successful foreign-owned businesses however, particularly when heavily concentrated in small towns like Otavalo,

Essentials

▶▶ The gringo trail

There exists in Ecuador a well defined route for many travellers. It runs roughly from north to south through Otavalo, for its market; Quito, from which a climbing excursion may be taken; Baños, from which a jungle excursion may be taken; Riobamba, for the train ride; Cuenca, to visit Ingapirca; and Vilcabamba, for a well-deserved rest. This 'gringo trail' offers the best opportunities for socializing with other travellers, finding facilities and services geared specifically to foreign tastes and of course seeing a few of

the tourist highlights of the country.

There is however more – so much more – to be experienced in Ecuador. The country remains a treasure trove of spectacular places and unforgettable experiences, all waiting to be discovered and responsibly explored beyond the gringo trail. You are heartily encouraged to venture further afield and do some real exploring on your own, to get to know Ecuadoreans as well as fellow tourists and to take home a more sincere impression of the country.

Baños or Vilcabamba, have generated their share of envy and anti-gringo sentiment among some segments of the local population.

Ecuador as a whole remains, in many ways, a pleasant and thoroughly interesting place for a foreigner to make his or her home. It is not, however, without its important risks and challenges, for which the outsider must be well prepared. Come and enjoy an extended visit and get to know the country before making major life choices.

Safety

See page 30 for information on women travelling alone Ecuador lost its innocence during the 1990s, prior to which it had been a remarkable island of peace and tranquillity. The incongruously peaceful reputation still lingers however, leading some visitors to mistakenly let down their guard. Today, safe and hassle-free travels remain the rule in Ecuador but cannot be taken for granted, they require a conscious effort on the part of every visitor. Routine precautions are generally sufficient to ensure a wonderful visit but the consequences of carelessness can be very severe. Please be careful and have a great time.

Protecting money & valuables
Make photocopies of important documents and give them to your family, embassy and travelling companion, this will speed up replacement if documents are lost or stolen and will still allow you to have some ID while getting replacements

Keep all documents (including your passport, airline tickets and credit cards) secure and hide your main cash supply in several different places. If one stash is lost or stolen, you will still have the others to fall back on. The following means of concealing cash and documents have all been recommended: extra pockets sewn inside shirts and trousers; pockets closed with a zip or safety pin; moneybelts (best worn below the waist and never within sight); neck or leg pouches; and elastic support bandages for keeping money and travellers' cheques above the elbow or below the knee. Never carry valuables in an ordinary pocket, purse or day-pack. Cargo pockets on shorts or trousers are especially prone to being picked or slashed.

You should keep cameras in bags or briefcases and generally out of sight. Do not wear expensive wrist watches or any jewellery. Even prescription eyeglasses can be a target if they have expensive looking frames; take a spare set or your prescription just in case. If you wear a shoulder-bag in a market, carry it in front of you. Backpacks should be lockable but are nonetheless vulnerable to slashers: in crowded places wear your day-pack on your chest with both straps looped over your shoulders. Whenever visiting an area which is particularly unsafe (see below) take the bare minimum of belongings with you.

Hotel security The cheapest hotels are usually found near markets and bus stations but these are also the least safe areas of most Ecuadorean towns. Look for something a little better if you can afford it, and if you must stay in a suspect area, always return to your hotel before dark. It is best, if you can trust your hotel, to leave any valuables you don't need in their safe-deposit box. But always keep an inventory of what you have deposited. If you don't trust the hotel, change hotels to one you feel safe in. If there is only one choice for places to stay, lock everything in your pack and secure that in your room; a light bicycle chain or cable and a small padlock will provide at least a psychological deterrent for would-be thieves. Even in an apparently safe hotel, do not leave valuable objects strewn about your room. Would *you* be tempted to pocket a camera worth two years of your salary?

Pickpockets, bag snatchers and slashers are always a hazard for tourists, especially in crowded areas such as markets or the downtown cores of major cities. Keep alert and avoid swarms of people. Crowded city buses and the Quito trolley are another magnet for thieves. Criminal gangs, at times well armed, also operate in the larger cities of Ecuador, especially in poor neighbourhoods and at night. You should likewise avoid deserted areas, such as parks or plazas after hours. If someone follows you when you're in the street, slip into a nearby shop or hail a cab. If you are the victim of an armed assault, never resist or hold back your valuables; they can always be replaced but your health or life cannot. Always purchase travel insurance before visiting Ecuador.

Urban street crime

The old scam of smearing tourists with mustard, ketchup, shaving cream and almost anything else, in order to distract and rob them, is currently enjoying a revival, especially in Quito. An apparently well meaning bystander usually helps clean you up, while their accomplice expertly cleans you out. Ignore remarks like "Hey, what's that on your shoulder?" or "Have you seen that dirt on your shoe?", and move along quickly to a secure location. Furthermore, don't bend over to pick up money or other items in the street.

The smear campaign

Banditry on the roads of Ecuador is a serious problem and occurs mostly at night. Travel only by daylight. There is plenty of daytime service going everywhere, and you never have to take a night bus. Risking your life and all your belongings in order to save the cost of a night's accomdation is the ultimate in penny wise, pound foolish, thinking. Also see Bus travel tips (page 52) for important safety suggestions.

Highway robbery

Be especially careful arriving at or leaving from bus stations. They are obvious places to catch people (tourists or not) with a lot of important belongings. Do not set your bag down without putting your foot on it, even to just double check your tickets or look at your watch; it will grow legs and walk away. Day-packs are easy to grab and run with, and are generally filled with your most important belongings. Take taxis to and from bus stations in major cities (look on it as an inexpensive insurance policy).

The countryside and small towns are generally the safest areas of Ecuador, and fortunately account for the largest and most interesting parts of the country. The Galápagos Islands are also particularly safe. The big cities – Quito, Guayaquil, and to a lesser extent Cuenca – call for the greatest care. The coast is slightly more prone to violence than the highlands, but hard drinking at *fiestas* can bring out the worst in people anywhere. The northern border with Colombia, including the provinces of Esmeraldas, Carchi, and especially Sucumbíos, call for special precautions. Armed conflict and the drug trade in Colombia has affected all northern border areas. Do not travel to this region without first carefully enquiring about the current public safety situation.

Dangerous areas

Although drugs are readily available, anyone found carrying even the smallest amount may be automatically considered a trafficker. If arrested on any charge the wait for trial in prison can take several years. Your foreign passport will not shield you in this situation, indeed you may be dealt with more harshly because of it. Honest officials may wish to make an example of you, while corrupt ones will try to squeeze you or your family for as much money as they can. If you are unconvinced, then visit an Ecuadorean

Drugs

Almost all foreigners serving long sentences in Ecuador's squalid jails are there for possession of illegal drugs

prison to see for yourself. Your embassy or consulate can give you the names of citizens of your country serving sentences who would appreciate a visitor.

Some people come to Ecuador specifically to consume or buy drugs, and the *gringo* drug scene shifts from place to place every couple of years. Quito nightlife is always prone to drug problems and Montañita, on the Pacific coast, is currently among the worst spots in the country. The authorities carry out sporadic raids in these places, and nobody is spared. Although drug planting by police is rare in Ecuador, the greatest risk is where drugs are most common. Even if you are not personally involved with drugs, you place yourself at considerable risk by associating with Ecuadoreans or foreigners who are.

Police

Emergency police phone number: 911 in Quito, 101 elsewhere

A special tourist police (uniformed and identified by arm-bands) operates in old town Quito, Otavalo, Cotopaxi National Park and the Chimborazo Fauna Reserve as well as a few other locations; they may be approached for advice and assistance. Police on bicycles patrol some of Quito's parks, and mounted police sometimes do likewise in La Mariscal nightlife district. Almost all police officers are helpful and friendly to tourists.

Unfortunately institutional corruption, including police corruption, is an important problem in Ecuador. Tourists are seldom affected but should be sensitive to the situation. If you are asked for a bribe (the polite euphemism is *'algo para la colita'*, a little something for a soft drink), then it is best to play innocent; be patient and the official will usually relent. This will also discourage harassment of other *gringos*. Never offer to bribe a police officer: you don't know the rules, so don't try to play the game.

Con tricks involving real or fake police officers are uncommon in Ecuador. You should nonetheless be wary of 'plainclothes policemen', politely insist on seeing identification and know that you have the right to write it all down. Do not get in a cab with any police officer, real or not. Tell them you will walk to the nearest police station. The real police only have the right to see your passport (not your money, tickets or hotel room) but before handing anything over, ask why they need to see it and make sure you understand the reason. Do not hand over your identification freely and insist on going to the station first. On no account take them directly back to your lodgings. Be even more suspicious if they seek confirmation of status from a passer-by.

Social unrest

Ecuadorean society has a remarkably long fuse. Despite several episodes of political and social unrest in the late 1990s, these did not lead to bloodshed. The social climate stabilized between 2000 and 2002, but visitors should know how to react (and not overreact) in the event of social unrest. Strikes and protests are usually announced days or weeks in advance, keep abreast of the local news and make your travel plans accordingly. The most significant impact of strikes on tourists is the restriction of overland travel; activities in towns and especially the countryside often go on as usual. Stay put at such times and make the most of visiting nearby attractions, rather than trying to stick to your original itinerary or return to Quito at all costs; the situation will soon blow over.

The last word on safety

If you remember nothing else from all of the foregoing, keep the following basic precautions in mind: **use a moneybelt**, **travel only by daylight** and **don't mess with drugs**. Furthermore, a relaxed and confident attitude is by far your best defence. A friendly smile, even when you've just thwarted a thief's attempt, can help you out of trouble. You should take even more comfort from the fact that the overwhelming majority of people in Ecuador are exceptionally well meaning. They are far more likely to go out of their way to help you than to hurt you.

Where to stay

Ecuador has hotels to suit every budget and in many places there are establishments which offer excellent value while catering to international travellers' tastes, particularly where foreign tourists go and foreigners have opened facilities (for example Otavalo, Baños, Vilcabamba) and in larger towns and cities. The greatest selection and most upscale establishments are found in the largest cities and more popular resorts. In less visited places the choice of better class hotels may be limited, but friendly and functional family-run lodgings can be had almost everywhere.

There is no regulated terminology for categories of accommodations in Ecuador, but you should be aware of the generally accepted meanings for the following. *Hotel* is the generic term, much as it is in English. *Hospedaje* means accommodations, of any kind. *Pensión* and *residencial* usually refer to more modest and economical establishments. An *hostal* or *posada* (inn) may be an elegant expensive place, while *hosterías* or *haciendas* usually offer upmarket rural lodgings. A *motel* is not a 'motor hotel' as it is in North America, rather it is a place where couples go for a few hours of privacy.

Hotel owners may try to let their less attractive rooms first, but they are not insulted if you ask for a bigger room, better beds or a quieter area. In cities, remember that rooms away from the street will usually be less noisy. The difference is often marked. Likewise, if you feel a place is overpriced then do not hesitate to bargain politely. Always take a look at the rooms and facilities before you check in, there are usually several nearby hotels to choose from and a few minutes spent selecting among them can make the difference between a pleasant stay and miserable one.

In cheaper places, do not merely ask about hot water (or any water for that matter); open the tap and see for yourself. Tall travellers (above 180 cm) should note that many cheaper hotels, especially in the highlands, are built with the modest stature of local residents in mind. Make sure you fit in the bed and remember to duck for doorways.

Air conditioning is only of interest in the lowlands of the coast and Oriente. If you want an air conditioned room expect to pay around 30% extra, otherwise look for a place with a good fan or sea breeze, and mosquito net. Conversely, hot water is only necessary in the highlands, where almost all places have it. A cool shower feels refreshing in the steamy climate of the coast and jungle, where only expensive tourist lodgings would think of heating water. The electric showers frequently used in cheaper hotels should be treated with respect. If you do not know how to use them, then ask someone to show you, and always wear rubber sandals or thongs.

Most better hotels have their own restaurants serving all meals. Few budget places have this facility, though some may serve a simple breakfast. Better hotels will often have their own secure parking but even more modest ones can usually recommend a nearby safe public parking lot. Most places have sufficient room to safely park a bicycle or motorcycle.

Some hotels charge per person or per bed, while others have a set rate per room regardless of the number of occupants. If travelling alone, it is usually cheaper to share with others in a room with three or four beds.

Due to increasingly strict tax enforcement even some cheaper hotels now charge 12% *IVA* (VAT or sales tax), but enquire beforehand if this is already included in their price. At the higher end of the scale 22% (12% tax + 10% service) is usually added to the bill.

The cheapest (and often nastiest) hotels can be found around markets, bus and train stations. If you're just passing through and need a bed for the night, they may be OK. In small towns, better accommodation may be found around the main plaza.

When booking a hotel from an airport or bus station by phone, always talk to the hotel yourself; do not let anyone do it for you. You may be told the hotel of your choice is full and be directed to one which pays a higher commission. Likewise, make sure that taxi drivers take you to the hotel you want, rather the one they think is best.

Hotels
At New Year, Easter and Carnival accommodation can sometimes be hard to find and prices are likely to rise. It is advisable to book in advance at these times and during school holidays and local festivals

Essentials

Essentials

▶▶ Hotel prices and facilities

Prices are for two people sharing a double room, including taxes and service charges **LL** (US$150 and over) and **L** (US$100-149) Hotels in these categories are usually only found in Quito, Guayaquil, Cuenca and the main tourist centres. They should offer pool, gym or spa, all business facilities, meeting rooms, banquet halls, several elegant restaurants, bars and often a small casino. Most will provide a safe deposit box in each room. Another set of options in this price range – although sometimes cheaper – are haciendas (country estates), a number of which have opened their doors to tourists. They generally provide a gracious and very traditional atmosphere, excellent food, activities such as horseback riding and the opportunity to experience life as it was lived by the country's élite in centuries gone by. **AL** (US$66-99), **A** (US$46-65) and **B** (US$31-45) The better value hotels in these categories provide a good deal more than standard facilities and comfort. Most will include breakfast and many offer 'extras' such as international cable TV, minibar, and tea and coffee making

facilities. They may also provide their own airport transfers. Service is generally very good and most accept credit cards. **C** (US$21-30) Hotels in this category range from very good to functional. You can expect your own bathroom, plenty of hot water, a towel, soap and toilet paper, TV, communal sitting area and a reasonably sized, comfortable room. **D** (US$12-20) an **E** (US$7-11) In hotels in this range you can expect cleanliness, sometimes a private bathroom, hot water in the highlands, maybe a small TV, a fan in tropical areas, but no other frills. **F** (US$4-6) and **G** (US$3 and under) A room in these price ranges usually consists of little more than a bed and four walls, with barely enough room to swing the proverbial cat. The bathroom is shared and soap, towels, toilet paper or a toilet seat are seldom supplied. In colder regions they may not have enough blankets, so take your own or a sleeping bag. In the lowlands insects are common in cheap hotels, use the mosquito net if one is provided (or bring your own) and ignore the cockroaches – they are harmless.

Many cheap hotels (as well as simple restaurants and bars) have inadequate water supplies. Almost without exception used toilet paper should not be flushed, but placed in the receptacle provided. This is also the case in most Ecuadorean homes and may apply even in quite expensive hotels, when in doubt ask. Tampons and sanitary napkins should likewise be disposed of in the rubbish bin. Failing to observe this custom will block the drain, a considerable health risk.

Camping   Camping in protected natural areas can be one of the most satisfying experiences during a visit to Ecuador – see Trekking, page 79, for details. Organized campsites, car or trailer camping on the other hand are virtually unheard of. Because of the abundance of cheap hotels you should never *have to* camp in Ecuador, except for cyclists who may be stuck between towns. In this case the best strategy is to ask permission to camp on someone's private land, preferably within sight of their home for safety. It is not safe to pitch your tent at random near villages and even less so on beaches. Those travelling with their own trailer or camper van can also ask permission to park overnight on private property, in a guarded parking lot or at a 24-hour gas station (although this may be noisy). It is unsafe to sleep in your vehicle on the street or roadside.

Homestays   Homestays are a good idea and growing in popularity, especially with travellers attending Spanish schools in Quito. The schools can make these arrangements as part of your programme. You can live with a local family for weeks or months, which is a good way to practise your Spanish and learn about the local culture. Do not be shy to change families however, if you feel uncomfortable with the one you have been assigned. Look for people who are genuinely interested in sharing (as you should also be), rather than merely providing room and board. Try a new place for a week or so, before signing up for an extended period.

Getting around

Air

TAME (www.tame.com.ec) is the main internal airline. It offers return flights from Quito to Cuenca, Esmeraldas, Galápagos (Baltra and San Cristóbal, for details see page 407), Guayaquil, Lago Agrio, Loja, Macas, Manta, Portoviejo and Tulcán; also from Guayaquil to Cuenca, Loja, Machala and Galápagos. *Airline offices are given under each relevant town or city*

Smaller local airlines include *Aerogal* (aerogal@andinanet.net), which flies Quito-Guayaquil; *Austro Aereo*, operating between Quito, Cuenca, Guayaquil and Macas; as well as *Icaro* (T1-800-883567, www.icaro.com.ec), serving Quito, Coca, Cuenca, Guayaquil, Lago Agrio and Loja. A few military fights serve isolated communities in Oriente, but these are generally not open to foreigners. Air taxis and charters can be organized to any airstrip in the country; to the jungle best from Quito or Shell, to the coast best from Guayaquil.

Ecuador is a small country and internal airfares are generally less than US$60 one way for all destinations except Galápagos, although they may rise if there is an increase in fuel prices. Flying times are typically under one hour. Foreigners must pay more than Ecuadoreans for flights to Galápagos and the Oriente. Routes and frequencies change often and up-to-date information may not be available outside Ecuador, so always enquire locally.

Seats are not assigned on internal flights, including to the Galápagos. Passengers may have to disembark at intermediate stops and check in again, even though they have booked all the way to the final destination of the plane. Make sure you confirm and reconfirm reservations frequently in order to avoid being bumped off your flight.

Rail

Sadly, the spectacular Ecuadorean railway system has all but ceased operations. In 2002 tourist rides were being offered over the Devil's Nose from Riobamba to Sibambe and back. From Quito, the only service was a weekend excursion to the El Boliche station near Cotopaxi National Park. Trains were running 45 km out of Ibarra and just for one hour out of San Lorenzo. *See box Railway to the Sierra, page 229, for a history of the Ecuadorean railway*

Road

The road network is extensive and because the country is not large and travelling times in many parts are not excessive, getting around by public transport is easy. The Panamericana runs down the length of the Andes connecting all the major towns and cities. A curiosity is that almost any large paved road may be referred to by locals as *'La Pana'*. **The road network** *Throughout Ecuador, intercity travel by car or bus is safest during the daytime*

The state of Ecuador's roads is constantly changing due to the cyclical forces of nature and the lack of ongoing maintenance. Rainy seasons in general, and the *El Niño* climatic phenomenon in particular, can cause heavy damage in both the highlands and coast. When the roads reach an intolerable state, a reconstruction campaign is focused on the most heavily affected areas, but usually only the surface is repaired. These roads are then excellent for a while, until the cycle of deterioration begins all over again. At the close of this edition (late 2002) many coastal roads were excellent

▶▶ Bus travel tips

Travel only by daylight*. The risks are highest after dark, both for traffic accidents and for hold-ups. While the incidence of the latter is relatively low when you consider the number of buses on the road, highway banditry is a serious problem in Ecuador and its consequences can be particularly severe. Buses are usually held up by heavily armed gangs, never resist or hold back your valuables. Shootings and rapes have occurred during hold-ups and foreign women may be at higher risk. Under the circumstances, travelling overnight in order to save on hotel accommodations is a particularly poor strategy, besides you miss the views and arrive too tired to enjoy the next day's touring. Some of the better bus lines take precautions against hold-ups like not stopping to pick up passengers between towns at night, but they cannot guarantee your safety.*

Politely refuse any food, drink, sweets or cigarettes offered by strangers on a bus. These may be drugged as a way of robbing you. Such tricks are fortunately uncommon in Ecuador, but they do happen occasionally.

Always carry money and valuable documents in your money belt with you on the bus, but also pack a little spare cash and travellers' cheques in with your luggage. If you want to hold your seat at a stop, leave a newspaper or other insignificant item on it, never your bag.

Luggage can be checked-in with the larger bus companies and will be stowed in a locked compartment. On smaller buses it usually rides on the roof, in which case you should make sure it is covered with a tarpaulin to protect against dust and rain. In all cases it is your own responsibility to keep an eye on your gear, never leave it unattended at bus stations. Many travellers place their luggage in a costal (potato or flour sack) for bus rides, this helps keep it clean and makes it a bit less conspicuous.

Only the most modern buses have toilets on board; neither these nor the sanitary facilities at rest stops are likely to be spotlessly clean. Avoid the very back of the bus if you can, as you will be right next to the toilet and the ride can be particularly dusty and bumpy. Take warm clothing when travelling in the highlands.

It is always possible to buy food and drinks on the roadside, as buses stop frequently, but keep an eye out for hygiene and make sure you have small change on hand. Bus drivers usually know the best places for meal stops and some roadside comedores can be quite good. On a longer journey however, take snacks and a small bottle of mineral water just in case.

Despite all these caveats, bus travel in Ecuador can be safe, pleasant and lots of fun; an excellent way to get to know the country and its people. Bon voyage!

while those in the highlands were generally good. The Panamericana from Quito to Ambato was given in concession to a private firm, which made improvements and is collecting tolls (US$1.60 for 140 km). The same system has been applied to other major routes throughout the country, where tolls are now charged.

Several important roads, mostly paved, link the highlands and the Pacific coast. These include from north to south: Ibarra to San Lorenzo, Quito to Esmeraldas via Calacalí and La Independencia, Quito to Guayaquil via Alóag and Santo Domingo de los Colorados (the busiest highway in Ecuador), Latacunga to Quevedo via La Maná (beautiful and partly paved), Ambato to Babahoyo via Guaranda, Riobamba to Guayaquil via Pallatanga and Bucay, Cuenca to Guayaquil via Zhud and La Troncal, Cuenca to Guayaquil via Molleturo, Cuenca to Machala via Girón and Pasaje, and Loja to Machala or Huaquillas.

Santo Domingo de los Colorados is the hub of most roads on the coast of Ecuador. From Guayaquil, the coastal route south to Peru is a major artery. From Guayaquil north, there are now roads all the way to Mataje on the Colombian border.

On the eastern side of the Andes, the roads in Oriente are mostly unpaved and may be impassable due to landslides during the rainy season. The *Carretera Perimetral de la Selva* (jungle perimeter road, a seldom-used term) runs from Lago Agrio in the north to Zamora in the south, via Baeza, Tena, Puyo and Macas. Roads connect Coca to both Lago Agrio and Baeza. There are road links from the highlands to the jungle by the following routes, also from north to south: Quito to Baeza via Papallacta (upper half is paved), Ambato to Puyo via Baños (partly paved), Cuenca to Macas via Gualaceo (unpaved and rough but beautiful), and Loja to Zamora (fully paved). Those driving in the Oriente should be reasonably self sufficient and pay special attention to safety, especially in the province of Sucumbíos.

Bus

Bus travel is generally more convenient than in other Andean countries. Some companies have comfortable air conditioned units for use on their longer routes. Fares for these are higher and some companies have set up their own stations, away from the main bus terminals, exclusively for these better buses. Most buses, though, leave from the central bus terminal (*terminal terrestre*) in each town. They are small and fill up quickly, so leave at frequent intervals. These buses are sometimes crowded and tall people may find the lack of leg room uncomfortable. For more information see box, page 52.

Car

Driving in Ecuador has been described as 'an experience', partly because of unexpected potholes and other obstructions and the lack of road signs, partly because of local drivers' tendency to use the middle of the road. Some roads in Oriente that appear paved are in fact crude oil sprayed onto compacted earth. Beware the bus drivers, who often drive very fast and rather recklessly (passengers also please note).

There are only two grades of gasoline sold in Ecuador, 'Extra' (82 octane, currently US$1.12 per US gallon) and 'Super' (92 Octane, currently US$1.51 per US gallon). Both are unleaded. Extra is available everywhere, while super may not be available in more remote areas. Diesel fuel (currently US$0.90 per US gallon) is notoriously dirty and available everywhere. These prices are expected to increase in 2003.

The road maps published by *Ediguías* (Nelson Gómez) are probably the most useful (see Maps, page 42).

To rent, buy or bring? The big choice for would-be foreign motorists, is whether to rent a vehicle, buy one in Ecuador, or bring their own from home. Each option has its own advantages and drawbacks. Rentals are of course the most convenient for short term visitors, but they are quite expensive and the insurance deductibles are sky-high. If you will stay for a few months or longer, it can make sense to purchase a local car and

Essentials

sell it before you leave. Vehicles are relatively expensive in Ecuador but there are many used ones on the market and they tend to maintain their value. There will be paperwork involved with transfer of ownership, registration, insurance, etc, but this is not an insurmountable obstacle. Bringing your own vehicle from home makes sense if you are travelling through Ecuador as part of a longer journey, and offers the advantage of driving something you know and trust. It is not a good idea however to bring a car from abroad if you wish to stay only in Ecuador for an extended period, as the import procedures are prohibitively complex, time-consuming and expensive.

Preparation Preparing your own car for the journey is largely a matter of common sense. The lengths you go to should depend on what kind of roads you plan to travel: the fully paved Panamerican Highway (Panamericana) with service stations every few kilometres, or third-order tracks deep in the jungle. Obviously any part that is not in first class condition should be replaced. It's well worth installing extra heavy-duty shock-absorbers before starting out, because a long trip on rough roads in a heavily laden car will give heavy wear.

Take spare plugs, fan-belts and radiator hoses. Even though local equivalents for some models can easily be found in the larger cities, it is wise to take spares for those occasions when you might need them. You can also change the fanbelt after a stretch of long, hot driving to prevent wear (for example after 15,000 km/10,000 miles). If your vehicle has more than one fanbelt, always replace them all at the same time (make sure you have the necessary tools if doing it yourself).

If your car has sophisticated electrics, spare 'black boxes' for the ignition and fuel injection are advisable, plus a spare voltage regulator or the appropriate diodes for the alternator, and elements for the fuel, air and oil filters if these are not a common type. (Some drivers take a spare alternator of the correct amperage, especially if the regulator is incorporated into the alternator.)

Dirty fuel is a problem in Ecuador, so be prepared to change filters more often than you would at home: in a diesel car you will need to check the sediment bowl often, too. An extra in-line fuel filter is a good idea if feasible (although harder to find, metal canister type is preferable to plastic), and for travel on dusty roads an oil bath air filter is best for a diesel car. If venturing off the beaten track, it is wise to carry a machete, spade, jumper cables, tow rope and an air pump. Fit tow hooks to both sides of the vehicle frame. A 12 volt neon light for repairs will be invaluable.

Gas stations are so common throughout most of Ecuador that a spare fuel container is seldom required unless you visit particularly remote areas. It is a good idea, though, to keep your tank full as there are occasional gasoline shortages. If you want a fuel container, it should be steel and not plastic, and a siphon pipe is essential for those few places where fuel is sold out of the drum. For such expeditions, you should also take a 10 litre water container for yourself and your vehicle.

Security Apart from the mechanical aspects, spare no ingenuity in making your car secure. Use heavy chain and padlocks to chain doors shut, fit security catches on windows, remove interior window winders (so that a hand reaching in from a forced vent cannot open the window). All these will help, but none is foolproof. Anything on the outside – wing mirrors, spot lamps, motifs etc – is likely to be stolen too. So are wheels if not secured by locking nuts.

Try never to leave the car unattended except in a locked garage or guarded parking space. Remove all belongings and leave the empty glove compartment open when the car is unattended. Also lock the clutch or accelerator to the steering wheel with a heavy, obvious chain or lock. Street children will generally protect your car in exchange for a tip. Be sure to note down key numbers and carry spares of the most important ones (but don't keep all spares inside the vehicle).

Documents There are police checks on many roads in Ecuador and you will be detained if you are unable to present your documents. Always carry your passport and driving licence. An international drivers license is not, strictly speaking, required in Ecuador but it may nonetheless be helpful. You also need the registration document (title) in the name of the driver, or, in the case of a car registered in someone else's name, a notarized letter of authorization. The original invoice from when the car was purchased may also be required in order to ascertain its value. All documents must be originals accompanied by a Spanish translation, preferably certified by an Ecuadorean embassy or consulate.

The rules for bringing a foreign car into Ecuador are complex, change frequently and are inconsistently applied. Customs officials at points of entry seem to have absolute discretionary powers. It is therefore a game of chance: you could breeze through on a smile and a nod, or spend weeks and hundreds of dollars pursuing fruitless paperwork. Our most recent reports suggest the following.

In principle, a *carnet de passage en douane* is an indispensable requirement for bringing a car into Ecuador and the maximum allowable stay is 30 days. The *carnet* (sometimes locally called a *tríptico*) is an international customs document – a sort of passport for your car – issued by the automobile club of your home country (AAA, CAA, RAC, AA, etc) or the country where the vehicle is registered. The requirements for obtaining a *carnet* vary from country to country but usually involve leaving a deposit ranging from 100% to 400% of the value of the vehicle; enquire well before you travel. If you do not have a *carnet*, then regulations state that you can only cross Ecuador with your car from north to south, or vice versa, in a maximum of three days. You must be accompanied throughout this period by a customs officer and will be required to pay for their meals and accommodation.

In practice, some motorists travelling overland from both Colombia and Peru without a *carnet* were granted entry with their vehicles in 2002. They were not required to leave an official security deposit, nor were they asked for bribes. Customs officers were friendly and helpful. In some cases details of the vehicle were stamped into the owners passports, in others they were not. Up to 90 days stay was granted and they were permitted to leave through different borders than where they had entered. On departure, papers were sometimes not even asked for. At the same time, other travellers have faced long delays and great expense in the port of Guayaquil becuase they did not have a *carnet* for their vehicle. In the end, they were denied permission to travel in Ecuador and escorted to the Peruvian border.

If any conclusion can be drawn from recent experience, it is only that overland crossings (except Huaquillas-Aguas Verdes) may be easier than entry through sea ports, of which Guayaquil seems to be the most difficult.

Insurance for a foreign-registered vehicle against accident, damage or theft can only be arranged in the country of origin, not in Ecuador, but it is getting increasingly difficult to find agencies who offer this service. It is very expensive to insure against accident and theft, especially as you should take into account the value of the car increased by duties. If the car is stolen or written off you may be required to pay very high import duty on its value.

Shipping Prices vary but they are seldom cheap. Vehicles are generally shipped in a container, which reduces the risk of theft and damage. Sending a 20-ft container from Guayaquil to Panama, for example, cost US$1,000 in 2002. There are, in addition, many miscelaneous fees and charges which can easily add up to several hundred dollars. Shipping a vehicle through Guayaquil is hazardous due to theft; you will be charged by customs for every day the car is left there and will need assistance from an agent. Shop around and try to get a personal recommendation, as customs agents' services vary greatly in price and quality, some are listed in the Guayaquil chapter. Spare cash may be needed to expedite paperwork. Manta is a smaller, more relaxed and efficient alternative port, but it receives fewer ships so you may be faced with a longer wait. If bringing in a motorcycle by air it can take over a week to get it out of customs. You need a customs agent, who can be found around the main customs building near Quito airport; try to fix the price in advance. Best to accompany the agent all the time and a letter from the **Ecuadorean Automobile Club** (ANETA) may be helpful. For details of required documents, see above.

Car hire   Various international and local car hire companies are clustered around the airports of Quito, Guayaquil and Cuenca. It may be difficult to rent a vehicle in smaller cities however, where there are usually only a few rental cars available and these are often in use. Even in Quito, rental cars may be scarce during high season (June to September, and December to January), it is best to reserve in advance for these times. The names and addresses of agencies are given in the main text.

In order to rent a car in Ecuador you must be at least 21 years old and have an international credit card. Surcharges may apply to clients between age 21 and 25. You may pay cash, which is sometimes cheaper and may allow you to bargain, but they want a credit card for security. You may be asked to sign two blank credit card vouchers, one for the rental fee itself and the other as a security deposit, and authorization for a charge of as much as US$5,000 may be requested against your credit card account. These arrangements are all above board and the uncashed vouchers will be returned to you when you return the vehicle. Always make certain that you fully understand the rental agreement before signing the contract, and be especially careful when dealing with some of the smaller agencies. Also, check the car's condition, not forgetting things like wheel nuts, and make sure it has good ground clearance. Always garage the car securely at night.

Rates vary depending on the rental company and vehicle, but a small car suitable for city driving hired from a reputable agency currently costs about US$400 per week including unlimited mileage, all taxes and insurance. A sturdier four-wheel-drive can be three times as much.

Car hire insurance   Some car hire firms do not have adequate insurance policies and you will have to pay heavily in the event of an accident. Check exactly what the hirer's insurance policy covers. All policies include a deductible, which you will have to cover out-of-pocket. This deductible also varies with the agency and vehicle, up to to US$3,000 in the event of a minor accident and US$5,000 or more in the event of theft or complete destruction of the vehicle. Beware of being billed for scratches which were on the vehicle before you hired it.

Drive carefully   It is best to try and settle minor fender-benders amicably without notifying the police.
Defensive driving is especially important in Ecuador   In case of a serious accident it is common for both the drivers and vehicles to be detained. The ensuing judicial process can be long and complicated and, as a foreigner, you will be at a considerable disadvantage. For this reason, and because you are on unfamiliar turf, you should drive defensively at all times. Always be on the lookout for pedestrians, especially near elevated crosswalks which are seldom used. The recklessness of the locals should make you more, not less, careful.

Cycling   At first glance a bicycle may not appear to be the most obvious vehicle for a major journey, but given ample time and reasonable energy it most certainly is the best. It can be ridden, carried by almost every form of transport from an aeroplane to a jungle canoe, and can even be lifted across one's shoulders over short distances. Cyclists can be the envy of travellers using more orthodox transport, since they can travel at their own pace, explore more remote regions and meet people who are not normally in contact with tourists.

Choosing a bicycle The choice of bicycle depends on the type and length of expedition being undertaken and on the terrain and road surfaces likely to be encountered. Unless you are planning a journey almost exclusively on paved roads – when a high quality touring bike would probably suffice – a mountain bike is strongly recommended. The good quality ones (and the cast iron rule is never to skimp on quality) are incredibly tough and rugged, with low gear ratios for steep hills, wide tyres with plenty of tread for good road-holding, V-type brakes, and good geometry for improved stability. Although bikes and spares are available in the larger cities, high quality equipment is expensive and the cheap stuff does not last. Within reason, buy everything you possibly can before you leave home. Shop around carefully when buying parts in Ecuador, as prices vary greatly.

Bicycle equipment A small but comprehensive tool kit (to include chain rivet and crank removers, a spoke key and possibly a block remover), a spare tyre and inner tubes, a puncture repair kit with plenty of extra patches and glue, a set of brake blocks, brake and gear cables and all types of nuts and bolts, at least 12 spokes (best taped to the chain stay), a light oil for the chain (for example Finish-Line Teflon Dry-Lube), tube of waterproof grease, a pump secured by a pump lock, a Blackburn parking block (a most invaluable accessory, cheap and virtually weightless), a cyclometer, a loud bell, and a secure lock and chain. *Richard's Bicycle Book* makes useful reading for even the most mechanically minded. At the same time, avoid taking more tools and parts than you can reasonably carry or know how to use properly.

Luggage and clothing Strong and waterproof front and back panniers are a must. When packed these are likely to be heavy and should be carried on the strongest racks available. Poor quality racks have ruined many a journey for they take incredible strain on unpaved roads. A top bag cum rucksack (for example Carradice) makes a good addition for use on and off the bike; also backpacks with hydratation systems such as Camelback, Blackburn and Hydrapack. A Cannondale front bag is good for maps, camera, compass, altimeter, notebook and small tape-recorder. (Other recommended panniers are Ortlieb – front and back – which is waterproof and almost 'sandproof', Mac-Pac, Madden and Karimoor.) 'Gaffa' tape (duct tape) is excellent for protecting vulnerable parts of panniers and for carrying out all manner of repairs.

   All equipment and clothes should be packed in plastic bags to give extra protection against dust and rain. (Also protect all documents etc, carried close to the body from sweat.) Always take the minimum clothing. It's better to buy extra items en route when you find you need them. Generally it is best to carry several layers of thin light clothes than fewer heavy, bulky ones. Always keep one set of dry clothes, including long trousers, to put on at the end of the day. The incredibly light, strong, waterproof and wind resistant Gore-Tex jacket and overtrousers are invaluable, as are moisture-wicking T-shirts and long underpants. Training shoes can be used for both cycling and walking.

Useful tips Wind, not hills, is the enemy of the cyclist. Try to make the best use of the times of day when there is little; mornings tend to be best but there is no steadfast rule. The air in Ecuador's highlands can be very dry. Take care to avoid dehydration, by drinking regularly; a sip of water every 10 minutes is recommended, whether you are thirsty or not. In hot, dry areas with limited supplies of water, be sure to carry an ample supply. For food, carry a few staples (sugar, salt, dried milk, porridge oats, raisins, dried soups etc) and supplement these with local foods, of which there is no shortage.

   Give your bicycle a thorough daily check for loose nuts or bolts or bearings. See that all parts run smoothly. A good chain should last 3,000 km or more but be sure to keep it as clean as possible – an old toothbrush is good for this – and to oil it lightly from time to time.

Essentials

Remember that thieves are attracted to towns and cities, so when sight-seeing, try to leave your bicycle with someone such as a café owner or shopkeeper. Country people tend to be more honest and are usually friendly and very inquisitive. However, don't take unnecessary risks; always see that your bicycle is secure (most hotels will allow bikes to be kept in rooms).

Dogs can be vicious. If you see them approaching, then you should stop, dismount, and walk a few paces with the bike between you and the dogs. Once you are merely another pedestrian, they will usually relent. Otherwise, bend over to pick up a few stones, or just pretend if there are no stones nearby. Most dogs simply make a lot of noise without attacking. If you are bitten, however, then you must see a doctor because rabies is present in Ecuador.

Traffic on main roads can be a nightmare; it is usually far more rewarding to keep to the smaller roads or to paths if they exist. When riding in big cities like Quito, Ecuadorean cyclists recommend behaving like a car and occupying the entire lane; this is safer and drivers usually respect you. Use hand signals to indicate when turning or switching lanes. Most cyclists agree that the main danger comes from other traffic. A rearview mirror has been frequently recommended to forewarn you of vehicles which are too close behind. You also need to watch out for oncoming, overtaking vehicles, unstable loads on trucks, protruding loads etc. Make yourself conspicuous by wearing bright clothing and a helmet.

Most towns have a bicycle shop of some description, but it is best to do your own repairs and adjustments whenever possible. Big city bike shops may also have boxes/cartons in which to send bicycles home.

The Expedition Advisory Centre, administered by the Royal Geographical Society, 1 Kensington Gore, London SW7 2AR, T020-7591 3030, www.rgs.org/eac, has a useful monograph entitled *Bicycle Expeditions*, by Paul Vickers, which can be downloaded free from their website. In the UK there is also the **Cyclist's Touring Club** (CTC), Cotterell House, 69 Meadrow, Godalming, Surrey GU7 3HS, T01483-417217, www.ctc.org.uk, for touring and technical information. In addition to the *Ediguía*s road maps recommended for cars (see page 42), a series of very practical *hojas de ruta* are available from the **IGM** in Quito. They include detailed road maps and elevation profiles for routes between the major towns.

Hitchhiking   Public transport in Ecuador is so abundant that there is no need to hitchhike along the major highways. On small out-of-the-way country roads however, the situation can be quite the opposite, and giving passers-by a ride is common practice and safe for drivers and passengers alike, especially in the back of a pick-up or larger truck. A small fee is usually charged, best ask in advance. In truly remote areas there may not be enough traffic to make hitching worthwhile.

For obvious reasons, a lone female should not hitch by herself. Besides, you are more likely to get a lift if you are with a partner, be they male or female. The best combination is a male and female together. Three or more and you'll be in for a long wait. Your appearance is also important. Someone with matted hair and a large tattoo on their forehead will not have much success. Remember that you are asking considerable trust of the driver. Would you stop to pick up a suspicious looking character?

Motorcycling   People are generally very amicable to motorcyclists and you can make many friends by returning friendship to those who show an interest in you. Simple motorcycles are a common means of transport, often carrying an entire family, while fancy dirt bikes have become popular in recent years with some wealthy young Ecuadoreans.

The machine   It should be off-road capable: a good choice would be the BMW R80/100/GS for its rugged and simple design and reliable shaft drive, but a Kawasaki KLR 650s, Honda Transalp/Dominator, or the ubiquitous Yamaha XT600 Tenere would also be suitable. A road bike can go most places an off road bike can go at the cost of greater effort.

Preparations Fit heavy duty front fork springs and the best quality rebuildable shock absorber you can afford (Ohlins, White Power). Fit lockable luggage containers such as Krausers (reinforce luggage frames) or make some detachable aluminium panniers. Fit a tank bag and tank panniers for better weight distribution. A large capacity fuel tank (Acerbis), +300 mile/480 km range, is helpful if going off the beaten track. A washable air filter is a good idea (K&N), also fuel filters, fueltap rubber seals and smaller jets for high altitude Andean motoring. A good set of trails-type tyres as well as a high mudguard are useful. Get to know the bike before you go, ask the dealers in your country what goes wrong with it and arrange a link whereby you can get parts flown out to you (but beware of high customs duties). If riding a chain driven bike, a fully enclosed chaincase is useful. A hefty bash plate/sump guard is invaluable.

Spares Reduce service intervals by half if driving in severe conditions. Take oil filters, fork and shock seals, tubes, a good manual, spare cables (taped into position), a plug cap and spare plug lead. A spare electronic ignition is a good idea, try and buy a second hand one and make arrangements to have parts sent out to you. A first class tool kit is a must and if riding a bike with a chain then a spare set of sprockets and an 'o' ring chain should be carried. Spare brake and clutch levers should also be taken as these break easily in a fall. Parts may be few and far between, but mechanics are skilled at making do and can usually repair things. Castrol oil can be bought everywhere and relied upon. Take a puncture repair kit and tyre levers. Find out about any weak spots on the bike and improve them. Get the book for international dealer coverage from your manufacturer, but don't rely on it. They frequently have few or no parts for modern, large machinery.

Clothes and equipment A tough waterproof jacket, comfortable strong boots, gloves and a helmet with which you can use glass goggles (Halcyon) which will not scratch and wear out like a plastic visor. The best quality tent and camping gear that you can afford and a petrol stove which runs on bike fuel is helpful. Also see Camping, page 50.

Security Never leave a fully laden bike on its own. An Abus D or chain will keep the bike secure. Never leave the bike outside a hotel at night. Most hotels will allow you to bring the bike inside.

Dogs They are ubiquitous in Ecuadorean towns and the countryside, they love to chase bikes, and they have been known to bite riders. See precautions for cyclists, below. Although the greater speed of a motorbike provides some protection, you are by no means immune.

Documents Passport, driving licence and registration (title) documents are all necessary. The rules for bringing a motorcycle into Ecuador are, in principle, the same as those for a car (see above) but may sometimes be applied more leniently.

Taxis Taxis are a particularly convenient, safe and cheap transport option for tourists in the cities and towns of Ecuador. In Quito, all taxis must have meters by law; for details of taxi services in the capital see page 93. Meters are not used in other cities, where a flat rate is charged within the central part of town, generally under US$1 at the present time. Ask around to ascertain the going rate. All legally registered taxis have the number of their co-operative and the individual operator's number prominently painted on the side of the vehicle. Note these and the licence plate number if you feel you have been seriously overcharged or mistreated. You may then complain to the transit police or tourist office, but be reasonable as the amounts involved are usually small and the vast majority of taxi drivers are honest and helpful.

Keeping in touch

Communications

Internet

The internet is exceptionally accessible in Ecuador and has replaced postal and telephone services for most travellers

Quito claims to have more cyber cafés per capita than any other city in the world. This may be hard to prove, but there are so many Internet places in the larger cities and towns of Ecuador that you will undoubtedly be tripping over them. They are frequented not only by tourists, but also by many locals, and are sometimes crowded and noisy. Mind your belongings while you navigate, lest they do likewise.

Some form of Internet access may be found almost everywhere in Ecuador, except for the most remote locations in the Oriente. Both the cost and speed of access vary, with the best service available in Quito, Guayaquil and Cuenca. Hourly Internet rates currently range from about US$0.60 to US$3.

Since public internet access is so easy in Ecuador, there is really no need to bring your own laptop just to keep in touch. If you have your own computer and modem however, you can connect to CompuServe and America Online via the SCITOR network, the Quito dialup is 250 5000. This is usually expensive though, check prices with your ISP beforehand. For those planning an extended stay, there are also many local ISPs offering service throughout Ecuador.

Net to Phone

Almost every place that offers Internet will also have Net to Phone, and there are a few that offer only this service. Net to Phone rates are typically under US$0.20 per minute to North America and Europe, about half the price of calling by ordinary telephone. Audio quality varies, however, and background noise can be a problem in busy cyber cafés.

Post

Urgent or valuable documents should never be entrusted to the post office

During 1999-2002 the Ecuadorean post office was unreliable for both sending and receiving mail, a shame in view of its previously reasonable track record. We have received numerous reports of parcels, letters and especially postcards which never arrived, and *correo certificado* (registered mail) seemed even more prone to problems than ordinary airmail. Those items which did arrive, were at times delayed for several months. It is hoped that this situation will once again improve, but visitors are advised to seek advice from local residents before sending all but the most trivial items through the mail. National and international courier service is available as an alternative, for details see below.

Opening hours for post offices vary from town to town and from branch to branch. In Quito they are generally Monday-Friday 0800-1800 and Saturday 0800-1200. Postal branches in small towns may not be familiar with all rates and procedures. Your chances are better at the main branches in provincial capitals or, better yet, in Quito: at Colón corner Almagro in La Mariscal district, at the main sorting centre on Japón near Naciones Unidas (behind the CCI shopping centre), or at Ulloa y Ramírez Dávalos (Monday-Friday 0730-1600) for very large parcels.

Letters and postcards Ordinary airmail rates for up to 20 g are currently US$0.90 to the Americas, US$1.05 to the rest of the world. Registered mail costs an additional US$0.95 per item.

Parcels Up to 30 kg, maximum dimensions permitted are 70 by 30 by 30 cm. Current rates by air parcel post (nominally 12 days delivery): to the Americas US$14.55 for the first kg, US$4.45 for each additional kg; to the rest of the world US$23.90 for the first kg, US$12.85 for each additional kg. Current rates by SAL/APR (surface air lifted, nominally 40 days delivery) reduced priority service: to the Americas US$13.80 for the first kg, US$3.75 for each additional kg; to the rest of the world US$21.50 for the first kg, US$10.45 for each additional kg. There is no surface (sea) mail service from Ecuador.

Dialling codes ◀◀

09 Mobile numbers
Main cities
02 Quito
04 Guayaquil
07 Cuenca
Provinces
02 Pichincha
03 Bolívar, Chimborazo, Cotopaxi, Pastaza, Tungurahua
04 Guayas
05 Galápagos, Manabí, Los Ríos
06 Carchi, Esmeraldas, Imbabura, Napo, Orellana, Sucumbíos, Zamora Chinchipe
07 Azuay, Cañar, El Oro, Loja, Morona Santiago

Emergency and useful phone numbers
101 Police
102 Fire
131 Red Cross
911 All emergencies (Quito only)
100 Directory information
105 National operator
116/117 International operator

To make direct international calls from Ecuador dial **00** *followed by the country code, the area code (dropping any initial zeroes) and the local number.*
The country code for calling Ecuador is **+593**

Essentials

Receiving mail Letters can be sent to Poste Restante/General Delivery (*lista de correos*, but you must specify the postal branch in larger cities), some embassies (enquire beforehand), or, for card holders only, American Express offices. Foreign names can cause considerable confusion, for the smallest risk of misunderstanding, use the initial and surname only (for example J Smith). Regardless of where they are addressed to, parcels above 2 kg will generally arrive at the Correo de Ulloa in Quito to undergo customs inspection, Ulloa y Ramírez Dávalos, customs open Monday-Friday 0830-1200. Items sent to you by courier must have a specific street address (for example your hotel or embassy, not a PO Box) and will also be subject to customs inspection and possibly high duties. See Shipping goods to Ecuador, page 34. Never send anything to Ecuador by surface (sea) mail, it is unlikely to arrive.

Couriers Courier companies are the only safe alternative for sending or receiving valuable time-sensitive mail in Ecuador. For rapid and reliable international service, *DHL* has offices throughout the country; the most convenient locations in Quito include Colón 1333 y Foch and República 433 y Almagro, T2485100. They are expensive but very efficient and reliable. For courier service within Ecuador, *Servientrega* has offices throughout the country, reliable one to two day service is available to all areas, US$2-3 for up to 2 kg. There are many other courier companies operating in Ecuador, but quality of service and reliability vary greatly.

Telephone Ecuador's telephone system is currently operated by three regional state companies, whose names you should look for on telephone offices: *Andinatel* in the northern highlands and northern Oriente; *Pacifictel* on the coast, in the southern highlands and southern Oriente; and *ETAPA* in Cuenca. There are also two private companies, *Bell South* and *Porta*, which provide cellular phone service, including convenient but expensive debit card operated public cell phones. Since this system is wireless, public phones have been installed in previously inaccessible locations, such as the mountain shelter on Chimborazo. Public cell phones are also more economical than regular phones for calling other cellular numbers in Ecuador. Short term cell phone rentals are also available.

The service provided by all of the above is generally adequate, best in the larger cities, worst in small towns and villages. Most public cellular phones have their numbers posted and allow you to receive calls. So you can make a brief contact with home and have someone call you back.

Essentials

Debit cards for public cell phones may be purchased at kiosks and many small shops; they are specific to one company (ie you cannot use Porta cards in Bell South phones nor vice versa). There are also new conventional (ie non-cellular) coin and debit card operated public phones being installed by the state companies listed above. These were not yet oprational at the close of this edition.

The best places to make local, national or international calls are currently telephone company offices. There are several of these in all major cities and towns, with new ones opening all the time. The travelling text lists only the central telephone office in each town, but other offices provide identical prices and service. You are assigned a cabin, dial your own calls, and pay on the way out. For international calls however, you may be asked to specify how many minutes you would like to speak and pay in advance.

Rates fluctuate. Examples of current state phone company rates for calls made from their offices are: US$0.38 per minute to the USA, US$0.46 per minute to the UK or Australia. Hefty surcharges may be applied to calls made from hotels, ask for their rates in advance.

Country-direct access is available free of charge from private phones and telephone company offices throughout Ecuador (except Galápagos), although not every office knows about this nor are they familiar with the access numbers.

NB Telephone numbers in the provinces of Pichincha (02) and Guayas (04), as well as all cellular phone numbers (09), have seven digits, whereas all other phone numbers in Ecuador have only six digits. A seventh digit may be added to the latter in 2003.

Faxes may be sent and received at phone company offices, some post offices, hotels and many private locations. Shop around for the best rates.

Media

Newspapers The main newspapers in Quito are *El Comercio* and *Hoy*, in Guayaquil *El Universo*. All three are available nationwide as well as on-line (see websites, page 26). *El Mercurio* of Cuenca is also highly regarded. There are several smaller regional or local papers published in the provincial capitals. Foreign newspapers are only available in some luxury hotels and a few speciality shops in Quito and Guayaquil.

Radio South America has more local and community radio stations than practically anywhere else in the world, and Ecuador is well known in this field for the presence of pioneer evangelical broadcaster HCJB. A shortwave (world band) radio offers a practical means to brush up on the language, sample popular culture and absorb some of the richly varied regional music. International broadcasters such as the **BBC World Service** (www.bbc.co.uk/worldservice), the **Voice of America** (www.voa.gov), Boston (Mass)-based **Monitor Radio International** (operated by *Christian Science Monitor*, www.csmonitor.com) and the Quito-based **HCJB** (89.3 FM in Quito, 102.5 FM in Guayaquil), keep the traveller abreast of news and events, in both English and Spanish.

Compact or miniature portables are recommended, with digital tuning and a full range of shortwave bands, as well as FM, long and medium wave. Detailed advice on radio models and wavelengths can be found in the annual publication, *Passport to World Band Radio* (Box 300, Penn's Park, PA 18943, USA). Details of local stations are listed in *World TV and Radio Handbook* (WTRH), PO Box 9027, 1006 AA Amsterdam, The Netherlands, US$19.95. Both of these free wavelength guides and selected radio sets are available from the *BBC World Service Bookshop*, Bush House Arcade, Bush House, Strand, London WC2B 4PH, UK, T020-7257 2576, www.bbc.co.uk/worldservice

Food and drink

Ecuadoreans take their meals pretty seriously, not only for nutrition but also as a social experience. In all but the largest cities, most families still gather around the lunch table at home to eat and discuss the day's events. Sharing food is also a very important part of traditional celebrations and hospitality. A poor family, who generally must get by on a very basic diet, might prepare a feast for a baptism, wedding or high school graduation.

In many Ecuadorean homes, breakfast (*desayuno*) is fresh fruit juice, coffee, bread, margarine, and perhaps a little jam or white cheese. On the coast, a *ceviche* may be enjoyed with a cold drink at mid-morning. Lunch (*almuerzo*) is by far the most important meal of the day. It may begin with small appetizer, such as an *empanada*, followed by soup – compulsory and often the most filling course. Then comes a large serving of white rice, accompanied by modest quantities of meat, chicken or fish and some cooked vegetables or salad. Desert, if served at all, might be a small portion of fruit or sweets. Lunch is also accompanied by fruit juice or a soft drink. Supper (*merienda* or *cena*) is either a smaller repetition of lunch or a warm drink with bread, cheese, perhaps cold cuts, *humitas* or *quimbolitos*.

Ecuadorean cooking
A recommended cookbook is Comidas del Ecuador by Michelle Fried, available in Quito bookshops

Essentials

The details of the above vary extensively with each region based on custom and traditionally available ingredients The following are some typical dishes worth trying.

Regional specialties

In the highlands *Locro de papas* is a potato and cheese soup. *Mote* (white hominy) is a staple in the region around Cuenca, but used in a variety of dishes throughout the Sierra. *Caldo de patas* is cow heel soup with *mote*. *Llapingachos* (fried potato and cheese patties) and *empanadas de morocho* (a ground corn shell filled with meat) are popular side dishes and snacks. *Morocho*, on the other hand, is a thick drink or porridge made from the same white corn, milk, sugar and cinnamon. *Sancocho de yuca* is a meat and vegetable soup with manioc root. The more adventurous may want to try the delicious roast *cuy* (guinea pig), most typical of highland dishes. Also good is *fritada* (fried pork) and *hornado* (roast pork). Vegetarians can partake of such typically Andean specialties as *chochos* (lupins) and *quinua* (quinoa, a grain related to millet). *Humitas* are made of tender ground corn steamed in corn leaves, and similar are *quimbolitos*, which are prepared with white corn flour and steamed in *achira* leaves. *Humitas* and *quimbolitos* come in both sweet and savoury varieties.

On the coast Seafood is excellent and popular everywhere. *Ceviche* is marinated fish or seafood which is usually served with popcorn, *tostado* (roasted maize) or *chifles* (plantain chips). Only *ceviche de pescado* (fish) and *ceviche de concha* (clams), which are marinated raw, potentially pose a health hazard. The other varieties of *ceviche* such as *camarón* (shrimp/prawn), and *langostino* (jumbo shrimp/king prawn) all of which are cooked before being marinated, are generally safe delicacies, though you should always check the cleanliness of the establishment. *Langosta* (lobster) is an increasingly endangered species but continues to be illegally fished; so please be conscientious. Other coastal dishes include *empanadas de verde* which are fried snacks: a ground plantain shell filled with cheese, meat or shrimp. *Sopa de bola de verde* is plantain dumpling soup. *Encocadas* are dishes prepared with coconut milk and fish or seafood, which are very popular in the province of Esmeraldas. *Cocadas* are sweets made with coconut. *Viche* is fish or seafood soup made with ground peanuts, and the ubiquitous *patacones* are thick fried plantain slices served as a side dish.

In the Oriente Most dishes are prepared with *yuca* (manioc or cassava root) and a wide variety of river fish. *Ayampacos* are spiced meat, chicken or palm hearts wrapped in *bijao* leaves and roasted over the coals.

▶▶ Restaurant price categories

All of the following prices are based on a complete meal for one person including a non-alcoholic beverage, tax and service:
***Very expensive**: above US$20*

***Expensive**: US$10-20*
***Mid-range**: US$5-10*
***Cheap**: US$2-5*
***Seriously cheap**: less than US$2*

Special foods *Fanesca* is a fish soup with beans, many grains, ground peanuts and more, sold during Easter Week throughout the country. *Colada morada* (a thick dark purple fruit drink) and *guaguas de pan* (bread dolls) are made around the time of *Finados*, the day of the dead at the beginning of November. Special *tamales* and sweet and sticky *pristiños* are Christmas specialities.

Ecuadorean food is not particularly spicy. However, in most homes and restaurants, the meal is accompanied by a small bowl of *ají* (hot pepper sauce) which may vary greatly in potency. Those unfamiliar with this condiment are advised to exercise caution at first. *Colada* is a generic name which can refer to cream soups or sweet beverages. In addition to the prepared foods mentioned above, Ecuador offers a large variety of delicious temperate and tropical fruits, some of which are unique to South America.

Eating out
Upmarket restaurants add 22% tax and service to the bill

The simplest and most common eateries found throughout Ecuador are little family run *comedores* or *salones* serving only set meals: *almuerzos* and *meriendas* of the type described above. These currently cost US$1.50-3 and are easiest to find at midday. As long as the establishment is clean, you are unlikely to go wrong at one of these places, but you are unlikely to discover a hidden gastronomic treasure either. Make sure that juices are prepared with boiled or bottled water. One step up, and available in provincial capitals, are restaurants which serve both set meals (perhaps an *almuerzo ejecutivo* for lunch) and à la carte (at night). They may feature Ecuadorean or international food, more swank surroundings, and can be very good for around US$3-6. Outside main cities and resorts, the above are seldom supplemented by more than *chifas* (Chinese restaurants, some quite good, others terrible) and Italian or pizza places which tend to be OK; both generally in our mid-range price category. Vegetarians must be adaptable in small towns, but can count on the good will and ingenuity of local cooks.

In Quito, Guayaquil, Cuenca and the more popular tourist resorts, the sky is the limit for variety, quality, elegance and price of restaurant dining. You can find anything from gourmet French cuisine to sushi, upscale Ecuadorean *comida típica*, good vegetarian, plush cafés and neon-on-plastic North American burger chains. Splurge if you can, to make the most of dining out in a few the better places, which are still economical by international standards. Another class of restaurant, which has flourished specifically in areas frequented by foreigners, serves undifferentiated tourist fare: a little Mexican, a little vegetarian, a little of everything but nothing in particular. Their mid-range prices and familiar looking menus may attract some tourists, but you can usually do better elsewhere. On the periphery of cities are many *paradores*, places where Ecuadorean families go on weekends to enjoy typical dishes or grilled meat. These can provide good quality and value for about US$4-8.

At the low end of the price range, every market in Ecuador has a section set aside for prepared foods. You always take a chance eating in a market, but if a place is clean then you might still find a tasty nourishing meal for under US$1.50. Food vendors in the street, however, who have no way to properly wash their hands or utensils, should be avoided. You will not save money by getting sick.

Bakeries, of which there are many, and a few very good ice-cream parlours round out the Ecuadorean eating scene.

The variety of tropical fruits on offer in Ecuador is bewildering. Not surprisingly, then, **Drink** fruit juices are wonderful here. Among the most popular are *naranjilla*, *maracuya* (passion fruit), *tomate de arbol*, *piña* (pineapple), *taxo* (another variety of passion fruit) and *mora* (blackberry). But anything can be made into a mouth-watering *jugo* (juice prepared with water) or *batido* (prepared with milk). A note of caution, however. Make sure the place is clean and the juice is made with boiled or bottled water, and ask for your drink *sin hielo* (without ice, which may be made from tap water). The usual soft drinks, known as *colas*, are widely available. On the downside, this is not coffee paradise. Instant coffee or liquid concentrate is common, so ask for *café pasado* if you want real filtered coffee. Places where you can get a decent cup of coffee are few and far between outside Quito and the more popular tourist spots.

As for alcohol, the main beers are Pilsener, Biela and Club, all of which are reasonable. Some Quito bars have good microbrews and also offer a wide selection of foreign beers. Good quality Argentine and Chilean wines are available in the larger cities and generally cheaper than European or US ones. *Aguardiente* (literally 'fire-water') is potent unmatured rum, also known as *paico* and *trago de caña*, or just *trago*. *Chicha*, a native beverage fermented from corn in the highlands (*chicha de jora*), and from *yuca* or *chonta* palm fruit in Oriente, is not for those with a delicate stomach.

Shopping

Almost everyone who visits Ecuador will end up buying a souvenir of some sort from *For more details of* the vast array of arts and crafts (*artesanías*) on offer. The most colourful places to shop *handicrafts and where* for souvenirs, and pretty much anything else in Ecuador, are the street markets which *to find them, see* can be found absolutely everywhere. The country also has its share of shiny, modern *Arts and crafts (page* shopping centres, especially in Guayaquil and the capital, but remember that the high *442). For local markets* overheads are reflected in the prices. *and shops see under*

Otavalo's massive market is the best-known place for buying wall hangings and *the relevant town, city* sweaters. Another market, at Saquisilí, south of Quito, is renowned for shawls, blankets *or village* and embroidered garments. Fewer handicrafts can be found on the coast, but this is where you can buy an authentic Panama hat at a fraction of the cost in Europe. The best, called *superfinos*, are reputed to be made in the little town of Montecristi, but the villages around Cuenca claim to produce superior models. Cuenca is a good place to buy Panama hats, and other types of hat can be bought throughout the Andes. Ecuador also produces fine silver jewellery, ceramics and brightly painted carvings, usually made from balsa wood. Particularly good buys are the many beautiful items fashioned from *tagua*, or vegetable ivory. By purchasing these you are promoting conservation of the rainforests where the *tagua* palm grows.

All manner of *artesanías* can be bought in Quito, either on the street or in any of the shops. There's not actually much difference in the price. The advantage of buying your souvenirs in a shop is that they'll usually package your gifts well enough to prevent damage on the flight home. Craft cooperatives are also a good place to shop, since there is a better chance that a fair share of the price will go to the artisan.

Stall holders in markets expect you to bargain, so don't disappoint them. Many tourists **Bargaining** enjoy the satisfaction of beating down the seller's original price and finding a real 'bargain', but don't take it too far. Always remain good natured, even if things are not going your way (remember that you're on vacation and they're working). And don't make a fool of yourself by arguing for hours over a few cents. The item you're bargaining for may have taken weeks to make and you're probably carrying more cash in your wallet than the market seller earns in a month.

Essentials

Photography Kodak Ektachrome is available but Fuji Sensia and Konica are the most common brands of slide film. A variety of colour print film is sold in Ecuador, but always be sure to check the expiry date. If you are a serious photographer, then it is best to bring all your supplies from home.

Machine processing for colour prints is available in most towns but the results are usually no better than fair. Colour slide and black and white processing is harder to find, and may be of even lower quality. A highly recommended professional lab for all types of work is run by Ronald Jones in Quito and among the commercial labs, Difoto is recommended, see page 123.

Modern airport X-ray machines are supposed to be safe for any speed of film, but it is worth trying to avoid X-rays as the doses are cumulative. Many airport officials will allow film to be passed outside X-ray arches; they may also hand-check a suitcase with a large quantity of film if asked politely. Or use a commercially available lead-lined pouch. Avoid sending film home by mail, both because of X-rays and because the post office is unreliable.

Cameras, lenses and film should be protected in humid areas such as Oriente by putting them in a plastic bag, preferably along with a pouch of silica gel or dry rice.

Holidays and festivals

Festivals are an intrinsic part of Ecuador's social fabric and for many the highlight of the year. For a description of the most important festivals, see under Festivals, page 445. The dates of local festivals are given under each town. The main holidays are given below.

1 January, *New Year's Day*; **6 January**, *Reyes Magos y Día de los Inocentes*; **27 February**, *Día del Civismo*; *Carnival*, Monday and Tuesday before Lent; **Easter**, *Holy Thursday; Good Friday; Holy Saturday*; **1 May** *Labour Day*; **24 May**, *Battle of Pichincha, Independence Day; Corpus Christi*, 40 days after Easter; **10 August**, *first attempt at independence*; **9 October**, *Independence of Guayaquil*; **12 October**, *Columbus' arrival in America*; **2 November, Finados**, *All Souls' Day*; **3 November**, *Independence of Cuenca*; **6 December** *Foundation of Quito*; **25 December** *Christmas Day*.

Sport and special interest travel

Birdwatching

Ecuador is one of the richest places in the world for birds, and some of the planet's most beautiful species can be found here

The lowlands are rich in cotingas, manakins, toucans, antbirds and spectacular birds of prey, while the cloud forests are noted for their abundance of hummingbirds, tanagers, mountain toucans and Cock of the Rock. As a result of this wonderful avian diversity, a network of birding lodges has sprung up and ecotourism has never been easier.

Here we list the best lodges and roads for birding according to their biological region; both the sites and the regions are more fully described in the main text. For further information about Ecuador's wonderful biodiversity, see Flora and fauna, page 456. Within each region described below, the sites are listed from north to south.

See Books, page 463, for further reading

Western lowlands & lower foothills Bilsa (400-700 m), a virgin site in Esmeraldas province, contains even the rarest foothill birds (such as Banded Ground-cuckoo and Long-Wattled Umbrellabird), though access can be an ordeal in the wet season. This site has 305 known species.

Aldea Salamandra (200 m) on the Calacalí-Esmeraldas road offers cabins with access to several forest reserves nearby.

Tinalandia (700-900 m) near Alluriquín on the Alóag-Santo Domingo road is a great introduction to the world of tropical birds. There are lots of colourful species (more than 360 have been seen here) and they are easier to observe here than at most other places, but some of the larger species have been lost from this area. The lodge itself is very accessible and comfortable.

Río Palenque (200 m) between Santo Domingo and Quevedo is one of the last islands of western lowland forest. It is a very rich birding area, with 370 species. It has begun to lose some species because of its isolation from other forests.

Parque Nacional Machalilla (0-850 m) on the coast near Puerto López has lightly disturbed dry forest and cloud forest, with many dry-forest specialties. The higher areas are slightly difficult to access. There are 115 known species here.

Ecuasal ponds (0 m), on the Santa Elena peninsula, which hold a variety of seabirds and shorebirds; famous for their Chilean Flamingos and other migratory species.

Cerro Blanco (250-300 m) just outside Guayaquil is one of the best remaining examples of dry forest. There have been breeding Great Green Macaws on occasion, and even Jaguars have been spotted. It has 190 known species of birds.

Manta Real (300-1,200 m) is a rainforest-to-cloud forest transition area on the Guayaquil-Cuenca road, with some very rare birds endemic to southwestern Ecuador and adjacent Peru. There are 120 species known from the area.

Manglares-Churute (50-650 m) just southeast of Guayaquil contains a dry-to moist forest and a mangrove forest. The bird list includes only 65 species but the area is poorly studied.

The petrified forest of **Puyango** (300-400 m) has live trees as well, and typical dry forest birds. It has 130 known species.

Páramo del Angel (2,500-4,500 m) south of Tulcán is a spectacular grassland dotted with tall tree-like herbs called *frailejones*; 160 bird species are known from here. **Western Andes**

Cerro Golondrinas (2,000-4,000 m) is near the Páramo del Angel, and there are highly recommended guided treks available through both.

Intag Cloud Forest Reserve (1,800-2,800 m), **Junín Community Reserve** (1500-2200 m), **Alto Chocó** and **Siempre Verde** are all cloud forests near the Reserva Ecológica Cotacachi-Cayapas, with a full set of cloud forest birds. Access is via Otavalo.

Los Cedros Reserve (1,000-2,700 m) near the Cotacachi-Cayapas Ecological Reserve has excellent forest over an interesting range of elevations. Populations of many bird species are higher here than in more accessible places.

Yanacocha (3,300-4,000 m) is a surprisingly well preserved high elevation forest on the west side of the Pichincha volcano. Access is from Quito.

The Nono-Mindo road (1,500-3,400 m) is a famous birding route starting from Quito and passes through a wide variety of forest types. It is somewhat disturbed in its higher sections but quite good in its lower half, where there are now several excellent lodges.

Tandayapa Lodge (1,700 m) on the Nono-Mindo road is well done, easily accessible and comfortable. Serious birders seeking rarities will benefit from the knowledgeable guides who can show practically any species they are asked to find. There are 318 species that have been seen here.

Bellavista (1,800-2,300 m) on the Nono-Mindo road is a perfectly situated lodge with colourful easy-to-see birds, and plenty of rarities for hardcore birders.

El Pahuma (1,600-2,600 m) is an easy day trip from Quito (about an hour) on the Calacalí-Esmeraldas road, with lots of birds and even an occasional Spectacled Bear. A visitor centre with lodging is under construction, along with a botanical garden. A preliminary survey found about 130 species of birds here.

Maquipucuna (1,200-2,800 m) just off the Calacalí-Esmeraldas road has extensive forest, and cabins for guests. There are about 300 species here.

Mindo (1,300-2,400), the most ecotourism-conscious town in Ecuador (see page 146) has many good lodges. Even the road into town (easily reached from Quito

In two hours) Is excellent for good views of beautiful birds like quetzals and tanagers. More than 400 species occur in the whole area.

The Chiriboga road (900-3,200 m) from the south of Quito to near Santo Domingo is good for birds in its middle and lower sections, but it can be very muddy; a four-wheel-drive vehicle is recommended. Guajalito (1,900-2,400 m) is situated half-way down the Chiriboga Road and could be used as a base and as a place to do forest-interior birding.

La Hesperia (1,000-2,000 m) off the Aloag-Santo Domingo road has good mid-elevation forest (which is otherwise hard to reach in the west) and good facilities.

Otonga (800-2,300 m) is a private reserve rising into the mountains south of the Aloag-Santo Domingo road. The bird life here is known for not being shy, especially the Dark-backed Wood-Quails.

Chilla, Guanazán, Manú, and Selva Alegre (2,800-3,000 m), on the road from Saraguro to the coast, have remnant forests and good birds.

Piñas Forest/Buenaventura (800-1,000 m) 24 km north of the road from Loja to the coast is an important area for bird conservation, since there are few remaining tracts in the area. Many rare birds are present. Piñas has over 310 bird species.

Guachanamá Ridge (2,000-2,800 m) between Celica and Alamor in extreme southwest Ecuador contains many rare southwestern endemic birds.

Sozoranga-Nueva Fátima road (1,300-2,600 m) near the Peruvian border in Loja has remnants of a wide variety of mid-elevation forests, and has many southwest endemics. There are 190 known species in the area.

Inter-Andean forests & páramos   Guandera (3,100-3,800 m), near the Colombian border, has beautiful temperate forest with Espeletia *páramo* and many rare birds.

Pasochoa (2,700-4,200 m) provides a very easy cloud forest to visit just south of Quito. Not virgin, but lots of birds (about 120 species).

Parque Nacional Cotopaxi (3,700-6,000 m), 1½ hours south of Quito, is a spectacular setting in which to find birds of the high arid *páramo*. There is also a birdy lake and marsh, Limpiopungo. About 90 species are known from the park.

Parque Nacional Cajas (3,000-4,500 m) has extensive *páramo* and high elevation forest, accessible from Cuenca. It has 125 known species, including Condor and the Violet-tailed Metaltail, a hummingbird endemic to this area.

The Oña-Saraguro-Santiago road (2,000-2,600 m) between Cuenca and Loja has great roadside birding in high-elevation forest remnants. About 145 species have been seen here.

Eastern Andes   Papallacta (3,000-4,400 m), 1½ hours east of Quito, has a dramatic cold wet landscape of grassland and high elevation forest. Condors are regular here, along with many other highland birds.

Guango (2,700 m) is a new lodge with good birding in temperate forest below Papallacta. 95 high-elevation species have been found here so far.

Baeza (1,900-2,400 m), about two hours east of Quito, has forest remnants near town which can be surprisingly birdy. The road to the antennas above town is especially rich.

San Isidro (2,000 m), half an hour from Baeza just off the Baeza-Tena road, is a comfortable lodge with bird-rich forests all around, and wonderful hospitality. The bird list exceeds 260 species.

SierrAzul (2,200-2,400 m), 12 km beyond San Isidro, protects a slightly higher elevation; good birds and some endangered mammals. About 140 bird species seen here so far.

Guacamayos Ridge (1,700-2,300 m) on the Baeza-Tena road has excellent roadside forest rich in bird life.

San Rafael Falls (1,400 m) on the Baeza-Lago Agrio road is a very good place to see Cocks-of-the–Rock and other subtropical birds. Access is an easy walk once you reach the site. Over 200 bird species have been found there, and the true total is certainly higher.

The Loreto road (300-1,400 m) connecting the Baeza-Tena road to Coca makes a fabulous subtropical transect with many very rare birds. More than 300 species have been found there.

The Baños area (1,500-5,000 m) has good forests at a wide range of elevations, though much of it can only be reached after serious hiking.

The Gualaceo-Limón road (1,400-3,350 m) northeast of Cuenca has perhaps the best roadside birding on the east slope, in a spectacular natural setting. It is not well studied, but already the bird list exceeds 200 species. A complete list will probably exceed 300 species.

Parque Nacional Podocarpus (950-3,700 m) near Loja is one of the most diverse protected areas in the world. There are several easy access points at different elevations. The park is very rich in birds, including many rarities and some newly discovered species; there could be up to 800 species in the park!

The Loja-Zamora road (1,000-2,850 m): some segments of the old road (parallel to the current one) are very good for birds. A total of 375 species have been found along the new and old roads.

Cuyabeno lodges (200-300 m) in the northern Oriente are located in seasonally flooded forests not found elsewhere, and lots of wildlife. These lodges have well over 400 species of birds. **Oriente jungle**

Rio Napo area lodges (200-300 m) in the north and central Oriente provide a wide spectrum of facilities and prices, in forest ranging from moderately disturbed to absolutely pristine. Some of these lodges are among the most bird-rich single-elevation sites in the world, with lists exceeding 550 species.

Archidona/Tena/Misahuallí area lodges (300-600 m) in west-central Oriente are much easier and cheaper to reach than other sites, and the lodges are especially comfortable. The forest in this area is somewhat disturbed however, so larger birds and mammals are scarce or absent.

Pastaza area lodges (200-300 m) in the southern Oriente have a slightly different set of birds than the other areas, and a different cultural environment.

Only the inhabited islands may be visited without taking an organized and guided tour. To visit the uninhabited ones independently, you have to obtain scientific permission, which is difficult. **The Galápagos**

See also the Galápagos chapter, page 389

There is great pleasure in coming to grips with tropical birds on your own, but a good professional bird guide can show you many more species than you will find by yourself. The quality of guides varies greatly; if you choose to take a guided tour, make sure you get a guide who knows bird calls well, since this is the way most tropical birds are found. There are excellent professional bird tour companies in Europe and the US; in addition, there are some Ecuadorean companies which specialize in bird tours. Price is usually a good indicator of quality. **Guided tours**

See Special interest tour operators, page 24, for a selection of Quito birding companies

Natural habitat is quickly being destroyed in Ecuador, and many birds are threatened with extinction. Responsible ecotourism is one way to fight this trend; by visiting the lodges listed above you are making it economically feasible for the owners to protect their land instead of farming or logging it. Another way you can help protect important Ecuadorean forest tracts is by donating to foundations that buy land for nature **Conservation issues** reserves. The **Jocotoco Foundation** specializes in buying up critical bird habitat in Ecuador; it is a small, lean foundation directed by the world's top experts on South American birds (for example Robert Ridgely, author of *Birds of South America*, and Neils Krabbe, co-author of *Birds of the High Andes*). Their work deserves support. For more information see www.jocotoco.org

Climbing

Outrageously easy access makes Ecuador a fantastic place to get some high altitude climbing experience

See Books, page 463, for further reading

Ecuador's mountains are one of its greatest attractions and there are 10 summits over 5,000 m high, of which nine have glaciers, with routes ranging from easy snow-plods to hard and technical routes. Michael Koerner, in his *The Fool's Climbing Guide to Ecuador and Peru*, wrote: "The mountains are beautiful but above all exotic. On the same climb one can fight tropical vegetation, stroll up a glacier, and look down the crater of a live volcano." From Quito, using public transport, you can arrive at the base of seven of the country's big 10 mountains the same day and summit the next day – after you have acclimatized.

Acclimatization means letting your body adapt to the high altitude. No one should attempt to climb over 5,000 m until they have spent at least a week at the height of Quito (2,800 m) or equivalent. Many of the sub-5,000 m mountains are enjoyable walk-ups and a number of the big 10 are suitable for beginners, while others are technically challenging and only suitable for experienced mountaineers.

NB Deglaciation is rapidly altering the face of Ecuador's highest mountains. Neither the descriptions provided in this book, nor those in specialized climbing guides, can be assumed to remain correct. Conditions and routes are constantly changing. Even experienced mountaineers should not attempt to climb in Ecuador without first consulting their local colleagues about current conditions. Beginners should never attempt a glaciated summit without a competent local guide.

The big ten   If you've never climbed and want to suck some air at high altitude, **Cotopaxi** (5,897 m) is your best bet. While not, as often stated, the highest active volcano in the world, Cotopaxi is undoubtedly one of the most beautiful mountains in the world and the view down into the crater from the rim is unforgettable. Access is easy: you drive to 4,600 m in three hours from Quito, and the normal route is suitable for complete beginners climbing with a competent guide. Starting in Quito, you spend one night at the hut, climb the next morning and are back in town that afternoon. On the down side, Cotopaxi is the most climbed mountain in the Andes, the hut is often crowded and so is the normal route. (See also page 196.)

The lowest of the big 10, **Tungurahua**, at 5,016 m, is not a good first climb because you start in the resort town of Baños at 1,800 m, leaving a massive 3,200 m of ascent to the summit. If you do climb Tungurahua you must have crampons and ice axe and be roped up to cross the summit glacier. **NB** At the close of this edition Tungurahua was dangerous and off-limits to climbers due to volcanic activity. (See Baños, page 220, for details.)

Ecuador's highest peak, the giant **Chimborazo**, at 6,310 m, was long considered the highest mountain on Earth. It is, if you measure its height from the centre of the planet. Stand on the summit and thanks to the equatorial bulge you are closer to the stars than at any other point on the Earth's surface. However, the climb is long – 1,300 m of ascent from the hut – and cold. Due to ash fall from Tungurahua and the effects of the tropical sun, there are at times impassable *penitentes* – conical ice formations – near the summit. (See also page 232.) Opposite Chimborazo is **Carihuairazo** (5,020 m), which is technically more interesting than its neighbour.

Other mountains regularly climbed include **Cayambe** (5,789 m), the only place on the planet where the latitude is 0° and so is the temperature. It's a technically easy climb but dangerous, because of the large number of crevasses and the fact that its eastern location means that cloud rolls in most days from the jungle, reducing visibility to another zero. (See also page 163.)

Access to **Antisana** (5,705 m) has improved dramatically with the opening of a new road. You can now drive to base camp in three hours from Quito, but you must obtain permission beforehand from a local landowner. The normal route is technically easy but, as with Cayambe, it is dangerous due to the large number of crevasses.

Iliniza Norte (5,116 m) is the only one of the big 10 that does not have a glacier. It is a rock scramble but parts of the route are exposed, unstable and dangerous. You need a rope and the experience to use it or hire a guide. Opposite Iliniza Norte is **Iliniza Sur** (5,263 m), which is beautiful but technically challenging and only for experienced climbers. (See page 195.)

The least climbed of the big 10 are **El Altar** (5,319 m) and **Sangay** (5,323 m). El Altar is a spectacularly beautiful blown-out volcano with an emerald-green crater lake and nine separate peaks, all of them technically difficult (see page 233). Sangay is the world's most continuously active volcano. The route is long – 5-7 days – and technically easy, but extremely dangerous due to the likelihood of being hit by lumps of rock being ejected from the volcano. (See page 234.)

The normal routes (and huts) on Cotopaxi, Chimborazo, and Iliniza Norte can be crowded. Outside these three you are likely to have the mountains to yourself, and if you climb any route other than the normal route on these three you will also keep away from the crowds.

Apart from the big 10 there are many other mountains worth climbing in Ecuador, whether you are acclimatizing for the bigger peaks, don't like the ice and snow or just want to try something different. Around Otavalo are three mountains: Ecuador's 11th highest peak **Cotacachi** (4,939 m) which is made of loose and dangerous rock, **Imbabura** (4,630 m), a walk-up best started from the La Esperanza to the north, and **Fuya Fuya** (4,263 m), the highest point of the massive Mojanda volcano. (See page 174, and note public safety problems in this area.)

Other mountains

Above Quito are the Pichinchas: **Guagua** (4,794 m) and **Rucu** (4,790 m). Guagua is a good acclimatization climb, but enquire beforehand about the current level of volcanic activity. Unfortunately, Rucu should not be climbed due to continuous problems with muggers, sometimes armed. (See page 155.)

In the Cotopaxi national park are the triple peaked **Rumiñahui** (4,722 m) and **Sincholagua** (4,901 m). For Rumiñahui Norte and Sincholagua, a rope and helmet are essential to reach the summits. Rumiñahui Central is the easiest scramble, starting from Limpiopungo, while Rumiñahui Sur is climbed from the northwest via Machachi and Pansaleo (see page 197). Opposite, on the other side of the central valley, is **Corazón** (4,791 m), which is a long but easy walk-up and gives fantastic views of Cotopaxi and the Ilinizas.

Two of the most esoteric peaks in Ecuador are **Sara Urcu** (4,676 m) and **Cerro Hermoso** (4,571 m). Sara Urcu is south of Cayambe. Whymper climbed it in 1880 but the climb was not repeated until 1955. It has Ecuador's lowest and easternmost glacier. You thrash about in the wet and vegetation for several days while your ice axe and crampons rust, before getting to the glacier and putting them on. It is very easy to get extremely lost in this area. A map and compass and the ability to use them are essential. A GPS is recommended. Map reading is also a requirement for **Cerro Hermoso**, the highest point of the mysterious Llanganates range, where dense vegetation and complicated topography allegedly help conceal 750 tons of Inca gold collected for Atahualpa's ransom and stashed after his murder (see box, Cursed treasure, page 429). The peak is a walk-up, once you've found it. Access is easier from the north but it is still a five-day plus expedition and only for the fit, acclimatized and experienced.

To the east, in the jungle, are two active volcanoes **Reventador** (3,562 m) and **Sumaco** (3,900 m), whose position was not determined until 1921. These two can be climbed if you like hot and sweaty conditions and have your machete-user's licence to hack your way through the vegetation to get to base of the volcanoes. Note however that Reventador errupted spectacularly at time of going to press: don't climb without checking out the latest situation. (See also page 364.)

When to climb   There are two climbing seasons in Ecuador: June to August and December to February. Allegedly, the eastern cordillera is drier December-February and the western cordillera June-August (though it is often windy in August) and Cotopaxi has more clear days than any other peak. It is best to avoid the wetter seasons March-May and September-November. However, the weather can be good or bad on any day of the year and it is worth remembering that Cotopaxi has been climbed on every day of the year and that Whymper's grand tour in 1880, when he made seven first ascents, was December to July. Bad weather is just predominant for the mountains on the eastern side of the eastern cordillera (for example El Altar, Sangay, Llanganates, Sara Urcu). Being on the equator, days and nights are 12 hours long. As a result, climbs are attempted all year round all over the country.

More important than the time of year is the time of day. You should aim to reach the summit of any of the snowcapped peaks at 0700 so that descent is completed well before midday. As the equatorial sun warms the snow it attains the consistency of sugar which makes it hard going and also dangerous, and avalanches are far more likely. On top of this, any rock held in place by ice will start its gravity-induced downward journey once the sun has melted the cementing ice.

Nights and early mornings are generally clear. However, cloud normally comes in by midday if not earlier, often reducing visibility to zero. This is another reason to climb at night but if the route is not tracked out by previous parties it is worth marking the way with flags; white footsteps in white snow in a white-out are difficult to follow. The weather tends to be better at full moon and the equatorial moon is so strong that you do not need to use your headtorch if climbing by moonlight, from full moon down to half moon.

Sunburn & altitude
In good weather the heat is incredible: you want to strip off but if you do so you will get the worst sunburn of your life

Ultra violet light at high altitude on or near the equator is very, very strong. Without proper eye protection it is possible to get snowblindness after as little as 15 minutes above 5,000 m. It does not matter if it is sunny or cloudy, in fact more UV light is reflected on cloudy days. Snowblindness is not normally apparent until the night after the damage has been done. The pain has been described as what it must be like to have acid or boiling water poured into your eyes. The next day, the victim often cannot see and will have to be led down the mountain. Snowblindness counts as a permanent eye injury – part of the retina is burnt out – which means victims are more susceptible in the future. Wear sunglasses that give 100 protection against UV light. Ski goggles with 100 UV protection lenses are useful for cloudy days, bad weather, and as spares in case you break or lose your glacier glasses. Sunburn is a serious business at high altitude and will happen on completely overcast days. The power of the equatorial sun reflecting off snow will burn the skin under the chin, up the nostrils and behind the ears, so remember to apply protection to all these areas. Use weatherproof sun block with a rating of factor 25 or higher.

Guides & rescue   **ASEGUIM (Asociación Ecuatoriana de Guías de Montaña)**, the Ecuadorean mountain guides association, was formed in 1993 and has very high standards for its members who have a rigorous training programme monitored by mountain guides from the French national mountain training school ENSA. Another advantage of climbing with ASEGUIM guides is that should you need rescuing they have the best and fastest rescue organization in the country. The usual cost is around US$1,500 per rescue, but can be much higher. All ASEGUIM guides carry a two-way radio. There is no helicopter rescue and, as yet, little cooperation from the army, police or government. If you will be climbing extensively in Ecuador, it is a good idea to register with your embassy or consulate and advise them of any insurance you may have to cover the costs of rescue or repatriation by air ambulance. The first place the authorities usually contact in the event of an emergency involving a foreign climber is the embassy of their home country. In an emergency ASEGUIM may be reached through *Safari Tours* (T02-2552505) or *Compañía de Guías de Montaña* (T02-2504773), both in Quito.

Equipment Everything you might lose, break or forget is usually available from one of the Quito climbing and outdoor shops, but sometimes none of them will have what you want. Gear from the US tends to be cheaper in Ecuador than in Europe but European gear tends to be very expensive. A number of shops hire gear as do agencies for their clients, but always check the condition of rented equipment very carefully before you take it out.

Mountain refuges These are mainly of international standard with many improvements in recent years. Most provide the basic services: electric light; running water; and cooking facilities. They usually have a warden throughout the main climbing season. Nightly tariffs are usually US$10-20.

Rock & ice climbing courses Courses are offered on Cayambe, Cotopaxi and Chimborazo. There is usually only one per year, but ASEGUIM might organize others if there is sufficient interest; ie if a reasonable number of tourists organize themselves into a group. *Safari* run an ice glacier school, the only one in the country (see Tour operators in Quito, page 127).

Diving and snorkelling

The coast of Ecuador is a paradise for divers, combining both cool and warm water dive destinations in one of the most biologically diverse marine environments on earth. The Galápagos Islands are undoubtedly the most popular destination, but diving in lesser known waters such as those off the central coast of Ecuador has been gaining popularity in recent years. The secluded coves of Isla de la Plata, 45 km off the coast of Machalilla National Park, contain an abundance of multicoloured tropical fish which make diving and snorkelling a great experience. Colonies of sea lions can be seen, as well as migrating humpback whales, from late June to September, and many species of marine birds.

For a detailed description of Galápagos dive sites and marine life, see page 405

The Galápagos Islands are well known for their distinctive marine environments and offer more than 20 dive sites including opportunities for night diving. Each island contains its own unique environment and many are home to underwater life forms endemic to this part of the world.

Diving is becoming more popular with tourists since the cost of doing a PADI course in Ecuador is relatively low. There are several agencies in Quito which feature diving and full instruction on their programmes. Equipment can be hired, but it is advisable to check everything thoroughly. The larger bookshops also stock diving books and identification guides for fish and other marine life. Among the agencies specializing in diving are *Quasar Nautica* and *Tropic Ecological Adventures* (see starting page 127 for their addresses). See also the Galápagos chapter, page 419, for diving agencies in Puerto Ayora.

Horse riding

See Special interest
tour operators,
page 24, for a
selection of companies
in Ecuador
specializing in
horse-trekking trips

The horse was only introduced to South America during the Spanish conquest but it has become an important part of rural life throughout Ecuador. Horse riding, whether for a brief excursion or a multi-day trek, is an excellent way to get to know the countryside, its people and local equestrian traditions. Horse rentals are available in many popular resort areas including Otavalo, Baños and Vilcabamba (see the corresponding sections in the travelling text). Visits to haciendas throughout the country also usually offer the possibility of horseback riding.

Hot springs

Ecuador is located on the 'Ring of Fire' and has many volcanoes: active, dormant and non-active (dead). Hot springs are associated with all three, although they are mostly found with the older volcanoes where sufficient time has elapsed since the last eruptions for water systems to become established. There are several areas where you can look for hot springs:

1 On the coastal lowlands, pressure from the collision of the continental and oceanic plates causes friction and heat is dissipated into the water system. Many of these springs have a high mineral content and these sulphurous waters are frequently praised for their curative properties. Very few are large enough to warrant development. Temperatures range from 20°C to 30°C.

2 At the foot of the Andes, water temperatures are elevated by pressure caused by plate tectonics. South of Guayaquil there are several springs with minimal or no development, all-in temperature ranges from 40°C to 55°C. To the north of Guayaquil there are fewer springs and the temperatures are much lower.

3 In the Andes above 1,500 m most of the springs are directly associated with older volcanic action. The vast majority of Ecuadorean hot springs are found in the Andes north of Riobamba and up to Colombia. To the south of Riobamba the only major hot springs are a few kilometres south of Cuenca.

4 The few springs at the foot of the Andes in the upper Amazon are mostly associated with secondary ridges of mountains, and the heat source seems to be pressure caused by uplifting and folding. None of these has been developed and access to all is difficult.

5 In the craters of Alcedo Volcano, in the Galápagos Islands, and Guagua Pichincha, direct contact with heat sources causes rainwater to boil. In the Galápagos this produces an intermittent geyser. On Pichincha, prior to the 1999 eruptions, a small hot stream with minimal mineral content flowed down from the active crater. **NB** At the close of this edition the crater of Guagua Pichincha was dangerous and off limits to visitors due to volcanic activity.

Here is a selection of Ecuador's best springs, from north to south.

Aguas Hediondas are about 1½ hours west of Tulcán, see page 189.

Chachimbiro   is accessed from Ibarra, see page 182.

Nangulví can be reached from Otavalo, see page 164.

Oyacachi   These springs have recently undergone development. There is public transport from Cayambe to Canguahua hourly; beyond there, only infrequently, but rental trucks are available. Alternatively, hire a horse or walk about 25 km. Several families in the village will provide floors to sleep on, or you can ask to sleep in one of the churches or in the school.

The hot springs at **Papallacta**, the best developed site in the country, can be visited in a day trip from Quito, as can the more modest ones at **El Tingo** and **La Merced**. See page 154 for details about Papallacta.

The hot springs of **Baños** (Tungurahua) are the best known in Ecuador. There are four separate bathing complexes here, and the town of Baños is overflowing with *residencias*, *pensiones*, guest houses, restaurants and activities, all of which can be full during national holidays, especially Carnival. See page 213.

Palitahua About one hour south of Baños on the flanks of Tungurahua, these springs are a couple of hours' walk up from the village of Puela. Tucked into a narrow mountain valley, surrounded by forest and below a cold waterfall, are three water sources, the two hotter ones contained in small cement tanks.

At the close of this edition the Palitagua area was dangerous and off-limits to visitors due to the volcanic activity of Tungurahua

Essentials

El Placer Access to this spring takes a couple of days' trekking, but it's well worth the effort. It is located in Sangay National Park by the headwaters of the Río Palora. Access is from the village of Alao, which is in turn reached from Riobamba. The trail is clear and easy to follow. The pool has been enlarged and deepened and a new refuge built to shelter about 15 people. Take food, adequate clothing, sleeping bags, mats, etc.

There is another **Baños**, near Cuenca, which has the hottest commercial springs in the country. It is only 10 minutes by city bus from the city, see page 255.

Baños San Vicente These springs are close to Salinas and Libertad on the coast. They are famed for the curative properties of the warm mud lake which people slide into before baking themselves dry. There are also several indoor pools of different temperatures, some steam rooms and massage facilities. Take a bus running between Guayaquil and Libertad and get off about 15 km east of Santa Elena. Small trucks and cars pick up passengers at this junction. There are a couple of small hotels in the village.

Yanayacu Two hours east of Guayaquil on the road to Cuenca is the village of Cochancay. About 1 km up the hill from the village there is a small turning on the left; this is the old unpaved road to the mountains. About 1 km along the road there is another turning to the left which leads down to the Baños of Yanayacu. There are numerous small and medium-sized hot pools on a rock outcrop beside the Río Bulu Bulu. The small *residencia* here has a few rooms and food on the weekend.

Mountain biking

More and more people come to Ecuador to ride through the spectacular mountain scenery or along the coastal roads. The upper Amazon basin also offers a relatively traffic-free route from north to south.

See Quito Sport, page 126, for agencies offering mountain bike tours and bike shops. See also Cycling, page 56

What many people don't take into account is the frequently extreme conditions in which they find themselves biking. Dehydration can be a very real issue when cycling at high altitudes or in the hot tropical lowlands. Bottled water is available at many small stores in villages, but along some of the more spectacular routes they are few and far between. A water pump or other sterilizing systems should always be carried. Sunscreen is essential at high altitudes even on cloudy days. Wrap around sunglasses help to restrict the amount of dust which gets into the eyes.

When planning routes it is best to use 1:50,000 topographical maps. The IGM in Quito also produces a series of very practical *hojas de ruta* which include elevation profiles. You should in addition seek a little local knowledge, since maps are not updated frequently and new roads are often not indicated, nor are landslides which may make certain routes impassable. Maps do not always distinguish between cobbled and good *lastre* (gravel) graded surfaces. The latter are normally far superior for biking and should be taken where possible.

Departing from Quito in northerly and southerly directions it is difficult to avoid the busy paved Panamericana for about the first 30 km. For those going south the **Machachi** area makes a good destination for a first day. To the north a lot of traffic can be avoided by biking to **Mitad del Mundo**, an easy first day, and then taking the old

Routes

road with its dramatic scenery via **San José de Minas** to travel to the **Otavalo** area. Those who wish to stay on the paved road should consider **Guayllabamba** (easy) or **Cayambe** (via Otón, with lovely views but harder) a first day destination.

The road **east from Baños** toward the jungle is very popular and beautiful, and there are ample opportunities to rent bikes here. Unfortunately holdups of bikers have (rarely) taken place on this route, so enquire about public safety before heading out. In general, for biking just like for hiking, the farther from the main gringo trail, the safer you are.

Trying to cover too great a distance, especially at the beginning of a trip, is a common mistake; 40-50 km a day is a respectable distance to cover at altitudes above 2,500 m. Beyond 50 km from Quito the traffic decreases and more alternative roads become available. In many areas the Panamericana is paralleled by older cobbled or dirt roads, with very little traffic.

General advice A good bike lock should be considered essential equipment, the best will be long enough to pass through both wheels and the frame. Most bus lines will carry bicycles on the roof racks for little or no extra charge. It is advisable to supervise the loading and assure that the derailer is not jammed up against luggage which might damage it. If you can, take some cardboard to protect the bike while it rides the bus. If you take a long journey with major altitude changes let a little air out of the tyres especially when going from lower to higher altitudes. Bikes may be taken on commercial flights in place of a suitcase, always double check that there will be space. Routes to the Jungle have more luggage restrictions, as do those to the Galápagos.

Paragliding and hang-gliding

These are pretty special activities amid the high mountains, and its devotees can sometimes be seen in the rays of the afternoon sun drifting off Pichincha toward Quito. The sports are also practiced at several other highland locations as well as at Crucita and Canoa on the Pacific coast. In **Quito** *Escuela Pichincha de Vuelo Libre*, Carlos Endara Oe3-60 y Amazonas, T02-2256592 (office hours) T09-9478349 (mob), parapent@uio.satnet.net, is a good point of contact. The school offers complete courses as well as tandem flights for novices. Speak to Enrique Castro here, he can also advise about other sites and contacts in **Ibarra**, **Ambato**, **Riobamba** and **Cuenca**. In **Crucita**, Raul Tobar at *Hostal Voladores*, T05-676200, hvoladores@hotmail.com, offers tandem flights, three-day paragliding and five-day hang gliding courses.

Rafting and kayaking

See Special interest tour operators, page 24, for a list of agencies in Quito, Tena and Baños

Ecuador is a whitewater paradise. Warm waters, tropical rainforest and dozens of accessible rivers concentrated in such a small area have made the country a 'hotspot' for rafters and kayakers the world over. Regional rainy seasons occur at different times throughout the year so the action never stops – there's always a river to run.

Rafting is an activity open to almost anyone with a sense of adventure. Worldwide the sport continues to grow, as is the case in Ecuador, with the majority of participants first-timers. No previous rafting experience is needed to join a trip if each boat has an experienced guide at the helm. Trips can run from one to six days.

Rafting trips are offered by operators in Quito, Tena and Baños with guides, equipment, transport and food provided. Although not new, the rafting industry has until recently remained relatively undeveloped. Standards vary so it is really important to ask a few questions before booking a trip. The most important things to look for are experienced guides and top notch equipment. Without exception, the reputable companies are run by foreign or foreign-trained Ecuadorean guides. Many guides now have a license issued by the Ministry of Tourism but be warned that as there are no controls in place this does not guarantee that safety standards are always met. Ask about the guides' rafting, river rescue and first aid training, about the rafting and personal safety equipment, if they carry first aid, raft repair and river rescue kits, if they utilize safety kayakers and have on-river emergency communications. Although there are some inherent dangers in river running, these are the factors that make a rafting trip relatively safe.

Kayakers find the biggest problem is choosing which of the dozens of enticing rivers to run in the time they have available. The following river descriptions include the most popular runs. However as new rivers are being 'opened' every year the list is by no means exhaustive. For information on river conditions, the ins and outs of travelling with kayaks, rental of kayaking equipment and guiding services, contact the **Quito KA Kayak Club** (www.quitokayakers.tripod.com) or *Yacu Amu Rafting/Ríos Ecuador* (see below). 'Learn to' courses may be offered that give newcomers the chance to find out what they've been missing out on. There's no better place to learn this exciting sport than on Ecuador's warm tropical rivers.

The majority of Ecuador's whitewater rivers share a number of characteristics. Plunging off the Andes the upper sections are very steep creeks offering, if they're runnable at all, serious technical grade V, suitable for expert kayakers only. As the creeks join on the lower slopes they form rivers navigable by both raft and kayak (ie less steep, more volume). Some of these rivers offer up to 100 km of continuous grade III-IV whitewater, before flattening out to rush towards the Pacific Ocean on one side of the ranges or deep into the Amazon Basin on the other.

Grades

Unfortunately, some of Ecuador's rivers are severely polluted. Water quality may vary significantly depending on such factors as proximity of towns, local agricultural practices, last rainfall, river volume, and the relative proportions of surface and ground water. It's a complex equation but as a general rule the rivers running straight off the eastern and western slopes of the Andes are less subject to pollution than the highland rivers which drain some of the most densely populated regions of the country before their descent into the jungle or to the Pacific.

Water quality
Always ask about water quality before signing up for a trip

Owing to their proximity to Quito, the **Blanco** river and its tributaries are the most frequently run in Ecuador. There is almost 200 km of raftable whitewater in the Blanco valley, with the Toachi/Blanco combination and the Upper Blanco being the most popular day trips. The former starts as a technical grade III-IV run, including the infamous rapids of the El Sapo canyon, before joining the Blanco where big waves abound year round. The latter is probably the world's longest day trip – 47 km of non-stop grade III-IV rapids in a little over four hours on the river (February-June only). Trips are also offered on the Caoni (grade II-III) and Mulate (III) rivers.

In addition to those already mentioned, kayakers have a number of other possibilities to choose from depending on the time of year and their skills and experience. The **Mindo** (III-IV), **Saloya** (IV-V), **Pachejal** (III-IV), **Upper Caoni** (IV), **Pilatón** (IV-V), **Damas** (IV-V) and **Upper Toachi** (IV-V) are all options.

Pacific Coast rivers

The waters of the Quijos river and its tributaries are a whitewater playground. Within a 30 km radius of the town of El Chaco you'll find everything from steep, technical grade V creek runs to big volume, roller coaster grade III and IV. The Quijos (IV-V) has quickly earned the reputation of a classic for rafting and kayaking, boasting challenging whitewater and spectacular canyon scenery. Other popular kayaking runs can be found on

Quijos river

the **Papallacta** (V), **Cosanga** (III-IV) and **Oyacachi** (IV) tributaries. Day tripping is the norm on the upper runs although further downstream a two day trip is possible starting near the town of El Reventador. At the end of the upper section the collected waters of the Quijos catchment plunge dramatically over **San Rafael Falls**, which at 145 m is the highest waterfall in Ecuador. Access to the Quijos valley is generally easy as it forms the main corridor from Quito down into the jungle. The most popular put ins and take outs are accessible by road although putting in for the run from El Reventador requires a 40 minute scramble down muddy slopes from the main road.

The best time to dip your paddle depends on how hard you want to push yourself. The rainy season on the eastern slopes generally runs from March to September so at this time you can expect high flows and truly continuous whitewater (for expert kayakers only). The rest of the year, the dry season, is when the commercial rafting and kayaking operators run trips. During these months there's still plenty of action and water and air temperatures are more comfortable.

Oriente

Enquire about public safety before visiting any of these areas near the Colombian border

About 1½ hours from Lago Agrio the **Upper Aguarico** river, from Puerto Libre to Lumbaquí, offers big volume grade II-III rapids. A short distance to the south the clear waters of the **Dué** river (III-IV), a major tributary of the Aguarico, run refreshingly cool off the flanks of Volcán El Reventador. Both rivers are best run between February and July. Regular rafting departures are not offered on either river but special trips can be arranged through one of the Quito-based operators.

In the jungle surrounding Tena, the **Napo** river and its tributaries offer a tremendous amount of whitewater in a small area. It's very easy to spend a week based here and paddle a different river every day. The grade III **Upper Napo** or **Jatunyacu**, the most popular rafting trip, is runnable year round, while the gem of this region, the **Misahuallí** (IV), is rafted during the drier months from October to March. This river passes through pristine jungle in a remote canyon, the highlight being the heart-stopping portage around **Casanova Falls**.

Additional kayaking options include various sections of the Misahualli, **Jondachi**, **Anzu** and **Hollín** rivers. Difficulty is very much water level dependent but most are grade IV or V when they have sufficient water to paddle.

Pastaza

This is generally not run on the lower reaches although a canyon between Shell and the Puyo-Macas road bridge contains some good grade IV rapids at high levels. The most popular trip out of Baños is a 1½-hour run on the grade II-III **Patate** river, a highland tributary of the Pastaza. It should be noted that the upper reaches of the Patate drain the city of Ambato to which are added the denim-blue waters of Pelileo, jean capital of Ecuador. Another tributary, the **Topo** (grade V), has been reported by some expert kayakers to be the best steep creek run in the country.

Upano

The vertical walls of the Namangosa Gorge are covered by a thick layer of primary rainforest broken only by the waters spilling spectacularly off the lip of the gorge

Best known for the **Namangosa Gorge** in which dozens of waterfalls plummet up to 100 m into the river, to date this spectacle has been witnessed by few river runners. While the gorge is undoubtedly the highlight, what makes a journey down the Upano special is witnessing the changing character of an Amazonian river. Trickling from a string of mountain lakes the Upano quickly gathers force, carving a path southward through the province of Morona Santiago. As it rushes past Macas it is shallow and braided. Picking a route from the myriad channels is a real challenge; make the wrong choice and an unscheduled portage will result.

The pace steadily increases until the river plunges into the magnificent Namangosa Gorge. Some falls cascade down staggered cliffs while others freefall into the jungle below. This 'Lost World' atmosphere is made even more daunting by the seething rapids below. The rapids are big class IV with lots of funny water including raft-flipping boils and kayak(er)-swallowing eddylines.

Once out of the gorge, the river broadens and deepens to become a calm but powerful giant on its way to meet the mighty Amazon.

Five and six day rafting trips start near Macas. A few kayakers have attempted the upper reaches of the river and returned with stories to be filed under E for epic. The run from Macas to the end of the gorge is about 120 km and takes four to five days. Some choose to continue another day or so further downstream to the village of Santiago Mayatico which is the final possible take-out. From here it's only a few miles as the toucan flies to the border with Peru.

Recommended months are October to February and this is when commercial trips are offered. During the rest of the year the river can flood unexpectedly. In fact during April and May, when the river peaks, the gorge fills so much that a local Shuar indian once travelled upstream to Macas in a motorized canoe.

Surfing

Ecuador has a few select surfing spots which are becoming increasingly popular with aficionados of the sport as well as with foreign and Ecuadorean tourists who just want to be part of the scene. On the mainland, from north to south, are: **Mompiche** (Esmeraldas), south of Muisne; **San Mateo** (Manabí), south of Manta; **Montañita** (Guayas), between Olón and Manglaralto; and **Playas** near Guayaquil. In Galápagos, there is good surfing at **Playa Punta Carola** outside Puerto Baquerizo Moreno on San Cristóbal Island. Waves are generally best from December to March, except at Playas where the surfing season is usually from June to September.

Trekking

Ecuador's varied landscape, diverse ecological environments, and friendly villagers within a compact area, make travelling by foot a refreshing break from crowded buses. Although the most commonly travelled routes are in the Sierra, there are also a few excellent trekking opportunities on the Coast and in the Oriente. Likewise you can descend from the windswept *páramo* through Andean Slope cloud forest to tropical rain forest and hence observe most of the ecosystems of Ecuador during a single excursion.

See Books, page 464, for further reading and for details of the authors' book Trekking in Ecuador

Many hikes pass through protected areas which are managed by the Ministerio del Ambiente. Approximately 15% of continental Ecuador lies within national parks, ecological reserves and recreation areas, but most of these are threatened by development pressures. The only mainland parks that are adequately staffed and have reasonable infrastructure are **Cotopaxi**, **Cajas**, **Podocarpus** and **Machalilla**. Excellent trekking opportunities are to be found, however, in the countryside throughout Ecuador, whether or not the land is part of a park or resrve.

The official entrance fees for parks and conservation units range from US$5 to US$20 for foreigners (much less for Ecuadoreans). They vary from park to park, see National Parks, page 459, for a complete list. In any event, the less-visited parks and less-used park entrances will have no one around to collect the fee.

It is still the ruggedness and lack of access, however, that protects most of these areas from environmental impacts and makes them so appealing to wilderness travellers. There are not nearly as many well-marked trails as you would find in national parks in developed countries. In some places ancient routes have been used for thousands of years by *campesinos* and are relatively easy to follow. In other areas you may be bush-whacking through the forest with a machete. A basic knowledge of how to ask for directions in Spanish and map and compass skills are perhaps the most important elements to a successful trek. It is also possible to hire experienced guides (US$50-100 per day) from the major cities or less expensive local *campesino* guides (US$10-25 per day) if you are unsure about the route.

Topographic maps should be purchased at the **IGM** in Quito (see page 42). The 1:50,000 scale maps are most useful, of which there is coverage of most of the country. For more remote locations bring a handheld GPS, but remember that this is no substitute for comprehensive navigation and map-reading skills.

It is best to bring trekking equipment from home, but if you are travelling light most gear can be purchased or hired at outfitters in Quito. Check rented gear very carefully.

Guiding & equipment rental Quito companies which offer guiding services include: *Angermeyer's*, *Compañía de Guias de Montaña*, *Pamir*, *Safari*, *Sierra Nevada*, *Surtrek* and *Vasco Tours*. Complete contact information is found under Quito Tour operators, page 127. For a complete list of Quito shops which sell or rent gear, see Camping, climbing and trekking equipment, page 123. Guides and gear can also be hired at agencies in Otavalo, Latacunga, Baños, Riobamba, Cuenca, Loja and Vilcabamba.

Equipment The standard hiking shoe for Ecuador is the rubber boot, which is worn by most *campesinos* while working in the countryside. Travellers may balk at using footwear that only costs US$5 and can be purchased in any town, but they keep feet warm and dry through muddy terrain, unlike conventional leather or goretex hiking boots. As long the trail is not rocky they are also very comfortable. Note, however, that very large sizes may be hard to find. **All drinking water must be boiled or treated.** Iodine tablets are easy and reliable but may be difficult to locate in Quito. Common stove fuels which may be found in Ecuador include white gas (this may be difficult, try Kywi hardware stores in Quito), kerosene (most hardware stores), and gas canisters (outfitters listed above). All gasoline in Ecuador is unleaded and may be burnt by some stoves.

Altitude sickness (locally called *soroche*) can be a problem for recent arrivals, and dehydration can affect anyone. It is important to drink lots of water and not push yourself too hard when you have just arrived. If an accident occurs self-evacuation may be quickest, but rescues can be arranged with ASEGUIM, see Guides and rescue, page 72.

Hazards
For information on sunburn and altitude, see Climbing, page 72, and Health, pages 86 and 88

NB Some of the more popular hikes in the country such as Laguna Cuicocha, Lagunas de Mojanda and especially Rucu Pichincha (best avoided) have experienced armed robberies. The basic rule of thumb is that the farther off the beaten gringo track, the safer you are. It is important to always enquire locally about the safety of a particular trek.

Hiking in the Sierra is mostly across high elevation *páramo*, through agricultural lands, and past indigenous communities living in traditional ways. There are outstanding views of glaciated peaks in the north and precolumbian ruins in the south. On the coast there are only a few areas developed for hiking ranging from dry forest to coastal rain forest. The Oriente is mostly virgin tropical rain forest and offers excellent hiking even outside the protected areas. The forest canopy shades out the brushy vegetation, making cross-country travel relatively easy. Since there are no vantage points to get a bearing it is also easy to get lost, and a GPS does not work in a dense forest. Local guides are therefore required because of this difficulty in navigation and because you will be walking on land owned by indigenous tribes. The Andean Slopes are steep and often covered by virtually impenetrable cloud forests and it rains a lot. Many ancient trading routes head down the river valleys. Some of these trails are still used. Others may be overgrown and difficult to follow but offer the reward of intact ecosystems. You may be travelling across land that is either owned outright by indigenous people or jointly managed with the Miniterio de Ambiente. It is important to be respectful of the people and request permission to pass through or camp. Sometimes a fee may be charged by locals but it is usually minimal.

Different terrains

Although each region has its own wet and dry seasons, the climate is inherently unpredictable and, as a trekker, you must be prepared for all conditions at any time of the year. See pages 20 and 456 for further details.

Climate

There are three treks described in detail in the main text. These are: **Cajas National Park** (page 257); **Saraguro to Yacuambi** (page 260); and the **Inca trail to Ingapirca** (page 241). **NB** Volcán Reventador erupted spectacularly at the time of going to press. It is currently dangerous to climb or trek near El Reventador.

Trek descriptions

Volunteer programmes

'Voluntourism' has been growing in popularity in Ecuador, attracting many visitors – from students to retirees. It is a good way to become more intimately acquainted with the country (blemishes and all) and, at the same time, to try and lend a hand to its people. If you are seriously interested in volunteering, you should research organizations before you leave home. Try to choose a position which matches your individual skills. Think carefully about the kind of work that you would find most satisfying, and also be realistic about how much you might be able to achieve. The shorter your stay, the more limited should be your expectations in all regards. You must speak at least basic Spanish, and preferably a good deal more, in order to work effectively in a local community setting. Also remember that you are volunteering in order to get to know and help the 'real Ecuador' and that conditions can sometimes be pretty harsh. In almost all cases you will have to pay your own airfare, and also possibly contribute toward your room and board. For information about visas for longer stays, see page 33. There are a number of different areas where voluntary work is possible. We list a few here but **South American Explorers** in Quito (see page 25) has details of many other opportunities.

Essentials

Environmental conservation   **Corporación Ornitológica del Ecuador (CECIA)** works with bird conservation in the Quito area and other locations in Ecuador. Volunteer opportunuies vary according to their current projects and requirements. Contact CECIA in Quito, La Tierra 203 y Los Shyris, T/F02-2271800, cecia_de@uio.satnet.net, www.cecia.org

Funadción Arcoiris works with a variety of nature conservation and sustainable community development projects in the far south of the country. Contact them at Segundo Cueva Celi 03-15 y Clodoveo Carrión (PO Box 11-01-860), Loja, T/F07-577499, www.arcoiris.org.ec

Fundación Jatun Sacha has six different sites at which volunteers can work, all in exceptional natural areas. Note that this is a large organization. Volunteer programs are just one small part of what they do and volunteers must be prepared to work independently. We have received mixed reports. Contact: Fundación Jatun Sacha, Pasaje Eugenio de Santillán N34-248 y Maurian (PO Box 17-12-867), Quito, T02-2432246, F2453583, www.jatunsacha.org

Fundación Maquipuicuna supports the conservation of biodiversity and sustainable use of natural resources. They need help with reforestation, trail building, environmental education and organic gardening at their reserve northwest of Quito. Contact: Fundación Maquipuicuna, Baquerizo Moreno E9-153 y Tamayo (PO Box 17-12-167), Quito, T02-2507200, F2507201, maqui@ecua.net.ec, www.maqui.org

Fundación Natura is a large Ecuadorean NGO which promotes environmental awareness and education. They require volunteers to assist at their Pasochoa reserve south of Quito, where volunteers may help with the with reforestation. Contact: Fundación Natura, Av República 481 y Almagro (PO Box 17-01-253), Quito, T02-2503391, natura@fnatura.org.ec, www.ecua.net.ec/fnatura/

Rainforest Concern, a British charity, works with various environmental projects in Ecuador, including reforestation in Santa Lucía cloud forest as well as buying and protecting rainforest in Oriente. Contact Fiona Pérez in Quito, T2457143; or Peter Bennett, 27 Lansdowne Crescent, London W11 2NS, T020-7229 2093, F020-7221 4094, www.rainforestconcern.org

Río Muchacho Organic Farm, in the coastal province of Manabí, is a small organization which works with local education, community development and sustainable agriculture. They offer a variety of flexible volunteer experiences. Contact Nicola Mears or Darío Proaño in Bahía de Caráquez, Bolívar 902 y Arenas, T/F691412, www.riomuchacho.com

Jungle guiding The best way to learn about the rainforest is to become a guide at one of the lodges. Qualified field biologists with good interpersonal skills are always in demand, especially if they know birds well. The job can be difficult but will leave a lasting imprint on your life. Check with any of the lodges listed in the Oriente chapter. You should carefully enquire about the terms in advance.

Teaching   **Intercambio Selvático (Jungle Exchange)** seeks to help indigenous communities by teaching them the basics of the English language to maximize their effectiveness in the tourist industry. Volunteers do not need to be qualified teachers but must have an excellent command of the language, an outgoing spirit and a concern for the survival of Amazon cultures and ecosystems. Minimum of one month's commitment. Contact: Chris Canaday, Quito, T02-2447463.

Street children   **Centro de Hospedería La Tola/Los Niños Migrantes** provides overnight shelter for homeless children and is also an educational centre for older children, teaching them skills such as carpentry. Volunteers should be able to make a commitment of at least three months. Contact: Valparaiso 887 y Don Bosco (PO Box 17-11-117), Quito, T02-2581312, F2223426.

Health

It should be no surprise that the health care in the region is varied: there are some decent private and government clinics/hospitals, which more often than not follow the more aggressive American style of medicine (where you will be referred straight to a specialist), but as with all medical care, first impressions count. If a facility is grubby and staff wear grey coats instead of white ones, then be wary of the general standard of medicine and hygiene. Its worth contacting your embassy or consulate on arrival and asking where the recommended (ie those used by diplomats) clinics are. Providing embassies with information on your whereabouts can also be useful if a friend/relative gets ill at home and there is a desperate search for you around the globe. You can also ask them about locally recommended do's and don'ts. If you do get ill, and you have the opportunity, you should ask your medical insurer whether they are satisfied that the medical centre or hospital that you have been referred to is of a suitable standard.

Written by Dr. Charlie Easmon; see Acknowledgements, page 478, for his biography

Essentials

Before discussing the disease-related health risks involved in travel within Ecuador, remember to try to avoid road accidents. You can reduce the likelihood of accidents by not drinking and driving, wearing a seatbelt in cars and a helmet on motorbikes.

Disease risk

The greater disease risk in Ecuador is caused by the greater volume of disease carriers in the shape of mosquitoes and sandflies. The key viral disease is **Dengue fever**, which is transmitted by a mosquito that bites during the day. The disease is like a very nasty form of the 'flu with two-three days of illness, followed by a short period of recovery, then a second attack of illness. Westerners very rarely get the worst haemorrhagic form of the disease. Bacterial diseases include **tuberculosis** (TB) and some causes of the more common traveller's diarrhoea. The parasitic diseases are many but the two key ones are **malaria** and South American trypanosomiasis (known as **Chagas Disea**se). The latter kills fit, young South American footballers.

Before you go

Ideally, you should see your GP or travel clinic at least 6 weeks before your departure for general advice on travel risks, malaria and vaccinations. Make sure you have **travel insurance**, get a **dental check** (especially if you are going to be away for more than a month), know your own **blood** group and if you suffer a long-term condition such as diabetes or epilepsy make sure someone knows or that you have a **Medic Alert** bracelet/necklace with this information on it.

Vaccinations

Polio   Recommended if nil in last 10 years
Tetanus   Recommended if nil in last 10 years (but 5 doses is enough for life)
Typhoid   Recommended if nil in last 3 years
Yellow Fever   It is best and easiest to get vaccinated. Hovever, it is true that there is no significant risk in the Galapagos Islands and high altitude resorts near Quito but few travellers will have a trip that does not include risk areas.
Rabies   Recommended if travelling to jungle and/or remote areas
Hepatitis A   Recommended as the disease can be caught easily from food/water

Further information

Organizations & websites

Foreign and Commonwealth Office (FCO)
This is a key travel advice site, with useful information on the country, people, climate and lists the UK embassies/consulates. The site also promotes the concept of 'Know Before You Go', and encourages travel insurance and health advice. It has links to the Department of Health travel advice site, listed below **www.fco.gov.uk**

Department of Health Travel Advice

This excellent site is also available as a free booklet, the **T6**, from Post Offices. It lists the vaccine advice requirements for each country. **www.doh.gov.uk/traveladvice**

Medic Alert (UK)

This is the website of the foundation that produces bracelets and necklaces for those with existing medical problems. Once you have ordered your bracelet/necklace you write your key medical details on paper inside it, so that if you collapse, people can identify the possible cause of this. **www.medicalalert.co.uk**

Blood Care Foundation

The Blood Care Foundation is a Kent-based charity "dedicated to the provision of screened blood and resuscitation fluids in countries where these are not readily available." They dispatch non-infected blood to your hospital/clinic. The blood is flown in from various centres around the world. **www.bloodcare.org.uk**

Public Health Laboratory Service

This site has up-to-date malaria advice guidelines for travel around the world. It gives specific advice about the right drugs for each location. It also has useful information for those who are pregnant, suffering from epilepsy or planning to travel with children. **www.phls.org.uk**

Centers for Disease Control and Prevention (USA)

This site from the US Government gives excellent advice on travel health, has useful disease maps and details of disease outbreaks. **www.cdc.gov**

World Health Organisation

The WHO site has links to the WHO Blue Book on travel advice. The book, which used to be Yellow, lists the diseases in different regions of the world. It describes vaccination schedules and makes clear which countries have Yellow Fever Vaccination certificate requirements and malarial risk. **www.who.int**

Tropical Medicine Bureau (Ireland)

This Irish based site has a good collection of general travel health information and disease risks. **www.tmb.ie**

Fit for Travel

This site from Scotland provides a quick A-Z of vaccine and travel health advice requirements for each country. **www.fitfortravel.scot.nhs.uk**

British Travel Health Association

This is the official site of an organization of travel health professionals. **www.btha.org**

NetDoctor

This general health advice site has a useful section on travel and has an 'ask the expert', interactive chat forum. **www.Netdoctor.co.uk**

Travel Screening Services

This is the author's website. A private clinic dedicated to integrated travel health. The clinic gives vaccine, travel health advice, email and SMS text vaccine reminders and screens returned travellers for tropical diseases. **www.travelscreening.co.uk**

Books & leaflets *Traveller's Health* edited by **Dr Richard Dawood** is at last re-published and is the car-manual for your off-the beaten track trip. *The Travellers Good Health Guide* by **Dr Ted Lankester** (ISBN 0-85969-827-0). *Expedition Medicine* (The Royal Geographic Society) Editors **David Warrell** and **Sarah Anderson** (ISBN 1-86197-040-4). *International Travel and Health World Health Organisation*, Geneva (ISBN 92-4-1580267). *The World's Most Dangerous Places* by **Robert Young Pelton**, **Coskun Aral** and **Wink Dulles**. (ISBN 1-566952-140-9). *The Travellers Guide to Health* (T6) can be obtained by calling the Health Literature Line on T0800-555777. Advice for travellers on avoiding the risks of HIV and AIDS (Travel Safe) available from **Department of Health**, PO Box 777, London SE1 6XH. **The Blood Care Foundation**. Order form PO Box 7, Sevenoaks, Kent TN13 2SZ, T44-(0)1732-742427.

Anti-malarials Important to take for the key areas. Specialist advice is required as to which type to take. General principles are that all except Malarone should be continued for four weeks after leaving the malarial area. Malarone needs to be continued for only seven days afterwards (if a tablet is missed or vomited seek specialist advice). The start times for the anti-malarials vary in that if you have never taken Lariam (Mefloquine) before it is advised to start it at least two to three weeks before the entry to a malarial zone (this is to help identify serious side-effects early). Chloroquine and Paludrine are often started a week before the trip to establish a pattern but Doxycycline and Malarone can be started only one to two days before entry to the malarial area.

What to take
It is risky to buy medicinal tablets abroad because the doses may differ and there may be a trade in false drugs

Ciproxin (Ciprofloaxcin) A useful antibiotic for some forms of travellers' diarrhoea (see below).

Immodium A great standby for those diarrhoeas that occur at awkward times (ie before a long coach/train journey or on a trek). It helps stop the flow of diarrhoea and in my view is of more benefit than harm. (It was believed that letting the bacteria or viruses flow out had to be more beneficial. However, with Immodium they still come out, just in a more solid form.)

MedicAlert These simple bracelets, or an equivalent, should be carried or worn by anyone with a significant medical condition.

Mosquito repellents Remember that DEET (Di-ethyltoluamide) is the gold standard. Apply the repellent every 4-6 hours but more often if you are sweating heavily. If a non-DEET product is used check who tested it. Validated products (tested at the London School of Hygiene and Tropical Medicine) include Mosiguard, Non-DEET Jungle formula and non-DEET Autan. If you want to use citronella remember that it must be applied very frequently (ie hourly) to be effective. If you are a popular target for insect bites or develop lumps quite soon after being bitten, carry an Aspivenin kit. This syringe suction device draws out some of the allergic materials and provides quick relief.

Pain killers Paracetomol or a suitable painkiller can have multiple uses for symptoms but remember that more than eight paracetomol a day can lead to liver failure.

Pepto-Bismol Used a lot by Americans for diarrhoea. It certainly relieves symptoms but like Immodium it is not a cure for underlying disease. Be aware that it turns the stool black as well as making it more solid.

Sun Block The Australians have a great campaign, which has reduced skin cancer. It is called Slip, Slap, Slop. Slip on a shirt, Slap on a hat, Slop on sun screen.

For longer trips involving jungle treks taking a clean needle pack, clean dental pack and water filtration devices are common-sense measures.

Travel with Care, Homeway, Amesbury, Wiltshire SP4 7BH, T0870-7459261, www.travelwithcare.co.uk, provides a large range of products for sale.

Essentials

An A-Z of health risks

Altitude sickness

Symptoms: This can creep up on you as just a mild headache with nausea or lethargy. The more serious disease is caused by fluid collecting in the brain in the enclosed space of the skull and can lead to coma and death. There is also a lung disease version with breathlessness and fluid infiltration of the lungs.

Cures: The best cure is to descend as soon as possible.

Prevention: Get acclimatized. Do not try to reach the highest levels on your first few days of arrival. Try to avoid flying directly into the cities of highest altitude. Climbers like to take treatment drugs as protective measures but this can lead to macho idiocy and death. The peaks are still there and so are the trails, whether it takes you a bit longer than someone else does not matter as long as you come back down alive.

Chagas disease

Symptoms: The disease occurs throughout South America, affects locals more than travellers, but travellers can be exposed by sleeping in mud-constructed huts where the bug that carries the parasite bites and defaecates on an exposed part of skin. You may notice nothing at all or a local swelling, with fever, tiredness and enlargement of lymph glands, spleen and liver. The seriousness of the parasite infection is caused by the long-term effects which include gross enlargement of the heart and/or guts.

Cures: Early treatment is required with toxic drugs.

Prevention: Sleep under a permethrin treated bed net and use insect repellents.

Dengue fever

Symptoms: This disease can be contracted throughout South America. In travellers this can cause a severe 'flu-like illness which includes symptoms of fever, lethargy, enlarged lymph glands and muscle pains. It starts suddenly, lasts for two to three days, seems to get better for two to three days and then kicks in again for another two to three days. It is usually all over in an unpleasant week. The local children are prone to the much nastier haemorrhagic form of the disease, which causes them to bleed from internal organs, mucous membranes and often leads to their death.

Cures: The traveller's version of the disease is self limiting and forces rest and recuperation on the sufferer.

Prevention: The mosquitoes that carry the Dengue virus bite during the day unlike the malaria mosquitoes. Which sadly means that repellent application and covered limbs are a 24 hour issue. Check your accommodation for flower pots and shallow pools of water since these are where the dengue-carrying mosquitoes breed.

Diarrhoea & intestinal upset
This is almost inevitable. One study showed that up to 70% of all travellers may suffer during their trip

Symptoms: Diarrhoea can refer either to loose stools or an increased frequency; both of these can be a nuisance. It should be short lasting but persistence beyond two weeks, with blood or pain, require specialist medical attention.

Cures: Ciproxin (Ciprofloaxcin) is a useful antibiotic for bacterial traveller's diarrhoea. It can be obtained by private prescription in the UK which is expensive, or bought over the counter in South American pharmacies. You need to take one 500mg tablet when the diarrhoea starts and if you do not feel better in 24 hours, the diarrhoea is likely to have a non-bacterial cause and may be viral (in which case there is little you can do apart from keep yourself rehydrated and wait for it to settle on its own). The key treatment with all diarrhoeas is rehydration. Try to keep hydrated by taking the right mixture of salt and water. This is available as Oral Rehydration Salts (ORS) in ready-made sachets or can be made up by adding a teaspoon of sugar and a half teaspoon of salt to a litre of clean water. Immodium and Pepto- Bismol provide symptomatic relief.

Prevention: The standard advice is to be careful with water and ice for drinking. If you have any doubts then boil it or filter and treat it. There are many filter/treatment devices now available on the market. Food can also transmit disease. Be wary of salads, re-heated foods or food that has been left out in the sun having been previously cooked. There is a simple adage that says wash it, peel it, boil it or forget it. Also be wary of unpasteurized dairy products, these can transmit a range of diseases from brucellosis (fevers and constipation), to listeria (meningitis) and tuberculosis of the gut (obstruction, constipation, fevers and weight loss).

Symptoms: Hepatitis means inflammation of the liver. Viral causes of the disease can **Hepatitis** be acquired anywhere in South America. The most obvious symptom is a yellowing of your skin or the whites of your eyes. However, prior to this all that you may notice is itching and tiredness.
Cures: Early on, depending on the type of hepatitis, a vaccine or immunoglobulin may reduce the duration of the illness.
Prevention: Pre-travel hepatitis A vaccine is the best bet. Hepatitis B (for which there is a vaccine) is spread through blood and unprotected sexual intercourse, both of these can be avoided. Unfortunately there is no vaccine for hepatitis C or the increasing alphabetical list of other Hepatitis viruses.

Symptoms: A skin form of this disease occurs in Ecuador. If infected, you may notice a **Leishmaniasis** raised lump, which leads to a purplish discoloration on white skin and a possible ulcer. The parasite is transmitted by the bite of a sandfly. Sandflies do not fly very far and the greatest risk is at ground level, so if you can avoid sleeping on the jungle floor, do so. There is another rarer form which is casued by a sub species of the parasite, this affects the musocal tissues such as lips and nose. Treatment and mode of transmission are the same.
Cures: Several weeks treatment is required under specialist supervision. The drugs themselves are toxic but if not taken in sufficient amounts, recurrence is more likely.
Prevention: Sleep above ground, under a permethrin treated net, use insect repellent and get a specialist opinion on any unusual skin lesions as soon as you can.

Malaria risk is about 50% of the deadly *P. falciparum* type. Malaria exists at altitudes less **Malaria &** than 1,500 m all year round. The highest risk areas are El Oro, Esmeraldas and Manabi and **insect bite** some of the Amazon river tributaries. If you only visit Quito, the Galapagos and certain **prevention** central highland tourist areas (eg Cotopaxi volcano), the risk of malaria is negligible.
    The choice of malaria drug depends on where you will travel, which type of malaria you may be exposed to, and your medical/psychological history. Always check with your doctor or travel clinic for the most up-to-date advice.

Symptoms: Malaria can cause death within 24 hours. It can start as something just resembling an attack of flu. You may feel tired, lethargic, headachy; or worse, develop fits, followed by coma and then death. Have a low index of suspicion because it is very easy to write off vague symptoms, which may actually be malaria. Whilst abroad and on return get tested as soon as possible, the test could save your life.
Cures: Treatment is with drugs and may be oral or into a vein depending on the seriousness of the infection. Remember ABCD: Awareness (of whether the disease is present in the area you are travelling in), Bite avoidance, Chemoprohylaxis, Diagnosis.
Prevention: This is best summarized by the B and C of the ABCD, bite avoidance and chemoprophylaxis. Wear clothes that cover arms and legs and use effective insect repellents in areas with known risks of insect-spread disease. Use a mosquito net dipped in permethrin as both a physical and chemical barrier at night in the same areas. Guard against the contraction of malaria with the correct anti-malarials (see above). Some would prefer to take test kits for malaria with them and have standby treatment available. However, the field tests of the blood kits have had poor results: when you have malaria you are usually too ill to be able to do the tests correctly enough to make the right diagnosis. Standby treatment (treatment that you carry and take yourself for malaria) should still ideally be supervised by a doctor since the drugs

themselves can be toxic if taken incorrectly. The Royal Homeopathic Hospital in the UK does not advocate homeopathic options for malaria prevention or treatment.

Schisto-somiasis & Fasciola hepatica
These two flukes both occur in Ecuador. A fluke is a sort of flattened worm. Schistosomiasis can be acquired through wading through stagnant water and swimming in such waters. Symptoms: The liver fluke may cause jaundice, gall stone symptons, right-sided abdominal pain, liver test abnormalities and changes in the white cell pattern of the blood. Schistosomiasis can cause a local skin itch at first exposure, fever after a few weeks and much later diarrhoea, abdominal pain and spleen or liver enlargement.
Cures: A single drug cures Schistosomiasis. The same drug can be used for the liver fluke but this infestation is much more difficult to treat.
Prevention: Avoid infected waters, be careful with unwashed vegetables (especially in the Altiplano), check the CDC, WHO websites and a travel clinic specialist for up-to-date information on the whereabouts of the disease.

Sun protection
Follow the Australians with their Slip, Slap, Slop campaign
Symptoms: White Britons are notorious for becoming red in hot countries because they like to stay out longer than everyone else and do not use adequate sun protection. This can lead to sunburn, which is painful and followed by flaking of skin. Aloe vera gel is a good pain reliever for sunburn. Long-term sun damage leads to a loss of elasticity of skin and the development of pre-cancerous lesions. Many years later a mild or a very malignant form of cancer may develop. The milder basal cell carcinoma, if detected early, can be treated by cutting it out or freezing it. The much nastier malignant melanoma may have already spread to bone and brain at the time that it is first noticed.
Prevention: Sun screen. SPF stands for Sun Protection Factor. It is measured by determining how long a given person takes to 'burn' with and without the sunscreen product on. So, if it takes 10 times longer to burn with the sunscreen product applied, then that product has an SPF of 10. If it only takes twice as long then the SPF is 2. The higher the SPF the greater the protection. However, do not just use higher factors just to stay out in the sun longer. 'Flash frying' (desperate bursts of excessive exposure), as it is called, is known to increase the risks of skin cancer.

Underwater health
Symptoms: If you go diving make sure that you are fit do so. The **British Scuba Association** (BSAC), Telford's Quay, South Pier Road, Ellesmere Port, Cheshire CH65 4FL, UK, T01513-506200, F506215, www.bsac.com, can put you in touch with doctors who do medical examinations. Protect your feet from cuts, beach dog parasites (larva migrans) and sea urchins. The latter are almost impossible to remove but can be dissolved with lime or vinegar. Keep an eye out for secondary infection.
Cures: Antibiotics for secondary infections. Serious diving injuries may need time in a decompression chamber.
Prevention: Check that the dive company know what they are doing, have appropriate certification from BSAC or **Professional Association of Diving Instructors** (PADI), Unit 7, St Philips Central, Albert Road, St Philips, Bristol BS2 0TD, T0117-3007234, www.padi.com, and that the equipment is well maintained.

Sexual health
If you do stray, consider getting a sexual health check on your return home
The range of visible and invisible diseases is awesome. Unprotected sex can spread HIV, Hepatitis B and C, Gonorrhea (green discharge), chlamydia (nothing to see but may cause painful urination and later female infertility), painful recurrent herpes, syphilis and warts, just to name a few. You can cut down the risk by using condoms, a femidom or avoiding sex altogether.

Quito

Introducing Quito

Few cities have a setting to match that of Quito, the second highest capital in Latin America. It sits on a long narrow shelf running north to south, wedged between the slopes of the volcano Pichincha (4,794 m) to the west and a low ridge to the east.

Quito is a city of many faces. The Old City, a UNESCO World Heritage Trust site, is the colonial centre, where pastel-coloured houses and ornate churches line a warren of steep and narrow streets. The New City extends north of the colonial city and is an altogether different place. Its broad avenues are lined with fine private residences, parks, embassies and villas. Here you'll find Quito's main tourist and business area: banks, tour agencies, airlines, language schools, smart shops and restaurants, bars and cafés, and a huge variety of hotels and cheap *residenciales*, in the district known as La Mariscal, and further north as far as Avenida Naciones Unidas. Quito's working class neighbourhoods stretch to the south of the Old City, while suburban sprawl fills the valleys to the east. In the far north and south are relatively small industrial zones.

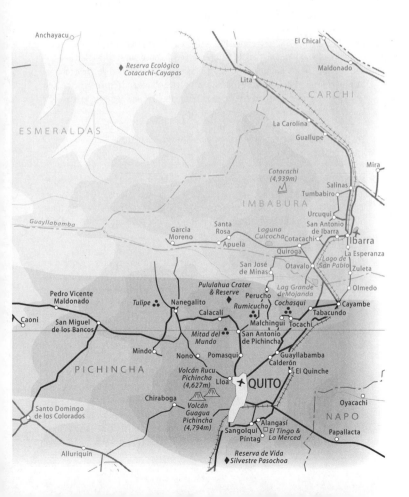

Quito

Things to do in Quito

- Stroll through the colonial heart of the **Old City**, page 97.
- Admire the views from the top of **Panecillo**, page 99.
- Enlighten yourself at the **Museo Nacional del Banco Central** (housed in the Casa de la Cultura), page 101.
- Let yourself be a tourist at **Mitad del Mundo**, page 141.
- Enjoy a nature excursion to **Mindo** or surroundings, page 146.
- Relax in the thermal baths of **Papallacta**, page 154.

Ins and outs

Getting there

Phone code: 02
Colour map 2,
grid C4
Population:
city proper 1,460,000
Altitude: 2,850 m

Air Quito's airport, Mariscal Sucre, lies only about 5 km to the north of La Mariscal, the main hotel district. The easiest way to get to your hotel is by taxi, which is recommended as safe, relatively cheap and reliable (see below). Taxis can be caught outside international arrivals. For full details of transport to and from the airport and other airport facilities, see Touching down, on page 41. For car hire companies, see page 133. For full details of flights into and out of Quito, see Getting there by air, page 37. For ground transportation see Getting around, below.

Terminal Terrestre and its surroundings are unsafe. Pay close attention to your belongings at all times, as robberies are common

Bus The main bus station (Terminal Terrestre) is at Maldonado and Cumandá, south of Plaza Santo Domingo, in the Old City. Most long distance bus services start and end here, and this is really the only place to get information on bus schedules. Several companies with long-distance luxury coach services have offices and terminals in the New City. (See also under Transport on page 132.) From the Terminal Terrestre to anywhere in the city, take a taxi, or the trolley bus (see below).

Train There is no regular passenger service. See Excursions, page 155, for details of tourist rides from Quito.

Getting around

See also Transport, page 132

Bus There are 2 levels of city buses, *ejecutivos* are red, take only sitting passengers (not always respected) and charge US$0.20. There are few *populares* left, these are light blue, cost US$0.14, can get very crowded. *Interparroquial* buses are pink, these run to the outer suburbs, including the valleys of Tumbaco and Los Chillos and to Mitad del Mundo.

The trolley bus is not designed for heavy luggage and can be very crowded at peak hours. Beware of pickpockets

Trolley bus 'El Trole' is an integrated transport system of trolley buses, running on exclusive lanes across the city from north to south, and feeder bus lines (*alimentadores*, painted green), serving suburbs from the northern and southern terminals and from El Recreo station. It runs along Av 10 de Agosto in the north of the city, C Guayaquil (southbound) and C Flores (northbound) in the Old City, and mainly along Av Pedro Vicente Maldonado in the south (see map on page 94). The northern station, Terminal Norte, is north of 'La Y', the junction of 10 de Agosto, Av América and Av de la Prensa; at El Recreo, on Av Maldonado is an important transfer station, known as Terminal Sur, and the southern terminus, Morán Valverde, is in Ciudadela Quitumbe in the far south of the city. The main bus terminal is served both northbound and southbound by the Cumandá stop, at Maldonado y 24 de Mayo. From the Terminal Norte, a feeder line marked 'Aeropuerto' goes near the airport. Some trolleys run the full length of the line, while others run only a section, the destination is marked in front of the vehicle. There is a special entrance for wheelchairs. ■ *Mon-Fri 0500-0000, weekends and holidays 0600-2200. US$0.20. Trole information, T2665015.*

Flying into Quito at night

Quito airport is normally open from 0400 to 0000 and most flights from North America arrive between 2100 and midnight. If a flight to Quito is delayed much after midnight, then it is usually diverted to land in Guayaquil. Most Quito airport services are closed at night and it can be difficult to make a phone call. There is nowhere to wait until dawn and it can get quite cold outside.

There is only one adequate hotel right by Quito airport, two blocks south of the national departures terminal. You are much better off, however, selecting a couple of hotels near one another in the New City, and taking a taxi to check them out. There is no bus service after about 2000 and walking is out of the question.

Try to team up with at least one other traveller and ask one of the many taxis to take you to your hotel of first choice. One person can remain with the luggage in the cab while the other checks out the hotel; if it is unsuitable or there is no vacancy, have the cab take you to the next place on your list. If you are in a group of six or more the Trans-Rabbit van service from the airport can be a good deal.

In the words of an old saying, 'All dogs look black at night'. Remember that it is always intimidating to arrive in an unfamiliar place after dark. Spend a bit more for safe and comfortable accommodation for your first night in Quito. After a good sleep, you will quickly get your bearings the next morning.

Ecovía   The 'Ecovía' is a bus transport system also running on exclusive lanes from north to south. It goes along Av 6 de Diciembre, from La Marín near the Old City to Av Río Coca in the north. Pending the arrival of special buses, trolley vehicles were running this route in late 2002 in the wrong (left) lane – be careful when you cross! ■ *0600-2200 daily. US$0.20.*

Taxi   Taxis are a safe, cheap and efficient way to get around the city. From the airport to the New City costs US$3-4, to the Old City US$4-5; from the Terminal Terrestre to the New City is US$3; and journeys around the New City cost from US$0.80. Expect to pay around 50-100% more at night. There is no increase for extra passengers. At night it is safer to use a radio taxi, there are several companies including: *Taxi Amigo,* T2222222/2333333, *City Taxi*, T2633333 and *Central de Radio Taxis*, T2500600. To hire a taxi by the hour costs from US$5 in the city.

Motoring   The city's main arteries run north south and traffic congestion along them is a serious problem. Note that there is a ring road around Quito, and a bypass to the south via the Autopista del Valle de Los Chillos and the Carretera de Amaguaña.

Quito is a long, narrow city, stretching from north to south for over 35 km, and east to west only between 3 and 5 km. The best way to get oriented is to look for Pichincha, the mountain which lies to the west of the city. The El Panecillo hill is a landmark at the south end of the Old City.

The areas of most interest to visitors are the colonial city, with its many churches, historical monuments, museums and some hotels, best accessed by trolley; La Mariscal or Mariscal Sucre district, which extends east from Av 10 de Agosto to Av 12 de Octubre, and north from Av Patria to Av Orellana, where you find many more hotels, restaurants, bars, discos, travel agencies and some banks; and the environs of Parque La Carolina, north of La Mariscal as far as Av Naciones Unidas and from Av 10 de Agosto east to and Av Eloy Alfaro, where the newer hotels, restaurants, main banking district, airline offices and a number of shopping malls are located. Efforts are being made to revitalize the Old City.

Orientation & safety
See page 42, for advice on maps

Quito

Quito orientation

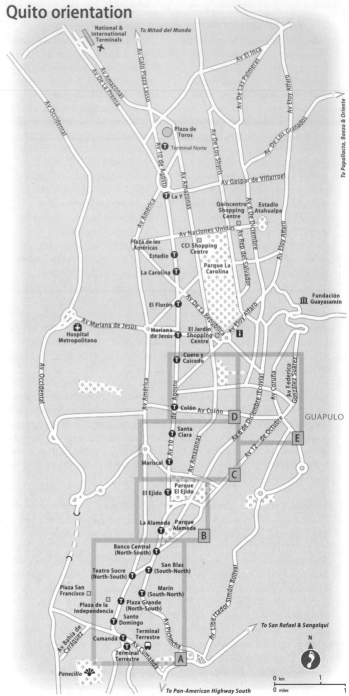

GUAPULO

Detailed maps
A Quito Old City,
    page 98
B South from El Ejido,
    page 105
C El Ejido north to
    Colón, page 106
D North from Colón,
    page 107
E Northeast of
Mariscal, page 113

24 hours in Quito

If you only do one thing in Quito then make sure it's a tour of the Old City. Here you can wander up and down a maze of steep cobbled streets jam-packed with indigenous street vendors as you admire the stunning colonial architecture.

Start in Plaza de la Independencia, the heart of the old colonial part of the city, and from there proceed to Plaza de San Francisco, dominated by its impressive church and monastery. Then head down to Plaza de Santo Domingo, where there's another fine colonial church to see.

For a wonderful view of the city and encircling volcanoes and mountains, take a taxi up to the top of Panecillo, which is instantly recognizable by the statue of the Virgen de Quito on top.

By now you'll no doubt be feeling peckish so catch the Trole to La Mariscal neighbourhood in the New City for lunch. The ever-popular Chez Alain, *or* Grain de Café *are both good choices and great value.*

After lunch, you might want to indulge in a little culture, so get yourself down to the Casa de la Cultura in Parque El Ejido, where you can bone up on archaeology, indigenous costumes, musical instruments and Modern Art, as well as many temporary exhibits.

Need a breather? Take a break for coffee and postcard writing at Super Papa. *Don't forget to check their chock-a-block bulletin board, before catching up on your emails in one of the city's myriad cybercafés.*

If you feel like something typically Ecuadorean for Dinner try Mama Clorinda, *or maybe* El Hornero *for pizza. Then it's time to sample Quito's nightlife.* Turtle's Head Bar *and* Ghoz *are perennial gringo faves, but if you want to experience a night of hot and sweaty salsa, head down south to* Macks, *where you can wiggle your hips with the best of them.*

Street numbers In 1998, the city introduced a new street numbering system. The north-south axis is C Rocafuerte. All streets north of this street are lettered N and numbered in sequence, and likewise streets running south, which are lettered S. The east-west axis is Av 10 de Agosto, C Guayaquil and C Maldonado; streets running east are lettered E and numbered in sequence, and those running west are lettered Oe (*oeste*). Street numbers are followed by a dash, then the individual building number, indicating the distance in metres from the corner – eg E5-127, or N12-43. This system was partly implemented in the north, but ran into major difficulties in the Old City as streets are not perpendicular. Renumbering then stopped. At the time of writing, both numbering systems are in operation. The addresses listed below use both systems.

Public safety Theft and violent crime are serious hazards. Both the Old and New Cities (including La Mariscal) are dangerous at night and pickpockets are active at all hours. Take the necessary precautions: watch your belongings at all times, avoid crowds, use taxis at night and whenever you carry valuables. Be careful on crowded buses and on the Trole. Even more caution is required around the Terminal Terrestre and La Marín. Do not walk through city parks in the evening or even in daylight at quiet times. This includes Parque La Carolina, where joggers are advised to stay on the periphery at such hours. The parks are quite safe and pleasant however when frequented by locals, such as on weekends. Also beware of young children selling flowers, groups of them occasionally swarm tourists and find a way to their belongings. The **Policía de Turismo** has its headquarters at Reina Victoria y Roca, T2543983. Members of the **Policía Metropolitana**, who patrol the Old City on foot, speak some English, are very helpful and will accompany visitors if they wish (no charge, but a tip is welcome).

See also Safety, page 46

Visiting **Panecillo** has long been considered a risky business, but neighbourhood brigades are patrolling the area and a have improved public safety; they charge visitors

US$0.20 per person. However, taking a taxi up is a lot safer than walking. Do not carry valuables and seek local advice before going on foot.

Pichincha volcano Guagua Pichincha is an active volcano, its crater is located 14 km west of Quito. The crater is a 800-m-deep breached caldera open to the west (ie facing away from Quito). Eruptions during 1999 made for some unforgettable photos but caused only minor inconvenience to the city, in the form of light ash fall. There has been no visible volcanic activity since then, and scientists indicate that seismic activity remained very low from Mar 2002 to the close of this edition.

Climate Quito is within 25 km of the equator, but it stands high enough to make its climate much like that of spring in England; the days pleasantly warm and the nights cool. Because of the height, visitors may initially feel some discomfort and should slow their pace for the first day or so. The mean temperature is 13°C; rainfall, 1,473 mm. The rainy season is Oct-May, with a lull in Dec, and the heaviest rainfall in Apr, though heavy storms in Jul are not unknown. Rain usually falls in the afternoon. The day length (sunrise to sunset) is almost constant throughout the year. Quito suffers from air and noise pollution, principally due to traffic congestion. These are worst at rush hours and especially severe during the Christmas shopping season. During school holidays, July-Sep, the air is considerably better.

Tourist information The **Cámara Provincial de Turismo de Pichincha (CAPTUR)** has information offices at international arrivals in the airport (daily 0730-1430 and 1730-0000), in the New City in Parque Gabriela Mistral at Cordero y Reina Victoria (Mon-Fri 0900-1700, T2551566), and in the Old City at edif Perez Pallares, Venezuela y Chile (Mon-Fri 0900-1700, T2954044). Service is helpful and friendly, some staff speak English, maps are sold. The **Empresa de Desarrollo del Centro Histórico** has an information office at international arrivals in the airport (daily 0900-2300) and a kiosk in the Old City, Chile y Venezuela, opposite Plaza de la Independencia (daily 0930-1700). Staff speak some English and French, sell maps, offer information and walking tours of the colonial city. The **Ministerio de Turismo** is located at Eloy Alfaro N32-300 (between República and Los Shyris), T2507559/560, F2229330, mtur1@ec-gov.net) Information counter downstairs. Mon-Fri 0830-1700.

Reservation centre *Cultura Reservation Center*, at Café Cultura, Robles 513 y Reina Victoria, T2504078, F2224271, www.cafecultura.com Gives information and books services.

History

Archaeological studies suggest that the valley of Quito and the surrounding areas have been occupied for some 10,000 years. The remains of ancient Paleoindian peoples, nomadic hunters who used obsidian, to make stone tools, have been found at various sites around town. During the subsequent Formative era, pre-Ecuadorian peoples began to settle in villages, till fields and make ceramics. One of the best-known Formative sites of highland Ecuador is located in northwest Quito, in Cotocollao.

Quito is named after the Quitus, a tribe which inhabited the region in pre-Inca times. By the beginning of the 16th century, the northern highlands of Ecuador were conquered by the Incas and Quito became the capital of the northern half of the empire under the rule of Huayna Capac and later his son Atahualpa. As the Spanish conquest approached, Rumiñahui, Atahualpa's general, razed the city, to prevent it from falling into the invaders' hands.

The colonial city of Quito was founded by Sebastián de Benalcázar, Pizarro's lieutenant, on December 6, 1534. It was built at the foot of Panecillo on the ruins of the ancient city, using the rubble as construction material and today you can still find examples of Inca stonework in the façades and floors of some colonial buildings such as the Cathedral and the church of San Francisco. Following the conquest, Quito became the seat of government of the **Real Audencia de Quito**, the crown colony, which governed current day Ecuador as well as parts of southern Colombia and northern Peru.

The city changed gradually over time. The Government Palace, for example, was built in the 17th century as the seat of government of the Real Audiencia, yet changes were introduced at the end of the colonial period and the begining of the republican period in the 19th century.

The 20th century saw the expansion of the city both to the north and south, first with the development of residential neighbourhoods and later with a transfer of the commercial and banking heart of the city north of the colonial centre. In 1978, Quito was declared a UNESCO World Heritage Trust site. In the 1980s and 1990s the number of high-rise buildings increased, the suburban valleys of Los Chillos and Tumbaco to the east of town were incorporated into a new **Distrito Metropolitano**, and a number of new poor neighbourhoods sprawled in the far north and south. The city continues to grow, and at the start of the millennium Quito stretched over 35 km from north to south.

Quito

Sights

Old City

On Sundays the Old City is closed to vehicles and fills with pedestrians, locals as well as tourists. This is an excellent time to visit. The **Empresa de Desarrollo del Centro Histórico** offers guided walking tours along two circuits in the colonial city. These include visits with English-speaking guides, who are part of the Metropolitan Police Force, to museums, plazas, churches, convents and historical buildings. ■ *Tue-Sun at 1000, 1100 and 1400. US$10, includes museum entrance fees. T2586591. At Plaza de la Independencia, Chile y García Moreno, ground floor of the Palacio Arzobispal.*

Guided walking tours

The heart of the colonial city is Plaza de la Independencia or Plaza Grande, dominated by the **Cathedral**, built 1550-62, with grey stone porticos and green tile cupolas. The portal and tower were only completed in the 20th century. On its outer walls are plaques listing the names of the founding fathers of Quito. Inside is the tomb of the independence hero, General Antonio José de Sucre, in a small chapel tucked away in a corner, and a famous Descent from the Cross by the Indian painter Caspicara. There are many other 17th and 18th century paintings and some fine examples of the works of the Quito School of Art (see Painting and sculpture, page 451). The interior decoration, especially the roof, shows Moorish influence. ■ *Mon-Sat 1000-1600. US$1.*

Plaza de la Independencia

Beside the Cathedral, around the corner, is **El Sagrario**, originally built in the 17th century as the Cathedral's main chapel and is very beautiful. It has some impressive baroque columns, its inner doors are gold plated and built in the Churrigueresque style. ■ *Mon-Sat 0800-1800, Sun 0800-1330. Free.*

Facing the Cathedral is the **Palacio Arzobispal**, the Archbishop's palace. The Empresa de Desarrollo del Centro Histórico offers guided tours of the Old Town from here; for details see above. Part of the building now houses shops. Next to it, in the northwest corner, is the former **Hotel Majestic**, with an eclectic façade, including baroque columns. Built in 1930, it was the first building in the old city with more than two stories; today it houses municipal administrative offices. On the east side of the Plaza is the new concrete **Municipio** which fits in surprisingly well.

The low colonial **Palacio de Gobierno**, silhouetted against the flank of Pichincha, is on the west side of the Plaza. It was built in the 17th century and remodelled in neoclassical style by Carondelet, president of the Crown Colony and later by Flores, first president of the Republic. On the first floor is a gigantic mosaic mural of Orellana navigating the Amazon. The ironwork of the balconies looking over the Plaza are from the Tuilleries in Paris, sold by the French government shortly after the French Revolution. ■ *Visits with special*

Quito Old City

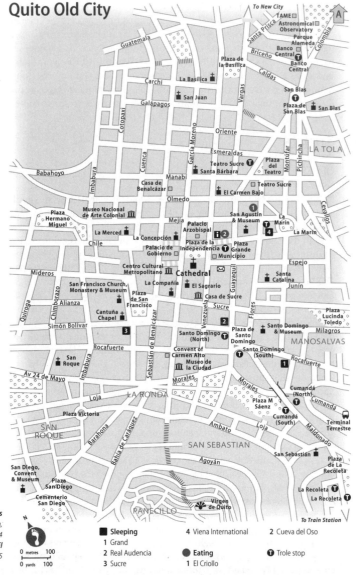

N

0 metres   100

0 yards   100

■ **Sleeping**
1 Grand
2 Real Audencia
3 Sucre

4 Viena International

● **Eating**
1 El Criollo

2 Cueva del Oso

Ⓣ Trole stop

permit only, Tue and Thu, 0930-1230. A written request, addressed to the Jefe de la Casa Militar, must be presented at the gate several days in advance.

Calle Morales, the main street of La Ronda district, is one of the oldest streets in the city, worth seeing for its narrow cobbled way and wrought-iron balconies. It is better known as **Calle La Ronda** and is now part of a red light district, beware of pickpockets.

La Ronda
The area should be avoided after dark

From Plaza de la Independencia two main streets, Calle Venezuela and García Moreno, lead south towards Panecillo (see below) to the wide Avenida 24 de Mayo.

Plaza de San Francisco (or Bolívar) is west of Plaza de la Independencia. On the northwest side of this plaza is the great church and monastery of the patron saint of Quito, San Francisco (see below).

San Francisco & Santo Domingo

Plaza de Santo Domingo (or Sucre), to the southeast of Plaza San Francisco, has the church and monastery of Santo Domingo and the Chapel of the Rosary. In the centre of the plaza is a statue to Sucre, pointing to the slopes of Pichincha where he won his battle against the Royalists. On the south side of the plaza is the **Arco de la Capilla del Rosario**, one of the city's colonial arches. Going through it you enter **La Mama Cuchara** (the 'great big spoon'), a dead-end street which conserves its colonial flavour.

El Panecillo (the little breadloaf) lies to the south of the Plaza de San Francisco. Gazing benignly over the Old City from the top of Panecillo is the impressive statue of the Virgen de Quito, a replica of the painting by Legarda found in the San Francisco Church. Mass is held in the base on Sunday. There is a good view from the observation platform up the statue. ■ *1030-1730 daily. US$0.20. Entry to the interior of the monument is US$1.*

Panecillo
From its top, there is a fine view of the city below and the encircling cones of volcanoes and other mountains

NB It is not safe to walk up the Panecillo by the series of steps and paths which begin on García Moreno (where it meets Ambato). See Public safety above. You should take a taxi up and down, which costs US$3, including time at the top to admire the spectacular view.

Outside the Old City

Between the old and new towns is Parque la Alameda at the northern end of the Old City, which has the oldest astronomical observatory in South America. ■ *Sat 0900-1200*. There is also an impressive monument to Simón Bolívar, various lakes, and in the northwest corner is *el churo*, a spiral lookout tower with a good view.

Parque la Alameda

In El Ejido, on the south side of Avenida Patria in the New City, there are exhibitions of paintings on the weekend, when the park fills with local families, as does **La Carolina** park, north of Avenida Eloy Alfaro and between Avenida Amazonas and Avenida de Los Shyris. You can also enjoy aerobics, boating and horse riding in Carolina on Sunday (but see Orientation and safety on page 93). The **Parque Metropolitano**, east of Estadio Atahualpa, is reputed to be the largest urban park in South America and is good for walking, running or biking through the forest. There are some picnic areas with grills. On Sundays (during the school year September-June), there are birdwatching tours, call CECIA (T2271800) for further information. Take the Ecovía along 6 de Diciembre to the stadium (Naciones Unidas stop) and walk 30 minutes uphill or a bus along Eloy Alfaro to Plaza Costa Rica from where it is a 20-minute walk to the park.

El Ejido, La Carolina & Parque Metropolitano

Quito

Quito

Guápulo
Popular with Quito's bohemian community and a worthwhile place to visit

The beautiful district of Guápulo is perched on the edge of a ravine on the eastern fringe of the city, overlooking the Río Machángara. To get there, take bus Hospital del Sur-Guápulo from Calle Venezuela by Plaza de la Independencia, Guápulo-Dos Puentes eastbound along Avenida Patria, or walk down the steep stairway which leads off Avenida González Suárez, near the *Hotel Quito*. One of the main points of interest is the **Santuario de Guápulo** and adjoining museum (see museums below). This 17th-century church, built by Indian slaves and dedicated to Nuestra Señora de Guápulo, is well worth seeing for its many paintings, gilded altars, stone carvings and, above all, the marvellously carved pulpit by Juan Bautista Menacho, one of the loveliest in the whole continent.

Churches

There are 86 churches in Quito; if you don't have much time, make sure you visit San Francisco, Santo Domingo and La Compañía

Beware of unofficial guides who offer to show you the churches in order to practise their English and later ask for money

San Francisco, Quito's largest church, is said to be the first religious building constructed in South America by the Spanish, in 1553 and the founding spot for the famous Quito School of Art. The two towers were felled by an earthquake in 1868 and rebuilt. A modest statue of the founder, Fray Jodoco Ricke, the Flemish Franciscan who sowed the first wheat in Ecuador, stands at the foot of the stairs to the church portal. Worth seeing are the fine wood carvings in the choir, a magnificent high altar of gold and an exquisite carved ceiling. The church is rich in art treasures, the best known of which is *La Virgen de Quito* by Legarda, which depicts the Virgin Mary with silver wings. The statue atop Panecillo is based on this painting. There are also some paintings in the aisles by Miguel de Santiago, the colonial *mestizo* painter. His paintings of the life of Saint Francis decorate the monastery of San Francisco close by, where the collection of painting and sculpture by artists of the Quito School of Art was renovated in 1994. (See museums below) ■ *Mon-Fri 0800-1200, 1500-1800, Sat-Sun 0900-1200. US$1*. Adjoining San Francisco is the **Cantuña Chapel** which has impressive sculptures. ■ *Mon-Fri 0800-1200 and 1500-1800, Sat-Sun 0900-1700.*

Completed around 1620, the church and monastery of **Santo Domingo** has a carved Moorish ceiling over its large central nave and rich wood carvings. In the main altar is an impressive silver throne, *el trono de la Virgen*, weighing several hundred pounds. To the right of the main altar is the remarkable **Capilla del Rosario**, built atop the arch of the same name. Santo Domingo housed the Colegio Mayor de San Fernando, where Latin and philosophy were taught in colonial days, today it houses a fine religious art museum (see below). ■ *Mon-Fri 0800-1230 and 1700-1830.*

The fine Jesuit church of **La Compañía**, on Calle García Moreno, one block south of Plaza de la Independencia, has the most ornate and richly sculptured façade and interior. Several of its most precious treasures, including a painting of the Virgen Dolorosa framed in emeralds and gold, are kept in the vaults of the Banco Central and appear only at special festivals. Replicas of the impressive paintings of hell and the final judgement by Miguel de Santiago can be seen at the entrance. Extensive restoration was completed in 2002. ■ *Mon-Sat 1000-1300, Mon-Fri 1400-1700. US$1.*

La Merced, not far away to the north, was built at the beginning of the 17th century, in baroque and moorish style, to commemorate Pichincha's eruptions which threatened to destroy the city. General Sucre and his troops prayed here for the wellbeing of the nation, following the decisive battle which gave Ecuador its independence in 1822. In the adjacent monastery of La Merced is Quito's oldest clock, built in 1817 in London. Fine cloisters are entered through a door to the left of the altar. La Merced church contains many splendidly elaborate styles, the main altar has wood carvings by Legarda; note the statue of Neptune on the main patio fountain. ■ *Mon-Sat 0600-1200, 1230-1800.*

Many of the heroes of Ecuador's struggle for independence are buried in the monastery of **San Agustín** on Flores y Chile. The church has beautiful cloisters on three sides where the first act of independence from Spain was signed on 10 August 1809, it is now a national shrine. The church was extensively renovated due to earthquake damage, the wood carved columns and gilded altars are among the few remains of the original 16th-century construction. The monastery was once the home of the Universidad de San Fulgencio, Quito's first university, founded in the 16th century, it has a large collection of paintings by Miguel de Santiago and an attractive fountain made from a single block of stone. ■ *Mon-Sat 0700-1300. Undergoing restoration in 2002.*

The **Basílica del Voto Nacional**, on Plaza de la Basílica (Calle Venezuela y Carchi), is very large, has many gargoyles, stained glass windows and fine, bas-relief bronze doors. Underneath is a large cemetery. Construction started in 1926 and took 72 years; some final details remain unfinished due to lack of funding. It is possible to go up to the tower, where there is also a cafeteria. The views of the city are magnificent. Recommended. ■ *0930-1730 daily. US$2.*

Other churches of note include **San Diego** (see museums), **La Concepción**, at Mejía y García Moreno, and **San Blas**, at Guayaquil y 10 de Agosto.

Museums

Quito prides itself on its art and the city's galleries, churches and museums boast many fine examples. Check museum opening times in advance.

Opposite **Parque El Ejido**, at the junction of 6 de Diciembre and Avenida Patria, there is a large complex housing the Casa de la Cultura and the museum of the Banco Central del Ecuador (entrance on Patria).

Casa de la Cultura
The place to go if you only have time for one museum

Of the many great museums in Quito, perhaps the most comprehensive is the **Museo Nacional del Banco Central del Ecuador**. It has three floors, with five different sections. The **Sala de Arqueología** is particularly impressive. It consists of a series of halls with exhibits and illustrated panels with explanations in English as well as Spanish. It covers successive cultures from 4000 BC to AD 1534 with excellent diagrams and extensive collections of beautiful precolumbian ceramics. The **Sala de Oro** has a good collection of pre-hispanic gold objects. The remaining three sections house art collections. The **Sala de Arte Colonial** is rich in paintings and sculptures especially of religious themes. The **Sala de Arte Republicano** houses works of the early years of the Republic. The **Sala de Arte Contemporáneo** presents contemporary art. There are also temporary exhibits, videos on Ecuadorean culture, a bookshop and a cafeteria which serves good coffee. For guided tours in English, French or German call ahead and make an appointment. Highly recommended. ■ *Tue-Fri 0900-1700, Sat-Sun 1000-1600. US$2, US$1 for students with ISIC or university student card. T2223259.*

The **Casa de la Cultura Ecuatoriana** hosts many temporary exhibits and cultural events. In addition, the following permanent collections are presented in museums belonging to the Casa de la Cultura: **Museo de Arte Moderno**, paintings and sculpture since 1830; **Museo de Traje Indígena**, a collection of traditional dress and adornments of indigenous groups; **Museo de Instrumentos Musicales**, an impressive collection of musical instruments, said to be the second in importance in the world. ■ *Undergoing renovations in 2002. T2223392 (ext 320).*

In the colonial city **Museo Nacional de Arte Colonial** features a small collection of Ecuadorean sculpture and painting, housed in the 17th-century mansion of Marqués de Villacís, which also has an attractive patio and fountain. ■ *Undergoing restoration in 2002. T2282297. Cuenca y Mejía.*

Housed in the restored 16th-century Hospital San Juan de Dios, a beautiful building, is the **Museo de la Ciudad**. It takes you through Quito's history from pre-hispanic times to the 19th century. ■ *Tue-Sun 0930-1730. US$3, students US$1.50, English, French, German or Italian guide service $4. T2283882. García Moreno 572 y Rocafuerte.*

Museo del Convento de San Francisco has a fine collection of religious art; there are pieces by many renowned local and European artists. The architecture of the convent is also of interest. ■ *Tue-Sat 0900-1800, Sun 0900-1300. US$2.50. T2281124. Plaza de San Francisco.*

In the restored monastery of **San Diego** (by the cemetery of the same name, just west of Panecillo) is the **Museo de San Diego**, guided tours (Spanish only, 40 minutes) take you around four patios where colonial architecture, sculpture and painting are shown. Of special interest are the gilded pulpit by Juan Bautista Menacho and the Last Supper painting in the refectory, in which a *cuy* and *humitas* have taken the place of the paschal lamb. ■ *0930-1300, 1430-1730 daily. US$2. T2952516. Calicuchima 117 y Farfán, entrance to the right of the church.*

Museo de San Agustín has an interesting exhibition of religious art and restoration work. ■ *Mon-Sat 0900-1200 and Mon-Fri 1500-1700. US$2. T2580263. Chile y Guayaquil..* There is a similar collection in the **Museo Dominicano Fray Pedro Bedón** on Plaza Santo Domingo, named after the friar and painter who created the first brotherhood of indian painters. Bedón's work and that of other renowned colonial artits is displayed. ■ *Mon-Fri 0900-1200. US$2. T2288865. Plaza de Santo Domingo. .*

An impressive colonial building which belonged to the Jesuits, later housing the royal Cuartel Real de Lima and most recently the municipal library, was restored and reopened in 2000 as the **Centro Cultural Metropolitano**. It houses several temporary exhibits (*free*) and the **Museo de Cera** depicting the execution of the revolutionaries of 1809. The museum, housed in the original cell, is well worth a visit, but is not for the claustrophobic. ■ *Tue-Sun 0900-1630. US$0.50. Espejo y García Moreno near Plaza de la Independencia.*

Museo Histórico Casa de Sucre is the beautiful, restored house of Sucre, with a museum about life in the 19th century and Sucre's role in Ecuador's independence. ■ *Tue-Fri 0830-1600, Sat-Sun 1000-1600. US$1. T2952860. Venezuela 573 y Sucre.*

The **Casa de Benalcázar**, built in the 18th century on land that belonged to Sebastián de Benalcázar, the Spanish founder of Quito, now houses the Instituto Ecuatoriano de Cultura Hispánica. The house with a courtyard and some religious statues and paintings is open to the public. Its façade was part of the Quito house of inquisition. ■ *Mon-Fri 0900-1300, 1400-1730. Free. T2288102. Olmedo y Benalcázar.*

Museo Manuela Sáenz, a tribute to a legendary *Quiteña* who played an important role in the struggle for independence. Some of her personal belongings as well as works of art and weapons are on display. ■ *Mon-Fri 0830-1300, 1400-1730. US$1. Junín y Montúfar.*

Casa Museo María Augusta Urrutia, the home of a *Quiteña* who devoted her life (1901-1987) to charity, shows the lifestyle of 20th century aristocracy, with furniture of the colonial and republican period. ■ *Tue-Sun 0900-1700. US$2.50. García Moreno 760 y Sucre. T258 0103.*

The **Museo Camilo Egas**, in the restored house of this 20th century (1889-1962) Ecuadorean artist, has different exhibitions during the year. ■ *Mon-Fri 1000-1300. US$0.75. T2954511. Venezuela 1302.*

The **Museo Jijón y Caamaño**, housed in the library building of the **In the New City** Universidad Católica, has a well displayed private collection of archaeological objects, historical documents, paintings by reknowned Ecuadorian artists. ■ *Mon-Fri 0800-1300, 1400-1600. US$0.60. T2565627 (ext 1242). 12 de Octubre y Roca.* The **Museo Weilbauer**, also at the university, has an important archaeological collection from many cultures, in all regions of Ecuador, a photo collection from Oriente and a library. ■ *Restoration due to be completed by 2003. T2565627 (ext 1369). 12 de Octubre y Carrión.*

The **Museo Antonio Santiana**, at the Escuela de Ciencias Sociales (Facultad de Filosofía y Letras) of the Universidad Central, has a history and ethnology collection with information on aboriginal cultures. ■ *0900-2000 daily, except during school holidays, at Ciudadela Universitaria. T2236973.*

Museo de Artesanía has a good collection of Indian costumes and crafts, with helpful guides and a shop. Several times a year they hold fairs, when artisans are on site to show and sell their wares. ■ *Mon-Fri 0800-1600. 12 de Octubre 1738 y Madrid.*

Museo de Ciencias Naturales, at the east end of Parque La Carolina, has a collection of stuffed Ecuadorian fauna and flora. ■ *Mon-Fri 0830-1630, Sat 0900-1300. US$2, students US$1. T2449824. Rumipamba 341 y Los Shyris.*

Museo del Colegio Mejía has natural science and ethnographic exhibits. ■ *Mon-Fri 0700-1300, 1530-2000. Ante y Venezuela.*

Vivarium, run by Fundación Herpetológica Gustavo Orces, is an organization whose aims are to protect endangered species through a programme of education. They have an impressive number of South American and other snakes, reptiles and amphibians, and run a successful breeding programme. You can take photos of the boa constrictors. Staff are friendly and there are good explanations in Spanish (information is available on request in English, French and German). ■ *Tue-Sat 0900-1245, 1430-1745, Sun 1100-1745. US$2 (children half price). T2230988. Reina Victoria 1576 y Santa María.*

The **Museo Amazónico** has interesting displays of Amazonian flora and fauna and tribal culture and shows the effects of oil exploration and drilling. There is also a bookstore (most books in Spanish). ■ *Mon-Fri 0800-1300, 1400-1600, Sat-Sun 0900-1300. US$1, children and seniors US$0.50. T2506247/2562633. Centro Cultural Abya Yala, 12 de Octubre 1430 y Wilson.*

In San Rafael, just east of the city is **La Casa de Kingman Museo**. The home of **In the suburbs** this renowned painter, unchanged from when he lived, is now open to the *For museums at* public. In addition to a collection of the artist's own work, you can see colo- *Mitad del Mundo,* nial, republican and 20th-century art. ■ *Thu-Fri 1000-1600, Sat-Sun* *see Around Quito* *1000-1800. US$1.50, students US$1, children under 7 free. T2861065.* *below* *Portoviejo y Dávila, 1 block from the San Rafael park, Valle de los Chillos, fpak@uio.satnet.net Take a taxi or a Sangolquí bound bus from La Marín as far as the San Rafael park. New in 2002.*

There is a fine museum in Bellavista in the northeast of Quito, **Museo Guayasamín**. As well as the famous artist's works there is a precolumbian and colonial collection, which is highly recommended. You can buy works of art and jewellery. Ask to see the whole collection as only a small portion is displayed in the shop. ■ *Mon-Fri 0900-1330, 1500-1830. US$2. T2446455. Bosmediano 543, Bellavista, near the Ecuavisa TV station. Easiest to take a taxi here, or try the Batán-Colmena bus, marked Bellavista.*

The **Museo Fray Antonio Rodríguez** in Guápulo, has three halls with religious art and furniture, from the 16th to the 20th centuries. Guided tours (Spanish only) include a visit to the beautiful Santuario de Guápulo (see Sights above). ■ *0900-1800 daily. T2565652. New in 2001.*

Cima de la Libertad is a history museum on the flanks of Pichincha, at the site of the 1822 Battle of Pichincha, with a great view. ■ *Tue-Fri 0800-1600, Sat 1000-1500. US$1, children and seniors US$0.25. The Tourist Office recommends taking a taxi there as the suburbs are dangerous. A good idea is to take the Trole south to El Recreo and a taxi from there.*

Museo-Biblioteca Aureliano Pólit is in the former Jesuit seminary north of the airport. It has a unique collection of antique maps of Ecuador. ■ *Mon-Fri 0800-1700. José Nogales y Francisco de Arco, Cotocollao.*

Excursions There are numerous rewarding day-trips that can be made using Quito as your base. Most famous of these is the trip to **Mitad del Mundo**, 23 km north of Quito. See Around Quito, page 141 and beyond, for this and other excursions, including visits to the volcanic crater of **Pululahua**; walking and birdwatching around **Mindo** on the western slopes of Pichincha; exploring the **Valle de los Chillos**; relaxing in the thermal baths of **Papallacta**; and taking the tourist train to **Cotopaxi**.

Essentials

Sleeping

Choosing a hotel in Quito
Read this first
■ *on maps*
Price codes:
see inside front cover

There are over 250 hotels in Quito, of which we list about half. With so much accommodation being offered, you can find a good place to stay regardless of your tastes or budget, but some travellers are bewildered by the huge selection. To narrow your search, read up on the city, its neighbourhoods and hotels before you arrive.

There are not many good places to stay near the bus station and even fewer by the airport. This is more than compensated for, however, by the abundance of cheap taxis. Think ahead about what type of lodgings and what part of town best suit you, and take a cab to your first choice. Many Quito hotels are easily contacted by phone or email for advance reservations, although this is seldom required. Also see Hotel prices and facilities (page 50) and Flying into Quito at night (page 93).

Quito's many hotels may be categorized by a combination of their style, price and location.

International hotel chains and business hotels Quito is well supplied with these, all in the New City. They occupy the highest end of the price range, and often charge foreign guests considerably more than they charge locals. *Swissôtel* stands out in this group for its opulence and excellent service, as does *Hotel Quito* for its lovely views. Most others are cut from a common mold: large modern buildings, elegant expensive restaurants and bars, small casinos, all services and comforts. They look and feel like big busy hotels anywhere in the world, with little that is distinctively Ecuadorean.

Upscale inns and bed and breakfasts *Quiteño* hospitality excels in this class of select establishments. Scattered throughout the New City, they include elegant little places like *La Cartuja, Hostal de La Rábida* and *Villa Nancy* (on Muros). Some are in beautifully refurbished private homes. These gems are expensive, but usually offer a great deal in return: personal service in tasteful, tranquil and very comfortable surroundings.

La Mariscal By far the greatest number of lodgings are concentrated here, between Av Patria to the south and Av Orellana to the north, Av 10 de Agosto to the west and Av 12 de Octubre to the east. This is Quito's tourist neighbourhood *par excellence* – the place for those who want to be in the heart of the action. Here you will be surrounded by restaurants, bars, nightlife, tour agencies, craft shops, cyber-cafés, Spanish schools, and even laundromats. With so much going on, it is not surprising that parts of La Mariscal are noisy, nor that this is where thieves can find the highest concentration of tourists. Hotels in La Mariscal come in all shapes, sizes and prices, and the greatest number of budget places are found here. Shopping around is essential to obtain good value in La Mariscal, especially since there is a rapid turnover of establishments. At the same time, the area also has its share of repeatedly recommended favourites, places like *Casa Sol*, *Casa Helbling*, *Posada del Maple* and *Amazonas Inn*.

La Floresta Situated east of La Mariscal, this is an older residential neighbourhood which offers a variety of accommodations in more relaxed surroundings. Many places here are family run and their setting affords a glimpse of the day-to-day lives of ordinary *Quiteños*. Examples include *Ciprés* and *Casona de Mario*.

The Old City Hotels here, rather like the *Centro Histórico* itself, have an air of faded glory. Some are clustered around the bus terminal, while others are found near the district's many colonial plazas. There are a couple of good comfortable places in the Old City, like *Real Audiencia* and *Vienna Internacional*, alongside some of the cheapest and most basic digs in town (where you might have to share the facilities with short-stay couples). Although the selection of restaurants in the Old City is limited, and it is not safe at night, staying here provides an interesting insight into the often overlooked, but very typical, way of life in Quito's historical heart.

Between the Old and New Cities (including the area west of La Mariscal) This is indeed a grey zone, with neither the charm of colonial Quito, nor the vibrant tourist scene of La Mariscal, nor the tranquillity of La Floresta. It is, nonetheless, home to some particularly good-value accommodations, such as *Marsella*, *Kinara* and *Margarita*, all very popular with travellers.

Other locations With the rapid growth of the New City, lodgings are also striking out beyond their traditional bounds. North of La Mariscal, and in a few off-the-beaten-track locations, are interesting options for those who prefer not to be surrounded by other hotels. Parking is also generally less complicated in these

Quito

South from El Ejido

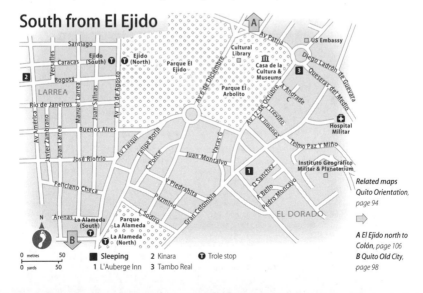

Related maps
Quito Orientation,
page 94

A El Ejido north to
Colón, page 106
B Quito Old City,
page 98

0 metres 50
0 yards 50

■ **Sleeping**   2 Kinara   ❶ Trole stop
1 L'Auberge Inn   3 Tambo Real

out-of-the-way places, especially if you have a large vehicle. In this category, *San Jorge* has the distinction of offering the only rural accommodations within easy reach of Quito. *Casa de Guápulo*, on a steep hillside (not an easy drive), likewise provides unusual and very attractive surroundings.

Apart-Hotels and suites These furnished apartments are a good choice for longer stays and for families. Some also rent by the day. They usually include a living room and fully equipped kitchen, with all utensils. There is a good selection located throughout the New City, with a broad range of prices and facilities. Apartments for rent (mostly unfurnished) are also advertised in *El Comercio* and *El Hoy* as well as their on-line editions (see websites, page 26).

Private homes To really get to know life in Quito, consider boarding in a private home. You can take your meals with the family, discuss the latest gossip, and find out what people think about themselves and their city. Such homestays are especially popular among visitors taking Spanish classes, and can be arranged in advance by Spanish schools. Price and quality vary greatly, however, so always try a week or less, before signing-up for a longer homestay.

International hotel chains & business hotels **LL** *Swissôtel*, 12 de Octubre 1820 y Cordero, T2566497, F2569189. Includes buffet breakfast, Japanese, French and Italian restaurants, also bar, deli and café, state-of-the-art fitness centre, business centre, 3 non-smoking floors and disabled facilities, superb 5-star accommodation. **LL-L** *Hilton Colón*, Amazonas y Patria, T2560666, F2563903, www.hilton.com Excellent Italian restaurant and 24-hr

El Ejido north to Colón

Related map
Quito Orientation,
page 94

A North from Colón,
page 107
B Northeast of
Mariscal, page 113
C South from El Ejido,
page 105

0 metres   50
0 yards   50

■ **Sleeping**
1 Alameda Real *B2*
2 Café Cultura *C2*
3 Casa Helbling *B3*
4 Chalet Suisse *A3*
5 El Cafecito *A3*

6 El Centro del Mundo *A3*
7 El Kapulí *B2*
8 El Taxo *A2*
9 Hilton Colón *C2*
10 Hostelling
   International *B2*
11 Hothello *C2*
12 Hostal Tierra Alta *B3*
13 Plaza Internacional *C2*
14 Posada del Maple *A3*
15 Queen's Hostal *B3*
16 Rincón de Castilla *B1*

17 Río Amazonas *A3*
18 Sebastián *A3*
19 Sierra Madre *B3*
20 Villantigua *C2*

● **Eating**
1 Adam's Rib *A3*
2 Alkerke *B2*
3 El Hornero *B2*
4 El Maple *A3*
5 Grain de Café *B2*
6 Il Grillo *A3*

7 Il Risotto *B3*
8 Magic Bean *A2*
9 No Bar *A3*
10 Reina Victoria *B2*
11 Shorton Grill *A3*
12 Super Papa *B2*
13 Terraza del Tártaro *B3*
14 Tex Mex *B2*

🚇 Trole stop

cafeteria, pool, internet, casino. One of Quito's first luxury hotels, renovated and run by the international chain. **LL-L** *Marriott*, Orellana 1172 y Amazonas, T2972000, F2972041, www.marriotthotels.com Breakfast included for executive rooms and suites, several restaurants with international and Ecuadorean food, pool and spa, internet, the most modern and grandiose of the luxury hotels.

L *Akros*, 6 de Diciembre N34-120 y Checoslovaquia, T2430600, F2431727, akros@ hotelakros.com Includes welcome cocktail and buffet breakfast, excellent restaurant and bar, internet, spacious rooms. **L** *Crown Plaza*, Shyris 1757 y Naciones Unidas, T2445305, F2251958, admihote@accessinter.net, www.crowneplaza.com Includes buffet breakfast, internet, near shopping and Parque La Carolina. **L** *Dann Carlton*, República de El Salvador 513 e Irlanda, T2448808, F2448807, reservas@ danncarlton.com.ec Includes breakfast, international restaurant, internet, business centre and spa. **L** *Howard Johnson*, Alemania E5-103 y República, T2265265, F2264264, www.enebro.net/howardjohnson/ Includes breakfast, 24-hr restaurant, gym, internet, modern and functional. **L** *Mercure Alameda*, Roca 653 y Amazonas, T2562345, F2565759, reservas@grandhotelmercure-alameda.com.ec Includes buffet breakfast, restaurant and 24-hr cafeteria, bought-out by international chain and being refurbished in 2002. **L** *Radisson*, 12 de Octubre 444 y Cordero, World Trade Center, T2233333, F2235777, www.radisson.com/quitoec Includes breakfast, sushi bar, grill, and international restaurants, spa, business center. **L** *Sheraton Four Points*, Naciones Unidas y República de El Salvador, T2970002, F2433906, sheraton@uio.satnet.net, www.sheraton.com Includes breakfast, international restaurant and bar, gym, travel agency, business center, craft shop.

AL *Reina Isabel*, Amazonas 842 y Veintimilla, T2544454, F2221337, www.hotelreinaisabel.com Includes breakfast, restaurant, parking, very nice, modern. **AL** *República*, República y Azuay, T2436553, hrep@impsat.net.ec Internet, parking, functional. **AL** *Río Amazonas*, Cordero E4-375 y Amazonas, T2556667, F5256670, www.hotelrioamazonas.com Restaurant, internet, parking, pleasant, full facilities. **AL** *Sebastián*, Almagro N24-416 y Cordero, T2222400, F2222500, hotelsebastian@ hotelsebastian.com Restaurant, internet, parking, comfortable and very good. **AL-A** *Hotel Quito*, González Suárez N27-142 y 12 de Octubre, T2544600, F2567284,

Quito

North from Colón

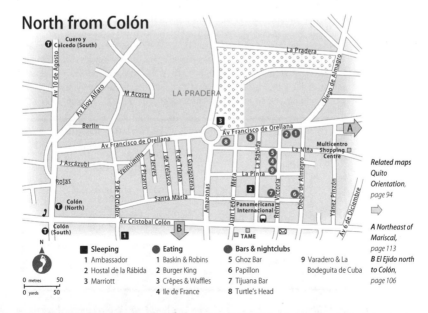

Related maps
Quito
Orientation,
page 94

A Northeast of
Mariscal,
page 113

B El Ejido north
to Colón,
page 106

0 metres 50
0 yards 50

■ **Sleeping**
1 Ambassador
2 Hostal de la Rábida
3 Marriott

● **Eating**
1 Baskin & Robins
2 Burger King
3 Crêpes & Waffles
4 Ile de France

● **Bars & nightclubs**
5 Ghoz Bar
6 Papillon
7 Tijuana Bar
8 Turtle's Head

9 Varadero & La
Bodeguita de Cuba

www.orotels.com Includes buffet breakfast, good restaurant, pool open to non-residents, internet, parking, on a hillside above the New City, lovely views.

A *Chalet Suisse*, Reina Victoria N24-191 y Calama, T2562700, F2563966. Includes breakfast, excellent restaurant, rooms to street are noisy. A *Tambo Real*, 12 de Octubre y Patria, T2563820, F2554964, reservac@hoy.net Includes breakfast, restaurant, internet, parking, convenient for US embassy.

Upscale inns L *Mansión del Angel*, Wilson E5-29 y J L Mera, T2557721, F2237819. Includes breakfast, **& bed &** refurbished old building, very elegant, lovely atmosphere. **AL** *Café Cultura*, Robles **breakfasts** E6-62 y Reina Victoria, T2504078, F2224271, www.cafecultura.com Restaurant, parking, beautiful rooms and garden, but reports of variable service. **AL** *Mi Casa*, Andalucía N24-151 y Francisco Galavis, T/F2225383, micasa@ecuanex.net.ec Includes large breakfast, comfortable rooms and suites, gardens, sauna, small quiet place, family run, multilingual owner. **AL** *Villa Nancy*, Muros 146 y 12 de Octubre, T2562473, F2562583, www.villanancy.com Includes breakfast, small lobby bar, internet, includes airport transfers, quiet, homey and comfortable, helpful multilingual staff. Recommended. **AL-A** *Sierra Madre*, Veintimilla 464 y Luis Tamayo, T2505687, F2505715, www.hotelsierramadre.com Restaurant, parking, fully renovated old-style villa with sun roof, comfortable.

A *Hostal de la Rábida*, La Rábida 227 y Santa María, T/F2221720, larabida@uio.satnet.net Good restaurant, parking, Italian run, bright, comfortable. Recommended. A *La Cartuja*, Plaza 170 y Washington, T2523577/3721, cartuja@uio.satnet.net, www.hotelacartuja.com Includes breakfast, restaurant, beautifully decorated, spacious comfortable rooms, safety deposit boxes, garden, very helpful and hospitable. Highly recommended. A *Los Alpes*, Tamayo 233 y Washington, T2561110, F2561128, www.hotellosalpes.com Includes breakfast, excellent restaurant, pleasant and comfortable, popular. A *Santa Bárbara*, 12 de Octubre N26-15 y Coruña, T2225121, F2275121, santabarbara@porta.net Includes breakfast, parking, beautiful refurbished colonial-style house, English, French and Italian spoken. A *Satori*, Pedro Ponce Carrasco 262 y Almagro, T/F2239575, info@satoriecuador.com Includes breakfast, restaurant, on quiet side street, good rooms, pleasant, comfortable. A *Villantigua*, Washington E9-48 y Tamayo, T2528564, alariv@uio.satnet.net Furnished with antiques, suites with fireplace more expensive, quiet, multilingual staff.

La Mariscal A *Embassy*, Wilson E8-22 y 6 de Diciembre, T2563103, F2563192, hembassy@interactive.net.ec Restaurant, parking, well furnished rooms, also suites with kitchens (more expensive). A *Vieja Cuba*, Almagro 1212 y La Niña, T2520738, viejacuba@andinanet.net Includes breakfast, restaurant, internet, parking, very stylish, great attention to detail, new in 2002. B *Ambassador*, 9 de Oct 1052 y Colón, T2561777,

F2503712, hambassadorquit@yahoo.com Cafeteria, good. **B** *Caimán*, Rodríguez 270 y Reina Victoria, T2567616, hcayman@uio.satnet.net Includes breakfast, parking, sitting room with fireplace, clean and good. **B** *La Casa Sol*, Calama 127 y 6 de Diciembre, T2230798, F2223383, info@lacasasol.com Includes breakfast, small place with courtyard, 24-hr cafeteria, very helpful, English and French spoken. Highly recommended. **B** *Fuente de Piedra*, JL Mera 721 y Baquedano, T2900323, fuente2@ecuahotel.com Includes breakfast, pleasant and comfortable, cheaper annexe nearby. **B** *Hothello*, Amazonas N20-20 y 18 de Septiembre, T/F2565835, www.cometoecuador.com Includes breakfast, café, modern, heating, multilingual staff. **B** *Jardín del Sol*, Calama 166 y Almagro, T2230941, F2230950, h.j.sol@uio.satnet.net Includes breakfast, snack bar, internet, parking, modern and nice. **B** *Orange Guest House*, Foch 726 y Amazonas, T2569960, angerme1@angermeyer.com.ec Includes breakfast, small sitting room, part of Angermeyer tour agency. **B** *Plaza Internacional*, Plaza 150 y 18 de Septiembre, T/F2505075, hplaza@uio.satnet.net Restaurant, parking, comfortable, multilingual staff, very helpful. **B** *Sierra Nevada*, Pinto E4-50 y Cordero, T2553658, F2554936, snevada@accessinter.net Includes breakfast, restaurant, parking, part of Sierra Nevada Expeditions tour agency, multilingual staff, gardens and terraces, climbing wall.

C *Alcalá*, Luis Cordero E5-48 y Reina Victoria, T2227396. Includes breakfast, same owners and facilities as as Posada del Maple (see below). **C** *Alston Inn*, J L Mera N23-41 y Veintimilla, T2229955, F2222721, alston@uio.satnet.net Parking, English spoken. **C** *Casa Helbling*, Veintimilla E8-166 y 6 de Diciembre, T2226013, casahelbling@ accessinter.net Laundry and cooking facilities, parking, helpful, German spoken, family atmosphere, good information, tours arranged. Recommended. **C** *Crossroads*, Foch N5-23 y J L Mera, T2234735, info@crossroadshostal.com Excellent rooms, cheaper in dorm, parking. **C** *Cumbres*, Baquedano 148 y 6 de Diciembre, T2562538. Includes breakfast, hotel rooms and 1 mini-apartment with kitchen, parking. **C** *Gnomo*, Cordero

E4-148 y Foch, T2528298. Includes breakfast, small clean place, family atmosphere. **C** *Palm Garten*, 9 de Octubre 923 y Cordero, T2523960, F2568944. Restaurant, parking, beautiful old house, very clean. **C** *Posada del Arupo*, Juan Rodríguez E7-22 y Reina Victoria, T2557543. Includes breakfast, laundry and cooking facilities, very clean, English and French spoken, same owners as Posada del Maple (see below). **C** *Rincón Escandinavo*, Leonidas Plaza N24-306 y Baquerizo Moreno, T2225965, F2540794, hotelres@porta.net, www.escandina vohotel.com Restaurant, small, modern, well-furnished, English spoken. **C** *Villa Nancy*, Carrión 335 y 6 de Diciembre, T2563084, villa_nancy@yahoo.com Includes breakfast, shared bath, travel information. **C-D** *Posada del Maple*, Rodríguez E8-49 y Almagro, T2544507, www.posadadelmaple.com Includes breakfast, restaurant, cheaper with shared bath, laundry and cooking facilities, warm atmosphere, free tea and coffee. **C-D** *Rincón de Bavaria*, Páez 232 y 18 de Septiembre, T2509401. More expensive rooms include breakfast, restaurant, large rooms. **C-D** *The Magic Bean*, Foch 681 y J L Mera, T2566181, magic@ecuadorexplorer.com Includes breakfast, good restaurant, cheaper in dorm, good beds, American owned, popular.

D *Adventure*, Pinto 570 y Amazonas, T2226340, rfcedeno@interactive.net.ec Cheaper with shared bath, cooking facilities, simple and clean, terrace, helpful. **D** *Amazonas Inn*, Pinto 471 y Amazonas, T2225723. Carpeted rooms, some are sunny, those on first floor are best, very clean and friendly. Recommended. **D** *Cafecito*, Cordero 1124 y Reina Victoria, T2234862, cafecito@ecuadorexplorer.com Vegetarian restaurant, shared bath, hot water if you ask for it, room called 'tomato' has a nice balcony, Canadian-owned, relaxed atmosphere but noisy at night. **D** *Calima*, Cordero E1-21 y 10 de Agosto, T2540891, vnburneo@interactive.net.ec Bright, cheery and modern, new in 2002. **D** *Emerald*, Veintimilla 1069 y Amazonas, T2564700, F2564746. Includes breakfast, some rooms with fridge more expensive, modern and friendly. **D** *Esmeraldas*, 6 Diciembre 1554 y Ventimilla, T254 2771. Ample parking, comfortable, friendly, family run, good value. **D** *Estancia San Martín*, Rodríguez 245 y Reina Victoria, T2509669, h_esanmartin@hotmail.com Includes breakfast, cooking facilities, reliable. **D** *Hostelling International*, Pinto 325 y Reina Victoria, T2543995, F2508221. Includes breakfast, cafeteria, cheaper in dormitory with lockers and shared bath, coin-operated washing machines, large hostel with capacity for 75, US$1 discount for IYHF members. Recommended. **D** *Kapulí*, Robles 625 y Amazonas, T/F2221872, sunlight87@ hotmail.com Laundry and cooking facilities, private rooms and 2 larger ones with several beds and shared bath, English spoken, very helpful. **D** *Loro Verde*, Rodriguez 241 y Almagro, T2226173. Includes breakfast, cooking facilities, clean and friendly. **D** *Nassau*, Pinto E4-340 y Amazonas, T2906645. Sitting room, friendly and helpful. **D** *Pickett*, Wilson 712 y J L Mera, T2551205. Includes breakfast, laundry facilities, carpeted rooms, popular. **D** *Queen's Hostel/Hostal De La Reina*, Reina Victoria N23-76 y Pinto, T255 1844, F240 6690, queen@uio.telconet.net Cafeteria, laundry and cooking facilities, sitting room with fireplace, nice. Recommended. **D** *Quinta Ecológica*, Cordero 1951 y Páez, T2551269, came@uio.satnet.net Parking, a renovated mansion, quieter rooms at rear. **D** *Taxo*, Foch 909 y Cordero, T2225593, hostaleltaxo@yahoo.com Shared bath, internet, cooking facilities, hostel-type, large family house, open fire, good meeting place, helpful. **D** *Tierra Alta*, Wilson E7-79 y Almagro, T2235993. Cheaper with shared bath, laundry and cooking facilities, parking, helpful. **D** *Titisee*, Foch E7-60 y Reina Victoria, T2529063, hostal_titisee@hotmail.com Cheaper with shared bath, cooking facilities, nice large rooms, lounge. Recommended. **D** *Vagabundo*, Wilson E7-45 y Almagro, T2226376, vagabundoecuador@hotmail.com Restaurant serving good set meals, some rooms with private bath, cooking facilities, parking, OK. **D-E** *Centro del Mundo*, Lizardo Garcia 569 y Reina Victoria, T2229050. Cheaper with shared bath, simple. **D-E** *Florencia*, Reina Victoria N21-248 y Roca, T2230489. Cheaper with shared bath, parking, simple but OK, garden, good value. **D-E** *Galería*, Calama 233 y Almagro, T250 0307. Snack bar, internet, cooking facilities, English spoken. **D-E** *Lafayette*, Baquedano 358 y J L Mera, T2224529. Cheaper with shared bath, carpeted and very clean. Recommended.

E *Bask*, Lizardo García 537 y Reina Victoria, T2503456, hostalbask@latinmail.com Cafeteria, private bath, hot water, cooking facilities, free coffee, nice atmosphere. **E** *Gan Eden*, Pinto 163 y 6 de Diciembre, T2223480, ganeden163@hotmail.com Restaurant serves cheap breakfast and good Israeli food, cheaper with shared bath, hot water, cooking facilities, double rooms or dorm, very helpful. **E** *Tortuga Verde*, J L Mera N24-41 y Pinto, T2556829. Includes breakfast, some rooms with private bath, also dormitory, hot water, cooking facilities, airport transfer, tours, very popular with young backpackers, noisy, Swiss run, English, German and French spoken, friendly.

A *La Villa*, Toledo 1455 y Coruña, T2222755, F2226082, nevadatu@uio.satnet.net, **La Floresta**
www.travelguides.com/home/lavilla/Includes breakfast, restaurant, carpeted rooms
and suites with minibar, European-style building. **B** *Floresta*, Isabel La Católica 1015 y
Salazar, T2225376, F2250422, floresta@impsat.net.ec Includes breakfast, restaurant,
parking, very quiet. **B-D** *Aleida's*, Andalucía 559 y Salazar, T2234570, aleidas@
ecuanex.net.ec Cheaper with shared bath, internet, 3 types of rooms.

D *Casona de Mario*, Andalucía 213 y Galicia, T/F2230129, lacasona@punto.net.ec
Shared bath, laundry and cooking facilities, sitting room, big garden, book exchange,
popular. Recommended. **D** *Ciprés*, Lérida 381 y Pontevedra, T2549558, F2502234,
turisavn@ecuanex.net.ec Includes breakfast, cheaper in dorm with shared bath, cooking facilities, parking, transport to airport or bus terminal if staying 3 days, very helpful.
Recommended. **E** *Casa de Eliza*, Isabel La Católica N24-679, T2226602, manteca@
uio.satnet.net Laundry and cooking facilities, shared rooms and bath, very popular
and homey, no smoking.

C *Real Audiencia*, Bolívar Oe3-18 y Guayaquil at Plaza Santo Domingo, T2950590, **The Old City**
F2580213. Includes breakfast, restaurant/bar on top floor, spacious, well furnished
rooms, great views. Highly recommended. **C** *San Francisco de Quito*, Sucre 217 y
Guayaquil, T2287758, F2951241. Includes breakfast, converted colonial building,
attractive patio but can be noisy at night. **C** *Viena Internacional*, Flores 600 y Chile,
T2959611, F2954633. Good restaurant, nice rooms, English spoken.

D *Auca Continental*, Sucre 314 y Venezuela, T2952240. Simple. **D** *Cumandá*,
Morales 449 y Maldonado near Terminal Terrestre, T2956984, www.hotel-
cumanda.com Restaurant, parking, comfortable, excellent service, noisy area but quieter at the back. **D** *Plaza del Teatro*, Guayaquil 1373 y Esmeraldas, T2959462. Restaurant, parking, carpeted rooms, stylish, good service. **D-E** *Huasi Continental*, Flores 322
y Sucre, T2957327. Restaurant, cheaper
with shared bath, simple.

E *Catedral Internacional*, Mejía 638 y
Cuenca, T2955438. Hot water, good
rooms. **E** *Posada Colonial*, Paredes 188 y
Rocafuerte, T2282859. Some rooms with
private bath, hot water, parking, beautiful
old building. **E** *Reina de Quito*,
Maldonado 2648 y Portilla, near bus ter-
minal and Ministry of Defence,
T/F2950347. Private bath, hot water,
great views from terrace, army-run. **E** *San
Blas*, Pasaje España E1-38 entre Caldas y
Fermín Cevallos, on Plaza San Blas,
T2281434. Private bath, hot water, laundry and cooking facilities, terrace, great
value but also used for short stays.
E-F *Grand Hotel*, Rocafuerte 1001 y
Pontón, near the bus terminal, T2959411.
Cafeteria, cheaper with shared bath, hot
water, laundry and cooking facilities,
some rooms are dingy but others OK,
friendly and helpful. Recommended.

F *Guayaquil*, Maldonado 3248 y
Morales, near the bus terminal, T2959937.
Private bath, hot water, basic.
F *Montúfar*, Sucre 160 y Montúfar,

Hostal La Villa

*You will be delighted with
our warm atmosphere and
european style, you will
feel right at home.*

*Services: Restaurant,
24hr room service,
laundry, fax and internet.*

*All rooms have a
private bathroom, minibar
and cable TV*

*Toledo 1455 and
Coruña Ave.
Tel: 22222755/2227747
Fax: 2226082
Email:
nevadatu@uio.satnet.net
Quito - Ecuador*

Quito

Quito

T2284644. Cheaper with shared bath, hot water, simple, good value. **G** *Sucre*, Bolívar 615 and Cuenca, Plaza San Francisco, T2954025. Shared bath, hot water, laundry facilities, a bit noisy, terrace with great views over the Old City, very cheap and basic, often full, also used for short stays.

Between the Old & New Cities (including the area west of La Mariscal)   **D** *Carrión*, Carrión 1259 y Versalles, T2548256, F2909769. Café and bar, laundry facilities, garden, good value, fills early. **D** *Deja Vu*, 9 de Octubre 599 y Carrión, T2224483. Includes breakfast, cheaper with shared bath, family run, friendly and helpful. **D** *Kinara*, Bogotá 534 y América, T2228524, kinara@andinanet.net Includes breakfast, laundry and cooking facilities, library, English/French spoken, free tea and coffee, spotless. Highly recommended. **D** *L'Auberge Inn*, Colombia 1138 y Yaguachi, T2552912, www.ioda.net/auberge-inn Restaurant, cheaper without bath, parking, duvets on beds, garden, lovely terrace and communal area, helpful, good atmosphere. **D** *Majestic*, Mercadillo 366 y Versalles, T2543182, F2504207, hmajestic@accessinter.net Cafeteria and bar, parking, well-furnished and quiet. **D** *Rincón de Castilla*, Versalles 1127 y Carrión, T2224312, F2548097. Restaurant, shared bath, laundry and cooking facilities, parking, a bit dingy. Owner speaks German, French and English. **D** *Versalles*, Versalles 1442 y Mercadillo, T2526145, hotversa@ecnet.ec Restaurant serves breakfast daily and lunch on weekdays, nice and clean.

D-E *Bambú*, Solano 1758 y Colombia, T2226738. Cheaper with shared bath, laundry and cooking facilities, garden with hammocks, family run, monthly rates US$90-$130, good value. **D-E** *Marsella*, Los Ríos 2035 y Espinoza, T2955884. Includes breakfast, cheaper with shared bath, parking, good rooftop terrace with views, top floor rooms best but noisy. Good value, very popular and often full by 1700. **E** *Hostal del Hoja*, Gerónimo Leyton N23-89 y La Gasca, T2560832, delhoja@mixmail.com Includes breakfast, shared bath, hot water, cooking facilities, dorms, small place, very helpful. **E** *Margarita*, Los Ríos 1995 y Espinoza, T2950441. Private bath, hot water, parking, good beds, sheets changed daily, great value. Highly recommended.

Other locations   **AL** *San Jorge*, Km 4 Vía Antigua Cotocollao – Nono, T2494002, F2565964, www.hostsanjorge.com.ec Restaurant, pool, sauna and turkish bath, parking, on a traditional farm in the Bosque Protector Pichincha, quiet, peaceful, horse riding and birdwatching, all within easy reach of Quito. Recommended. **AL** *Sol de Quito*, Alemania N30-170 y Vancouver, T2541773, www.soldequito.com Restaurant, internet, parking, friendly and helpful. Recommended. **A** *Pradera*, San Salvador 222 y Pasaje Martín Carrión, T2226833, F2227309, hpradera@uio.satnet.net Includes breakfast, restaurant, parking, comfortable, quiet, residential area.

B *Chevalier*, Inglaterra N31-173 y Mariana de Jesús, T2220917, thierrychevalier@ hotmail.com Includes breakfast, quiet area. **B** *Eco Karmel*, Italia 875 y Alemania, T2553444, shaed4@punto.net.ec Includes breakfast, sitting room, terrace, quiet area.

B *Finlandia*, Finlandia 227 y Suecia, T2244288. Includes breakfast, parking, lovely, new in 2002. **B** *Hostal La Carolina*, Italia 324 y Vancouver, T2542471, F2222744, hoscarol@uio.satnet.net Includes breakfast, restaurant, internet, parking, helpful, ask for quiet rooms at the back. **B** *Portón*, San Javier 203 y Orellana, T2231712, F2232662, elporton@rdyec.net Includes breakfast, cafeteria, rooms in rustic style cabins and suites, room service, small, quiet and friendly.

C *Barón Carondelet*, Barón de Carondelet 318 y Naciones Unidas, T/F2921569. Includes breakfast, internet, in modern commercial area. **C** *Ébano*, Amazonas 3009 y Rumipamba, T2248523, hostalebano@andinanet.net Includes breakfast, parking, comfortable, nice sitting room, family run. **C** *FerReisen*, Azuay 147 y Amazonas, T2242682, F2269907, www.ferreisen.de Includes breakfast, internet, ample parking, on a quiet side-street, German and English spoken, friendly. **C-D** *Paraná*, Amazonas N48-243 y Río Curaray, near airport, 2 blocks south of national departures terminal, 1245/818. Cheaper with shared bath, modern, clean and bright, new in 2002.

D *Casa de Guápulo*, C Leonidas Plaza (Guápulo), T/F2220473. Includes breakfast, restaurant and bar, parking, peaceful area, multilingual staff, free transfer to airport. **D** *Casa Girasol*, Jorge Juan 30/110 y Cuero y Caicedo, T/F2238292, mhomberger@ access.net.ec Includes good breakfast, shared bath, laundry and cooking facilities, good place, owners also operate Galápagos tours and guide nature trips. **D** *Nuestra Casa*, Bartolomé de las Casas 435 y Versalles, T2225470, mlo@ uio.satnet.net Shared bath, laundry and cooking facilities, converted family house, dinner available, camping in garden. Recommended. **D** *Vizcaya*, Rumipamba 1726 y Manuela Sáenz, opposite Colegio San Gabriel's coliseum, T2452252, racincs@ uio.satnet.net Includes breakfast, evening meal on request, laundry facilities, parking, reservations essential, comfortable beds, English spoken, kind family. **E** *Casa Paxee*, Romualdo Navarro 326 y La Gasca, T2500441. Includes breakfast, private bath, hot water, laundry and cooking facilities, 3 rooms only, discounts for longer stays.

Northeast of Mariscal

Sleeping
1 Hotel Quito
2 Radisson
3 Swissôtel
4 Villa Nancy

3 Cocina de Kristi
4 La Viña
5 Sake
6 Taco Factory

Eating
1 Avalon
2 Clancy's

Bars & nightclubs
7 Bierkeller
8 Pobre Diablo

N
0 metres   50
0 yards   50

LL-L *Sofitel Quito*, 12 de Octubre y Salazar, T2564456, F2564563. Includes buffet breakfast, elegant restaurant with panoramic views, internet, luxury 1 and 2 bedroom suites, long term rentals available. **AL** *American Suites*, Eloy Alfaro 3333 y Correa, T2275120, F2275117, www.americansuites.com Restaurant, pool and sauna, internet, parking, modern, from US$2,200. **AL** *Colina Suites*, La Colina N26-119 y Orellana, T2234678, F2566189, www.lacolinasuites.com Includes buffet breakfast, cafeteria, small spa, internet,

Apart-Hotels & suites
US$ prices quoted are for monthly rentals

Related maps
Quito Orientation, page 94

A El Ejido north to Colón, page 106
B North from Colón, page 107

Quito

parking, includes aiport pick-up or drop-off, from US$2,000. **A** *Apart-Hotel Amaranta*, Leonidas Plaza N20-32 y Washington, T2560585. Includes breakfast, good restaurant, parking, comfortable, well-equipped suites, from US$1,600. **A** *Apart-Hotel Antinea*, Rodríguez 175 y Almagro, T2506839, F2504404, www.hotelantinea.com Includes breakfast, parking, suites and apartments, lovely rooms, from US$800.

C *Apartamentos Modernos*, Amazonas N31-75 y Mariana de Jesús, T2233766 (ext 800), F2233766 (ext 807), modernos@uio.satnet.net Convenient location near El Jardín Mall and Parque La Carolina, English and German spoken, impeccably clean, from US$450, parking, good value. **C-D** *Apartamentos Colón*, Plaza 326 y Robles, T2563183. Hot water during limited hrs, parking, simple appartments from US$400. **D** *Apart-Hotel Mariscal*, Robles 958 y Páez, T2544179, F2222446, amariscal@ gye.on.net.ec Parking, simple rooms and apartments, from US$300.

Private homes *Sra Anita Gomezjurado*, Julio Zaldumbide N24-741 entre Miravalle y Coruña, near Hotel Quito, T2237778, anezkaslatinkova@hotmail.com **E** per person half board in rooms with private bath, hot water, includes laundry service and airport pick-up. In quiet, residential neighbourhood, convenient for Universidad Católica, German, Czeck, and some English spoken, friendly, clean. *Sra Rosa Jácome*, edif Doral Mariscal, Mercadillo y Páez, T2503180 (evenings), 1 double room with bath and 2 singles, **F** per person, use of kitchen and phone, she will arrange outings and is friendly and helpful, airport pick-up. *Sra Leonor de Maldonado*, Hungría N31-192 y Mariana de Jesús, 1 block west of Amazonas, T2256489, maldonado_maria_@hotmail.com One double room with private bath, **E** per person full board, includes laundry service and airport transfers. Daughters speak English and French, they can accompany visitors to local sights. *Dra Cecilia Rivera*, Salazar 327 y Coruña, T2569961, ceciriverin@hotmail.com **D** per person full board, **E** per person half board. Hot water, good views across the valley, quiet, airport pick-up.

Eating

● *on maps*
Price codes:
see inside front cover

Dining in Quito is excellent, varied, and increasingly cosmopolitan. The vast majority of restaurants are in the New City, where almost any type of cuisine can be found, to suit any budget. Those in the Old City tend to offer only local and fast food. Many restaurants throughout the city close on Sun evening. **NB** Restaurants with stickers indicating acceptance of credit cards do not necessarily do so. In many of the more expensive restaurants 22% tax and service is added to the bill. There are a number of restaurants in the food courts of shopping malls, for their addresses see Shopping below. The following list is by type and all restaurants are in the New City unless otherwise stated. In all cases, assume good food, service and value.

Ecuadorean
There are many places throughout the city serving almuerzos, set lunches, for about US$1.50-2.50

Expensive *La Choza*, 12 de Octubre N24-551 y Cordero, T2230839. Good music and special décor. Mon-Fri 1200-1600, 1900-2230, Sat-Sun 1200-1630. *El Níspero*, Valladolid N24-438 y Cordero, T2226398. Meat and seafood specialties. 1200-1600 daily, Tue-Sat also 1900-2300. *Rincón de La Ronda*, Belo Horizonte 406 y Almagro, T2540459. Very good local and international food, huge Sun buffet, Sun night folklore show. Touristy. Daily 1200-2300. **Expensive to mid-range** *La Querencia*, Eloy Alfaro N34-194 y Catalina Aldaz. Good views and atmosphere. Tue-Sat 1200-1600, Sun 1200-1600. **Mid-range** *Mama Clorinda*, Reina Victoria 1144 y Calama, T2544362. A la carte and set meals. Filling, good value. Sun-Mon 1200-1700, Tue-Sat 1200-2100. *El Pajonal*, Homero Salas Oe5-69 y El Altar, near the airport, T2449816. Very good food, live music on Fri and Sat night. Tue-Thu 1000-2200, Fri-Sat 1000-0200, Sun 1000-1600. **Cheap** *Los Adobes*, La Terraza Quicentro Shopping, T2254917. Traditional meals, specially 'fritada'. Sun-Thu 1000-2000, Fri-Sat 1000-2100.

There has been something of a fast food explosion in Quito and you can find most of the better-known US outlets here. All the shopping centres have food courts with a variety of fast food outlets including traditional Ecuadorean, Chinese and Italian food in addition to the ubiquitous hamburger, pizza, etc.

Fast food
For pizza restaurants also see below

Expensive *Chalet Suisse*, Reina Victoria N24-191 y Calama, T2562700. Good steaks, also some Swiss dishes, good quality. Daily 1100-1500, 1900-2300. *Chantilly*, Roca 736 y Amazonas and Whymper 394. Good restaurant and bakery. Tue-Sat 1200-1500, bakery 1700-2100. *Ile de France*, Reina Victoria N26-143 y la Niña, T2553292. French-Swiss cuisine and fondue bar, very good. Daily 1230-1500, 1830-0000. *Raclette*, Eloy Alfaro 1348 y Andrade Marín, T2237753. Swiss specialties including raclette, fondue, some international dishes. Alpine décor. Mon-Sat 1230-2300, Sun 1200-1600. *Rincón de Francia*, Roca 779 y 9 de Octubre, T2554668. Excellent, reservation essential, slow service. Mon-Fri 1200-1600, 2000-2300, Sat 1200-1530, 2000-2200. *Swiss Corner*, Los Shyris 2137 y El Telégrafo, T2468007. Swiss dishes, also delicatessen and pastry shop. Mon-Sat 0700-2030, Sun 0700-1600. **Cheap** *Chez Alain*, Baquedano y JL Mera, T2903192. Choice of good quality set meals. Mon-Fri 1200-1600. Recommended.

French & Swiss

Expensive *Hansa Krug*, Salazar 934 y 12 de Octubre, T2237334. Typical German fare, great variety of dishes, very good. Mon-Sat 1200-1500, 1800-2300, Sun 1200-1600. *Muckis*, in El Tingo, T2861789, see Excursions east of Quito.

German

Expensive *Columbus*, Amazonas 1539 y Santa María, T2540780, and Amazonas 3463 y Atahualpa, T244 4859. Mon-Sat 1200-0200, Sun 1200-2200. *Rincón del Gaucho*, Almagro 422 y García, T2547846. Very tasty meat, salad bar. Daily 1200-2300. *Shorton Grill*, Calama E7-73 y Almagro, T2523645, and Urrutia N14-233 y Eloy Alfaro, T2247797. Meat and seafood, salad bar, large portions, smart decor. Expensive. Daily 1200-2300. *Los Troncos*, Los Shyris 1280 y Portugal, T2437377. Good Argentine grill, serves beef, chicken, pork, fish, salads. Small and friendly. Mon-Sat 1000-2200, Sun 1000-1600. **Mid-range** *La Casa de Mi Abuela*, JL Mera 1649 y la Niña, T2565667. Very good meat and salads. Mon-Sat 1100-1430, 1900-2200, Sun 1100-1430. *Columbia*, Colón 1262 y Amazonas and Tarqui 851 y 10 de Agosto, T2249239. Popular. Daily 1100-1500, 1900-2200.

Grill

Cheap *Ariana Tandoori*, Reina Victoria y Foch. Varied menu, good. Mon-Sat 0900-0100. *Chandani Tandoori*, JL Mera N24-277 y Cordero, T222 1053. Simple little place, with good authentic cuisine, good variety and value. Recommended. Mon-Sat 1100-2230, Sun 1200-1500.

Indian

All of the luxury class hotels have very good international restaurants (see Sleeping above). The *Swissôtel* has several superb restaurants including Japanese, Swiss, grill and a cafeteria with excellent breakfast, lunch and afternoon-tea buffets. The *Hilton Colón* has a 24-hr cafeteria with an excellent lunch buffet, daily except Sat, and an excellent Italian restaurant. In the *Hotel Quito*, the rooftop restaurant has excellent views and serves a buffet breakfast and lunch and à la carte dinner.
    Expensive *Amadeus Restaurant and Pub*, Coruña 1398 y Orellana, T2230831. Very good international cuisine and concerts, usually 2300 on Fri, rather formal. Can work out very expensive. Tue-Sat 1200-1600 and 1900-2300. *Bambú Bar*, Francisco Andrade Marín N32C-133 y Almagro, T2237436. Good quality and service, some seafood specialties. Daily 1100-1700. *Cantagallo* Los Laureles E14-138 y Eloy Alfaro, T2434672. Excellent food, a number of seafood and highbrow dishes, live music, great atmosphere. Very expensive. Mon-Sat 1200-1530, 1900-2300, Sun 1200-1600. *Cocina de Kristy*, Whymper y Orellana. Upmarket, great view from

International

the terrace and equally great food. Recommended. Tue-Sat 1230-1600, 1800-2300, Sun 1230-1600. *La Escondida Bar & Grill*, General Roca N33-29 y José Bosmediano, T2242380. California style cooking, meat, trout. Young crowd, informal atmosphere. Sun-Fri 1230-1530, Mon-Fri 1700-2300. Recommended. *Oscar*, Gonzalez Suárez 1100 y Bejarano, T2230295. Meat and fish specialties in elegant atmosphere. Mon-Sat 1200-1530, 1900-2300. *Terraza del Tártaro*, Veintimilla 1106 y Amazonas (no sign), at the top of the building, T2527987. Excellent views, pleasant atmosphere. Recommended. Mon-Sat 1200-1600, 1800-2200, Sun 1200-1600. *La Viña*, Isabel la Católica y Cordero, T2566033. Extensive and unusual menu, beautifully presented and excellent food. Highly recommended. Tue-Sat 1200-1500, 1900-2300, Sun 1200-1600. *El Zócalo*, JL Mera y Calama. Varied menu. Lively atmosphere, live music on Fri night, terrace, a meeting place for young people. Mon-Thu 1200-1500, 1900-2200, Fri 1200-1500, 1900-0100.

Mid-range *Cafetería Stop*, Amazonas N24-15 y Moreno Bellido, T2567960. International and Chilean dishes. Mon-Sat 1100-1500, 1700-2200, Sun 1000-1600. *Clancy's*, F Salazar y Toledo, T2554278, good food and service. Daily 1200-2400. *Crêpes & Waffles*, La Rábida 461 y Orellana, T2500658. Succulent savoury crêpes and salads and delicious desserts. Mon-Thu 1200-2130, Fri-Sat 1200-2330, Sun 1200-2130. Recommended. **Mid-range to cheap** *Cafetería Sutra*, Calama 380 y JL Mera, top floor. Very good food, snacks, drinks, friendly, nice vibe, popular meeting place. Tue-Sat 1600-2200. *Grain de Café*, Baquedano 332 y Reina Victoria, T2565975. Good, cheap, meat or vegetarian set lunches, good cakes and coffee, cocktails, good service. Mid-range for à la carte. Mon-Sat 0700-2200. Recommended.

Italian **Expensive** *La Briciola*, Toledo 1255 y Cordero, T2547138. Extensive menu, excellent food, homey atmosphere. Daily 1230-1500, 1930-2300, closed Sun. *Il Grillo*, Baquerizo Moreno 533 y Almagro, T2225531. Great pizzas, upmarket style. Mon-Fri 1200-1500, 1900-2300, Sat 1900-2300. *Pavarotti*, 12 de Octubre 1955 y Cordero, above *Restaurant La Choza*, T2566668. Creative cuisine and very attentive service. Recommended. Tue-Sat 1200-1600, 1900-2300, Sun 1200-1600. *Il Risotto*, Pinto 209 y Almagro, T2220400. Very popular and very good. Mon-Sat 1200-1500, 1900-2200, Sun 1200-1530. *La Scala*, Salazar y 12 de Octubre. Good atmosphere. *Siboney*, Eloy Alfaro y 6 de Diciembre. Homemade pasta, great huge pizzas. Mon-Sat 1600-2200, Sun 1000-1600. *La Trattoria de Renato*, San Javier y Orellana, T2541648. Nice atmosphere. Mon-Sat 1200-1500, 1830-2200, Sun 1200-1500. **Mid-range** *Capuletto*, Eloy Alfaro N32-544 y Los Shyris, T2550611. Excellent fresh pasta and desserts, Italian deli, lovely outdoor patio with fountain. Mon-Sat 0900-0000, Sun 0900-2200. Recommended. *Spaghetti*, Plaza de las Américas, at Av América y República, near Naciones Unidas, T2260340, and Orellana 1171 y La Rábida, T255 2570. Very good. Mon-Sat 1230-2300, Sun 1230-2200.

Latin American **Expensive** *La Bodeguita de Cuba*, Reina Victoria 1721 y la Pinta, T2542476. Good Cuban food. Good music and snacks at the *Varadero* bar next door (see Bars below). Mon-Sat 1200-1500, 1830-2300. *Churrascaría Tropeiro*, Veintimilla 564 y 6 de Diciembre, T2548012. Brazilian-style, salad bar and *espeto* grill, *feijoada completa* on weekends. Mon-Sat 1200-1500, 1900-2200, Sun 1200-1500. **Mid-range** *La Guarida del Coyote*, Av Eloy Alfaro E25-94 y Portugal, T2467882, Carrión 619, T2503293, and Japón 542, T2252453. Excellent Mexican Food, live music. Mon-Sat 0900-2300. *Rincón Ecuatoriano Chileno*, 6 de Diciembre y Orellana. Delicious, very good value, small, busy on weekends. Recommended. Daily 1200-1600. *Tex Mex*, Reina Victoria 847 y Wilson, T2527689. The Tex Mex Mixto is especially recommended. Lively atmosphere, draught beer. Mon-Sat 1300-2200.

Mid-range *Aladdin*, Almagro y Baquerizo Moreno, T2229435. Varied menu. Daily **Middle Eastern**
1030-2330, Fri and Sat until 0100, Sun until 2130. **Cheap** *El Arabe*, Reina Victoria 627 y
Carrión, T2549414. Good food. Mon-Sat 1130-0000. *Gan Eden*, Pinto 163 y 6 de
Diciembre, T2223480. Israeli meals and snacks, falafel. Daily 0800-2200.

Expensive *Casa de Asia*, Eloy Alfaro 3027 y Germán Alemán, T2464517. Excellent, **Oriental**
authentic Korean and Japanese food, nicely presented, pricey drinks. Tue-Sat
1200-1600, 1830-2200, Sun 1130-1600. *Sake*, Paul Rivet N30-166 y Whymper,
T2524818. Sushi bar and other Japanese dishes. Very trendy, great food, nicely decorated. Mon-Sat 1200-1530, 1900-2300. Sun 1230-1600. Recommended. *Shogun*,
Calama E5-10 y Jl Mera, T2906200. Sushi bar. Mon-Sat 1230-1600, 1800-0000. *Siam*,
Calama E5-104 y JL Mera. Good Thai food, slow service, nice balcony. Mon-Sat
1200-2300, Sun 1200-1600. *Thai-an*, Eloy Alfaro N34-230 y Portugal, T2446639. Excel-
lent Thai food and ambience. Mon-Sat 1200-1600, 1900-2300, Sun 1200-1600.
Expensive to mid-range *Happy Panda*, Cordero E9-348 e Isabel la Católica,
T2547322. Excellent Hunan specialties. Tue-Sat 1600-2200. **Mid-range** *Chifa
Asiático*, Robles y Páez. Authentic Chinese cuisine. Mon-Sat 1200-1600, 1900-2200,
Sun 1200-1700. *Fuji*, Robles 538 y JL Mera, T2529634. Japanese food. Mon-Sat
1130-1530, 1830-2200, Sun 1130-1600. *Hong Kong*, Wilson 246 y Tamayo, T2234332.
Good. Daily 1200-1600, 1900-2200. *Hong Tai*, La Niña 234 y Yanez Pinzón. Good
authentic cuisine. Tue-Sat 1300-1500, 1900-2300, Sun 1300-1600. *Pekín*, Whimper
300 y Orellana, T2235273. Excellent food, very nice atmosphere. Mon-Sat 1200-1500,
1900-2230, Sun 1200-2030. **Mid-range to cheap** *Chifa China*, Carrión Oe2-82 y
Versalles, T2229954. Good. Mon-Sat 1200-1600, 1900-2200, Sun 1200-1700.

There are many good pizzerías, most with several outlets and a home delivery service **Pizza**
(phone numbers given below). The most centrally located ones are listed. Prices are
generally **mid-range**. *Le Arcate*, Baquedano 358 y JL Mera, T2237659. Wood oven
pizza, good, excellent banana flambé, same management as *Il Risotto*. 1100-1500,
1800-2300, closed Mon. *Domino's*, Coruña 1239 y San Ignacio, T2508506. More expensive than average. *Ch Farina*, Carrión, entre JL Mera y Amazonas, T2558139, and
Naciones Unidas y Amazonas (open 24 hrs), T244 4400. Fast service, good, popular.
El Hornero, Veintimilla y Amazonas, República de El Salvador y Los Shyris and on Gonzalez Suárez, T1-800-500500. Very good wood oven pizzas, try one with *choclo* (fresh
corn). 1200-2300. Recommended. *Pizza Hut*, JL Mera 566 y Carrión, T2500143,
Naciones Unidas y Amazonas, T2454288, and at several shopping centres. *Pizza Net*,
Calama E5-37 y JL Mera, T2238128. Large screen TV, internet.

Expensive *Avalón*, Orellana 155 y 12 de Octubre, T2509875. Excellent food, also **Seafood**
meat dishes, upmarket. Tue-Sat 1200-1500, 1800-2300, Sun 1200-1700. *La Canoa* *Be selective when*
Manabita, Calama y Reina Victoria. Great seafood and very clean. Daily 1200-2100. *choosing a seafood*
El Cebiche, JL Mera 1236 y Calama, T2526380, and on Amazonas 2428 y Moreno *restaurant, visitors*
Bellido, T250 4593. Delicious *ceviche*. Tue-Sun 1000-1600. *Cebiches y Banderas de la* *have become ill*
Foch, 12 de Octubre 1533 y Foch, T2526963. *Delmónicos*, Mariano Aguilera 331 y *after eating at some*
Pradera, T2544200. Very good seafood. Daily 1230-1500, 1930-2300, closed Sun eve- *of the cheaper*
ning. *La Jaiba*, Reina Victoria N25-20 y Colón, T2543887. An old favourite, varied menu, *establishments*
good service. Mon 1100-1530, Tue-Sat 1100-1600, 1900-2100, Sun 1100-1630.
Mare Nostrum, Foch 172 y Tamayo, T2528686. Very upmarket, fine ambiance. Very
expensive. Daily 1200-2300. *Puerto Camarón*, 6 de Diciembre y Granaderos, Centro
Comercial Olímpico, T2265761. Good quality, varied menu. Tue-Sat 1000-1500,
1800-2100, Sun 1000-1600. Recommended. *Las Redes*, Amazonas 845 y Veintimilla,
T2525691. Lovely atmosphere. Expensive. Recommended. Mon-Sat 1000-1600.
Mid-range *Barlovento*, 12 de Octubre 2511 y Orellana, T2223751. Seafood, also

Quito

Ecuadorean food, outside seating. Daily 0900-1900. *Cebiches de la Rumiñahui*, 7 branches including **Real Audiencia** Real Audiencia N59-121 entre Av del Maestro y Tufiño, T2599888 (the original branch and less clean); *La Carolina*, Nuñez de Vela E3-73 y Amazonas, T2263463; *Quicentro Shopping Centre*, T2452814. All are popular for *ceviche*, seafood and fish. Daily 1200-2000. *Las Palmeras*, Japón N36-87 y Naciones Unidas, opposite Parque la Carolina, T2458439. Very good *comida Esmeraldeña*, try their *viche*, outdoor tables, good value. Daily 0800-1800.

Spanish   **Expensive** *El Mesón de Triana*, Isabel La Católica 1015 y Salazar, T2502844. Varied Spanish and international menu, tapas, nice décor with Talavera ceramics. Mon-Fri 1200-1500, 1900-2300, Sat 1200-15000. *La Paella Valenciana*, República y Almagro. Huge portions, superb fish, seafood and paella. Very expensive. Tue-Sat 1200-1500, 1900-2300, Sun 1200-1600. *La Vieja Castilla* La Pinta 435 y Amazonas. Typical Spanish food. Mon-Sat 1200-1500, 1900-2200.

US   **Expensive** *Hunters*, 12 de Octubre 2517 y Muros, T2234994. BBQ wings, ribs, beer, drinks. Tue-Sat 1200-1600, 1930-2300, Sun 1200-1530. *The Magic Bean*, Foch 681 y JL Mera, T2566181. Good food, large portions, outdoor eating, specializes in fine coffees and natural foods, more than 20 varieties of pancakes, good salads, gets very busy. Recommended. Mon-Sat 1200-1530, 1900-2200, Sun 1200-1530. *Red Hot Chilli Peppers*, Foch 713 y JL Mera. Amazing fajitas, the best daiquiris in town, friendly. Mon-Sat 1200-2200. **Mid-range** *Adam's Rib*, Calama E6-15 y Reina Victoria, T2563196. American ribs, steaks, good BBQ, great pecan pie, a popular meeting place for American expats. Mon-Fri 1200-2230, Sat closed, Sun 1200-2100. Happy hour 1730-2100. *American Deli*, República de El Salvador 1058 y Naciones Unidas, T2451252, also at Mall El Jardín and Centro Comercial Iñaquito. Sandwiches, hamburgers, desserts. Daily 1300-2100. *Mango Tree Café*, Foch 721 y Amazonas. Salads, fruit juices, coffee, homemade bread and bagels, nice patio and décor. Closed Sun and holidays. *Roasters*, República N6-238 y Eloy Alfaro, behind El Jardín Mall, T2227766. American franchise serving roast chicken, also nice corn bread. Take out and home deliveries. Tue-Sat 1230-1500, 1900-2230, Sun 1230-1600. *Sports Planet*, at Plaza de las Américas, Av América y Naciones Unidas, T2267790. Bar and restaurant. The complex also houses cinemas and other restaurants. *TGI Friday's*, at Quicentro Shopping, T2264636. American franchise, food and drinks. Daily 1200-2200. *The Taco Factory*, at Whymper y Paul Rivet. Generous portions, US TV. **Cheap** *Bagel Connection*, Reina Victoria y Pinto. Breakfast, bagels with a variety of spreads. Mon-Sat 0800-1900, Sun 0830-1300. *Fried Bananas*, JL Mera y Roca, T2562003. Funky little café, great menu, good salads. Mon-Sat 1100-2200.

Vegetarian   **Mid-range** *Le Champignon*, Robles 543 y JL Mera, T2543284. Nice atmosphere. Mon-Sat 1200-1600, 2000-2300, Sun 1200-1530. *Las Ensaladas/Mi Frutería*, Quicentro Shopping. Gorgeous fresh fruit salads and coastal Ecuadorean food. Daily 1000-2200. **Cheap** *Manantial*, 9 de Octubre 591 y Carrión and Cordero 1838 y 9 de Octubre. Good set lunch. *El Maple*, JL Mera y Calama, T2231503. Varied menu, good meals and fruit juices, set lunches, stylish décor. Recommended. Daily 0730-2330. *El Marquez*, Calama y Almagro. Good set lunch served Mon-Fri and other dishes. Mon-Fri 1200-2200, Sat 1200-1600. *Viejo Arribal*, JL Mera y Foch. Good, varied menu.

In the Old City   **Expensive** *La Cueva del Oso*, Edificio Pérez Pallares, Chile 1046 y Venezuela, across from the Plaza de la Independencia, T2572786. In elegant covered courtyard, art deco interior, great atmosphere. Mon-Sat 1200-0100. *Las Cuevas de Luis Candelas*, Benalcázar 713 y Chile, T2287710. Open since 1963, Spanish and Ecuadorean dishes served in a nice atmosphere with flamenco music. Mon-Sat 1200-1530, 1900-2300,

Sun 1200-1600. **Mid-range** *La Chimenea*, Díaz de Pineda 545 y Pedro Dorado, La Villaflora, south of the colonial city, T2264287. Excellent meat and steaks. Daily 1100-2300. **Cheap** *El Criollo*, Flores 731 y Olmedo, T2289828. Tasty chicken specialities, clean. Mon-Sat 1200-1900, Sun 1200-1600. *Chifa El Chino*, Bolívar y Venezuela, T2218679. Chinese food, good lunch. *Govinda*, Esmeraldas y García Moreno. Vegetarian dishes. Daily 1200-2100.

Bangalô, Foch 451 y Almagro, T2501332. Excellent cakes, quiches, coffees. Great atmosphere, good jazz at weekends. Mon-Sat lunchtime and 1600-2000. *Books & Coffee*, JL Mera 12-27 y Calama, T2528769. Capuccino, espresso, book exchange, local newspapers, a good place to sit and write. Mon, Tue and Sat 0900-2000, Wed-Fri 0900-2300. *El Cafecito*, Luis Cordero 1124 y Reina Victoria, at the hotel. Pancakes, set meal of the day and the best chocolate brownies. Daily 0900 until late. *Café Amazonas*, Amazonas y Roca. Good coffee, popular with locals. Mon-Sat 1700-2200. *Café Cultura*, Robles 513 y Reina Victoria, at the hotel. Relaxed atmosphere, tasteful décor, excellent cakes and homemade bread, good service. Daily 0800-1130, 1500-1700. Recommended. *Café Galletti*, Amazonas 1494 y Santa María. Great coffee bar, New York owner. Recommended. *Super Papa*, JL Mera 761 y Baquedano. Stuffed baked potatoes, some vegetarian, sandwiches and salads, excellent cakes, takeaway service, great breakfasts, popular for notices and advertisements. Cheap. Mon-Fri 0700-2130, Sat-Sun 0700-2000. *Hothello*, Amazonas N20-20 y 18 de Septiembre, at the hotel. Parisian style café, serves sandwiches. 0700-2200. *Lennon*, Calama 434 y Amazonas, T2906193. Coffee bar, nice atmosphere. Recommended. Mon-Sat 1700-2300. *Omi*, Amazonas 2487 y Mariana de Jesús, T2545791. Popular upscale meeting place, smokey. Mon-Fri 1600-2300. *Sapo Cancionero*, Almagro 1550 y Pradera. Café bar, live music Thu and Fri starting 2030. Tue-Sat 1600-0000. *Sun Café*, Reina Victoria 1343 y Rodríguez, T2236085. Generous portions. English spoken, occasional films shown and live entertainment. Tue-Sat 1700-0100. *Tianguez*, Reina Victoria 1780 y la Niña, at Plaza San Francisco and on Rafael León Larrea (behind *Hotel Quito*). Good café and shop, run by Fundación Sinchi Sacha. *Yogurt Persia*, Reina Victoria y Luis Cordero and Mariana de Jesús y Amazonas. Delicious home-made yoghurt with fresh fruit, small menu. Mon-Sat 1200-1900.

Cafés

In the Old City *Café Condal*, Sucre 350 y García Moreno, T2565244. Cappuccino, snacks, also internet. Mon-Fri 1000-1700. *Café Modelo*, Sucre y García Moreno. Cheap breakfast. *Café Royal*, Portoviejo 161, T2521320. Very good breakfasts. Mid-range prices. Tue-Sat 1000-1700, Sun 1000-1500. *Cafetería Imperio*, Pasaje Amador, García Moreno 858 y Sucre, B-9, T2583370. Very good coffee and snacks, reasonable prices. Tue-Sat 1000-1700, Sun 1000-1500. *Jugos Naturales*, Oriente 449 y Guayaquil. Safe juices and extracts. *Tianguez*, Plaza de San Francisco, T2954326. Good coffee, snacks, sandwiches. Popular with visitors, also sells crafts. Cheap. Daily 0900-1830. *Viena*, Chile y Flores. For breakfast and Ecuadorean food. Mon-Sat 1200-1600.

Quito seems to have a good bakery on every street corner. A few of the most outstanding include: *La Cosecha*, Los Shyris y El Comercio, try their garlic breads. *Cyrano*, Portugal y Los Shyris, excellent pumpernickel and whole wheat breads, outstanding pastries. *Sal y Pimienta* at the *Hilton Colón* and other locations. *Swissôtel* has its own bakery with excellent speciality breads and pastries.

Bakeries

Corfú, Portugal y Los Shyris, next to Cyrano, excellent and pricey. *Helados de Paila*, Los Shyris, opposite and just north of the grandstands. Good sherbet from local fruits, just like in Ibarra. *Gelateria Uno*, 6 de Diciembre, Centro Comercial Olímpico, north of the stadium. Very good Italian ice-cream. At the south end of the same shopping centre is *Venezia*, Italian ice-cream, also coffee, snacks and pizza.

Ice-cream parlours

Quito

Bars and nightclubs

Bars

Quito's nightlife is largely concentrated in La Mariscal A 2002 municipal ordinance requires all establishments to close by 0100, however, this is not strictly enforced

NB Bars and nightclubs are subject to frequent drug raids by police: don't risk it (see Drugs, page 47). You can also be arrested for not having your passport. A photocopy of the passport and entry stamp may suffice, but it depends on the particular police officer; see Spot checks on page 30. Note also that the word nightclub in Ecuadorean usage can mean brothel.

Acústica, Portugal y Eloy Alfaro, T2453466. Varied music, shows at 2230 and 0030. Thu-Sat 2100-0200. *Alkerke*, Baquedano 340 y Reina Victoria. Good bar-café. Mon-Fri 1230-1600, Thu-Sat 1900-0200. *Bierkeller*, Muros y González Suárez, T2232435. Steaks, German sausages and *parrilladas*, good salads, imported German beer, pool and darts, good atmosphere, live music on Fri. Variable schedule, usually from 1900, call for reservations, Austrian owner, *Taberna Austriaca* bar upstairs. *La Boca del Lobo*, Calama 284 y Reina Victoria, T2234083. Café-bar, snacks and meals at mid-range prices, very laid-back, good meeting place, nice atmosphere, trendy young bar. Mon-Sat 1700-0000. *Bogarín*, Reina Victoria N24-217 y Lizardo García, T2555057. Café-bar, snacks, live music. Tue-Sat 1800-0200. *Café Toledo 1*, Toledo 720 y Lérida and number 2, Francisco Salazar y Tamayo. Café-bar, live music every night. Open from 1700. *La Cascada Mágica*, Foch 476 y Almagro, T2527190. Pool (billiards), air-hockey and other games, live music Tue, Thu and Sat. 1700-0200. *Ghoz Bar*, La Niña 425 y Reina Victoria, T2239826. Swiss owned, excellent Swiss food, pool, darts, videos, games, music, German book exchange, pricey. Open 1800 onwards. *Kings Cross Bar*, Reina Victoria 1781 y La Niña. Good BBQ most nights. Recommended for old hippies. *Kizomba*, Almagro y L García. Brazilian music, good atmosphere, friendly staff, dancing at weekends, good *caipirinhas*. Highly recommended. *Matices Piano Bar*, Isabel La Católica y Cordero, T2555020. Excellent food, live piano music, owner is a well known local pianist and composer, Dr Nelson Maldonado. Mid-range prices. Open 1630-0200. *Matrioshka*, Pinto 376 y JL Mera, T2552668. Gay and lesbian bar. Wed-Sat from 1900, but only gets started around 2200. *No Bar*, Calama y JL Mera. Good mix of latin and Euro dance music on weekdays, always packed on weekends, entry US$4 at weekends, happy hour 1800-2000. Open till 0200, closed on Sun. *Papillon* and *Tijuana Bar* are at Santa María and Reina Victoria, they are popular with local yuppies. *Patau's*, Wilson y JL Mera. Good drinks, pool table, happy hour all night Mon, loud music, dancing. A special place for those who want to show off their dancing skills, owner speaks English and German. Open 2030-0200, closed Sun. *El Pub*, San Ignacio y González Suárez. English menu, including fish and chips. *El Pobre Diablo*, Isabel La Católica y Galavis, 1 block north of Madrid, T2235194. Good atmosphere, relaxed and friendly, jazz music, sandwiches and Ecuadorean snacks, a good place to hang out and chill. Mon 1800-0200, Tue-Sat 1100-0200. *Reina Victoria Pub*, Reina Victoria 530 y Roca, T2226369. English style pub, good selection of microbrews and of Scottish and Irish single malt whiskeys, moderately priced bar meals, darts, happy hour 1800-2000, relaxed atmosphere, fireplace, popular meeting point for British and US expats. Mon-Sat from 1700. *La Trastienda*, Toledo 708 y Lérida, T2524655. Varied music, live shows. Wed-Sat 2000-0300. *The Turtle´s Head Bar*, La Niña 626 y JL Mera, T2565544. Amazing microbrews, great fish and chips, chicken curry, also serves Sun lunch, pool table, darts. Mon-Sat 1700-0200, Sun 1200-0200. *Varadero*, Reina Victoria 1721 y La Pinta, T2542575. Bar-restaurant, live Cuban music Wed-Sat, meals and snacks, good cocktails, older crowd and couples. Mon-Fri 1200-0000, Sat 1800-0300.

Nightclubs

Many of the bars turn into informal discos after 2200

Cerebro, 6 de Diciembre y Los Shyris, Sector El Inca. Large disco, they have contests and occasionally well known artists performing. Private disco for well-off Ecuadorians but will let others over 18 in, very expensive. Thu-Sat 2000-0100. *Cool Antro*, Ponce Carrasco 282 y Almagro, T2239627. Latin music and some tecno, ladies night on Thu until 2320. Thu-Sat 2100-0300. *Macks*, Maldonado y Pujilí, in the south near El Recreo Trole stop. Fine mix of music and people, huge, 5 dance halls, the 'in' place in 2002. Wed-Sat 2000-0200. *Mayo 68*, Lizardo García 662 y JL Mera. Salsoteca, small, an absolute must for all you authentic salseros. Highly recommended. *Le Pierrot*, Carrión N22-54 y Amazonas. *Seseribó*, Veintimilla y 12 de Octubre, T2563598. Caribbean music and salsa. Thu-Sat 2100-0100, US$6. Recommended. *Tabujas*, Almagro y La Niña. *Vauzá*, Tamayo y F Salazar. Varied music. Large bar in the middle of the dance floor, mature crowd. Wed-Sat 2100-0100.

Entertainment

There are always many cultural events taking place in Quito, usually free of charge. See the listings section of *El Comercio* and other papers for details, especially on Fri. Aug is a particularly active month, see festivals below.

Art galleries *Art Forum*, JL Mera N23-106. Fundación Guayasamín, in Bellavista, see Museums above. **Galería Pomaire**, Amazonas 863 y Veintimilla, T2540074. **La Galería**, Juan Rodríguez 168 y Almagro, T2225807. **Posada de las Artes Kingman**, Almagro 1550 y Pradera, T2526335. **Viteri**, Orellana 473 y Whimper, T2561548.

Cinema
Films listed daily in Section C or D of El Comercio

First run movies at: *Cinemark*, at Plaza de las Américas, Av América y República, T2260301, www.cinemark.com.ec Multiplex, many salons, restaurants in the same complex, US$3.90, or US$2.50 on Wed. *Multicines*, CCI, Amazonas y Naciones Unidas (in the basement), T1-800-352463. Excellent selection of movies, 8 salons, same price as *Cinemark*. *Multicines*, El Recreo, at El Recreo Trole stop in the south of the city. Same movies as in *CCI*, 10 salons, convenient if staying in the Old City, US$3.10 or US$2.50 on Wed. *Universitario*, Av América y Av Pérez Guerrero, Plaza Indoamérica, Universidad Central, US$1. *24 de Mayo*, Granaderos y 6 de Diciembre, US$2.
The **Casa de la Cultura** (see Museums) has a film library and often has film festivals or shows foreign language films.

Dance classes
One-to-one or group lessons are offered for US$5-6 per hr

Ritmo Tropical, Av 10 de Agosto 1792 y San Gregorio, edif Santa Rosa, oficina 108, T2227051. Teaches salsa, merengue, cumbia, vallenato and folkloric dance. *Son Latino*, Reina Victoria 1225 y García, T2234340, specializes in several varieties of salsa, 10-hr programs cost US$40. *Tropical Dancing School*, Foch E4-256 y Amazonas, T2224713, salsa, merengue and cumbia.

Music

Local folk music is popular and the entertainment, as well as the venue, are known as a *peña*. Most *peñas* do not come alive until 2230. *Dayumac*, JL Mera y Carrión. This meeting place for local music groups is dark and bohemian, and warms up after 0000. Fri-Sat 2100-0200. *Ñucanchi*, Av Universitaria 496 y Armero, T2540967. Tue-Sat 2000-0200. *Pacha Camac*, Washington 530 y JL Mera, T2234855. Wed-Sat 1900-0300.
The *Orquesta Sinfónica Nacional* presents weekly concerts on Fri evenings. Since the Teatro Sucre is being restored (see below), concerts are held at *Teatro Politécnico*, Queseras del Medio, opposite Coliseo Rumiñahui, or in one of the colonial churches. Call for information, T2565733, US$2. There are concerts on Tue evenings, 3 times per month, Oct-Dec and Feb-Aug, at the *Auditorio de las Cámaras* (Chamber of Commerce), Amazonas y República. Information, T2260265/6 (ext 231).
Popular concerts are held at the *Plaza de Toros*, Amazonas y Juan de Azcaray, in the north or at the *Coliseo Rumiñahui*, Toledo y Queseras del Medio, La Floresta. Tickets are sold in advance and go fast for the better known groups.

Quito

Folk dance shows   The Ecuadorean folk ballet 'Jacchigua' performs at *Teatro Aeropuerto*, Juan J Pazmiño y Av de la Prensa (just south of the airport), T2506651 (ext 121). Wed and Fri at 1930. Entertaining, colourful and touristy, reserve ahead, US$12. *Teatro Humanizarte*, Leonidas Plaza N24-226 y Baquerizo Moreno, T2226116. Presents the 'Miércoles Andino', Andean folk ballet every Wed at 1930, US$5. Plays and comedies are also often in their repertoire.

Theatre   *Teatro Sucre*, at Plaza del Teatro, Manabí between Flores and Guayaquil, T2281644, was built in the 1880s. Its interior is small and distinguished. It is undergoing long-term restorations and closed in 2002. *Teatro Bolívar*, Flores 421 y Junín, T2582486. Another classic theatre in the Old City. It was damaged by fire in 1999, but despite restoration work there are still theatrical presentations, the proceeds being used for the renovations. Call to enquire if a performance is on. *Teatro Charles Chaplin*, Cordero 1200 y JL Mera, has regular theatrical presentations on weekends, check the paper for events. *Teatro Prometeo*, adjoining the Casa de la Cultura Ecuatoriana, 6 de Diciembre y Tarqui. *Agora*, the open-air theatre of the Casa de la Cultura, at 12 de Octubre y Patria, stages many concerts. There are also plays at the *Patio de Comedias*, 18 de Septiembre, between Amazonas and 9 de Octubre. *Centro Cultural Afro-Ecuatoriano* (CCA), Tamayo 985 y Lizardo García, T2522318. Sometimes has cultural events and published material, and is a useful contact for those interested in the black community.

Festivals

For details of national festivals see page 66   In Quito *años viejos* are on display throughout the city before New Year's; a good spot to see them is on Amazonas, between Patria and Colón. Water throwing is common at *Carnival*. The solemn *Good Friday* procession in the Old City is most impressive, with thousands of devout citizens taking part. **24 May** is Independence, commemorating the Battle of Pichincha in 1822 with early morning cannonfire and parades; everything closes. **Aug** is *Mes de Arte y Cultura*, organized by the municipality, with cultural events, dancing and music in different places throughout the city.

The city's main festival, *Día de Quito*, is celebrated throughout the week ending **6 Dec**. It commemorates the founding of the city with elaborate parades, bullfights, performances and music in the streets. It is very lively and there is a great deal of drinking. The main events culminate on the evening of Dec 5, and the 6th is the day to sleep it all off; everything (except a few restaurants) closes. Foremost among **Christmas** celebrations is the *Misa del Gallo*, midnight mass. Over Christmas Quito is crowded and the streets are packed with beggars, street vendors and shoppers.

Shopping

In the Old City, streets are lined with shops of every imaginable kind   Trading hours are generally 0900-1900 on weekdays, although some shops close at midday, as they do in smaller cities. Saturday afternoon and Sunday most shops are closed. The Old City remains a very important commercial area. Outside the colonial centre, especially to the north, much of the shopping is now done in shopping centres (malls), which are as insipid as anywhere else in the world. These are usually open Mon-Sat 1000-2000 and Sun 1000-1400. They include: *Mall El Jardín*, Amazonas between Mariana de Jesús and República; *Centro Comercial Iñaquito*, known as CCI, Amazonas and Naciones Unidas; *Quicentro Shopping*, Naciones Unidas between Los Shyris and 6 de Diciembre; *El Bosque*, Av Occidental and Carvajal, to the northwest; *El Recreo*, Av Maldonado at the Trole stop, in the south of the city.

Bookshops   *Libri Mundi*, JL Mera N23-83 y Veintimilla, T2234791. Excellent selection of Spanish, English, French and also some Italian books. Sells a wide selection of guidebooks including several Footprint titles including the Ecuador & Galápagos Handbook and the South American Handbook. Knowledgeable and helpful staff. It has a noticeboard of what's on in Quito. Very highly recommended. Open Mon-Sat 0800-1800. There is also a branch at Quicentro Shopping, open daily. *Mr. Books*, Mall El Jardín, 3rd floor, T2980281. Excellent bookshop, good selection, many in English including Footprint travel guides. Open daily. Recommended. *The Travel Company*, JL Mera 517 y Roca and JL Mera 1233 y Lizardo García. For books (second-hand at No 1233), postcards, T-shirts and videos. Recommended. *Imágenes*, 9 de Octubre y Roca. For books on Ecuador and art, also postcards. *Libro Express*, Amazonas 816 y Veintimilla, T2548113, also at Quicentro Shopping and El Bosque. Has a good stock of maps, guides and international magazines. *Librería Selecciones*, Veintimilla E5-27 y Amazonas. Nice stock of magazines. *Confederate Books*, Calama 410 y JL Mera, T252 7890. Has an excellent selection of second-hand books, including travel guides, mainly in English but German and French are also available. Open 1000-1900. *Libros para El Alma*, Almagro 129 y Pinto, T2226931. Also has café and library and will even organize jungle trips. *Abya-Yala*, 12 de Octubre 14-30 y Wilson, T2506247. Good for books about indigenous cultures and anthropology. Also has an excellent library and museum (see Museums above). *Biblioteca Luz*, Oriente 618 y Vargas. Runs a book exchange (mainly Spanish), for which they charge US$2. There is a bookshop at *Centro Comercial Popular*, Flores 739 y Olmedo, T2212550. Sells half-price books and magazines, some French and English books, also book exchange. Foreign newspapers are for sale at news-stands in luxury hotels and in some shops along Amazonas. *Lufthansa* will supply German newspapers if they have spare copies.

Camera repairs & equipment *Difoto*, Amazonas 893 y Wilson, T2224676. Good quality processing. Recommended. *Foto Imágen*, Mariana de Jesús E5-11 e Italia, T2469762. Camera sales and repairs. *Kis Color*, Amazonas 1238 y Calama. Better quality for 24-hr printing than 1-hr service, passport photos in 3 mins. *Ecuacolor/Kodak*, Amazonas 888 y Wilson, Orellana 476 y 6 de Diciembre, and 10 de Agosto 4150 y Atahualpa and at several shopping centres. A highly recommended professional lab for slides and prints is that of *Ron Jones*, Lizardo García E9-104 y Andrés Xaura, 1 block east of 6 de Diciembre, T2507622, helpful and informative. *Color Power*, Vancouver 505 y Alemania, T2568287. Good lab. *Fotomania*, 6 de Diciembre N19-23 y Patria, T2547512. For new and second-hand cameras, also for black and white developing. Lots of shops on Amazonas sell film, but always check the expiry date. In the Old City: *Suba Foto*, Maldonado 1371 y Rocafuerte. Sells second-hand cameras. *Foto Estudio Grau*, Bolívar 140 y Plaza Santo Domingo. For repairs and parts.

Camping, climbing & trekking equipment *Los Alpes*, Reina Victoria N23-45 y Baquedano, T/F2232362. Equipment sale and hire, guides for climbing and trekking. *Altamontaña*, Jorge Washington 425 y 6 de Diciembre, T2524422. Imported climbing equipment for sale, equipment rental, good advice, experienced climbing and trekking guides. *The Altar*, JL Mera 615 y Carrión, T2523671. Equipment rental at good prices. Imported and local gear for sale. *Altu Sport*, JL Mera N23-15 y Veintimilla, T2903654. *Andísimo*, 9 de Octubre 479 y Roca, T2508347. Equipment rental and some for sale, guiding service for climbing and trekking. *Antisana*, Centro Comercial El Bosque, ground floor, T2451605. Local and imported equipment, no rentals. *Aventura Sport*, Quicentro Shopping, top floor, T2924373. Tents, good selection of glacier sunglasses, upmarket. *Camping Sports*, Colón 942 y Reina Victoria, T2521626. Local and imported equipment, no rentals. *Equipos Cotopaxi*, 6 de Diciembre 927 y Patria, T2500038. Ecuadorean and imported gear for sale, no rentals. Lockable pack covers, made to measure can be ordered here. *The Explorer*, Reina Victoria E6-32 y Pinto, T2550911. Reasonable prices for renting or buying, very helpful, will buy US or European equipment. Offers guiding service for climbing, trekking and jungle. *Tatoo*, Wilson y JL Mera, T2904355. Quality backpacks and outdoors clothing.

Camping fuel   *Bluet Camping Gas* is generally available in the above shops. White gas is sometimes available at **Kywi** hardware stores, at Centro Comercial Olímpico, 6 de Diciembre, 2 blocks north of the stadium (and several other locations), ask for *'combustible para lámparas Coleman'*. It is better to have a multifuel stove, but some white gas stoves (eg the SVEA Optimus 123) will also burn unleaded gasoline, which is available at service stations everywhere. For hiking boots try **Calzado Beltrán**, Cuenca 562, in the Old City, and other shops on the same street, also see the Shopping section for Ambato.

Foodstuffs   *Supermaxi* supermarkets at CCI, El Bosque, Centro Comercial Plaza Aeropuerto (Av de la Prensa y Homero Salas), at the Multicentro shopping complex on 6 de Diciembre y La Niña, about 2 blocks north of Colón, Mall El Jardín and El Recreo. This is a very well stocked supermarket and department store with a wide range of local and imported goods, not cheap. All branches are open Mon-Sat 1000-2000, Sun 1000-1300. *Mi Comisariato* is another supermarket and department store at Quicentro Shopping and García Moreno y Mejía in the Old City. *La Feria* supermarket, Bolívar 334, between Venezuela and García Moreno. Sells good wines and spirits, and Swiss, German and Dutch cheeses. **Supermercado Santa María** with good prices, Av Iñaquito y Pereira and Versalles y Carrión. Macrobiotic food is available at **Vitalcentro Microbiótico**, Carrión 376 y 6 de Diciembre. *Sangre de Drago*, the Indian cure-all, is sold in markets and at homeopathic pharmacies.

Handicrafts   Typical Ecuadorean *artesanías* include: wood carvings, wooden plates, silver of all types, textiles, buttons, toys and other objects fashioned from tagua nuts, hand-painted tiles, naïve paintings on leather, Panama hats, hand-woven rugs and a variety of antiques dating back to colonial times.

A large selection can be found at the **Mercado Artesanal La Mariscal**, on Jorge Washington, between Reina Victoria and JL Mera. This interesting and worthwhile market, which occupies most of a city block, was built by the municipality to house street vendors. ■ *Daily 1000-1800*. There are also souvenir shops on García Moreno in front of the Palacio Presidencial in the colonial city. At Parque El Ejido (Av Patria end), artists sell their crafts and paintings on weekends. Indigenous garments (for natives rather than tourists) can be seen and bought on the north end of the Plaza de Santo Domingo and along the nearest stretch of C Flores.

The following craft shops have been recommended, but this list is far from comprehensive. *Hilana*, 6 de Diciembre 1921 y Baquerizo Moreno. Beautiful and unique 100% wool blankets in Ecuadorean motifs, excellent quality, purchase by metre possible. *Folklore*, Colón E10-53 y Caamaño, near *Hotel Quito,* T2541315, the store of the late Olga Fisch. It stocks a most attractive array of handicrafts and rugs, and is distinctly

Quito

expensive, as accords with the designer's international reputation. Branch store at *Hotel Hilton Colón*, where *El Bazaar* also has a good selection of crafts. *Productos Andinos*, Urbina 111 y Cordero, T2224565. An artisans' co-operative selling a great variety of good quality items. *Camari*, Marchena 260 y Versalles. Direct sale shop run by an artisan organization. *La Bodega Exportadora*, JL Mera 614 y Carrión. Recommended for antiques and handicrafts, as is *Renacimiento*, Carrión y JL Mera. *Fundación Sinchi Sacha*, Reina Victoria 1780 y La Niña, and Plaza San Francisco, co-operative selling select ceramics and other arts and crafts from the Oriente. Recommended. *Marcel Creations*, Roca 766, entre Amazonas y 9 de Octubre. Good panama hat selection. *Artesanías Cuencanas*, Av Roca 626 entre Amazonas y JL Mera. Friendly, knowledgeable, wide selection. *Galería Latina*, JL Mera 823 y Veintimilla, T2221098. Fine selection of alpaca and other handicrafts from Ecuador, Peru and Bolivia. Occasionally visiting artists demostrate their crafts. *Centro Artesanal*, JL Mera 804. *El Aborigen*, Washington 536 y JL Mera. *Écuatolklore*, Robles 609 entre Amazonas y JL Mera (also stocks guidebooks). *The Ethnic Collection*, Amazonas N2163-A y Robles (corner), PO Box 17-03-518, T2500155, www.ethniccollection.com Wide variety of clothing, leather, bags, jewellery, balsa wood and ceramic items from across Ecuador. *Antigüedades el Chordeleg*, at Hilton Colón. For goldwork and antiques. *Handicrafts Otavalo*, Sucre 255 and García Moreno. Good selection, but expensive. *Amor y Café*, Foch 721 y JL Mera. Quality ethnic clothing. *Los Colores de la Tierra*, JL Mera 838 y Wilson. Hand-painted wood items and unique handicrafts.

For **T-shirts**: *Coosas*, JL Mera 838 and Quicentro Shopping. Outlet for Peter Mussfeldt's attractive animal designs (bags, clothes, etc). *Hyla*, JL Mera N24-12 y Wilson. Nice designs. *Nomada*, Foch 499 y Almagro and at Palacio Arzobispal, Plaza de la Independencia, T290 9488. Excellent quality T-shirts at factory prices. *Rooan*, JL Mera 517A Y Roca. Very good but expensive.

Leather goods can be found at *Chimborazo*, Amazonas y Naciones Unidas (next to El Espiral shopping centre) and *Aramis*, Amazonas 1234. *Su Kartera*, Sucre 351 y García Moreno, T2512160, also at Veintimilla 1185, between 9 de Octubre y Amazonas. Manufacturers of bags, briefcases, shoes, belts etc.

Jewellery *H Stern's*, has stores at the airport, *Hotel Hilton Colón* and *Hotel Quito*. *Hamilton*, 12 de Octubre 1942 y Cordero. Fine silver and gold crafts and jewelery, native designs. *Alquimia*, Juan Rodríguez 139. High quality silversmith. *Jewelry & Design*, Mall El Jardín, local 166. *Taller Guayasamín*, in Bellavista (see Museums above). *Edda*, Tamayo 1256 y Cordero. Custom-made jewellery. Recommended. *Argentum*, JL Mera 614. Reasonably priced. *La Guaragua*, Washington 614 y Amazonas. Also sells *artesanías* and antiques, excellent selection, reasonable prices. *Tinta*, JL Mera 1020 y Foch, good selection of silver jewellery, reasonable prices, good service. *Jeritsa*, Veintimilla E4-162 y Amazonas, good selection of gold and silver items, good prices and service.

Markets For fruits and vegetables and to get the overall *mercado* experience, the main markets are: *Mercado Central*, Av Pichincha y Olmedo, in the Old City, Teatro Sucre Trole stop southbound or San Blas northbound; *Mercado Santa Clara*, Versalles y Ramírez Dávalos, Santa Clara Trole stop, *Mercado Iñaquito*, Iñaquito y Villalengua, west of Amazonas, La Y Trole stop.

Watch your belongings & pockets at all markets

Mercado Ipiales, on Chile uphill from Imbabura, where clothing, appliances and stolen goods are sold (a particularly unsafe area). *Plaza Arenas* on Vargas, next to Colegio La Salle or along 24 de Mayo and Loja uphill from Benalcázar, is where you are most likely to find your stolen camera for sale (also try *Grau*, a camera shop on Plaza Santo Domingo, on your left as you face the church and *Fotomania*, 6 de Diciembre N19-23 y Patria). Not surprisingly, these are unsafe parts of town.

Sport

Ball games   The city's parks are filled on weekends with locals playing ball games. Professional **football** (soccer) is played at Estadio Atahualpa, 6 de Diciembre y Naciones Unidas and at Estadio Casa Blanca, in Carcelén to the north. Schedules vary, check the newspapers. **Basketball** and **volleyball** are played in the Coliseo Julio César Hidalgo on Av Pichincha and Coliseo Rumiñahui on Toledo y Queseras del Medio. Informal 'ecuavolley' is played in all neighbourhood parks. A local game, *pelota de guante* (glove ball), is played on Sat afternoons and Sun at Estadio Mejía and in Parque El Ejido. Friendly games of **rugby** are played when there are enough people, see notice-board at the *Reina Victoria Pub*. **Tennis** is played on courts at Parque La Carolina, otherwise at a number of private clubs.

Climbing   Climbs and trekking tours can be arranged in Quito and several other cities. The follow-
& trekking   ing Quito agencies have all been recommended to us - see Tour operators below for
See Special interest   their contact details. *Safari Tours*, uses only ASEGUIM guides for climbing, maximum 2
travel, pages 70   climbers per guide, has own transport and equipment, large and small groups, several
and 79, for more   languages spoken, very knowledgeable, well organized and planned. *Safari* also runs a
information   high altitude glacier school, with courses of 3-5 days with bilingual guides. *Surtrek* Arranges guided climbs of most peaks, also rents and sells equipment, uses ASEGUIM guides, 1 guide per 2 climbers, large and small groups. *Compañia de Guías*, English, German, French and Italian spoken. All ASEGUIM guides: Julio Mesías, Cesar Román, Edison Salgado, Diego Zurita. *Sierra Nevada* Chief guide Freddy Ramírez uses mostly ASEGUIM guides and is fluent in French, English and German, he has his own equipment, and takes mostly large groups. *Pamir Travel and Adventures* Chief guide Hugo Torres is very experienced and speaks English. *Vasco Tours*, Juan Medina is very experienced and professional. Independent guides do not normally provide transport or a full service (ie food, equipment, insurance) and without a permit from the Ministerio del Ambiente, they might be refused entry to the national parks. The following independent guides have been recommended: *Eduardo Agama*, T2905258, *Cosme León*, T2603140. *Iván Rojas* T2558380, *Benno Schlauri*, T2340709.

Climbing clubs   The Quito climbing clubs welcome new members, but they do not provide guiding services. Do not expect to get a free mountaineering trip from them. It is not really worth joining if you are in Ecuador for only a few weeks. There are active climbing clubs at the following institutions: *Colegio San Gabriel*, *Universidad Católica*, *Club Nuevos Horizontes* (Colón 2038 y 10 de Agosto, T2552154) and *Club Sadday* (Alonso de Angulo y Galo Molina).

Equipment   Stores which sell climbing and camping equipment (see Shopping above) also rent some items and can be a source of general information. They are often looking for used European/North American equipment, contact them if you wish to sell before leaving.

Mountain   **Tours**   There are specialized agencies offering one or several day biking tours, a num-
biking   ber of other agencies also offer cycling tours or rent bikes. *The Biking Dutchman*, Foch
See Special interest   714 y JL Mera, T2542806, after hours T09-9730267 (mob), F2567008,
travel, page 75, for   www.bikingdutchman.com The pioneers of mountain biking in Ecuador, one and
more information on   several day tours, great fun, good food, very well organized, English, German and
mountain biking   Dutch (of course) spoken. Recommended. *Aries*, Wilson 578 y Reina Victoria, T/F2906052, after hours T09-9816003 (mob), www.ariesbikecompany.com 1-2 day tours, all equipment provided. *Safari* (see Tour operators below) biking tours, rents bikes and has free route planning.

Bicycle shops   *Bike Stop*, 6 de Diciembre 3925 y Checoslovaquia, T2255404. Stocks a wide range of bikes. *Bicisport*, in Quicentro Shopping, top floor, and 6 de

Diciembre 6327 y Tomás de Berlanga, T2460894. Stocks imported high quality bikes and parts. *Bike Tech*, 6 de Diciembre N39-59 y El Telégrafo, T2263421. A meeting place for long distance bikers. Owner Santiago Lara has informal 'meets' almost every weekend, anyone is welcome, no charge, they ride 20 or more routes around Quito. They also have a good repair shop and cheap parts. They are friendly and glad to advise on routes. Recommended. *Ciclo Vivas* 6 de Diciembre 2810 y Orellana, T2566100. Stocks Jamis, Shimano and Wheeler. *Sobre Ruedas*, Av 10 de Agosto N52-162, Ciudadela Kennedy, T2416781. Repairs, tours, rentals and sales.

Bowling At El Molinón, Amazonas y Eloy Alfaro. **Bullfighting** At Plaza de Toros Iñaquito, Amazonas y Tomás de Berlanga, during the first week of December for *fietas de Quito*. Tickets on sale at 1500 the day before the bullfight, you may have to buy from touts. The Unión de Toreros, Edif Casa Paz, Av Amazonas, has information on all bullfights around the country; these take place all year. They do not have details of the parochial *toros de pueblo*, these take place during each village's *fiestas patronales*. **Bungee jumping** *Bungee Zone*, Pinto 163 y 6 de Diciembre, T2223480, T09-9032355 (mob), US$55, for 2 jumps. Be mindful of safety however, as accidents have occurred. **Jogging** The Hash House Harriers is a club for runners and walkers which meets fortnightly. Enquire at *Reina Victoria Pub*, T2226369. **Paragliding** *Escuela Pichincha de Vuelo Libre*, Carlos Endara Oe3-60 y Amazonas, T2256592 (office hrs), T09-9478349 (mob) (after hours), parapent@uio.satnet.net Offers complete courses for US$350-500 and tandem flights for US$40-60. **Snorkelling** *El Globo* shops, 10 de Agosto y Roca, Amazonas y Gaspar de Villaroel and Venezuela 936, stock snorkelling gear, as do *Importaciones Kao*, Colón y Almagro, at Quicentro Shopping and at El Bosque.

Other activities

Swimming There is a cold spring-water pool on Maldonado beyond the Ministry of Defence building. A public heated, chlorinated pool is in Miraflores, at the upper end of Av Universitaria, a 10-min walk from Amazonas. Open Tue-Sun 0900-1600. There is another public pool at Batán Alto, on Cochapata, near 6 de Diciembre and Gaspar de Villaroel. **Whitewater rafting** For complete information on rafting and kayaking, see under Special interest travel, page 76. The *Quito Kayakers* is a club of whitewater fans who meet on weekends to enjoy kayaking and rafting. More information at http://quitokayakers.tripod.com or at the *Reina Victoria Pub*, T2226369.

Swimming cap, towel and soap are compulsory for admission to public swimming pools

Tour operators

The following companies have all been recommended at some time. Many are clustered in the Mariscal district, especially along Av Amazonas between Colón and Patria, where you are encouraged to have a stroll and shop around. Most Quito agencies sell a variety of tours in all regions of Ecuador; they may run some of those tours themselves, while they act as sales agents for others. Those offering a variety of tours are listed under General tours below. Galápagos operators with offices in Quito are listed separately. See also Sport, page 126, for companies specializing in climbing/trekking, river rafting or mountain biking. Choosing a responsible tour operator is very important, not only as a way of getting the best experience for your money, but also to limit impact on areas you will visit and ensure benefits for local communities. See Responsible tourism, page 44.

When booking tours, note that national park fees are rarely included. For park fees, see page 462

Advantage Travel, El Telégafo E10-63 y Juan de Alcántara, T2462871, F2437645, www.advantagecuador.com Run tours to Machalilla and Isla de la Plata. Also operate 4-5 day jungle tours on the *Manatee* floating hotel, on the Río Napo (new in 2002). *Amerindia*, Montúfar E15-14 y La Cumbre, Bellavista, T2270550, F2436625, www.quasarnautica.com Land operators for *Quasar Náutica*, full range of tours including visits to historic sites, haciendas, national parks and jungle lodges. *Alta Montaña*, JL Mera 12-27 y Calama, T2528769, donoso@andinanet.net For

General tours

Also see Jungle lodges, page 358

climbing and trekking. *Anaconda Travel*, Foch 635 y Reina Victoria, 1st floor, T/F2224913, anacondaec@andinanet.net Run *Anaconda* lodge in the upper Napo, jungle trips, sell good value trips to Galápagos and tours to all other destinations. *Andes Adventures*, Baquedano E5-27 y JL Mera, T2222651, F2523837. Climbing, trekking, rafting, jungle tours, tourist-class Galápagos cruises. *Andísimo*, 9 de Octubre 479, T2508347, www.andisimo.com Trekking, climbing and other tours, equipment sale and rental. *Campus Trekking*, Joaquina Vargas 99 y Abdón Calderón, Conocoto, T/F2340601, campus@pi.pro.ec, www.campustrekking.com Trekking and climbing, cultural tours (markets, museums, archaeology), multilingual service. *Canodros*, Portugal 448 y Catalina Aldaz, T2256759, www.canodros.com, www.galapagosexplorer.com Luxury Galápagos cruises and jungle tours in the Kapawi Ecological Reserve (details in Macas section, see page 384), also have an office

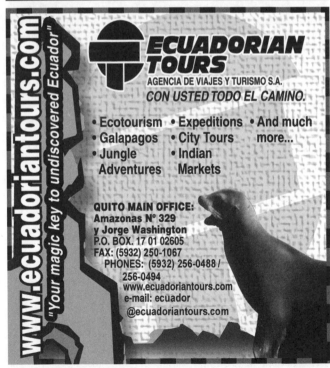

in Guayaquil. *Coltur*, Páez 370 y Robles, T2221000, F2502449, coltur@uio.satnet.net Tours to Galápagos, Amazon, also general travel agency. *Compañía de Guías de Montaña*, Jorge Washington 425 y 6 de Dicembre, T/F2504773, guiasmontania@accessinter.net, www.companiadeguias.com Climbing and trekking specialists, but also sell other tours. *Dracaena*, Pinto 446 y Amazonas, T2546590, dracaena@andinanet.net, www.amazondracaena.com Run very good jungle trips in Cuyabeno, also day tours, climbing trips. *Ecoventura*, Almagro N31-80 y Whymper, T/F2231034, lulym@uio.satnet.net, www.ecoventura.com Miami office: Galapagos Network, USA and Canada toll-free T1-800-633-7972, info@galapagosnetwork.com Operate excellent Galápagos cruises and sell tours throughout Ecuador. *Ecuadorian Alpine Institute*, Ramírez Dávalos 136 y Amazonas, of 102, T2565465, F2568949, www.volcanoclimbing.com Individual or group ascents, customized itineraries, multilingual guides. *Ecuadorian Tours* (American Express representative), Av Amazonas 329 y J Washington, several other locations, T2560488, F2501067, www.ecuadoriantours.com Tours in all regions and airline tickets. *Elinatour*, Wilson 413 y 6 de Diciembre, T2900350, F2232690, elinasp@uio.satnet.net Sells jungle, Galápagos and other tours, combined tours with other Andean countries. Very helpful. *Emerald Forest Expeditions*, Pinto E4-244 y Amazonas, T2541278, F2541543, emerald@ecuanex.net.ec, www.emeraldexpeditions.com Jungle tours to *Pañacocha Lodge*, 4-7 day jungle trips, also have office in Coca. *Enchanted Expeditions*, Foch 726 y Av Amazonas, PO Box 17-1200599, T2569960, T2221305, F2569956, www.enchantedexpeditions.com Operate Galápagos cruises in various categories, jungle trips to Cuyabeno and mountain tours. *Explorandes*, Wilson 537 y Diego de Almagro, T2556936, F2556938, explora@hoy.net .Trekking, rafting, climbing, jungle tours. *Explorer Tours*, Reina Victoria 1235 y Lizardo García, T2508871, F2222531, beniet@uio.satnet.net, www.galapagoslastminute.com Agents for *Sacha Lodge* and *La Casa del Suizo* on the upper Río Napo, first rate educational jungle tours, also sell Galápagos tours. *Galasam*, Amazonas 1354 y Cordero, T2507080/81, F2567662, www.galasam.com Full range of tours in highlands, jungle trips to their own lodge on the Río Aguarico, Galápagos trips. *Green Planet*, JL Mera N23-84 y Wilson, T2520570, greenpla@interactive.net.ec Ecologically sensitive jungle tours in Cuyabeno and in the Tena area, friendly staff and guides, good food. Recommended. *Kapok Expeditions*, Pinto E4-225, T/F2556348, www.kapok expeditions.com Jungle tours to Cuyabeno and Yasuní, trekking, Machalilla, hacienda tours (participate in daily farm activities). *Kempery Tours*, Pinto 539 y Amazonas, T2226583, F2226715, www.kempery .com Good value tours, 4-14 day jungle trips in Huaorani territory and Galápagos cruises; sell horse ridding, climbing and trekking trips, multilingual service. *Klein Tours*, Eloy Alfaro N34-151 y Catalina Aldaz, T2267080, F2442389, www.kleintours.com Galápagos and mainland tours, tailor-made, English,

French and German spoken. *KBtours*, Marco Aguirre 648, T2241209, kbtours@hotmail.com Quito city tours, Quito surroundings, Indian markets and Cotopaxi. *Metropolitan Touring*, República de El Salvador N36-84, also Amazonas 239 y 18 de Septiembre and several other locations, T2988200, F2464702, www.metropolitan-touring .com A very large organization. Run Galápagos cruises, also arranges climbing, trekking expeditions led by world-known climbers, as well as city tours of Quito, Machalilla National Park, private rail journeys, jungle camps. *Native Life*, Foch E4-167 y Amazonas,T/F2229077, natlife1@ natlife.com.ec Run tours to their *Nativo Lodge* in the Cuyabeno Reserve, sell climbing and other highland trips. Recommended. *Pablo Prado*, Rumipamba 730 y República, T2446954, pradopa@ uio.satnet.net Custom made tours for photographers and nature lovers. *Palmar Voyages*, Alemania 575 (N31-77) y Mariana de Jesús, T2569809, palmarvoyages@andinanet.net, www. palmarvoyages.com Small specialist company, custom itineraries to all areas, trips to *Cuyabeno Lodge*, Galápagos, good rates. *Pamir Travel and Adventures*, JL Mera 721 y Ventimilla, T2542605, F2547576. Galápagos cruises, climbing tours and jungle tours. *Positiv Turismo*, Voz Andes N41-81, T2440604, F2257883, www.positivturismo.com Swiss-Austrian-run company offers trips to Galápagos, cultural trips, trekking and special interest tours. *Rainforestur*, Av Amazonas 420, between Robles and Roca, T2239822, rainfor@interactive. net.ec, also have an office in Baños. Offers climbing and jungle trips to Cuyabeno and the Puyo area. *Ranft Turismo*, Los Shyris y Río Coca, edif Eurocentro, T2255954, F2432622, www.ranfturismo. com Trips to Galápagos, Andes and Amazon. *Safari*, Calama 380 y JL Mera, T2552505, USA/Canada toll free T1-800-4348182, T2552505, F2223381, www.safari.com.ec Run by Jean Brown and Pattie Serrano, both knowledgeable and informative. Excellent adventure

travel, customized trips, mountain climbing, cycling, rafting, trekking and Oriente jungle including Huaorani territory. They also book Galápagos tours, run a high-altitude glacier school and are an excellent source of travel information. Open 7 days a week 0900-1900. Highly recommended. *Sierra Nevada*, Pinto 637 y Amazonas, T2553658, F2554936, snevada@accessinter.net Specialized adventure tours (climbing, trekking, whitewater rafting) and jungle expeditions. *Sudamericana de Turismo*, Av Amazonas 400 y Robles, T/F2233233. Tours in all regions of Ecuador, English and German spoken. *Surtrek*, Amazonas 897 y Wilson, T2561129, F2561132, www.surtrek.com Climbing and trekking expeditions, jungle and Galápagos tours, also flights. *Terracenter*, Reina Victoria 1343 y J Rodríguez, T/F2507858. Wide variety of tours, including to the Galápagos and Oriente. *Tropic Ecological Adventures*, Av República E7-320 y Almagro, edif Taurus, Apto 1-A, T2225907, F2560756, tropic@uio.satnet.net, www.tropiceco.com Run by Andy Drumm and Sofía Darquea, naturalist guides with many years experience in Galápagos, who work closely with conservation groups. Winners of awards for responsible tourism in 1997, 2000. Their ecologically responsible and educational tours are recommended for anyone seriously interested in the environment. Part of each fee is given to indigenous communities and ecological projects. Also sell Galápagos and highland trips run by ecologically sensitive operators. *TruColorsTravel*, Mariscal Foch 831 y Amazonas, T2906409, T09-802279 (mob), www.horseecuador.com, www.truecolorstravel.com Horse-riding treks of 1-11 days, including Inca Trail, rides between haciendas , volcano paramo rides, cloud forest trails. *Vasco Tours*, Calama E7-49 y Reina Victoria T/F2540227, vascotours @andinanet.net Run by Juan Medina, a very knowledgeable guide. Jungle, climbing and trekking tours, day trips, Galápagos cruises. *Zenith Travel*, Juan Leon Mera 453 y Roca, Chirboga Building, 2nd floor, T2529993, F2905595, www.zenithecuador.com

Quito

Galápagos operators

For more details of tours to the Galápagos, see page 407

For operators whose contact information is not listed here, see General tours above

Andando Tours, Coruña N26-311 y Orellana, T2566010, F2228519, www.andandotours.com Run the first class vessel *Sagita* and are agents for the *Andando* and *Samba*, in the same category. *Canodros* Operate the *Galapagos Explorer II*, a large, luxury cruise ship, with a good track record in environmental protection. **Ecoventura/Galápagos Network** Operate 4 luxury class 20-passenger motor yachts and a 48-passenger ship. **Ecuagal**, Amazonas 1125 y Foch, T2229579, F2550988. Operate the *Floreana*, a tourist superior class boat. **Enchanted Expeditions**, operate the luxury *Beluga* and first class *Cachalote* and are agents for the tourist superior *Angelito* and tourist class *Sulidae*. **Etnotur**, Luis Cordero 13-13 y JL Mera, T256 4565, F2502682, etnocru@uio.satnet.net English spoken. Operate the tourist superior catamaran *Amará*. **Galacruises Expeditions**, Jorge Washington 748 b/, Av Amazonas and 9 de Octubre, T/F2556036, www.galapagosseaman.com.ec Owners of the *Sea Man* yacht, offer diving and nature cruises. **The Galápagos Boat Company**, Calama 980, T2508316, F2220426, admin@safari.com.ec. Broker for up to 74 boats in the islands, will find you the best deals around. **Galasam**, good value Galápagos tours in their fleet of 10-16 passenger motor yachts, ranging from the luxury *Millenium* catamaran, to tourist class vessels. For representatives abroad see www.galasam.com **Galextur**, Portugal 600 y 6 de Diciembre, T2269626, ingmar1@attglobal.net, www.hotelangermeyer.com Run 4-8 day land based tours with daily sailings to different islands. Good service. **Kempery Tours**, operate the 16-passenger, tourist superior sailboat *Angelique*, refurbished in 2002. **Klein Tours**, operate the luxury 90-passenger *Galapagos Legend* and 3 yachts for 16-32 passengers. **Quasar Náutica**, Montúfar E14-15 y La Cumbre, Bellavista, T2441550, T2446996, F2436625, www.quasarnautica.com 7-10 day naturalist and diving cruises on 8-16 berth luxury sail and power yachts with multilingual guides. Also a 48-passenger vessel, the *Eclipse*. UK agent: Penelope Kellie, T01962-779317, F779458, pkellie@yachtors.u-net.com; US agent: T1-800-2472925, F1-305-5927060, tumbaco@gate.net Highly recommended. **Rolf Wittmer**, Foch E7-81 y Almagro, T2526938, F2228520, www.rwittmer.com Run 2 first class yachts, *Tip Top II* and *III*.

Transport

Local

See also Ins and outs, page 92

Bus All tickets are bought on the buses; the exact fare is sometimes expected. Buses are very slow in the Old City owing to traffic jams. Many bus lines go through *La Marín* (officially called Plaza San Martín) at the north end of the Old City. Extra caution is advised here: it is a rough area, pickpockets abound and it should be avoided at night.

Suburban service: buses for destinations near Quito leave from 'La Marín'; a few others leave from Larrea y Asunción for destinations to the north, and from Villaflora for destinations to the south.

Don't ask the price if the meter is running as this will offend bona fide drivers

Taxis All taxis must have working meters by law, so make sure the meter is running (drivers sometimes say their meters are out of order). If the meter is not running, fix the fare before getting in. Insist that the taxi drops you precisely where you want to go.

All legally registered taxis have large numbers prominently displayed on the side of the vehicle and on a decal on the windshield. They are safer and cheaper than unauthorized taxis. Note the registration and the licence plate numbers if you feel you have been seriously overcharged or mistreated, then complain to the transit police or tourist office. But be reasonable and remember that most taxi drivers are honest and helpful.

For trips outside Quito, agree taxi tariffs beforehand. Expect to pay US$70-85 a day. Outside the luxury hotels, cooperative taxi drivers have a list of agreed excursion prices and most drivers are knowledgeable. Arrangements can also be made through the radio taxi numbers listed under Ins and outs (page 93). For taxi tours with a guide, try Hugo Herrera, T2267891/2236492 who speaks good English and is recommended.

Bus The main Terminal Terrestre for all national services is in the Old City, on Maldonado (see Ins and outs, page 92). There is a 24-hr luggage store which is safe, US$1.75 per day. There are company booking offices in the terminal but staff shout destinations of buses leaving and you can hop on board and pay later; but confirm the fare in advance. For the less frequent routes, or at busy times of the year (long weekends or holidays), consider purchasing your ticket a day in advance, but this is usually not necessary. See under the relevant destinations for fares and schedules.

Long distance
Watch your belongings at the Terminal Terrestre at all times

Quito's Terminal Terrestre is neither particularly safe nor pleasant, so try to spend as little time here as possible. If going to the Terminal Terrestre by taxi, you can pay the driver a little extra to take you inside directly to the departure ramps, to avoid walking through the station. This is an especially good idea at night or very early in the morning. When arriving in Quito by bus, you and your luggage will be unloaded next to a large taxi rank. Cab drivers wait for the buses; choose one, either agree to use the meter or agree on a price, and get going. If you have almost no luggage and know Quito well, then there is a trolley stop right outside the bus station which is convenient, but riding the trolley with a backpack is not recommended because of crowding and theft.

Several companies now run better quality coaches on their longer routes. Those with stations in the new city are: *Flota Imbabura*, Manuel Larrea 1211 y Portoviejo, T2236940, for Cuenca and Guayaquil; *Transportes Ecuador*, JL Mera 330 y Jorge Washington, T2503642, to Guayaquil; *Panamericana Internacional*, Colón 852 y Reina Victoria, T2501585, for Huaquillas, Machala, Cuenca, Loja, Guayaquil, Manta and Esmeraldas.

Bus *Panamericana Internacional* (see previous paragraph) also run an international service: daily to **Bogotá**, changing buses in Tulcán and Ipiales, US$65, 28 hrs; to Lima, changing buses in Aguas Verdes and Túmbes, US$60, 38 hrs. *Ormeño Internacional*, from Perú, has an office on Los Shyris N34-432 y Portugal, opposite Parque la Carolina, T2460027. They go twice per week to **Lima**, US$55, 36 hrs, **Santiago**, US$130, 4 days, and **Buenos Aires**, US$190, 1 week. For these and other South American destinations, it is cheaper to take a bus to the border and change there.

International

The main car hire companies are at the airport: *Avis* (T2440270), *Budget* (T2459052), *Ecuacars* (T2247298), *Expo* (T2433127), *Localiza* (T1-800-562254) and *Sicorent* (T2432858). City offices: *Budget*, Colón y Amazonas, T2221814. *Ecuacars*, Colón 1280 y Amazonas, T2529781. *Expo*, Av América N21-66 y Bolívia, T2228688. *Localiza*, 6 de Diciembre E8-124 y Veintimilla, T2505986. *Trans-Rabbit*, in the international arrivals section of the airport, rent vans for 8 -14 passengers with driver for trips in Quito and out of town, T2276736, US$12 per hr. *Budget* and *Ecuacar* have been particularly recommended as being helpful. For rental prices and procedures, see Car hire, page 56.

Car hire

AMIPA, *Auxilio Mecánico Inmediato para Automóviles*, T2924461, T09-9734222 (mob). Reliable roadside mechanical assistance in the Quito metropolitan area (including Los Chillos and Tumbaco valleys), service for members and non-members.

Car & motorcycle repairs
For dealers with repair shops see the yellow pages under motocicletas and motos

Car repairs New car dealers have repair shops specializing in the brands they sell, a list can be found in the yellow pages under *automotores*. Other recommended shops are: *Alvarez Barba*, 10 de Agosto N51-97, T2472568, for BMW, Jeep, Mercedes Benz, Peugeot, Porche, Volvo. *Atlas*, Inglaterra 533 y Vancouver, T2234341, Land Rover specialists. *Autocom*, Eloy Alfaro y de las Anonas, T2412461, for Land Rover and Hyundai. *Automobile*, Río Coca 500 y Colimes, T2442196, for Jeep, Fiat, Chevrolet and many Japanese brands. There are several repair shops along the same street. *Dar Car's*, 6 de Diciembre 7758, T2412221, for many Japanese brands, Jeep and Ford. *Euro Servicio*, Los Shyris y Río Coca, T2432033, for BMW, Mercedes Benz and Porsche, very busy. *Kosche*, Eiffel 138 y Los Shyris, T2442204. BMW and Mercedes Benz specialists, but will also do other brands. *The Paint Bull*, 10 de Agosto N32-163 y Rumipamba, T2551212,

Quito

for American brands, Toyota and Fiat. *Ponce Yépez*, 10 de Agosto 9085, T2400222, for VW. *SERR*, de las Azucenas y Las Higueras, T2257926, for Land Rover. *Slip*, de las Azucenas y Eloy Alfaro, for Range Rover.

Motorcycle repairs Sr Lother Ranft, at *Euro Servicio* (see above), is a bike enthusiast and can get BMW motorcycle parts from Germany in 2 weeks. *Juan Molestina*, 6 de Diciembre y Bélgica, fuel and travel equipment shop, helpful for motorbike spare parts.

Train Regular passenger service has been discontinued throughout the country: see Getting around, page 51. For information on the tourist train from Quito to Cotopaxi, see page 155.

Directory

Airline offices **Domestic** *Aerogal*, Amazonas 7997 opposite the airport, T2257202. *Austro Aéreo*, Amazonas 7565 y Río Curaray, 2271536. *Icaro*, Palora 124 y Amazonas, near airport, T2450928, T1-800-883567. *TAME*, Amazonas 13-54 y Colón, Colón y La Rábida and 6 de Diciembre N26-112, T2909900. **International** *ACES*, Naciones Unidas y Amazonas, edif Banco La Previsora, Torre B, #411, T2466461. *Aero Continente*, Amazonas N22-118 y Veintimilla, T2902160. *Aeropostal*, Eloy Alfaro N32-564 y Bélgica, Edif Loveina, ground floor, T2268936. *Air France*, 12 de Octubre N24-562 y Cordero, World Trade Center, Torre A, #710, T2221605. *American Airlines*, Amazonas 4545 y Pereira, T2260900. *Avensa/Servivensa*, Portugal 794 y República de El Salvador, T2253972. *Avianca*, República de El Salvador 780 y Portugal, edif Twin Towers, mezzanine, T2264392. *Continental Airlines*, 12 de Octubre 1830 y Cordero, World Trade Center, #1108, also Naciones Unidas y República de El Salvador, edif City Plaza, ground floor, T2557170. *Copa Airlines*, República de El Salvador 361 y Moscú, edif Aseguradora del Sur, T2273829. *Cubana*, Los Shyris N32-14 y Almagro, edif Torre Nova, p1, T2902369. *Iberia*, Eloy Alfaro 939 y Amazonas, edif Finandes, p5, T2566009. *KLM*, 12 de Octubre y A Lincoln, edif Torre 1492, #110, T2986828. *Lan Chile*, Amazonas y Pasaje Río Guayas, edif Rumiñahui, by Parque La Carolina, T2458168, T1-800-526328. *Lufthansa*, Amazonas N49-107 y Río Palora, near the airport, T2258456. *TACA*, República de El Salvador N35-67 y Portugal, T2923170. *Varig*, Portugal 794 y República de El Salvador, edif Porto Lisboa, T225 0126.

Banks
For the best way to bring your funds, see Money, page 35

Banks are generally open Mon-Fri 0830-1800 and some also on Sat 0900-1300. Service for cash advances and TC exchange is usually only Mon-Fri until about 1500 (the earlier the better). Expect queues and paperwork at all banks. The procedures and commissions indicated below are subject to frequent change. The *American Express* representative is *Ecuadorean Tours*, Amazonas 329 y Jorge Washington, T2560488. Replaces lost Amex TCs and sells TCs to Amex card holders, but does not exchange TCs or sell them for cash. Mon-Fri 0830-1700. *Banco del Austro*, Amazonas y Santa María. Cash advances on Visa. Mon-Fri 0830-1700. *Banco de Guayaquil*, Colón y Reina Victoria, 3rd Floor. Amex and Visa TCs, 1% commission. Cirrus, Maestro or Plus ATM with maximum withdrawal of US$100, cash advances on Visa, fast and efficient. *Mastercard* headquarters, Naciones Unidas 825, next door to Banco del Pacifico. Cash advances, efficient service. Mon-Fri 0830-1700. *Banco del Pacífico*, main branch at Naciones Unidas between Los Shyris and Amazonas, also Amazonas y Roca, Mall El Jardín and Centro Comercial El Bosque. Amex TCs in US$ only, maximum US$200 per day, US$5 charge per transaction, also Mastercard and Visa through Cirrus and Maestro ATMs. *Banco del Pichincha*, Amazonas 13-54 y Colón, Venezuela y Espejo, half block from Plaza de la Independencia and many other branches. Cash through Cirrus ATM only. *Mutualista Pichincha*, 18 de Septiembre y JL Mera, García Moreno 1130 y Chile and other branches. Cash advances on Mastercard 0900-1630. *Produbanco*, Amazonas N35-211 y Japón (opposite CCI), Amazonas y Robles (also open Sat 0900-1300), Benalcazar 852 y Olmedo (cash advances only) and at the airport. Cash and TCs in various currencies, 1-2% commission, good service, cash advance on Mastercard. Mon-Fri 0830-1500.

Casa de Cambio *Vazcambios*, Amazonas y Roca, at *Hotel Mercure Alameda*, T2225442. Charges 1.8% commission for US$ TCs, 2% for TCs in other currencies. Also changes other currencies and sells TCs. Mon-Fri 0845-1745, Sat 0900-1300.

Internet Quito has very many cyber cafés, particularly in the Mariscal tourist district. Rates start at about US$0.60 per hr, but US$1 per hr is more typicial. Since there are so many to choose from, you can select a cyber café to suit your particular mood – do you prefer to surf to the sounds of classical music or heavy metal? Some places get crowded, smoky, and very noisy – especially distracting for net to phone. Also remember that internet access is cheapest and fastest in Quito, Guayaquil and Cuenca, more expensive and slower in small towns and more remote areas.

Communica-tions
Watch your belongings while in the internet cafés, there have been some reports of theft

Post There are 22 postal branches throughout Quito, opening times vary but are generally Mon-Fri 0800-1800, Sat 0800-1200. In principle all branches provide all services, but your best chances are at Colón y Almagro in the Mariscal district, and at the main sorting centre on Japón near Naciones Unidas, behind the CCI shopping centre. Very large parcels may have to be sent from Ulloa y Ramírez Dávalos (Mon-Fri 0730-1600). The branch on Eloy Alfaro 354 y 9 de Octubre is especially chaotic and unhelpful, best avoided. There is also a branch in the Old City, on Espejo, between Guayaquil y Venezuela, and between the old and new towns at Ulloa and Ramírez Dávalos, behind the Mercado Santa Clara. This is the centre for parcel post, and you may still be directed there to send large packages. *Poste Restante* is available at the post offices at Espejo and at Eloy Alfaro. All *poste restante* letters are sent to Espejo unless marked 'Correo Central, Eloy Alfaro', but you are advised to check both *postes restantes*, whichever address you use. For those with an Amex card, letters can be sent care of *American Express*, Casilla 17-01-0265, Quito. *South American Explorers*, see page 25, holds mail for members.

See Post, page 60, for rates, procedures and precautions

Telephone National and international calls can be made from the **Andinatel** offices at Av 10 de Agosto y Colón; in the Old City at Benalcázar between Chile and Mejía; the Terminal Terrestre; and the airport (above international departures). All open 0800-2200. New calling centres are operating throughout the city, and more were opening in late 2002. Look for the blue and orange Andinatel signs, prices are the same as in the offices mentioned above. For information about making long distance calls from Bell South and Porta public phones, see Telephone services, page 61.

Argentina, Amazonas 477, 8th floor, T2562292, 0900-1600. **Austria**, Gaspar de Villaroel E9-53 y Los Shyris, p3, T2443272, 1000-1200. **Belgium**, JL Mera N23-103 y Wilson, T2545340. Mon-Thu 0900-1200, Mon-Wed 1430-1700. **Bolivia**, Eloy Alfaro 2432 y Fernando Ayarza, T2244830, 0800-1600. **Brazil**, Amazonas1429 y Colón, edif España, p9, T2563086, 0900-1500. **Canada**, 6 de Diciembre 2816 y Paul Rivet, edif Josueth González p4, T2232114, 0900-1200. **Chile**, Juan Pablo Sanz 3617 y Amazonas, edif Xerox p4, T2249406, 0800-1700. **Colombia** (consulate), Atahualpa 955 y República, p3, T2458012, 0830-1330. **Germany**, Naciones Unidas y República de El Salvador, edif City Plaza, T2970820, 0830-1130. **Ireland**, Ulloa 2651 y Rumipamba, T2451577, 0900-1300. **Israel**, 12 de Octubre y Salazar, edif Plaza 2000, p9, T2238055, 1000-1300. **Italy**, La Isla 111 y H Albornoz, T2561077, 0830-1230. **Japan**, JL Mera N19-36 y Patria, edif Corporación Financiera Nacional, p7, T2561899, 0930-1200, 1400-1700. **Netherlands**, 12 de Octubre 1942 y Cordero, World Trade Center, p1, T2229229, 0830-1300, 1400-1730. **Norway** and Sweden, Pasaje Alfonso Jerves 134 y Orellana, T2509514, 0900-1200. **Paraguay**, 12 de Octubre y Cordero, edif World Trade Center, p9,

Embassies & consulates
All open Mon-Fri unless otherwise noted

T2231990, 0830-1330. **Peru**, República de El Salvador 495 e Irlanda, edif Irlanda, T2468410, 0900-1300, 1500-1800. **Spain**, La Pinta 455 y Amazonas, T2564373, 0900-1200. **Switzerland**, Juan Pablo Sanz 120 y Amazonas, edif Xerox, p2, T2434948. **United Kingdom**, Naciones Unidas y República de El Salvador, edif Citiplaza, p14, T2970800, Mon-Thu 0830-1230, 1330-1700, Fri 0830-1330. **Uruguay**, 6 de Diciembre 2816 y Paul Rivet, edif Josueth González, p9, T2544228, 0900-1500. **USA**, 12 de Octubre y Patria, T2562890, 0800-1230, 1330-1700. **Venezuela**, Los Cabildos 115 e Hidalgo de Pinto, Quito Tenis, T2444873, 0915-1215.

Foreign cultural centres *Alliance Française* at Eloy Alfaro 1900. French courses, films and cultural events.*Casa Humboldt*, Vancouver y Polonia, T2548480. German centre, films, talks, exhibitions.

Language courses Quito has become one of the most important centres for Spanish language study in all of Latin America, with over 100 schools operating in the city. Students range from executives pursuing an intensive period of technical training to travellers beginning an extended journey with a few informal classes. Many people combine language study with touring and opportunities for cross-cultural exposure, and some schools are well set up to organize this. Homestays with an Ecuadorean family are often part of the experience. There are schools and programs to suit every taste and budget, far too many to list here. Instead we will try to focus on how to choose a language school, and list just a few of those which have received consistently favourable recommendations.

If you are short on time then it can be a good idea to make your arrangements from home, either directly with one of the schools or through an agency such as *AmeriSpan Unlimited*, USA and Canada toll-free T1-800-879-6640, www.amerispan.com, who can offer you a wide variety of options. If you have more time and less money, then it may be cheaper to organize your own studies after you arrive. You can try one or two places without committing yourself for an extended period. *Internacional de Español (IE)*, Pinto E4-358 y Amazonas, T2564910, www.diplomaie.com is an organization which groups Spanish schools, they can provide general information, books and a list of schools. *South American Explorers* also provides its members with a list of recommended schools and these may give club members discounts.

Identify your budget and goals for the course: rigorous grammatical and technical training, fluent conversation skills, getting to know Ecuadoreans or just enough basic Spanish to get you through your trip. Visit a few places to get a feel for what they charge and offer. Prices vary greatly, from US$4 to US$10 per hr, but you do not always get what you pay for. If you book for a longer period, you may get a discount. There is also tremendous variation in teacher qualifications, infrastructure and resource

Quito

materials. A great deal of emphasis has traditionally been placed on one-to-one teaching, but remember that a well structured small classroom setting, such as that provided by the *Universidad Católica* (see below), can also be very good.

The quality of homestays likewise varies, the cost including meals running from US$12 to US$25 per day. Try to book just one week at first to see how a place suits you, don't be pressed into signing a long term contract right at the start. For language courses as well as homestays, deal directly with the people who will provide services to you, and avoid local intermediaries.

Finally, remember that Quito is not the only place in Ecuador where you can study Spanish. Although some of the best schools are located in the capital there are also good options in Otavalo, Baños, Cuenca and elsewhere (listed in the corresponding sections of the text). Do you prefer the cosmopolitan bustle and nightlife of Quito, or the clean air and tranquillity of a smaller town?

The following are some of the recommended Spanish schools in Quito. **In the New City** *Academia de Español Amistad*, Pasaje Manuel Salcedo N14-56 y Montevideo, T2221092, F2545576, www.amistad-spanish.com *Academia de Español Equinoccial*, Roca 533 y JL Mera, T/F2564488, www.ecuadorspanish .com Small school. *Academia de Español Quito*, Marchena 130 y 10 de Agosto, T2553647, F2506474, www.academiaquito.com.ec *Academia Latinoamericana*, José Queri 2 y Eloy Alfaro, T2452824, F2231102, www. latinoschools.com *Amazonas Spanish School*, Washington 718 and Amazonas, edif Rocafuerte, p3, T2527509, F2504654, www.eduamazonas.com *American Spanish School*, 9 de Octubre 564 y Carrión, T2229166, F2229165, as.school@ accessinter.net *Bipo & Toni's Academia de Español*, Carrión 300 y L Plaza, T/F2556614, T/F 2500732, www.bipo.net *Centro de Español Vida Verde*, 18 de Septiembre E4-135 y Amazonas, T2237709, F2568501, www.vidaverde .com Lessons in Quito or while travelling in Ecuador with your teacher, a percentage of the profits is donated to socially and environmentally responsible projects. *Cristóbal Colón*, Colón 2088 y Versalles, T2562485, F2222964, www.southtravel.com *Estudio de Español Pichincha*, Andrés Xaura 182, entre Lizardo García y Foch, T2528051, F2601689, www.pichinchaspanishschool.com *Galápagos Spanish School*, Amazonas 258 y Washington, 2nd floor, T2565213, www.galapagos.edu.ec *Instituto Superior de Español*, Darquea Terán 1650 y 10 de Agosto, T2223242, F2221628, www.instituto-superior.net They also have a school in Otavalo (Sucre 1110 y Morales, 2nd floor, T922414, F922415), in Galápagos (advanced booking required) and can arrange voluntary work. *La Lengua*, Colón 1001 y JL Mera, p8, T/F2501271, www.la-lengua.com (Switzerland T/F8510533, peter-baldauf@bluewin.ch). *Mitad del Mundo*, Gustavo Darquea Terán Oe2-58 y Versalles, p2, T2546827, F2567875, www.mitadmundo.com.ec Repeatedly recommended. *Simón Bolívar*, Leonidas Plaza 353 y Roca, T/F2236688, www.simon-bolivar.com Have their own travel agency. *Sintaxis*, 10 de Agosto 15-55 y Bolivia, edif Andrade, p 5, T2520006, www.sintaxis.net Repeatedly recommended. *South American Language Center*, Amazonas 1549 y Santa María, T2544715, T/F2226348 (UK 020-8983 6724), www.southamerican.edu.ec *Spanish Lessons*, Lizarazo N23-28 y C Zorilla, La Gasca, T2557529, gmarr@interactive.net.ec Provide individual or group classes at students' homes or hostels. *Switzerland Spanish School*, Calama E4-68 y JL Mera, p2, T/F2508665, www.geocities.com/switzerspanish *Universidad Católica*, 12 de Octubre y Roca, contact Carmen Sarzosa, T2228781, csarzosa@puceuio.puce.edu.ec

In the Old City *Los Andes*, García Moreno 1245 y Olmedo, p2, T2955107, has schools outside Quito and can arrange volunteer work. *Beraca School*, García Moreno 858 between Sucre and Espejo, Pasaje Amador, p3, T2288092, beraca@

interactive.net.ec It has a second location in the new town. *San Francisco*, Sucre 518 y Benalcázar (Plaza San Francisco), p3, T2282849, sanfranciscoss@latinmail.com

Recommended course books *Español, Curso de Perfeccionamiento*, by Juan Felipe García Santos (Universidad de Salamanca, Sep, 1990). *Español, Español* (a grammar text) and *Ejercicios, Ejercicios*, both published by *Internacional de Español* (see above).

Laundromats There are many around La Mariscal, wash and dry costs about US$0.80 per kg, some deliver pre-paid laundry. Several are clustered around the corner of Foch and Reina Victoria and along Pinto. *Lavandería*, Olmedo 552, in the Old City. **Dry cleaning** *Martinizing*, 1-hr service, 12 de Octubre 1486, Diego de Almagro y La Pradera, and in 6 shopping centres, plus other locations, expensive. *La Química*, Mallorca 335 y Madrid and Olmedo y Cotopaxi in the Old City. *Norte*, Amazonas 7339, 6 de Diciembre 1840 y Eloy Alfaro, and Pinzón y La Niña.

Laundry

The *Instituto Geográfico Militar* is on top of the hill to the east of Parque El Ejido. From Av 12 de Octubre, opposite the Casa de la Cultura, take Jiménez (a small street) up the hill. After crossing Av Colombia continue uphill on Paz y Miño behind the Military Hospital and then turn right to the guarded main entrance. You have to deposit your passport or identification card. There is a beautiful view from the grounds. Map and aerial photo indexes are all laid out for inspection. The map sales room (helpful staff) is open Mon-Fri 0800-1600. Map and geographic reference libraries are located next to the sales room.

Maps
For more information on maps and guide books, see page 42

Dentists Drs Sixto y Silvia Altamirano, Amazonas 2689 y República, T2244119. Excellent. *Dr Fausto Vallejo*, Madrid 742 (1 block from the end of the Colón-Camal bus line), T2554781. Very reasonable. *Dr Roberto Mena*, Coruña E24-865 e Isabel la Católica, T2559923. Speaks English and German. *Dr Víctor Peñaherrera*, Coruña 1898, T2234284. Speaks English.

Medical services
For all emergencies in Quito call 911. See also Health, page 83

Doctors Most embassies have the telephone numbers of doctors who speak non-Spanish languages. The following are recommended.

General practice and internal medicine: *Dr Wilson Pancho*, República de El Salvador 112, T2463139/2469546. Speaks German. *Dr John Rosenberg*, Med Center Travel Clinic, Foch 476 y Almagro, T2261677 in the morning, T2521104 in the afternoon, paging service T2227777 (beeper 310), internal and travel medicine with a full range of vaccines, speaks English and German, very helpful. *Dr Rodrigo Sosa Cevallos*, Alemania 144 y Eloy Alfaro, T2525102. English-speaking.

Dermatology: *Dr Rodrigo Armijos*, at the pathology laboratory in the Medical Faculty of the Universidad Central, entrance below Iquique y Sodiro. For treatment of leishmaniasis and other tropical cutaneous horrors, he is a researcher developing a vaccine for leishmaniasis. *Dra Mónica Santamaría*, edif Diagnóstico 2000 on Mariana de Jesús, 1 block below Hospital Metropolitano, T2460404. For all skin problems. Speaks English and some French.

Gynaecology: *Dr Juan Molina*, Centro Médico Meditrópoli, Mariana de Jesús opposite Hospital Metropolitano,, T2432171/2260581, speaks German and English.

Paediatrics: *Dr Ernesto Quiñones*, at Centro Materno Infantil, Manuel Barreto 167 y Coruña, at north end of Coruña, T2232956/2564538. Speaks English and Italian. *Dr Guillermo Luna*, Av América 4343 y Hernández de Girón, T2245317. Speaks English.

Urology: *Dr Wilson Vargas Uvidia*, Centro Médico Metropolitano, Mariana de Jesús y Calle A, Oficina 102, T2267777, T2431100 (home). Speaks English and French.

Hospitals Among the recommended health centres are: *Hospital Voz Andes*, Villalengua Oe2-37 y 10 de Agosto, T2262142 (reached by Trole, la Y stop). Emergency room, quick and efficient. American, British and Ecuadorean doctors and nurses on staff, fee based on ability to pay, run by Christian HCJB organization, has out-patients department, T2439343. *Hospital Metropolitano*, Mariana de Jesús y Av Occidental, just east of the western city bypass, T2261520, ambulance T2265020. Catch a Quito Sur-San Gabriel bus along Av América, or the Trole (Mariana de Jesús stop) and walk up or take a cab from there. Very professional and recommended, but prices are almost the same as in the USA. *Clínica Pichincha*, Veintimilla E3-30 y Páez, T2562296, ambulance T2501565. Another very good, expensive hospital. *Clínica Pasteur*, Eloy Alfaro 552 y 9 de Octubre, T2234004. Also good and cheaper than the above. *Novaclínica Santa Cecilia*, Veintimilla 1394 y 10 de Agosto, T2545390, emergency T2545000. Reasonable prices, good.

Medical laboratories All the hospitals listed above have reliable laboratories for all tests. Other reliable labs include *Dra Johanna Grimm*, República de El Salvador 112 y Los Shyris, edif Onyx, p3, T2462182. English and German spoken. *Dr Jaime Silva*, at Medcenter, Foch 476 y Almagro, T2521104.

Opticians *Optica Los Andes*, several locations including 10 de Agosto 520 y Arenas, T2545159 and Quicentro Shopping. Professional. *Optica Gill*, Amazonas 1068, opposite the British Council, English spoken, glasses, contact lenses, helpful.

Pharmacies *Fybeca* is a reliable chain of 33 pharmacies throughout the city. Their 24-hr branches are at Amazonas y Tomás de Berlanga near the Plaza de Toros, and at Centro Comercial El Recreo in the south. *Farmacia Colón*, 10 de Agosto 2292 y Cordero, T2226534, also 24 hr. Check the listing of *farmacias de turno* in *El Comercio* on Sat for 24-hr chemists during the following week. Always check expiry dates on any medications and avoid purchasing anything that requires refrigeration in the smaller drug stores.

Places of worship Joint Anglican/Lutheran service is held (in English) at the *Advent Lutheran Church*, Isabel la Católica 1419, Sun 0900. A *Synagogue* is located in the far north of the city, for information contact T2483800.

Useful addresses **Immigration Offices** See Getting in, Extensions, page 32. **Police** Criminal Investigations are at Cuenca y Mideros, in the Old City. To report a robbery, make a *denuncia* within 48 hrs; if one officer is unhelpful, try another. Thefts can also be reported at the **Policía Judicial**, Roca y JL Mera. If you wait more than 48 hrs, you will need a lawyer. **Policía de Turismo** is at Reina Victoria y Roca, T254 3983.

Around Quito

Mitad del Mundo and surroundings

Some 23 km north of Quito is the Mitad del Mundo Equatorial Line Monu- **Equator**
ment at an altitude of 2,483 m near San Antonio de Pichincha. The location of **monument**
the equatorial line here was determined by Charles-Marie de la Condamine *Colour map 2, grid B4*
and his French expedition in 1736, and agrees to within 150 m with modern
GPS measurements. A paved road runs from Quito to the Monument, which
you can reach by a 'Mitad del Mundo' bus (US$0.34, one hour) from Avenida
América y Pérez Guerrero, by the Universidad Central or further north along
Avenida América or Avenida Occidental. An excursion to Mitad del Mundo
by taxi, with a one hour wait and a visit to Pululahua, is about US$30 per taxi.
Just the taxi ride from the New City costs about US$12.

The monument forms the focal point of the **Ciudad Mitad del Mundo**, a
park and leisure area built as a typical colonial town, with restaurants, gift
shops, a post office with philatelic sales, travel agency, pavilions showing the
history of the French scientific expedition and a numismatic collection and so
on, all run by the Consejo Provincial de Pichincha. There are free live music
and dance demonstrations on Sundays and holidays (1300-1800). It is all
rather touristy but the monument itself has an interesting ethnographic
museum inside. A lift takes you to the top, then you walk down with the
museum laid out all around with exhibits of different indigenous cultures
every few steps. ■ *Mon-Thu 0900-1800, Fri-Sun 0900-1900 (very crowded on
Sun). US$0.50, includes entrance to the pavilions; entry to the ethnographic
museum US$3 (includes guided tour of museum in Spanish or English, guides are
found near the entrance to the complex or at the information booth); parking
US$1. T2394806.*

There is a Planetarium with 30-minute shows (Tue-Sun 0900-1600, US$1,
group of 15 minimum) and an interesting model of colonial Quito, about 10 sq
m, with artificial day and night, which took seven years to build, also of
Manhattan (New York, USA); both are very impressive (daily 0900-1700, US$1).

Just north of the complex is **Museo Inti-Ñan**, eclectic, entertaining and
interesting. It shows different experiments relating to the equator and exhibits
about native life. Recommended. ■ *0900-1800 daily. US$2. A bit difficult to
find, from the complex entrance follow the main road north (toward Calacalí) for
about 200 m, look for a small sign and lane to your left, English, French and
Hebrew speaking guides. T2395122.*

Sleeping C *Hostería Alemana*, on Av Manuel Córdoba Galarza, the approach road
from Quito, 700 m south of the complex, T2394243. Very good restaurant.
C *Rancho Alegre*, in San Antonio, opposite the church, new hotel in 2002.
D *Residencial Mitad del Mundo*, Av Equinoccial, 3 blocks from the complex, in San
Antonio de Pichincha. Simple. D *Sol y Luna*, Av Equinoccial 1272, 3 blocks from monu-
ment, T2394979. Private bath, hot water, breakfast available.

Eating Expensive *El Cráter*, on the rim of the crater of Pululahua (see below),
signed access before (east) the road to the *mirador*, T239399. Popular upscale restaurant, international and Ecuadorian food, excellent views. Daily 1230-1700. *Equinoccio*,
Av Manuel Córdoba Galarza, just north of the equator complex, T2394091. Ecuadorian
food, live music on Sun, also issues certificates for their guests. Daily 1000-1600.
Mid-range *Vicente's*, Av Equinoccial, 6 blocks down from the complex, in the town of

San Antonio. Ecuadorian food, also fish. **Cheap** *Balcón del Mundo*, at the complex, overlooking the square. Good for coffee and traditional snacks, and to see the shows.

Tour operators *Calimatours*, Manzana de los Correos, Oficina 11, at Mitad del Mundo complex, T2394796, calima@andinanet.net Runs tours to Pululahua and Rumicucho, offers general information, very helpful, open daily 0900-1800, some English spoken. Recommended.

Pululahua A few kilometres beyond the Equator Monument, off the road to Calacalí, is the Pululahua crater, which is well worth visiting. Try to go in the morning, as there is often cloud later. In the crater, with its own warm microclimate, is the hamlet of Pululahua, surrounded by agricultural land and to the west of it, the **Reserva Geobotánica Pululahua**. The crater is open and drops to the west; the climate gets warmer and the vegetation more lush as you descend. There are two access points to the crater, one road leads to the *mirador*, a lookout on the rim, with wonderful views of the agricultural area in the crater floor. From here a rough track leads down into the crater. It's a half hour walk down, and one hour back up. A second much longer road allows you to drive into the crater. For a very scenic but long (15-20 km) walk, go down from the *mirador*, beyond the village of Pululahua turn left and follow the second access road mentioned (see description below) back up to the rim and the main highway.

Access and transport Continue on the road past the Monument towards Calacalí. After nearly 5 km (one hour's walk) the road bears left and begins to climb steeply. A smaller paved road to the right leads to the *mirador*. There are infrequent buses to Calacalí which will drop you at the fork, from where it is a 30-minute walk. There is plenty of traffic at weekends for hitching a lift. A taxi to the *mirador* from Mitad del Mundo costs US$5. *Calimatours* (see above) runs tours to Pululahua which include a walk on the rim (one hour for US$4, two hours for US$8).

To drive to the reserve, continue beyond the turn-off for the *mirador*, 8 km from Mitad del Mundo, take the turn-off to the right past the gas station; it is 2.4 km to the Moraspungo Park gate, where the park entrance fee (US$5) is paid, and a very scenic drive into the crater begins. In 8 km you reach the valley floor. From there you can turn right towards the village of Pululahua, or left and continue downhill to the sugar-cane growing area of Nieblí. There are two cabins near the Moraspungo entrance: US$5 per person, take sleeping bag, warm clothing and food. There is no public transport to the reserve.

Other excursions near Mitad del Mundo Also in the vicinity of the Mitad del Mundo Monument, 3 km from San Antonio, are the Inca ruins of **Rumicucho**. Built on a magnificent location, with views south to Quito and to the north, it is a sample of one of the most common Inca site types in the northern Andes, the fortress. It was built over pre-existing structures and is believed to have guarded a pass from the north. The site was excavated and partially restored by the Banco Central. Pre-Inca ceramics, weaving implements and ceremonial objects were found here. Unfortunately the site was looted. Today you can only see remains of walls, probably pre-Inca, on five levels of terraces. The site is administered by the local community. Celebrations are held here during the equinoxes. ■ *US$0.50, tour from Mitad del Mundo with Calimatours US$7, includes entry fee. Taxi from Mitad del Mundo, about US$10. Books about this site by Eduardo Almeida.*

In Quito's northwestern suburb of **Cotocollao** is the archaeological site of the same name, dating back over 3,000 years to the Formative period. Ash found covering this settlement suggests that it might have been abandoned around 2,300 years ago, after a particularly strong eruption of nearby Volcán Pululahua. There is a small site museum, **Museo de Sitio de Cotocollao**, with ceramics, burrials and a scale model of the ancient village. ■ *Near the Museo-Biblioteca Aureliano Pólit, see Museums above.*

About 8 km from Quito on the road to San Antonio de Pichincha, is the village of **Pomasqui**, near where was a tree in which Jesus Christ appeared to perform various miracles, El Señor del Arbol, now enshrined in its own building. In the church nearby is a series of paintings depicting the miracles (mostly involving horrendous road accidents), which is well worth a visit. You may have to find the caretaker to unlock the church.

From San Antonio a dirt road heads north towards **Perucho**. South of Perucho another road turns sharply southeast to **Guayllabamba** via **Puéllaro** (eat at the house on the plaza which is also a radio/TV workshop). A left turn (northeast) off this road, just before Guayllabamba, goes to **Malchinguí**, **Tocachi** and **Cayambe** (see page 161).

The Equator line also crosses the Panamericana 8 km south of Cayambe, where there is a concrete globe beside the road. Take a Cayambe bus (two hours, US$0.80) and ask for Mitad del Mundo by Guachala. For nearby accommodation, see *Hostería Guachala*, under Cayambe (page 162).

North of Quito

The Quito municipal zoo is situated in the small town of Guayllabamba, 45 minutes north of the capital, see page 160. The zoo is spacious and well designed and a visit to it makes a worthwhile family outing. It gets quite warm in Guayllabamba, so take something to drink. ■ *US$2, children and seniors $1.40. To get there, take a Flota Pichincha bus from América y Colón.*

Guayllabamba Zoo

Northwest of Quito

Despite their proximity to the capital, the western slopes of **Pichincha** and its surroundings are surprisingly wild, with fine opportunities for walking and especially birdwatching. There are four roads that drop into the western lowlands from Quito. Each has a unique character, and each has interesting ecotourism reserves. The northernmost, the **Calacalí-La Independencia-Esmeraldas road**, starts by the Mitad del Mundo monument, goes through Calacalí, Nanegalito (two basic hotels, better is **E** *Don Fabara* next to the church, shared bath, hot water), San Miguel de los Bancos and several other towns, before joining the Santo Domingo-Esmeraldas road at La Independencia. This is the simplest of the four roads to drive, since it is paved and traffic is light. Note that markers along the road refer to the distance from the toll booth outside Quito, on the way to Mitad del Mundo. Parallel to this road is the much rougher **Nono-Mindo road**, famous for its excellent birdwatching. This road begins off Avenida Occidental, Quito's western ring road; you must ask for directions to find it. At the beginning of this road is *Hostería San Jorge*, above Quito (see Quito Sleeping, page 112). There are several connections between the paved Calacalí road and the rough Nono-Mindo road, so it is possible to drive on the paved road most of the way even if your destination is one of the lodges on the Nono-Mindo road. The remaining two roads are described under Southwest of Quito below.

The Noroccidente, as this region is known, offers many attractions and new tourism developments are opening up throughout the area. The major reserves off the paved road are **Maquipucuna** and **El Pahuma**; the major

Colour map 2, grid B4

lodges on the Nono-Mindo road are **Tandayapa** and **Bellavista**. Both roads meet just before the turn-off to **Mindo**, a town with many more lodges. Along the Calacalí-La Independencia road, west of the Mindo turn-off, are a number of additional lodges.

Reserves & lodges

The **Reserva Orquideológica El Pahuma** has 600 ha. It is an interesting collaboration between a local landowner and the Ceiba Foundation for Tropical Conservation. Less than one hour from Quito on the Calacalí-La Independencia road, El Pahuma features an orchid garden and an orchid propagation program. Trails start at 1,900 m and go to 2,600 m. Birds such as mountain toucans and tanagers are present, and Spectacled Bear have been seen. ■ *US$2, guide US$2.50 per day*. The information centre is on the south side of the road, 30 km from Mitad del Mundo. There is parking on the north side of the road, take any bus bound for Nanegalito or points west. Accommodation in simple but nice lodge at the information centre: **C** in private room with shared bath and cold water, **E** per person in dorm, meals available. Very rustic accommodation in a cabin, 2 hours climb from the entrance, no facilities, **F** per person including entry fee. Camping **G** per person. Contact Alejandro Trillo, T2252053, T09-9196747 (mob), or see www.ceiba.org

The **Tandayapa Lodge** is on the Nono–Mindo road and can be reached in 1½ hours from Quito via the Calacali-La Independencia road; take the signed turn-off to Tandayapa at Km 52, just past *Café Tiepolo*. At the intersection with the Nono-Mindo road turn right. It is longer but more scenic to take the Nono road all the way from Quito. This is a very comfortable lodge at about 1,700 m, with trails going higher. The lodge is owned by dedicated birders who strive to keep track of all rarities on the property; they can reliably show you practically any of 318 species, even such rare birds as the White-faced Nunbird or the Lyre-tailed Nightjar. Recommended for serious bird watchers. ■ *Contact T02-2225180 (Quito), T09-735536 (mob), www.tandayapa.com Accommodation in **L** range, including 3 meals.*

The **Maquipucuna Reserve** contains 4,500 ha, surrounded by an additional 14,000 ha of protected forest. It can be reached in two hours from Quito with a private vehicle. The cloud forest at 1,200-2,800 m contains a tremendous diversity of flora and fauna, including over 325 species of birds. Especially noteworthy are the colourful tanager flocks, mountain-toucans, parrots and quetzals. The reserve has trails ranging in length from 15 minutes to all day. There is also a research station and an experimental organic garden. ■ *US$5, guide US$10 per day for group of 5. Accommodation in our **L** range, including 3 meals, options with*

shared bath and/or without meals are cheaper. Contact Fundacion Maquipucuna, Baquerizo Moreno E9-153 y Tamayo, Quito, T2507200, F2507201, www.maqui.org Take the Calacalí-La Independencia road, at Nanegalito turn right on a dirt road to Nanegal; keep going until a sign on the right for the reserve (before Nanegal). Pass through the village of Marianitas and it's another 20 mins to the reserve. The road is poor, especially in the Jan-May wet season, 4WD vehicles recommended. By public transport, take a bus to Nanegalito (43 km from Mitad del Mundo) and hire a truck, US$20, or arrange transport with Maquipucuna in Quito, return service from your hotel in Quito US$100 for 4, they can also pick you up in Nanegalito, US$20.

Near Maquipucuna are a couple of community conservation and eco-tourism projects. By the upper elevation border of Maquipucuna, to the southeast, is **Yunguilla**, reached by pick-up truck from Calacalí, with a cabin for visitors (**C** *Tahuallullu* includes three meals) and guiding service for treks in the forest and down to Maquipucuna (US$10 per person). ■ *Further information from Germán Collaguazo, T09-9580694 (mob), yunguilla@yahoo.com* To the east of Maquipucuna in a beautiful tract of cloud forest is **Santa Lucía**, with a cabin for visitors. The British organization Rainforest Concern is involved with this reserve and offers volunteer programmes (see page 81). ■ *Information from Francisco Molina, T2866695 in Marianitas, or Paulina Tapia T2573904 in Quito, administrador@santa-lucia.org, www.santa-lucia.org Three day visit* **AL** *per person full board, take a truck from Nanegalito, from the entrance to Maquipucuna it is one hour walking to the cabin.*

Bellavista is located at Km 68 at the top of the Tandayapa Valley on the old Nono-Mindo road. This dramatic dome-shaped lodge is perched in beautiful cloud forest. Faster access is recommended along the Calacalí-Esmeraldas road. Various access options: shortest is via Km 52 just after a bridge 4 km before Nanegalito, also at Km 62 (past Nanegalito) - usually all roads are accessible to normal vehicles, all have Bellavista signs. The reserve is part of a mosaic of private protected areas dedicated to conservation of one of the richest accessible areas of west slope cloud forest. Bellavista at 2,200 m is the highest of these, and the easiest place to see the incredible Plate-billed Mountain-Toucan. Over 300 species of birds have been seen in the Tandayapa Valley, including large numbers of hummingbirds drawn to the many feeders at the lodge. The area is also rich in orchids and other cloud forest plants. Recommended. ■ *L Accommodation with private bath, hot shower, and full board (good vegetarian food); AL private room or dormitory with shared bath. Camping also possible, US$5 per person. A biological station on the property is available for researchers, E per person without meals. Package tours can be arranged including transport from Quito; to get there on your own take a bus to Nanegalito and hire a pick-up truck, US$15-20, or get off at Km 52 taking the dirt road to the left (coming from Quito). For reservations, T2232313 or T09-9490891 (mob) in Quito or email info@bellavistacloudforest.com.*

In the village of **Tulipe**, northwest of Nanegalito, are a series of large **Tulipe** stone-lined pools and feeder canals which are unique in Ecuador. These were **archaeological** first studied in 1982; in 2002, the Fondo de Salvamento (Fonsal) from the **site** Municipio de Quito was conducting further studies and restoration. To date, their origin or probable use has not been determined. The stonework could suggest Inca influence, however the material recovered in excavations is pre-Inca. They could have been ceremonial pools, bathing pools or pools used as mirrors to study the stars. ■ *The site is not yet officially open, but you can ask permision to enter from the people who own the property. La Armenia is a village 3 km east of Nanegalito along the main road, here a secondary road goes west towards Pacto. Tulipe is 9 km from the turn-off along this road.*

Sleeping and eating Tulipe only has a simple shop for provisions. The closest accommodation is at Nanegalito or 1 km east of the Pacto turnoff is **C** *Hostería El Rosal*, on the Calacalí-La Independencia road, T2862691, cabin or rooms with bath, cheap restaurant with set meals and à la carte, pool, horses.

Transport Transportes Otavalo, in Quito, from Asunción y Manuel Larrea, 5 daily, morning ones at 0630, 1000, 1200, US$1.50, 2 hrs, also interparroquiales from Miraflores, by the Universidad Central. Last one returns to Quito at 1530.

Mindo

Phone code: 02
Population: about 1,800 including surroundings
Altitude:1,250 m

Mindo is a small town surrounded by dairy farms, rivers and lush cloud forest climbing the western slopes of Pichincha. It is an excellent base for many outdoor activities: walking, horse-riding, bathing in waterfalls, tubing (floating down the river in inner tubes), bird and butterfly watching, etc. Some 19,200 ha, ranging in altitude from 1,400 to 4,780 m (the rim of the crater of Guagua Pichincha), have been set aside as a nature reserve, **Bosque Protector Mindo-Nambillo**. The reserve features spectacular flora and fauna, beautiful cloud forest and many waterfalls. Access to the reserve proper is restricted to scientists, but there is a buffer zone of private reserves which offers many opportunities for exploring.

Mindo was much in the spotlight in 2002. The Ecuadorean government pushed through a project to build a new oil pipeline right through the heart of the reserve, despite the scientifically founded objections of local and international environmental groups. A number of foreign environmentalists were deported and construction began with a swath being bulldozed through the primary cloud forest. Despite the damage done, this has not diminished the area's many attractions.

Environmental groups and reserves. There are several environmental groups working in the Mindo area, these operate private reserves, most of which abut on the main reserve. Some of the lodges such as Mindo Garden, El Monte and Séptimo Paraiso also own private reserves. They all run tours on their properties.

Amigos de la Naturaleza de Mindo runs the **Centro de Educación Ambiental (CEA)**, 4 km from town, within a 17-ha buffer zone at the edge of the reserve. There are simple accommmodations and well maintained trails. ■ *US$1, lodging E-F per person; package with accommodation, full board and excursion C per person (guide included when there are minimum 3 passengers); camping US$2 per person. Take food if you wish to prepare your own, there are good kitchen facilities. Volunteer programmes can be arranged. All arrangements have to be made in advance, contact in Mindo: Amigos de la Naturaleza de Mindo, 1½ blocks from the parque central, T/F2765463.*

Acción por la Vida is an environmental group which runs **La Isla**, a 12-ha forest reserve on the Río Saguambi. There is a camping area with cooking facilities and a covered dining area, and several waterfalls which are used for rappelling. ■ *US$2 (includes camping), rappel US$7 (includes entry fee). It is a 40-min walk to the camping area and about 1 hr from there to the waterfalls. Visits only with local guides, information and booking through César Fiallo, El Bijao, T2765470.*

Fundación Puntos Verdes is an environmental organization which works on conservation, reforestation programmes, education, waste management, etc. with communities along the Calacalí-La Independencia road. They operate from **Finca Mindo Lindo**, a 7-ha reserve, 1 km west of the Mindo turn-off, and also run volunteer programmes. For contact information see Sleeping below.

The Mindo area is a birdwatchers paradise. A total of 350 species of birds have been identified and this is one of the best places in the country to see Cock-of-the-rock, Golden-headed Quetzal and Toucan-Barbet. The steep access road into town is particularly good for birdwatching, as is the private 'Yellow House Trail' (*Hacienda San Vicente*, see Sleeping below). The area is also rich in insects and a fine sample can be admired at the *Caligo Butterfly Farm*, 3 km from town on the road to Mindo Garden, where the stages of metamorphosis are well displayed and explained (English spoken), a great place to photograph butterlies. Recommended. ■ *0900-1500 daily. US$3. T2440360, caligobutterfly@hotmail.com* There are a couple of orchid gardens in Mindo. *Armonía*, two blocks from the church, by the stadium, at Cabañas Armonía, has a collection of regional orchids displayed on trees. ■ *US$1*.

Several waterfalls can be visited, these are on private land. Since the owners cut and maintain access trails, they charge an entrance fee. On the Río Nambillo is the **Cascada de Nambillo** ■ *US$5, US$3 for students. 4 hrs return*. On a small tributary of the Nambillo are the **Cascadas La Primavera**, three scenic falls, nearby are a shelter and a place to camp. ■ *US$3, camping US$3. 5-6 hrs return*. The **Cascadas de San Antonio**, where you can go rapelling, are on the Río Saguambi and the **Cascada de Azucar** is along one of its tributaries. Both are within the La Isla Reserve and can be only visited with a guide (see above). There is a Tourist Information Office at the main park, with information about attractions in the area and hotels. Here you can pay the entry fee for the waterfalls and obtain directions on how to reach them or hire a guide.

A very popular activity in the Mindo area is *regattas*, the local name for inner-tubing, floating down a river on a raft made of several inner tubes tied together. The number of tubes that can run together depends on the water level. Several local agencies and hotels offer this activity for US$4-6. It is usually done on the Río Mindo, but the experts also run the Río Blanco, where competitions are held during the local holidays.

One of the many nice roads for walking starts by the highschool near the entrance to town and heads west to an area known as Cunuco. Here is **Finca La Palma**, T2492940, a working farm with fish ponds by the Río Mindo. There is a cheap restaurant featuring tilapia, a camping area with tents, horses for rent, inner-tubing and swimming in the river. Entry is US$1, **E** for camping in their tents, cheaper if you bring your own, horses US$4 per hour.

Mindo & area sleeping

LL *Sachatamia*, 1 km E of Mindo turn-off on Calacalí-La Independencia road, T2765436. Includes 3 meals, small pool, rooms and cabins, walking trails, birdwatching, new in 2002. **L** *El Monte*, 2 km form Mindo on road to CEA, then cross river on cable car near the butterfly farm, best to contact office in town beforehand, T2765427, mindo@ecnet.ec, www.ecuadorcloudforest.com Includes 3 meals and some (but not all) excursions, birdwatching, tubing, walking, swimming. Horse riding and English-speaking guide extra. **L** *Mindo Gardens*, 3 km form Mindo on road to CEA, T2252488. Includes 3 meals, very good food, expensive restaurant open to the public, also snack bar serving pizza, comfortable, tastefully decorated cabins, beautiful setting, good birdwatching.

AL *El Carmelo de Mindo*, in 32 ha reserve, 1 km W of town, T2765449. Includes 3 meals, restaurant, pool and river bathing, rooms, cabins, and tree-house, camping U$5 pp, excursions, fishing, horse riding, mid-week discounts. **A** *Curiquindi Huasi*, 3 km from Mindo on road to Cunuco, T2431772 (Quito) or leave message at Mindo, T2765456. Includes breakfast, comfortable cabins for up to 4, nice grounds near Río Mindo, new in 2002. **A** *Finca Mindo Lindo*, 1 km W of the Mindo turn-off along the Calacalí-La Independencia road, T2455344, puntos_verdes@hotmail.com Includes breakfast, other meals available, day visits and overnight stays, relaxing, guided tours. **A** *Séptimo Paraiso*, 2 km from Calacalí-La Independencia road along Mindo access road, then 500 m right on a small side road, well signed, T09-934133 (mob), info@septimoparaiso.com, www.septimoparaiso.com Includes breakfast, expensive restaurant, pool, ample parking, all wood lodge, comfortable rooms, lovely grounds in a 300 ha reserve with walking trails. On it's own, isolated from Mindo town, new in 2001.

B *Hacienda San Vicente*, 'Yellow House', 500 m south of the plaza. Includes 3 meals, excellent food, family-run, friendly, nice rooms, good walking trails nearby, good value. Recommended. **C** *Jardín de Orquideas*, 2 blocks from church, follow signs, T2765471, info@mindo-mundo.com, http://mindo-mundo.com Includes breakfast, pricey restaurant, vegetarian meals available, nice atmosphere, beautiful gardens. **C-D** *El Descanso*, 300 m from main street, take first right after bridge, T2765383, www.eldescanso.net Cheaper in loft with shared bath, ample parking, nice house, comfortable and friendly, new in 2001. **D** *Paulin*, on main road at entrance to town, T2765379. Snack bar and bakery, electric shower, nice cabin for up to 6, friendly. **D-E** *Arco Iris*, Quito y 9 de Octubre, on main Plaza, T/F2765445, albertmind@yahoo.com.ar Restaurant downstairs, cheaper with shared bath, simple, clean, OK.

E *El Bijao*, Av Quito, near entrance to town, T2765470. Good restaurant, cheaper with shared bath, hot water, laundry facilities, simple but nice, family run, very friendly, knowledgeable and helpful, good value. Recommended. **E** *Guadual*, Av Quito, near entrance to town, T2765382. Shared bath, cold water, small simple rooms with mosquito nets, family run. **E** *Saguambi*, by Río Saguambi, 10-min walk from town. Private bath, cold water, simple cabins with porch. **E-F** *Casa de Cecilia*, 2 blocks from Plaza, T2765453, casadececilia@gmx.net Cheap meals available, shared bath, hot water, internet, US$2 for use of kitchen, cheaper in dorm with matresses on floor, pleasant atmosphere, popular with volunter groups, very friendly. Recommended. **F** *Familia Pérez*, by Río Saguambi, 10-min walk from town. Shared bath, cold water, very basic rooms in private home. **F** *Flor del Valle*, on lane beside church. Shared bath, hot water, good value, basic.

Eating The lodges outside town have good restaurants, *Mindo Garden* fires a pizza oven in the evenings. In town most restaurants are along Av Quito, the main street. *Arco Iris*, at the park, set lunches, very cheap. *Armonía*, by the hotel and orchid garden, vegetarian set lunch and mid-range prices for à la carte. *El Bijao*, at the hotel, very good set lunches and à la carte, also brekfast, cheap. *Bambú*, by the main park, very cheap set lunches, cheap pizza and à la carte. *El Chef*, very good set meals and à la carte, meat specialties, cheap. *San Francisco*, à la carte, OK, cheap.

Festivals   May 18 is Mindo's fiesta and **Sep 6** is the festival in honour of la Virgen del Cisne. During the weekends closest to these dates there are sporting events, regattas, masses and partying.

Shopping   *Productos Lácteos Guerrero*, on the main park, sell very good dairy products and special jams made from regional fruits.

Transport   From **Quito**, *Cooperativa Flor del Valle* (Cayambe), M Larrea y Asunción (not from the Terminal Terrestre), T2527495. Daily at 0800 and 1530, additional service

Sat-Sun at 0900. From Mindo to Quito, daily 0630 and 1400, Sat-Sun also at 1500, US$2, 2½ hrs. The weekend buses fill quickly, buy ahead. *Cooperativa Kennedy* from **Santo Domingo** at 0720, 1140 and 1400, to Santo Domingo at 0700, 1300 and 1700, US$3.50, 3½ hrs. If buses to Quito are booked, try taking a Santo Domingo bound bus as far as the main highway or to **San Miguel de los Bancos** and transfer there. The most direct access from Quito is along the Calcalí-La Concordia road; at Km 79 to the south is the turn-off for Mindo. It is about 8 km down a side road to the town.

Mindo can also be reached on a 3-day walk from the town of Lloa (10 km west of the the southern end of Quito). See Lloa, page 156. **NB** Check about the current level of volcanic activity of Guagua Pichincha before undertaking this trek. Also be careful fording the Río Cristal.

Internet At *El Bijao* and *La Casa de Cecilia*, see Sleeping above, US$3-4 per hr.

Beyond the turn-off for Mindo the main road continues to descend westward to San Miguel de los Bancos, Pedro Vicente Maldonadao and Puerto Quito before joining the main road from Santo Domingo to Esmeraldas at La Independencia. The climate here is subtropical and there are a growing number of tourist developments in the area. There are frequent buses along this route, noted in the San Miguel de los Bancos section below, but serving the other towns as well. Due to the oil pipeline construction, many of the economy hotels in the area were fully booked in late 2002.

Los Bancos, as the locals call it, is a pleasant market town, surrounded by farms. It is perched on a ridge top above the Río Blanco and has a nice climate. A dirt and gravel road goes south from town and then splits into two branches, right to Santo Domingo via Valle Hermoso and left to Alluriquín (see southwest of Quito, below). Just west of town is *Productos Lácteos Guerrero*, good dairy products and jams made of unusual local fruits such as *arashá*.

San Miguel de los Bancos
Phone code: 02
Population: about 3,000
Altitude: 1,060 m

A nice day excursion from Los Bancos is to **Cascada La Sucia**. Take a bus or *ranchera* bound for Alluriquín (Reina de las Mercedes company, a couple daily, get current schedule in town) and get off at the bridge over the Río Blanco, about 15 minutes from Los Bancos. Just after crossing the bridge, turn left on a small dirt road and walk past the hamlet of Río Blanco (no services) for 2 km, through pleasant country filled with butterflies and birds. At the end of the road, turn left and descend to ford a small river, a tributary of the Blanco. Just upstream is a lovely cascade which spills into a great swimming hole. Remember to leave enough time to catch a vehicle back to Los Bancos. The last one goes by the bridge at about 1730, but enquire ahead. Otherwise it is a 5-km walk uphill from the bridge to town. Take water and sun protection, it gets quite warm.

Sleeping and eating **D-E** *Rancho Ilusión*, 2 km west of town at Km 97, T09-9589320 (mob), in pleasant country setting, with bath, hot water, restaurant with German specialties; good value. **D** *La Trainera*, on the main street, T2770278, **E** with shared bath, hot water. **F** *Pensión San Miguel*, on the main street, T2770232, shared bath, cold water, newer rooms with bath in back, very basic, firendly. *Il Grillo*, on the main street, set lunch and à la carte, pizza, cheap. *El Remanso del Valle*, just west of town, roadside eatery, mid-range prices for à la carte.

Transport Frequent service passing through from/to **Quito**, US$1.90, 2½ hrs. To **Santo Domingo**, frequent along the main road, 2 daily via Valle Hermoso, US$2.50, 3 hrs. To **Alluriquín**, 4 daily on the secondary road. To **Mindo**, 3 daily, US$0.80, ½ hr.

Quito

Buses bound for Esmeraldas pass through here or take a Santo Domingo bus and transfer at La Independencia.

Pedro Vicente
Maldonado
Phone code: 02
Population:
about 3,900
Altitude: 610 m

Pedro Vicente Maldonado is a small supply town in a subtropical cattle ranching area. A secondary road goes from here northwest to the Río Guayllabamba. The main road bypasses town to the south. About 8 km west of PV Maldonado along the main road, is Finca San Carlos. Within the farm is **Laguna Azul**, a lovely pool at the base of a striking 35-m waterfall on the Río Negro. ■ *Finca San Carlos, Km 144 (124 on old sign), T2765346, US$1, 15-min walk, local children will show you the way and expect a tip.*

Sleeping and eating **LL** *Arasha*, 4 km west of PV Maldonado, at Km 141, T2765347, arasharv@interactive.net.ec   Resort and spa, with pools, waterfalls (artificial and natural), jaccuzzi and hiking trails, world class chef and kitchen (meals not included in price of accommodation), tours. Elegant and very upmarket. Quito office T2253937, F2260992. **C** *Posada el Horizonte*, 1.5 km east of PV Maldonado, T2252412, T09-9702350 (mob). Tastefully decorated cabins on a working ranch, some with kitchen and fridge, restaurant, pool, horse-riding, excursions. **E** *Sander*, on the main street, T2392206, with bath, cold water, **F** with shared bath, basic. **F** *El Principe*, on the main street, T2392210, with bath, cold water, basic, restaurant with good very cheap set meals.

Accessed from PV Maldonado is **A** *Reserva Río Guaycuyacu*, an exotic fruit farm with 400 varieties of fruit and birdwatching. Includes 3 hearty vegetarian meals a day, maximum 8 guests. One-month agricultural apprenticeships can be arranged. From PV Maldonado take a *ranchera* to Cielo Verde (0600, 1300 and 1600, returning 2 hrs later, US$2, 2 hrs), from where it is a 30-min hike. Booking essential, write to: Galápagos 565, Quito, guaycuyacu@yahoo.com

Puerto Quito
Phone code: 02
Population:
about 2,300
Altitude: 400 m

On the shores of the lovely Río Caoni is Puerto Quito, a small town which was once intended to be the capital's port. The main road bypasses the centre of town to the south. Along the Caoni and other rivers in the region are several reserves and resorts. This is a good area for birdwatching, swimming in rivers and natural pools, walking, kayaking, or simply relaxing in pleasant natural surroundings.

Sleeping and eating **D** *Grand Hotel Puerto Quito*, along the highway bypass, T09-970 6337 (mob), with bath, hot water, restaurant, pool, sauna, nice views of the river, rafting trips, new in 2001. Good value. **E** *Bambú*, on the main street, T2765251, with bath, some rooms with fan, restaurant, parking. **F** *Las Palmas*, on the main street, T2765260, shared bath, basic, restaurant. There are several simple comedores along the main street.

Lodges and reserves About 2 km east of Puerto Quito, is **C** *Hostería Loro Verde*, T2765239. Cabins for 6 on the shores of the Caoni, pool, horses, the restaurant is at the roadside, the cabins 500 m from there along a small dirt road. Run down and overpriced.

About 2½ km east of Puerto Quito, a dirt road goes southeast, 650 m along it is **A** *Aldea Salamandra*, T2561146 (ext 294) (Quito), aldeasalamandra@yahoo.com   A 5-ha forest reserve with simple bamboo and thatch cabins, in a lovely setting by the river. Price includes all meals and excursions, just accomodations in **D** range. Some cabins with private bath, cold water, mosquito nets, some have balconies with hammocks, one nice tree house directly over the river, nice open-air dining area. About 1½ km past Aldea Salamandra, along the same road is **A** *La Isla*, T2765281, T2463641 (Quito).

On an island between the Caoni and Achiote rivers, a variety of cabins from simple tree-houses to more comfortable cottages, with bath, cold water, price includes meals and excursions, just accommodations in **B** range, pool, rafting and kayaking, horse riding, ample grounds.

About 6 km east of Puerto Quito, a dirt road goes southeast towards Paraíso Alto, 4 km from the turnroff is the small village of Caoni. Across a pedestrian bridge from Caoni is **L** *Kaony Lodge,* T09-9739262 (mob), T2544892 (Quito), info@kaonylodge.com Comfortable bamboo and thatch cabins with fan, hot water, pool, horses (extra charge). Price includes 4 meals (lunch to lunch on second day) and excursions, accommodations and breakfast only in the **A** range. Nice grounds along the Río Caoni.

About 7 km south of Puerto Quito, along the main road to La Independencia, is the village of Puerto Rico. Here a dirt road goes southeast. About 6 km from the turn-off is **AL** *Shishink,* T2245128 (Quito), www.cascadazul.com A resort with thatched cabins with bath and hot water. Price includes meals and excursions, there is also an option to stay in tents. A day visit, including lunch costs US$30 per person. There are waterfalls, natural pools, caves and opportunities for outdoor activities.

The Calacalí road meets the Santo Domingo-Esmeraldas road 28 km southwest of Puerto Quito. Just south of the junction, on the way to Santo Domingo, is the village of **La Independencia** and 5 km further south the town of **La Concordia**, see Santo Domingo to the coast, page 307. Some 22 km from Puerto Quito and 6 km east of the junction of the Calacalí road with the Santo Domingo-Esmeraldas road is **A** *Cabañas Don Gaucho,* T/F2330315 (Quito), www.ecuador-sommerfern.com Comfortable, well furnished rooms with bath and hot water, fan, balcony, includes breakfast, restaurant specializing in Argentinian *parrilladas,* nice grounds on the shores of the Río Salazar. Tours to tropical forest, fruit plantations, Colorado Indians.

Southwest of Quito

Just south of Quito are two other roads to the western lowlands, the **Chiriboga road** and the main **Alóag-Santo Domingo road**. The Chiriboga road is complicated to find; go to Quito's southern neighbourhood of Chillogallo and then on to San Juan de Chillogallo. There is irregular bus service on the first half of the Chiriboga road, but it is often muddy and difficult, especially November to April when a four-wheel drive is needed. See Quito to Santo Domingo, page 304, for a description of the Santo Domingo road.

Guajalito is a rustic lodge on the the Chiriboga road. It is surrounded by a very large forest reserve, with a wide variety of birds. This would be a good base for birdwatching along the road and for getting inside the forest, which is normally impossible elsewhere because of steepness or deforestation. Accessible by bus from Chillogallo. Price is in our **B** range, meals included. Reservations are required, T2600531, vlastimilz@mail.usfq.edu.ec

Otonga is an extensive private reserve near **Las Pampas**, south of the Alóag-Santo Domingo road. There is a basic shelter about two hours' walk from the end of the side road which branches off the Santo Domingo road at **Union de Toachi**. Much of the forest is virgin and rich in unusual orchids, gesneriads, and birds. Bring a sleeping bag and flashlight. Price **D** includes basic food. Contact the Tapias or Dr Onore in Quito, T2567550.

La Hesperia is an old hacienda with new facilities for ecotourism. Some of the hacienda is still used for farming and raising cattle, but most of it has been

Nature reserves

kept in forest. There are many birds (such as Cock-of-the-rock) and even some monkeys. Most of the forest is at around 1,500-2,000 m, with a mild pleasant climate. Access is from the Aloag-Santo Domingo road 8 km past **Tandapi**. Prices in our **L** range. Reservations required, contact Juan Pablo Játiva, Quito, T2241877, T09-9227509 (mob).

Tinalandia, near Santo Domingo, is one of the best places to see many species of birds with minimal effort. Complete details are given under Santo Domingo de los Colorados, page 304.

East of Quito

To the east of Quito lie a series of valleys which are gradually being developed into suburbs. The rate of population growth in this area between 1990 and 2001 was 3.8%, among the highest in the country. **Ilaló**, an extinct volcano, with some planted forests and walking trails, divides this area into two sections. To the south is the Valle de los Chillos. To the north the valleys Cumbayá, Cunuyacu, Tumbaco, Puembo and Pifo; these are joined by the Vía Interoceánica, the road leading east from Quito to Papallacta, Baeza and the northern Oriente.

Valle de los Chillos The Valle de los Chillos lies southeast of the centre of Quito. Once the city's market garden, it still holds a few undeveloped spots which are favourites for weekend recreation among Quiteños. There are a few options for accommodation here, a good choice for those who prefer a slightly milder climate and tranquillity. The main access artery is the Autopista General Rumiñahui, which starts at El Tébol, east of the Terminal Terrestre. Transport to all destinations in this area leaves from La Marín in Quito, US$0.35.

Sangolquí
Phone code:02
Population: 57,000
Altitude: 2,500

Sangolquí is the largest city in the Valle de los Chillos, it has a pleasant park and a nice church. There is a busy Sunday market (and a smaller one on Thursday) and few tourists. On two traffic circles east of town are tile sculptures by the well known 20th-century artist Gonzalo Endara Crow: an ear of corn, the main crop of the valley, and a hummingbird.

Sleeping and eating AL *La Carriona*, Km 2½ via Sangolqui-Amaguaña, T2331974, lacarriona@accessinter.net In a beautiful colonial hacienda, some rooms in the old hacienda house, others in more modern section but in the same style, includes breakfast, with pool, spa, includes horse riding. **AL** *Hostería Sommergarten*, Chimborazo

248 y Riofrío, Urbanización Santa Rosa, T2330315, F2332761, www.ecuador-sommerfern.com Comfortable bungalows in nicely kept grounds, price includes breakfast, restaurant, pool, sauna, tours and transport available. Along the Sangolquí-Amaguaña road are a number of *paradores*, roadside restaurants, serving typical Ecuadorean food, some only open at weekends when they are all busy. *Los Tres Guabos*, with 2 restaurants, 1 open daily, is recommended. The local Sangolquí specialty is *hornado*, baked pork served with *llapingachos* (potato patties).

Northeast of Sangolquí, also in the valley of Los Chillos, are the thermal pools of **El Tingo** and **La Merced**. These thermal pools are among the easiest to get to, and are both within 30-40 minutes of Quito. There are numerous complexes all with comfortably warm water for swimming, entry fee US$0.60. Both are extremely crowded at the weekend. At El Tingo, there is excellent food and a good atmosphere at the German-owned *Mucki's Garden* restaurant, T2320789. About 4 km past La Merced is **Ilaló**, privately owned pools, admission US$2. These are cleaner, with fewer mosquitoes and people, but also best on weekdays. Take a 'La Merced' bus from La Marín. They leave about every 30 minutes throughout the day. **El Tingo & La Merced hot springs**

From **Alangasí**, along the road to La Merced, a good paved road branches 10 km southeast to **Píntag**, which can also be reached from Sangolquí. The road then turns to rough gravel and divides, the right fork goes to the base of Sincholagua (4,899 m), the left fork goes to Laguna La Mica at the base of the snow-covered volcano Antisana (5,704 m). This magnificent area for hiking and camping, where condors may be seen, is part of **Reserva Ecológica Antisana**. There are no services, so visitors must be self-sufficient. Access requires passing through the private *Hacienda Antisana*, a permit from the landowner is required (US$10); enquire beforehand in Píntag, Sr José Delgado, T2435828. See also Trek of the Condor below.

Towards the south end of Valle de Los Chillos is the **Refugio de Vida Silvestre Pasochoa** (formerly known as Bosque Protector Pasochoa), 45 minutes southeast of Quito by car. This park preserves a remnant of native mountain forest. The reserve, situated between 2,700 m and 4,200 m, is classified as humid Andean forest. It has more than 120 species of birds (unfortunately some of the fauna has been frightened away by the noise of the visitors) and 50 species of trees. This is a good place for a family picnic or an acclimatization hike close to Quito. There are walks between 30 minutes and eight hours. ■ *Run by Fundación Natura, República 481 y Almagro, T2503391. US$7, it can be touristy at weekends. Shelter US$3 per person, has cooking facilities and hot shower, take sleeping bag, it gets very cold. Camping US$0.75 per person. There are no shops, take food and water.* **Pasochoa**

Transport From Quito buses run from La Marín to Amaguaña, US$0.35 – ask the driver to let you off at the 'Ejido de Amaguaña'. From there follow the signs for Pasochoa. It's an 8-km walk, with not much traffic for hitching, except at weekends. By car, take the highway to Los Chillos; at San Rafael (second traffic light) continue straight on towards Sangolquí and on to Amaguaña. About 1½ km past Amaguaña turn left onto a cobblestone road and follow the signs to Pasochoa. Tours from Quito cost US$40 per person. Since the road from Amaguaña to the reserve is poor, Quito taxis do not like to go there; you can hire one to Amaguaña (US$20) and take a pick-up from there. A pick-up truck from Amaguaña is about US$6 for up to 3 people. There is a Bell South public phone at the information centre, take a debit card so you can request a pick-up on the way out, Cooperativa Pacheco Jr in Amaguaña, T2877047.

Tumbaco &
surroundings
Phone code: 02

Like los Chillos, the valleys north of Ilaló have suburban developments and also recreational opportunities. Tumbaco is the main town in this area. The main access to this area, the Vía Interoceánica, starts at the partidero a Tumbaco, where Avenida 6 de Diciembre and Avenida Almagro come together, however the initial segment was closed for reconstruction in 2002. An alternate access is along Avenida de los Granados further north. Buses to this area leave from the partidero a Tumbaco, San Martín stop on the Ecovía. Buses to Oriente leave from the Terminal Terrestre. **Cumbayá**, in the first valley east of Quito, has a number of good restaurant options, generally concentrated around the Cumbayá suburban shopping centre.

Sleeping and eating L *Cuevas de Alvaro*, 10 km east of Pifo on the way to Papallacta. The price includes 3 meals, excursions and use of horses. All rooms are in caves, built right into the rock. An interesting concept. It is a good spot to see condors at certain times of the year. Advance reservations required, T2547403, F2228902, birdecua@hoy.net

Papallacta
Phone code: 06
Altitude: 3,200 m

Papallacta is a village 64 km east of Quito, along the Vía Interoceánica, the road to Oriente. It is on the eastern slopes of the range, an attractive area where you leave the *páramo* for more humid cloud forests. The region has wonderful thermal baths and offers good walking within the **Reserva Ecológica Cayambe-Coca**. The once popular **Trek of the Condor** is no longer feasible because land owners along the route do not permit trespassing.

The **Termas de Papallacta** are the most attractively developed set of hot springs in Ecuador. The hot water is channelled into three pools large enough for swimming, three smaller shallow pools and two tiny family-size pools. There is also a steam room, hot showers and two cold plunge pools as well as access to the river. The baths are crowded at weekends but usually quiet through the week. The view, on a clear day, of Antisana from the Papallacta road or while enjoying the thermal waters is superb. The Termas de Papallacta complex includes an extension of land following the Río Papallacta upstream from the baths to forested areas. There are well maintained trails, entry US$1. Access to the complex is along a secondary road branching off the Via Interoceánica, 1 km west of Papallacta. It is 1 km uphill from the turn-off to the complex. ■ *0700-2100, US$5, children under 12 half price.*

There are additional pools at the *Hotel Termas de Papallacta* and in the other hotels on the road to the Termas, all for exclusive use of their guests. More springs in this area provide the village of Papallacta with abundant hot water and fill three simple but clean pools at the **Balneario Municipal**, below the village towards the river. ■ *US$2, children and seniors US$1.*

The **Fundación Ecológica Rumicocha** has a small office on the main street in the village, run by Sra Mariana Liguia, who is friendly. There are leaflets on the Cayambe-Coca reserve. ■ *0800-1200, 1400-1600.*

Sleeping and eating **Within the Termas complex**: 6 cabins each holding up to 6 people, US$115 per cabin. A good but expensive restaurant serves trout and other dishes. Reservations T320621 or in Quito T2504787, www.papallacta.com.ec Across the road from the main pools is **AL** *Hotel Resort Termas de Papallacta*, also part of the Termas complex. Comfortable rooms for 2-4, heated with thermal water, some rooms for 2 have a private jacuzzi, indoor and outdoor pools, good expensive restaurant. Reservations at same numbers as above.

Along the access road to the Termas: **D** *La Choza de Don Wilson*, at the junction of the main road with the road to the Termas, T320627, private bath, hot water, good restaurant with set meals and à la carte, pool, spa, friendly service. **D** *Hostal*

Antisana, shared bath, restaurant, clean, simple, 1 small pool. **D** *Pampas de Papallacta*, T320624, private bath, hot water, sitting room, cheap restaurant with set meals and à la carte, jacuzzi, covered and outdoor pools, helpful. Also several cheap, simple places to eat – trout is the local speciality.

In the village   D *El Arriero*, opposite the Balneario Municipal, T320640, includes breakfast and entry to the municipal baths, with bath, hot water, jacuzzi and steam bath planned. Very helpful, new in 2002. **F** *Residencial El Viajero*, on the main road, very basic, shared bath, restaurant with reasonable meals, avoid the rooms in the old building. **E** *Hotel Quito*, on the main road, with private bath, cheaper without, clean and friendly, popular restaurant. **E** *Saudi*, at the east end of town near the school, T320694, new in 2002. There are also a couple of shops with basic supplies.

Transport   Many buses a day pass Papallacta on their way to and from Lago Agrio, Coca or Tena (drivers sometimes charge full fare). From Quito, 2 hrs, US$1.50. If going to the Termas, ask to be let off at the turn-off to the springs before town; it is then a short 30-min walk up the hill to the complex. Travelling back to Quito at night is not recommended.

East of Papallacta is **L** *Guango Lodge*, including three good meals. Situated in temperate forest, Grey-breasted Mountain-toucans are regularly seen here along with many other birds. Reservations needed, Quito T2547403, F2228902, www.ecuadorexplorer.com/sanisidro

Birding at Guango

South of Quito

South of Quito lies the lush agricultural area of Machachi, with lovely views of the surrounding peaks, the area can be enjoyed on foot or horse. Beyond is Parque Nacional Cotopaxi, a very popular destination, tours are arranged by Quito agencies. Details are found in the Central Highlands chapter.

A tourist train runs from Quito to the Cotopaxi station in **Area Nacional de Recreación El Boliche**, abutting on Parque Nacional Cotopaxi, Saturday and Sunday at 0800, returning at 1430. The ride takes three hours, so it gives you time to walk around and enjoy the views. Dress warmly and take lunch. ■ *US$4.60 return, children under 12 US$2.30. Tickets must be purchased in advance at Bolívar 443 y García Moreno, T258 2927 (Mon 1300-1630, Tue-Fri 0800-1600), you need passport number for all the tickets you purchase and the persons age. Last minute sales at the station are only for boxcars, same price. If you wish to return by bus, it is a 2-km walk from the Cotopaxi station to the Panamericana. The lovely but run down Quito railway station is 2 km south of the Old City, along the continuation of C Maldonado, reached by trolley, Chimbacalle stop if northbound, Machángara if southbound, and walk uphill along Maldonado. El Boliche park entrance fee US$10.*

Train ride to Cotopaxi

Climbing near Quito

Cruz Loma is the low, southern one of the two antenna-topped peaks overlooking Quito from the west (to the north is a peak with loads of antennas, known as Las Antenas). **Rucu Pichincha** (4,627 m) can be seen from some parts of Quito, and can be climbed either via Cruz Loma or via its neighbouring hill to the north. Unfortunately, public safety along all of the above routes is so poor that you are advised not to climb here. A large group does not confer protection.

Cruz Loma & Rucu Pichincha
Unfortunately, both these climbs have severe public safety problems

**Guagua
Pichincha**
*Enquire about
volcanic activity
before climbing*

After almost 350 years of dormancy, Guagua Pichincha renewed its volcanic activity in 1999. The level of activity subsequently diminished, but descent into the crater remains dangerous because of the loose rock and poor trail conditions. Descending to the crater floor is not recommended and, in particular, should never be undertaken during the rainy season. The caretakers at the *refugio* (shelter) can give you first hand up-to-date information concerning conditions. Climbing to the *refugio* and crater rim is currently safe but you should always enquire beforehand, since volcanic activity can change at any time. The National Geophysics Institute provides volcanic activity updates in Spanish at www.epn.edu.ec

To climb Guagua Pichincha volcano (4,794 m), go to the town of **Lloa**, from where a four by four track goes almost to the *refugio* at the rim of the crater, just below the summit at 4,800 m. Depending on road conditions you might be able to get a pick-up from Lloa to the *refugio*. If walking you will need all day to make it up to the *refugio*. Set off early.

Lloa is a small, friendly village set in beautiful surroundings. The road to the summit is signposted from the right-hand corner of the main plaza as you face the volcano, and is easy to follow. There are a couple of forks, but head straight for the peak each time. It can take up to eight hours to reach the *refugio*, allowing for a long lunch break and plenty of rests. The *refugio*, which is maintained by the Defensa Civil, is manned and will provide a bed and water for US$5 per person. The warden has his own cooking facilities which he may share with you. It gets very cold at night and there is no heating or blankets. Be sure to keep an eye on your things. Entry to the *refugio* on a day visit is US$1.

The walk from the *refugio* to the summit is very short. You can scramble a bit further to the 'real' summit (above the *refugio*) which is tricky but worth it for the views; many other volcanoes can be seen on a clear morning.

The descent back to Lloa takes only three hours, but is hard on the legs. There is a restaurant in Lloa, on the main road to Quito, which sells good soup. The last bus for Quito leaves Lloa around 1830, or walk a few hundred metres down the main road until you reach a fork. Wait here for a truck, which will take you to the outskirts of the city for around US$1. A taxi from the southern outskirts to the New City costs around US$5.

Transport to Lloa A school bus makes 4-5 trips a day, back and forth between Lloa and Quito, starting at 0600 in Lloa. The first one leaves Quito around 0700, the last one returns from Lloa about 1830, US$0.35, 30 mins. This bus goes from C Angamarca, at the entrance of the neighbourhood called Mena 2 in southwestern Quito. To get there, take an *alimentador* bus from El Recreo stop on the Trole, or any Chillogallo bound bus, one goes along 12 de Octubre in the New City. Ask to be let off at El Triángulo, the intersection of Av Mariscal Sucre and the road to Lloa. Walk 1 block west (up) to where the Lloa bus stops. It might also be possible to catch a lift on a truck (dump trucks go to a mine near Lloa on weekdays). A taxi to Lloa costs around US$15.

Northern Highlands

Introducing the Northern Highlands

North from Quito to the border with Colombia is an area of great natural beauty and cultural interest. The landscape is mountainous, with views of Cotacachi, Imbabura, Chiles and glacier-covered Cayambe, interspersed with lakes. This is also a region renowned for its *artesanía*. Countless villages specialize in their own particular craft, be it textiles, hats, woodcarvings, bread figures or leather goods. And, of course, there is Otavalo, with its outstanding Saturday market, a must on everyone's itinerary.

The Panamericana, fully paved, runs northeast from Quito to Otavalo (94 km), Ibarra (114 km), and Tulcán (240 km), from where it continues to Ipiales in Colombia. Secondary roads go west from all these cities, and descend to subtropical lowlands. From Ibarra a paved road runs northwest all the way to the Pacific port of San Lorenzo. To the east is the impressive snow capped cone of Cayambe (5790 m), part of the Reserva Ecológica Cayambe-Coca.

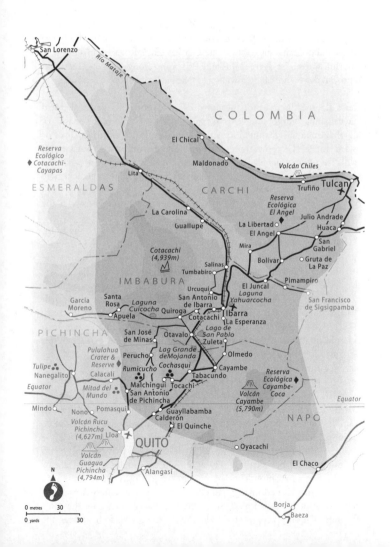

Things to do in the Northern Highlands

· Take in **Otavalo market** with all five senses, page 166.
· Enjoy a boat ride on **Cuicocha crater lake**, page 175.
· Admire the pre-Inca pyramids of **Cochasquí**, page 160.
· Savour an *helado de paila* (sorbet) in Ibarra, page 180.
· See the *frailejones* at **Reserva Ecológica El Angel**, page 184.
· Visit **Tulcán cemetery**, 'so beautiful it invites one to die', page 188.

Quito to Cayambe

Calderón
Colour map 2, grid B5

Some 32 km north of Quito's centre, and 5 km from the periphery, Calderón is the place where figurines are made of bread dough and glue. You can see them being made, though not on Sunday, and prices are lower than in Quito. Especially attractive is the Nativity collection. Prices range from about US$0.50 to US$8. The figures can be seen in the cemetery on 1-2 November, when the graves are decorated with flowers, drinks and food for the dead. (See also Arts and Crafts, page 443.) The Corpus Christi processions are very colourful. Many buses leave from Santa Prisca and along Avenida América in Quito, but drivers are often unwilling to take backpackers at rush hour.

Guayllabamba
Colour map 2, grid B5

After Calderón the road for the north descends into the spectacular arid Guayllabamba gorge and climbs out again to the fertile oasis of **Guayllabamba** village, noted for its avocados and delicious *chirimoyas* or custard apples (**D** *Hostería Guayllabamba*, cabins on eastern outskirts of town). The Quito municipal zoo is located in Guayllabamba (worthwhile, see page 143). The area is also a popular destination for Quiteños, who flock here on weekends to eat *comida típica*, especially *locro de papas*, in a number of good *paradores*. Along the road to Cayambe, 2 km north of town is the **Bosque de Bromelias**, a small protected area.

At Guayllabamba, the highway splits into two branches. To the right, the Panamericana runs northeast to Cayambe. The left branch goes towards the town of **Tabacundo**, from where you can rejoin the Pamamericana travelling east to Cayambe or northeast to Cajas. Many buses take the latter route, which is faster. There is an access road from Tabacundo to the **Lagunas de Mojanda**, see page 174. About 4 km north of Tabacundo by the village of Tupigachi is **AL** *Hostería San Luís*, T02-2360464, F2360103, haciendahosteriasanluis@andinanet.net In a hacienda, all rooms with large fireplaces, good restaurant, price includes breakfast, use of horses, mountain bikes, fishing, pool, spa, games room. There are great views of Cayambe.

Tolas de Cochasquí archaeological site

About 10 km past Guayllabamba on the road to Tabacundo and 8 km before Tabacundo, just south of the toll booth, a cobbled road to the left (signed Pirámides de Cochasqui) leads to **Tocachi** and further on to the Tolas de Cochasquí archaeological site, administered by the Consejo Provincial de Pichincha. The protected area contains 15 truncated clay pyramids, nine with long ramps, built between AD 900 and 1500 by Indians of the Cara or Cayambi-Caranqui nation. The pyramids are covered by earth and grass but a few have been excavated, giving a good idea of their construction. Among the many pre-Inca mounds found in northern Ecuador, these are the most ellaborate. The site is considered by many archaeologists to have been the ceremonial center of a large cultural area extending from Quito to north of Ibarra in the centuries immediately preceding the Inca conquest. Festivals take place with dancing at the equinoxes and solstices. There is a site museum with interesting historical explanations in Spanish. The views from the pyramids, south to Quito, are marvellous. ■ *0830-1630. US$3. Visits to the pyramids are guided. Take a bus that goes on the Tabacundo road and ask to be let off at the turn-off. From there it's a pleasant 8-km walk through an agricultural landscape. If you arrive at the sign around 0800, you could get a lift from the site workers. A taxi or pick-up from Cayambe costs US$10.*

Two-day horse-riding tours from Cayambe to Cochasquí are offered by Shungu Huasi (see Cayambe below). It is an interesting ride, crossing lovely scenery and a couple of microclimates from the lush green plains of Cayambe to the bleak hills of Cochasquí. ■ *US$124, includes guide, 2 nights accommodation and meals.*

Sleeping and eating C *Centro Turístico Quilango*, opposite the Cochasquí site, T02-2237842, F2520852 (Quito). Includes breakfast, **A** with half board, simple cabins with electric shower, restaurant, camping US$6 per tent, local crafts shop, tours of Cochasquí and vicinity, new in 2002.

El Quinche
Colour map 2, grid B5

About 6 km southeast of Guayllabamba, along the road to Pifo, is the small village of El Quinche, where there is a huge sanctuary to Nuestra Señora del Quinche in the plaza. It has nice stained-glass windows, a lovely carved wooden entrance and a very large gold altar. The image was the work of the sculptor Diego Robles around 1600 in Oyacachi. It was brought to El Quinche because the local Indians did not wish to worship the image. There are processions on 21 November in El Quinche. There are many paintings illustrating miracles, ask the caretaker for the details. There is a bus service from Guayllabamba and direct buses from Quito via Cumbayá and Pifo. There are several restaurants and simple places to stay, including **D** *El Puchito*, by the main park, T02-2387227, with bath and hot water, restaurant.

Near el Quinche, on a hill called Pambamarca, with magnificent views to Quito and, on a clear day, even as far as the coastal plain, is the fortress of **Quitoloma**. This is one of the largest pre-Columbian fortresses of the new world, with two concentric walls and ditches, one of numerous fortresses in this area. Some of these may have been originally built by the Cayambe and Caranqui inhabitants, but most were built (or at least rebuilt and reoccupied) by the Incas. These are not public sites, they belong to the communities. To visit them, ask for instructions and permission in nearby villages.

Cayambe

Cayambe, on the eastern (righthand) branch of the Panamericana, 25 km northeast of Guayllabamba, is dominated by the snow capped volcano of the same name. The surrounding countryside consists of a few remaining dairy farms and a great many flower plantations. Roses and carnations are grown for export and have turned Cayambe into a boom town. As a result rural property values have soared and the indiscriminate use of agro-chemicals is doing great damage. The area is noted for its *bizcochos*, which are small shortbread-type biscuits served with *queso de hoja*, tasty string cheese. Market day is Sunday, along Calle Rocafuerte. There is a fiesta in March for the equinox with plenty of local music. Inti Raymi during the summer solstice blends into the San Pedro celebrations around 29 June.

Phone code: 02
Colour map 2, grid B5
Population: 30,450
Altitude: 2,850 m

On the edge of town are the pyramids of Puntiachil, an important but poorly preserved archaeologic site of the Cayambe culture in the late pre-Inca era. There are several large mounds and a large occupation area. Studies suggest it probably was a political and ceremonial centre. ■ *Entrance at Olmedo 702, US$1 includes guided tour in Spanish, there is also a small private museum.*

There are excellent horse-riding tours with *Shungu Huasi* (see Sleeping below), US$40 per day, including guide. Of particular interest is a two-day tour to Cochasquí (see page 160), US$124 including two nights accommodation and all meals.

Sleeping

Hotels may be full on Fri during Jun-Sep and during the week before Valentine's Day (high season at the flower plantations)

A *Jatun Huasi*, Panamericana Norte Km 1½, T2363775, F2363832, jatunhuasi@ hotmail.com Includes breakfast, restaurant, indoor pool, parking, north American motel style, rooms with fireplace and frigo-bar, new in 2001. B *Hacienda Guachala*, south of Cayambe on the road to Cangahua, T2363042, F2362426, guachala@ uio.satnet.net Spring-fed swimming pool, parking, a beautifully restored hacienda (dating to 1580), basic but comfortable rooms with fireplaces, delicious food, good walking, horses for rent, excursions to nearby pre-Inca ruins. Highly recommended. C *Shungu Huasi*, 1 km northwest of town, T/F2361847, shungu@hoy.net Excellent Italian restaurant, parking, comfortable and friendly, nice setting, offers horse-riding excursions. Recommended.

D *Cabañas de Nápoles*, Panamericana Norte Km 1, T2360366. Good restaurant, laundry facilities, parking, OK cabins near highway. D *Gran Colombia*, Panamericana y Calderón, T2361238, F2362421. Restaurant, parking, OK, modern but noisy. E *Crystal*, 9 de Octubre 215 y Terán, T2361460. Cheaper with shared bath, hot water, simple, small rooms, new in 2002. E *Mitad del Mundo*, Panamericana a little south of town, T2360226. Restaurant, cheaper with shared bath, pool (open weekends), laundry facilities, parking, good value.

Eating

There are a number of roadside cafés along the Panamericana serving the local specialty, bizcochos y queso de hoja (biscuits and string cheese)

Mid-range *Bon Bini*, on the Panamericana, just north of the Shell station, T2360272, international food, upscale. *Casa de Fernando*, Panamericana Norte Km 1½. Varied menu, good. *El Molino*, Panamericana Norte, Km 3. Excellent breakfasts, French cuisine, cosy atmosphere. Open for lunch and early dinner. *Shungu Huasi*, at the hotel, excellent authentic Italian cuisine in very pleasant surroundings, also serves breakfast, good service. Recommended. 0830-2200, closed Tue. **Cheap** *Aroma Cafetería*, Bolívar 404 y Ascázubi. Large choice of set lunches and à la carte, variety of desserts, very good. Recommended. Open until 2100, Sun until 1800, closed Wed. **Seriously cheap** *La Casa Vieja*, Ascázubi 908 y Sucre, good local snacks such as humitas and quimbolitos, fruit juices, breakfasts, set lunches.

Transport

Direct **bus** with *Flor del Valle*, leaves from M Larrea y Asunción in **Quito**, every 10 mins, 0500-1900, US$1, 1½ hrs. Cayambe station is at Montalvo y Junín. Some Quito-Otavalo buses stop in Cayambe. They depart every few minutes from the Terminal Terrestre in Quito. To **Otavalo**, from traffic circle at the corner of Bolívar and Av Natalia Jarrín, US$0.60, 40 mins. To **Olmedo**, buses from corner Restauración y Vivar, every 30 mins, 0630-1830, US$0.40, 45 mins. To **Ibarra**, transfer in Otavalo, frequent service, or Olmedo-Ibarra at 0700 and 1230 only. To **Tabacundo**, from Libertad y Av Natalia Jarrín, every 5 mins, US$0.17, 20 mins.

Directory

Banks *Banco del Pacífico*, Junín y Panamericana, TCs. **Communications** Internet: *Caffé.Net*, Bolívar 404 y Ascázubi, US$1 per hr. **Post**: Rocafuerte y Sucre, 2nd floor of Centro Comercial. **Telephone**: *Andinatel*, Sucre y Rocafuerte.

Reserva Ecológica Cayambe-Coca

Cayambe is a good place to access the western side of the Reserva Ecológica *Colour map 2, grid B5* Cayambe-Coca which spans the Cordillera Oriental and extends down to the eastern lowlands. Park entry US$10.

At 5,790 m, Cayambe is Ecuador's third-highest peak. About 1 km south of **Cayambe** Cayambe is an unmarked cobbled road heading east via Juan Montalvo, lead- **Volcano** ing in 26 km to the Ruales-Oleas-Berge refuge at about 4,800 m. The *refugio* *The highest point in* costs US$17 per person per night; it can sleep 37 people in bunks, but bring a *the world which lies directly on the Equator* sleeping bag, as it is very cold. There is a kitchen, fireplace, and eating area with tables and benches, running water, electric light and a radio for rescue. It is named after three Ecuadorean climbers killed by an avalanche in 1974 while pioneering a new route up from the west.

This is now the standard route, using the refuge as a base. The route heads off to the left of a rocky outcrop immediately above the *refugio*. To the right of the outcrop is an excellent area of crevasses, seracs and low rock and ice walls for practising technical skills. The climb is heavily crevassed, especially near the summit, there is an avalanche risk near the summit and southeasterly winds are a problem. It is more difficult and dangerous than either Chimborazo or Cotopaxi. An alternative route is to the northeast summit (5,570 m), which is the most difficult, with the possible need to bivouac.

Transport How close to the refuge you will be able to get by vehicle depends on the condition of the road at the time and the type of vehicle. Most can go as far as the *Hacienda Piemonte El Hato* (at about 3,500 m) from where it is a 3-4 hr walk, sometimes longer if heavily laden, and the wind can be very strong, but it is a beautiful walk. Regular pick-ups can often make it to 'la Z', a sharp curve on the road from where it is a 30-min walk to the *refugio*. 4WDs can often make it to the *refugio*. Pick-ups can be hired by the market, corner Junín y Ascázubi, US$30, 1½-2 hrs. It is difficult to get transport back to Cayambe. A milk truck runs from Cayambe's hospital to the hacienda at 0600, returning between 1700-1900. An alternative route is via Olmedo (see below), through *Hacienda La Chimba* to Laguna San Marcos. This gives access to the northeast summit.

An adventurous trek takes you from the highlands to the Oriente lowlands in **Oyacachi to** three to four days. Starting in the village of Oyacachi at 3,100 m, it follows the **El Chaco trek** Oyacachi river first along the north bank and later on the southern bank, crossing several tributaries along the way (a pulley may be necessary for these crossings). The walk ends at El Chaco, at 1,550 m, on the western shore of the Quijos river and along the Baeza-Lago Agrio road. The season for this walk is November to February, it is impassable during the rainy season.

Transport Take a truck from Cayambe to Oyacachi via Cangahua, a very scenic route. From El Chaco there is bus service to Quito via Baeza or to Lago Agrio in the northern Oriente.

Cayambe to Otavalo

Two routes can be taken from Cayambe to the north. To the east is a cobbled road, the very scenic *carretera vieja* or old road, which runs to **Olmedo**. There are no hotels or restaurants in Olmedo, but there are a couple of shops and lodging may be available with the local nuns. There is also an Andinatel office, in the old Tenencia Política, on the plaza. The surrounding countryside is pleasant for strolling. A road runs east from Olmedo to the scenic **Laguna San Marcos**, popular with fishermen, 40 minutes by car, three hours on foot. Pick-ups can be hired in Olmedo, US$10. Note that San Marcos is part of a waterworks project and access may be restricted, enquire in Cayambe.

After Olmedo the road is not so good (four-wheel drive vehicles are recommended). It is 9 km from Olmedo to **Zuleta**, where beautiful embroidery is done on napkins and tablecloths. There is a *feria* on Sunday. You can see the beautiful *Hacienda Zuleta* of the former president Galo Plaza, which offers exclusive accommodation. Advance arrangements are required: book through Quito agencies or www.zuleta.com About 15 km beyond Zuleta is La Esperanza (see Excursions from Ibarra, page 181), 8½ km before Ibarra.

To the west, the main paved road heads north from Cayambe and crosses the *páramo* at the Nudo de Cajas, where it meets the Guayllabamba-Tabacundo road and suddenly descends to the basin of Lago San Pablo and beyond to Otavalo.

An **alternative route** from Quito to Otavalo is via San Antonio de Pichincha, past the Inca ruins of Rumicucho (see page 142) and San José de Minas. The road curves through the dry but impressive landscape down to the Río Guayllabamba, then climbs again, passing some picturesque oasis villages. After Minas the road is in very bad condition and a jeep is necessary for the next climb and then descent to join the Otavalo-Selva Alegre road about 15 km west from Otavalo. The journey takes about three hours altogether and is rough, hot and dusty, but the scenery is magnificent. This is a great biking route since there is little traffic. In **San José de Minas** is E *La Carreta*, on the plaza, with hot shower, restaurant, clean. In the valley below, at Cubi there are warm springs. Buses to San José de Minas leave from Asunción y Larrea and from Anteparra y San Blas in Quito.

Otavalo

Phone code: 06
Colour map 2, grid B5
Population: 31,100
Altitude: 2,530 m

Otavalo is set in beautiful countryside which is well worth exploring. The town itself is nothing to write home about, consisting as it does of rather functional modern buildings. There are efforts underway to make this tourist centre more eye-catching, but visitors still don't come here for the architecture. Otavalo is one of South America's most important centres of ethno-tourism and its enormous Saturday market, featuring a dazzling array of textiles and crafts, is second to none. Absolutely not to be missed. It's best to travel on Friday, in order to avoid overcrowded buses on Saturday and to enjoy the nightlife. For those interested in learning more about how local crafts are made, a visit to surrounding villages can be interesting.

Ins & outs
See Transport,
page 171,
for further details

Getting there The bus terminal is at Atahualpa and Ordoñez in the northeast of the city and just off the Panamericana (see map). Through buses going further north drop you at the highway which is not recommended. Near the terminal is a lifelike monument, showing Otavaleños performing a traditional dance. There are few hotels around the bus terminal; walk about 6 blocks into the centre, taxis and city buses are also avalable. There is no longer a train service to Otavalo.

Getting around The centre is bounded by the Río El Tejar to the west and the disused rail tracks in the east. It is quite small and you can walk between the *artesanías* market at Plaza de Ponchos and the produce market at Plaza 24 de Mayo. The livestock market is more of a hike.

The Otavaleños

In a country where the term indio *can still be intended as an insult and a few highland Indians continue to address whites as* patroncito *(little master), the Otavaleños stand out in stark contrast. They are a proud and prosperous people, who have made their name not only as successful weavers and international businessmen, but also as unsurpassed symbols of cultural fortitude. Today, they make up the economic elite of their town and its surroundings.*

There is some considerable debate over the origin of the Otavaleños. In present-day Imbabura, pre-Inca people were Caranquis, or Imbaya, and, in Otavalo, the Cayambi. They were subjugated by the Caras who expanded into the highlands from the Manabí coast. The Caras resisted the Incas for 17 years, but the conquering Incas eventually moved the local population away to replace them with vassals from Peru and Bolivia. One theory is that the Otavaleños are descended from these forced migrants and also Chibcha salt traders from Colombia, while some current-day Otavaleños prefer to stress their local pre-Inca roots.

Otavalo men wear their hair long and plaited under a black trophy hat. They wear white, calf-length trousers and blue ponchos. The women's colourful costumes consist of embroidered blouses, shoulder wraps and a plethora of gold coloured necklace beads. Their ankle-length skirts, known as anacos, *are fastened with an intricately woven cloth belt or* faja. *Traditional footwear for both genders is the* alpargata, *a sandal whose sole was originally made of coiled hemp rope, but today has been replaced by rubber.*

Impeccable cleanliness is another striking aspect of many Otavaleños' attire. Perhaps the most outstanding feature of the Otavaleños, however, is their profound sense of pride and self-assurance. This is aided not only by the group's economic success, but also by achievements in academic and cultural realms. All families speak Quichua as their first tongue and Spanish as their second, although the former is losing ground with some young people. It is ironic perhaps that these fascinating people, whom many tourists come to regard as typical representatives of Ecuador's highland Indians, are in fact so atypical.

Northern Highlands

Tourist office and information *Cámara Provincial de Turismo de Imbabura*, Bolívar 8-14 y Montalvo, Mon-Sat 0900-1200, Mon-Fri 1500-1700, general information about attractions, hotels in Otavalo and region. **Maps**: the IGM produces a detailed tourist map of the province of Imbabura. There is also a handy pocket map from *Ediguias*, with good maps of the province and city maps of Otavalo and Ibarra.

See also www. otavalo-web.com www.otavalosonline .com

Sights

While most visitors come to Otavalo to meet its native people and buy their crafts, you cannot escape the influence of the modern world here, a product of the city's very success in trade and tourism. The streets are lined not only with small kiosks selling homespun wares, but also with wholesale warehouses and international freight forwarders, as well as numerous hotels, cafés and restaurants catering to decidedly foreign tastes.

Otavalo is a generally safe town but beware pickpockets, especiallly in crowded markets

In the Plaza Bolívar is a statue of Rumiñahui, Atahualpa's general. There was outrage among indigenous residents over suggestions that the monument be replaced with a statue of Bolívar himself, symptomatic of the ongoing rivalry between native Otavaleños and their *mestizo* neighbours.

Markers

The artesanías industry is so big that the Plaza de Ponchos is now filled with vendors every day of the week

The Saturday market actually comprises four different markets in various parts of the town and the central streets are filled with vendors. The *artesanías* (crafts) market (0700-1800) is based around the Plaza de Ponchos (officially called Plaza Centenario). The livestock sections begin at 0500 and last until 1000. Large animals are traded outside town in the Viejo Colegio Agrícola, west of the Panamericana. To get there, go west on Calle Colón from the town centre. The small animal market is held either north of the Plaza de Pochos (corner 31 de Octubre y Quito) or on Atahualpa by the bus terminal. The produce market (0700-1400) is in Plaza 24 de Mayo.

Polite bargaining is appropriate in the market and in the shops

The Otavaleños sell goods they weave and sew themselves, as well as *artesanías* from throughout Ecuador, Peru and Bolivia. *Mestizo* and indigenous vendors from Otavalo, and from elsewhere in Ecuador and South America, sell paintings, jewellery, shigras, baskets, leather goods, woodcarvings from San Antonio de Ibarra and the Oriente, ceramics, antiques and almost anything else you care to mention. The *artesanía* market has more selection on Saturday but prices are a little higher than other days when the atmosphere is more relaxed. Indigenous people respond better to photography if you buy something first, then ask politely. Reciprocity and courtesy are important Andean norms.

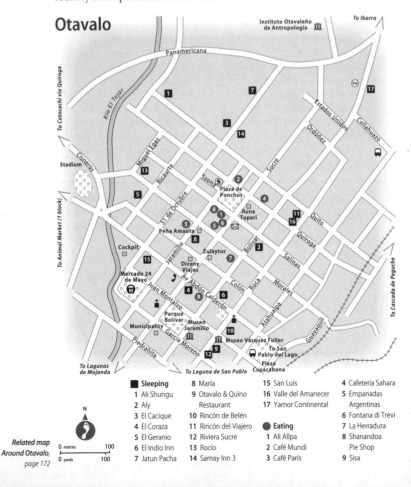

Otavalo

■ **Sleeping**	8 María	15 San Luis	4 Cafetería Sahara
1 Ali Shungu	9 Otavalo & Quino	16 Valle del Amanecer	5 Empanadas
2 Aly	Restaurant	17 Yamor Continental	Argentinas
3 El Cacique	10 Rincón de Belén		6 Fontana di Trevi
4 El Coraza	11 Rincón del Viajero	● **Eating**	7 La Herradura
5 El Geranio	12 Riviera Sucre	1 Ali Allpa	8 Shanandoa
6 El Indio Inn	13 Rocío	2 Café Mundi	Pie Shop
7 Jatun Pacha	14 Samay Inn 3	3 Café París	9 Sisa

Related map
Around Otavalo,
page 172

N

0 metres   100
0 yards   100

Related map Around Otavalo, page 172

Northern Highlands

Instituto Otavaleño de Antropología has a library, an archaeological **Museums** museum with artefacts from the northern highlands, a collection of musical instruments, as well as a good ethnographic display of regional costumes and traditional activities. ■ *Visits by appointment, Mon-Fri 0800-1200, 1430-1830. Free T920321. Av de los Sarances west of the Panamericana Norte.*

Museo Arqueológico César Vásquez Fuller has an excellent collection from all over Ecuador and is recommended. ■ *Mon-Sat 1400-1800. US$1. The owner gives free tours. Roca y Montalvo.*

Museo Victor Alejandro Jaramillo has a small collection of regional ceramic and stone pieces. It was renovated in 1998. Recommended. ■ *Thu-Sat 1000-1300, 1500-1700. Bolívar, off Parque Central.*

Museo de Tejidos El Obraje, shows the process of traditional Otavalo weaving from shearing to final products. Traditional weaving lessons are available. ■ *Mon-Sat 1000-1200, 1500-1700. US$2. T920261. Sucre 608.* There is another weaving museum in Peguche, see Weaving villages, below.

Essentials

■ on map, page 166

A *Ali Shungu*, Quito y Miguel Egas, T920750, www.alishungu.com Good restaurant with live music at weekends, parking, nice rooms, lovely garden, no smoking, safe deposit boxes, US run, no credit cards, small surcharge for TCs. Recommended. **B** *El Indio Inn*, Bolívar 904 y Calderón, T920325. Restaurant, rooms and suites, spotlessly clean, attractive. **B** *Yamor Continental*, Av Paz Ponce de León y Jacinto Collahuazo, near bus terminal, T920451, F920982. Restaurant, pool, parking, pleasant gardens, comfortable.

Sleeping
Price codes: see inside cover Hotels may be full on Fri nights, before market, when prices go up

C *El Coraza*, Calderón y Sucre, T/F921225, coraza@ecuahotel.com Good restaurant, nice rooms, quiet and comfortable. Recommended. **C** *Doña Esther*, Montalvo 4-44 y Roca, T920739, ilderoma@yahoo.com Good pizzeria downstairs, simple rooms in nicely restored colonial house, overpriced. **C** *Hotel Otavalo*, Roca 504 y J Montalvo, T923712, F920416. Good breakfast, pricey restaurant, refurbished colonial house, large rooms, patio, good service, helpful.

D *Cabañas El Rocío*, Barrio San Juan W of Panamericana, near stadium, T920584. Parking, ask at Residencial Rocío. Helpful owners, attractive, gardens, views. **D** *El Indio*, Sucre 1214 y Salinas, near Plaza de Ponchos, T920060. Restaurant, cheaper with shared bath, OK. **D** *Jatun Pacha*, 31 de Octubre 19 entre Quito y Panamericana, T922223, F922871. Includes breakfast, nice, modern, cheaper in dorm, discount for IYHF card holders, bicycle rentals. **D** *Rincón de Belén*, Roca 8-20 y J Montalvo, T/F921860. Grill downstairs, OK, modern. **D** *Samay Inn 1*, Abdón Calderón 10-05 y Sucre, T/F922871. Cooking facilities, older place but OK. **D** *Samay Inn 2*, Colón y Roca, T/F922995. Clean, modern and comfortable. **D** *Valle del Amanecer*, Roca y Quiroga, T920990, F920286. Includes breakfast, good restaurant, internet, small rooms, courtyard, popular and overpriced, mountain bike hire.

D-E *Aly*, Salinas y Bolívar, T921831. Restaurant, nice, modern, new in 2001. **D-E** *Rincón del Viajero*, Roca 11-07 y Quiroga, T921741, rincondelviajero@ hotmail.com Includes breakfast, cheaper with shared bath, laundry facilities, parking, rooftop hammocks, sitting room with fireplace, US run, friendly. Recommended. **D-E** *Riviera Sucre*, García Moreno 380 y Roca, T/F920241. Good breakfasts, cafeteria, cheaper with shared bath, laundry facilities, book exchange, nice garden, friendly, good meeting place.

E *Chukito's*, Bolívar 10-13 y Morales, chukitos@hotmail.com Private bath, hot water, internet, modern, new in 2001. **E** *El Geranio*, Ricaurte y Colón, T920185, hgeranio@hotmail.com Restaurant, cheaper with shared bath, hot water, laundry and cooking facilities, quiet, family run, helpful, popular. Good value, recommended.

E *Kikinpaq*, Sucre 1414 y Quiroga, near Plaza de Ponchos, T922408. Restaurant, private bath, hot water, parking, OK. E *Los Ponchos Inn*, Sucre y Quiroga by Plaza de Ponchos, T/F923575. Restaurant, private bath, hot water, internet, view of plaza. E *María*, Jaramillo y Colón, T/F920672. Private bath, hot water, modern, convenient, cafeteria. Good value. Recommended. E *Samay Inn 3*, 31 de Octubre 901 y Quito, T922438. Private bath, hot water, parking, a bit run down.

E-F *La Cascada*, Sucre 506 y Colón, T920165. Cheaper with shared bath, hot water, basic. E-F *Los Andes*, Sucre y Quiroga by Plaza de Ponchos, T921057. Restaurant, cheaper with shared bath, hot water, internet, modern. E-F *Rocío*, Morales y Egas, T920584. Cheaper with shared bath, hot showers, helpful, popular, good value.

F *Colón*, Colón 7-13, T924245. Cheaper with shared bath, hot water, simple, good. F *El Cacique*, 31 de Octubre y Quito, T921740, F920930. Private bath, hot water, parking, spacious, nice rooftop area. F *La Herradura*, Bolívar 1005 y Colón, T923418. Restaurant, shared bath, hot water, cheap and basic. F *Samac Tarina*, Calderón 713 y 31 de Octubre, T920182. Shared bath, hot water, helpful, basic. F *San Luis*, Abdón Calderón 6-02 y 31 de Octubre, T920614. Shared bath, basic, family run.

■ *on map,*
Around Otavalo,
page 172

Out of town L *Hacienda Pinsaquí*, Panamericana Norte Km 5, 300 m north of the turn-off for Cotacachi, T946116, www.haciendapinsaqui.com Includes breakfast, restaurant, beautiful antiques, lovely dining room, lounge with fireplace, colonial ambience, gardens, horse riding. A *Casa Mojanda*, Vía Mojanda Km 3, T09-9731737 (mob), www.casamojanda.com Includes breakfast, beautiful setting on 10 ha of farmland and forested gorge, organic garden, including all meals, comfortable, quiet, library, horse riding, mountain bikes. Highly recommended. B *La Casa de Hacienda*, entrance at Panamericana Norte Km 3, then 300 m east, T946336, F923105. Includes breakfast, restaurant, parking, tasteful cabins with fireplace, advance resrvations required for horse riding. B *Las Palmeras*, outside Quichinche, 15 mins by bus from Otavalo, T922607, palmeras@cusin.com.ec, www.laspalmerasinn.com Includes breakfast, restaurant, cheaper with shared bath, parking, rural setting, nice grounds, English owned, friendly, new in 2002. B *Troje Cotama*, 4 km north of Otavalo by Carabuela, T/F946119. Restaurant, converted grain house, very attractive, fireplace in rooms, good food, Dutch, English and German spoken, advance reservations required.

C-D *Aya Huma*, on the railway line in Peguche, T922663, F922664, ayahuma@imbanet.net Restaurant, cooking facilities, quiet, pleasant atmosphere, Dutch run, live folk music on Sat. Highly recommended. D *Cabañas de Miriam*, Valle del Tambo 137, Vía a Mojanda, take city bus for Punyaro, T920421. Laundry and cooking facilities, simple furnished cabins, meals available, caters to longer stays. D *La Luna de Mojanda*, Vía Mojanda Km 2, T/F09-9737415. Restaurant, run by young Argentine couple, organize cheap 4WD tours, games room and library, taxi service to Otavalo, English/German spoken, good restaurant. Recommended. **D** *Peguche Tío*, near centre of the village of Peguche, T/F922619. Includes breakfast, restaurant, internet, nice lounge with fireplace, decorated with works of art, interesting museum, sports fields, caters to groups.

Ecuadorean Cheap *El Indio*, Sucre y Salinas. Good fried chicken (weekends especially) and steaks, local speciality *fritada* (fried pork). *Mi Otavalito*, Sucre y Morales. Good for lunch also international food à la carte. *La Herradura*, Bolívar 10-05. Good set meal and à la carte, outdoor tables. *Cafetería Camba Huasi*, Bolívar y J Montalvo. Self service, varied food, good coffee. *Aly Micuy*, at Aly Hostal, Salinas y Bolívar. Set meals and à la carte, vegetarian dishes available.

Eating
● *on map, page 166*
All of the following restaurants are cheap unless indicated otherwise

    French Expensive *Café París*, Modesto Jaramillo 5-69 y Morales. Excellent authentic French cooking.

    International Mid-range *Ali Shungu*, at the hotel (see above) serves all meals, wide variety including vegetarian. Recommended. 0700-2100. **Cheap** *Ali Allpa*, Salinas 509 at Plaza de Ponchos. Good value set meals and à la carte, trout, vegetarian, meat. Recommended. *Café Mundi*, Quiroga 608 y Jaramillo, Plaza de Ponchos. Nice atmosphere, varied menu, vegetarian available. 0700-2200. *Geminis*, Morales between Sucre and Jaramillo, T922980. Excellent food, good atmosphere and music. Highly recommended. *Oraibi*, Colón y Sucre. Vegetarian meals, salads, quiche, pleasant courtyard, snacks, live music Fri and Sat evenings. *SISA*, Abdón Calderón 409 entre Bolívar y Sucre, T920154. Coffee shop, cappuccino, excellent food in clean restaurant upstairs, reports of slow service, also bookstore, cultural centre shows weekly international films, live music Fri-Sun. 0700-2200.

    Italian Mid-range *Fontana di Trevi*, Sucre 12-05 y Salinas, 2nd floor. Good pizza and pasta, nice juices, friendly service. *Il de Roma*, J Montalvo 4-44. Good food, warm atmosphere. *Pizza Siciliana*, Morales 5-10 y Sucre. Large pizzas, vegetarian dishes, good juices.

    Mexican *Tabasco's*, Sucre y Salinas, Plaza de Ponchos, Good food, nice views.

    Middle Eastern *Cafetería Sahara*, Quiroga 4-18 y Sucre, T922212. Good for falafel and humus, fruit and vegetable juices, water pipes, Arabic coffee and sweets. Small portions, cushions on the floor for sitting.

    Oriental *Chifa Long Xiang*, Quito y Roca. Good Chinese, new in 2001.

    Seafood *Quino*, Roca 740 y Juan Montalvo. Typical coastal cooking, good value.

Cafetería Shanandoa Pie Shop, Salinas y Jaramillo. Good pies, milk shakes and ice-cream, expensive, popular and friendly meeting place, recommended for breakfast, book exchange, daily movies at 1700 and 1900. *Café San Seba's*, Quiroga entre Roca y Bolívar. Bakery with good coffee, meals, open late, *Deli* next door serves breakfast, pizza, pasta. *Empanadas Argentinas*, Morales 502 y Sucre. Good savoury and sweet *empanadas*. *Terraza Café Sol*, Jaramillo at Plaza de Ponchos, top of tall building. Snacks, breakfast and meals, good views of the plaza and mountains. Open only Sat. *Huaqui Inti*, Salinas at Plaza de Ponchos. Popular with foreigners, live music on weekends. *Plaza Café*, Sucre 1115 y Morales. Good food and atmosphere.

Cafés & bars

Peña Amauta, Morales 5-11 y Jaramillo, T922475. Good local bands, friendly and welcoming, mainly foreigners. *Peña la Jampa*, Jaramillo 5-69 y Morales, T922988. Popular. *Peña Tucano*, Morales 10-80 y 31 de Octubre. *Habana Club*, Quito y 31 de Octubre. Lively disco, cover US$1. *Maracaná*, Salinas 6-12 y Jaramillo. Disco, young crowd. On Fri and Sat nights there are nightlife tours on a chiva (open-sided bus with a musical group on board), it stops at the Plaza de Ponchos and ends its route at the *Habana Club*.

Entertainment
Otavalo is generally safe until 2200. Avoid deserted streets and plazas. Peñas are open on Fri and Sat from 2200, entrance US$2

Northern Highlands

Festivals Indigenous celebrations overlap with *mestizo* Catholic holidays, prolonging festivities for a week or more. If you wish to visit fiestas in the local villages, ask the musicians In the tourist restaurants, they may invite you; outsiders are not always welcome. The music is good and there is a lot of drinking, but transport back to Otavalo is hard to find.

At the **end of Jun** the *Inti Raymi* celebrations of the summer solstice (**21 Jun**), are combined with the *Fiesta de San Juan* (**24 Jun**) and the *Fiesta de San Pedro y San Pablo* (**29 Jun**). There are bullfights in the plaza and regattas on the beautiful Lago San Pablo, 4 km away (see Around Otavalo below for transport). These combined festivities are known as *Los San Juanes* and participants are mostly indigenous. The celebration begins with a ritual bath in the Peguche waterfall (a personal spiritual activity, best carried out without visitors and certainly without cameras). Most of the action takes place in the smaller communities surrounding Otavalo. Groups of musicians and dancers compete with each other as they make their way from one village to another over the course of the week; there is much drinking along the way. In Otavalo, indigenous families have costume parties, that at times spill over onto the streets. In the San Juan neighbourhood, near the Yanayacu baths, there is a week-long celebration with food, drink and music.

The *Fiesta del Yamor* and *Colla Raimi* (fall equinox or festival of the moon) are held during the **first 2 weeks of Sep**. This is the largest festivity in the province of Imbabura, it takes place in several cities and is mainly a *mestizo* celebration. Special *yamor chicha* is prepared from 7 varieties of corn and served to the participants. Local dishes including *llapingachos* and *fritada* are cooked, also amusement parks are set up, bands play in the plaza and there is much dancing. Other events include bullfighting (corner 31 de Octubre y Quito), fireworks and sporting events, including swimming and reed boat races across Lago San Pablo.

Mojandas Arriba is an annual 2-day hike from Quito over Mojanda to reach Otavalo for the **31 Oct** foundation celebrations commemorating the day Simon Bolívar elevated Otavalo to the status of a city. It is walked by hundreds each year and follows the old trails with an overnight stop at Malchinguí. *Pawkar Raimi* is a festival held in Peguche during Carnival with much music, food and drinking.

Shopping *Tagua Muyu*, Sucre 10-11 y Colón, is good for *tagua* (vegetable ivory) carvings.
Otavalo can seem like a giant souvenir shop at times. As well as the market, there are countless shops selling sweaters, tapestries and other souvenirs *Galeria de Arte Quipus*, Sucre y Morales, and *Galeria Inti Ñan*, Salinas 509 y Sucre, Plaza de Ponchos, are both good for paintings with native motifs. *Palos de Lluvia*, Morales 506 y Sucre, is good for rain sticks and other crafts. *Hilana*, Sucre esquina Morales, sells wool blankets. *The Book Market*, at Jaramillo 6-28 y Salinas, is highly recommended for buying, selling or exchanging books in English, French, German and other languages at cheap prices. Guidebooks, maps, postcards, CDs and cassettes. *SISA*, see Eating above, has a good bookshop. *El Salinerito*, Bolívar 10-08, for good cheese and cold cuts.

Sport **Mountain bikes** For hire at *Jatun Pacha* (see Sleeping above), US$3 per hr, US$12 per day, includes helmet. *Taller Ciclo Primaxi*, García Moreno y Atahualpa 2-49 and at the entrance to Peguche, has good bikes for rent, US$1 per hr. Recommended. *Hostal Valle del Amanecer* (see above). US$8 per day. Some tour operators also rent bikes and offer cycling tours, see below.

On the Panamericana, *Yanayacu* has 3 swimming pools, volleyball courts and is full of locals on Sun. *Neptuno*, at Morales and Guayaquil, also has a popular pool. Near the market, on Quiroga y Sucre, a ball game is played in the afternoons called *pelota de mano*. It is similar to the game in Ibarra (described on page 180) except that the ball is about the size of a table-tennis ball, made of leather, and hit with the hands, not a bat. There is a cockpit (*gallera*) at 31 de Octubre y Montalvo, fights are on Sat and Sun 1500-1900, US$0.50.

All agencies offer similar tours and prices. One-day tours with English-speaking guides **Tour operators**
to artisans' homes and villages, which usually provide opportunities to buy handicrafts
cheaper than in the market, cost US$15-20 per person. Day-trips to Cuicocha or
Mojanda, US$20-30. Horse-riding tours around Otavalo: 5 hrs to Tangali thermal
springs US$20; full day to Cuicocha crater lake US$35. Other destinations are the Intag
subtropical region, Nangulví and Chachimbiro thermal baths. There is variation in the
duration of the tours, find out before signing up. *Chachimbiro Tours*, Colón 412 y
Sucre, T923633. Trips to the *Complejo de Ecoturismo Chachimbiro* 1 hr northwest of
Otavalo (thermal baths, spa, see Excursions from Ibarra, page 181). *Diceny Viajes*, Sucre
10-11 y Colón, T921217, zulayviajes@hotmail.com Run by Zulay Sarabino, an indigenous Otavaleña, English and French spoken, native guides knowledgeable about the
area and culture, climbing trips to Cotacachi volcano, favourable reports. Recommended. *Eden Travel*, Salinas 503 at Plaza de Ponchos, T923611. Bike rentals US$7 per
day, cycling tours US$25 per day. *Intiexpress*, Sucre 11-10, T921436, F920737, also on
Bolívar y Salinas esquina, T921588. Recommended for horse-riding tours, US$20 for 5
hrs, US$35 full day, ask them to prepare the horses before you arrive or time is wasted,
good for those with or without experience, beautiful rides. *Intipungo*, Sucre y Abdón
Calderón, T921171, F921888. For airline reservations, *DHL/Western Union* representa-
tive, also tours. *Leyton's Tours*, Quito y Jaramillo, T922388, leytontour@yahoo.com
Horseback and bicycle tours. *Runa Tupari*, Sucre y Quiroga, Plaza de Ponchos
T/F925985, www.runatupari.com Trips to community inns in the Cotacachi area,
U$$15 per person per day, half board, includes transport (see Cotacachi below), also
the usual tours at higher-than-average prices, English and French spoken. *Suni Tours*,
García Moreno 313 y Atahualpa, T920624 or T09-9933148 (mob), F923383, sunitour@
yahoo.com, www.geocities.com/sunitour Interesting itineraries, trekking and
horse-riding tours, climbing, trips to Intag, Piñán, Cayambe, Oyacachi. English spoken,
guides carry radios. Recommended. *Yuraturs*, Morales 505 y Sucre, T/F921861,
www.yuratours.com For reservations and tours. *Zulaytur*, Sucre y Colón, 2nd floor,
T921176, F922969. Run by Rodrigo Mora. English spoken, information, map of town,
slide show, horse-riding, tours, interesting day tour of local artisan communities. Their
tours, especially the latter, have been repeatedly recommended.

Bus From **Quito**, Terminal Terrestre, take a *Cooperativa Otavalo* or *Cooperativa Los* **Transport**
Lagos bus, as they are the only ones which go into Otavalo; other companies bound for
Ibarra or Tulcán will drop you off on the highway, which is not safe after dark. From the
Terminal in Quito, buses go along the Av Occidental and later Av de la Prensa in
Cotocallao, where you can also get on. Every 10 mins, US$1.60, 2 hrs. **Taxi** A fast and
efficient alternative with *Supertaxis Los Lagos* (in Quito at Asunción 3-82, T256 5992; in
Otavalo at Roca 8-04, T923203) who will pick you up at your hotel (in the New City
only); hourly 0800-1900 (less often on weekends), 2 hrs, US$6 per person, buy ticket at
their office the day before travelling. A regular taxi costs US$40 one way, US$60 return
with a couple hours wait, US$80 for a full day with a visit to Cotacachi and other sites.
Hotel Ali Shungu (see above) runs a shuttle bus from any hotel in the New City, Quito, to
Otavalo, US$17 per person. It's not restricted to *Ali Shungu* guests.

Other buses To **Ibarra**, every 15 mins, US$0.32, 40 mins. To **Tulcán**, via Ibarra, fre-
quent departures. To **Cayambe**, every 15 mins, US$0.60, 45 mins. To **Cotacachi**, every
15 mins (some via Quiroga), US$0.20, 30 mins. To the communities around Lago San
Pablo there's frequent service, US$0.18. To **Peguche**, take a city bus (blue), every
15 mins, US$0.12. To **Apuela** and other points in the Intag area, see page 177.

Banks *Banco del Pacífico*, Bolívar 614 y García Moreno, Mastercard ATM. *Banco del* **Directory**
Pichincha, Bolívar y Piedrahita, TCs 1% commission. *Vaz Cambios*, Jaramillo y Saona, *Spanish classes cost*
Plaza de Ponchos. TCs 1.85% commission, also change Euros and Colombian Pesos. *about US$4 per hr*

Northern Highlands

Northern Highlands

Communications Internet: many in town especially along C Sucre, US$1.20 per hr. **Post**: corner of Plaza de Ponchos, entrance on Sucre, 1st floor. **Telephone**: *Andinatel*, Calderón between Jaramillo and Sucre. 0800-1245, 1300-1845, 1900-2145. **Language schools** *Academia de Español Mundo Andino*, Salinas 404 y Bolívar, T/F921801, espanol@interactive.net.ec *Fundación Jacinto Jijón y Caamaño*, Bolívar 8-04 y Montalvo, p 2, T920725. Spanish and Quichua lessons. *Instituto Superior de Español*, Sucre 11-10 y Morales, 2nd floor, T992414, F922415, institut@superior.ecuanex.net.ec (see also Language courses, Quito, page 136). **Laundry** *Tecno Clean*, C Olmedo 32. Dry cleaning. *Colón*, Colón y Jaramillo, US$0.90 per kg or US$2.50 per machine. *New Laundry*, Roca y Quiroga, at Hostal Valle del Amanecer. US$1.20 per kg.

Around Otavalo

Weaving villages The Otavalo weavers come from dozens of communities, but it is easiest to visit the nearby towns of Peguche, Ilumán, Carabuela and Agato which are only 15-30 minutes away and all have a good bus service. Buses leave from the terminal and stop at Plaza Copacabana (Atahualpa y Montalvo). You can also take a taxi or go with a tour.

In **Ilumán**, the Conterón-de la Torre family of *Artesanías Inti Chumbi*, on the northeast corner of the plaza, gives backstrap loom weaving demonstrations and sells crafts. There are also many felt hatmakers in town who will make hats to order. In **Agato**, the Andrango-Chiza family of *Tahuantinsuyo Weaving Workshop* gives weaving demonstrations and sells textiles. In

Around Otavalo

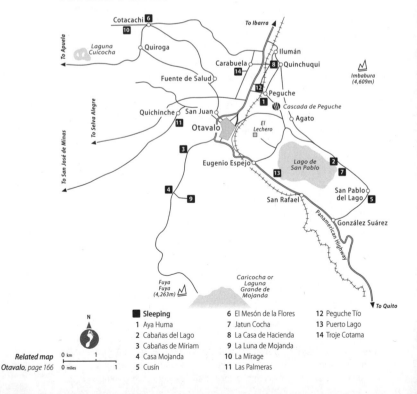

■ Sleeping	6 El Mesón de la Flores	12 Peguche Tío
1 Aya Huma	7 Jatun Cocha	13 Puerto Lago
2 Cabañas del Lago	8 La Casa de Hacienda	14 Troje Cotama
3 Cabañas de Miriam	9 La Luna de Mojanda	
4 Casa Mojanda	10 La Mirage	
5 Cusín	11 Las Palmeras	

Related map
Otavalo, page 166

0 km 1
0 miles 1

Carabuela many homes sell crafts including wool sweaters. Carlos de la Torre, a backstrap weaver, can be found above the Evangelist Church. In **Peguche**, the Cotacachi-Pichamba family, off the main plaza behind the church, sells beautiful tapestries, finished with tassels and loops, ready to hang. At the entrane to Peguche is **Galería Peguche Huasi**, an interesting museum about the native way of life and weaving tradition. T922620.

To get to this waterfall, situated near the village of Peguche, follow the old railway track through the woods in the direction of Ibarra until the track drops away to the left and a dirt path continues up the hill towards the waterfall. The patch of eucalyptus forest near the base of the falls is a popular spot for weekend outings and picnics. Allow 1-1½ hours each way. A wooden bridge at the foot of the falls leads to a steep path on the other side of the river which leads to Ibarra. From the top of the falls (left side) you can continue the walk to Lago de San Pablo (see below).

Cascada de Peguche
The tracks go through an unsafe neighbourhood which can be avoided by taking a bus to the trailhead near Peguche

About 4 km north of Otavalo are cold ferrous baths at the **Fuente de Salud**, said to be very curative, but opening hours are very irregular.

There is a network of old roads and trails between Otavalo and the Lago de San Pablo area, none of which takes more than an hour or two to explore. It is worth walking either to or back from Lago de San Pablo for the views. The walk there via *El Lechero* (a large tree, considered sacred among indigenous people) is recommended, though you will be pestered by children begging. The trail starts at the south end of Calle Morales in Otavalo. The walk back via the outlet stream from the lake, staying on the right hand side of the gorge, takes two to three hours, and is also recommended, or you can flag down a passing bus. Alternatively, take a bus to San Pablo, then walk back towards the lake. The views of Imbabura are wonderful. To explore the lake itself, boats can be hired at *Cabañas del Lago* or *Puerto Lago* (see Sleeping below).

Lago de San Pablo
Colour map 2, grid B5

Robberies of lone walkers have been reported, best go in a group

Sleeping Around the lake: **L** *Hostería Cusín*, in a converted 17th-century hacienda on the east side of the lake, San Pablo del Lago, T918013, F918003, www.haciendacusin.com.ec 25 rooms with fireplaces, includes breakfast, fine very expensive restaurant, sports facilities (horses, mountain bikes, squash court, pool, games room), library, large screen TV, lovely courtyard and garden, book in advance, British run, German also spoken, Hacienda.
   AL *Hostería Puerto Lago Country Inn*, Panamericana Sur, Km 5½ y Lago San Pablo

■ *on map, Around Otavalo, page 172*

Northern Highlands

Northern Highlands

on the west side of the lake, T920920, F920900, www.puertolago.net Rooms and suites in a beautiful setting, a good place to watch the sunset, very hospitable, good expensive restaurant (try trout in walnut sauce), boats, kayaks and water skis for rent. **AL** *Hostería Jatun Cocha*, Panamericana Km 5½, on the east side of the lake, T/F918191, www.ranfturismo.com Tasteful rooms with fireplaces, includes breakfast and dinner. On the lakeshore, kayaks, windsurfing, pool, sauna, bicycles. **AL-A** *Cabañas del Lago*, on northeast side of the lake, T/F918001 (in Quito, T2435936), www.lagosanpablo.itgo.com Nice rooms, cabins with fireplace and suites, on the lakeside, expensive restaurant, nice garden, boats and pedalos for hire.

From **San Pablo del Lago** it is possible to climb the **Imbabura** volcano, at 4,630 m and almost always under cloud – allow at least six hours to reach the summit and four hours for the descent. An alternative access, preferred by many, is from La Esperanza, south of Ibarra (see page 181). Easier, and no less impressive, is the nearby **Cerro Huarmi Imbabura**, 3,845 m. Buses from Otavalo to San Pablo del Lago leave every 30 minutes, more often on Saturday, from the bus terminal (US$0.18). A taxi costs US$4.

Lagunas de Mojanda

For safety reasons, go with a tour or request an escort at the Otavalo police station

Southwest of Otavalo are the impressive **Lagunas de Mojanda**, accessed by a cobbled road from Otavalo or a path from Cochasquí. Note however that there have been several reports of **armed hold-ups** of campers by Mojanda and those travelling the nearby roads. Some visitors have been badly hurt. Independent travel is therefore not recommended here.

Caricocha (or Laguna Grande de Mojanda) is a crater lake 18 km away from and 1,200 m higher than Otavalo. About 25 minutes' walk above Caricocha is **Laguna Huarmicocha** and a further 25 minutes is **Laguna Yanacocha**. Take a warm jacket, food and drinks; there is no entrance fee. The views on the descent are excellent.

From Caricocha the route continues south about 5 km before dividing: the left-hand path leads to **Tocachi**, the right-hand to **Cochasqui** (see page 160). Both are about 20 km from Laguna Grande and offer beautiful views of Quito and Cotopaxi (cloud permitting). You can climb **Fuya Fuya** (4,263 m) and **Yanaurco** (4,259 m), but the mountain huts on the shore of Laguna Grande and on the path to Fuya Fuya are derelict. (See Out of town, page 168, for hotels on the way to Mojanda.) Take a tent, warm sleeping bag, and food; there is no accommodation. Or take a Quito bus as far as Tabacundo, hitch to Lagunas (difficult at weekends), then walk back to Otavalo by the old Inca trail, on the right after 2-3 km. A taxi or camioneta from Otavalo is US$8 one way, arrange your return trip in advance but don't pay ahead.

Cotacachi

Phone code: 06
Population: 7,376
Altitude: 2,440

Regional information from: www.cotacachi.gov.ec

West of the Panamericana between Otavalo and Ibarra is Cotacachi, where leather goods are made and sold. The collapsible leather duffle bags are recommended. Credit cards are widely accepted but there's a hefty surcharge. There is also access along a cobbled road directly from Otavalo via Quiroga.

The **Museo de las Culturas**, García Moreno 13-41, off the main plaza, has good displays about early Ecuadorean history, regional crafts and indigenous traditions. Some English explanations. ■ *Tue-Fri 0900-1200, 1400-1700 , Sat 1400-1700 , Sun 1000-1300 . US$1.* **Huilla Cuna**, 10 de Agosto y Sucre, is an art gallery.

Local festivals include *Inti Raymi* (the sun and corn harvest festival held during the June solstice) and *La Jora* held at the September equinox.

To promote rural and ethno-cultural tourism, the municipality has set up an interesting series of country inns in nearby villages. Visitors experience life with a native family by taking part in daily activities. The comfortable inns have space for three, fireplace, bathroom and hot shower. US$15 per person including breakfast and dinner and transport from Otavalo. Arrange with *Runa Tupari* or other agencies in Otavalo.

Sleeping LL *La Mirage*, 500 m west of town, T915237, F915065, mirage1@ mirage.com.ec, www.larc1.com Converted hacienda with luxurious facilities. Includes breakfast and dinner, lovely restaurant, pool and gym, , beautiful gardens, antiques, conference facilities and spa. **AL** *La Banda*, 750 m west of town, T915176, F915873. Includes breakfast, restaurant, country estate style, best for weekends and holidays. **B** *Mesón de las Flores*, García Moreno 1376 y Sucre, T916009, F915828. Converted ex-hacienda off main plaza, restaurant, meals on a beautiful patio, live music at lunch Sat-Sun. Recommended.

C *Sumac Huasi*, Montalvo 11-09 y Moncayo, T915873. Includes breakfast, large modern rooms, nice but overpriced. **D** *Munaylla*, 10 de Agosto y Sucre, T916169, munaïlla@prodigy.net Modern, comfortable, friendly, new in 2001. **D** *Plaza Bolívar*, Bolívar 12-26 y 10 de Agosto, 3rd floor, T915755, F915149. Internet, indoor parking, refurbished older building, friendly. Recommended. **E** *Bachita*, Sucre 16-82 y Peñaherrera, T915063. Private bath, hot water, simple, quiet and friendly.

■ *on map, Around Otavalo, page 172*

Eating A local speciality is *carne colorada* (spiced pork, although restaurants catering to tourists may also use beef). *Asadero La Tola*, Rocafuerte 018 y 9 de Octubre, grill in an old courtyard. *Inty Huasi*, Bolívar 11-08 y 10 de Agosto, cheap set meals and mid-range for à la carte. *El Leñador*, Sucre 1012 y Montalvo, varied menu, mid-range prices. *El Viejo Molino*, Parque San Francisco next to Banco del Pichincha, good value and quality, set meals and à la carte, cheap. Recommended. *Swisscoffee*, Bolívar 13-04, snacks, sandwiches, coffee, juices; books for sale.

Transport Buses: terminal at 10 de Agosto y Salinas by the market. To **Otavalo**, every 10 mins, service alternates between the Panamericana and Quiroga roads, US$0.20, 20 mins. To **Ibarra**, every 15 mins, US$0.35, 45 mins. To **Quito**, transfer in Otavalo. **Pick-ups**: to **Cuicocha** from the market, US$5 one way, US$8 return with short wait.

Communications Internet: *Hotel Plaza Bolívar*, US$1.50 per hr. Telephone: *Andinatel*, Sucre y García Moreno.

This lovely crater lake lies about 15 km beyond Cotacachi, past the town of Quiroga, at an altitude of 3,070 m. The area has been developed for tourism and is part of the **Reserva Ecológica Cotacachi-Cayapas**, which extends from Cotacachi volcano to the tropical lowlands on the Río Cayapas in Esmeraldas. The US$5 park fee need not be paid if only visiting the lake. A visitors' centre has good natural history and cultural displays (entry US$1). The lake's two islands are closed to the public for biological studies. Motor boat rides around the islands, US$1.20 per person, minimum five persons.

Laguna Cuicocha
Colour map 2, grid B5

There is a well-marked, 8-km path around the lake, which takes four to five hours and provides spectacular views of the Cotacachi, Imbabura and, occasionally, glacier-covered Cayambe peaks. The best views are to be had in the early morning, when condors can sometimes be seen. There is a lookout at 3 km, two hours from the start. It's best to do the route in an anticlockwise direction and take water and a waterproof jacket. Entry to the path US$1.

Always enquire about safety before walking around the lake

Warnings There have been armed robberies of people walking around the lake. Do not take valuables. The public safety situation varies with time and the efforts of the authorities, so always enquire locally before heading out. Do not eat the berries which grow near the lake, as some are poisonous.

Northern Highlands

Cerro Cotacachi (4,944 m), north of the lake, is also part of the reserve. To climb it, it's best to approach from the ridge, not from the side with the antenna which is usually shrouded in cloud. Detailed maps of the region can be bought from the IGM in Quito. Climbing tours to Cotacachi are available through *El Mirador* (see Sleeping below) and Otavalo agencies.

Sleeping and eating   At the lakeshore by the pier is *El Muelle*, a restaurant overlooking the lake, expensive. **D** *El Mirador*, above the restaurant and pier, follow trail, T648039. Rooms withfireplace and electric shower, restaurant at mid-range prices, friendly service, camping possible, excellent views, hikes arranged with knowledgeable guide up Cotacachi or to Piñán lakes, but you must be fit, return transport provided to Quiroga, US$4, or Otavalo, US$7.

Transport   Buses from Otavalo to **Quiroga**, US$0.15. Bus Cotacachi-Quiroga US$0.15; taxi or *camioneta* Quiroga-Cuicocha US$3, Cotacachi-Cuicocha US$5. Alternatively, hire a taxi (US$10) or a *camioneta* (US$7) in Otavalo for Laguna Cuicocha. The 3-hr walk back to Cotacachi is beautiful. After 1 km on the road from the park entrance, turn left (at the first bend) on to the old road. You can also walk from Otavalo.

Intag area
Colour map 2, grid B4
Several reserves have been created in this area to protect its rich cloud forests

To the northwest of Otavalo lies the lush subtropical region of Intag, after the river of the same name. One access to this area is along the road that follows the southern edge of Cuicocha, crosses the western range and gradually descends to the southwest.

The hamlet of **Santa Rosa**, 35 km from Cuicocha, is at the heart of several reserves. There is a women's cooperative, their *cabuya* (sissal) wares are sold in town. In the **Intag Cloud Forest Reserve**, one hour's walk from Santa Rosa, is a friendly lodge with good vegetarian food. The reserve contains primary cloud forest at 1,800-2,800 m, and there is a trail to Los Cedros (see below). The owners are very involved in community environmental work, see www.decoin.org ■ *The lodge only accepts groups of 6 or more and specializes in university groups. Prices depend on group size, about US$45 per person per day. Reservations by mail only: Casilla 18, Otavalo, or through Safari Tours in Quito.*

Just east of Santa Rosa, a poor road turns north. This is the access to **Reserva Alto Chocó**, 30 minutes' walk from the turn-off. Accommodation is in simple rooms, **F** per person, no meals. There are some trails through forest to waterfalls, a reforestation project is underway and they welcome volunteers. ■ *Run by Fundación Zoobreviven, Marco Pavón, Quito T2235366.* Accessed by the same road, 1½ hours' walk from the turn-off, is **Reserva Siempre Verde**.

Apuela is a small town 46 km from Cuicocha. **Defensa y Conservación Ecológica de Intag (Decoin)**, an NGO working on conservation through community projects, has an office uphill from the plaza. ■ *Thu-Sun. T648593, www.decoin.org* Beyond Apuela, 5 km south, are the thermal baths of **Nangulví**. As with most developed springs in the country they tend to be busy at weekends. There are four hot pools here and one large cold one for plunging. ■ *US$0.32.* The area is relaxed and pleasant for walking, with a waterfall one hour away. Between Apuela and Nangulví, a side road goes to **Peñaherrera**, down which is the **Tolas de Gualimán arcaheological site**, several mounds with ramps, from the Caranqui culture. The main road continues southwest beyond Nangulví, one hour's driving to **García Moreno**.

Beyond García Moreno is the **Junín Cloud Forest Reserve**, a 800-ha forest at 1,500-2,000 m. The local community is trying ecotourism as an alternative to forest destruction and has built **A** accommodations. From García Moreno, the lodge can be reached by a 1½-hour truck ride or four-hour hike depending on road conditions (worst January-April). When hiking in, mules carry your luggage. There are good walking possibilities, including a trail to Los Cedros (see below). ■ *Further information from www.decoin.org*

On the southwest boundary of Reserva Cotacachi-Cayapas is **Los Cedros Research Station**, 6,400 ha of pristine cloud forest famous for the number of new orchid species discovered there. Bird life is abundant, and large species are more common and less shy than in many other places. Nice **A** facilities, including meals. Volunteer program US$250 per month, minimum stay one month. Access involves a four to five hour walk from **Chontal**, north of **Pacto** and west of **García Moreno**, which can be reached by bus from Quito. Trans Minas from Anteparra y Pedro Fermín Cevallos, San Blas, daily at 1100 and 1500, sometimes also at 0600 (US$3.50, four hours). ■ *Reservations necessary, in Quito contact: T2231768, cibt@ecuanex.net.ec, www.ecole-adventures.com*

Sleeping and eating **Apuela**: **E** *Pradera Tropical*, near the school (no sign, ask), T648557. Rustic cabins for 3, private bath, cold water, friendly. **F** *Fanicita*, on Plaza, T648552. Shared bath, electric shower, basic. **F-G** *Residencial Don Luís*, uphill from Plaza. Basic, cold showers, fairly clean, friendly. **Nangulví**: **D** *Cabañas Río Grande*, next to the baths, Otavalo T920442, Otavalo. Comfortable log cabins for 4 (price per cabin), private bath, restaurant. **G** *Complejo Ecoturístico Nangulví*, at the municipal baths, basic rooms with bunk beds, private bath, cold water, restaurant. **Other locations**: **G** *Parador Valle Hermoso*, in Valle Hermoso, between Apuela and Nangulví, basic rooms in family home and meals. **F** *Cabañas Monterrey*, in Pilambiro Bajo, north of Nangulví, simple cabins. **D** *Gualiman*, up the road to Peñaherrera. Cabins overlooking the Nangulví area, near the archaeological site. *Cabañas Monserath*, in Peñaherrera.

Transport From Otavalo, *Trans Otavalo* to **García Moreno** at 0800, 1000 and 1400; *Trans 6 de Julio* to **Barcelona** (turn-off past Nangulví) at 1200 and to **Peñaherrera** at 1500. **Apuela** US$1.38, 2½ hrs, **Nangulví** US$1.50, 3 hrs, **García Moreno**, US$2, 4 hrs.

Just west of the Panamericana, 11 km north of the turn-off for Cotacachi, is **Atuntaqui**, a quiet, pretty town with many sweater factories. Its *fiesta* is around 2 March. It can also be reached from Cotacachi via a secondary road, good for cycling or walking. Here is *El Manantial*, a swimming pool and sauna.

North of Otavalo

Ibarra

Once a pleasant colonial town (founded in 1606), Ibarra is the main commercial centre of the northern highlands, with an increasingly big city feel. It has many good hotels and restaurants. Prices are lower than Otavalo and there are fewer tourists. The city has an interesting ethnic mix, with blacks from the Chota valley and Esmeraldas alongside Otavaleños and other highland Indians, mestizos and Colombian immigrants.

Phone code: 06
Colour map 2, grid B5
Population: 108,600
Altitude: 2,225

Getting there There is no central bus terminal. Buses leave from their own terminals all near the train station and obelisk: *Andina/Aerotaxi*, Borja y Velasco, for Quito and Guayaquil; *Expreso Turismo* and others at Moncayo y Flores, for Quito and Tulcán; *Trans Otavalo*, Av Vacas Galindo cuadra 3 (beside the railway track), for Otavalo; *Valle del Chota*, Colón near the obelisk, for San Lorenzo; *Espejo*, Pérez Guerrero y Cabezas, for Tulcán; *CITA*, Flores y Velasco, for Ambato (bypassing Quito).

Ins & outs
See Transport, page 181, for further details

Getting around No problem here as the city is compact although the Santo Domingo church is a few blocks from the centre.

Tourist information *Ministerio de Turismo*, García Moreno 744, p 2, by Parque de la Merced, T958547, F958759. Very helpful; free city map and leaflets available, English spoken. Mon-Fri 0830-1300, 1400-1700. *Cámara Provincial de Turismo de Imbabura*, Oviedo y Bolívar, of 102, T/F642531. Regional information, very helpful, Spanish only. Mon-Fri 0900-1300, 1430-1800. *Municipio de Ibarra*, Sucre y P Moncayo, at Plazoleta Francisco Calderón, T955051. Spanish only. Mon-Sat 0800-1630, Sun 0900-1300.

Sights

The city has two fine plazas with flowering trees. On **Parque Pedro Moncayo** stand the Cathedral, the Municipio and the Gobernación. One block away, at Flores y Olmedo, is the smaller **Parque de la Merced**, named after its church.

Some interesting paintings are to be seen in the church of **Santo Domingo** and its museum of religious art. On the premisses is also a small zoo. ■ *0800-1800 daily. US$0.60. At the north end of Simón Bolívar.* At the small Parque Abdón Calderón is the **San Agustín** church. On Sucre, at the end of Avenida A Pérez Guerrero, is the **Basílica de La Dolorosa**, damaged by an earthquake in May 1987, but reopened in December 1992. A walk down Pérez

Ibarra

	Sleeping ■	3 El Chivo Loco	3 Expreso Turismo
	1 El Retorno	4 Heladería Rosalía	(Quito, Tulcan)
	2 Hostal Madrid	Suárez	4 San Lorenzo (Bus 6)
	3 Imbabura	5 Los Almendros	5 Trans Andina
	4 Madrid	6 Mesón Colonial	(Quito, Guayaquil)
	5 Montecarlo	7 Mr Peter's	6 Trans Otavalo
	6 Residencial Colón	8 Pizza El Horno	(Otavalo)
	Eating ●	Buses 🚌	
	1 Café Floralp	1 CITA (Ambato direct)	
	2 Casa Blanca	2 Espejo (Tulcán)	

Guerrero leads to the bustling, large, covered **Mercado Amazonas** on Sánchez y Cifuentes, by the railway station, open daily, busiest at the weekend. The **Museo Arqueológico de la Sierra Norte,** run by the *Banco Central del Ecuador,* has interesting displays about the pre-Inca cultures of the northern highlands, explanations in Spanish and English. There is also a hall for temporary art exhibits, a library and a bookshop. ■ *Mon-Sat, 0830-1330, 1430-1630 . US$0.50. T952777. Sucre 7-21 y Oviedo.*

Essentials

Along the Pan-American Highway south towards Otavalo are several **country inns,** some in converted haciendas. From south to north are: **L** *Vista del Mundo,* Panamericana at Pinsaquí toll, halfway between Otavalo and Ibarra, T946333, F946109, www.thegoldenspa.com   Luxury hotel, includes dinner, elegant expensive restaurant, spa (US$85 per person), and convention centre, built around the theme of world peace. Unusual and interesting. **B** *Natabuela,* Panamericana Sur Km 8, T932032, F932482, sproano@andinanet.net   Restaurant, covered pool, sauna, parking, comfortable rooms. **B** *Chorlaví,* Panamericana Sur Km 4, T932222, F932224. In an old hacienda. Includes breakfast, expensive restaurant with excellent *parillada,* pool, parking, popular, busy on weekends, folk music and crafts on Sun. **B** *Rancho Carolina,* Panamericana Sur Km 4, next to Chorlaví, T932444, F932215, ranchoc@andinanet.net   Includes breakfast, restaurant, small pool, parking, a bit faded. **D** *San Alfonso de Moras,* Panamericana Sur Km 3, T932499. Restaurant, parking, modest cabins, a bit run down.

In town   A *Ajaví,* Av Mariano Acosta 16-38 y Circunvalación, along main road into town from south, T955221, F952485. Restaurant, pool, parking, comfortable. **B** *El Prado,* in Barrio El Olivo, off the Panamericana at Km 1, T/F959570. Includes breakfast, restaurant, pool, luxurious, set in fruit orchards. **C** *Montecarlo,* Av Jaime Rivadeneira 5-61 y Oviedo, T958266, F958182. Includes breakfast, restaurant, heated pool open weekends only, parking, a better class hotel near bus stations.

D *El Dorado,* Oviedo 5-47 y Sucre, T950699, F958700, hostalnet@latinmail.com   Restaurant, parking, a bit run down. **D** *Hostal Madrid,* Olmedo 8-69 y Moncayo, T644918, F955301. Parking, modern and comfortable. Recommended. **D** *Hotel Madrid,* Moncayo 7-41 y Olmedo, T959017, F950796. Comfortable. **D** *Royal Ruiz,* Olmedo 940 y P Moncayo, T641999, F644644. Restaurant, parking, carpeted rooms. **E** *El Retorno,* Pasaje Pedro Moncayo 4-32 entre Sucre y Rocafuerte, T957722. Restaurant, cheaper with shared bath, hot water, nice views from terrace, good value. Recommended. **E** *Ibarra,* Obispo Mosquera 6-158 y Sánchez y Cifuentes, near market, T955091. Restaurant, private bath, hot water, OK. **E** *Imbabura,* Oviedo 9-33 y Narváez, T950155, F958877. Shared bath, hot water, nice colonial building with patio, large simple rooms, small private museum, popular with travellers, very friendly, good value. Highly recommended. **E** *Nueva Colonial,* Olmedo 5-19 y Grijalva, away from centre, T952918. Restaurant, private bath, hot water, old colonial building, a bit run down. **E** *Residencial Madrid,* Oviedo 85-7 y Olmedo, T951760. Private bath, hot water, simple. **E** *Vaca,* Bolívar 7-53 y Moncayo, T955844. Private bath, hot water, older but well cared for. **E-F** *Colón,* Narváez 8-62, T958695. Cheaper with shared bath, hot water, laundry facilities, basic and friendly.

Expensive   The restaurants at *Chorlaví* and *Ajaví* are recommended, but can be crowded with tour buses on Sat lunchtime. **Mid-range**   *Café Floralp,* García Moreno 4-30 y Sucre. A variety of crêpes, fondue, good breakfast, bread, has its own cheese factory, yoghurt, cold cuts, excellent coffee, good selection of Chilean wines, the 'in place' to meet and eat, Swiss-owned. Warmly recommended. *Los Almendros,* García Moreno 3-80. Set lunches and à la carte. *Mesón Colonial,* Rocafuerte 5-53, at Parque Abdón

Sleeping
■ *on map*
Price codes:
see inside front cover

Note the 3 Madrids, they are quite different from one another

Eating
● *on map*
There are many restaurants on Olmedo between Flores and Oviedo

Northern Highlands

Calderón. Also in a colonial house, extensive à la carte menu, good food and service, closed Sun. Recommended. **Mid-range to cheap** *Gourmet de Luc*, Olmedo 9-48, at *Hotel Royal Ruiz*. Cheap set lunch and mid-range à la carte, slightly upscale. *Pizza El Horno*, Rocafuerte 6-38 y Flores. Good pizzas and Italian dishes, live music Sat night, closed Mon. *Mr Peter's*, Sucre 5-36, opposite Parque Pedro Moncayo. Good pizza, wide choice of snacks and meals, good service, nice atmosphere, open 1100-2200. **Cheap** *Café Pushkin*, Olmedo 7-75. For breakfast, with good bread, opens 0730, a classic. *Casa Blanca*, Bolívar 7-83. Excellent, family run, located in colonial house with seating around a central patio with fountain, delicious food, closed Sun. Warmly recommended. *Chifa Muy Bueno*, Olmedo 7-23. Chinese, does a good *chaulafan*. *Chifa Nueva*, Olmedo 7-20, reasonable Chinese food, large portions. *El Chagra*, Olmedo 7-44. *Platos típicos*, good trout. Recommended. *Pizzeria Charlotte*, Jaime Rivadeneira 228 y Elías Almeida. Pizza and Italian dishes, in residential neighbourhood west of the centre, popular with locals, daily 1600-2230. **Seriously cheap** *El Cedrón*, Olmedo 7-45. Set meals. *La Tertulia*, Olmedo 8-84. Set meals. *El Chivo Loco*, P Moncayo 12-68 y Flores, opposite Expreso Turismo bus station. Good set meals.

There are several excellent *heladerías* serving *helados de paila*, home-made fruit sherbets, including: *Heladería Rosalía Suárez*, Oviedo y Olmedo, an Ibarra tradition since 1896, very good, try the *mora* (raspberry) or *guanábana* (soursop) flavours. Highly recommended. *La Bermejita*, at Olmedo 7-15. Directly opposite is *Hielo y Dulce*, at Olmedo 7-08.

Local specialities These include walnut nougat (*nogadas*) and bottled blackberry syrup concentrate (*arrope de mora*); quality varies, ask to try a sample before you buy. These are both made locally and sold in the small shops along Olmedo 700 block. The best selection of these, plus others such as guava jam, are to be found in the line of kiosks opposite the Basílica de la Merced. *Helados de paila* made in large copper basins (*pailas*, see above), are available in many *heladerías* throughout the town.

Bars & nightclubs *El Encuentro*, Olmedo 9-59. Piano bar, interesting drinks, very popular, pleasant atmosphere, unusual décor. *El Zarape*, on Circunvalacíon. *Peña* and Mexican restaurant. Discos include: *Sambuca*, Oviedo y Olmedo, and *Studio 54* at Laguna Yaguarcocha.

Festivals *Fiesta de los Lagos* is held over the last weekend of **Sep**, Thu-Sun, commemorates the foundation of Ibarra, it begins with *El Pregón*, a parade of floats through the city. On **16 Jul** is the festival in honour of the *Virgen del Carmen*. *El Retorno* on **28 Apr** celebrates the return of the people of Ibarra to their city after four years absence following the 1868 earthquake. There are music festivals, bull fights, parades and sporting events.

Shopping There are a number of good supermarkets in the centre of town: *Akí*, Bolívar y Colón. *Supermaxi*, south of the centre on Eugenio Espejo. *Supermercado El Rosado*, at Olmedo 9-46. *Supermercado Universal*, Cifuentes y Velasco. *Mi Supermercado*, Bolívar 7-83.

Sport **Paddle ball** A unique form of paddle ball is played on Sat and Sun near the railway station and other parts of town; ask around for details. The players have huge spiked paddles for striking the 1 kg ball. On weekdays they play a similar game with a lighter ball. *Balneario Primavera*, Sánchez y Cifuentes 3-33. **Turkish bath** Heated pool, Turkish bath, also offers aerobics classes and remedial massage, for membership T957425. Also *Baños Calientes*, at Sucre 10-68. **Tennis** *Ibarra Tennis Club*, at Ciudad Jardín, T950914. **Paragliding** is possible from Ibarra; enquire with *Escuela de Vuelo Pichincha* in Quito for local contacts. See page 76.

Nevitur, Bolívar 7-35 y Oviedo, T958701, F640040. Excellent guides, vans for trips **Tour operators**
throughout the country. *Turismo Intipungo*, Rocafuerte 6-08 y Flores, T957766,
F955270, intiibr@interactive.net.ec Regional tours. *Metropolitan Touring*, Flores 5-76
y Sucre, see Quito.

Bus To/from **Quito**, *Expreso Turismo* or *Aerotaxi*, frequent service, US$2, 2½ hrs. **Transport**
Shared taxis with **Supertaxis Los Lagos** (in Quito at Asunción 3-81, T2565992; in Ibarra *See Around Ibarra*
at Flores 924 y Sánchez Cifuentes, Parque La Merced, T955150) who will pick you up at *below for details of*
your hotel (in the New City only) hourly 0800-1900 (less often on weekends), buy ticket *the tourist train*
at their office the day before travelling, US$6 per person, 2½ hrs. To **Tulcán**, *Expreso
Turismo*, hourly, US$2, 2½ hrs. To **Otavalo**, *Trans Otavalo*, frequent service, US$0.32, 40
mins. To **Cotacachi**, US$0.35, 45 mins, some continue to **Quiroga**. To **Lita** and **San
Lorenzo**, *Valle del Chota* and other companies, see Ibarra to the Coast, page 183. To
Ambato, *CITA* goes via El Quinche and bypasses Quito, 5 daily, US$4, 5 hrs. **Train** Reg-
ular passenger service from Ibarra has been discontinued.

Banks *Banco del Pacífico*, Olmedo y P Moncayo, TCs. *Banco del Austro*, Colón 7-51, **Directory**
VISA. *Banco del Pichincha*, Bolívar y Mosquera, VISA. **Communications** Internet:
Several in centre, prices around US$1 per hr. **Post**: Flores opposite Parque Pedro
Moncayo, 2nd floor. **Telephone**: *Andinatel*, Sucre 4-56, past Parque Pedro Moncayo.
Opens 0800. **Language courses** *Centro Ecuatoriano Canadiense de Idomas (CECI)*,
Pérez Guerrero 6-12 y Bolívar, T951911, US$3 per hr. *CIMA*, Obelisco Casa No 2, 2nd
floor. **Medical services** *Clínica Médica del Norte*, at Oviedo 8-24, T955099. Open 24
hrs. **Useful addresses** Immigration: Olmedo y LF Villamar, T951712.

Around Ibarra

Along the start of the spectacular route to San Lorenzo, a motorized rail-car **Train ride**
(*autoferro*) runs 45 km out of Ibarra, about two hours to Primer Paso, just **from Ibarra**
past Tulquizán. It is an interesting excursion through nice scenery. The *If there are heavy*
autoferro stays for a few hours before returning, so you can spend some time *rains service can be*
at Hostería Tulquizán (across the river, see Ibarra to the Coast, page 183) or *interrupted, check*
explore the surroundings. This is a transition zone between the higlands and *ahead if it is running*
coast. From Tulquizán you can also continue by bus to San Lorenzo or
return by bus to Ibarra. Train enthusiasts may wish to visit the railway yards
beyond the station, with several old locomotives. ■ *The autoferro runs when
there are enough passengers (15 people going one way or fewer return).
Mon-Fri at 0700, returning at 1400, Sat-Sun and holidays at 0800, returning
at 1600. US$3.80 one way. Tickets can be purchased 30 mins before departure
or the day before. The train station is near the obelisk, T955050, open daily
0700-1200 and 1400-1800.*

About 10 minutes south of Ibarra, just off the Panamericana between **San Antonio**
Otavalo and Ibarra, this village is well known for its wood carvings. The **de Ibarra**
trade is so successful that the main street is lined with galleries and bou-
tiques. Bargaining is difficult, but it is worth seeing the range of styles and
techniques and shopping around. The following workshops are worth visiting: Moreo Santacruz, Osvaldo Garrido in the Palacio de Arte, Luís Potosí
and Gabriel Cevallos.

Close to Ibarra, 10 km directly south on the road to Olmedo, this pretty village **La Esperanza**
is set in beautiful surroundings on the pre-Inca road which goes to Cayambe.
Ask in La Esperanza for makers of fine clothes and embroidery.

You can climb **Cubilche** volcano in three hours from La Esperanza for beautiful views. From the top you can walk down to Lago San Pablo, another three hours.

You can also climb **Imbabura** volcano more easily than from San Pablo del Lago. Allow 10-12 hours for the round trip, take a good map, food and warm clothing. The easiest route is to head right from *Hotel Casa Aída*, take the first road to the right and walk all the way up, following the tracks up past a water tank. It's a difficult but enjoyable walk with superb views; watch out for some loose scree at the top. You can go back to La Esperanza from the summit or go on to Otavalo, which is about another 3-4 hours.

Sleeping **E** *Casa Aída*. With bath, clean, hot water, friendly, Aída speaks some English and cooks good vegetarian food. Next door is **F** *Café María*. Basic rooms, will heat water, friendly, helpful, use of kitchen, laundry facilities. The bus from Parque Germán Grijalva in Ibarra passes the hotels, US$0.30, 30 mins. A taxi from Ibarra is US$6.

Urcuquí   Urcuquí is a pretty little town with a basic hotel and a park. On Sunday the locals play unusual ball games. To get there, a bus from Ibarra leaves from the open space opposite *Supermaxi*. Urcuquí is the starting point for walking to the Piñán lakes.

Chachimbiro   About two hours' drive on a bumpy track northwest from Ibarra, in the parish of Tumbabiro, are the clean, hot mineral swimming pools of Chachimbiro. These are part of the *Complejo de Turismo Ecológico Chachimbiro*, run by *Fundación Cordillera*. The complex is part of a project to encourage sustainable development and environmental education in the region. *Proyecto Chachimbiro* has made many improvements including trails, organic gardens and a medical centre for treatment in the thermal waters. Weekends can be quite crowded. There is one exceedingly hot pool for therapy and several of mixed water for soaking and playing. There are **D** cabins in the complex with private bath and jacuzzi and simpler **E** ones with shared bath. There are also two restaurants. ■ *Entry to the recreational pools US$1, to the medicinal pools and spa US$2.50. There is a bus daily direct to the complex from the Expreso Turismo terminal on Calle Flores in Ibarra; be there by 0700 as it leaves when full. Tours are available from Chachimbiro Tours in Otavalo (see page 171)*

Laguna   Laguna Yahuarcocha is a popular weekend recreation spot for *Ibarreños* who
Yahuarcocha   go to paddle on the lake, ride a bike, eat tilapia, or party at one of the discotheques. The beauty of the lake has been disfigured by the building of two motor-racing circuits around its shores. The smaller one is closed to vehicles and used by cyclists. The lake is gradually drying up with *totora* reeds encroaching on its margins. They are woven into *esteras* (mats) and sold in huge rolls at the roadside. Reed boats can sometimes be seen. The lively weekend atmosphere at the lake hides its more sombre past. Yahuarcocha means 'blood lake', and was the site of a decisive battle which the Incas won over the native Caranquis, a nation which resisted the Inca conquest for a long time.

It is possible to walk the 4 km to Yahuarcocha in about 1½ hours. Follow Calle 27 to the end of town, cross the river and walk to the right at the first junction. At the end of this road, behind two low buildings on the left, there is a small path going steeply uphill. There are beautiful views of Ibarra and then, from the top of the hill, over the lake surrounded by mountains and the village of the same name. ■ *Entry to Yahuarcocha for vehicles US$0.30, boat rental US$1, frequent buses from the market area in Ibarra.*

Sleeping and eating All with lovely views over the lake. **B** *Rancho Totoral*, T/F955544. Ample rooms, restaurant with excellent cooking, many local dishes (mid-range to expensive), golf course, beautiful, tranquil during the week. **C** *Parador El Conquistador*, T953985, carpeted rooms, large restaurant with mid-range prices, disco Thu-Sat. Recommended. **C** *Imperio del Sol*, T959794, rooms and restaurant at mid-range prices. On weekends there are food stalls near the village of Yahuarcocha serving tilapia.

Ibarra to the Coast

The train ride from Ibarra to the Pacific coast has been replaced by a very scenic fully paved road which takes you to the ocean in as little as four hours. Completed in 2002, this is the northernmost route connecting the highlands with the Pacific. Although it is has opened new opportunities for communities along the way, there is also increased logging and accelerated destruction of the remaining forests in Ecuador's unique Chocó Bioregion.

The road starts from the Panamericana, 24 km north of Ibarra. It goes by the town of **Salinas**, then drops northwest following the valley of the Río Mira to the subtropical lowlands. About 15 minutes beyond Salinas is **Tulquizán**, here is **C** *Hostería Tulquizán*, T641989 Ibarra, a resort by the river, full board, pool, horses. Lower down, 39 km from the Salinas turn-off, are the villages of **Guallupe**, **El Limonal** and **La Carolina**, separated by a stream and the Río Mira, from where you can visit the Cerro Golondrinas cloud forest. Here are **D** *Bospas Farm*, 800 m from the village. Private bath, full board, also offer volunteer opportunities on experimental organic farm. Contact Piet Sabbe, bospas22@hotmail.com **D** *Martyzu*, has pool and restaurant. Better is **E** *El Limonal*, T648688, with private bath, three pools, restaurant. In 28 km, the road reaches **Lita** (altitude 512 m), a town near the old railway line, with good swimming in the river. There is a basic, adequate **F** residencial and several restaurants along the road. It is 66 km from Lita to **Calderón**, where this road meets the coastal highway comming from Esmeraldas. About 7 km beyond is **San Lorenzo** (see page 352).

Bus To **San Lorenzo** from Ibarra, *Coop Valle de Chota* (Colón near the obelisk, 4 daily), **Transport** *Coop Espejo* (Av Pérez Guerrero y Cabezas, by the Mobil gas station, 6 daily) and a few others serve this route, US$4, 3½ hrs. There are additional buses which go only as far as **Lita**, 2 hrs, US$2, and weekend buses direct to **Las Peñas**, a beach south of San Lorenzo, US$4, 4 hrs.

North to Colombia

The Panamericana goes past Laguna Yahuarcocha and the turn-off to San Lorenzo before descending to the hot dry Chota valley. About 30 km north of Ibarra, at Mascarilla, is a police checkpoint (have your documents at hand), after which the highway divides.

One branch follows an older route northeast through Mira and El Angel to Tulcán on the Colombian border (see below). This road is paved and in good condition as far as El Angel, but deteriorates rapidly thereafter. The El Angel-Tulcán section is unpaved and in very poor condition but the scenery is beautiful. It is often impassable beyond Laguna El Voladero.

The second branch, the modern Panamericana, in excellent shape but with many heavy lorries, runs east through the Chota valley to Juncal, before turning north to reach Tulcán via Bolívar and San Gabriel. A good paved road runs between Bolívar and El Angel, connecting the two branches. A second lateral road, between San Gabriel and El Angel, requires a four-wheel drive vehicle and is often impassable during the rainy season.

The El Angel route to the border

Mira
Phone code: 06
Colour map 2, grid B5
Population: 2,900

Along the old route, which climbs steeply from Mascarilla, is the town of Mira, 15 km past the fork. Some of the finest quality woollens come from this part of the country and are sold for export and in Otavalo. Locally you can find them up the hill opposite the bus stop. There are two festivals held each year, on 2 February and 18 August, with fireworks and free flowing Tardón, the local *aguardiente*. **F** *Residencial Mira*, 1 block from the park, behind the Municipio, T280228. Basic but clean, good beds. There are very few restaurants. Bus from Ibarra, every 30 minutes (US$1, one hour). From El Angel, every 30 minutes (US$.50, 20 minutes).

El Angel
Phone code: 06
Colour map 2, grid B5
Population: 4,400
Altitude: 3,000 m

Some 20 km northeast of Mascarilla is El Angel, a sleepy highland town that comes to life during its Monday market. It is the birthplace of José Franco, designer of the famous topiary in the Tulcán cemetery, and the main plaza retains a few trees that were originally sculpted by him.

Sleeping and eating A *Hostería El Angel*, at entrance to village, T/F977584, www.ecuador-sommerfer.com Includes breakfast, meals available on request, parking, caters to groups, reservations required, contact Quito T/F2221480. Offers trips into reserve (see below). **E** *Asadero Los Faroles*, José Grijalva 5-96 on the plaza, T977144. Above restaurant, shared bath, hot water, simple rooms in family home. Eating places include *Asadero Los Faroles*, downstairs from the hotel. Roast chicken and trout, cheap set meals. Several other chicken places in town. The shops are well stocked.

Transport *Trans Espejo*, hourly to **Quito**, US$3, 4 hrs. To **Ibarra**, US$1.10, 1½ hrs. To **Tulcán**, at 0730 daily, US$1.20, 1½ hrs. *Trans Mira*, hourly to **Mira**, **Ibarra** and **Tulcán**.

La Calera

About 3 km south of town, along the road to Mira, is the turn-off for the thermal baths of **La Calera**. From here a steep but good cobbled road descends for 6½ km into a lovely valley to the baths themselves, with good views along the way. There are two pools with warm water in pleasant surroundings, admission US$0.50. The baths are deserted during the week, when only the smaller pool is filled. There is no public transport; hire a taxi from El Angel, US$4 one way. The baths are crowded with locals on weekends and holidays, when transport costs US$0.50 per person. With a sleeping bag it is possible to stay the night in the main building, but take food.

Reserva Ecológica El Angel
Colour map 2, grid B5

El Angel is the main access point for this reserve, created in 1992 to protect 15,715 ha of *páramo* ranging in altitude from 3,400 to 4,768 m. The reserve contains the southernmost large stands of the velvet-leaved *frailejón* plant, also found in the Andes of Colombia and Venezuela. Also of interest are the spiny *achupallas* with giant compound flowers, related to the *Puya Raymondi* of Peru and Bolivia. The wildlife includes *curiquingues* (birds of prey), deer, foxes, and a few condors. There are several small lakes in the reserve. It can be very muddy during the rainy season; the best time to visit is May to August. ■ *The Ministerio del Ambiente's park office is at the Municipio. T/F977597. Information and pamphlets are available. Park entry fee US$10.*

Excursions into the reserve From El Angel follow the poor road north towards Tulcán for 16 km to **El Voladero** ranger station where a self-guided trail climbs over a low ridge (30 minutes' walk) to two crystal clear lakes. Camping is possible here, but you must be self-sufficient and take great care not to damage the surroundings. Pick-ups/taxis can be hired in the main plaza of El Angel for a day-trip to El Voladero; US$15 return with short wait.

The Lagunas Verdes area is close to the Colombian border, for safety reasons travel here is not recommended

A longer route follows an equally poor road to **Cerro Socabones**, beginning in the town of **La Libertad**, 3½ km north of El Angel. This route climbs gradually to reach the high *páramo* at the centre of the reserve and, in one hour, the **El Salado** ranger station. Another hour ahead is **Socabones**, from where you can trek or take pack animals to the village of **Morán** (local guide Hugo Quintanchala can take you further through the valley). Many paths criss-cross the *páramo* and it is easy to get lost. Transport from El Angel to Cerro Socabones, US$25 return. A helpful driver is Sr Calderón, T977274.

A third access to the reserve is from the north along the Tulcán-Tufiño-Maldonado road (see below) from which the Lagunas Verdes (green lakes) can be seen.

In the Morán area, at 2,800 m is A *Cotinga Lodge*, rustic cabin with bunk beds, includes breakfast. The area has lovely cloud forest. Contact information as for *Hostería El Angel*, above. Beyond the Morán valley, in the forested hills towards the Mira valley, is the Cerro Golondrinas Cloudforest. Further information from *La Casa de Eliza* in Quito (see page 111).

The Panamericana to the border

Following the Panamericana east past Mascarilla into the Chota valley for 2 km is the turn-off for the town of El Chota with the **Honka Monka** museum of Afro-Ecuadorean culture. Sugar cane is grown in this area. A further 8 km leads to a series of tourist complexes popular with vacationing Colombians and Ecuadoreans who come down from the highlands for the warmer temperatures and *sabor tropical*.

**El Chota
& Juncal**
*Phone code: 06
Colour map 2, grid B5
Altitude: 1,700 m*

Sleeping AL *Oasis*, T/F941200, roasis@uio.satnet.net Price includes 3 meals and tour, cabins for up to 5 and mini-cabins for 2, facilities include 3 large pools (one is a wave pool), waterslide, playground, several snack bars, disco, good restaurant with live music on weekends, day use US$5 per person. Tours throughout the region in a *chiva*. **B** *Aruba*, T941146. Modern, small pool, restaurant offering cheap set lunches and à la carte at mid-range prices. **B** *Hostería El Kibutz*, Km 37, T/F942340, comfortable cabins for up to 5 with fridge, pool, smaller and more relaxed than some of the others. There are many more.

Just beyond is **El Juncal**, the turn-off east to Pimampiro, after which the highway turns north to cross the Río Chota into the province of Carchi and begins its steep climb out of the valley.

The quiet town of Pimampiro lies 8 km off the Panamericana along a paved road. The surrounding countryside offers excellent walking. There is a Sunday market. **F** *Residencial* is run by the Hurtado family on Calle Flores. It has no sign so ask around; it is basic and friendly, but has a poor water supply. *El Forastero*, on the corner of Flores and Olmedo, serves good food. Buses from Ibarra, *Cooperativa Oriental* from the same station as *Expreso Turismo*, P Moncayo y Flores, leave every 20 minutes (US$0.80, 1¼ hours).

Pimampiro
Colour map 2, grid B5

Nueva América & Laguna Puruhanta South of Pimampiro is the town of Mariano Acosta, beyond which is **Nueva América**, a small community at 3,400 m which has developed a tourism project. They have a house for visitors (US$6 per person, take a warm sleeping bag), can provide meals, and guides. The scenery along the route to town is very nice and views of Cayambe once you get there are magnificent. Near town is the 502-ha Bosque Nueva América, a cloud forest reserve with trails. The community also runs a medicinal plants project.

Nueva América is along one of the access routes to **Laguna Puruhanta**, a magnificent lake surrounded by forest, popular with fishermen. It is part of Reserva Ecológica Cayambe-Coca. The walk to the lake along the Río Pisque is very nice but quite demanding, weather conditions can be harsh and the trail muddy, there are a couple of river crossings on single log bridges. Allow three or more days for the excursion and take a tent, sleeping bag, warm waterproof clothing, food, stove and fuel. In Nueva América you can hire a guide and pack animals, although the latter can only go part of the way. ■ *Several days advance notice are required for all services from Nueva América, call the Unidad de Medio Ambiente, Municipio de Pimampiro, T937117 (ext 16).*

Transport There are buses and pick-ups from Pimampiro to Mariano Acosta, US$0.50, 1½ hrs. In Mariano Acosta you can hire a pick-up to Nueva América, US$6-8, 45 mins, or walk 2½ hrs uphill, ask for the path out of Mariano Acosta. You can also hire a pick-up from Pimampiro to Nueva América.

Bolívar
Phone code: 06
Colour map 2, grid B5
Population: 4,400

A further 17 km north is Bolívar, a neat little town with houses and the interior of its church painted in lively pastel colours, a well kept plaza and a Friday market. The basic **F** *Hospedaje* is run by Sra Lucila Torres, on Julio Andrade s/n, one block north of the plaza, T287212. There is no sign; shared bath, cold water. *Restaurant Los Sauces*, by the highway, serves good cheap food. Recommended. There's a good bakery on the main plaza at García Moreno esq Julio Andrade.

La Paz
Colour map 2, grid B6

About 5 km north of Bolívar is the turn-off east for the town of La Paz, from which a steep but good cobbled road descends for 5 km to the **Gruta de La Paz**. Views along the road are breathtaking, including two spectacular waterfalls. The place is also called *Rumichaca* (Quichua for stone bridge) after the massive natural bridge which forms the *gruta* (grotto). Not to be confused with the Rumichaca on the Colombian border.

The entire area is a religious shrine, receiving large numbers of pilgrims during Holy Week, Christmas, and especially around 8 July, feast day of the Virgen de La Paz. In addition to the chapel in the grotto itself, there is a large basilica, a Franciscan convent, a guest house for pilgrims, a restaurant and shops selling religious articles. These are open on weekends and pilgrimage days only; there are very few visitors at other times. It is possible to camp for free opposite the convent. The river which emerges from the grotto is rather polluted, and the sewer smell detracts from its otherwise great natural beauty.

There are clean thermal baths (showers and one pool) just below the grotto, open Wednesday to Sunday (crowded at weekends), admission US$0.50, showers US$0.25. Look for the caretaker if the gate to the pool is locked. Several scenic trails through the valley start from behind the hotel.

Transport There is public transport to La Paz from **Tulcán** on Sat and Sun. Also vans from **San Gabriel**, US$0.60 per person (20 minimum) on weekends. It costs US$6 to hire a vehicle during the week. A second, signposted access road to La Paz goes from the Panamericana, 3 km south of San Gabriel.

About 10 km north of La Paz is San Gabriel, an important commercial centre. The spectacular 60-m high **Paluz** waterfall is 4 km north of town, beyond another smaller waterfall. Follow Calle Bolívar out of the main plaza and turn right after the bridge. It's well worth the walk. There is a rather chilly 'thermal' bath along the way.

San Gabriel
Phone code: 06
Colour map 2, grid B6
Population: 12,600

Sleeping and eating D *Casa de los Abonos*, Mejía y Los Andes, above the agricultural supply shop, T291832. Includes breakfast, modern, clean, best in town. F *Residencial Ideal*, Montúfar 08-26, T290265. Private bath, electric shower, cheaper with shared bath, basic. There are other cheap and basic places to stay. For eating, try *Asadero Pío Riko*, Bolívar 10-15. Chicken and others. *Super Burguer*, Montúfar 09-34, set meals, very cheap *Heladería Zanzibar*, Colón 3-16. For ice-cream.

Transport To **Tulcán**, vans and jeeps US$0.60, shared taxis US$0.80, all from the main plaza. To **Quito**, buses, US$3, 4 hrs.

About 20 km east of San Gabriel is the tiny community of Mariscal Sucre, also known as Colonia Huaquenia, which has no tourist facilities but is very hospitable. It can be reached by taxi from San Gabriel in one hour; sometimes shared four-wheel drive vehicles also go there, which are a cheaper option. This is the gateway to the **Guandera Reserve and Biological Station**, part of the Jatun Sacha Foundation's system of reserves. It includes over 1,000 ha of Frailejon *páramo* and twisted mossy temperate forest. There are rare birds like the Chestnut-bellied Cotinga and Crescent-faced Antpitta and many orchids. There is a **C** guest house 30 minutes' walk from Mariscal Sucre. It is very cold at night so bring warm clothes. Reservations and further information about visits and volunteer programmes from Jatun Sacha Foundation in Quito (see Volunteer programmes, page 81).

Mariscal Sucre

This small town before Tulcán (F *Residencial Julio Andrade*, on the Panamericana, T973474, shared bath, simple) is the access for **El Carmelo** and **La Bonita**. The former is a back way for contraband into Colombia, the latter is on a new road into Sucumbíos province, which should eventually connect with the Baeza-Lago Agrio road at Lumbaquí; very scenic. Trans Sucumbios buses go from here to La Bonita, four hours.

Julio Andrade
Enquire about public safety (see Dangerous areas, page 47) before entering this area straddling Carchi and Sucumbios

Tulcán

The El Angel road and the Panamericana join at Las Juntas, 2 km south of Tulcán, a commercial centre and capital of the province of Carchi. It is always chilly. To the east of the city is a bypass road going directly to the Colombian border. There is a great deal of informal trade here with Colombia, a textile and dry goods fair takes place on Thursday and Sunday.

Phone code: 06
Colour map 2, grid A6
Population: 47,100
Altitude: 2,960

Tourist information Unidad de Turismo, at the Municipio, Olmedo y Ayacucho opposite Plaza de Independencia, T980487. Helpful, Spanish only, Mon-Fri 0800-1300, 1500-1800. Information office at the border, open Mon-Fri 0830-1700.

Ins & outs

Safety Tulcán and the traditionally tranquil border province of Carchi have seen an increase in tension due to drug trafficking and the *guerrilla* conflict in neighbouring Colombia (see Dangerous areas, page 47). Do not travel outside town (except along the Panamericana) without enquiring in advance about current conditions. It is also prudent not to wander about late at night. The area around the bus terminal is unsafe.

Northern Highlands

Tulcán

Sights The centre is long and narrow, stretching along Calle Sucre which goes by the main square, **Plaza de la Independencia**, and along Calle Bolívar, one block west. The bus terminal is some distance to the south and transport to the border leaves from **Parque Ayora**, five blocks north of the main square. Parque Ayora has an amazing cantilevered statue of Abdón Calderón and his horse leaping into mid-air. Two blocks away is the **cemetery**, where the art of topiary is taken to incredible, beautiful extremes. Cypress bushes are trimmed into archways and fantastic figures of animals, angels, geometric shapes and so on, in *haut* and *bas* relief. Note the figures based on the stone carvings at San Agustín in Colombia, to the left just past the main entrance. To see the various stages of this art form, go to the back of the cemetery where young bushes are being pruned. The artistry, started in 1936, is that of the late Sr José Franco, now buried among the splendour he created. His epitaph reads: 'In Tulcán, a cemetery so beautiful that it invites one to die!' The tradition is carried on by his sons.

Sleeping
■ *on map*
Many hotels are along C Sucre

C *Machado*, Bolívar y Ayacucho, T984221, F980099. Includes breakfast, parking, comfortable. **C** *Sara Espíndola*, Sucre y Ayacucho, on plaza, T985925, F986209. Includes breakfast, nice restaurant, parking, comfortable rooms, helpful staff, best in town.

D *Lumar*, Sucre y Rocafuerte, T980402. Modern, clean, comfortable. **D** *Park Hotel*, across from bus station, T987325. Restaurant, clean, modern, small rooms, traffic noise all night, new in 2002. **D** *Rossy*, Sucre y Chimborazo, north of centre, T987649. Restaurant, simple, modern, new in 2001. **D** *Torres de Oro*, Sucre y Rocafuerte, T980296. Includes breakfast, restaurant, parking, modern, clean, nice. **D** *Unicornio*, Sucre y Pichincha, T982713. Chifa downstairs, OK.

E *Frailejón*, Sucre y Rocafuerte, T981129. Restaurant, private bath, hot

7 Sáenz Internacional
8 Sara Espíndola
9 Torres de Oro
10 Unicornio & Chifa
   Pak Choy

■ Sleeping
1 Colombia
2 Florida
3 Frailejón
4 Lumar
5 Machado
6 Rossy & Lucero
   Princess

● Eating
1 Antojitos Express
2 Café Tulcán
3 El Patio
4 La Fonda Paisa
5 Los Arrieros
6 Los Leños
7 Mama Rosita

water, parking, OK. **E** *Los Alpes*, JR Arellano next to bus station, T982235. Restaurant, private bath, hot water, OK, good value. **E** *Lucero Princess*, Sucre y Chimborazo, north of centre, T981523. Restaurant, private bath, hot water, parking, OK. **E** *Sáenz Internacional*, Sucre y Rocafuerte, T981916, F983925. Private bath, hot water, very nice, modern, good value. Recommended. **E-F** *Florida*, Sucre y 10 de Agosto, T983849. Cheaper with shared bath, hot water, modern section at back, good value. **F** *Colombia*, Colón 52-017 y Ayacucho, T982761. Shared bath, hot water, parking, clean, simple. **F** *Karina*, Sucre y 10 de Agosto, T984930. Private bath, hot water, basic.

Mid-range Upscale restaurant at *Hotel Sara Espíndola*, cheap set lunch, otherwise mid-range prices. **Cheap and seriously cheap** *Mama Rosita*, Sucre entre Boyacá y Atahualpa, typical Ecuadorian dishes. *Los Leños*, Olmedo y Ayacucho, seriously cheap set meals and cheap à la carte. *Antojitos Express*, Olmedo y Ayacucho, next door to *Hotel Sara Espíndola*, set meals very cheap. *Café Tulcán*, Sucre 52-029 y Ayacucho, café, snacks, desserts, juices. You can find Colombian specialities, all cheap, at *Los Arrieros*, Bolívar 51-053, *El Patio*, Bolívar 50-050 y 10 de Agosto, and *La Fonda Paisa*, Bolívar 50-032 y Pichincha. *Casa China*, at the bus terminal, serves Chinese food at cheap prices. There are a few other *chifas* and many cheap broiled chicken places in town.

Eating
● *on map*

Air *TAME*, Sucre y Ayacucho, T980675, flies Mon, Wed and Fri to **Quito**, US$33, and to **Cali**, Colombia, US$78, comfirm schedules and prices in advance. The airport is on the road to Rumichaca, the Colombian border.
    Bus The bus terminal is 1½ km uphill, south of the centre. It's best to take a taxi or a bus, US$1 from Parque Ayora. There is frequent service to Quito and all destinations along the way. To **Quito**, US$3.70, 5 hrs. To **Ibarra**, US$2, 2½ hrs. To **Otavalo**, US$2.50, 3 hrs. To **Guayaquil**, 20 a day, US$10, 11 hrs. To **Huaquillas**, on the Peruvian border, with *Panamericana Internacional*, 1 luxury coach a day, US$15, 17-18 hrs; with *Trans Gacela* US$14.

Transport

Banks *Banco del Austro*, Bolívar y Ayacucho, for Visa. *Banco del Pichincha*, at Plaza de la Independencia, Visa. Few places accept credit cards. There is nowhere in Tulcán to change TCs. Street changers at Plaza de la Independencia deal in Colombian Pesos. **Communications** Internet: prices around US$3 per hr, 1 by terminal and a couple near the Plaza de la Independencia. **Post**: Bolívar 53-27. **Telephone**: Olmedo y Junín and at bus terminal. **Colombian Consulate** Bolívar y Junín, visas require up to 20 days, Mon-Fri 0800-1300, 1430-1530.

Directory

Around Tulcán

To the west of Tulcán, along the Colombian border, lies a scenic area of rivers and waterfalls and further on *páramos* with geothermal activity at the foot of Volcán Chiles. This is also the access to the northern section of Reserva Ecológica El Angel. **Warning** Do not visit areas along the Colombian border without first enquiring about public safety (see Dangerous areas, page 47).

By far the best hot springs of the region are Aguas Hediondas (stinking waters). The baths are deserted on weekdays. Condors can sometimes be seen hovering above the high cliffs surrounding the valley. The area has been developed with indoor and outdoor pools, and camping is possible but bring all gear and food. **Warning** The area around the source is walled off because of extremely dangerous sulphur fumes (deaths have occured in the past), never attempt to enter.

Aguas Hediondas
A complex of pools fed by a stream of boiling sulphurous mineral water in a wild, impressive, lonely valley

Northern Highlands

Transport Buses leave for Tufiño every 2 hrs from opposite Colegio Nacional Tulcán, C R Sierra, US$0.80, 45 mins; it's a rough road with a military checkpoints. Last bus back at 1700. Follow the winding road 3 km west of Tufiño, to where a rusting white sign marks the turn-off to the right. From here it is 8 km through strange scenery to the magnificent natural hot river. Only the midday Tulcán-Tufiño bus goes up the hill to the turning to Aguas Hediondas.

Volcán Chiles & Lagunas Verdes Past the turn-off for Aguas Hediondas the road climbs to the *páramo* on the southern slopes of **Volcán Chiles**, whose summit is the border with Colombia. The volcano can be climbed in about six hours, but this border area is unsafe. To the south lies the Reserva Ecológica El Angel and the Lagunas Verdes (see page 184). The road then begins its long descent to **Maldonado** and Chical in the subtropical lowlands. One bus leaves from opposite Colegio Nacional Tulcán, Calle Sierra, daily at noon (US$4, five hours), returning early the next morning. Note safety warnings, above.

Frontier with Colombia

Leaving Ecuador Minivans from Tulcán to the border leave when full from Parque Ayora near the cemetery, 15 minutes, US$0.60. Shared taxis leave from the same area, US$0.70. A taxi from anywhere in Tulcán to the border costs US$3.50. A taxi from the bus terminal to Parque Ayora, US$0.80, there are also city buses from the terminal to Parque Ayora, but these may be too crowded for luggage. It's a short walk across the bridge from the Ecuadorean side to the Colombian side.

At the border At the close of this edition, the border was open 0600-2200; 24-hr service might resume in the following months. It is a well organized border. There is an *Andinatel* office for phone calls, a tourist information office with maps and general information (Mon-Fri 0830-1700) and a snack bar. Try to ask for 90 days on entering Ecuador if you need them, although you will most likely be given less.

NB You are not allowed to cross to Ipiales for the day without having your passport stamped. Both Ecuadorean exit stamp and Colombian entry stamp are required. The Colombian border complex is well organized. There is a Telecom office for phone calls.

Exchange The many money changers on both sides of the border will exchange US dollars cash and Colombian Pesos. Always do your own arithmetic and beware of tricks.

Into Colombia About 2 km from the border bridge is the Colombian town of **Ipiales**, 'the city of the three volcanoes'. It has an Indian market every Friday morning. There is a good selection of hotels and transport links by air and road into Colombia are frequent. About 7 km east of Ipiales is the famous Sanctuary and pilgrimage centre of **Las Lajas**, on a bridge over the Río Guáitara, which is definitely worth a visit for its architecture and setting. For more details see the *Colombia Handbook* or *South American Handbook*.

Southern Colombia has been a centre of that country's guerrilla conflict. Always enquire about public safety before entering Colombia

Transport Just north of the international bridge you will find transport for Ipiales. Minivans and shared taxis for US$0.30, taxi to the centre US$1.85, and taxi to the bus terminal US$2.25.

Central Highlands

Introducing the Central Highlands

South from Quito is some of the loveliest mountain scenery in Ecuador. This part of the country was named the 'Avenue of the Volcanoes', by the German explorer, Alexander Von Humboldt, and it is easy to see why. An impressive roll call of towering peaks lines the route south: Cotopaxi, the Ilinizas, Carihuairazo and Chimborazo, to name but a few. This area obviously attracts its fair share of trekkers and climbers, while the less active tourist can browse through the many colourful Indian markets and colonial towns that nestle among the high volcanic cones.

Baños, named and famed for its thermal baths, is a spa popular with tourists and Ecuadoreans alike on the main road from the Central Highlands to the Oriente jungle. It is the base for activities ranging from mountain biking to café lounging, and Ecuador's latest attraction: volcano watching.

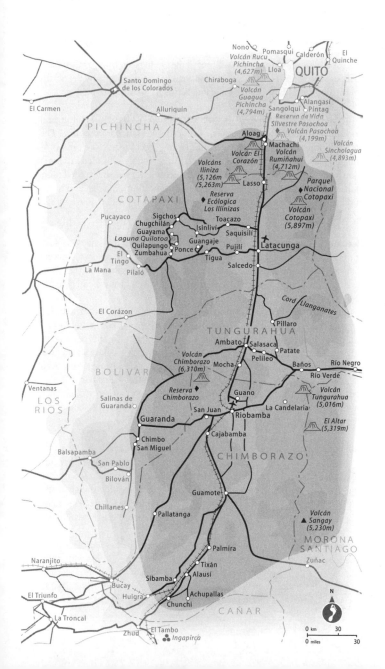

★ Things to do in the Central Highlands

- Climb **Cotopaxi**, one of the world's highest active volcanoes, page 195.
- Explore the popular **Quilotoa Circuit**, page 202.
- Savour the Provençal cuisine at *Mariane's* in Baños, page 216.
- Make a trekking excursion alongside **Chimborazo** or through **Parque Nacional Sangay**, page 232.
- Ride the train over the **Devil's Nose**, page 227.

The Panamericana climbs gradually out of the Quito basin towards Cotopaxi. At Alóag, a road heads west to Santo Domingo de los Colorados and the northern Pacific Lowlands; this is the main link between coast and mountains.

Machachi
Phone code: 02
Colour map 4,
grid A6
Population: 12,500
Altitude: 2,900 m

In a valley nestled between the summits of Pasochoa, Rumiñahui and Corazón, lies this town, with good views from its pleasant *parque central*. The area is famous for its mineral water springs and icy cold, crystal clear swimming pool. ■ *0800-1530 daily*. The water, 'Agua Güitig', is bottled in a plant 4 km from the town and sold throughout the country. Free, self-guided tours of the plant can be made 0800-1200 (take identification). Machachi is in the middle of an important dairy area. An annual highland rodeo, El Chagra, is held during the third week of July.

Sleeping   In town: **E** *Castillo del Valle*, Panamericana at 'P&S' gas station, south of town, T2314807. Private bath, hot water, parking, comfortable and good value, but out of the way. **E** *Estancia Real*, Luis Cordero y Panzaleo, 3 blocks east of park, T2315760. Private bath, hot water, parking, OK. **F** *Miravalle*, Luis Cordero y Barriga, east of centre, T2315222. Shared bath, hot water, basic.

Out of town: **D** *La Estación de Machachi*, 3 km west of the Panamericana, by railway station outside the village of Aloasi, T2309246 or T02-2447052 (Quito). Parking, lovely old home, fireplaces, hiking access to Volcán Corazón, advance reservations required. **D** *Tambo Chisinche*, 200 m east of the Panamericana, entrance 5½ km south of Machachi (small sign), T2315041. Includes breakfast, shared bath, spartan but clean, offers horse riding on Rumiñahui, advance reservations required. **E** *Papa Gayo*, in Hacienda Bolívia, 500 m west of the Panamericana, T2310002, h_eran@yahoo.com Restaurant, cheaper with shared bath, hot water, parking, chilly old farmhouse, nice communal area and library, friendly, arranges excursions, popular.

Eating   *Café de la Vaca*, 4 km south of Machachi on the Panamericana. Very good lunches and dinners using fresh produce from the farm. Pricey. Open Wed-Sun. *El Pedregal*, Colón 4-66, 1 block from the park. Roast chicken. Good, mid-range prices, log-cabin style. *El Chagra*, take the road that passes in front of the church, on the right-hand side and it's about 5 km further on. Good Ecuadorean food. *Kibi's Burguer*, Colón y Mejía, 1 block from the park. Snacks, fruit salads. Popular with locals. Cheap.

Transport   **Bus** to **Quito**, 1 hr, US$0.45, from Av Amazonas 1 block south of the park – *Ejecutivos* go to the Terminal Terrestre, *Populares* to El Recreo, 2-3 blocks north of the Trole station of the same name. To **Latacunga**, from obelisk at the Panamericana, 1 hr, US$0.45. To **El Chaupi**, from Av Amazonas opposite the market, every ½ hr, US$0.20. **Taxi** to **Cotopaxi**, about US$30 per car.

Reserva Ecológica Los Ilinizas

Machachi is a good starting point for a visit to the northern section of the Reserva Ecológica Los Ilinizas, a 150,000 ha nature reserve created in 1996 to preserve remnants of western slope forest and *páramo*. It includes El Corazón, Los Ilinizas and Quilotoa. The area is suitable for trekking and the twin peaks of Iliniza are popular among climbers. ■ *US$5.* *The southern section is accessed from Latacunga, see Quilotoa Circuit (page 202)*

Access is through a turn-off west of the Panamericana 6 km south of Machachi, from where it is 7 km to the village of El Chaupi. A dirt road continues from here to 'La Vírgen' (statue) about 9 km beyond. Nearby are some woods where you can camp. It takes three hours to walk with a full pack from 'La Vírgen' to the *refugio*, a shelter below the saddle between the two peaks, at 4,750 m.

Iliniza Norte (5,105 m) can be climbed without technical equipment in the dry season but a few exposed, rocky sections require utmost caution. Allow two to four hours for the ascent from the refuge, and take a compass as it's easy to mistake the descent. Iliniza Sur (5,245 m) is a four-hour ice climb. There are some steep, technical sections on this route, especially a 50-65° 400-m ice slope, and full climbing gear and experience are absolutely necessary. Climbing the Ilinizas
Also see Climbing, page 66

Sleeping *Refugio*, the shelter is fully equipped with beds for 12 and cooking facilities, take a mat and sleeping bag because it fills quickly, US$8 per person per night (the caretaker locks the shelter when he is out). **C** *Hacienda San José del Chaupi*, 3 km southwest of El Chaupi, T09-9713986 (mob). Includes breakfast, meals available on request, parking, converted farmhouse and cabins, horse riding, call in advance. **E-F** *Posada El Chaupi*, in front of bus-stop, T2860830. Meals with family on request, shared bath, electric shower, run by the Salazar family, basic and very friendly. *La Llovizna*, behind the church, T2314927 or T09-9699068 (mob). Restaurant, private bath, OK but not always open, try to call in advance.

Transport There is a frequent bus service from in front of Escuela Lequerica in Machachi to **El Chaupi**, 0600-1930 (30 min, US$0.30), from where you can walk to the shelter in 7-8 hrs. Horses can be hired at *Hacienda San José* or ask around the village. A pick-up from Machachi can be taken to 'La Virgen' (about 45 mins, US$10) from where it is a 3-hr walk to the refuge.

Parque Nacional Cotopaxi

Cotopaxi volcano (5,897 m) is at the heart of this beautiful national park and is one of the prime tourist destinations in the country. If you only climb one of Ecuador's many volcanoes, then this should probably be the one. Many agencies run tours here.

There are three entrances to Parque Nacional Cotopaxi. **The first entrance**, 16 km south of Machachi along the Panamericana, starts at a sign for the Clirsen satellite tracking station, which cannot be visited. This route goes past Clirsen and the old Cotopaxi railway station, then via **Area Nacional de Recreación El Boliche**. There is a shared entry fee for El Boliche and Cotopaxi; you should only pay once, but enquire beforehand on site. Follow the route for over 30 km along a signposted dirt road to reach the museum and Limpio Pungo plateau described below. Getting there
Colour map 4, grid A6

The second (main) entrance lies about 9 km further south along the Panamericana and is marked by a small Parque Nacional Cotopaxi sign; it is 6 km north

Central Highlands

of Lasso. Turn east off the Panamericana at the sign; nearly 1 km beyond, turn left at a T-junction and a few hundred metres later turn sharp right. Beyond this the road is either signed or you take the main fork. This is the main entrance and it is quicker and easier to follow than the first route. It leads first to a gate (see Park fees below), then climbs to a small museum and on to the plateau and lake of Limpio Pungo (3,850 m). Past Limpio Pungo the road deteriorates and a branch right climbs steeply to a parking lot at 4,600 m. From here it is 30 mins to 1 hr on foot to the *José Ribas* refuge, at 4,800 m (beware of altitude sickness). Walking from the Panamericana to the refuge takes an entire day or more, and may exhaust you for the climb to the summit. Entry to the refuge costs US$1, or US$12 to stay overnight (see Sleeping below).

The third entrance is from the north. Cyclists should consider this approach, rather than from the west, because the latter route is too soft to climb on a bike. From Machachi it is 13 km on a cobbled road, then 2 km of sand to Santa Ana del Pedregal. A further 5 km of sand leads to the park entrance, then it is 15 km to the car park. The last 7 km are steep and soft. The descent takes 1½ hrs, as opposed to 7 hrs going up. Quito operators run bicycling tours here.

If you don't have a car it is best to take a **Quito-Latacunga** bus (or vice-versa) and get off at **Lasso** (see below). Do not take an express bus as you can't get off before Latacunga. A pick-up truck from Lasso to the parking lot at 4,600 m costs US$25 for 4-6 people, one-way. If you don't arrange transport for the return you can sometimes get a cheaper ride down in a pick-up which has just dropped off another party. Alternatively, get off the bus at the second entrance described above and hitchhike into the park from there. This is usually possible on weekends. Frequently, but not always, there are pick-ups waiting for passengers at this entrance, US$20 for 4-6 people, US$40 return including wait; agree on the price beforehand. There is sometimes also a van for 10 passengers, US$10 per person. Pick-up trucks are also available from Latacunga for about US$25 round trip (ask at the Hotels *Estambul* or *Tilipulo* in Latacunga).

Climbing Cotopaxi

It is advisable to seek information from Quito tour operators or climbing clubs. Also see Climbing, page 66

Check out snow conditions with the guardian of the refuge before climbing. In 1996, a freak avalanche buried about 30 people on the patio behind the refuge. The ascent from the refuge takes 5-8 hours. It's best to start climbing at 0100 as the snow deteriorates in the sun. A full moon is both a practical and magical experience. Equipment and experience are required. Take a guide if you're inexperienced on ice and snow. Agencies in Quito and throughout the Central Highlands offer Cotopaxi climbing trips. Climb the sandy slope above the hut and head up leftwards on to the glacier. The route then goes roughly to the right of Yanasacha (a bare black rock cliff) and on to the summit. Allow 2-4 hours for the descent.

In addition to the normal route, above, Cotopaxi may also be climbed from the south. A private shelter was under construction on the south face in 2002. Contact Eduardo Agama in Quito, T02-2905258, F2903164, agama@accessinter.net

The best season is December to April. There are strong winds and clouds from August to December but the ascent is still possible for experienced mountaineers. The route is more difficult to find on Cotopaxi than on Chimborazo and the snow and ice section is more heavily crevassed and is also steeper, but the climbing time is less.

A four-wheel drive vehicle is advised as parts of the road are washed out

From the left branch at the fork for the José Ribas refuge, a narrow dirt road continues north and east along the *páramo*, making an incomplete clockwise circuit around the Cotopaxi volcano. Beautiful views and the undeveloped **El Salitre** archaeological site can be found in this area. The Inca fortress at El Salitre apparently guarded a pass from the eastern slopes of the Andes, which can be seen south of the site. Just north of Cotopaxi are the peaks of

Sincholagua (4,893 m), **Rumiñahui** (4,712 m) and **Pasochoa** (4,225 m). To the southeast is **Qulindaña** (4,878 m).

Rumiñahui can be climbed from the park road, starting at Laguna Limpio Pungo. The area around the base of the mountain is excellent for birdwatching and it is possible to see several species peculiar to the *páramo*. Watch out for wild horses, mountain lions and, most of all, wild bulls. From Laguna Limpio Pungo to the mountain base takes about 1-1½ hours.

Climbing Rumiñahui
Also see Climbing, page 66

The climb itself is straightforward and not technical. There is no difficulty, though it is quite a scramble on the rockier parts and it can be very slippery and muddy in places after rain. There are three summits: **Cima Máxima** is the highest, at 4,722 m; **Cima Sur** and **Cima Central** are the others. The quickest route to Cima Máxima is via the central summit, as the climb is easier and not as steep. There are excellent views of Cotopaxi and the Ilinizas. From the base to the summits takes about 3-4 hours. Allow around 3-3½ hours for the descent to Limpio Pungo.

This is a good acclimatization climb. Take cold/wet weather gear. Even outside the winter months there can be showers of sleet and hailstones.

Park essentials

Visitors to Parque Nacional Cotopaxi must register at the main entrance and pay the entrance fee of US$10. The park gates are open 0700-1500, although you can stay until 1800. The park administration and a small museum are located 10 km from the park gates, just before the plateau of Laguna Limpio Pungo, where wild horses may be seen. The museum has a 3D model of the park and stuffed animals. It is open 0800-1200 and 1300-1700. On the pine-forested lower slopes you may see the llamas which were bred by the park authorities and released in the park. Their numbers are diminishing, however, as they are prey to an increasing number of mountain lions.

Park fees & facilities

Inside the park There are 2 very run-down *cabañas* and some campsites (US$2 per tent, no facilities), at La Rinconada and Cóndor Huayco, both between the museum and Laguna Limpio Pungo; camping is not permitted around the lake itself. It is very cold, water needs to be purified, and food should be protected from foxes. The *José Ribas* refuge has a kitchen, water, and 30 bunks with mattresses. It costs US$12 per person per night, bring a sleeping bag and mat, as well as a padlock for your excess luggage when you climb; or use the lockable luggage deposit, US$2.50.

Sleeping

Outside the park To the east of the Panamericana and south of the park is a rounded hill known as Cerro Callo or Cerro San Agustín, a volcanic outcrop, once thought to be a prehistoric burial site. At its base are 2 nearly complete Inca buildings and the remains of several others incorporated into **LL** *Hacienda San Agustín de Callo*, entrance from the Panamericana just north of the southern park entrance, marked by a painted stone, it is 10-min ride from the highway, T03-719160, www.incahacienda.com Suites with fireplaces in room and bath, bathtub, breakfast and dinner included. Horse rides and bicycles US$10 per hr. For day visitors, there is a very expensive restaurant serving meals in 1 of the more complete Inca rooms, or pay US$7 just to enter. To the southeast of the park lies an area of rugged *páramos* and mountains dropping down to the jungle. The area has several large haciendas which form the *Fundación Páramo*, a private reserve with restricted access. Here is **L** *Hacienda Yanahurco*, T02-2241593 (Quito), F2445016, yanahurco@impsat.net.ec Ranch style rooms with bath, hot water, fireplace or heater, meals, 2-4 day programs, all-inclusive. Yearly rodeo in Nov. **B** *Cuello de Luna*, 2 km northwest of park entrance on a dirt road, T09-9700330 (mob),

At altitudes of 3,100-3,800 m, all these inns are good for acclimatization

T02-2242744 (Quito), F2464939, www.cuellodeluna.com Meals available at mid-range prices, parking, comfortable rooms with fireplaces, cheaper in dorm (a very low loft). **B** *Tambopaxi*, within the park at 3,750 m, 3 km south of the northern entrance (1 hr drive from Machachi) or 4 km north (left) of the turn-off for the climbing shelter, T02-2224241 (Quito). Rooms with several beds, duvet blankets, shared bath with hot shower, good restaurant serving expensive set meals and Swiss specialties, llama trekking, camping US$5 per person. **B** *Volcanoland*, between El Pedregal and the northern access to the park, www.volcanoland.com, includes breakfast. Transport from Quito and complete packages available at extra cost. **D** *Huagra Corral*, 200 m east along southern park entrance road, T09-9801122 (mob). Includes breakfast, restaurant, some rooms with private bath, parking, convenient location for those arriving late at highway turn-off, friendly and helpful, good value.

Lasso

Phone code: 03
Colour map 4, grid A6
Altitude: 3,000 m

The old railway tracks and the Panamericana cross one another at Lasso, a small town with a milk bottling plant, 33 km south of Alóag. It has some simple *comedores*, including *Express*, by the railway station, which serves Ecuadorean food, simple hardy meals. In the surrounding countryside are several *hosterías*, converted country estates offering accommodations and meals. Along the Panamericana are *paradores* or roadside restaurants.

Sleeping **B** *Hostería La Ciénega*, 2 km south of Lasso, west of the Panamericana, T719052, hcienega@uio.satnet.net Nice rooms with heater or fireplace, good expensive restaurant, horse riding (US$2 per hr). Reservations recommended Thu-Sun. In a historical hacienda reached via an avenue of massive, old eucalyptus trees. There are nice gardens and a private chapel. It belongs to the Lasso family (whose land once spread from Quito to Ambato), but is administered by others. A camioneta from here to the refuge parking area on Cotopaxi costs US$35. **C** *Posada del Rey*, facing La Ciénega, T719319. Carpeted rooms, mid-range restaurant with choice of 3 set meals, covered pool. Clean but a bit characterless and overpriced. **C** *Hostería San Mateo*, 4 km south of Lasso on the west side of the Panamericana, T/F719471, san_mateo@ yahoo.com Bright rooms with bath, pricey restaurant with set meals and à la carte, horse riding included. Small but nice, with friendly service, adjoining working hacienda can be visited. **E** *Cabañas los Volcanes*, at the south end of Lasso, T719524. Nice rooms with shared bath, hot water, transport to mountains, new in 2001.

Eating places include *Parador La Avelina*, on the Panamericana, 5 km south of Lasso. Cafeteria known for its cheese and ice-cream. A traditional stop for Ecuadoreans travelling this route. *Parador Chalupas*, opposite La Avelina. Similar cafeteria.

Latacunga

Phone code: 03
Colour map 4, grid A6
Population: 52,000
Altitude: 2,800 m

The capital of Cotopaxi Province, Latacunga, was built largely from the local light grey pumice and the colonial character of the town has been well preserved. Cotopaxi is 29 km away and dominates the city. Many other mountains can also be seen on a clear day and the wind sweeping off them is cold. The architecture, scenery and climate are well complemented by the local people, making Latacunga a thoroughly authentic highland town.

Ins & outs   **Getting there** The road from Quito enters from the north. A few simple hotels and restaurants are dotted along the highway, with better quality and more selection in the centre. **Getting around** The centre is compact and it is quite pleasant to walk around it.

Sights

The central plaza, **Parque Vicente León**, is a colourful and beautifully maintained garden with tall palm trees. It is locked at night. There are several other gardens in the town including **Parque San Francisco** and **Lago Flores**, also known as La Laguna. On Avenida Amazonas, by the Palacio de Justicia, is an interesting statue of a market vendor.

Casa de los Marqueses de Miraflores, at Sánchez de Orellana y Abel Echeverría, is housed in a restored colonial mansion with a lovely inner courtyard and gardens. Some of the rooms have been converted into a modest museum and it includes exhibits about the Mama Negra celebrations (see below), colonial art, archaeology, numismatics and a library. The house itself is worth a visit. ■ *Mon-Fri 0800-1200,1400-1800. Free. T801410.*

Casa de la Cultura was built in 1993 around the remains of a Jesuit monastery and incorporates the old Monserrat watermill. The finely designed modern building contains an excellent museum with precolumbian ceramics, weavings, costumes and models of festival masks. There is also an art gallery, library and theatre. Week-long festivals with exhibits, concerts and so on, are held here around 1 April (Fiesta de la Provincia), 9 August (Día de la Cultura) and 11 November (Fiesta de Latacunga). ■ *Tue-Fri 0800-1200, 1400-1800, Sat 0800-1500. US$1. T813247. Antonia Vela 3-49 y Padre Salcedo.*

Escuela Isidro Ayora, Quijano y Ordóñez y Tarqui, and the **cathedral** both have museums.

Latacunga

■ **Sleeping**	7 Llacta-Cunga	13 Santiago
1 Amazonas & El Salto	8 Los Nevados	14 Tilipulo
2 Central	9 Makroz	
3 Cotopaxi	10 Quilotoa	● **Eating**
4 El Alamo	11 Rodelú	1 Cafetería El Pasaje
5 Estambul	12 Rosim & Pizzería Los	2 Chifa China &
6 Jaqueline	Sabores de Italia	Chifa Fortuna

3 El Mashca
4 Los Copihues
5 Pingüino
6 Pizzería Buon
Giorno
7 Rosita

0 metres 100
0 yards 100

N

Essentials

Sleeping
■ on map
Price codes:
see inside front cover

C *El Márquez*, Roosevelt y Márquez de Maenza, in La Laguna neighbourhood, T811150, F813487. Restaurant, parking, bright, quiet, modern, but out of the way. **C** *Makroz*, Valencia 8-56 y Quito, T800907, F807274. Restaurant (closed Sun), parking, modern, comfortable, new in 2002. Recommended. **C** *Rodelú*, Quito 16-31, T800956, F812341, rodelu@uio.telconet.net Good restaurant (closed Sun), comfortable and popular, but some rooms small and a bit overpriced.

D *Central*, Sánchez de Orellana y Padre Salcedo, T802912. Cafeteria, a bit faded but friendly. **D** *Cotopaxi*, Padre Salcedo 5-61 on Parque Vicente León, T801310. Cafeteria, hot water after 0700, OK, rooms with view over plaza are noisy on weekends. **D** *El Alamo*, 2 de Mayo 8-01 y Echeverría, T812043. Helpful, area gets busy on market days. **D** *Estambul*, Belisario Quevedo 6-46 y Padre Salcedo, T800354. Cheaper with shared bath, long popular with travellers, quiet. Recommended. **D** *Llacta-Cunga*, Eloy Alfaro 79-213 (Panamericana, note hotel *Ilinizas* in same building is not as nice), T802372, F800635. Restaurant, parking, comfortable, helpful, fine views. **D** *Quilotoa*, Julio Andrade 1-08 y Eloy Alfaro (Panamericana), T801866. A bit out of the way but good value. **D** *Rosim*, Quito 16-49 y Padre Salcedo, T802172, F800853. Carpeted rooms, quiet and comfortable. **D** *Tilipulo*, Guayaquil y Belisario Quevedo, T810611, hoteltilipulo@ hotmail.com Cafeteria, comfortable, popular, helpful. Recommended.

All cheaper with
shared bath

E *Santiago*, 2 de Mayo 7-16 y Guayaquil, T802164. Comfortable, good value. **E-F** *Amazonas*, Valencia 4-36 y Amazonas on Plaza El Salto, T812673. Electric shower, simple but OK, overlooking market, noisy. **E-F** *Los Nevados*, Av 5 de Junio 53-19 y Eloy Alfaro, near bus terminal, T800407. Restaurant, hot water, parking, clean, modern, spacious rooms, good value but unpleasant area. **F** *El Salto*, Valencia 4-37 on Plaza El Salto, T803578. Small rooms, noisy, very basic but friendly. **F** *Jaqueline*, Antonia Vela 9-34, T801033. Shared bath, dodgy electric shower, very basic.

Eating
● on map
Price codes:
see inside front cover
Note that most places
are closed Sun

Expensive *Finca Parador Don Diego*, south of the train station and the Rumipamba bridge on the Panamericana. Trout, steak, chicken. Clean, classy, great service. **Mid-range** *Los Copihues*, Quito 14-25 y Tarqui. International menu, 4 course set lunch, good, generous portions. Mon-Sat 1000-2200. Recommended. *Rodelú* (see hotel above). Good breakfasts, steaks and pizzas, popular with travellers. *Chifa China*, Antonia Vela 6-85 y 5 de Junio, Chinese food, large portions. Daily to 2230. *Chifa Fortuna*, Antonia Vela 6-91, Chinese food, good quality. Daily 1100-2230. *Pizzería Los Sabores de Italia*, Quito 16-57 next to Hotel Rosím. Good pizza and Italian dishes, popular. Daily 1300-2300. **Cheap** *Pizzería Buon Giorno*, Quito 16-57. Great pizzas and lasagne, large selection. Open late. *El Mashca*, Valencia 41-54. Chicken. Good value. Open until 2200. Recommended. *Pingüino*, Quito 73-106, 1 block from Parque Vicente León. Good milk shakes and coffee. *Cafetería El Pasaje*, Padre Salcedo 4-50, on pedestrian mall. Snacks, burgers, coffee. Closed Sun. *Café Precolombino*, Belisario Quevedo 5-56 y Padre Salcedo. Breakfast, desserts and sweets. Closed Sun.

A **local specialty** is *chugchucaras*, a deep-fried assortment of pork, pork skins, potatoes, bananas, corn, popcorn, and *empanadas* – the ultimate high-cholesterol snack! The best are at *Rosita* Eloy Alfaro 31-226 on the Panamericana, very popular; also at *Don Pancho*, Quijano y Ordoñez y Rumiñahui; there are many others. Also try *allullas con queso de hoja*, biscuits with string cheese.

Bars &
nightclubs

Beer Center, Sánchez de Orellana 74-20. Bar and disco. Good atmosphere, young crowd. *Galaxy*, Barrio El Calvario, on a hill to the east of the centre. Disco, varied music, nice atmosphere. *Kahlúa Bongo Bar*, Padre Salcedo 4-56, on pedestrian mall. Bar. Wed-Sat 1900-0100. *Taberna La Mama Negra*, Padre Salcedo 4-49.

The *Fiesta de la Mama Negra* is held on **24 Sep**, in homage to the Vírgen de las **Festivals**
Mercedes. It celebrates the black slaves brought by the Spanish to work on the plantations and is similar to the *morenada* at Oruro in Bolivia. There is dancing in the streets
with colourful costumes, head-dresses and masks. Market vendors are among the
most enthusiastic participants in this event. The *civic festival of Mama Negra* is on the
first Sun in Nov, when all the elected officials of the Municipio participate.

Handicrafts Regional items include *shigras* (finely stitched colourful straw bags) and **Shopping**
'primitivist' paintings. *Azul*, Padre Salcedo 4-20, on pedestrian mall, ceramics, bronze
and wooden items. *La Mama Negra*, Padre Salcedo 4-43, on pedestrian mall. **Markets** There is a Sat market on the Plaza de San Sebastián at Juan Abel Echeverría.
Goods for sale include *shigras*, reed mats, and homespun wool and cotton yarn. On C
Guayaquil, between Sánchez de Orellana and Quito, is the Plaza de Santo Domingo,
where a Tue market is held. The main fruit and vegetable market, the *mercado central*
or Plaza El Salto, is between Félix Valencia and 5 de Junio. Market days are Tue and Sat,
but there is also daily trading. **Supermarkets** *Aki*, Av Rumiñahui y Unidad Nacional,
southeast of centre, largest. *Rosim*, Quito 16-37, is also well stocked.

All operators and some hotels offer day-trips to Cotopaxi (US$25 per person) and Quilotoa **Tour**
(US$35 per person, includes lunch and a visit to a market town if on Thu or Sat); prices for 3 **operators**
or more people. Climbing trips to Cotopaxi run from US$120 per person for 2 days (includes *Many are*
equipment, park entrance fee, meals, refuge fees), minimum 2 people. Trekking trips to *closed Sun*
Cotopaxi, Ilinizas, etc US$30-40 per person, per day. *Estambul Tours*, at *Hotel Estambul*,
T800354. Fausto Batallas, pleasant, experienced and knowledgeable. *Metropolitan
Touring*, Guayaquil y Quito, T802985, makes airline reservations. *Neiges*, Guayaquil 5-19 y
Quito, T/F811199. Day-trips and climbing. Fredy Parreño. *Ruta de los Volcanes*, Padre
Salcedo 4-55 y Quito, T812452. Day trips, tour to Cotopaxi follows a secondary road
through interesting country, instead of the Panamericana. *Selvanieve*, Belisario Quevedo y
Guayaquil, various tours, helpful. *Tovar Expediciones*, Guayaquil 5-38 y Quito, T811333.
Climbing and trekking. Fernando Tovar is an ASEGUIM mountain guide.

Bus Buses to Quito, Ambato, Guayaquil, Quevedo and all regional destinations such as **Transport**
Saquisilí, Zumbahua, Chugchilán and Sigchos leave from the **terminal terrestre** on the *Note that on*
Panamericana. Long distance interprovincial buses which pass through Latacunga, such as *Thursdays many*
Quito-Cuenca, Quito-Riobamba, etc do not go into the terminal. During the day *buses to nearby small*
(0600-1700) they go along a bypass road called Av Eloy Alfaro, to the west of the *communities leave*
Panamericana. To try to get on one of these buses during daytime you have to ask for the *from the Saquisilí*
Puente de San Felipe, 4 blocks from the terminal. The bus terminal has some shops, a bak- *market instead of*
ery, cafeteria, restaurant and a municipal tourist information office on the second floor. The *Latacunga*
tourist office is staffed by local high school students, friendly but limited information, Spanish only, open daily 0900-1800. To **Quito**, every 15 mins, US$1.40, 1½ hrs. To **Ambato**,
every 10 mins, US$0.80, 45 mins. To **Saquisilí**, every 20 mins (see below). To **Quevedo**,
hourly, US$3, 5 hrs. *Cooperative Santa*, Eloy Alfaro 28-57 y Vargas Torres, 3 blocks north of
the terminal terrestre along the Panamericana, T811659, serves **Cuenca**, US$8, 9 hrs; **Loja**,
US$10, 12 hrs; and **Guayaquil** via Riobamba and Pallatanga, US$5.50, 6 hrs. See Quilotoa
Circuit below for buses to Zumbahua, Quilotoa, Chugchilán, and Sigchos.

Banks Banco de Guayaquil, General Maldonado y Sánchez de Orellana, for TCs, Visa **Directory**
and MC. **Communications** Post Office and Andinatel: both at Belisario Quevedo y
Maldonado. **Internet**: prices around US$1.50 per hr. **Hospital** at southern end of
Amazonas y Hnos Páez, good service. **Laundry** *Lavandería*, General Maldonado 5-26,
$1 per kg, Mon-Fri 0800-1330, 1500-1800, Sat 0800-1200. **Parking** *Parqueadero Cen-
tral J S*, Quito y Echeverría, ample.

Central Highlands

The Quilotoa Circuit

This is a popular route with visitors, yet preserves an authentic feel in the many small villages and vast expanses of open countryside. You could easily spend a few days or more hiking, horse riding, visiting indigenous markets or just relaxing. The scenery is grand and varied, ranging from the immense Río Toachi Canyon, through patchwork fields and high páramo to cloud forest. There are several good little hostels in the area and an interesting 'hostel-hopping' trek is described in Trekking in Ecuador *(see page 464 for further details).*

All bus times quoted are approximate, as buses are often late owing to the rough roads or too many requests for photo stops

A popular and recommended round trip is from Latacunga to Pujilí, Zumbahua, Quilotoa crater, Chugchilán, Sigchos, Isinliví, Toacazo, Saquisilí and back to Latacunga, which can be done in two to three days by bus. Some enjoy riding on the roof for the views and thrills, but hang on tight and wrap up well. The whole loop covers around 200 km and can be covered in a car or by taxi in 7-8 hours of non-stop driving, but it is a long, hard trip. A better idea is to break it up into two to three days or more. There is accommodation in Saquisilí, Sigchos, Chugchilán, Laguna Quilotoa, Isinliví and Zumbahua.

Festivals in all the villages are quite lively and include *Año Nuevo* (New Year), *Domingo de Ramos* (Palm Sunday), *Carnaval* (Mardi Gras), *Semana Santa* (Easter Week), *Corpus Cristi, Mama Negra,* and *Finados* (Day of the Dead). Life in these small villages can be very quiet, so people really come alive during their festivals, which are genuine and in no way designed to entertain tourists.

Biking around Quilotoa

This is a great route for biking and only a few sections of the loop are cobbled or rough. The best access is from Lasso or Latacunga. Between **Toacazo** and **Sigchos** on the newer northern route there's quite a lot of cobble. Taking the

Quilotoa Circuit

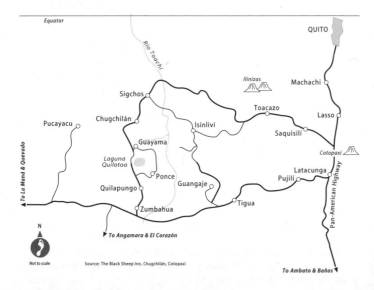

Source: The Black Sheep Inn, Chugchilán, Cotopaxi

Not to scale

older southern route via Isinliví avoids most of it, but there's a rough 4 km stretch coming down from **Güingopana** (the stunning views almost compensate). The route north from near **Guangaje** to **Guantualo** and **Isinliví** is good, hard-packed earth. From there to Sigchos is good gravel, then to Chugchilán and up to Quilotoa on gravel. It makes four days of good riding in beautiful surroundings.

From Saquisilí there are a series of little lanes which take you up to Yanaurco Alto and then either over Güingopana to Isinliví or south to Cruz Blanco near Guangaje. There's no accommodation here, but with a sleeping bag you can sleep overnight in the local school.

From Zumbahua an interesting route goes south. Take the main road towards Quevedo, turn south at **Apagua** on the pass and then climb to the pass above **Angamarca**. There is one dip on the road at a tiny village, then it is a major descent to Angamarca. You will find a small and very basic *pensión* on the plaza, or ask at the church. Below Angamarca, 3 km downhill, is the village of **Shuyo**, with a small shop with rooms used by bus drivers; if you arrive early there is usually space.

The road continues to **El Corazón** (*Hotel Cotopaxi*). From here you can freewheel down to **Moraspungo** (several *pensiónes*) and Quevedo, or continue through the mountains to **Facundo Vela** and up to Radio Loma and into **Salinas** (of cheese fame, see page 223). This latter route has a long tough uphill section from Facundo Vela, and sleeping bags are needed to sleep in village schools or the church.

Latacunga to Zumbahua

A fine paved road leads west to **Pujilí** (15 km, bus US$0.25) which has a beautiful church (but it's closed most of the time). There is some local ceramic work, a good market on Sunday, and a smaller one on Wednesday. Beware of local illicit liquor and pickpockets. The town boasts excellent Corpus Christi celebrations with masked dancers (*danzantes*) and *castillos*, 5-20 m high poles which people climb to get prizes suspended from the top (including sacks of potatoes and live sheep!). **E** *Residencial Pujilí*, Rocafuerte, half a block from the highway, T723648, simple, with bath, restaurant.

Pujilí
Phone code: 03
Population: 6,800

The road goes on over the Western Cordillera to Zumbahua, La Maná and Quevedo on the coastal plain (see page 309). This is a great downhill bike route. Quevedo can also be reached by turning off this road through El Corazón. *Transportes Cotopaxi* (Calle 5 de Junio 53-44) runs several buses daily to El Corazón via Angamarca (a spectacular ride).

This small indigenous village lies 500 m north of the main Latacunga-Quevedo road, 65 km from Pujilí. It has an excellent hospital, a school and a large church with woodcarvings by local artisans. It is quite sleepy for most of the week, but comes alive on weekends, festivals and market day, Saturday. The market starts at 0600, and is only for local produce and animals, interesting and best before 1000. Friday nights involve dancing and drinking. Take a windbreaker, as it can be windy and dusty. Many interesting crafts are produced by the Indians in the neighbouring valley of Tigua, such as primitivist paintings on leather, hand-carved wooden masks and baskets.

Zumbahua
Phone code: 03

Sleeping and eating E *Cóndor Matzi*, shared bath, hot water, best place around, reserve ahead, meals US$4. **E** *Richard's*, modern, clean, hot showers. **E** *Res Oro Verde*, first place on the left as you enter town, has small store and restaurant.

F *Pensión Quilotoa*, grey building at the bottom of the plaza, small sign, hot shower. **F** *Pensión Zumbahua*, at the top of the plaza, many rooms. There are a couple of others in the **E-F** range. You can find a cheap meal in the market. Just below the plaza is a shop selling dairy products and cold drinks.

Transport Bus: many daily on the Latacunga-Quevedo road, being paved in 2002 (buses run 0500-1900, 2 hrs, US$1). The noon bus continues up to **Laguna Quilotoa** along a fully paved road (2½ hrs from Latacunga, US$1.20). Buses on Sat are packed full; ride on roof for best views, get your ticket the day before. A **pick-up** truck can be hired from Zumbahua to Quilotoa for US$10-15; also to Chugchilán for around US$30-35. On Sat mornings there are many trucks leaving the Zumbahua market for Chugchilán which pass Quilotoa. **Taxi**: day-trip by taxi to **Zumbahua, Quilotoa**, return to Latacunga is US$40.

Quilotoa

Phone code: 03
Colour map 4,
grid A5
Altitude: 3,850 m

Zumbahua is the point to turn off for a visit to Quilotoa, a volcanic crater filled by a beautiful emerald lake, to which there is a steep path from the rim. From the rim of the crater several snowcapped volcanoes can be seen in the distance.

The crater is reached by a paved road which runs north from Zumbahua. It's about 12 km and takes 3-5 hours to walk, or 20 minutes by car. There's a 300-m drop down from the crater rim to the water. The hike down takes about 30 minutes (an hour or more to climb back up). The trail starts to the left of the parking area down a steep, canyon-like cut. You can hire a mule to ride up from the bottom of the crater, but arrange it before heading down. Bring drinking water as there's none at the top of the crater and the water in the lake is salty and sulphurous.

You can walk right round the crater rim in 6-7 hours, but parts of the path are very slippery and dangerous. Enquire locally beforehand and take a stick to fend off dogs on the road. Also be prepared for sudden changes in the weather. During the wet season, the best views are in the early morning.

Everyone here tries to sell the famous naïve Tigua pictures and carved wooden masks. The best artists are the Toaquiza family, at Chimbacucho, by the road at Km 53 on the way to Zumbahua. The father, Julio, began the paintings at the request of the late Olga Fisch, founder of the exclusive handicrafts store in Quito. Julio's sons and daughters are now regarded as the most accomplished of the Tigua painters, with exhibitions in the USA and Europe. Try to spread your business as people here are very poor.

Take a good sleeping bag as it gets cold

Sleeping D *Cabañas Quilotoa*, T812044. Owned by Humberto Latacunga. Basic, very cold, wool blankets, electric shower, includes breakfast and dinner, Humberto will lead treks and provide mules, he is a good painter and has a small store. **E** *Hostal Quilotoa*, owned by José Guamangate. Very basic, giant fireplace, offers bicycle rental, food, paintings and excursions. **F** *Refugio Quilotoa*, owned by Jorge Latacunga. You sleep on mats on the floor, he will cook food and take you on a day trek round the lake if you wish, he also paints masks. Camping is possible here. Also *Zhalaló*, a 40-min walk east of village, in the Ponce area T02-246 7130 (Quito). Restaurant with access to the lake; cabins are under construction, temporary accommodations may be offered.

Transport From the terminal terrestre in Latacunga there is a daily noon **bus** to **Quilotoa**, US$1.20, 2½ hrs. Note that this leaves from Latacunga, not Saquisilí market, even on Thur. Return bus to Latacunga passes Quilotoa daily at 0530. Another daily bus, *Trans Vivero*, takes teachers to schools in **Zumbahua** and **Quilapungo** (US$2.20), leaving Latacunga at 0600 and arriving at 0750 in Zumbahua and 0815 in Quilapungo, from where it is about a 1-hr walk to the crater. Alternatively, **hitch** a truck on Sat morning from Zumbahua market bound for Chugchilán and you'll be dropped close to the volcano. Hitching a return trip should not be left till late in the afternoon. Buses bound for **Chugchilán** or **Sigchos** will drop you 5 mins from the crater.

It is 22 km (six hours' walk) by road from the Quilotoa crater to Chugchilán, a small poor village in a beautiful setting. There is a Sunday market. **Chugchilán**

Sleeping B-C *The Black Sheep Inn*, a few mins below the village, T814587, www.blacksheepinn.com Run by Andy Hammerman and Michelle Kirby, private rooms or cheaper in dorm for up to 6. Includes excellent vegetarian dinner plus breakfast or lunch, drinking water and hot drinks all day, hot showers, book exchange, organic garden, sauna, 5% discount for ISIC, seniors or SAE members, llama treks, horse riding arranged, a good base for hiking. Highly recommended, reservations advised. **D** *Hostal Mama Hilda*, 100 m from centre of village towards Sigchos, T814814. Shared bath, hot water, cheaper in dorm, homey, includes dinner and breakfast, good food, warm atmosphere, arrange horse-riding and walking trips. Highly recommended. **D** *Hostal Cloud Florest*, next to *Mama Hilda*, T814808. Includes dinner and breakfast, shared bath, hot water, delicious local food, helpful owners, new in 2001.

Transport Buses depart daily from **Latacunga** terminal terrestre to Chugchilán, at 1030 via Sigchos, at 1100 via Zumbahua; on Thu from Saquisilí market via Sigchos around 1130. Confirm details in advance. Either route 4 hrs, US$1.80. Buses return to Latacunga at 0300, via Sigchos, at 0400 via Zumbahua. Milk truck to Sigchos around 1100. On Sat also **pick-ups** going to/from market in Zumbahua and Latacunga.

Continuing from Chugchilán the road runs through Sigchos, with its Sunday market. The road east to Toacazo is cobbled and from there to Saquisilí it is paved. Sigchos is the main starting point for hiking in the Río Toachi Canyon, but this can also be done from Chugchilán. **Sigchos**

Sleeping and eating E *Residencia Sigchos*. Basic but clean, large rooms, shared bath, hot water downstairs. **E** *Hostal Tungurahua*. Shared bath, hot water. Cheap accommodation at the *Casa Campesina*, take sleeping bag. There are a few restaurants in Sigchos, but ask in advance for food to be prepared.

Transportt Six daily **buses** to and from **Latacunga** (see Chugchilán above), US$1.40, 2 hrs. On Wed to **Pucayaco**, via Chugchilán, Quilotoa and Zumbahua at 0400, 9 hrs (returns Thu at 0400); and to **La Maná**, via Chugchilán, Quilotoa and Zumbahua at 0500, 9 hrs (returns Thu at 0500 and Sat at 0400).

Southeast from Sigchos, off the main Quilotoa circuit, is Isinliví, with its colourful Christmas fiestas. There are some spectacular hikes and bike rides in the area and several *pucarás* (hill fortresses). Also here is an excellent carpentry workshop to visit and some birdwatching. The Monday market at nearby **Guantaló** is also an attraction; there is plenty of transport. You can hike from here to the *Black Sheep Inn*, or vice versa, in three hours. A longer hike is to Yanuarco volcano, which will take a full day. Alternatively, catch a morning bus to Güingopana and hike the ridge route from the pass. **Isinliví**

Sleeping D-E *Llullu Llama* ('baby llama', pronounced zhu-zhu-zhama), T814790. Nicely refurbished house, private rooms or cheaper in dorm, shared bath (with great views!), hot water, meals available, a lovely spot. Recommended.

Transport Two **buses** serve Isinliví: from **Latacunga** at 1100 via Sigchos and 1300 direct, on Thu both leave from **Saquisilí** market around 1100, Sat and Sun both from Latacunga at 1100, US$1.80, 3 hrs, confirm details in advance. One bus returns to Latacunga at 0330, the second at variable hrs, enquire locally.

Saquisilí
Population: 5,200

Some 16 km south of Lasso, and 6 km west of the Panamericana, is this small but very important market town. Its Thursday market (0700-1400) is famous throughout Ecuador for the way in which its seven plazas and most of its streets become jam-packed with people, the great majority of them local Indians with red ponchos and narrow-brimmed felt hats.

Dan Buck and Anne Meadows describe the market thus: "Trucks brimming with oranges and yellow and red bananas; reed mats, fans and baskets. Beef, pork and mutton parts are piled on tables. Indian women squat down beside bundles of onions, radishes and herbs and little pyramids of tomatoes, mandarin oranges, potatoes, okra and avocados. *Cabuya* ropes are laid out like dead snakes, and a food kiosk every few metres offers everything from full *almuerzos* to *tortillas de papa*."

The best time to visit the market is between 0900 and 1200, be sure to bargain. The animal market is a little way out of the village and it's best to be there before 0700. Saquisilí has colourful Corpus Christi processions.

Sleeping and eating C *Rancho Muller*, 5 de Junio y González Suárez at south end of town. Expensive restaurant, parking, cabins, German run, owner organizes tours and rents vehicles. F *San Carlos*, Bolívar opposite the parque central, T721057. Private bath, electric shower, parking, view of plaza, good value, but watch your valuables. G *Pensión Chavela*, Bolívar by main park, T721114. Shared bath, cold water, very basic but friendly. G *Salón Pichincha*, Bolívar y Pichincha. Restaurant, shared bath, hot water, cheap and basic. *El Refugio*, half a block from crafts market, set meals and à la carte. *El Trébol*, 24 de Mayo near craft market. Cheap set meals. *La Abuela*, 24 de Mayo 5-60. Set meals and snacks. Very cheap.

Transport Frequent **bus** service between **Latacunga** and Saquisilí, US$0.25, 20 mins. Many buses daily to/from **Quito**, 0530 onwards, US$1.50, 2 hrs. Buses and trucks to many outlying villages leave from 1000 onwards. Bus tours from Quito cost about US$45 per person, **taxis** charge about US$60, with 2 hrs wait at market.

Salcedo
Population: 10,000

About 11 km south of Latacunga is Salcedo, with good Thursday and Sunday markets. The town's Mama Negra festival is on 1 November.

Sleeping A *Hostería Rumipamba de las Rosas*, in Rumipamba, 1 km north of town, T726128, F727103. Nice rooms and suites, swimming pool, good expensive restaurant. In pleasant country setting with gardens, a lake with boats, and sport fields. Highly recommended. F *Residencial Central*, Bolívar y Sucre, 1 block from main park. Small rooms, cheaper with shared bath.

Eating Mid-range *Casa del Marquez*, García Moreno y Quito, at north end of town. International food, set lunch and à la carte, bar. Very good, recommended. 0800-2400. *Ritz*, Bolívar y Sucre. Chicken. *Marisquería Tiburón*, Sucre opposite main park. Seafood. 0800-2100. **Seriously cheap** *Rocío*, García Moreno y Vicente León, 1 block north of park. Simple set meals.

Ambato

The capital of the Province of Tungurahua, Ambato is the main commercial hub of the central highlands, an important centre for the leather industry and a major market for nearby fruit growing valleys. It was almost completely destroyed in the great 1949 earthquake and has, therefore, lost the colonial charm found in other Andean cities. The city comes alive during festivals, especially Carnival, and market days. The Monday market is so busy in fact that Lunes de Ambato *(an Ambato Monday) has become synonymous with an unbearably hectic day anywhere in Ecuador.*

Phone code: 03
Colour map 4, grid B5
Population: 154,000
Altitude: 2,700 m

Getting there The main bus station is on Av Colombia y Paraguay, 2 km north from the centre. Town buses go there from Parque Cevallos in the city centre.

Ins & outs
See Transport, page 210, for further details

Getting around Ambato is a pleasant town to wander around. Many hotels are conveniently placed within a block or two of the centre, while others are in the quiet residential neighbourhood of Miraflores. Motorists driving through Ambato to other cities should avoid going into the centre as traffic is very congested. The *paso lateral*, a new bypass road running east of the city, is due to open in 2003.

Tourist information The helpful *Ministerio de Turismo* is next to the *Hotel Ambato*, Guayaquil y Rocafuerte, T821800. Open Mon-Fri 0800-1200, 1400-1800.

Central Highlands

Ambato

Sleeping
1 Ambato
2 Bellavista
3 Cevallos & El Alamo
  Chalet Restaurant
4 Gran
5 Guayaquil & Nueve
  de Octubre
6 Pirámide Inn
7 San Ignacio
8 Señorial

Eating
1 Café Marcelo's
2 El Coyote Disco Club
3 El Gaucho
4 Gran Alamo
5 La Buena Mesa
6 Mama Miche
7 Nueva Hong
  Kong

0 metres   100
0 yards   100

Sights

Because of its many orchards, flower and tree-lined avenues, parks and gardens, Ambato's nickname is 'the city of fruits and flowers'. Since it is the birthplace of the writers Juan Montalvo, Juan León Mera and the artist Juan Benigno Vela, it is also known as the 'city of the three Juanes'. On a clear day Tungurahua and Chimborazo can be seen from the city.

The modern cathedral faces the pleasant **Parque Montalvo**, where there is a statue of the writer Juan Montalvo (1832-89) who is buried in a memorial in a neighbouring street. His house (Bolívar y Montalvo) is open to the public. ■ *US$1. T824248.*

In the **Colegio Nacional Bolívar** is the **Museo de Ciencias Naturales Héctor Vásquez** with stuffed birds and other animals, botany samples, a small ethnographic collection and items of local historical interest. ■ *Mon-Fri 0800-1200 and 1400-1730, closed for school holidays. US$1. T827395. Sucre entre Lalama y Martínez.*

The **Quinta de Mera** is an old mansion set in beautiful gardens in Atocha suburb. ■ *Wed-Sun 0830-1600. US$1. Bus from Espejo y 12 de Noviembre.*

Out along the Río Ambato, a pleasant walk from the centre, is the prosperous suburb of Miraflores, which has several hotels and restaurants. Buses leave from the centre to Avenida Miraflores. Ambato is an important centre for the manufacture of leather goods and has some excellent tourist shops – look for colourful and good-quality cloth shoulder bags.

The main market, one of the largest in Ecuador, is held on Monday, and there are smaller markets on Wednesday and Friday. They are interesting, but have few items specifically for the tourist. Most of the action takes place in the streets, although there are also two market buildings.

Excursions

A couple of interesting excursions are to **Picaihua** (frequent buses) to see the local work from cabuya fibre, and to **Pinllo** to see the leather work. At **Píllaro**, 10 km to the northeast of the city, there is a bull run and fight in early August. Buses leave from the corner of Colón and Unidad Nacional, near Parque La Merced in the Ingahurcu neighbourhood (30 minutes, US$0.30).

Essentials

Sleeping
■ *on map*
Price codes:
see inside front cover

A *Ambato*, Guayaquil 01-08 y Rocafuerte, T412006, F412003, hambato@hotmail.com Includes breakfast, good restaurant, parking, casino, squash court. Best in town. Recommended. **A** *Hostería Loren*, C Los Taxos, southwest of centre in Ficoa neighbourhood, T/F846165. Includes breakfast, restaurant, parking, spacious rooms, residential area, modern, comfortable, but out of the way. **A** *Miraflores*, Av Miraflores 2-27, T843224, F844395. Includes breakfast, good restaurant, parking, heating, refurbished. **A-B** *Florida*, Av Miraflores 1131, T843040, F843074. Includes breakfast, restaurant with good set meals, parking, pleasant setting.

B *De las Flores*, Av El Rey y Mulmul, near bus station, T/F851424. Includes breakfast and dinner, cafeteria, modern and nice. **B** *Diana Carolina*, Av Miraflores 05-175, T/F821539. Includes breakfast, restaurant, pool and spa, modern, good views. **B** *Villa Hilda*, Av Miraflores 09-116 y Las Lilas, T840700, F420255. Includes breakfast, good restaurant, parking, classic old hotel with big garden. **C** *Pirámide Inn*, Cevallos y Mariano Egüez, T842092, F421066. Includes breakfast, cafeteria, parking, comfortable, owner speaks English and Italian. **C** *Señorial*, Cevallos y Quito, T825124, F829536. Restaurant, good.

Galápagos Wildlife

Lava Lizard (previous page) There are seven different species of this genus (Microlophus) endemic to Galápagos
Giant Tortoise (right and below) The oldest Giant Tortoise or 'Galápago' (Geochelone elephantopus) on the islands is thought to be 170 years old, born a few years before Charles Darwin's visit to the Galápagos

Marine Iguana (above) This endemic species (Amblyrynchus cristatus) could be as much as nine million years old, even older than the islands existing today.
Land Iguana (right) Two species of land iguana are found on the islands, Conolphus pallidus and subscristatus). Though less gregarious since the outlawing of feeding by visitors, the land iguana can still be seen at close quarters

Reptiles

The reptiles found on the Galápagos are represented by five families: **iguanas**, **lava lizards**, **geckos**, **snakes** and, of course, the **giant tortoises**. Of the 27 species of reptiles on the islands, 17 are endemic.

The Galápagos and the Seychelles are the only two island groups in the world which are inhabited by giant tortoises. The name Galápagos derives from the subspecies Saddleback tortoise (*galápago* means saddle). Fourteen subspecies of tortoise have been discovered on the islands, though now only 11 survive, including Lonesome George, a subspecies all by himself.

Giant Tortoises
Geochelone
elephantopus

No one knows the maximum age of these huge reptiles, though the oldest inhabitant of the Darwin Research Station may be as old as 170 (old enough to have met Darwin himself). Perhaps this longevity is due to their living a peaceful life, free from the stresses of modern living. Basically, all they do is eat, sleep and mate.

This latter activity takes place during the wet season from January to March. Later, between February and May, the females head down to the coast to search for a suitable nesting area. The female digs a nest about 30cm deep, lays between three and 16 eggs - depending on the species - then covers them with a protective layer of urine and excrement. Three to eight months later, the eggs hatch, usually between mid-January and March.

In the past, the tortoise population on the islands was estimated at 250,000, but during the 17th and 18th centuries thousands were taken aboard whaling ships. Their ability to survive long periods without food and water made them the ideal source of fresh meat on long voyages. Black rats, feral dogs and pigs, introduced to the islands by pirates, also affected the population by feeding on their eggs and young, until, in 1980, only 15,000 remained.

The Darwin Research Station is now rearing young in captivity for re-introduction into the wild, giving visitors the opportunity to see them close up. To see them in the wild, you can go to the tortoise reserve on Santa Cruz, visit the Los Galápagos site on San Cristóbal or make the long climb up to Volcán Alcedo on Isabela, the island with the largest tortoise population.

Of the eight species of marine turtles in the world only one is found on the islands - the Pacific green turtle. Mating turtles are a common sight around December and January, especially in the Caleta Tortuga Negra, at the northern tip of Santa Cruz. Egg laying usually takes place between January and June, when the female comes ashore to dig a hole and lay 80-120 eggs under cover of darkness. The white sand beach on Floreana is a popular egg-laying spot. After about two months the hatchlings make the hazardous trip across the beach towards the sea, also after dark, in order to avoid the predatory crabs, herons, frigates and lava gulls on the lookout for a midnight feast.

Marine Turtles
Chelonia mydas

This prehistoric-looking endemic species is the only sea-going lizard in the world. The marine iguana is, in fact, from another era. It could be as much as nine million years old, making it even older than the islands existing today. They are found along the coasts of most islands and gather in huge herds on the lava rocks. They vary greatly in size, from 60 cm for the smallest variety (Genovesa island) up to 1 m for the largest (Isabela island). Their black skin acts as camouflage and allows the iguana to absorb more heat during its exposure to the fierce equatorial sun, although those on Española have red and green

Marine Iguanas
Amblyrynchus
cristatus

Galápagos Wildlife

Red-footed booby *(right)* *Of the three species of booby found on the islands, the Red-footed booby is the only one to nest in trees, thanks to the fact that its feet are adapted to gripping branches*
Masked booby *(below)* *Masked boobies are most commonly seen on Española and Genovesa Islands*

Galápagos penguin *(above)* *Although distinctly ungraceful on land, underwater these penguins are speedy and agile and can be seen breaking the surface, like dolphins*
Blue-footed booby *(right)* *Best known for their comical and complicated courtship 'dance'*

Galápagos Wildlife

colouration. The marine iguana's flat tail is ideal for swimming. But though they can dive to depths of 20 m, and can stay underwater for up to one hour at a time, they prefer to feed on the seaweed on exposed rocks at low tide. Overzealous photographers should note that they frequently spray a salt excess through their nostrils to warn off any unwanted intruders.

There are officially two species of land iguana found on the islands: *conolphus subcristatus* is yellow-orange coloured and inhabits Santa Cruz, Plaza, Isabela and Fernandina islands, while the other, *conolphus pallidus*, is whitish to chocolate brown and found only on Santa Fé. The latter is the biggest land iguana, with the male weighing six to seven kilograms and over a metre in length. Their numbers have been greatly reduced over the years as the young often fall prey to rats and feral animals; the chances of survival for a young land iguana in the wild is less than 10 per cent. Though less gregarious since the outlawing of feeding by visitors, the land iguana remains a friendly little chap and can be seen at close quarters. It now feeds mainly on the fruits and yellow flowers of the prickly pear cactus.

Land Iguana
Conolphus pallidus **or** *subcristatus*

Birds

Sea birds were probably the first animals to colonize the archipelago. Half of the resident population of birds is endemic to the Galápagos, but only five of the 19 species of sea birds found on the Galápagos are unique to the islands. These are: the Galápagos penguin, the flightless cormorant, the lava gull, the swallowtail gull and the waved albatross. The endemism rate of land birds is much higher, owing to the fact that they are less often migratory. There are 29 species of land birds in the Galápagos, 22 of which are endemic.

This is the most northerly of the world's penguin species and breeds on Fernandina and Isabela islands, where the Humboldt Current cools the sea. The penguin population is small (under 1,000 in 2000) and fluctuates in response to the El Niño cycle. They may appear distinctly ungraceful on land, hopping clumsily from rock to rock, but underwater they are fast and agile swimmers and can be seen breaking the surface, like dolphins. The best time to see them in the water is between five and seven o'clock in the morning.

Galápagos penguin *Spheniscus mendiculus*

This is one of the rarest birds in the world, with an estimated population of 800 pairs. It is found only on Fernandino island and the west coast of Isabela, where the nutrient-rich Cromwell Current brings a plentiful supply of fish from the central Pacific. Though it has lost the ability to fly, partly due to the lack of predators, the cormorant still insists on spreading its wings to dry in the wind, proving that old habits die hard.

Flightless Cormorant *Nannopetrum harrisi*

The largest bird in the Galápagos, with a wing span of 2½ m, is a cousin of the petrels and the puffins. It is not only endemic to the archipelago but also to the island of Española, for this is the only place in the world where it breeds. Outside the April to December breeding season, the albatross spends its time gliding majestically across the Pacific Ocean, sometimes as far as Japan. It returns after six months to begin the spectacular courtship display, a cross between an exotic dance and fencing duel, which is repeated over and over again. Not surprisingly perhaps, given the effort put into this ritual, albatrosses stay faithful to their mate for life.

Waved Albatross *Dimeda irrorata*

Both the Great Frigatebird, *Fregata minor,* and Magnificent Frigatebird, *Fregata magnificens,* are found on the Galápagos. These 'vultures of the sea' have a wingspan as big as that of the albatross and spend much of their time aloft, gliding in circles with

Frigatebird

their distinctive long forked tail and angled wings. Having lost the waterproofing of its black plumage, the frigate never lands on the sea, instead it pursues other birds – in particular boobies - and harasses them for food, or catches small fish on the surface of the water with its hooked beak. During the courtship display, the male of both species inflates a huge red sac under its throat, like a heart-shaped scarlet balloon, and flutters its spread wings. This seduces and attracts the female to the nest, which the male has already prepared for the purpose of mating. This amazing ritual can be seen in March and April on San Cristóbal and Genovesa, or throughout the year on North Seymour.

Unlike the Great Frigatebird, the Magnificent Frigatebird is an 'inshore feeder' and feeds near the islands. It is very similar in appearance, but the male has a purple sheen on its plumage and the female has a black triangle on the white patch on her throat.

Boobies These are very common in the islands. Three species are found in the Galápagos: the blue-footed, red-footed and masked booby. The name is thought to derive from their extreme tameness, which led to many being killed for sport in earlier times.

The most common booby is the **Blue-footed booby**, *Sula nebouxii*. This is the only booby to lay more than one egg at a time (three is not unusual) though if food is insufficient the stronger firstborn will kick its siblings out of the nest. Unlike its red-footed relative, the blue-footed booby fishes inshore, dropping on its prey like an arrow from the sky. They are best known for their comical and complicated courtship 'dance'.

The **Red-footed booby**, *Sula sula*, is the only Galápagos booby to nest in trees, thanks to the fact that its feet are adapted to gripping branches. It is light brown in colour, although there is also a less common white variety. The largest colony of red-footed boobies is found on Genovesa island.

The **Masked booby**, *Sula dactylactra*, is the heaviest of the three boobies and has a white plumage with a distinctive black mask on the eyes. Like its blue-footed cousin, the white or masked booby nests directly on the ground and surrounds its nest with waste. It chooses to fish between the other two boobies, thus illustrating the idea of the 'ecological niche'.

Mammals

The number of native mammals in the archipelago is limited to two species of bats, a few species of rats and, of course, sea lions and seals. This is explained by the fact that the islands were never connected to the mainland. Since the arrival of man, however, goats, dogs, donkeys, horses and the black rat have been added to the list and now threaten the fragile ecological balance of the islands.

Sea Lion
Zalophus
californianus As the scientific name suggests, the Galápagos sea lion is related to the Californian species, though smaller. They are common throughout the archipelago, gathering in large colonies on beaches or on the rocks. The male, which is distinguished from the female by its huge size and domed forehead, is very territorial, especially at the beginning of the May to January mating season. He patrols a territory of 40 to 100 sq m with a group of up to 30 females, chasing off intruders and also keeping an eye on the young, which may wander too far from the safety of the beach. Those which are too tired or old to hold a territory gather in 'bachelor clubs'.

Sea Lion *(left) The male sea lion (Zalophus californianus) is very territorial, especially during mating season*
Waved Albatross *(below) The spectacular courtship of the Waved albatross (Dimeda irrorata) is part exotic dance, part fiery duel*

Great Frigatebird *(above) During courtship displays, the male inflates a huge red sac under its throat and flutters its spread wings*
Sally lightfoot crab *(left) These colourful and ubiquitous crabs stand out brightly as they scurry about on the dark volcanic rocks*

Galápagos Wildlife

The friendly and inquisitive females provide one of the main tourist attractions, especially when cavorting with swimmers. One of the sea lion's favourite games is surfing the big waves and another popular sport is 'water polo', using a marine iguana instead of a ball.

Sea lion colonies are found on South Plaza, Santa Fé, Rábida, James Bay (Santiago island), Española, San Cristóbal and Isabela.

Fur Seal
Arctocephalus
galapaoensis

Fur seals and sea lions both belong to the Otaridae or eared seal family. The fur seal's dense, luxuriant pelt attracted great interest and the poor creature was hunted almost to extinction at the beginning of the 20th century by whalers and other skin hunters. Fortunately, these *lobos de dos pelos* (double-fur sea wolves), as they are known locally, survived and can be seen most easily in Puerto Egas on Santiago island, usually hiding from the sun under rocks or lava cracks. The fur sea lion is distinguished from the sea lion by its smaller size, its pointed nose, big round sad moist eyes, larger front flippers and more prominent ears.

Marine Life

The Galápagos are washed by three currents: the cold Humboldt and Cromwell currents, and the warm El Niño. This provides the islands with a rich, diverse and unique underwater fauna. The number of species of fish has been estimated at 306, 17 % of which are endemic, though recent research suggests this number could exceed 400. Among the huge number of fish found in the islands' waters, there are 18 species of morays, five species of rays (stingrays, golden ray, marbled ray, spotted eagle ray and manta rays) and about 12 species of sharks. But not to worry, there have been no reported shark attacks on humans! The most common sharks are the white-tip reef shark, the black-tip reef shark, two species of hammerheads, the Galápagos shark, the grey reef shark, the tiger shark, the hornshark and the whale shark.

Among the marine mammals, at least 16 species of whales and seven species of dolphins have been identified. The most common dolphins are the bottle-nosed dolphin, *Tursiops truncatus,* and the common dolphin. Whales include the sperm whale, humpback whale, pilot whale, the orca and the false killer whale, Sei whale, Minke whale, Bryde's whale, Cuvier's beaked whale and the blue whale. These whales can be seen throughout the islands, but most easily to the west of Isabela and Fernandina. The waters are also rich in seastars, sea urchins, sea cucumbers and crustaceans, including the ubiquitous and distinctive Sally lightfoot crab.

D *Bellavista*, Oriente y Napo Pastaza, by stadium, T851542. Good. **D** *Cevallos*, Montalvo y Cevallos, T842877. Includes breakfast, restaurant, parking, good. **D** *Gran Hotel*, Lalama 10-45 y Rocafuerte, T824235, F825915. Friendly. **D** *Imperial Inn*, 12 de noviembre 24-92 y Av El Rey, near bus terminal, T844837. Restaurant, fridge, OK. **D** *San Ignacio*, Maldonado y 12 de Noviembre, T842370. Cafeteria, good value. **D-E** *Royal*, Cevallos 05-60 y Vargas Torres, T823528. Comfortable, modern, good value, new in 2002.

E *Madrid*, Juan Cajas y Cumandá, near bus station, T828679. Restaurant and disco, cheaper with shared bath, hot water, OK. **E** *Portugal*, Juan Cajas 01-36 y 12 de Noviembre, near bus station, T822476. Private bath, hot water, good value. **E-F** *Guayaquil*, JL Mera 7-86 y 12 de Noviembre, T823886. Cheaper with shared bath, hot water, renovated in 2002, simple but good. **F** *Nueve de Octubre*, JL Mera 326 y 12 de Noviembre, T820018. Shared bath, hot water, basic.

There are other cheap residenciales and restaurants around Parque 12 de Noviembre, but this area is not safe at night

Expensive *La Buena Mesa*, Quito 924 y Bolívar, T824332. French. Recommended. *El Gaucho*, Bolívar y Quito, T828969. Grill.

Mid-range *Bom Bocado*, Av Los Guaytambos next to *Supermaxi* supremarket in the susburb of Ficoa. Brazilian *churrascaría*. *El Alamo Chalet*, Cevallos 1719 y Montalvo, T824704. Ecuadorean and international food. Set meals and à la carte, Swiss-owned, good quality. 0800-2300, Sun until 2200. A little more expensive is *Gran Alamo*, Montalvo 520 y Sucre, T820806. International, meat, chicken, seafood. 1200-2230, Sun until 1600. *Farid*, Bolívar 705 y JL Mera, T824664. Grilled meat served in middle eastern sauces. *Miramar*, Quito y Rocafuerte. Good seafood. *El Coyote Disco Club*, Bolívar y Guayaquil. Mexican-American food, disco at weekends. *Cominos*, Guayaquil 9-34 y Bolívar. Good pizza. *La Fornace*, Cevallos 1728 y Montalvo, wood oven pizza. There are also several other pizzerías on Cevallos.

Cheap Two good cheap chifas are *Gran Pacífico*, Mariano Egüez y 12 de Noviembre, and *Nueva Hong Kong*, Bolívar 768 y Martínez. *Mama Miche*, 13 de Abril y JL Mera, Centro Comercial Ambato. 24-hr cheap cafeteria.

Eating
● *on map, page 207*
Price codes:
see inside front cover

Café Marcelo´s, Rocafuerte y Castillo, T828208. Good cheap cafetería, 0900-2100. *Pasterlería Quito*, JL Mera y Cevallos, good for breakfast.

Cafés

El Coyote, Bolívar y Guayaquil. *Cow-Boys*, Paccha y Los Incas. *Ilusiones*, Qis Quis y Madrid. *Exis*, Av El Rey y Floreana.

Bars & nightclubs

Ambato has a famous festival in **Feb or Mar**, the *Fiesta de frutas y flores*, during carnival when there are 4 days of bullfights, parades and festivities. It is impossible to get a hotel room unless you book ahead. The town has taken the bold step of prohibiting water-throwing at carnival (see Festivals, page 445).

Festivals

Supermercado, Centro Comercial Ambato, Parque 12 de Noviembre, or *Supermaxi*, Centro Comercial Caracol, Av de los Capulíes y Mirabeles, in Ficoa, for buying provisions. Good leather hiking boots from *Calzado Piedrahita*, Bolívar 15-08 y Lalama. Also quality footwear at *Calzados Cáceres*, Cevallos y Mariano Egüez. You can find leather jackets, bags and belts on Vela between Lalama and Montalvo. There are many stores for leather shoes along Bolívar.

Shopping

Metropolitan Touring, Bolívar 19-22 y Castillo, T824084, F829213 and in Centro Comercial Caracol, for airline tickets. *Coltur*, Cevallos 15-57; 471 y Castillo and Páez 370 y Robles, T548219, F502449. *Ecuadorean Tours*, Cevallos 428. Amex agent, but does not change TCs.

Tour operators

Central Highlands

Transport   **Car hire** *Localiza*, Juan Cajas y 12 de Noviembre, near the bus terminal, T849128.

Bus To **Quito**, 2½ hrs, US$2. To **Guayaquil**, 6 hrs, US$5. To **Cuenca**, 7 hrs, US$6. To **Baños**, 1 hr on a good paved road, US$0.60. To **Riobamba**, 1 hr, US$1. To **Guaranda**, 2 hrs, US$1.50. To **Latacunga**, 45 mins, US$0.80. To **Santo Domingo de los Colorados**, 4 hrs, US$2.65. To **Tena**, 6 hrs, US$4. To **Puyo**, US$2.50, 3 hrs. To **Macas**, 6½ hrs, US$6. To **Esmeraldas**, 8 hrs, US$6. To **Loja**, 12 hrs, US$9. To **Machala**, 7 hrs, US$6.

Directory   **Airline offices** *TAME*, Sucre 09-62 y Guayaquil, T826601. **Banks** *Banco de Guayaquil*, Sucre y JL Mera. Visa. *Banco del Pacífico*, Cevallos y Lalama, and Cevallos y Unidad Nacional. Visa and TCs. *Produbanco*, Montalvo y Sucre. MasterCard and TCs. *Banco del Pichincha*, Lalama y Cevallos, on Parque Cevallos and Av El Rey y Av de las Américas, near the bus terminal. Visa and TCs. **Communications** Internet: several in the centre of town, along Castillo, also Montalvo. Rates about US$1.20 per hr. Post: Castillo y Bolívar, at Parque Montalvo, 0730-1930. **Telephone**: *Andinatel*, Castillo 03-31 y Rocafuerte, 0800-2130.

To the east of Ambato, an important road leads to Salasaca, Pelileo and Baños, and then on along the Pastaza valley to Shell and Puyo, from where there is access to other cities in the Oriente (see page 379).

Salasaca   Salasca is a small, modernized village, 14 km from Ambato. The Salasaca Indians wear distinctive black ponchos with white trousers and broad white hats. Some anthropologists think they might be descendants of *mitimaes*, vassals brought by the Incas from Bolivia. Most are farmers, but they are best known for weaving *tapices*, wall hangings with remarkable bird and animal shapes. Prices are somewhat cheaper than in Quito, and the selection is much better. If you have the time you can order one to be specially made. This takes four to six weeks, but is well worth the wait. You can watch the Indians weaving in the main workshop opposite the church. Fine backstrap weaving can also be seen at Alonso Pilla's, just off the main road (signed). He also runs a small hostel, **E** *Runa Huasi*, 1 km north off main highway, look for signs and ask around, T09-9840125 (mob). Shared bath, kitchen facilities, simple and friendly, nice views. Alonso's daughter guides walks in the area.

Pelileo   Pelileo, 5 km beyond Salasaca, is a lively little market town which has been *Phone code: 03*   almost completely rebuilt on a new site since the 1949 earthquake. In all, *Population: 9,000*   Pelileo has been destroyed by four earthquakes during its 400-year history. *Altitude: 2,500 m*   The town springs to life on Saturday, the main market day. This is the blue jean manufacturing capital of Ecuador, with lots of clothing for sale everywhere. There are good views of Tungurahua from the plaza. The town's *Fiesta* is held on 22 July. Regular buses make the half-hour journey from Ambato and Baños. There is **E** *Hostal Pelileo*, Eloy Alfaro 641, T871390, shared bath, hot water, and several simple restaurants near the bus terminal.

Patate   About 8 km northeast from Pelileo on a paved side-road is Patate, a sleepy lit- *Phone code: 03*   tle town at the centre of the warm, fruit-growing Patate valley. It has a *Population: 1,800*   well-kept main park and a modern church. The fiesta of Nuestro Señor del *Altitude: 2,213 m*   Terremoto is held on the weeekend of **February 4**, featuring a parade with beautiful floats made with fruit and flowers, reportedly the most elaborate in Ecuador. Arepas, sweets made of squash (unrelated to the Colombian or Venezuelan variety), are the local delicacy; sold around the park

Sleeping and eating   A *Hacienda Los Manteles*, in the Leito Valley, on the road to El Triunfo, T870123, T/F02-2505230 (Quito). Converted farm with great views of Tungurahua and Chimborazo, restaurant, offers hiking and horse riding. **A** *Hostería Viña del Río*, 3 km from town along the old road from Patate to Baños, T/F870139. Cabins for 4-8, restaurant, pool, sauna, games room, horse riding. Busy at weekends, US$3 per day for the use of the facilities. **E** *Jardín del Valle*, M Soria y A Calderón, 1 block from the main park, T870209, nicely furnished, good breakfast available, good value. Recommended. **F** *Hospedaje Altamira*, Av Ambato y J Montalvo, on the road from Pelileo, shared bath, hot shower, basic. *Los Arupos*, a restaurant at the park, set meals.

From Pelileo, the road gradually descends to Las Juntas, the meeting point of the Patate and Chambo rivers to form the Río Pastaza. About 1 km further east, the junction with the road from Riobamba is marked by a large sculpture of a macaw and a toucan – the spot is locally known as *los pájaros* (the birds). The road from Ambato then continues along the lower slopes of the volcano Tungurahua to Baños (25 km from Pelileo). The road gives good views of the Pastaza gorge and the volcano.

Due to landslides and volcanic activity the road from Los pájaros to Riobamba was impossible to all vehicles in 2002

Baños

The town of Baños, with its beautiful setting and pleasant sub-tropical climate, is a major holiday resort. It is bursting at the seams with hotels, residenciales, restaurants and tour agencies. The sidewalks of the main street, Calle Ambato, are lined with outdoor cafés and teem with visitors on a Saturday night. Ecuadoreans flock here on weekends and holidays for a dip in the hot springs, to visit the basilica, and to enjoy the melcochas *(toffees), while escaping the Andean chill. Foreign visitors are also frequent; using Baños as a base for trekking, organizing a visit to the jungle, making local day-trips on horseback or by mountain bike, or just plain hanging out. The town's landmarks include the* Parque de la Basílica, Parque Central *and the* Manto de la Vírgen *waterfall. The Río Pastaza rushes past Baños to the Agoyán waterfalls 10 km further down the valley, nearly dry now because of the construction of a hydroelectric dam. The whole area has a relaxing sub-tropical climate, but it can be cool during the rainy season, usually May to October, especially July and August.*

Phone code: 03
Colour map 4, grid B6
Population: 10,500
Altitude: 1,800 m

Ins and outs

The bus station is on the Ambato-Puyo road (Av Amazonas) a short way from the centre. On the 2nd floor is the information office. Its patio is the scene of vigorous volleyball games most afternoons. The road from Ambato enters the city from the west, crosses the Riachuelo Bascún and continues to the east along the southern bank of the Río Pastaza towards Puyo.

Getting there
See also Transport, page 219

Baños is an easy place to get around, with most hotels centrally located. A unique feature is the presence of sidewalk ramps, which make the centre of town wheelchair accessible. City buses run throughout the day from Alfaro y Matrtínez east to Agoyán. There is less frequent service west to El Salado and the zoo. Baños is generally safe and tranquil but occasional robberies have been reported along some of the walking trails near town, usually on busy weekends and holidays.

Getting around

The Municipal tourist office is on the 2nd floor of the bus terminal; 0800-1300, 1400-1700 (1600 Sat and Sun). There are also several private 'tourist information

Tourist information

offices' run by travel agencies near the bus station. The latter offer high-pressure tour sales, maps and pamphlets. Local artist, J Urquizo, produces an accurate pictorial map of Baños, 12 de Noviembre y Ambato, also sold in many shops.

Volcanic activity

Volcanic hazards
The National Geophysics Institute provides volcanic activity updates in Spanish at www.epn.edu.ec

Baños is nestled between the Río Pastaza and the Tungurahua volcano, only 8 km from its crater. After over 80 years of inactivity, Tungurahua began venting steam and ash in 1999 and the town was evacuated because of the threat of a major eruption between October and December of that year. Volcanic activity gradually diminished during 2000, former residents and tourists returned, and Baños recovered its wonderful resort atmosphere. At the close of this edition (October 2002) volcanic activity continues at a generally low level, but occasionally intensifies to produce notable explosions which affect the upper parts of the cone. Tungurahua is closed to climbers and the road from Baños to Riobamba is impassable because of damage caused by debris flows, but all else is normal. Since the level of volcanic activity can change, you might wish to enquire locally before visiting Baños.

Baños

Sleeping	
1	El Castillo C4
2	El Rey B2
3	Flor de Oriente B2
4	Hostal Cultural C4
5	Inti Raymi B2
6	Isla de Baños C2
7	La Floresta C2
8	La Petite Auberge & Le Petit Restaurant C3
9	Los Nevados B4
10	Monte Selva C2
11	Palace C4
12	Pensión Patty B3
13	Plantas y Blanco C3
14	Posada El Marqués C4
15	Princesa María B1
16	Rosita C3
17	Sangay C4
18	Santa Clara C4
19	Santa Cruz C3
20	Timara C2
21	Villa Gertrudis C3

Eating	
1	Café Blah Blah B2
2	Café Hood B2
3	Casa Hood C3
4	Closerie des Lilas B3
5	Deep Forest Café C2
6	Donde Marcelo B3
7	El Jardín C3
8	Higuerón C3
9	Inca Flame B3
10	La Casa Vieja de Düsseldorf B3
11	Mariane C2, C3
12	Pancho Villa C3
13	Rico Pan B2
14	Rincón de Suecia C3

Bars	
15	Bamboos
16	Hard Rock Café
17	La Burbuja
18	Peña Ananitay
19	Peña Canela y Clavo

The positive side of the reactivation of Tungurahua is that the Baños area has acquired an important new attraction: volcano watching, which can be enjoyed from Baños, Patate, Pelileo and several other nearby locations. With clear weather and a little luck, the visitor can experience the unforgettable sight of mushroom clouds being expelled from the crater by day, and occasionally even red-hot boulders tumbling down the flanks of the volcano at night. *Trekking in Ecuador* (see page 464 for further details) describes an interesting volcano-watching route which can be accessed from Baños or Riobamba.

Volcano watching

Sights

The **Manto de la Virgen** waterfall at the southeast end of town is a symbol of Baños. The **Basílica** attracts many pilgrims. The paintings of miracles performed by Nuestra Señora del Agua Santa are worth seeing and there is a museum with stuffed birds and Nuestra Señora's clothing. ■ *0700-1600. US$0.50.*

Waterfall & basílica

Six sets of thermal baths are located in and around town. The brown colour of the water is due to its high mineral content. The **Baños de la Virgen** are by the waterfall opposite the *Hotel Sangay*. The water in the hot pools is changed daily, and the cold pool is chlorinated. It's best to visit very early in the morning before the crowds (open 0430-1700). Two small hot pools are open in the evenings only (1800-2200) and their water is also changed daily. The **Piscinas Modernas**, with a water slide, are next door and are open weekends and holidays only (0800-1700).

Hot springs
Each of the baths, which can get very crowded at weekends and holidays, charge US$2 for foreigners

The **El Salado** baths (several hot pools with water changed daily, plus icy-cold river water) are 1½ km from the centre, off the Ambato road (0430-1700). If walking from town, take a trail that starts at the west end of Martínez and crosses the Bascún river; the baths are at the top of the road on the west side of the river. **NB** This is a high risk area during volcanic activity.

This is a high risk area during volcanic activity

The **Santa Clara** baths, at the south end of Calle Rafael Vieira (formerly Santa Clara), are tepid, popular with children and have a gym and sauna, open weekends and holidays (0800-1800). **Eduardo's** baths are next to Santa Clara, with a 25-m cold pool (the best for swimming laps) and a small warm pool (0800-1800). Entry to pools only US$1, spa US$2.50. The **Santa Ana** baths, with hot and cold pools, just east of town on the road to Puyo, are open weekends and holidays (0800-1700).

Excursions

There are many interesting **walks** in the Baños area. The **San Martín shrine** is a 45 minute easy stroll from town and overlooks a deep rocky canyon with the Río Pastaza rushing below. Beyond the shrine, crossing the San Martín bridge to the north side of the Pastaza, is the **zoo**, with a large variety of regional animals, in well designed enclosures. Recommended. ■ *0800-1800. US$1.* Across the road is the **vivarium**, with a collection of snakes, ■ *US$0.75.* Some 50 m beyond the zoo is a path to the **Inés María waterfall**, a thundering, but sadly polluted, cascade. The road continues on the north side of the Pastaza to the village of **Lligua** which straddles the river of the same name. A trail leads uphill from Lligua two to three hours to **Las Antenas**, a good place for viewing Tungurahua.

Central Highlands

Caution is advised near the San Francisco bridge as well as on the paths to Bellavista and Runtún. Visitors have occasionally been robbed in these locations

You can also cross the Pastaza by the **Puente San Francisco** pedestrian suspension bridge, behind the kiosks across the main road from the bus station (a larger vehicular bridge was under construction here in 2002). From here a series of trails fans out into the surrounding hills, offering excellent views of Tungurahua from the ridgetops in clear weather. A total of six bridges span the Pastaza near Baños, so you can make a round trip.

On the hillside behind Baños, it is a 45-minute hike to the statue of the Virgin, with good views of the valley below. Take the trail at the south end of Calle JL Mera, before the street ends, take the last street to the right, at the end of which are stairs leading to the trail. A steep path continues along the ridge, past the statue. Another trail begins at the south end of JL Mera and leads to the *Hotel Luna Runtún*, continuing on to the village of Runtún (5-6 hour round trip).

Along the same hillside, starting at the south end of Calle Maldonado, the path to the left leads to the **Bella Vista cross**. It's a steep climb, 45 minutes to one hour, and there's a cafeteria along the way. You can also continue from the cross to the *Hotel Luna Runtún*.

Essentials

Sleeping
■ *on map, page 212*
Price codes:
see inside front cover.
Baños can get very crowded and noisy on public holidays, especially Carnival and Holy Week, when hotels are fully booked and prices rise

Baños is so amply supplied with accommodation in all categories that we cannot list every establishment. Many cheaper places are found around both parks, and north of C Ambato toward the bus terminal.

LL *Luna Runtún*, Caserío Runtún Km 6, T740882, F740376, www.lunaruntun.com Includes dinner and breakfast, restaurant, internet, beautiful setting overlooking Baños, very comfortable rooms with balconies, gardens, excellent service, English, French and German spoken, hiking, horse-riding and biking tours, travel agency, sports and nanny facilities. Recommended.

A *Cabañas Bascún*, Vía El Salado, west of town, T740334, F740740. Includes breakfast, good restaurant and service, pool, parking, comfortable cabins for 5, spa, tennis.

A-C *Sangay*, Plaza Ayora 101, next to waterfall and thermal baths, T720917, F740490, www.sangayspa.com Includes buffet breakfast, good restaurant, pool and spa open to non-residents 1600-2000 (US$3.50), parking, tennis and squash courts, attentive service, 3 categories of rooms, massage service. Recommended.

B *Monte Selva*, Halflants y Montalvo, T740566, F740244. Includes breakfast, restaurant, warm pool, parking, cabins, bar, spa, excellent service. **B** *Palace*, Montalvo 20-03, T740470, F740291, hotelpalace@hotmail.com Includes breakfast, restaurant, pool, sauna and jacuzzi, parking, nicely old-fashioned, front rooms with balcony, pleasant garden, friendly. **B-C** *La Petite Auberge*, 16 de Diciembre y Montalvo, T/F740936.

Includes breakfast, good French restaurant, parking, rooms with fireplace, patio, French run, quiet.

C *Casa Nahuazo*, Via a El Salado, below the baths, T740315. Includes breakfast, parking, quiet country house, pleasant surroundings. **C** *La Floresta*, Halflants y Montalvo, T740457, F740717. Includes excellent breakfast, good restaurant, parking, comfortable rooms, nice garden, friendly. Recommended. **C** *Villa Gertrudis*, Montalvo 2975, T740441, F740442. Includes breakfast, pool open to non-residents (US$1.50), parking, classic old resort, lovely garden, reserve in advance. **C-D** *Hostal Cultural*, Pasaje Velasco Ibarra y Montalvo, T740083. Includes breakfast, restaurant, nice sitting room, more expensive rooms have fireplace. **C-D** *Isla de Baños*, Halflants 1-31 y Montalvo, T/F740609. Includes European breakfast, internet, German run, nice atmosphere, pleasant garden. Recommended

D *El Carruaje*, Martínez y 16 de Diciembre, T740913. Laundry facilities, cooking facilities, comfortable. **D** *El Edén*, 12 de Noviembre y Montalvo, T740616, hostaleleden@ andinanet.net Restaurant, parking, wheelchair accessible, patio, balconies, nice. **D** *El Oro*, Ambato y JL Mera, T740933. With bath, includes breakfast, laundry facilities, cooking facilities, good value, popular. Recommended. **D** *Flor de Oriente*, Ambato y Maldonado on Parque Central, T740418, F740717. Parking, very good but can be noisy at weekends. **D** *Inti Luna*, Via a El Salado, below the baths, T741341. Quiet, comfortable, good value. **D** *Posada El Marqués*, Pasaje Velasco Ibarra y Montalvo, T740053, F741710. Spacious, good beds, garden, quiet area. Recommended. **D** *Santa Cruz*, 16 de Diciembre y Martínez, T740648. Modern and comfortable. Good value. Recommended.

D-E *El Belén*, Reyes y Ambato, T741024. Cooking facilities, parking, nice, helpful. **D-E** *Hospedaje 5 B*, Runtún above Luna Runtún, T09-944 9067 (mob). Meals available, cheaper with shared bath, well equipped kitchen facilities, parking, modern rooms with views of Baños or Tungurahua, pleasant but out of the way, new in 2001. **D-E** *Plantas y Blanco*, 12 de Noviembre y Martínez, T/F740044. Excellent breakfast in rooftop cafeteria (not included), cheaper with shared bath, French run, steam bath 0730-1100 (US$3). Recommended. **D-F** *Santa Clara*, 12 de Noviembre y Montalvo, T740349. Cheaper with shared bath, laundry facilities, cooking facilities, parking, simple rooms and nice cabins, garden.

E *Buena Vista*, Martínez y Pastaza, T740263. Private bath, hot water, quiet, simple, good value, new in 2001. **E** *Casa Blanca*, Maldonado y Oriente, T740092. Cafeteria, private bath, hot water, modern, sauna and hydro-massage (US$2). **E** *El Castillo*, Martínez y Rafael Vieira, T740285. Restaurant, private bath, hot water, parking, simple, quiet, friendly. **E** *Inti Raymi*, Maldonado y Espejo, T740332. Private bath, hot water, cooking facilities, garden, nice. **E** *Los Nevados*, Ambato 1 block east of the Basílica, T740637. Private bath, hot water, friendly. **E** *Monik's*, Ambato y Pastaza, T740428. Private bath, hot water, OK. **E** *Montoya*, Oriente y Maldonado, T740640. Private bath, hot water, modern. **E** *Princesa María*, Rocafuerte y Mera, T741035. Private bath, hot water, laundry facilities, cooking facilities, budget travellers' meeting place, popular. Good value, highly recommended.

E-F *Dinastía*, Oriente y Alfaro, T740933. Private bath, hot water, nice, quiet. **E-F** *El Rey*, Oriente y Reyes, T740322. Cheaper with shared bath, hot water, OK. **E-F** *Rosita*, 16 de Diciembre y Martínez, T740396. Private bath, hot water, a kitchen for every 2 rooms, OK. **F** *Carolina*, 16 de Diciembre y Martínez, T740592. Private bath, hot water, cooking facilities, terrace, friendly, good value. **F** *Pensión Patty*, Alfaro 556 y Oriente, T740202. Shared bath, lukewarm water, cooking facilities, ground-floor rooms poor, otherwise acceptable, family-run, long popular, very basic. **F** *Timara*, Maldonado 381 y Martínez, T740599. Shared bath, hot water, laundry facilities, cooking facilities, small and simple, nice garden.

Long term Rentals are ususally posted on the many bulletin boards in Baños hotels and restaurants; look and ask around.

Eating
● on map, page 212
Price codes:
see inside front cover.
There are restaurants
for all tastes and
budgets, many close
by 2130

Most establishments serve international food intended for foreign visitors, at mid-range prices. Those serving local fare and set meals are usually cheap or very cheap.

Ecuadorean C Ambato has many restaurants serving cheap set meals and local fare. The *picanterías* on the outside of the market serve local delicacies such as *cuy* and *fritada*. *Ambateñito*, Ambato y Eloy Alfaro. Good set meals and barbecued chicken. *La Puerta de Alcalá*, Av Amazonas (main highway), half a block downhill from the bus terminal. Good value set meals.

French *Mariane*, Martínez y 16 de Diciembre and Halflants y Rocafuerte, opposite *Andinatel*. Excellent authentic Provençal cuisine, large portions, pleasant atmosphere, good value and attentive service, mid-range prices, open daily 1800-2300. Highly recommended. *Le Petit Restaurant*, 16 de Diciembre y Montalvo, T740936. Vegetarian dishes, meats, fondue. Parisian owner, excellent food, great atmosphere. Expensive. Open 0800-1500, 1800-2200, closed Mon. *Closerie des Lilas*, Alfaro y Oriente, T741430. Simple but good. Open 1100-2300.

International On C Ambato are several popular restaurants, some with outdoor seating. Between Halflants and Eloy Alfaro are: *La Abuela*, small, good pizzas, good breakfasts. *La Calderada*, varied menu. *La Casa Vieja de Düsseldorf*, varied menu. Good value. *Caña Mandur*, set meals and à la carte. *Mama Inés*, popular. *Pepos*, varied menu. Other locations: *Deep Forest Café*, Rocafuerte y Halflants, at Parque Central. Middle Eastern and Greek specialties, vegetarian dishes. Good falafel and desserts, good breakfast. Open 0730-2100. *Donde Iván*, Halflants y Montalvo, at Hospedaje La Floresta. Ecuadorean and international food, excellent breakfast. *Donde Marcelo*, Ambato near 16 de Diciembre. Good breakfasts, friendly gringo bar upstairs. *Higuerón*, Arrayanes y Oriente. Good European, local and vegetarian food, nice garden, friendly. Open daily 0900-2230. *El Jardín*, 16 de Diciembre y Rocafuerte. some vegetarian food, juices and bar. Good atmosphere and nice garden. *Manantial*, Martínez y 16 de Diciembre. Dishes from all over the continent, specialty is 'elephant's ears', a thin piece of meat which covers your entire plate.

Italian *La Bella Italia*, 16 de Diciembre entre Montalvo y Martínez. Pasta. OK. *Bon Giorno*, Rocafuerte y 16 de Diciembre. Good, authentic dishes. *Buono Pizza*, Ambato y Alfaro, T740430. Pizza and Pasta. *Caesar´s*, Martínez y Halflants. Pizza. Wood oven. *Pizzería Napolitano*, 12 de Noviembre y Martínez. Pizza and pasta, pleasant atmosphere, pool table. *Il Pappagallo*, Martínez y 16 de Diciembre. Pasta.

Mexican *Pancho Villa*, 16 de Diciembre y Martínez. Good quality and service. Highly recommended. Open 0730-2130.

Vegetarian *Café Hood*, Maldonado y Ambato, at Parque Central, T740537. Some meat dishes. Excellent food, English spoken, always busy, closed Tue. *Casa Hood*, Martínez between Halflants and Alfaro. Varied menu including Indonesian and Thai dishes, some meat dishes, juices, good desserts. Travel books and maps sold, book exchange, repertory cinema, popular. Recommended. *El Paisano*, Rafael Vieira y Martínez. Variety of herbal teas and meals.

Cafés *Café Blah Blah*, good coffee, snacks, small, cosy, popular meeting place. Open 0900-2100. *Rico Pan*, Ambato y Maldonado across from Parque Central. Cheap breakfasts, hot bread, good fruit salads and pizzas, also meals. Open Mon-Sat 0700-2100, Sun 0700-1300. *Pancho's*, Ambato y Pasaje Ermita de la Virgen, west of the market. Snacks, coffee. Friendly. Open late 0800-2300.

Local specialities Look out for jaw-sticking toffee (known as *melcocha*) and the less sticky *alfeñique* made in ropes in shop doorways; another local speciality is *caña de azucar* (sugar cane), sold in pieces or as *jugo de caña* (cane juice).

Córdova Tours (see below) has a *chiva* (open sided bus) cruising town, playing music, it will take you to different night spots. *Peña Canela y Clavo*, Rocafuerte y Maldonado, at the Parque Central. Good atmosphere. Open 1900-2400. *Hard Rock Café*, Alfaro y Ambato, a favourite travellers' hangout, fantastic *piña colada* and juices. *Peña Ananitay*, 16 de Diciembre y Espejo. Good live music and dancing. *La Burbuja*, Ciudadela El Rosario, off Calle Ambato, east of the Basílica. Disco. *Bamboos Bar*, Alfaro y Oriente, popular for *salsa*, live on weekends *Coco Bongo*, Montalvo y 16 de Diciembre. Bar, snacks and pool hall. *Kasbah*, Alfaro y Oriente. Latin music, pool table, snacks and pizza. Open 1900-0200.

Bars & nightclubs
Many bars along Eloy Alfaro between Ambato and Oriente

Cinema   Films are shown at *Casa Hood* (see Eating above).

Entertainment

Oct *Nuestra Señora de Agua Santa,* with several daily processions, bands, fireworks, sporting events and general partying throughout the month. Week long celebrations ending **16 Dec**, the town's anniversary, with parades, fairs, sports and cultural events and much partying. On the evening of **15 Dec** are the *verbenas* when each *barrio* hires a band and there are many street parties.

Festivals

There are craft stalls at Pasaje Ermita de la Virgen, off C Ambato, by the market. For painted balsa-wood birds see *Recuerdos*, at the south end of Maldonado, where you can see crafts-people at work. Shops with a large selection of crafts include: *Tucán*, Maldonado y Ambato; *Monilu*, Alfaro y Oriente, good quality handicrafts and T-shirts, reasonable prices; *Las Orquídeas*, Ambato y Maldonado, also at Halflants y Montalvo (*Hotel La Floresta*), large selection; *Taller Arte*, Ambato y Halflants. T-shirts can be brought from *Latino Shop*, Montalvo y Rafael Vieira. Nice tagua (vegetable ivory made of palm nuts) crafts can be found at 3 shops on Maldonado between Oriente and Espejo, where you can see how the tagua is carved. Ask for the weaver José Masaquiza Caizabanda, Rocafuerte 2-56, who sells Salasacan weaving, gives demonstrations and explains the designs, materials, etc to visitors. *Galería de Arte Contemparáneo Huillac Cuna*, Rafael Vieira y Montalvo, has modern art exhibits and sells paintings including some from well known artists and coffee-table books. Crafts and musical instruments from the Oriente at *Pusanga Women's Cooperative*, Eloy Alfaro y Martínez. Leather shops on Rocafuerte between Halflants and 16 de Diciembre. *Tucán Silver*, Ambato corner Halflants, for jewellery.

There is a fruit and vegetable market all day Sun and Wed morning, in Plaza 5 de Junio on C Ambato y JL Mera. A smaller daily market is held at the Mercado Central on Ambato y Alfaro.

Book exchange *Artesanía El Tucán*, *Casa Hood* restaurant and *Rico Pán Café*.

Camping equipment *Varoxi*, Maldonado 651 y Oriente, quality backpacks, repairs luggage. Recommended.

Shopping

Safety A number of potentially hazardous activities are currently in vogue in Baños, including old favourites such as mountaineering and white water rafting, as well as more recent adrenaline-sports like canyoning and bridge jumps. You should be aware that safety standards for these sports vary greatly from agency to agency, and may be completely different from standards in other parts of the world. It is your personal responsibility to ascertain the quality of equipment and the qualifications of guides. There is seldom any recourse in the event of a mishap and you undertake such activities entirely at your own risk.

Canyoning This is an exciting new sport which involves rappelling down steep river gorges, above and in the water (note safety, above). Contact Franco at *Pequeño Paraíso*, Rio Verde (see below), T09-9819756, US$35.

Climbing See warning under Climbing Tungurahua, page 220. For companies offering climbs on nearby peaks, see Tour operators below.

Sport

Central Highlands

Cycling The road east toward the jungle is very beautiful and popular for mountain biking, see East of Baños (below). *Hotel Isla de Baños* runs cycling tours with good equipment. Bike rentals from *Adrián Carrillo*, 12 de Noviembre y Martínez, mountain bikes and motorcycles (reliable machines with helmets). Many other places rent bikes but the quality is variable; check brakes and tyres, find out who has to pay for repairs, and insist on a helmet, puncture repair kit and pump. Bicycles cost from US$4 per day; moped US$5 per hr; motorcycles US$10 per hr.

Hiking There are innumerable possibilities for walking and nature observation, near Baños and east towards Oriente (see below). Local agencies offer treks in the area.

Horse riding *Hotel Isla de Baños*, horses for rent; 6 hrs with a guide and jeep transport costs US$25 per person, English and German spoken. *Caballos José*, Maldonado y Martínez, T740746, flexible hrs; and *Angel Aldaz*, Montalvo y JL Mera (on the road to the statue of the Virgin). *Ringo Horses*, 12 de Noviembre y Martínez (*Pizzeria Napolitano*), nice horses, very well looked after. There are several others, but check their horses as not all are well cared for. Rates average US$5 per hr.

See also Rafting, page 76

River rafting Note that the Chambo, Patate and Pastaza rivers are all polluted. Also note safety, above; fatal rafting accidents have taken place here (not with the agencies listed). *Río Loco*, Ambato y Alfaro, T/F740929, riolocot@yahoo.com, half day, US$30, US$60 for full day (rapids and calm water in jungle), US$120 per person for 2 days with camping. Also *Geotours*, see below.

Tour operators There are many tour agencies in town, some with several offices, as well as 'independent' guides who seek out tourists on the street, or in hotels and restaurants. The latter are generally not recommended. Quality varies considerably; to obtain a qualified guide and avoid unscrupulous operators, it is best to seek advice from other travellers who have recently returned from a tour. We have received some critical reports of tours out of Baños, but there are also highly respected and qualified operators here. In all cases, insist on a written contract and, if possible, try to pay only half the fare up-front. See also Safety, under Sport, above. Most agencies and guides offer trips to the jungle (US$25-$50 per person per day in 2002) and 2-day climbing trips to Cotopaxi (about US$120 per person) and Chimborazo (about US$130 per person). There are also volcano watching, trekking and horse tours, in addition to the day-trips and sports mentioned above.

The following agencies and guides have received positive recommendations but the list is not exclusive and there are certainly others. *Rain forestur*, Ambato y Maldonado, T/F740743, www.ecuador-paginaamarilla.com/rainforestur.htm Run by Santiago Herrera, guides are knowledgeable and environmentally conscious. *Córdova Tours*, Maldonado y Espejo, T740923. Tours on board their *chiva Mocambo*, an open-sided bus (reserve ahead): waterfall tour, along the Puyo road to Río Verde, 0930-1430, US$8; Baños and environs, 1600-1800, US$5; night tour with music, 2100-2300, US$3 (they will drop you off at the night spot of your choice). *Deep Forest Adventure*, Rocafuerte y Halflants, next to Andinatel, T741815, deepforestadventure@ hotmail.com Eloy Torres, speaks German, English and French, jungle and trekking tours. *Geotours*, Ambato next to Banco del Pichincha, T741344, geotours@ hotmail.com Geovanny Romo. Small, experienced agency offering jungle and horseback tours, and rafting. *Explorsierra*, Alfaro 556 y Oriente, T740628, explorsierra1@ hotmail.com Guido Sánchez. Climbing, trekking, jungle and volcano-watching tours. *Expediciones Amazónicas*, Oriente 11-68 y Halflants, T740506. Run by Hernán and Dosto Varela, the latter is a recommended mountain guide, also offer trekking and jungle trips. *Willie Navarrete*, at *Café Higuerón*, T09-932411 (mob), is a highly recommended guide for climbing, an ASEGUIM member. *Huilla Cuna*, there are 3 agencies of the same name: at Rocafuerte y Ambato, T741086, Byron Castillo, helpful and knowledgeable, jungle and mountain tours; at Ambato y Halflants, T741292, huilacuna@

yahoo.es, Marcelo Mazo organizes jungle trips; and at Rafael Vieira y Montalvo, T740187, Luis Guevara runs jungle and mountain trips.

Car hire 4WD vehicles with driver can be rented from *Córdova Tours* (see Tour operators above), US$80 a day.

Bus To/from **Quito**, via Ambato, US$2.50, 3½ hrs, best service with *Transportes Baños* half hourly, recommended. Going to Quito sit on the right for views of Cotopaxi, and buy tickets early for weekends and holidays. To **Ambato**, US$0.60, 45 mins. To **Riobamba**, landslides caused by Tungurahua's volcanic activity have closed the direct Baños-Riobamba road until further notice, buses go via Ambato, US$1.60, 2 hrs. To **Latacunga**, US$1.50, 2-2½ hrs. To **Puyo**, US$1.50, 2 hrs. Pack your luggage in plastic as it all goes on top of the bus. Puyo-bound buses stop at the corner of Av Amazonas (highway) and Maldonado, opposite the terminal. To **Tena**, US$3.50, 5½ hrs. To **Misahuallí**, change at Tena, or at the Río Napo crossing (see page 376). To **Macas**, US$3.50, 7 hrs, some direct buses or change at Puyo (sit on the right). To **Coca**, 2 daily, US$10, 11 hrs.

Banks *Banco del Pacífico*, Martínez y Rocafuerte by the Parque Central, TCs and Mastercard ATM, Mon-Fri 0845-1600. *Banco del Pichincha*, Ambato y Halflants, TCs and VISA, Mon-Fri 0900-1300. *Distracturs*, Ambato y Halflants, 2.5% commission on TCs. *Don Pedro*, Ambato y Halflants, hardware store opposite Banco del Pichincha, 2% conmission on TCs.

Communications Internet: There are many cyber cafés in town, US$2 per hr. **Post:** Halflants y Ambato across from Parque Central. **Telephone:** *Andinatel*, Halflants y Rocafuerte by Parque Central, international calls. .

Language classes. *Baños Spanish Center*, Antonio Páez y Oriente, T740632, elizbasc@uio.satnet.net Elizabeth Barrionuevo, English and German speaking, flexible, salsa lessons. Recommended. *Spanish School 16 de Diciembre*, Montalvo 5-26 y Rafael Vieira, T740232. José M Eras, English speaking retired teacher. *International Spanish School*, 16 de Diciembre y Espejo, T/F740612. Martha Vaca F. *Instituto de Español Alternativo IDEA*, Montalvo y Alfaro, T/F740799. *Raíces Spanish School*, Av 16 de Diciembre y Pablo A Suáres, T/F740090, racefor@hotmail.com

Laundry Municipal washhouse next to the Virgen baths, US$1 a bundle, or do it yourself for free. *La Herradura*, Martínez y Alfaro, US$0.80 per kg. Several hotels have laundry service, eg *Monik's* and *El Marqués*, see Sleeping for addresses. Many others.

Therapeutic massage *Massage and Body Work*, Alfaro y Matrtínez, T741071. Swedish and Thai massage, US$20 per hr. *Stay in Touch*, Martínez entre Alfaro y 16 de Diciembre, T09-9208000 (mob). Various techniques, US$20 per hr. Also at *Hotel Sangay*.

Transport
See also Ins and outs, page 211

Directory

Rates for Spanish lessons in 2002 ranged from US$4-5 per hr

East of Baños

The road from Baños to Puyo (58 km) is very scenic, with many waterfalls tumbling down to the Pastaza. The first half to Río Negro is unpaved and can get muddy when it rains, the remaining half is paved and in good condition. The area has excellent opportunities for walking and nature observation.

About 17 km from Baños is the town of **Río Verde** at the junction of the Verde and Pastaza rivers, with several snack bars and simple restaurants. The Río Verde has crystalline green water and forms several waterfalls along its course, the most spectacular of which is **El Pailón del Diablo** (the devil's cauldron). Cross the Río Verde on the road and take the path to the right after the church, then follow the trail down towards the suspension bridge over the Pastaza, for about 20 minutes. Just before the bridge take a side trail to the right (signposted) which leads you to a viewing platform above the falls; there is a kiosk selling drinks and snacks.

The **San Miguel falls**, smaller but also nice, are some five minutes' walk along a different trail. In town cross the bridge and take the first path to the right.

Take any of the buses bound for Puyo from the corner of Maldonado y Amazonas (main highway), across from the bus terminal (US$0.50, 30 minutes). *Córdova Tours* offer a tour to Río Verde, stopping at several sites along the way, on a *chiva* (see Tour operators above). For a thrill (not without its hazards), ride on the roof. A worthwhile trip is to cycle to Río Verde and take a bus back to Baños. Leave your bike at one of the snack bars while you go to the falls (tip expected). It is also possible to cycle all the way to Puyo (4-5 hours); the entire route from Baños is very scenic.

There are excellent hiking opportunities up the Río Verde. The trail on the west side of the river begins at the town park. This trail makes a good day trip. There is basic lodging three hours up the trail; ask about Angel's cabins at the store just east of the town square.

At 2¼ km east of Río Verde is **Machay**, where several waterfalls can be seen, another lovely area for walking. About 10 km beyond is the larger village of **Río Negro**, from where there is access to the southeastern region of Parque Nacional Sangay. See page 383 for the section closer to Puyo.

Sleeping   **B** *Pequeño Paraíso*, 1½ km east of Río Verde, west of Machay, T09-9819756 (mob), www.geocities.com/pequeno_paraiso/ Nicely furnished, comfortable cabins, abundant hot water, includes breakfast and dinner. Lovely surroundings, tasty vegetarian meals with homemade bread, small pool, climbing wall, Swiss-run. Camping possible. Recommended. **D** *Indillama*, by the San Miguel falls, T09-9785263 (mob). Nice cabins, hot water, restaurant, includes breakfast. Beautiful surroundings, German-run.

Climbing Tungurahua

Colour map 4, grid B6   **Warning** Due to the reactivation of the volcano, Tungurahua has been officially closed to climbers since 1999. There is nobody to stop you from entering the area, but the dangers of being hit by flying volcanic bombs are very real. Those who ignore this warning do so at considerable risk to their lives. Unless volcanic activity has completely ceased, do not be talked into climbing to the *refugio*, crater or summit. To obtain impartial information, try the municipal tourist office at the Baños bus station; never rely exclusively on an agency who is trying to sell you a climbing tour. At the same time, remember that Tungurahua was a reasonably safe and popular climb for many decades. If the volcano calms down, then in all likelihood it will be reasonably safe once again. We do not describe details of the climb since these are likely to change once the mountain is re-opened to visitors.

Ambato to Guaranda

To the west of Ambato (see above, page 207), a paved road climbs through tilled fields, past the *páramos* of Carihuairazo and Chimborazo, to the great *arenal*, a high desert at the base of Chimborazo where *vicuñas* may be seen. Some 50 km from Ambato (44 km before Guaranda) is the access to Mechahuasca, one of the areas where *vicuñas* were reintroduced to the **Reserva de Producción de Fauna Chimborazo**. The turn-off left is marked by a large orange sign. About 13 km further is the intersection with the *arenal* road, to the south it leads to the Chimborazo *refugios* (page 232) before meeting the Guaranda-Riobamba road at **San Juan**. From the *arenal* the road from Ambato drops to Guaranda in the Chimbo valley; some parts are badly potholed and in need of repair.

Guaranda

This quaint, quiet town, capital of Bolívar Province, proudly calls itself 'the Rome of Ecuador' because it is built on seven hills. The town maintains its colonial flavour, and there are many fine, though fading, old houses along the cobbled streets with narrow sidewalks. There are nice views of the mountains all around, with Chimborazo towering above. The climate can be very pleasant with warm days and cool evenings; however, the area is also subject to rain and fog. Although not on the tourist trail, there are many sights worth visiting in the province, for which Guaranda is the ideal base.

Phone code: 03
Colour map 4, grid B5
Population: 21,000
Altitude: 2,650 m

Guaranda is connected by a paved road to Ambato and southwest to Babahoyo and by a narrow but spectacular dirt road to Riobamba. This latter route is known as the Gallo Rumi, so named because of a rock that is said not only to resemble a rooster but also, in a high wind, to sound like one! Until the beginning of the 20th century Guaranda was the main crossroads between Quito and Guayaquil, but with the construction of the railroad and later the opening of newer, faster roads, it has since stagnated.

For tourist information, the *Oficina Municipal de Información Turística*, García Moreno entre 7 de Mayo y Convención de 1884, has useful information and maps about the city and province. It can also arrange guided tours, horse riding and camping in the area. Spanish only. ■ *Mon-Fri 0800-1200, 1400-1800.*

Sights

Central Highlands

Guaranda

Selva Alegre
Plaza 15 de Mayo
Manuela Cañizares
Las Mariantas
Plaza Roja
Mons Cándido Rada
Av Guayaquil
To Ambato
Azuay
Convención de 1884
7 de Mayo
9 de Abril
Salinas
Gen Enríquez
Eloy Alfaro
MO Carvajal
Joaquín Galarza
Sucre
Municipio
García Moreno
Parque Libertador Simón Bolívar
Pichincha
10 de Agosto
Cathedral
Olmedo
Amazonas
Ambato
Terminal Terrestre
Vicente Rocafuerte
Espejo
Solanda
To Riobamba & Babahoyo

N
0 metres 100
0 yards 100

Sleeping	4 Ejecutivo	**Eating**
1 Acapulco	5 La Colinaí	1 Balcón Cuencano
2 Bolívar	6 Rosa Elvira	2 Juad's
3 Cochabamba	7 Sante Fé	3 Rumipamba

Locals traditionally take an evening stroll in the palm-fringed main plaza, **Parque Libertador Simón Bolívar**, with a modern statue of Bolívar. Those with an eye for detail will notice that the blade is missing from his sword; every year during Carnival the city places a new blade, which is promptly removed by the university students. Around the park are the municipal buildings with an attractive courtyard, paintings in the Salón de la Ciudad and good views from the tower (open Mon-Fri 0800-1200, 1400-1800), several colonial homes, and a large stone **Cathedral**, with a nice marble altar, wooden ceiling and stained glass windows.

Towering over the city, atop one of the hills, is an impressive statue of '**El Indio Guaranga**', a local Indian leader after whom the city may have been named. The site offers fine views of the city, the surrounding hills and the summit of Chimborazo. A cultural centre at the base of the sculpture includes a regional ethnographic and history **museum** (open Wed-Sun 0800-1200, 1400-1700), art gallery and auditorium. To get there, take a taxi (US$0.80); take a 'Guanujo' bus to the stadium and walk 10 minutes from there; or walk 45 minutes from the centre, follow García Moreno to the west end and continue up via the cemetery. Beyond El Indio Guaranga, 2 km towards the Río Salinas is **El Troje**, where you can camp by the river (make arrangements at the tourist office, see above). Walking two hours upriver along the narrow canyon you reach the 8-m high waterfall of **El Infiernillo**.

The **Escuela de Educación de la Cultura Andina** (Universidad de Bolívar), 7 de Mayo y Olmedo, has an anthropology museum with pre-Inca and Inca collections. ■ *Mon-Fri 0800-1200,1400-1800. Free.*

Market days are Friday and Saturday (larger), when many indigenous people in typical dress from the nearby communities can be seen trading at the market complex at the east end of Calle Azuay, by Plaza 15 de Mayo (9 de Abril y Maldonado), and at Plaza Roja (Avenida General Enríquez). These markets are colourful and interesting. There is also a small daily market at **Mercado 10 de Noviembre** (Sucre y Espejo), busiest on Wednesday.

Sleeping
■ *on map, page 221*
Price codes:
see inside front cover

B *La Colina*, Av Guayaquil 117, T/F980666. Restaurant mediocre and expensive but good for Sun lunch, small covered swimming pool, parking, high up on hill, bright and attractive, restful, lovely views, best in town. **D** *Bolívar*, Sucre 704 y Rocafuerte, T980547. Good cheap restaurant (closed Sun), cheaper with shared bath, simple but pleasant, small courtyard. **D** *Cochabamba*, García Moreno y 7 de Mayo, T981958, F982125, vviteriv@gu.pro.ec Very good expensive restaurant (best in town), parking, a bit faded but good service. **D** *Ejecutivo*, García Moreno 803 y 9 de Abril, T982044. Shared bath, simple but OK. **D** *Santa Fé*, 10 de Agosto y 9 de Abril, T981526. Restaurant, cheaper with shared bath, electric shower, very thin walls, sometimes noisy but friendly. **F** *Acapulco*, 10 de Agosto y Amazonas. Restaurant, cheaper with shared bath, small rooms, basic. **F** *Rosa Elvira*, Sucre 606. Shared bath, hot water, basic.

Eating
● *on map, page 221*
Price codes:
see inside front cover.
Most restaurants are
closed on Sun

Expensive *Cochabamba*, at *Hotel Cochabamba*. International food. Best in town, closed Sat evening and Sun. Recommended. *La Colina*, at *Hotel La Colina*, international food. Best for Sun lunch when they expect local families, otherwise mediocre. **Mid-range** *Pizza Buon Giorno*, Av Circunvalación 2 blocks from Plaza Roja on the way to the bus terminal. Pizza and salads. *Balcón Cuencano*, Convención de 1884 entre García Moreno y Azuay. Breakfast, lunch and dinner, set meals and à la carte, good. **Cheap** *Bolívar*, Sucre 706, at Hotel Bolívar. Good value set meals. Has a nice display of Andean musical instruments, closed Sun. Recommended. *Marisquería El Conchal*, Plaza Roja. Good *ceviche de pescado, camarones* and *mixtos*. Closed evenings but open Sun. *Rumipamba*, Gen Enríquez 308, Plaza Roja. Fresh fruit juices, grilled chicken, set meals and à la carte. Many simple *comedores* around Plaza Roja serve **seriously cheap** set meals.

Juad's Pastelería, Convención de 1884 y Azuay. Cappuccino, hot chocolate, sand- **Cafés**
wiches, fruit salad, pastries. Very good, popular, best selection early in the day, closed
1300-1500 and Sun. Recommended. *Heladería El Pingüino*, Sucre accross from Parque
Bolívar. Factory ice cream. A popular meeting place in the evenings. *Salinerito*, Plaza
Roja. Salinas cheese shop also serves coffee and sandwiches. Closed Sun.

Balcones de la Pila Disco Bar, Pichincha y García Moreno. Varied music, drinks, snacks. **Bars &**
No Bar, Sucre entre Manuela Cañizares y Azuay. Salsa, rock, drinks. *Patatús*, García **nightclubs**
Moreno entre Sucre y Pichincha. Varied music, drinks, snacks. *Discos are open on
Thu, Fri and Sat nights*

Carnival in Guaranda is among the best known in the country. People of all walks of life **Festivals**
share the festivities; parades, masks, dances, guitars, poetry and liquor fill the streets.
Taita Carnaval (Father Carnival), a landowner who sponsors the party, opens the celebrations when he makes his grand entrance into town. As in other parts of the country
water throwing (and at times flour, ink, etc) is common. In the surrounding countryside
the celebrations last for 8 days.

There are many well stocked shops in town. *Artesanías de PHD*, General Enríquez, **Shopping**
Plaza Roja. Crafts from co-operative in nearby Salinas, woollens, decorations. Open
Mon-Fri 0900-1300, 1430-1900, Sat 0900-1700. *Salinerito*, General Enríquez, Plaza
Roja, sells good quality cheese and other products from Salinas.

Cashcaventura, Convención de 1884 1112 y García Moreno (no sign), T/F980725. **Tour**
Diego Vargas. Guided tours to many destinations in the region including Chimborazo, **operators**
Salinas, nature reserves. *Delgado Travel*, García Moreno y 9 de Abril, T/F981719. Airline
tickets. Mon-Fri 0900-1700, Sat 0900-1200.

Buses The terminal is at Eliza Mariño Carvajal, on the way out of town towards **Transport**
Riobamba and Babahoyo. If you are staying in town ask to be dropped off closer to the
centre. Many daily buses to: **Ambato**, US$1.50, 2 hrs (beautiful views); **Riobamba**
(some along the Gallo Rumi road and others via the arenal), US$1.75, 2 hrs; **Babahoyo**,
US$2.50, 3 hrs; **Guayaquil**, US$3, 4 hrs; **Quito**, 3 companies run almost 30 daily services, US$3.50, 4-5 hrs.

Communications Post: Azuay y Pichincha. **Telephone**: *Andinatel*, Rocafuerte 508 y **Directory**
Sucre, 0800-2200 daily; and at the bus terminal. **Laundry** *La Primavera*, Ciudadela 1
de Mayo, T982538. Call for pick-up from your hotel, ask for Patricio Zurita.

North of Guaranda, 1½ hours by car along poor roads, is **Salinas de** **Around**
Guaranda (population: 5,000), in a picturesque setting with interesting geo- **Guaranda**
logical formations. This is the best example in Ecuador of a thoroughly
succesful community development project. Once a very poor village which
lived from salt mining, it now runs very succesful co-operative projects
including a dairy (Salinerito brand cheeses, among the best in the country), a
wool spinning and dyeing mill, and a sweets industry. It is a good area for
walking, horse riding and fishing. ■ *Entry fee to Salinas US$1, guided tour of
the community projects US$4.*

Sleeping D *Hotel Refugio Salinas*, T981266. With bath, hot water, cheaper with
shared bath or in dorm, meals available. F*Hostería Samilagua*, across the road from
the hotel, simple, new in 2001.

Central Highlands

Transport *Transportes Cándido Rada*, Mon-Fri to Salinas from Verbo Divino School at the top of Plaza Roja, at about 0600. From Parque Montúfar, Gen Salazar y Sucre, below the market, at 0700, and from Plaza 15 de Mayo at 1300, all US$1, 2 hrs. A taxi or pick-up truck from Plaza Roja costs US$10 (US$15-20 with wait included). Also enquire at the co-operative office or *Salinerito* cheese shop (Plaza Roja) about their vehicles going to Salinas.

The success achieved in Salinas is starting to spread. In the 1980s a group of people from Salinas migrated west and founded the town of **La Palma**, which has established a similar co-operative system. Further west, the village of **Chazo Juan** also has a dairy co-operative. Just east of La Palma is the **Bosque Peña Blanca**, a native cloud forest reserve with a spectacular 300-m high waterfall, La Chorrera. A dirt road links this area east to Salinas and west to **Echeandía**, 1½ hours by truck from Chazo Juan, three hours by bus from Guaranda. In Chazo Juan is **E** *La Granja*, bunk beds, cooking facilities, shared bath, an hour's walk from reserve. Echeandía has several basic **F** hotels and a couple of restaurants; *Amparito* is the best of both.

About two thirds of the province of Bolívar is in the foothills of the western *cordillera*, a region known as the *sub-trópico*. Remnants of cloud forest still cover some of the higher elevations of this transition zone between the slopes of Chimborazo and the coastal plain, while the lower reaches produce sugar cane and citrus. The area sees very little tourism but has great potential; recommended for off-the-beaten-track travellers. Several roads go from the highlands to the coast, all very scenic.

The bus ride to Babahoyo (see page 309) is beautiful. **Chimbo**, where fireworks and guitars are made, is 24 km south of Guaranda. Nearby there is an interesting church museum in **Huayco** (Santuario de Nuestra Señora de la Natividad), constructed around a 'Vatican Square', with interesting pre-Spanish artefacts. The main road continues through **San Miguel**, not far from the colonial town of **Santiago** with paintings in the church by a local artist and the **Bosque Protector Cashca Totoras**. It continues to **San Pablo**, skirting the forests of **Bosque de Arrayanes** and **San José de las Palmas**. Further on is **Bilován**, with the caves of **Las Guardias** to the west, and then **Balsapamba**, with waterfall and river beaches, before the road reaches the coastal plain at Babahoyo. The views along the way are magnificent. An older route known as *el torneado* runs from Chimbo to Balsapamba – it is very steep, narrow, there are innumerable hairpin bends and more wonderful views. At **Santa Lucía**, before reaching Balsapamba, is the interesting, Swiss-run Museo de las Culturas del Ecuador.

Ambato to Riobamba

After Ambato, the Pananamericana passes apple orchards and onion fields. Between Ambato and Riobamba is **Mocha**, where guinea-pigs (*cuy*) are raised for the table. You can sample roast *cuy* and other typical Ecuadorean dishes at stalls and restaurants by the roadside (*Mariadiocelina* is recommended). The valley's patchwork of fields gives an impression of greater fertility and prosperity than the Riobamba zone that follows. On the houses a small crucifix crowns the roof, where figurines of domestic animals are also found. At the pass there are fine views in the dry season of Chimborazo and its smaller sister mountain, Carihuairazo. For excursions in this area see page 233.

Riobamba

Riobamba is the capital of Chimborazo Province. It is built in the wide Tapi Valley and has broad streets and many ageing but impressive buildings. Because of its central location Riobamba and the surrounding province are known as Corazón de la Patria, *the heartland of Ecuador, while Mount Chimborazo has earned the epithet of* Sultana de los Andes *(the Sultan of the Andes).*

Phone code: 03
Colour map 4, grid B5

Riobamba has many good churches and public buildings, and magnificent views of five of the great volcanic peaks: Chimborazo, Altar, Tungurahua, Carihuairazo and, on occasion, Sangay. The city is the commercial centre for the Province of Chimborazo and an important centre of highland culture, both because of the many indigenous communities which live in the province and because of the city's self-styled European aristocracy.

Getting there Buses from Quito, Guayaquil and Ambato arrive at the well-run terminal terrestre on Epiclachima y Av Daniel León Borja. Buses from Baños and the Oriente arrive at the Terminal Oriental, at Espejo y Córdovez. A taxi between terminals costs US$0.80. The railway station remains a central landmark, but is used only for tourist rides (see Excursions below).

Ins & outs
See Transport,
page 231,
for further details

Getting around The city centre is compact and easy to walk around. City busses and taxis are available out to the terminal terrestre.

Tourist information *Ministerio de Turismo*, Av Daniel L Borja y Pasaje Municipal, in the Centro de Arte y Cultura, T/F941213. Open Mon-Fri 0830-1300, 1430-1800, very helpful and knowledgeable, English spoken.

Sights

Riobamba has several attractive plazas and parks. The main plaza is **Parque Maldonado**, with a statue to the local scientist Pedro Vicente Maldonado and some interesting wrought-iron fountains. Around it are the **Santa Bárbara Cathedral**, with a beautiful colonial stone façade and an incongrously modern wooden interior, the **Municipality** and several colonial buildings with arcades. Worth visiting is the house on the corner of Primera Constituyente and Espejo, beautifully restored in 1996, which houses the *SRI* (internal revenue service). **Parque Sucre** with a Neptune fountain is located two blocks to the southeast. Standing opposite, along Primera Constituyente, is the imposing building of Colegio Maldonado.

Four blocks northeast of the railway station is the **Parque 21 de Abril**, named after the city's date of independence. (The Batalla de Tapi was fought in the Riobamba valley, on 21 April 1822, when the Argentine General, Juan de Lavalle and 97 patriots defeated 400 Spanish troops.) The park (**La Loma de Quito**), affords an unobstructed view of Riobamba and its five volcanic peaks. It also has a colourful tile tableau of the history of Ecuador and is especially fine at sunset.

West of the centre, along Avenida Daniel León Borja, is **Parque Guayaquil**, the largest in the urban area, with a small lake, a band-shelland a good playground. A stylized Simón Bolívar, donated by Venezuela, adorns the traffic circle at Avenida Daniel L Borja and Zambrano.

Riobamba is an important market centre where indigenous people from many communities congregate. Saturday is the main market day when the city fills with colourfully dressed Indians from many different parts of the

Markets

Central Highlands

province of Chimborazo, each wearing their distinctive costume; trading overflows the markets and buying and selling go on all over town. Wednesday is a smaller market day. The 'tourist' market is in the small **Plaza de la Concepción** or **Plaza Roja**, on Orozco y Colón, south of the Convento de la Concepción (see below). It is a good place to buy local handicrafts and authentic Indian clothing (Saturday and Wednesday only, 0800-1500).

The main produce markets are **San Alfonso** (Argentinos y 5 de Junio) which on Saturday spills over into the nearby streets and also sells clothing, ceramics, baskets and hats, and **La Condamine** (Carabobo y Colombia) open daily, largest market on Fridays. Other markets in the colonial centre are **San Francisco** and **La Merced**, near the churches of the same name.

Museums   **Convento de la Concepción** has been carefully restored and functions as a religious art museum. It is a veritable treasure chest of 18th-century religious art. The priceless gold monstrance, Custodia de Riobamba Antigua, is the museum's greatest treasure, one of the richest of its kind in South America. The museum is well worth a visit. The guides are friendly and knowledgeable (tip expected). ■ *Tue-Sat 0900-1200, 1500-1800. US$4. T965212. Orozco y España, entrance at Argentinos y J Larrea.*

Museo del Banco Central, opened in 2002, has well displayed exhibits of archaeology and colonial art. ■ *Mon-Sat 0830-1330, 1430-1630. US$0.50.T965501. Veloz y Montalvo.*

Riobamba

■ **Sleeping**
1 Chimborazo Internacional *C2*
2 El Cisne *C1*
3 Imperial *C4*
4 Los Shyris *C4*
5 Montecarlo & Cafetería Montecarlo *C5*
6 Riobamba Inn *C4*
7 Rocío *D3*
8 Tren Dorado *C4*
9 Whymper *C3*
10 Zeus *D2*

Museo Histórico Córdoba-Román is a private museum which includes a photo collection, paintings, sculptures, furniture and documents. ■ *Mon-Fri, 1000-1200, 1500-1700. US$1. Velasco 24-25 y Veloz.*

Excursions

Riding the rails from Riobamba over the Devil's Nose (*La Nariz del Diablo*) is extremely popular with tourists and, increasingly, with Ecuadorean families. It makes a great day-trip. The train leaves Riobamba on Wed, Fri and Sun at 0700, arrives in Alausí around 1100, reaches Sibambe about 1130-1200, and returns to Alausí by 1330-1400. From Riobamba to Sibambe and back to Alausí costs US$11; Alausí-Sibambe-Alausí US$7; Alausí back to Riobamba US$3.40. Tickets are sold the day before departure, or the same morning starting around 0600; passport required to purchase tickets. Seats are not numbered, so best arrive early. Riding on the roof is fun, but hang on tight and remember that it is very chilly early in the morning. It's also a good idea to sit as far back on the roof as possible to avoid getting covered in oil from the exhaust. On the days when the train is not running, you can still experience the Devil´s Nose and the scenery, by walking along the tracks down from Alausí; a pleasant day trip. Horseback rides in the area are also offered (see Alausí, page 235).

The Devil's Nose train ride
See also box Railway to the Sierra, page 229

The train service is subject to frequent disruptions and timetables are always changing, best enquire locally about current schedules. The railway administration office is on Espejo, next to the Post Office, where information is available during office hours, T960115, or at the station T961909.

Metropolitan Touring (see Tour operators below) operates a private *autoferro* on the Riobamba-Sibambe route. They require a minimum number of passengers but will run any day and time convenient to the group. Approximately US$120 per person.

Guano is a quiet sisal-working, leather and carpet-weaving town of 7,000 inhabitants, 8 km north of Riobamba. There are lovely views of El Altar from the plaza. Chimborazo and Tungurahua can also be seen from a nearby hilltop. Rugs have been produced here since colonial times when, under the *encomiendas* system, local Indian slaves were trained in this art. You can have rugs made to your own design. There are a number of shops selling rugs, leather goods, and other crafts. You can see how the rugs are made on Calle Asunción, the road that comes in from Riobamba.

Guano

Eating and sleeping D *Quinta Karen Estefanía*, Calle Esmeraldas,

● **Eating**
1 Ashoka *C5*
2 Cabaña Montecarlo *C5*
3 Che Carlitos *C5*
4 Chifa Joy Sing *D4*
5 El Delirio *C4*
6 La Pizzería de Paolo *D1*
7 Luigi's
8 Mónaco Pizzería *C3*

Central Highlands

T900040. Private bath, hot water, pool, sauna and restaurant (Sat-Sun only), pleasant surroundings, a local weekend place. **E** *Bummen*, Hidalgo y 20 de Diciembre by the plaza, shared bath, hot water, simple. **E** *Residencial La Chilenita*, Tomás Ramírez y Juan Montalvo, across from the market, hot water, some rooms with private bath. *Oasis*, at the main park, serves very cheap set meals. Buses for Guano leave from the Mercado Dávalos, García Moreno y New York, every 20 minutes 0600-2200, US$0.20, last bus returns to Riobamba at 1800. Taxi US$3.

Cacha   In Cacha, a small Indian town southwest of Riobamba, the descendants of the indigenous ruling family still live. There have been many articles and books written about the 'Daquilemas'. Textiles and excellent honey are produced here and sold in the Sunday market.

Essentials

Sleeping   **AL** *La Andaluza*, 16 km north of Riobamba along the Panamericana, T949370,
■ *on map, page 226*   F949375, www.hosteria-andaluza.com Includes breakfast, good restaurant, parking,
Price codes: nice rooms in old hacienda with heaters and roaring fireplaces, lovely views, good
see inside front cover   walking. **A** *Abraspungu*, Km 3 on the road to Guano, T940820, F940819,
Many of the   www.hosteria-abraspungu.com Excellent restaurant, parking, beautiful house in
upmarket hotels are   country setting. Recommended.
located out of town

B *Chimborazo Internacional*, Los Cipreses y Argentinos, T963475, F963473, www.hotelchimborazo.com Includes breakfast, overpriced restaurant, parking, spacious rooms, comfortable but starting to show its age, sometimes noisy because of disco. **B** *El Troje*, 4½ km on the road to Chambo, T960826, F964572, gerencia@eltroje.com Good restaurant, pool and suana, internet, parking, nice rooms, good views. **B** *Zeus*, Av Daniel L Borja 41-29, T968036, F962292. Restaurant, parking, jacuzzi, gym, bathtubs with views of Chimborazo! Recommended.

C *El Cisne*, Av Daniel L Borja y Duchicela, T964573, F941982. Restaurant, parking, mixed reports. **C** *El Galpón*, Argentinos y Zambrano, T960981, F960982, www.hotelgalpon.com Restaurant and bar, parking, on a hill overlooking the city, spacious rooms, a bit faded, sometimes noisy because of disco. **C** *Montecarlo*, Av 10 de Agosto 25-41 entre García Moreno y España, T960557, F961577, montecarlo@laserinter.net Includes breakfast, restaurant, nice house in colonial style, some mattresses are poor.

D *Camino Real*, Av de la Prensa y Calle D, opposite bus terminal, T/F962365. Restaurant, OK. **D** *Canadá*, Av de la Prensa 23-31 y Av Daniel L Borja, near bus terminal, T964676, F946677, melissa16ec@yahoo.com Includes breakfast, parking, clean, modern and friendly. **D** *Glamour*, Primera Constituyente 37-85 ente Brazil y Zambrano, T944406, F944407. Restaurant, bright and comfortable but a bit out of the way. **D** *Humboldt*, Av Daniel L Borja 35-48 y Uruguay, T961788, F940814. Laundry facilities, parking, clean but a bit rundown. **D** *Majestic*, Av Daniel L Borja 43-60 y La 44, not far from bus terminal, T968708. Cafeteria, electric shower, laundry facilities, parking, OK. **D** *Manabí*, Colón 19-58 y Olmedo, T967967, F942402. Restaurant, cheaper with shared bath, laundry facilities, basic but clean. **D** *Mashany*, Veloz 41-73 y Zambrano, T942914, F964606. Parking, modern and comfortable but a bit out of the way, new in 2001. **D** *Riobamba Inn*, Carabobo 23-20 y Primera Constituyente, T961696, F940974. Restaurant, laundry facilities, carpeted rooms, OK. **D** *Tren Dorado*, Carabobo 22-35 y 10 de Agosto, T/F964890. Restaurant, reliable hot water, laundry facilities, modern and nice, good value. Recommended. **D** *Whymper*, Av Miguel Angel León 23-10 y Primera Constituyente, T964575, F968137. Hot water 0600-0930, 1800-2130, laundry facilities, parking, spacious rooms, friendly, but just a little rundown.

Railway to the Sierra

◀◀

As you climb aboard for the Devil's Nose, consider the rich history of the train you are about to ride. What is today an exhilarating tourist excursion was once the country's pride and joy, and its construction was an internationally acclaimed achievement.

A spectacular 464 km railway line (1.067 m gauge), which ran from Durán up to Riobamba, was opened in 1908. It passed through 87 km of delta lands and then, in another 80 km, climbed to 3,238 m. The highest point (3,619 m) was reached at Urbina, between Riobamba and Ambato. It then rose and fell before reaching the Quito plateau at 2,857 m.

This was one of the great railway journeys of the world and a fantastic piece of engineering, with a maximum gradient of 5.5%. Rail lines also ran from Riobamba south to Cuenca, and from

Quito north to Ibarra, then down to the coast at San Lorenzo. There were even more ambitious plans, never achieved, to push the railhead deep into the Oriente jungle, from Ambato as far as Leticia (then Ecuador, today Colombia).

Sadly, time and neglect have taken their toll and today only a few short rail segments remain in service as tourist rides: from Ibarra to Tulquizán, from Quito to Parque Nacional Cotopaxi, and from Riobamba to Alausí and over the Devil's Nose to Sibambe. There has often been talk of reviving the Ecuadorean railway, and such talk persists. As time passes however, the tracks rust and the ties rot, that seems like an ever more remote possibility. Which is a great shame because a working railroad could serve Ecuador today as much as, if not more than, it did in the past.

Central Highlands

D-E *Imperial*, Rocafuerte 22-15 y 10 de Agosto, T960429. Cheaper with shared bath, hot water 24 hrs, good beds, basic, good views from the roof, loud music from bar on Fri and Sat nights, good value. **D-E** *Los Shyris*, Rocafuerte 21-60 y 10 de Agosto, T/F960323, hshyris@yahoo.com Cheaper with shared bath, hot water 0500-1100, 1700-2300, internet, laundry facilities, good rooms, service and value. Rooms at the back are quieter. **D-E** *Oasis*, Veloz 15-32 y Almagro, T961210, F941499. Hot water (not always reliable), laundry facilities, Some rooms with kitchen and fridge, parking, small and quiet, family run, nice garden, friendly. Recommended. **D-E** *Rocio*, Brasil y Av Daniel L Borja, T961848. Electric shower, parking, clean, nice, good value.

There are several cheap and basic hotels near the railway station. None are great, however, and the area is unsafe and noisy

Chinese *Chifa China*, Av Daniel L Borja 43-49, and *Chifa Joy Sing*, Guayaquil 29-27 y Carabobo. Both are OK.

Grill *Parrillada de Fausto*, Uruguay 2038 y Av Daniel L Borja. Good meat, nice atmosphere. *Che Carlitos*, Colón 22-44, entre 10 de Agosto y Primera Constituyente. Argentine owner, great *parrilladas*.

International and Ecuadorean *Luigi's*, Condorazo y Unidad Nacional. International meat and seafood, expensive and good. *El Delirio*, Primera Constituyente 2816 y Rocafuerte (Bolívar stayed in this house). Ecuadorean and international dishes, popular with tour groups and overpriced, closed Mon and Sun. *Cabaña Montecarlo*, García Moreno 21-40. Good food and service, large portions, serves lunch and dinner, cheap set meals and mid-range à la carte, recommended. *Cafetería Real Montecarlo*, 10 de Agosto 25-45 y García Moreno. Excellent food and service, nice atmosphere, good breakfasts, closed at midday. Ecuadorean food at *Restaurante Montecarlo*, Primera Constituyente y Pichincha, popular. *Tambo de Oro*, Carlos Zambrano 27-20 y Junín, near Hotel El Galpón. Good cheap set lunch and mid-range à la carte, open lunch only. *Bonny*, Diego de Almagro y Villarroel. Cheap set meals and very good seafood (mid-range, à la carte), very popular. Rcommended.

Eating

● *on map, page 226*
Price codes:
see inside front cover.
Most restaurants close by 2100 and on Sunday.
All prices are mid-range unless otherwise indicated

Italian *La Pizzería de Paolo*, Av Daniel L Borja corner Epiclachima, near the bus station. Good pizza and pasta. *Mónaco Pizzería*, Diego Ibarra y Av Daniel L Borja. Pizza and pasta, open evenings only. Popular and good value. Several other pizzerias in town.

Vegetarian *Ashoka*, Guayaquil 22-50 y Espejo. Good cheap set meals and à la carte, lunch only, closed Sun. *Natural Food*, Tarqui entre Veloz y Primera Constituyente, very cheap set meals, vegetarian available.

Snacks and coffee *Caffe Johnny*, Espejo 22-45 y Primera Constituyente. Breakfast from 0730, good, closed Sun. *Helados de Paila*, Espejo entre Guayaquil y 10 de Agosto. Home made ice-cream, good selection, café, sweets, popular. *Pynn's*, Espejo 21-20 y 10 de Agosto, T943259. Coffee, fruit salad, tacos, set lunches. Cheap.

Bakeries *Pan Van*, Primera Constituyente y Colón. Excellent quality and variety.

Bars & nightclubs *Gens-Chop Bar*, Av Daniel L Borja 42-17 y Duchicela. Bar, good music and sport videos, open daily, popular. Recommended. *Casa de la Cultura*, Rocafuerte y 10 de Agosto, sometimes has a good *peña* on Fri and Sat evenings, enquire in advance. *Unicornio*, St Armand y Av Lizarzaburo, Vía Ambato Km 1. Piano bar and salsoteca, open Thu-Sat. *Vieja Guardia*, good bar and open air disco at Av Flor 40-43 y Av Zambrano, US$1 cover. *Milenium*, Cdla Los Tulipanes, off Av de la Prensa, 3 blocks south of the bus terminal. Disco, pub, international music, popular, US$1.

Festivals *Fiesta del Niño Rey de Reyes* starts in Dec and culminates on **6 Jan**, with street parades, music and dancing throughout that period. Riobamba's independence day is **21 Apr**, celebrated for several days with lively parades, concerts, bullfights and drinking. Hotel prices rise and rooms may be difficult to find during this period. Festivals to celebrate the *Foundation of Riobamba* take place on **11 Nov**.

Shopping **Crafts** Crafts are sold Wed and Sat, 0800-1500, at Plaza Roja, see Markets above. Nice tagua carvings and other crafts are on sale at *Alta Montaña*, Av Daniel L Borja y Diego Ibarra, where you can see how the tagua is carved. *El Buho*, Primera Constituyente 36-31 y Brasil, large selection of regional crafts; workshop on the 2nd floor where you can see the artisans at work, open 1000-1900. Also at several shops on 10 de Agosto near the train station. *Almacén Cacha*, Orozco next to the Plaza Roja, a cooperative of native people from the Cacha area, sells good value woven bags, wool sweaters and other crafts, also excellent honey. Closed Sun-Mon. **Supermarkets** *La Ibérica*, Av Daniel L Borja 37-62. *Camari*, Espejo y Olmedo, opposite La Merced market. *Akí*, Colón y Olmedo.

Sport **Ball games** A local ball game, the *mamona*, in which a solid leather ball is hit with the palm of the hand, is played in the afternoons at the Plaza Roja and in San Alfonso on Sun. A game played with marbles can be seen at Parque Barriga on Av Miguel A León. **Climbing and trekking** Riobamba is an excellent starting point for Chimborazo, Carihuairazo, Altar and Sangay. See Tour operators and Excursions below. **Cockfights** At Gallera San Francisco, Alvarado y Olmedo, Sat at 1500 and during the city's fiestas. **Mountain biking** *Pro Bici*, at Primera Constituyente 23-44 y Larrea, T951760, F961923, www.probici.com Run by guide and mechanic, Galo Brito, bike trips and rental, guided tours with support vehicle, full equipment (use Cannondale ATBs), US$25-35 per person per day, excluding meals and overnight stays. Rental from US$10 per day. *Julio Verne* (see Tour operators below), rental US$10 per day, tours including transport, guide, meals, US$30 per day. **Swimming** There is a spa *CENAEST*, 5 de Junio y Villarroel, several pools kept at different temperatures, gym, cafeteria. Open daily 0600-1000, 1600-2200, US$4.

Most companies offer climbing trips (from US$180 per person for 2 days) and trekking (from US$50 per person per day). *Alta Montaña*, Av Daniel L Borja 35-17 y Diego Ibarra, T950601, F942215, aventurag@laserinter.net Trekking, climbing, cycling, birdwatching, photography and horse-riding tours in mountains and jungle, logistic support for expeditions, transport, equipment rental, English spoken. Recommended. *Andes Trek*, Colón 22-25 y 10 de Agosto, T940964, F940963, www.andes-trek.com Climbing, trekking and mountain-biking tours, transport, equipment rental, English and German spoken. *Coltur*, Av Daniel L Borja y Vargas Torres, T/F962662. Airline tickets. *Expediciones Andinas*, Vía a Guano, Km 3, across from *Hotel Abraspungo*, T964915, F969604, www.expediciones-andinas.com Climbing expeditions, operate Chimborazo Base Camp on south flank of mountain. Cater to groups, contact well in advance. Recommended. *Julio Verne*, Calle 5 de Junio 21-46 y 10 de Agosto, T/F963436, www.julioverne-travel.com Climbing, trekking, cycling, jungle and Galápagos trips, river rafting, transport to mountains, equipment rental, Ecuadorean-Dutch run, uses official guides. Recommended. *Metropolitan Touring*, Av Daniel L Borja y Miguel Angel León, T969600, F969601. Railway tours, airline tickets, DHL and Western Union representatives.

Tour operators
Many hotels offer tours, but note that not all are run by qualified guides. See also Guides, under Climbing and trekking around Riobamba, page 232

Bus From the main bus terminal: to Quito, US$3, 3½ hrs, about every 30 mins. To Guaranda, US$1.75, 2 hrs; the road is paved to San Juan, from where there are 2 routes, both very scenic: that via Gallo Rumi is unpaved, while the one via the arenal is partly paved (some *Flota Bolívar* buses take this route), sit on the right for the beautiful views on either route. To Ambato, US$1, 1 hr. To Alausí, every 30 mins, US$1.20, 2 hrs. To Cuenca, US$5, 6 hrs. To Guayaquil, via Pallatanga, frequent service, US$3.60, 4 hrs; really spectacular for the first 2 hrs.

From the Terminal Oriental: to Baños, landslides caused by Tungurahua's volcanic activity have closed the direct Baños-Riobamba road until further notice, buses go via Ambato (2 hrs, US$1.60). To Puyo, also via Ambato, US$3, 4 hrs direct.

Transport

Banks *Banco del Pacífico*, Av Miguel A León y Veloz, TCs and Mastercard ATM. *Banco del Pichincha*, Primera Constituyente y García Moreno, only Visa. *Banco de Guayaquil*, Primera Constituyente 2626 y García Moreno, TCs, Visa and Mastercard. *Vigo Rianxeira*, 10 de Agosto 25-37 y España, T968608, changes all US$ TCs (2% commission), Euros and other major currencies in cash only, friendly service, Mon-Fri 0830-1330, 1500-1800, Sat 0900-1230. Recommended. **Communications** Internet: rates about US$1 per hr. Post: 10 de Agosto y Espejo. Telephone: *Andinatel*, at Tarqui entre Primera Constituyente y Veloz, 0800-2200. Also at the bus terminal. **Laundry** *Lava Todo*, T940394, US$0.25/lb, including pick-up and delivery. **Useful addresses** Ministerio del Ambiente, for information about Parque Nacional

Directory

Central Highlands

Sangay, Av 9 de Octubre y Quinta Macají, at the western edge of town, north of the roundabout at the end of Av Isabel de Godin, T963779. Open Mon-Fri 0800-1300, 1400-1700, but rangers are only in the office in the early morning. From town take a city bus San Gerardo-El Batán.

Climbing and trekking around Riobamba

See also Climbing, page 70, and Trekking, page 79

Riobamba is a great starting point for many climbing and trekking expeditions. Chimborazo, Carihuairazo, El Altar, Sangay, Tungurahua, and the Inca Trail to Ingapirca can all be accessed from here. Tour agencies in Riobamba offer transport and trips to all the attractions, see Tour operators above. *Trekking in Ecuador* (see page 464) describes a set of four interconnecting routes in Sangay National Park, for up to three weeks of excellent hiking.

Guides
See also Riobamba tour operators, above

Enrique Veloz Coronado, Chile 33-21 y Francia, T/F960916, best reached after 1500, very helpful. His sons are also guides and work with him on climbing and trekking expeditions. **Marcelo Puruncajas** of *Andes Trek*, member of Aseguim, highly recommended, speaks English, when not leading tours uses good guides, also offers trekking, four-wheel drive transport and mountain biking. **Marco Cruz** of *Expediciones Andinas*, recommended, he is a certified guide of the German Alpine Club and considered among the best and most expensive guides. **Rodrigo Donoso** of *Alta Montaña* (see above), for climbing and a variety of trekking and horse-riding trips, speaks English.

Trekking including guide, transport, equipment, shelter and food will cost about US$50 per person per day, minimum two persons. Climbing with qualified guides costs about US$140 per person per day.

Youngsters of the communities of **Pulinguí San Pablo** and **La Chorrera**, 15 km north of San Juan, along the road to the Chimborazo climbing shelters, are being trained as *guías nativos*, native guides who lead visitors to the attractions at the base of Chimborazo. Simple accommodations are available in the village, see Sleeping below.

Chimborazo
Colour map 4, grid B5
Altitude: 6,310 m

This is a difficult climb owing to the altitude. No one without mountaineering experience should attempt it; rope, ice-axe and crampons must be used and acclimatization is essential. The best season is December and June-September. The two routes are up the southwest and northwest faces.

Southwest face

From the Whymper refuge to the summit the climb is eight to nine hours and the descent about four hours. The path from the hut to the glacier is marked but difficult to follow at midnight, so it's best to check it out the day before. The route on the glacier is easy to follow as it is marked with flags, though it can be tricky in cloud or mist. There are several crevasses on the route, so you need to rope up. There are three routes depending on your experience and ability. It is highly recommended to go with a guide and start at 2400 or 0100. There are avalanche problems on the entire mountain. *Penitentes* are conical ice formations which can obstruct the final part of the route.

Getting there The refuge is 56 km from Riobamba and takes about 1½ hrs. Access is through the scenic paved *arenal* road, which joins San Juan, on the Riobamba-Guaranda road, with the Ambato-Guaranda road, to the north. Vicuñas can be seen along this route. There are no direct buses so arrange transport with a tour operator or taxi from Riobamba (either costs about US$25 one way). You can also take a Guaranda-bound bus which takes the *arenal* route (ask, as not all go this way), alight at the turn-off for the refuge and hitch from there (better chance at the weekend) or walk the remaining steep 5 km, which gains 440 m in height.

Entrance fee   Chimborazo lies within the **Reserva de Producción de Fauna Chimborazo**. A US$10 entrance fee is charged at the turn-off for the refuges, from the *arenal* road.

Sleeping   The road ends at 4,800 m, at a large building, the *Hermanos Carrel refuge*. It has a guard, bunk beds with mattresses for 8, includes 1 private room for 2, dining area, cooking facilities, running water, toilet, electricity; bring food and warm gear, it gets very cold at night. In about 45 mins you can walk up to the *Edward Whymper refuge*, another building at 5,000 m, which was at the foot of the Thielman glacier, although this is receding. The same facilities are available here, with capacity for 40, in 5 separate rooms. Both refuges are managed by *Alta Montaña* and a small fee is charged for a day visit. Overnight stays are US$10. Take padlock for the small lockers under the bunks; the guards also have a locked room for valuables, and you can leave your gear with them. If there are only a few people, you will be given the key to your room.

Be careful with your belongings in the shelters, parked cars and throughout this area. Do not take any unnecessary valuables. Occasional thefts and rare armed robberies have been reported

In **Totorillas**, 7 km south of the turn-off for the refugios, is *Chimborazo Base Camp*, in a lovely valley at the foot of Chimborazo – you must make advance arrangements through *Expediciones Andinas* in Riobamba. The views are stunning. In the hamlet of **Puiguí San Pablo**, 1 km away, is **F** *Casa Cóndor*, the local community centre, with a couple of basic rooms with shared bath and bunk beds. Also more comfortable **E** cabins with bunk beds by the roadside. Take a warm sleeping bag.

Getting there   Take the Guaranda bus from Ambato along the new paved road or a truck along the spectacular old road (50 km) to the valley of Pogyos. At Pogyos (4,000 m) there is a house with a metal roof where you can hire mules to carry your luggage. Beware of pilfering from your bags on the ascent. Walk about 3 hrs to the *Fabián Zurita refuge* (4,900 m) which is uninhabitable. From the refuge to the summit is about an 8-hr climb; descent about 3-4 hrs. It's advisable to start at 2330-2400 at the latest. Take tents and water (obtainable at Pogyos). (We are grateful to Enrique Veloz Coronado, page 232, for much of this information.)

Northwest face (Pogyos route)

A good area to access Chimborazo for trekking is along the high *páramo* between its eastern slopes and Igualata. There are many walking opportunities here and it is a good area for acclimatization. You can make an excursion (Tuesday, Thursday and Friday) to see the *hieleros* who bring ice blocks down from the glacier to sell in the Riobamba market (Riobamba agencies offer this tour). Horses can be hired in **Urbina**, 2 km west of the Panamericana, about halfway between Ambata and Riobamba, and at the village of **12 de Octubre** to the north, ask for Daniel Villacís.

The Eastern slopes

Sleeping   D *Posada de la Estación*, T/F942215 (Riobamba), aventurag@laserinter.net Shared bath, hot water, good food, dining room with fireplace. A pleasant inn located in the converted station of Urbina at 3,619 m, once the highest point of the Ecuadorean railway. Clean, cold at night, tours, slide shows when the owner is in. Recommended.

El Altar is part of Sangay National Park (see below), the most popular trek is to its crater. In 2000 an exceptionally large avalanche spilled a great deal of water from the crater lake of El Altar. The flow of water and debris roared through the Collanes plain like an inland tidal wave, leaving much destruction in its wake. The resulting lunar landscape is striking.

El Altar
Colour map 4, grid B6
Altitude: 5,315 m

Central Highlands

The well-used track (very muddy in the wet season) leads up a steep hill past the *Hacienda Releche*, outside the little village of **Candelaria** (see Transport below). There are small signs at the only two turnings on the route. The track leads up a hill to a ridge where it joins a clearer track. This goes south first and then turns east up the valley of the Río Collanes. It is about six hours to the Collanes plain, where there are thatched-roof shelters (see Sleeping below), and another two hours to the crater which is surrounded by magnificent snow-capped peaks.

Note that rapid deglaciation is changing these climbing routes

Technical climbs For experienced ice climbers the Ruta Obispo offers grade 4 and 5 mixed ice and rock. **El Obispo** is the highest and most southerly of Altar's nine summits, at 5,315 m. Another technical route is to **El Canónigo** (5,260 m), the northernmost of the summits, mixed ice and rock, grade 4 and 5. Altar's seven other summits are, from north to south: **Fraile Grande** (5,180 m); **Fraile Central** (5,070 m); **Fraile Oriental** (5,060 m); **Fraile Beato** (5,050 m); **Tabernáculo** (5,100 m); **Monja Chica** (5,080 m); and **Monja Grande** (5,160 m). Details are given in *Ecuador: A Climbing Guide*, see page 463.

Sleeping E *Hostal Capac Urcu*, at *Hacienda Releche*, T949761 or T960848 (Riobamba). Bath, hot water, kitchen (extra) or good meals on request. Pleasant and relaxing. Recommended. The hacienda also rents horses for the trek to Collanes, US$5 each way. They likewise run an **E** *Refugio* in thatched-roof shelters up at Collanes, with kitchen, gas stove and all utensils. No hot water or blankets, take a warm sleeping bag.

Transport Don't confuse the mountain with the village of the same name. There is an El Altar signpost on the Riobamba-Baños road but this is not the route to the mountain. There are 2 buses a day from the Terminal Oriental in Riobamba, to Candelaria, US$1, 1½ hrs. Alternatively, take a bus from the same terminal to Penipe, every ½ hr, US$0.75, 45 mins, and hire a pick-up truck from there to Candelaria, US$10, 45 mins.

Sangay
For the lowland access to Parque Nacional Sangay see page 383

Sangay (5,230 m), one of the most active volcanos in the world, lies within **Parque Nacional Sangay**. Access to the mountain takes seven days and is only for those who can endure long, hard days of walking and severe weather. Sangay can be dangerous even on a quiet day and protection against falling stones is vital. With a little coaching a *mecánica* can make shields, such as arm loops welded to an oil drum top. December/January is a good time to climb Sangay. Agencies in Quito and Riobamba offer tours or you can organize an expedition independently. A guide is essential. Porters can be hired in the access town of Alao, reached by bus from Riobamba.

South of Riobamba

Cajabamba
Phone code: 03
Colour map 4, grid B5

In 1534 the original Riobamba was founded on this site, but in 1797 a disastrous earthquake caused a large section of the hill on the north side of the town to collapse in a great landslide, which can still be seen. It killed several thousand of the original inhabitants of Riobamba and the town was moved almost 20 km northeast to its present site. The new Riobamba has prospered, but Cajabamba has stagnated and is now a small, rather poor town. A colourful, Colta Indian market on Sunday is small but uncommercialized and interesting. The town is easily reached by bus from Riobamba (25 minutes, US$0.25). There are few restaurants out of town on the Panamericana towards Cuenca.

The road and railway skirt the shores of **Laguna de Colta**, just after the fertile Cajabamba valley. The lake and surroundings are very beautiful and just a short bus trip from Riobamba. At the edge of the village along the main road on the shore of Laguna de Colta is a small chapel, **La Balbanera**, dating from 1534, making it the oldest church in Ecuador, although it has been restored several times because of earthquakes. Just south of La Balbanera, 5 km south of Cajabamba, a paved highway branches southwest to **Pallatanga**, a small town with a pleasant subtropical climate. Here are **B** *Hostería El Valle*, west of town on the road to Bucay, T/F919216, cabins in a rural setting, includes 3 meals, pool, advance reservations required; **E** *Residencial Melita*, on main plaza, with private bath, electric shower, simple, family run and friendly; and many small *comedores* along the highway. The road continues from Pallatanga to Bucay, Milagro and Guayaquil.

Some 28 km south of Cajabamba is Guamote. It has an interesting and colourful market on Thursday with lots of animals and few tourists, and some good half day walks in the area. **D** *Ramada Inn*, Vela y Riobamba, T916242. Some rooms with private bath, hot water. There is also a basic *pensión* and *comedores* by the railway station. Many buses from Riobamba, especially on Thursday.

Guamote
Phone code: 03
Colour map 4, grid B5
Population: 2,000
Altitude: 3,050 m

South of Guamote is **Tixán**, which has a beautifully restored church and many old houses. It is the home of many workers in the nearby sulphur mines. The San Juan Bautista celebrations around 24 June are very colourful.

Between Guamote and Tixán is the well-signed turn-off to Osogoche, 32 km to the southeast. There is good trekking in the area. The hike to/from the paved road takes at least five hours across windswept *páramos* with views of Sangay on clear days. The Indians here still live in *chozas* (grass huts) and dress in traditional bright colours. You might arrange for pack animals and local guides, but take all food and camping equipment. The best season is November to early March. A small road connects this area with Achupallas (see Inca trail to Ingapirca, page 241).

Osogoche
This is a wild, cold and beautiful area of three large lakes with spectacular mountains towering overhead

Central Highlands

Alausí

Some 84 km south of Riobamba, Alausí sits at the foot of Cerro Gampala on a terrace overlooking the deep Chanchán gorge. The area enjoys a temperate climate and, in the heyday of the railroad, it was a popular holiday destination for Guayaquileños wishing to escape their hottest season. Many tourists join the train here for the amazing descent to Sibambe, via the famous *Nariz del Diablo* (Devil's Nose). There is also a road going from here to the Pacific lowlands through Huigra (basic lodgings and restaurants). The atmosphere in the town is laid-back and friendly. The colourful Sunday market, in the plaza by the church, just up the hill from the station, draws *campesinos* from the outlying villages. The town's *fiesta*, *San Pedro de Alausí*, is in late June.

Phone code: 03
Colour map 4, grid C5
Population: 5,500
Altitude: 2,250 m

The train runs Wed, Fri and Sun. It leaves Riobamba about 0700, arrives Alausí around 1100, gets to Sibambe almost an hour later, stops there for about 15 mins and returns to Alausí about 1330 for a lunch stop, returning to Riobamba at about 1700. From Riobamba to Sibambe and back to Alausí costs US$11; Alausí-Sibambe-Alausí US$7; Alausí back to Riobamba US$3.40. Tickets go on sale around 0900.

Train ride
Further information at the station, T930126

D-E *Panamericano*, 5 de Junio y 9 de Octubre, near the bus stop, T930278. Restaurant, cheaper with shared bath, OK, quieter rooms in back. **E** *Americano*, García Moreno 151, T930159. Private bath, hot water, a bit run down. **E** *Gampala*, 5 de Junio 122,

Sleeping

T930138. Restaurant, private bath, electric shower, simple but OK. **E** *Tequendama*, 5 de Junio 152, 1930123. Shared bath, electric shower, basic but clean. **E-F** *Aluusí*, 5 de Junio 142 y Orozco, T930361. Cheaper with shared bath, electric shower, simple, clean and friendly. *Europa*, 5 de Junio y Orozco, T930200. Closed for renovations in late 2002, will be very nice when finished.

Eating Alausí is not the culinary centre of Ecuador, but a few places serve decent meals, prices are very cheap: *Gampala*, at the hotel, set meals and à la carte, vegetarian on request, open 0700-2300. *Danielito*, opposite *Tequendama*. Popular for breakfast, will cook vegetarian meals, friendly. *El Flamingo*, Antonio Mora y 9 de Octubre, behind Hotel *Tequendama*. Good set meals, popular for lunch. *La Diligencia*, at railway station. Set meals and pizza. Several others.

Tour operator *Nariz del Diablo Devil's Nose*, 5 de Junio 132 y Pedro de Loza, T/F930240. Runs horse-back trips to the Devil's Nose.

Transport **Buses** To/from **Riobamba**, 2 hrs, US$1.20, 84 km, all paved. To **Quito**, buses from Cuenca pass through from 0600 onwards, about 20 a day (5½ hrs, US$5); or change in Riobamba. To **Cuenca**, 4 hrs, US$4. To **Cañar**, 7 daily, US$3, 2½ hrs. To **Ambato** hourly, 3 hrs, US$2.50. *Coop Patria* has a small office where you can buy bus tickets to Cuenca or Riobamba. Other cooperatives have no office, but their buses pass through town, some stop up at the highway and others outside the *Hotel Panamericano*.

Directory **Bank** *Banco de Guayaquil*, 5 de Junio near train station. TCs, Visa and Mastercard.

Chunchi
Phone code: 03
Population: 3,400
Altitude: 2,300 m

Chinchi, a friendly village with a Sunday market, is 37 km south of Alausí along the Panamericana. The local fiesta is celebrated on July 4. From here you can hike or cycle down the Huigra road to Chanchán, a scenic area. **D** *New Hotel* (no name yet), Bolívar y Manuel Reyes, near market, T936626, F936658. Private bath, hot water, modern, new in 2002. **E-F** *Residencial Patricia*, Bolívar, half a block from the main plaza, T936237. Cheaper with shared bath, OK. There are many restaurants along the highway, which are better than those in Alausí, and an incongruously large cyber café on the plaza, US$1.50 per hour. Buses leave from the plaza, several daily, to Riobamba.

Southern Highlands

Introducing the Southern Highlands

The convoluted topography of the Southern Highlands, comprising the provinces of Cañar, Azuay and Loja, reveals an ancient non-volcanic past distinct from its northern *Sierra* neighbours. The region is home to many treasures. Here are Ecuador's prime Inca site, one of its most spectacular national parks, and Cuenca, the focal point of *El Austro* (as this part of the country is called), which boasts some of the country's finest colonial architecture. The Cuenca basin is a major *artesanía* centre, producing ceramics, baskets, gold and silver jewellery, textiles and the famous Panama hat.

In addition to the cultural attractions mentioned above, a pleasant climate and magnificent scenery make the Southern Highlands ideal walking country. Vilcabamba, south of Loja, is a particularly suitable base for trekking and horseback excursions, with nearby undisturbed *páramo* and cloud forest which are home to many birds and other wildlife.

An extensive road network provides access to the Peruvian border at several different points. An increasing number of travellers are discovering these out-of-the-way crossings which link Ecuador with interesting areas in its neighbour to the south.

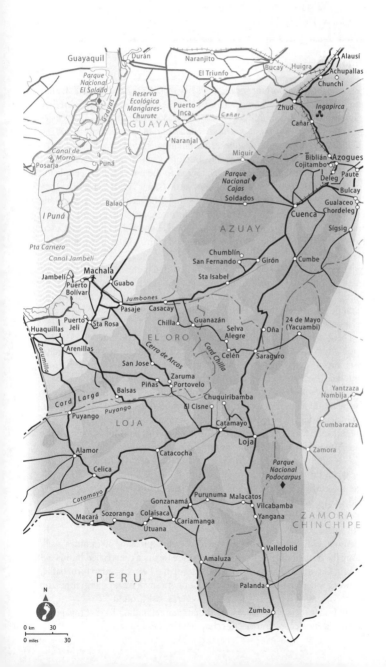

Things to do in the Southern Highlands

- Visit **Ingapirca**, Ecuador's most famous archaeological site, see page 240.
- Stroll through colonial **Cuenca**, see page 245.
- Indulge in dessert at *Heladería Holanda* in Cuenca, see page 251.
- Explore **Vilcabamba** and surroundings on horseback, see page 267.
- Enjoy the Sunday night roast chicken dinner at *Hostal Madre Tierra* in Vilcabamba, see page 269.

Ingapirca

Colour map 4, grid C5
Altitude: 3,160 m

Ecuador's most important Inca site lies between Alausí and Cuenca 8½ km east of Cañar. Access is from Cañar or El Tambo. The site is administered by the local Cañari community. ■ *Daily 0800-1800. Entry to the site is US$6, including entry to the site museum and a guided tour in Spanish (before 1700). A small café serves very cheap set lunches and photogenic llamas graze the grounds.*

Though famed as a classic Inca site, Ingapirca, which translates as 'Wall of the Inca', had probably already been sacred to the native Cañari people for many centuries years. It is also known as 'Jatun Cañar', great Cañar. The Inca Huayna Capac took over the site from the conquered Cañaris when his empire expanded North into Ecuador in the third quarter of the 15th century. Ingapirca was strategically placed on the Royal Highway that ran from Cusco to Quito and soldiers may have been stationed there to keep the troublesome Cañaris under control.

The site, first described by the French scientist Charles-Marie de la Condamine in 1748, shows typical imperial Cusco-style architecture, such as tightly fitting stonework and trapezoidal doorways, which can be seen on the 'Castillo' and 'Governor's House'. The central structure may have been a solar observatory.

There is considerable debate as to Ingapirca's precise function. Though popularly considered a fortress complex, this is contradicted by archaeologists. From what remains of the site, it probably consisted of storehouses, baths and dwellings for soldiers and other staff, suggesting it could have been a Royal *Tambo*, or Inn. It could also have been used as a sun temple, judging by the beautiful ellipse, modelled on the *Qoricancha* in Cusco. Furthermore, John Hemming has noted that the length is exactly three times the diameter of the semicircular ends, which may have been connected with worship of the sun in its morning, midday and afternoon positions.

A 10-minute walk away from the site is the **Cara del Inca** (face of the Inca), an immense natural formation in the rock looking over the landscape. Nearby is a throne cut into the rock, the **Sillón de Inga** (Inca's Chair) and the **Ingachugana**, a large rock with carved channels. This may have been used for offerings and divination with water, *chicha* or the blood of various sacrificial animals.

About 1 km down the hill off the road to Ingapirca, or 30 minutes' walk along the disused rail line from El Tambo, are the Inca ruins called **Baños del Inca** or **Coyoctor**. This massive rock outcrop has been carved to form baths, showers, water channels and seats overlooking a small plaza or amphitheatre; worth visiting. It is not easy to find, however, so ask around.

On Friday there is an interesting Indian market in the village at Ingapirca. There is a good co-operative craft shop next to the church.

Ingapirca village The most convenient place to stay. **B** *Posada Ingapirca*, 500 m uphill from the site, T215116, or T838508 (Cuenca), santaana@etapa.com.ec Comfortable rooms with bath, heating, includes breakfast. Good, expensive restaurant and well stocked bar. In a converted farm, good service, superb views. **E** *Inti Huasi*, at the entrance to the the village, T215171. Private bath, electric shower, parking, simple but nice. Restaurant serves cheap set meals. **E** *Sra Zoila Montero* rents rooms in the village, ask at *Restaurant El Turista*, shared bath, electric shower, basic.

El Tambo On the Panamericana 8 km northwest of Ingapirca, this is one of the access towns for the ruins (see below) but it has limited accommodation and services. **F** *Pensión Estefanía*, on main street, T233126. Shared bath, cold water in buckets only, very basic. The local *comedores* are also pretty basic. Cañar (see page 243), 7 km south of El Tambo on the Panamericana, is a better bet if you do not wish to sleep up in Ingapirca village.

Sleeping & eating
Phone code: 07

From the corner of 24 de Mayo and Borrero in **Cañar**, local **buses** leave every 20 mins for Ingapirca, 0600-1800, US$0.50, 1 hr; last bus returns from Ingapirca to Cañar at 1700. The same buses pass through El Tambo on their way to Ingapirca. Both Cañar and **El Tambo** have frequent bus services from Cuenca (US$1.40, 2 hrs), or you can get off any long-distance bus passing through Cañar or El Tambo (eg heading south from Quito or Riobamba). *Transportes Cañar* has 2 direct buses daily from Cuenca to Ingapirca, at 0900 and 1300, returning 1300 and 1600, US$2, 2 hrs. Agencies in Cuenca offer day tours to Ingapirca for US$35-45, including visits to other nearby sites (see page 253). It is a beautiful 4-hr, 16-km walk from Ingapirca to Cañar. The start of the road is clearly signposted, along the main street; take water.

Transport

Inca trail to Ingapirca

The popular three day hike to Ingapirca on an Inca trail starts at **Achupallas**, 25 km from Alausí. There are persistent beggars, especially children, the length of the hike. Don't encourage them with gifts, rather make a donation to a recognized project, charity or school (see Responsible tourism, page 44). Good camping equipment is essential. Take all food and drink with you as there is nothing along the way. A shop in Achupallas sells basic foodstuffs and on Saturday you can buy fresh vegetables at the market. Tour operators in Riobamba offer this trek for about US$150 per person, three days, everything included.

The IGM map (Juncal sheet, 1:50,000) is very useful; also a compass. The name Ingapirca does not appear on the Cañar 1:50,000 sheet; you may have to ask directions near the end

There is an irregular service from Alausí to Achupallas. A bus or pick-up truck leaves most days from in front of the *Residencial Tequendama* but the departure time varies, US$1, 1 hr, a nice ride. To hire your own pick-up costs US$10-15 for up to 4 passengers, you can bargain. Transport may be more frequent (and crowded) on Sat for the Achupallas market. Alternatively, take any bus along the Panamericana to **La Moya**, south of Alausí, at the turn-off for Achupallas. Here is **F** *Hospedaje La Moya*, 1 km north of town on the Panamericana. Private bath, electric shower, meals available on request, simple and friendly. Camping possible. Pick-up trucks go from La Moya to Achupallas, best on Thu and Sun, or you can hire one for about US$8. There is basic accommodation in Achupallas.

Getting there

The route
- Head for the arch with a cross at the top of the village. Follow the trail to the left of the arch and you'll soon pass the cemetery on the right.
- The track then deteriorates into a stony footpath and crosses the first footbridge. Continue on the trail which follows alongside the river.
- About 45 minutes out of the village cross the river again on another footbridge and follow the left bank of the Río Cadrul. Head for a pass ahead between **Cerro Mapahuiña** to the left (4,365 m) and **Cerro Callana Pucará** to the right.
- At the pass there is an awkward climb over what looks like a huge rockfall. This involves squeezing through a very tight gap, too narrow for you and your backpack at the same time.
- Soon after you need to cross the river to meet the trail on the other side. In the dry season it can be jumped.
- About 200 m further on the trail starts to leave the river and climb diagonally up the mountain. There is enough flat ground near the river to pitch a tent for the night, if you're not up to the steep climb.
- The trail climbs to 4,000 m before following the contours of the west side of the valley.
- Several kilometres later the trail reaches **Laguna Las Tres Cruces**. From the previous camping spot it is about three hours.
- Follow the trail beyond the lake and across the pass. Beyond the pass the trail is not very clear. It crosses some worn rocks and then climbs steeply to the top of the left hand ridge. The views from here are stupendous and make the previous day's hard walking suddenly seem worthwhile.
- Walk along the top of the ridge to the peak of **Quilloloma**. The trail becomes clear again and then descends sharply to the lush, marshy valley floor below. You can see the vestiges of the old Inca road running in a straight line across the valley floor to the remains of the foundations of an Inca bridge.
- Follow the Inca road to the river which you have to cross. The best place is a little upstream from the bridge, where it may be narrow enough to jump.
- There is a clear trail on the left hand side of the **Quebrada Espíndola** which leads past the southern shores of **Laguna Culebrillas** and to a ruined house.
- It is a comfortable day's hike from Laguna Las Tres Cruces to the ruined house. This is a good place to camp but don't leave your rubbish to accumulate with the rest, especially as part of the house is still, surprisingly, inhabited. The name of the ruined house is **Paredones de Culebrillas** (or simply Paredones).
- From the ruined house to the ruins of Ingapirca is a steady 5-6 hours, leaving you enough time to explore the ruins and then find a room for the night. Head southwest on the Inca road, which is at its full width of about 6-7 m. After a short while the trail turns south and continues across the marshy ground, through a landscape strewn with giant boulders.
- After 2-3 hours the trail fades out again. Walk in a southerly direction, keeping to the right and as high as possible above the river valley. Eventually you should see signs of cultivation and habitation.
- Pick up the trail (not the Inca road) and follow it past fields and houses to a road which winds its way up to the ruins of Ingapirca.

South to Cuenca

South of Riobamba, as the Panamericana approaches the southern highlands, it runs through bleak mountainous country alongside great canyons. The countryside is poor, dry, chilly and windswept, and the Indians withdrawn and wrapped-up. In the province of Cañar, natives are dressed in traditional garb with small white hats. At Zhud a paved road runs to Cochancay and La Troncal in the coastal lowlands, from where there are paved roads to Guayaquil and Machala. Towards Cuenca the road loses height and the land is more intensively farmed. There is an excellent four-lane highway which bypasses Biblián and Azogues and continues to Cuenca.

Some 67 km north of Cuenca and 36 km north of Azogues, Cañar is a cold colonial town and one of the access points for Ingapirca. It is famous for double-faced weaving, although this is now difficult to find. The jail, Centro de Rehabilitación Social, Colón y 3 de Noviembre, sells weavings made by prisoners. The market on Sunday, when indigenous inhabitants of surrounding rural communities flock to town, is very colourful and it is still relatively easy to find the Cañar hats for sale in several of the small stores in town.

Cañar
Phone code: 07
Colour map 6, grid A4
Population: 11,000
Altitude: 3,175 m

Sleeping and eating **E** *Irene*, 24 de Mayo, in the upper part of town, T236496. Shared bath, dodgy electric shower, parking, OK. **E-F** *Ingapirca*, Sucre y 5 de Junio, on the plaza, T235201. Cheaper with shared bath, electric shower, basic but OK. **F** *Mónica*, just off main plaza, T235486. Some rooms with private bath, electric shower, basic, mixed reports. Very cheap meals are available at *Los Maderos*, 1 block from plaza; and *Don Panchito*, 24 de Mayo, food OK but count your change.

It's a better idea to stay here, rather than El Tambo, if you do not wish to sleep up in Ingapirca village

Transport To **Ingapirca**, see above. Buses leave every 15 mins from 24 de Mayo to the Terminal Terrestre in **Cuenca**, US$1.20, 2 hrs; also 1 a day to **Quito**, 9½ hrs, US$9. **Bank** *Banco del Austro*, on plaza, Visa cash advances, morning only.

Between Cañar and Azogues is Biblián, with a sanctuary to La Virgen del Rocío, built into the rocks high above the village. It's a pleasant walk up with impressive views of the river valley and surrounding countryside. At Sageo is **E** *Hostería El Camping*, 3 km north of Azoguez, 2½ km south of Biblián, T240445. Private bath, hot water, pool, a local weekend place.

Biblián
Phone code: 07

The capital of the province of Cañar, Azogues is a busy city perched on a steep hillside above the Río Burgay, 31 km north of Cuenca. The Saturday market is colourful. Beautifully situated on a hill is the city's huge church and convent **San Francisco de la Virgen de las Nubes**.

    A relaxed excursion from Azogues is to the village **Cojitambo**, 20 minutes west on the road to **Deleg** (buses from terminal terrestre, US$0.25). There is good technical rock climbing on the cliffs behind Cojitambo, bring all your own gear. Or walk 1½ km along the road towards Deleg and take a turn-off left to follow trails to the summit. Small Inca/Cañari ruins are being restored near the top and there are grand views. Free admission, no services or facilities.

Azogues
Phone code: 07
Colour map 6, grid A4
Population: 28,000
Altitude: 2,500 m

Azogues Sleeping and eating **D** *Cordillera*, overlooking the former bus terminal, T240587. OK. **D** *Paraiso*, Váscones y Veintimilla, in La Playa sector north of town, T244729, F244927, hparaiso@cue.satnet.net Restaurant, parking, modern and comfortable, quiet neighbourhood, good value. **D** *Rivera*, 24 de Mayo y 10 de Agosto,

T248113. Restaurant, parking, modern. **D** *Santa María*, Serrano y Emilio Abad, T241883, F241210. Restaurant, OK. **E** *Chicago*, 3 de Noviembre y 24 de Mayo, T241040. Private bath, electric shower, basic. All of the following serve cheap meals. *Peleusí*, Emilio Abad y Sucre, T242611. Cafeteria, nice atmosphere, open 0900-1900, closed Sun. *El Padrino*, C Bolívar 609 y 10 de Agosto, T240534. Popular restaurant. *Ochenta y siete*, 3 de Noviembre y 24 de Mayo, next to *Hotel Chicago*, good restaurant. *Los Picantes de Azogues*, Bolívar y Azuay, popular. *Tatiana*, Serrano y Malo, set meals.

Transport The bus station is at the south end of town, near the highway. To **Cuenca**, every 10 mins, US$0.50, 30 mins. To **Quito**, US$10, 8 hrs. To **Guayaquil**, US$6, 4 hrs.

Cuenca

Phone code: 07
Colour map 6, grid A4
Population: 600,000
Altitude: 2,530 m

Cuenca is capital of the province of Azuay and the third largest city in Ecuador. The city has preserved much of its colonial air, with many of its old buildings constructed of the marble quarried nearby and recently renovated. The colonial centre is fairly compact and flat, making it easy to get around on foot. Most Ecuadoreans consider this their finest city and few would disagree. Its cobblestone streets, flowering plazas and whitewashed buildings with old wooden doors and ironwork balconies make it a pleasure to explore. In 1999 Cuenca was designated a World Heritage Trust site by UNESCO.

As well as being the economic centre of *El Austro*, as the Southern Sierra is called, Cuenca is also an intellectual centre. It has a long tradition as the birthplace of notable artists, writers, poets and philosophers, earning it the title 'Athens of Ecuador'. It remains a rather formal city, loyal to its conservative traditions. Everything closes for lunch between 1300 and 1500 and many places are closed on Sunday. The climate is spring-like, with chilly nights.

Ins and outs

Getting there
See Transport, page 253, for further details

The well-organized and policed Terminal Terrestre is on Av España, a 20-min walk northwest of the city centre and 5 mins' walk from the airport – both can be reached by city bus. The terminal for local or within-the-province buses is at the Feria Libre on Av las Américas. Many city buses also pass here, but note that this is an unsafe area.

Getting around The city is bounded by the Río Machángara to the north. The Río Tomebamba separates the colonial heart from the stadium, universities and newer residential areas to the south. Parque Nacional Cajas can be seen to the west of the city. Av las Américas is a ring road to the north and west, while to the south there is a new multi-lane bypass.

Tourist information *Ministerio de Turismo*, Sucre y Benigno Malo, on Parque Calderón next to the *municipio*, T839337, helpful. ■ *Mon-Fri, 0830-1700*. *Cámara de Turismo*, at the Terminal Terrestre, T868482. ■ *Mon-Fri 0700-2100, Sat 0800-2000, Sun 0800-1300*. *Asociación Hotelera de Cuenca*, Pres Córdova y Padre Aguirre, T836925. Information about accommodation. ■ *Mon-Fri 0830-1300, 1430-1800*.

Safety Cuenca is safer than either Quito or Guayaquil, but street crime does occur and routine precautions are advised. The city centre is deserted and unsafe after 2200. The area around El Puente Roto (south end of Vargas Machuca) is unsafe at night and around El Puente del Vado (Av 12 de Abril y Av Loja) is unsafe at all hours. Market areas, especially Mercado 9 de Octubre, call for caution at all times.

History

Cuenca was originally a Cañari settlement, dating from AD 500 to around 1480, called Guapondeleg, which roughly translates as 'an area as large as heaven'. The suffix 'deleg' is still found in several local place names, a vestige of the now extinct Cañari language.

Ingapirca and Tomebamba were, for a time, the hub of the northern part of the Inca empire

Owing to its geographical location, this was among the first parts of what is now Ecuador to come under the domination of the Inca empire, which had expanded north. The Incas settled the area around Cuenca and called it Tomebamba, which roughly translates as 'Valley of Knives'. The name survives as one of the region's rivers. Some 70 km north of Cuenca, in an area known as *Jatun Cañar*, the Incas built the ceremonial centre of Ingapirca, which remains the most important Inca site in the country (see page 240).

The city as it is today was founded by the Spanish in 1557 on the site of Tomebamba and named Santa Ana de los Cuatro Ríos de Cuenca. Cuenca then became an important and populous regional centre in the crown colony governed from Quito. The *conquistadores* and the settlers who followed them were interested in the working of precious metals, for which the region's indigenous peoples had earned a well deserved reputation. Following independence from Spain, Cuenca was capital of one of three provinces that made up the new republic, the others being Quito and Guayaquil.

Sights

On the main plaza, **Parque Abdón Calderón**, are both the Old Cathedral (closed for restoration in 2002), also known as **El Sagrario**, begun in 1557 when modern Cuenca was founded, and the immense 'New' **Catedral de la Inmaculada**. The latter was started in 1885 and contains a famous crowned image of the Virgin. It was the work of the German architect Padre Johannes Baptista Stiehle, who also designed many other buildings in the Cuenca area. It was planned to be the largest cathedral in South America but the architect made some miscalculations with the foundations and the final domes on the front towers could not be built for fear that the whole thing would come down. Modern stained glass, a beautiful altar and an exceptional play of light and shade inside the cathedral make it worth a visit. The Sunday evening worship is recommended.

El Sagrario was built on the foundations of an Inca structure and some of the Inca blocks are still visible facing the plaza. The French Geodesic Mission of 1736-44 came to Ecuador to measure the Equator, and probably also to see what the Spanish were up to. They used El Sagrario as one of the fixed points for their measurements.

Other churches which deserve a visit are **San Blas**, **San Francisco**, **El Cenáculo**, and **Santo Domingo**. Many churches are open at irregular hours only and for services, because of increasing problems with theft. The 17th-century church of **El Carmen de la Asunción** is close to the southwest corner of La Inmaculada and has a flower market in the tiny **Plazoleta El Carmen** in front. The church is open early in the morning and mid-afternoon, but the attached cloister of El Carmen Alto is closed as the nuns inside live in total isolation.

South of the city on Avenida Fray Vicente Solano, beyond the football stadium, is **El Turi church and mirador**, a 40-minute walk from the base or two hours from the colonial city (not safe after dark), or take taxi. It's well worth a visit for the great views and a tiled panorama explains what you see. There is an

Southern Highlands

orphanage attached to the church. There are good walks along attractive country lanes further south but do not take valuables.

There is a daily market in **Plaza Cívica** where pottery, clothes, guinea pigs and local produce, especially baskets, are sold. Thursday is the busiest.

The suburb of **San Joaquín**, out west near the tennis club, is famous for its basketwork. There are many houses where you can see the different types of baskets being made. Some of the styles, especially the ones with a waist, are made only in the Cuenca and Azogues areas.

Museums
The excellent **Museo del Banco Central 'Pumapungo'**, on the southeastern edge of the colonial city, is at the actual site of the Tomebamba excavations. A **Parque Arqueológico Pumapungo** is scheduled to open at the site in 2003. The **Museo Arqueológíco** contains all the Cañari and Inca remains and artefacts found here. Although the Ingapirca ruins are more spectacular, it is believed that Tomebamba was the principal Inca administrative centre in southern Ecuador. Other halls in the premises house the **Museo Etnográfico**, with information of the different cultures which make up Ecuador including a special collection of *tsantsas* (shrunken heads from Oriente), the **Museo de Arte Religioso**, the **Museo Numismático,** and temporary exhibits. There are also book and music libraries and free cultural videos and music events. ■ *Mon-Fri 0900-1800, Sat 0900-1300. US$2. T831255. C Larga y Huayna Capac. The entrance is on the far left of the building.*

About 300 m from the Pumapungo site there are excavations at the **Museo Manuel Agustín Landívar**, which reveal traces of Inca and Cañari civilizations and show how the Spanish reused the stonework. ■ *Mon-Fri, 0900-1300, 1500-1800, Sat 0900-1300. US$0.25. C Larga 287.*

The **Instituto Azuayo de Folklore** has an exhibition of popular Latin American arts and crafts. Through CIDAP (Centro Interamericano de Desarollo de Artes Populares), it supports research and promotes sales of artisans' works. There is also a library and a recommended crafts shop. ■ *Mon-Fri 0930-1300, 1430-1800, Sat 1000-1300. Free. Escalinata 303 y C Larga, extension of C Hermano Miguel.*

Museo de las Culturas Aborígenes A good private collection of precolumbian archaeology, in the house of Dr J Cordero López. There are guided tours in English, Spanish and French, refurbished in 2002. It's well worth a visit. ■ *Mon-Fri 0830-1230, 1430-1830, Sat 0830-1230. US$2. T811706. C Larga y Mariano Cueva.*

Museo del Monasterio de las Conceptas A well displayed collection of religious and folk art, and an extensive collection of lithographs by Guayasamín housed in a cloistered convent founded in 1599. ■ *Mon-Fri 0900-1730, Sat and public holidays 1000-1300. US$2.50. T830625. Hermano Miguel 6-33 between Pdte Córdova and Juan Jaramillo.*

The **Museo Municipal de Arte Moderno** has a permanent contemporary art collection and an art library. A biennial international painting competition is held here as well as other cultural activities worth attending. ■ *Mon-Fri 0830-1830, Sat 0900-1300, Sun 0900-1300. Free. T831027. Sucre 1527 y Talbot, on the Plaza San Sebastián.*

The **Museo de Esqueletología** has a small well designed collection of bird and animal skeletons, from a hummingbird to an elephant. ■ *Mon-Fri 0900-1330, 1500-1800. US$1. Sucre y Borrero.*

A lovely, restored colonial house is the **Casa Azul** on Gran Colombia 10-29 y Padre Aguirre, housing a travel agency, restaurant and a little museum.

The **Museo Remigio Crespo Toral**, housed in a beautifully restored colonial mansion, has various regional history collections, including a selection of gold objects from the Cañar and Chordeleg cultures. ■ *Closed for renovations in 2002. C Larga 7-07 y Borreo.*

The **Museo de Artes de Fuego** on Calle las Herrerías, or the blacksmith's road, has a display of wrought iron work and pottery. It is housed in a beautifully restored old building. Outside is a sculpture of a volcano and on special occasions the god Vulkan, wrapped in flames, comes out of the volcano. There is also a shop. ■ *Mon-Fri except for lunchtime and Sat morning. Las Herrerías y 10 de Agosto, across the river from the Museo del Banco Central.*

Essentials

LL-L *El Dorado*, Gran Colombia 787 y Luis Cordero, T831390, F831663, www.hoteldorado.com Good restaurant, cafeteria open all day, internet, excellent restaurant with good views. **L** *Oro Verde*, Ordóñez Lazo, T831200, F832849, ecovc@ gye.satnet.net Good restaurant, small pool, internet, on the road to Cajas, on a lagoon in the outskirts of town.

    AL *Crespo*, C Larga 793, T842571, F839473, info@hotel-crespo.com, www.ecuadorexplorer.com/crespo Restaurant, a/c, internet, parking, some nice rooms overlooking the river, others dark or with no windows. **AL** *Pinar del Lago*, Av Ordoñez Laso, next door to the *Oro Verde*, T837339, F842833, pinarlag@impsat.net.ec Includes breakfast, cafeteria, parking, carpeted rooms, good views of lake or river. **A** *El Conquistador*, Gran Colombia 665, T831788, F831291, www.hotelconquistador.com Includes buffet breakfast, good restaurant, internet, avoid back rooms Fri-Sat because of noise from disco, good value. **A** *Patrimonio*, Bolívar 6-22 y Hermano Miguel, T831126, F842163, patrimo@etapa.com Includes breakfast, restaurant, internet, modern, centrally located, new in 2001.

    B *Atahualpa*, Sucre 3-50 y Tomás Ordóñez, T831841, F842345. Includes breakfast, small restaurant and cafeteria, parking, good. **B** *El Molino*, out of town at Km 75 on Cuenca-Azogues road, T875367, F875358. Includes breakfast, restaurant, pool, parking, pleasant location near river, rustic style. Reservations advised. Recommended. **B** *El Quijote*, Hermano Miguel 9-58 y Gran Colombia, T843197, hquijote@ cue.satnet.net Restaurant, nicely restored old building with patio. **B** *Inca Real*, G Torres 8-40 entre Sucre y Bolívar, T823636, F840699, incareal@cue.satnet.net Includes breakfast, restaurant, internet, parking, comfortable. **B** *Italia*, Av España y Huayna-Cápac, T840060, F846475, hitalia@cue.satnet.net Includes buffet breakfast, restaurant, parking, modern, comfortable. **B** *La Orquidea*, Borrero 9-31 y Bolívar, T824511, F835844, orquihos@etapa.com.ec Refurbished colonial house, small patios, bright, good value. **B** *Nuestra Residencia*, Los Pinos 1-100 y Ordóñez Laso, T831702, F835576. Includes breakfast, small place with living room and bar, friendly, good atmosphere. **B** *Posada del Angel*, Bolívar 14-11 y Estévez de Toral, T840695, F821360, hdaniel@ cue.satnet.net Includes breakfast, internet, restored colonial house, comfortable. **B** *Presidente*, Gran Colombia 659, T831066, F842127. Includes breakfast, good restaurant, internet, parking, good value, comfortable, convenient location. **B** *Victoria*, C Larga 6-93, T827401, F838508, santaana@etapa.com.ec Good expensive restaurant, comfortable, modern, nice views, new in 2002.

    C *Alli Tiana*, Córdova y Padre Aguirre, T821955, F821788. Includes breakfast, restaurant, small rooms, good view. **C** *Chordeleg*, Gran Colombia 11-15 y Gral Torres, T822536, F824611, hostalfm@etapa.com.ec Includes breakfast, cafeteria, charming colonial house with courtyard. **C** *Macondo*, Tarqui 11-64 y Lamar, T840697, macondo@cedei.org Includes breakfast, cooking facilities, restored colonial house, US run. Highly recommended.

Sleeping
■ *on map, page 248*
Price codes:
see inside front cover
Cuenca has many hotels but they are often full, try booking in advance

Southern Highlands

D *Aranjuez*, Aranjuez 1-31 y Madrid, T820622. Modern and OK, new in 2001.
D *Cabañas Yanuncay*, C Cantón Gualaceo 21-49, between Av Loja and Las Américas (in Yanuncay), 10 mins by car from centre, T883716. Includes breakfast, home-cooked meals available, rustic cabins and rooms, nice setiing, English spoken, friendly and helpful. Recommended. **D** *Caribe Inn*, Gran Colombia 10-51 y Padre Aguirre, T835175, F834157. OK. **D** *Casa del Barranco*, Calle Larga 8-41 entre Benigno Malo y Luis Cordero, T839763, F822503. Restaurant, parking, some spacious rooms, pleasant views over river. **D** *Catedral*, Padre Aguirre 8-17 y Sucre, T823204. Includes breakfast, good restaurant, coffee shop opens 0700, internet, cheerful, spacious, modern, but not very warm, English spoken. **D** *El Monasterio*, Padre Aguirre 7-24 y Sucre, T843609, monasterio724@hotmail.com Internet, clean kitchen facilities, pleasant terrace with good views, popular. Recommended. **D** *Gran Hotel*, Torres 9-70 y Bolívar, T831934, F842127. Includes breakfast, restaurant, nice patio, popular meeting place. **D** *Milán*,

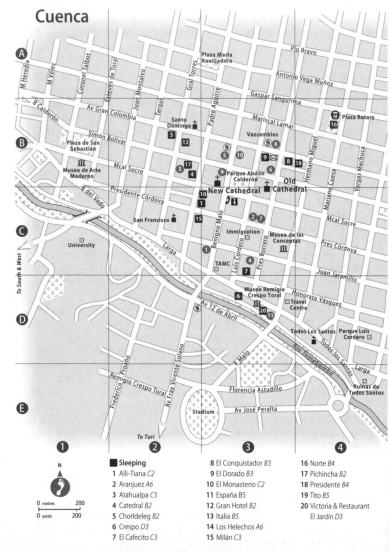

Cuenca

Sleeping
1 Alli-Tiana *C2*
2 Aranjuez *A6*
3 Atahualpa *C5*
4 Catedral *B2*
5 Chorldeleg *B2*
6 Crespo *D3*
7 El Cafecito *C3*
8 El Conquistador *B3*
9 El Dorado *B3*
10 El Monasterio *C2*
11 España *B5*
12 Gran Hotel *B2*
13 Italia *B5*
14 Los Helechos *A6*
15 Milán *C3*
16 Norte *B4*
17 Pichincha *B2*
18 Presidente *B4*
19 Tito *B5*
20 Victoria & Restaurant
   El Jardín *D3*

Pres Córdova 989 y Padre Aguirre, T831104, hotmilan@etapa.com.ec Includes breakfast, restaurant, internet, laundry facilities, view over market, rooms variable. **D-E** *El Cafecito*, Honorato Vásquez 7-36 y Luis Cordero, T832337, elcafec@cue.satnet.net Restaurant, cheaper in dorm, colonial house with patio, popular with travellers and noisy.

E *La Casa*, Hermano Miguel 4-19, T837347. Shared bath, hot water, internet, laundry and cooking facilities, will pick up from airport or bus station. **E** *Norte*, Mariano Cueva 11-63 y Sangurima, T827881. Good restaurant, cheaper with shared bath, hot water, renovated, large rooms, comfortable. The hotel is safe but it's in a dodgy area after dark. **E** *Pichincha*, Gral Torres 8-82 y Bolívar, T823868, F833695, karolina@etapa.com.ec Shared bath, hot water, internet, parking, spacious rooms, helpful. Recommended. **E** *Tinku*, C Larga 4-68 y Alfonso Jerves, T838520. Restaurant and bar, shared bath, hot water, internet, cooking facilities, colonial house, friendly and helpful.

Near the bus terminal C *Hurtado de Mendoza*, Huayna-Cápac y Sangurima, T843611, F831909, hostalhm@cue.satnet.net Includes breakfast, restaurant, parking, good. **D** *España*, Sangurima 1-17 y Huayna-Cápac, T831351, F846442, hespana@cue.satnet.net Good restaurant, internet, modern but rooms are a bit small. **D** *Tito*, Sangurima 1-49 y M Vega, T829734, F843577. Restaurant very good value, older place but refurbished. **D-E** *Los Helechos*, Gil Ramírez Dávalos y Del Chorro, T863401. Restaurant, cheaper with shared bath, parking, OK. Many others in this area, shop around.

Furnished apartments *El Jardín*, Av Pumapungo y Viracochabamba, T804103. Equipped apartments with cooking facilities, parking. US$495 per month. **B** *Apartamentos Otorongo*, Av 12 de Abril y Guayas, T811184, pmontezu @az.pro.ec A 10-15 min walk from centre, fully furnished flats for 4 with kitchenette, TV, phone. Cleaning service included, friendly owners, discount for longer stay.

Av Remigio Crespo, between the stadium and the coliseum, has a variety of *pizzerías*, *heladerías*, burger and sandwich bars, steak houses, bars and discos. The area is very popular with young people and lively at weekends. There are cheap *comedores* on the 2nd floor of Mercado Modelo, on 10 de Agosto y 18 de Noviembre.

Eating
● *on map*
Price codes:
see inside front cover
22% tax and service
is added in more
upmarket restaurants

● Eating
1 Café Austria *C3*
2 Chifa Pack How *C3*
3 El Túnel *B2*
4 Goura *C3*
5 Heladería Holanda *B3*
6 La Barraca *B3*
7 Los Capulíes *C3*
8 Los Pibes *B3*
9 Raymipampa *B3*
10 Tutto Freddo *B3*
11 Wunderbar *D3*

Southern Highlands

Expensive *Chifa Pack How*, Presidente Córdova 7-72 y Cordero. Good oriental cuisine. Recommended. *El Jardín*, in *Hotel Victoria*, C Larga 6-93. Lovely, elegant, good food, closed Sun-Mon. *La Rotond*, 12 de Abril y José Peralta, T888111. Excellent French and international cooking, elegant, good view of the river and residential area. *Los Capulíes*, Córdova y Borrero, T832339. Bar-restaurant, excellent Ecuadorean cuisine, friendly, lovely setting, Andean live music Thu-Sat 2030, reservations recommended at the weekend. *Molinos del Batán*, 12 de Abril y Puente El Vado, T811531. Ecuadorean. Good setting by river, good food. *Parrillada Argentina*, good grill, excellent service, also chicken, pizza, pasta, salads etc, open till late. *Rancho Chileno*, Av España, next to airport. Latin American. Good steak and seafood, slow service. *Villa Rosa*, Gran Colombia 12-22 y Tarqui. Very elegant, excellent food.

Mid-range *Balcón Quiteño*, Sangurima 6-49 y Borrero, T822581, and Av Ordoñez Lazo 311 y los Pinos, T825251. Ecuadorean. Popular with the locals after a night's hard partying. *Casa Grande*, San Joaquín-La Cruz Verde, T839992. Grill, good food and value. In picturesque San Joaquín district where flowers and vegetables are grown and baskets made. *Chifa Asia*, Cueva 11 s/n, entre 34 y 68. Oriental cuisine. Large portions. Recommended. *Coyote Flaco*, C Larga y Borrero. Mexican, OK atmosphere but small portions. *El Che Pibe*, Av Remigio Crespo 2-59. Latin American. *El Pedregal Azteca*, Gran Colombia 10-29 y Padre Aguirre. Good Mexican food. *El Mar*, Gran Colombia 20-33, T843522. Seafood. *El Paraíso*, Tomás Ordóñez 10-45 y Gran Colombi. Open Mon-Sat 0800-1600, good breakfast, excellent vegetarian food, cheap set lunch. *El Tequila*, Gran Colombia 20-59, T831847. Ecuadorean. Good local food, good value and service. *El Túnel*, Gral Torres 8-60, T823109. Quick service, romantic atmosphere, good, cheap lunch menu. *Gran Muralla*, Juan Jaramillo entre Benigno Malo y Luis Cordero. Oriental. *La Barraca*, Antonio Borrero 9-68 y Gran Colombia, opposite the Post Office, T829967. Breakfast, dinner, quiet music, coffee, excellent, open daily 0800-2300. *La Casa del Marisco*, Av Paucarbamba y Luis Moreno, T843522. Seafood. *La Napolitana*, Federico Proaño 4-20. Italian, nice atmosphere, good food. *Las Campanas*, Borrero 7-69 y Sucre, good Ecuadorean food, open until 0200. *A las Riberas del Guayas*, Bolívar 4-40 y Mariano Cueva. Ecuadorean. Coastal food. *Las Tres Caravelas*, part of hotel *El Conquistador*. Good value, Ecuadorean and international fare. Andean live music at weekends. *La Tasca*, Pasaje 3 de Noviembre bajos del Puente Roto. Cuban food. *La Viña*, Juan Jaramillo y Luis Cordero. Italian. *Los Pibes*, Gran Colombia 776 y Cordero, opposite *Hotel El Dorado*. Good pizzas and lasagne. *Los Sauces*, Bolívar 6-17. Original dishes. *NY Pizza*, Gran Colombia 10-43 y Padre Aguirre. Italian, good, especially the *calzones*. *Tuna*, Gran Colombia 8-80. Pizzas and trout, popular. **Weekends, holidays and by arrangement**: *Hacienda Sustag*, Km 17 via Joaquín-Soldados, T830834, F832340. Located in the countryside, a farm with beautiful landscapes, camping and picnic area, delicious Ecuadorean food. *Dos Chorreras*, via Cajas north road. Excellent for fresh trout.

Cheap *Caos*, J Jaramillo y Hermano Miguel. Good Italian food, pleasant atmosphere. Open Mon-Sat 1800-2400. *Goura*, Juan Jaramillo 7-27 y Borrero, vegetarian, good cheap set lunch and pizza, great fruit salad, good choice of à la carte dinners. Recommended. *Sol Oriental*, Gran Colombia y Vega. Oriental cuisine, large portions.

Cafés & snackbars *Café Austria*, Benigno Malo 5-99. Good cakes, pies, sandwiches, coffee, fruit, ice-cream, yoghurt, closed Mon. *Café Capuchino*, Bolívar y Aguirre. Open 0930, good hamburgers, real coffee and liqueur coffees. *Café Chordeleg*, Gran Colombia 7-87. Open 24 hrs, excellent breakfast. *Café Eucalyptus*, Gran Colombia 9-41 y Benigno Malo, T849157, www.cafeeucalyptus.com Tapas restaurant and bar, also offers full English breakfast, travel guide shop upstairs, detailed maps. A cozy hangout. *Cinema Café*, Luis Cordero y Sucre, above the *Casa de la Cultura* cinema, snacks, salads, popular. *The English Café & Bookshop*, C Larga 6-69. Breakfast, juices, snacks and sandwiches, British-Ecuadorean run, English books for sale, closed Wed. *Heladería Holanda*, Benigno Malo 9-51. Open 0930, yoghurt for breakfast, good ice-cream, fruit salads, cream cakes. Recommended. *Helados Honey*, Mcal Lamar 4-21. Clean, recommended milkshakes. *MiPan*, Pres Córdova 824 between Cordero y Malo (also Bolívar y Aguirre). Open 0730, excellent bread, cakes, tarts, doughnuts, tea, coffee and chocolate. *Monte Bianco*, Bolívar 2-80 y Ordóñez, near San Blas church, good cakes, ice-cream, open Sun. *Pity's*, 2 branches, Av Remigio Crespo Toral y Alfonso Borrero, and Ordóñez Lazo y Circunvalación. For sandwiches, hamburgers. Recommended. *Raymipampa*, Benigno Malo 8-59, T834159, on Parque Calderón, also at Sucre 9-13 y Benigno Malo and Remigio Crespo 1-20 y Av del Estadio. Open daily, very popular, especially at lunchtime, local dishes, good ceviche, crêpes, good ice-cream, clean, excellent value. *Tutto Freddo*, Benigno Malo entre Gran Colombia y Bolívar. Ice-cream, pizza and sandwiches. *Wunderbar*, Hermano Miguel y C Larga, behind the Instituto Azuayo de Folklore. German-run, good atmosphere, good food and coffee, also vegetarian, book exchange, German magazines.

Bars *Chaos*, Honorato Vásquez y Hermano Miguel, popular. *Tapas y Canciones*, Remigio Crespo y Galápagos, small quaint *peña*. *La Vitrola*, Av Ordóñez Lazo, 500 m from *Hotel Oro Verde*, T837197. Bar, restaurant and *peña* with Latin music, excellent atmosphere. **Bars & nightclubs**

Discos *Aazúcar*, Pasaje 3 de Noviembre y 12 de Abril, under the Puente Roto bridge. Latin and international music. Overpriced. *La Mesa Salsoteca*, Gran Colombia 3-36 entre Vargas Machuca y Tomás Ordóñez. No sign, latin music, very popular among locals and travellers. *Papa Galo*, Remigio Crespo y Galápagos, in the Zona Rosa, varied music, popular with local youth. *Pop Art*, Remigio Crespo y Solano, modern music. Also discos in the hotels *Conquistador* and *Alli-Tiana* (older crowd).

Cinemas Films (evening) at **Casa de la Cultura**, Luis Cordero y Sucre. *Teatro Cuenca*, P Aguirre 10-50. *Multicines*, Av José Peralta, complex of 5 theatres and food court. **Entertainment**

On **Christmas Eve** there is an outstanding parade, *Pase del Niño Viajero*, probably the largest and finest Christmas parade in all Ecuador. Children and adults from all the *barrios* and surrounding villages decorate donkeys, horses, cars and trucks with symbols of abundance. Young children dressed in colourful Indian costumes or as Biblical figures ride through the streets accompanied by musicians. The parade starts about 1000 at San Sebastián, proceeds along C Simón Bolívar, past Parque Calderón and ends at San Blas. In the days around Christmas there are also smaller *Pase del Niño* parades. **Festivals**

On **New Year's Eve**, as elsewhere in Ecuador, the festivities include the parading and burning at midnight of effigies called *Años Viejos* (some political, some fictional) which symbolize the old year.

Southern Highlands

On **10-13 Apr** is the *Foundation of Cuenca*. On **Good Friday** there is a fine procession through the town and up to the Mirador Turi. Cuenca hosts an internationally famous art competition every 2 years, *La Bienal*, which begins in **Apr** or **May**. Exhibitions occupy museums and galleries around the city for about 4 months. The whole event is coordinated by the Museo de Arte Moderno.

Septenario is the religious festival of *Corpus Christi* in **Jun**, and lasts a week. On Parque Calderón a decorated tower with fireworks attached, known as 'castillo', is burnt every night after a mass, 'vacas locas' or mad cows (people carrying a reed structure in the shape of a cow, with lit fireworks) run across the park, and hundreds of hot air paper balloons are released. A spectacular sight which is not to be missed. There are also dozens of dessert sellers and games in the streets.

On **3 Nov** is *Independence of Cuenca*, with street theatre, art exhibitions and night-time dances all over the city, including the **Puente Roto**, east of the Escalinata.

Shopping   **Bookshops**   *The English Café & Bookshop*, C Larga 6-69. See Cafés above.

Camping   Camping Gas is available at several locations; camping equipment can be found at *Bermeo Hnos*, Borrero 8-35 y Sucre, T831522, and *Créditos y Negocios*, Benigno Malo y Pdte Córdova, T829583.

Handicrafts   The Cuenca region is noted for its *artesanía*. Good souvenirs are carvings, leather, basketwork, ceramics, painted wood, onyx, woven stuffs, embroidered shirts and jewellery. There are many craftware shops along Gran Colombia, Benigno Malo and Juan Jaramillo alongside Las Conceptas. *Arte Artesanías y Antigüedades*, Borrero y Córdova, has some lovely textiles, jewellery and antiques. *Bazaar Susanita*, Benigno Malo 1092. For good woollen sweaters at reasonable prices. *Centro Cultural Jorge Moscoso*, Pres Córdova 6-14 y Hermano Miguel, T822114. Weaving exhibitions, ethnographic museum, antiques and handicrafts. *El Barranco*, Hermano Miguel 3-23 y Av 3 de Noviembre. Artisans' co-operative selling a wide variety of crafts. *El Tucán*, Borrero 7-35. Recommended. *Galápagos*, Borrero 6-75, excellent selection of crafts. There are several good leather shops in the arcade off Bolívar between Benigno Malo and Luis Cordero, the quality and price are comparable with Cotacachi, near Otavalo in Northern Ecuador. *Galería Claudio Maldonado*, Bolívar 7-75, has unique precolumbian designs in silver and precious stones. *Galería Pulla*, Jaramillo 6-90. Works by this famous painter, also has sculpture and jewellery. *Torres*, between Sucre y Córdova, or *Tarqui*, between Córdova and the river, for *polleras*, traditional Indian women's skirts. *Yapacunchi*, Luis Cordero y Bolívar. Also, good quality handicrafts are for sale in the *El Dorado hotel*. *Artesa*, L Cordero 10-31 y Gran Colombia. Several other branches around the city, sells modern Ecuadorean ceramics at good prices.

Jewellery   Prices are reported as high, so shop around. *Joyería Turismo*, owned by Leonardo Crespo, at Gran Colombia 9-31. Recommended. He will let wholesale buyers tour his factory. *Unicornio*, Gran Colombia y Luis Cordero. Good jewellery, ceramics and candelabras.

Markets   Sat is the busiest market day. There's an interesting market behind the new cathedral, and a *Centro Comercial* in the industrial park, with interesting shops. There is a well stocked supermarket behind *Residencial España*. *Supermaxi* is at Gran Colombia y Av de las Américas and on Av José Peralta, near the stadium.

Check the quality of Panama hats very carefully as some tend to unravel and shops are unwilling to replace or refund

Panama hats   Cuenca is a centre of the Panama hat industry. Manufacturers offer factory tours followed by visits to their showrooms where purchases can be made. The fist two listed are next to each other, behind the bus terminal. *Kurt Dorfzaun*, Av Gil Ramírez Dávalos 4-34, T807563, F807608, www.kdorfzaun.com Mon-Fri 0830-1200, 1500-1830. *Homero Ortega P e Hijos*, Av Gil Ramírez Dávalos 3-86, T801288, F867600, www.homeroortega.com *Exportadora Cuenca*, Mcal Lamar 3-80.

Photography   *Asefot*, Gran Colombia 7-18, T/F839342. Recommended for colour prints. *Ecuacolor*, Gran Colombia 7-44 y Cordero. Good service. *Foto Ortiz*, Gran

Colombia y Aguirre. Wide range of film, good same-day developing. Not recommended for slides.

Sport

Fishing The lakes at Parque Nacional Cajas offer trout fishing opportunities.

Horse riding Beatrice and Xavier Malo of *Montaruna Tours* (see *The Travel Center* under Tour operators, below) offer horse-riding trips (up to 10 days) from their hacienda outside Cuenca. Excellent horses, interesting itineraries, recommended.

Mountain biking *Biketa*, also in *The Travel Center* (see Tour operators, below), rents bikes for US$15 per day and offers cycle tours to Ingapirca and Cajas, US$45 per person per day. *Tecno Cyclo*, Remigio Tamariz 3-15, T839659, sells bicycles.

Trekking There are excellent hiking opportunities at Parque Nacional Cajas and other areas around Cuenca, see below.

Tour operators
Day tours to Ingapirca run US$35-45 per person, trekking in Cajas about US$35 per person per day. The cascada de Girón is another popular destination, see page 258

Apullacta, Gran Colombia y G Torres. Rent tents. *Ecotrek*, C Larga 7-100 y Luis Cordero, T842531, F835387, ecotrek@az.pro.ec Contact Juan Gabriel Carrasco. Trips to Kapawi (see page 384), great adventure travel, specializes in Shaman trips. *Enmotur*, Gran Colombia 10-45. Bus tours to Ingapirca. *Metropolitan Touring*, Sucre 6-62 y Hermano Miguel, T831463, and Remigio Crespo y A Cordero, T816937. Tours and airline tickets. *Río Arriba*, Hermano Miguel 7-14 y Pres Córdova, T840031, F830116, negro@az.pro.ec Recommended. *The Travel Centre*, Hermano Miguel 4-46 y C Larga, T823782, F820082. Three tour operators under one roof with lots of useful information, helpful staff, a pleasant sitting area, small library and bulletin boards. Recommended. The 3 operators are: *Biketa*, for mountain biking (see Sport above); *Montaruna Tours*, T/F846395, www.montaruna.ch, excellent horse-riding trips, Swiss-Ecuadorean run, English and German spoken, recommended; and *Terra Diversa*, www.terradiversa.com, trips to Ingapirca, Cajas, Inca Trail and other attractions, plus airline tickets. Packages combining the above activities (ie cycling, horse riding and trekking) and fixed-day departures to the most popular sites may be offered in 2003, enquire when you are in Cuenca.

Recommended guides *Luis Astudillo*, C Azuay 1-48 entre Guayas y Tungurahua, home T815234, best after 2030. Tours to Ingapirca, Cajas and other local attractions. *José Rivera Baquero*, Pedro Carbo 1-48 y Guapondelig. Extensive knowledge of Cuenca and its surroundings. *Eduardo Quito*, home T823018, F834202. Or Contact through *Ecuaturis*, Hermano Miguel y Gran Colombia, T826594, F829524. Own 4WD and offers special tours as a professionally qualified guide, transports up to 10 people, speaks good English. Highly recommended.

Transport

Local Bus: city buses US$0.20. **Taxi**: US$1 for a short journey; US$1.40 to the airport or bus station. **Car hire**: *Inter*, Av España, opposite the airport, T801892. *Localiza*, at the airport, T863902.

Southern Highlands

Long distance Air: to **Quito**, US$58, **Guayaquil**, US$39, and **Macas**, with *TAME*, *Austro Aéreo* and *Icaro*. Schedules change often so ask locally. Reconfirm all flights.

Bus: to **Riobamba**, 6 hrs, US$5. To **Ambato**, 7 hrs, US$7. To **Quito**, 10 hrs, US$10. To **Loja**, 5 hrs, US$6. To **Machala**, 4 hrs, US$3.60, sit on the left, wonderful scenery. To **Guayaquil**, via Zhud, 5 hrs, US$7. To **Guayaquil**, via Cajas and Molleturo, 3½ hrs, US$7. To **Cajas National Park**, 1 hr, US$1.50. To **Macas** via Guarumales or Limón, 8-10 hrs, US$7; spectacular scenery but prone to landslides, check in advance if roads are open. To **Huaquillas**, 6 hrs, US$5. To **Azogues**, every 10 mins, US$0.50, 30 min. To **Saraguro**, US$4.20, 3½ hrs. To **Gualaquiza**, in the southern Oriente, 6 hrs, US$5. To **Alausí**, 4 hrs, US$4; all Quito-bound buses pass through.

Directory **Airline offices** *TAME*, Benigno Malo 508 y C Larga, T843222. *Austro Aéreo*, Hermano Miguel 6-86 y Pres Córdova, T832677, F848659. *Icaro*, Av España 1114, T802700, F808261. *American Airlines*, Padre Aguirre y Lamar, T831699, F832024. *Iberia*, in the *Hotel El Dorado*.

Banks *Banco del Pacífico*, Benigno Malo 9-75. TCs only. *Banco del Austro*, Sucre y Borrero, T842492. Visa ATM. *Banco de Guayaquil*, Sucre entre Hermano Miguel y Borrero. For Visa, MC and TCs. *Banco del Pichincha*, Av Solano y 12 de Abril, no commission on TCs (this is subject to change), also Visa. *MasterCard* office at Bolívar y T Ordóñez, T883577, F817290. *Vaz Cambios*, Gran Colombia 7-98 y Cordero, T833434. Open on Sat morning, efficient. No Peruvian currency is available in Cuenca.

Communications **Internet**: rates US$0.70-1.00 per hr. **Post**:on corner of C Gran Colombia and Borrero. **Phone**: calls from either *Pacifictel*, Benigno Malo between Córdova and Sucre, or *ETAPA*, Benigno Malo 7-27 y Sucre.

Medical facilities *Clínica Los Andes*, Mariano Cueva 14-68 y Pío Bravo, T842942/832488, excellent care, clean, 24-hr service. *Clínica Santa Ana*, Av Manuel J Calle 1-104, T814068. *Clínica Santa Inés*, Av Daniel Córdova Toral 2-113, T817888, Dr Jaime Moreno Aguilar speaks English. *Hospital Monte Sinai*, Miguel Cordero 6-111 y Av Solano, near the stadium, T885595. *Farmacia Botica Internacional*, Gran Colombia 7-20 y Borrero. Experienced staff, wide selection.

Language courses *Fundación Centro de Estudios Interamericanos*, Gran Colombia 11-02 y Gral Torres, edif Assoc de Empleados, T839003, F833593, www.cedei.org Spanish and Quichua, free email service for students, accommodation at short notice, *Hostal Macondo* attached. Recommended. *Centro Abraham Lincoln*, Borrero y Honorato Vásquez, T830373. Small Spanish language section. *Sí Centro de Español e Inglés*, Hermano Miguel 6-86 y Pres Córdova, T846932, F836174, www.sicentro spanishschool.com Good, competitive prices, helpful, tourist information available. Recommended. *Contacto* Galápagos 5-75 y Esmeraldas, T882703. Spanish, Quichua and English lessons. *Estudio Internacional Sampere*, Hermano Miguel 3-43 y Calle Larga, T/F841986, samperec@samperecen.com.ec At the high end of the price range.

Hourly rates for classes US$4.50-8.00

Laundry *La Química*, Borrero 734 y Córdova. Same day service, dry cleaning, expensive. *Lavahora*, Honorato Vásquez 7-72 (next to *El Cafecito*), T823042. Same day service, helpful and efficient. Recommended. *Fast Klin*, Hermano Miguel 4-21 y Calle Larga. *Durán & Hijos*, Luis Cordero y Juan Jarmillo.

Useful addresses *Policía Nacional de Migración*, Luis Cordero 6-62 y Pres Córdova, T831020. For tourist visa extensions, Mon-Fri 0800-1230, 1500-1830.

Southern Highlands

Around Cuenca

There are sulphur baths at Baños, with its domed, blue church in a delightful landscape, 5 km southwest of Cuenca. Water temperatures at the source are measured at 76°C. There are four complexes: Rodas, Marchan, Familiar and Durán. The last are by far the largest and best maintained and, although associated with the *Hostería Durán*, they are open to the public. There are numerous hot pools and tubs and steam baths open from dawn till 2100 or 2200. They are very crowded at weekends. The country lanes above the village offer some pleasant walks. At the baths is **A** *Hostería Durán*, Km 8 Vía Baños, T892485, F892488. It has an expensive restaurant, its own well maintained and very clean pools (US$2.80 for non-residents), tennis courts and steam bath. There are also a couple of cheap and basic *residencias*.

Baños
The hottest commercial baths in Ecuador, so hot that there are steam baths at 3 of the complexes

Transport City buses marked Baños go to and from Cuenca every 5-10 mins, 0600-2330. To walk takes 1½ hrs.

East of Cuenca

Gualaceo is a thriving, modern town set in beautiful landscape, with a charming plaza and fine new church with splendid modern glass. Its Sunday market doesn't cater to tourists. Woollen goods are sold on the main street near the bus station, while embroidered goods are sold from a private home above the general store on the main plaza. Inexpensive good shoes are made locally.

From Gualaceo take a taxi to **Bulzhun** (10 minutes) where backstrap weavers make *macanas* (Ikat dyed shawls). From there walk back down to **Bulcay**, another weaving community, and catch a bus back to Cuenca. Buses leave from the Terminal Terrestre in Cuenca to Gualaceo every 30 minutes (US$0.50, 45 minutes).

Gualaceo
Phone code: 07
Colour map 6, grid A4
Population: 11,000
Altitude: 2,300 m

Sleeping and eating B *Parador Turístico*, T255010. Outside town, chalets, rooms, modern, nice, swimming pool, good restaurant, also has a lit minutetle handicrafts museum which is free during the week. On the same street but further down the hill is **D** *Molina*, T255049. Private bath, hot water, clean. **E-F** *Residencial Gualaceo*, Gran Colombia 302, T255006. Some rooms with private bath, lcean, friendly, camping possible. *Don Q*, The best place to eat in town, clean, fast service, good menu. *Borin Cuba*, Av Jaime Roldós, set meals.

Paute
Phone code: 07
Colour map 6, grid A4
Population: 5,100
Altitude: 2,200 m

Some 24 km north of Gualaceo, on the Río Palma, is Paute, home to the largest hydroelectric plant in Ecuador. Improved access roads have converted much of the original farmland into weekend home developments and the farming has been pushed onto the higher slopes, contributing to deforestation. The rainwater run-off now carries much more mud and soil which is quickly silting up the Paute dam, which has to be continually dredged to function.

Sleeping A *Hostería Huertos de Uzhpud*, T250339, huzhupud@cue.satnet.net In the beautiful Paute valley, rooms at back have best views. Swimming pool, sauna, horses, gardens full of orchids, quiet, relaxing. Recommended. On the edge of town is **C** *San Luis*, cabins. Also **E** *Residencial Cuticay*, T250133. Private bath, hot water, OK.

Chordeleg
Phone code: 07
Colour map 6, grid A4
Population: 2,400
Altitude: 2,400 m

A paved road runs 4 km south from Gualaceo to Chordeleg, a village famous for its crafts in wood, silver and gold filigree (though very little is available nowadays), pottery and panama hats. The village has been described as very touristy (watch out for fake jewellery). *Joyería Dorita* and *Joyería Puerto del Sol*, on Juan B Cobos y Eloy Alfaro, have been recommended. There are some good shops selling beautiful ceramics. Food can be had at the *Restaurante El Turista*. There is plenty of local transport, US$0.15 from Gualaceo market, every 30 minutes. Direct bus from Cuenca, one hour, US$0.60.

The church is interesting with some lovely modern stained glass. Chordeleg has a small Museo de Comunidad with fascinating local textiles, ceramics and straw work, some of which are on sale at reasonable prices. It's a good uphill walk from Gualaceo to Chordeleg, and a pleasant hour downhill in the other direction. With your own vehicle, you can drive back to Cuenca through San Juan and San Bartolomé, which is a lovely colonial town famous for guitar makers. Two small mines after this village welcome visitors.

Sígsig
Colour map 6, grid A4
Population: 3,400
Altitude: 2,500 m

South of Gualaceo, 83 km from Cuenca, is Sígsig, another good place to buy panama hats. There's a market on Sunday, one cheap *residencial*, and *Restaurante Turista*, which is OK. Buses from Cuenca, 1½ hours, US$1. There's an hourly bus from Chordeleg. A road has been built between Sígsig and Gualaquiza, along a beautiful and unspoilt route (see page 387). There is bus service along it from Cuenca, see above.

Parque Nacional Cajas

Colour map 6, grid A3

This national park, located 29 km west of Cuenca, is an easily accessible páramo and high elevation forest park speckled with over 250 lakes separated by rocky ridges. It is well managed because it is the source of Cuenca's drinking water and hundreds of Cuencanos go there on the weekends. It is small (29,000 ha), but most tourists do not travel far from the road so it is possible to find solitude. The park is a favourite for birders; 125 species have been identified here, including the Condor and many hummingbirds. The Violet-tailed Metaltail is a hummingbird endemic to this area; others which can be seen include: Shining Sunbeam, Veridean Metaltail, Sparkling Violet-ear and the Sword-Billed Hummingbird. The lakes also harbour Andean Gulls, Speckled Teal and Yellow-billed Pintails.

Getting there Cajas is on a main road from Cuenca to Guayaquil. From Cuenca's Terminal Terrestre take any Gauyaquil bus that goes via Molleturo (not Zhud), 1 hr, US$1.50. The park entrance fee is US$10. Near Laguna Toreadora is a visitors' centre and a *refugio* (see below)

Ins & outs

Getting around Travel is largely cross-country along way-trails or through the *páramo* grasses, so good maps are necessary. The following IGM 1:50,000 maps cover the whole park: Chaucha, Cuenca, San Felipe de Mollerturo and Chiquintad. Access to some drainages on the eastern edge of the park may be restricted.

Tourist information For more information contact **ETAPA** in Cuenca, Empresa de Telefonos, Agua Potable y Alcantarillado, T890418/831900. The **Ministerio del Ambiente** office in Cuenca, Bolívar 5-33, T823074, has limited information.

Treks in the park

There are some trails marked near the visitors' centre but they tend to peter out quickly. For an overnight trek you can follow the routes described below or, if you have adequate experience and equipment, head out on your own.

There have been several deaths from exposure so it is important to be prepared with proper clothing

On the opposite side of the lake from the *refugio* is **Cerro San Luis** (4,200 m) which may be climbed in a day, with excellent views. From the visitors' centre go anticlockwise around the lake; after crossing the outflow look for a sign 'Al San Luis', follow the yellow and black stakes to the summit and beware of a side trail to dangerous ledges.

A strong hiker with a good sense of direction can cross the park in two days. Since the altitude throughout the park is under 4,500 m there is no permanent snow, but it is cold at night and it can rain and hail. August and September are the driest months but hiking is possible all year round. The best time is August

Southern Highlands

Parque Nacional Cajas

to January, when you can expect clear days, strong winds, night-time temperatures of -8°C and occasional mist. From February to July temperatures are higher but there is much more fog, rain and snow. It is best to arrive in the early morning as it can get very cloudy, wet and cool after about 1300.

Migüir to Soldados trek
Along this path vegetation changes from second growth cloud forest to páramo

Continue past **Laguna Toreadora** on a paved road to the village of **Migüir**. In town ask for the trail that heads up to **Laguna Sunincocha**. The trail fades but stay on the south side of Laguna Sunincocha and follow drainage south past **Laguna Valeriana Yacu** to the pass. From here you can see **Laguna Inga Casa** and the Río Soldados drainage. It is about four to five hours to this pass from Migüir and there are good camping spots next to the lakes in the Río Soldados drainage. The walk out to **Soldados** along the Río Soldados the next day takes four to five hours. Since there are only four buses a week to Cuenca via Soldados you should not rely too heavily on transport out.

Ingañan Trail

It is also possible to follow the Ingañan trail, an old Inca pathway that used to connect Cuenca with the coast. It is in ill-repair or lost in places but there are some interesting ruins above **Laguna Mamamag**. You can access the Ingañan from the park headquarters or from **Migüir**. Beginning in Migüir follow an established path to **Laguna Luspa**. At Laguna Lupsa take a path on the north side of the lake which connects to a stream that flows into Laguna Luspa. From here head east on a trail eventually ascending to a divide where you will be able to see **Laguna Osohuaycu**. Continue down to Laguna Osohuaycu. The route passes to the north of Laguna Osohuaycu and then descends to **Laguna Mamamag** where you should stay on the south side of the lake. At the downstream end of the lake cross over the small ridge and descend steeply through cloud forest on an established trail. At the bottom of the hill follow the wide Inca road over pastures to **Laguna Llaviuco**. There is a gate where you should be able to get a ride with fishermen back to Cuenca or walk to the main road in about an hour. This trip takes two to three days.

Park essentials

Sleeping E per person *Refugio* at Laguna Toreadora. Cold, with bunk beds and cooking facilities. There are also 2 primitive shelters by the shore of the lake, a 20- and 40-min walk from the refuge. Take a warm sleeping bag and all supplies. Camping costs US$5. **Tour operators** See Cuenca tour operators, page 253, for further details of tours, some offering fishing at about US$35 per person per day.

Cuenca to Machala

From Cuenca the Panamericana runs south to La Y, about 20 km away. Here the road divides: the left branch continues as the Panamericana south to Loja and the right branch runs southwest through sugar cane fields to Pasaje and Machala on the coast. Although this is a major intersection it is not well signposted, so make sure you take the correct fork.

One hour from Cuenca along the right branch is **Girón** (2,100 m) whose beauty is spoiled only by a modern concrete church. After the battle on 27 February 1829 between the troops of Gran Colombia, led by Sucre, and those of Peru under Lamar, at nearby Portete de Tarqui, a treaty was signed in Girón. The building, **Casa de los Tratados**, is shown to visitors, as is the site of the Peruvians' capitulation; open daily 0800-1600, US$1. Ask directions to the beautiful **El Chorro** waterfall, a 6-km walk, with cloud forest above. Agencies in Cuenca also offer tours here.

From Girón trucks take passengers up a winding road to the hamlets of **San Fernando** (rooms at *La Posada*) and **Chumblín**. Friendly inhabitants will act as guides to three lakes high in the *páramo* where excellent trout-fishing is to be had. There is also rock-climbing on San Pablo, overlooking Lago Busa. Take camping gear. Return to the main road through Asunción. There's a beautiful downhill stretch for cyclists.

The route to the coast continues through the Yungilla valley and **Santa Isabel** (altitude: 1,800 m). There's accommodation at **C** *Sol y Agua*, below the village, T270596, F270436, rooms with fan and fridge, good restaurant, pool and water-slide, sports fields, disco, nice views, good service, a pleasant weekend place for *Cuencanos*; and **D** *La Molienda*, by Cataviña, just before Santa Isabel, T260217, restaurant and small pool, unattractive. There are many other small weekend farms. The road then descends through desert to the stark, rocky canyon of the Río Jubones.

The next town is **Casacay** (**D** *Hostería San Luis*, T915904, bath, fan, pool, simple), after which the road passes through lush banana plantations. Before Casacay, at a military checkpoint, a road climbs south to **Chilla** (see below).

In the lowlands is **Pasaje** (population: 45,000) with accommodation at **D** *San Martín*, Bolívar 616 y Olmedo, T915434, clean, cold water, air conditioning, best in town; and many basic *pensiones*. Buses travel west to Machala, north to Guayaquil via La Troncal, or south down the coast to Huaquillason for the Peruvian border (see page 298).

South of Cuenca

Southern Highlands

The road from Cuenca south to Loja is fully paved, though often in disrepair. It passes through bare sparsely populated country and offers lovely views. The road climbs south from La Y to the village of **Cumbe**, with its small, colourful Wednesday market. The road then rises to the Tinajillas pass (3,527 m). Further south at La Ramada a branch road forks left to the lovely, sleepy colonial town of **Nabón**, with its weekend market. There is fine hiking in the nearby valleys and several unexcavated ruins. A small *pensión* offers accommodation. With a rental car or bikes it is possible to do a loop rejoining the Panamericana at Oña, though this trip is best done in the dry season (June to September).

The road descends sharply into the warm valley of the Río León (Km 95, 1,900 m, the 'Grand Canyon' of Ecuador) before rising again to the small town of **Oña** (population 700, 2,300 m) at Km 105. Accommodation at **E** *Hotel Buenos Aires*, near the highway, shared bath, hot water, basic. Best to eat next door at *Restaurant Pana*, where the Alvarado sisters offer good traditional cooking and lots of friendly chatter in their outdoor kitchen – recommended for the food and the experience. Another recommended restaurant is *San Luis*, also by the highway. Oña is the starting point for the 5-7 day, 65-km 'Gold Rush Trail' to Zaruma (see page 296). This difficult and rewarding trek climbs 2,600 m from the valley of the Río León to mysterious rock formations atop Cerro de Arcos. See *Trekking in Ecuador* (page 464) for details. From Oña the road crosses into the province of Loja. It weaves and climbs south through highland *páramo* pastures and then descends towards Saraguro (Km 144).

This is a cold town, famed for its weaving and distinctive indigenous population. Here the Indians, the most southerly Andean group in Ecuador, dress all in black. They wear very broad flat-brimmed hard felt hats. The men are notable for their black shorts, sometimes covered by a whitish kind of divided apron, and a particular kind of saddle bag, the *alforja*, and the women for their

Saraguro
Phone code: 07
Colour map 6, grid B3
Population: 3,100
Altitude: 2,500 m

pleated black skirts, necklaces of coloured beads and silver *topos*, ornate pins fastening their shawls. Many of them take cattle across the mountains east to the tropical pastures above the Amazonian jungle. The town has a picturesque Sunday market and interesting mass. Above the altar of the church, with its imposing stone façade, are inscribed the three Inca commandments in Quichua: *"Ama Killa, Ama Llulla, Ama Shua"*. Do not be lazy, do not lie, do not steal. In the surroundings of Saraguro are several high elevation forest remnants, in which 145 species of birds have been identified. Birdwatching is good even along the main road both north and south of town.

Sleeping and eating D *Samana Wasi*, 10 de Marzo near Panamericana, T200315. Modern, new in 2002. **E-F** *Sara Allpa*, Antonio Castro y Loja, T200272. Cheaper with shared bath, electric shower, OK, new in 2002. **F** *Armijos*, Antonio Castro Y Azuay, T200306. Shared bath, hot water, basic. **F** *Saraguro*, Loja 03-2 y Antonio Castro, T200286. Shared bath, electric shower, clean, basic, friendly. Good value, recommended. Simple very cheap *comedores*, all on or near the park, include *Salón Cristal*, Azuay y Castro, *Reina del Cisne* and *Mama Cuchara*.

Transport Buses to **Cuenca**, service throughout the day, US$4, 3½ hrs. To **Loja**, US$1.40, 2 hrs. Dirrect to **Quito**, US$11, 12 hrs.

West from Saraguro From Saraguro a spectacular road (subject to landslides in the rainy season) runs through **El Pariso de Celén**, **Selva Alegre**, **Manu**, **Guanazán** and **Chilla** down to the coast. A bus goes to Manu throughout the year and to Guanazán in the dry season. Chilla is famous for its Church of the Virgin and pilgrims flock here in September from all over the country. The only place to stay is the *Casa de Huéspedes* (Pilgrims' Guest House) which is empty the rest of the year. This area has remnants of native forest between 2,800 and 3,000 m and good birdwatching possibilities.

Saraguro to Yacuambi trek

The best time to do this trek is during the dry season from August to December The trail from Saraguro to the jungle town of **Yacuambi** (called 28 de Mayo on some maps), is a classic old trading route down the eastern slope of the Andes to the jungle. It is perhaps one of the most delightful two to three day walks in Ecuador. It is prone to landslides in the rainy season, so ask about conditions before starting. In 2002 there were plans to build a road the length of this route. Until that happens, however, it will remain an excellent trek.

Saraguro to Yacuambi

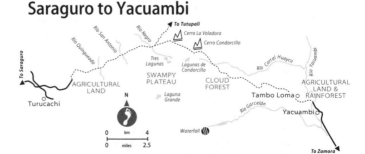

A wide track heads up from the agricultural lands surrounding Saraguro to an expansive swampy bench which is dotted with lakes and a few granite knolls. The track is well-constructed with several sections of stone paving (probably precolumbian) and an interesting stone bridge. The views from this low section of the Andes (3,400 m) into the Amazon Basin on a clear day are awe-inspiring. The path is obvious and still travelled by Saraguros and Oriente settlers. The difficulty of walking is moderate but be prepared for cold, rain and mud during the wet season.

The appropriate maps are IGM 1:50,000 Saraguro and San José de Yacuambi

Some food can be purchased in the shops in Saraguro but it is best to buy most supplies in a major city such as Cuenca or Loja. The friendly owner of *Residencial Armijos*, Rogelio Armijos, knows how to get to the beginning of this hike and will take you up in his truck for around US$10.

You can also catch any bus heading north on the Panamericana just beyond the town of **Urdaneta** (known locally as Paqulshapa) to the turn-off to the village of **Turucachi**. There is a fork in this road about 100 m from the Panamericana; go left towards an area called **Quingueado**. It is possible to drive as far as Quingueado.

From Quingueado the trail is an obvious white streak that heads down to **Río Quingueado** then up to a notch. The stone paving is present in this section and is often elevated because of erosion of the surrounding soil. Where the paving is missing years of mule and foot traffic have worn away a path that in places is entrenched 10 m into the hillsides. The trail eventually crosses the **Río San Antonio** and then comes to an interesting stone bridge across the boulder strewn **Río Negro**. It is worth stopping here to admire the craftsmanship of the bridge and perhaps take a dip in one of the cool stream pools.

From the Río Negro the trail climbs steeply and within 30 minutes comes to a Y; turn right and up. The trail to the left takes you to the village of **Tutupali** which also could make an interesting hike. Soon you are on a broad flat ridge and pass a glacial erratic (boulder) perched on a hill called **Cerro La Voladora**. Ambling along the granite knolls are views of the **Tres Lagunas** and other lakes on the plateau.

There are good camping spots at the edge of the Andean Slope about 6-8 hours from the landslide on the road. There is a small lake on the southeast side of **Cerro Condorcillo** which is a good source of water. Sunsets reflect off the lakes on the plateau and sunrises come up over the Amazon Basin. Although this is one of the lowest points along the crest of the Ecuadorean Andes the views are outstanding. The descent down to the cloud forest is magnificent. From the top on a clear day you can just glimpse where the trail heads through a notch in a ridge just above Yacuambi. The notch seems a short stroll but it is really a good 6-8 hours of knee pounding descents. The trail has some long sections of paving and seems to blend into the landscape of boulders and shrubby cloud forest vegetation as if in a Japanese garden.

About an hour from Cerro Condorcillo the trail crosses the **Río Corral Huaycu** and enters dense cloud forest. The descent is steep in places and deeply entrenched. Stay on the main path which generally sticks to the ridge crest. In the distance to the right there is a large waterfall above the **Río Garcelán valley**. As you descend it gets hot and humid but there are plenty of streams to refill water bottles. There is one ambiguous intersection about 4-5 hours from Cerro Condorcillo where you need to turn left. If you head straight you will climb for about five minutes then funnel into a steep deeply eroded trench – this is the wrong way.

Always take the most travelled path and do not be tempted to drop down to the pastures along the **Río Garcelán** since you will only have to climb back up

Southern Highlands

again to gct to Yacuambi. In the community of **Tambo Loma** there is electricity. Just beyond you pass through the notch with views of the wide Río Yacuambi (which means clear water in Quichua). From the notch you descend switchbacks to a suspension bridge over the Río Yacuambi. This is also a great spot to go for a swim.

The gravel road from **Zamora** ends at the bridge and from here it is about a 30-minute hike to the town of Yacuambi. There is one very basic hostel near the village plaza which also serves a good and cheap meal. *Unión Cariamanga* has a nightly bus Yacuambí-Saraguro, at 2000. Trucks leave in the mornings for the 2½-hour drive to Zamora. Once in Zamora there are hotels and numerous buses to Loja which is two hours away.

Loja

Phone code: 07
Colour map 6, grid B3
Population: 118,000
Altitude: 2,063 m

This friendly pleasant city, encircled by hills, is the provincial capital. Long isolated from other Ecuadorean centres, Loja is functionally as well as culturally self-sufficient. Although transport is now greatly improved, the city and province retain a unique character. There are fewer mestizos here than in other parts of Ecuador. The Saraguros are the only indigenous group and most Lojanos are of European stock dating back to early colonial days.

Ins & outs
See also Transport, page 265

Getting there The city can be reached by air from Quito or Guayaquil to Catamayo (known locally as La Toma), which is 35 km away by paved road (see page 271). The well organized bus terminal at Av Gran Colombia e Isidro Ayora is to the north of the centre. At the terminal is left luggage, an information desk, shops and *Pacifictel* office. There are frequent city buses to the centre. A taxi costs US$1.

Getting around The centre of Loja, which has most hotels and services, is compact and easy to walk around.

Loja

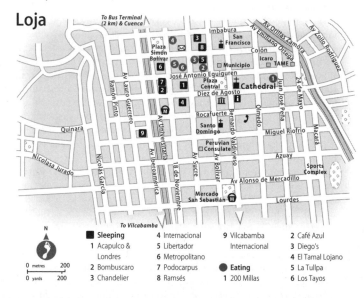

N

0 metres 200
0 yards 200

■ **Sleeping**
1 Acapulco &
   Londres
2 Bombuscaro
3 Chandelier
4 Internacional
5 Libertador
6 Metropolitano
7 Podocarpus
8 Ramsés
9 Vilcabamba
   Internacional

● **Eating**
1 200 Millas
2 Café Azul
3 Diego's
4 El Tamal Lojano
5 La Tullpa
6 Los Tayos

Tourist information *Ministerio de Turismo*, Sucre y Eguiguren, edif Banco de Fomento, piso 4, T572964, F570485, miturgfs@impsat.net.ec Open Mon-Fri 0830-1300, 1430-1730. *Loja tradición, cultura y turismo*, is a useful guidebook available at the *municipio* for US$5. *La Hora* and *Crónica* are local newspapers.

Loja was founded on its present site in 1548, having been moved from La Toma, and was rebuilt twice after earthquakes, the last of which occurred in the 1880s. The town has the distinction of being the first in the country to have electricity and it remains a progressive place. The central market is the cleanest in all of Ecuador and, in 2002, Loja won international awards for its beautiful parks and for recycling garbage.

In 2002 there were plans to build a hiking trail from Loja to Vilcabamba. Enquire locally

The surrounding province, on the other hand, has a bad reputation for unsustainable agricultural practices. These combined with cyclical droughts have made many Lojanos migrate over the years. Some became colonists in Oriente, hence the official name of Lago Agrio, capital of the province of Sucumbíos, is Nueva Loja. Today Lojanos are migrating further afield, to Europe and North America, in search of better economic opportunities.

Sights

At Puente Bolívar, by the northern entrance to town, is a fortress-like monument and a lookout over the city, known as **La Entrada de la Ciudad**. It has art exhibits at ground level and a small café upstairs, a good place to take pictures. ■ *0800-2100*.

The **Cathedral** and **Santo Domingo** church, Bolívar y Rocafuerte, have painted interiors. **El Valle** church, on the south edge of the city, is colonial, with a lovely interior. The **Museo Historia y Cultura Lojana del Banco Central** on the main plaza has exhibits of local art, archaeology, folklore and history. ■ *Mon-Fri 0800-1600*.

The central market, **Mercado Centro Comercial Loja**, 10 de Agosto y 18 de Noviembre, is worth a visit. It is clean, efficient and attractive. Saturday is the main market day. ■ *Mon-Sat 0600-1630, Sun 0600-1330*.

Loja is famed for its musicians and has one of the few musical academies in the country. Musical evenings and concerts are often held around the town. The city also boasts two universities, with a well-known law school. The Universidad Técnica, on the hill to the northeast of the centre, is the Open University for Ecuador, having correspondence students and testing centres scattered across the country and even in Spain and the USA. The Universidad Nacional has good murals on some of its buildings.

In the north of the city, a couple of blocks east of the Terminal is the **Parque Recreacional Jipiro**, a good place to walk and relax. A well maintained, clean park, with a small lake, sports fields, pools, an observatory and replicas of different cities, it is popular with Lojanos at weekends, when there are puppet shows, theatre and other activities. Take the city bus marked 'Jipiro', a five-minute ride from the centre. Camping is possible here, information from T583357, F571266.

Parks

Parque Educacional Ambiental y Recreacional de Argelia is superb, with trails through the forest to the *páramo*. It is 500 m before the police checkpoint on the road south to Vilcabamba, but poorly signposted so ask around. Take a city bus marked 'Argelia'. Across the road and 100 m south, the **Jardín Botánico Reynaldo Espinosa** has several cinchona trees. ■ *Mon-Fri 0800-1600. US$0.60.*

Essentials

Sleeping
■ on map, page 262
Price codes:
see inside front cover
Several Loja hotels
have web pages on
www.hotelesloja.
com.ec
There are few
good inexpensive
places to stay

A *Libertador*, Colón 14-30 y Bolívar, T570344, F572119, hlibloja@impsat.net.ec Includes buffet breakfast, good restaurant, pool and spa, parking, suites available, comfortable but can be noisy.

B *Bombuscaro*, 10 de Agosto y Av Universitaria, T577021, F577022, bombus@ impsat.net.ec Includes breakfast, comfortable rooms and suites, good service. Recommended. **B** *Grand Hotel Loja*, Av Iberoamérica y Rocafuerte, T586600, F575202, ghloja@impsat.net.ec Includes breakfast, spa, parking, nice.

C *Aguilera Internacional*, Sucre 01-08 y Emiliano Ortega, T572894, F584660. Includes breakfast, restaurant and bar, parking, nice rooms, comfortable. Recommended. **C** *Hostal del Bus*, Av 8 de Diciembre y Flores, across from bus station, T575100, F572297, hdelgado@impsat.net.ec Includes breakfast, restaurant, carpeted rooms and suites. **C** *Podocarpus*, Eguiguren 16-50 y 18 de Noviembre, T581428, F548912. Includes breakfast, restaurant, parking, modern and comfortable. **C** *Ramsés*, Colón 14-31 y Bolívar, T562290, F571402. Good restaurant, parking, modern. **C** *Vilcabamba Internacional*, Iberoamérica y Pasaje la FEUE, T573393, F561483. Includes breakfast, restaurant, pleasant, comfortable carpeted rooms, discount for Handbook users.

D *Acapulco*, Sucre 07-61 y 10 de Agosto, T570651, F571103. Includes breakfast, restaurant, 1st floor rooms are quieter. **D** *Chandelier*, Imbabura 14-82 y Sucre, T563061, F578233. Parking, OK. **D** *Metropolitano*, 18 de Noviembre 6-31 y Colón, T570007, F570244. OK, a bit refurbished in 2001. **D** *San Antonio*, 18 de Noviembre entre Quito y Valdivieso, T570237. Abundant hot water, parking, older building, rooms vary, all rather improvised but OK. **D** *San Luis*, Sucre 04-62 y Quito, T570370. Large rooms, simple, parking.

D-E *Carrión*, Colón 16-36 y 18 de Noviembre, T584548, F575429. Cheaper with shared bath, tiled floor, some rooms without windows but OK. **D-E** *Internacional*, 10 de Agosto 15-30 entre Sucre y 18 de Noviembre, T578486. Cheaper with shared bath, electric shower, older place but refurbished and OK. **F** *Londres*, Sucre 741 y 10 de Agosto. Shared bath, hot water, basic but clean.

Long stays **C** *Apart-Hotel Iberoamérica*, Av Iberoamérica y Manuel Ignacio Monteros, T574432, F570587. 1-3 bedroom apartments, US$300-480 per month.

Eating
● on map,
page 262

Mid-range *200 Millas*, Juan José Peña y 10 de Agosto. Good fish and seafood. *A lo Mero Mero*, Sucre y Colón 6-20. Good Mexican food and sandwiches. *Café Azul*, Eguiguren entre Bolívar y Sucre. Crêpes, salads, sandwiches, lasagna. Closed at midday. *Cevichería Las Redes*, 18 de Noviember entre Mercadillo y Lourdes. Seafood, some tables on patio. *Diego's*, Colón 14-88 y Sucre, 2nd floor, very good cheap set lunch and mid-range à la carte, very popular, open 0730-2200 daily. Recommended. *La Capiata*, Av Cuxibamba y Tena. Very good seafood. *Parrilladas El Fogón*, 8 de Diciembre y Flores, across from the bus station, good grill and salad bar. *Parrilladas Uruguayas*, Iberoamérica y J de Salinas. Opens 1700, good grilled meat, helpful owner. *Rincón de Francia*, B Valdiviezo y Eguiguren. Very good food, imaginative cooking, small portions. *Salud y Vida*, Azuay near Olmedo. Vegetarian. In **El Valle** area the *Colonial* and *La Lolita* are recommended, try their *cuy*.

Many other places
in the centre serve
seriously cheap set
meals of varying
quality

Cheap *Chifa El Arbol de Oro*, Bolívar y Lourdes, opposite Mercado San Sebastián. Good cheap Chinese food. *La Tullpa*, 18 de Noviembre 06-32 y Colón. Cheap set meals and good selection à la carte. *Los Tayos*, Sucre 06-55. Regional specialties, choice of cheap set meals, open Sun. *Plaza Inn*, Bolívar 07-57, at main park. Cheap fast food. Open 0900-2300. *Tamal Lojano*, 18 de Noviembre y Imbabura, cheap set lunches, very good tamales and other local snacks in the evening. Recommended.

Southern Highlands

Loja has many excellent bakeries and cafés. Lojanos often enjoy a warm drink and sweets in the evening, or one of the very popular *tamales* (see below). *Topoli*, Riofrío y Bolívar. Best coffee and yoghurt in town, good for breakfast (closed for lunch). *El Jugo Natural*, J Eguiguren 14-18 y Bolívar. Very good fresh juices and breakfast. Closed Sun. *Yogur & Helados*, 24 de Mayo y V Vivar, east of the centre. Good ice-cream and yoghurt. *Sinaí*, at main park, opposite the Catedral, popular ice-cream place. **Cafés, bakeries & snacks**

Local specialities *Tamales lojanos* are made of corn meal mixed with chicken or pork, onions, raisins and spices, steamed wrapped in *achira* leaves; very good. Another local dish is *repe*, a green banana soup made from a special type of banana which only grows in the south. *Cecina* is thinly cut meat, usually pork, cooked over open flames. Local buns made with raw sugar are called *bollos*.

El Viejo Minero, Sucre 10-76 y Azuay. Bar and café, popular with foreigners. Recommended. *Fiesta*, 10 de Agosto 10-59 y JJ Peña. Disco with 2 halls, one plays Latin music, the other Techno. *Music Bar*, JJ Peña y Azuay. Bar, good live music and atmosphere. *Siembra*, Prolongación 24 de Mayo, Ciudadela Zamora, pizzeria and bar. Popular with foreigners. *Unicornio*, Bolívar y 10 de Agosto, on the main plaza. Bar and snacks. **Bars & nightclubs**

The *Fiesta de la Virgen del Cisne* is held **16-20 Aug**, and the image of the Virgin remains in Loja until 1 Nov. The statue of the Virgen del Cisne spends a month each year travelling around the province and hundreds of the faithful walk in procession with it. The most important of these peregrinations is the 3-day, 70-km walk from El Cisne to Loja cathedral, which begins on **17 Aug**. Loja, Catamayo and El Cisne are crowded with religious pilgrims and Ecuadorean tourists during the last **2 weeks of Aug** and the **1st week of Sep** when it is very difficult to find a room and all prices rise. **Festivals**

The Mercado (see Sights above) is very well supplied. *Romar*, 18 de Noviembre y Eguiguren, is a well-stocked supermarket. Health food shop on 10 de Agosto behind the Catedral. Great choice of products. *Procuero*, Eguiguren entre Av Universitaria y 18 de Noviembre, for leather crafts. *Ilusion*, 18 de Noviembre y Eguiguren, for woollen sweaters. *Cer-Art Ceramics* sells precolumbian designs on mostly high-gloss ceramics, which are produced at the Universidad Técnica. Above the Universidad Técnica is the 'Ceramics Plaza', where you can buy directly from the crafts studio. A little higher on the same road is the *Productos Lacteos*, where you can buy excellent cheeses and fresh butter, all produced by the university and contributing to its finances. *Loaizacolor*, 10 de Agosto 13-20 for film and developing. **Shopping**

Aratinga Aventuras, Lourdes 14-80 y Sucre, T/F582434, jatavent@cue.satnet.net Specializes in birdwatching tours, overnight trips to cloud forest. Pablo Andrade is a knowlegeable guide. *Biotours*, 10 de Agosto y 24 de Mayo, T578398, F574696, biotours@loja.telconet.net City, regional and jungle tours, airline tickets. Friendly service. *Franky Tours*, 10 de Agosto 11-67 y Olmedo, T571031, F562554, fhidalgo@loja.telconet.net Local and regional tours, airline tickets. *Podocarpus Travel*, 10 de Agostso y Sucre, T/F588010, agpodo@impsat.net.ec City and regional tours, airline tickets. **Tour operators**

Local Bus: city buses US$0.15. **Car hire**: *Arricar*, in *Hotel Libertador*, T571443, F588014. *Bombuscaro Rent-a-Car*, in hotel of the same name, T/F577021. **Taxirutas** are shared taxis which run on a set route, their stops are clearly marked, US$0.20. **Transport**

Long distance Air: there are flights to **Quito** and **Guayaquil** with *TAME* and to Quito with *Icaro*. Flights are often cancelled due to strong winds and the airport is sometimes closed by 1000.

Southern Highlands

There is frequent service to most destinations, all buses leave from the terminal terrestre at the north of town

Bus To **Vilcabamba**, vans from the bus terminal every 15 mins, US$1, 1 hr; or taxirutas (shared taxis) along Av Iberoamérica. To **Cuenca**, 5 hrs, US$6. To **Saraguro**, 2 hrs, US$1.40. To **Machala**, 5 hrs, US$5. There are 3 different routes from Loja to Machala, with bus service along all of them; ask for the one you need. They are, from north to south: via Piñas, for Zaruma (see page 296) unpaved and rough but very scenic; via Balsas, fully paved and also scenic; and via Alamor, for Puyango petrified forest (see page 298), military checkpoints on route. To **Huaquillas**, US$4, 5 hrs direct; or get off at Machala crossroads and take a local bus from there. To **Zamora**, 2 hrs, US$2, a beautiful ride on a paved road (landslides possible with heavy rains). To **Macará**, 5 hrs, US$5, fully paved. To **Zumba** via Vilcabamba, with *Sur Oriente* (at 0800, 1730 and 2130 daily) and *Unión Cariamanga* (at 0530, 0900, 1200 and 1600 daily), 7 hrs, US$6, a rough but beautiful ride, prone to landslides with heavy rain. To **Quito**, US$12, 16 hrs (US$15 with *Panamericana Internacional* from *Gran Hotel Loja*, 1 a day). To **Guayaquil**, 8 hrs, US$8.

International buses To **Piura (Peru)**, with *Loja Internacional* at 0700, 1300 and 2130 daily, 8 hrs including border formalities, US$8. Also with the Peruvian bus company *Civa*, at 2130 daily.

Directory **Airline offices** *TAME*, 24 de Mayo y E Ortega, T573030, open Mon-Fri 0830-1600. *Icaro*, Eguiguren y Olmedo, T578416, F585955. **Banks** *Banco de Guayaquil*, Eguiguren y Valdivieso, TCs and Mastercard. *Banco del Austro*, Eguiguren 14-12 y Bolívar, Visa. *Mutualista Pichincha*, on plaza, Mastercard. There is nowhere to change Peruvian currency. **Communications** Internet: many internet cafés in town, price about US$1.50 per hr, which is much cheaper than in Vilcabamba – catch up on you email here. There is a cyber café a short walk from the bus terminal toward town. **Post**: Colón y Sucre. No good for sending parcels. **Telephone**: *Pacifictel*, Eguiguren entre Olmedo y Valdivieso. **Embassies and consulates** *Peru* Sucre 10-64 y Azuay, T571668, Mon-Fri 0830-1330.

Parque Nacional Podocarpus

Colour map 6, grid C4

One of the most diverse protected areas in the world

Spanning elevations between 950 and 3,700 m, this national park is particularly rich in birdlife, including many rarities and some newly discovered species; there could be up to 800 species in the park. It also includes one of the last major habitats for the spectacled bear. Podocarpus is divided into two areas, an upper premontane section with spectacular walking country, lush tropical cloud forest and excellent birdwatching, and a lower subtropical section, with remote areas of virgin rain forest and unmatched quantities of flora and fauna.

The park has easy access at several points. Both areas are quite wet, making hiking boots essential. The upper section is also very cold, so warm clothing and waterproofs are indispensable. ■ *Fee is US$10 in either area.*

Tourist information For a map of the area and further information, try the **Ministerio del Ambiente** in Loja, Sucre entre Quito e Imbabura, T/F585421, podocam@impsat.net.ec In Zamora contact the Ministerio at T/F605606. Conservation groups working in and around the park include: **Arcoiris**, Segundo Cueva Celi 03-15 y Clodoveo Carrión, T/F577499, www.arcoiris.org.ec; **Biocorp**, J A Eguigurten y Olmedo, T/F576696; **Fundación Ecológica Podocarpus**, Av 24 de Mayo, T571734; and **ama Podocarpus**, Clodoveo Carrión y Pasaje M de J Lozano, Ciudadela Zamora, T585924.

Upper premontane section Access to the upper section of the park is at Cajanuma, about 15 km south of Loja on the Vilcabamba road. Take a Vilcabamba van or *taxiruta*, get off in about 20 mins, US$1 – then it's an 8-km hike uphill to the guard station. It's possible to sleep here and there are cooking facilities. Direct transport is by taxi, about US$10 round trip or with a tour

Valley of the immortals?

◀◀

The tiny, isolated village of Vilcabamba gained a certain fame in the 1960s when doctors announced that it was home to one of the oldest living populations in the world. It was said that people here often lived to well over 100 years old, some as old as 135. Fame, though, turned to infamy when it was revealed that researchers had been given parish records which corresponded to the subjects' parents. However, given that first children are often born to parents in their teenage years, this still means that there are some very old people living in these parts.

There is also a high incidence of healthy, active elders. It's not unusual to find people in their 70s and 80s toiling in the fields and covering several miles a day to get there.

Such longevity and vitality is not only down to the area's famously healthy climate. Other factors must also be at play: physical exercise, strong family ties, a balanced diet low in animal fats and a lack of stress.

Attracted in part by Vilcabamba's reputation for nurturing a long and tranquil life, a number of outsiders – both Ecuadoreans and foreigners – have settled in the area. You will meet them, as many work in the tourist trade, or hear of them since some of their exploits have become local lore. What do you think? Will the gringos benefit from the unique serenity of the 'valley of the immortals' or have they brought with them the seeds of their own destruction?

from Loja. You can arrange a pick up later from the guard station. The southwestern section of the park can also be accessed through trails from Vilcabamba and Yangana.

There are two possible entrances to the lower subtropical section of the park. **Bombuscaro** can be reached from Zamora (see page 388). Take a taxi to the entrance, then walk 1 km to the refuge, camping is also possible. There are trails to explore beyond. The other entrance is at **Romerillos**, 2 hrs south of Zamora. A 3-5 day hike is possible into this part of the park, contact the **Ministerio del Ambiente** in Zamora (see above) or **Fundación Maquipucuna** in Quito, Baquerizo Moreno E9-153 y Tamayo, T2507200, F2507201, maqui@ecua.net.ec, www.maqui.org

Lower subtropical section

Vilcabamba

Once an isolated village, Vilcabamba has become increasingly popular with Lojanos on a weekend excursion as well as foreign visitors. It is a 'must' along the gringo trail from Ecuador to Peru or vice versa. There are many excellent places to stay and several good restaurants. The whole area is very beautiful and tranquil, with an agreeable climate. Right outside town, the Mandango trail is a popular and very scenic half-day hike. There are many other great day-walks and longer treks throughout the area as well as ample opportunities for horse riding. A number of beautiful private nature reserves are situated east of Vilcabamba, between it and Podocarpus National Park.

Phone code: 07
Colour map 6, grid C3
Population: 4,000
Altitude: 1,520 m

There is a tourist office on the main plaza next to *Pacifictel*, T580890, open 0800-1200, 1400-1800, closed Tue and Fri, friendly and helpful. **Avetur**, an association of Vilcabamba hotels and tour operators, has an information office in the Loja bus station.

Tourist information

Vilcabamba has become famous among travellers for its locally-produced hallucinogenic cactus juice called San Pedrillo. In addition to being illegal, it is more dangerous than it may seem because of flashbacks which can occur months or years after use. The resulting medical condition has been named the 'Vilcabamba Syndrome' and can affect sufferers for the rest of their lives. Tourist demand for San Pedrillo and other drugs is a problem in Vilcabamba. Don't get involved (see also Drugs, page 47).

Excursions

This is a splendid area for excursions. Most tours are on horseback to private reserves in the foothills east of town. Trekkers can continue on foot through orchid-clad cloud forests to the high cold *páramos* of Podocarpus National Park. Day-trips are also available. All of the tour operators mentioned on page 270 are recommended.

Essentials

Sleeping
■ *on map,*
Price codes:
see inside front cover

NB You may be approached in Loja bus terminal by people touting for hotels in Vilcabamba. Van or taxi drivers on commission may also suggest a particular establishment. There are so many great places to stay in Vilcabamba, however, that you are much better off choosing your own. Insist on being taken to the hotel of your choice or to the main plaza, from where you can safely and easily browse around.

Vilcabamba

Sleeping		11 Ruinas de Quinara	2 El Ché
1 Don Germán	5 Las Margaritas	12 Rumi Wilco	3 Huilcopamba
2 Hidden Garden &	6 Madre Tierra	13 Valle Sagrado	4 La Terraza
El Jardín Restaurant	7 Mandango		5 Natural Yogurt
3 Hostería Vilcabamba	8 Manolo's & Pizzería	● Eating	6 Shanta's
4 La Posada Real	9 Parador Turístico	1 Cafetería Solomaco	
	10 Paraíso		

Not to scale

A-C *Madre Tierra*, 2 km north on road to Loja, follow signs, T580269, F580687, www.madretierra1.com Includes breakfast and dinner, cheaper in dorm, pool, internet, laundry facilities, parking, variety of cabins from simple to nicely decorated new ones. Superb home cooking, vegetarian to order, non-residents must reserve meals a day ahead. Spa (extra charge), videos, horse rental, English and French spoken. Very popular and highly recommended. **B** *Hostería Vilcabamba*, by the northern bridge, T580271, F580273. Includes breakfast, good restaurant and bar, pool and spa, parking, comfortable rooms, good facilities, popular with Ecuadorean families. **C** *Ruinas de Quinara*, Diego Vaca de Vega east of centre, T580301, F580314, www.lasruinasdequinara.com Includes breakfast and dinner (vegetarian available), pool and sauna, internet, laundry facilities, parking, hammocks, videos, sports facilities. Looks OK but negative reports received. **C-D** *Cabañas Río Yambala*, Yamburara Alto, 4 km east of town, rio_yambala@yahoo.com, www.vilcabamba.cwc.net Includes dinner and breakfast, cheaper without meals, some kitchen facilities, cabins in a beautiful, tranquil setting. Access to Las Palmas private nature reserve, good birdwatching. Friendly owners: Charlie and Sarah. Highly recommended.

D *Izhcayluma*, 2 km south on road to Zumba, www.vilcabamba.de Includes breakfast, very good restaurant with European specialities, cheaper with shared bath, pool, parking, comfortable cabins, nice grounds, lovely views, German run, friendly and helpful. A bit out of the way but includes use of bikes to get to town, new in 2001. Recommended. **D** *Las Margaritas*, Sucre y Clodoveo Jaramillo. Includes good breakfast, pool, parking, very comfortable rooms, spacious, nice garden, family atmosphere, English and German spoken. Recommended. **D** *Parador Turístico*, at the southeast end of town, T/F673122. Includes breakfast, restaurant and bar, pool, parking, one of Vilcabamba's first hotels and still good. **D** *Paraíso*, 500 m north of town on road to Loja, T580266, F575429. Includes breakfast, restaurant, pool, parking, comfortable cabins. **D** *Posada Real*, Agua de Hierro s/n at northeast end of town, T580904, laposadareal@yahoo.com Includes breakfast, US$4 per day for use of kitchen, nice location and views, facilities are OK but overpriced.

D-E *Hidden Garden*, Sucre y Diego Vaca de Vega, T/F580281, hiddengarden@latinmail.com Includes breakfast, 1 room has bath, small pool, long popular, simple facilities, due for renovation in 2003. **D-E** *Rumi Wilco Ecolodge*, 10-min walk northeast of town (information at *Primavera* craft shop on main park), ofalcoecolodge@yahoo.com Cheaper with shared bath, laundry facilities, fully furnished kitchen, adobe cabins and a wooden one on stilts (the 'Pole House') in a 40-ha private nature reserve. Nice setting, friendly owners: Orlando and Alicia. Recommended. **E** *La Tasca*, 2 km east on road to Yamburara. Shared bath, cold water, modest kitchen, simple cabins on a steep hillside, great views, being refurbished in 2002. **E-F** *Mandango*, Guilcopamba y Juan Montalvo behind the market. Cheaper with shared bath, electric shower, small pool, laundry/cooking facilities, clean, friendly, rooms from simple to basic.

F *Don Germán*, Bolívar y Clodoveo Jaramillo (no sign), T673130. Shared bath, hot water, laundry/cooking facilities, simple, family run, friendly owner: Sra Líbia Toledo. **F** *La Florida*, 1 km east on road to Yamburara. Shared bath, hot water, cooking facilities, basic cabin, friendly. **F** *Manolo's*, past 2nd bridge east on road to Yamburara. Pizzeria, private bath, hot water, simple, good value. **F** *Valle Sagrado*, Sucre on main plaza, T580686. Cheaper with shared bath, electric shower, laundry/cooking facilities, parking, ample grounds, basic rooms and facilities.

Excellent meals are served at hotels *Madre Tierra* and *Izhcayluma*. A day's advance notice is required for non-residents wishing to eat at the former, both are highly recommended. The following are all on or near the plaza. *El Jardín*, Sucre y Agua de Hierro, next to Hidden Garden hotel. Excellent authentic Mexican food and drinks, pleasant atmosphere, tables in garden, attentive service. Highly recommended. *El Ché*, on Bolívar.

Vilcabamba experiences occasional water shortages; check that your hotel has a reliable supply

Eating
● *on map*
All prices are mid-range unless otherwise indicated

Argentine specialties, small place, good quality and generous portions, friendly owner. Recommended. *Natural Yogurt*, on Bolívar. Yogurt, crêpes, light fare. *Huilcopamba*, D Vaca de Vega y Sucre. Cheap set meals, good local food. *La Terraza*, D Vaca de Vega y Bolíva. International style. *Cafetería Solomaco*, Sucre y Luis Fernando de Vega. Breakfast, excellent home baked bread and pastries. Recommended. Several other restaurants on and near the plaza, including a couple of places serving very cheap set meals.

On the road to Yamburara are *Manolo's Pizzería* , just after 2nd bridge, pizzas, juices, sandwiches; and *Shanta's*, across the road from Ruinas de Quinara, specialties are trout and frog legs, pleasant atmosphere, friendly.

Shopping   There are a number of well stocked small shops in town. *Artesanías Primavera*, Diego Vaca de Vega y Sucre, on the main park, has crafts, T-shirts and homemade jams. *Artesanías Tucán*, Fernando del la Vega y Sucre. Assorted crafts.

Tour operators   *Caballos Gavilán*, Sucre y Diego Vaca de Vega, T580281, gavilanhorse@yahoo.com
Horse trekking tours   Run by New Zealander Gavin Moore, lots of experience, good horseman.
cost US$25-$30 per   *Caminatas Andes Sureños*, Bolívar by the plaza, T673147, jorgeluis222@latinmail.com
person per day,   Run by Jorge Mendieta, knowledgeable and friendly. *Centro Ecuestre*, Diego Vaca de
various trip length are   Vega y Bolívar, T/F673183, centroecuestre@hotmail.com A group of local guides,
available   friendly and helpful. *Orlando Falco* is an experienced English-speaking guide. Contact through *Rumi Wilco Ecolodge* (see Sleeping above) or *Primavera* craft shop on plaza. *Las Palmas*, a nature reserve run by Charlie and Sarah, at *Cabañas Río Yambala*, see Sleeping above. *Solomaco*, Sucre y Diego Vaca de Vega, T/F673186, solomaco@hotmail.com French-run by Bernard and Martine, friendly and helpful.

Transport   There are regular buses, vans and shared taxis to and from **Loja**, US$1, 1 hr. Vans and *taxirutas* leave from behind the market, buses pass along the highway. Loja-Zumba buses pass Vilcabamba about 1 hr after departure, see Loja Transport.

Directory   **Bank** TCs may sometimes be exchanged at hotel *Madre Tierra*, see Sleeping above, US$5 commission. **Communications** Internet: service is scarce, slow and expensive, about US$3 per hr. Better to do your email in Loja. **Telephone:** *Pacifictel*, Bolívar y Diego Vaca de Vega, near the park, poor service, long queues. **Laundry** *Shanta's*, see Eating above, US$3 per load.

South from Vilcabamba

Colour map 6, grid C3   A dirt road south continues from Vilcabamba to **Yangana**, **Valladolid**, **Palanda** and **Zumba**. All these small towns have very basic accommodation and simple places to eat. There are seven daily buses along this route, which is affected by landslides in wet weather, see Loja Transport above for further details. The scenery is wild and beautiful but marred by deforestation. If you leave Vilcabamba on the southbound bus that passes through between 0600 and 0700, then you can make it to San Ignacio, Peru, the same day and reach Chachapoyas the following day. This is faster and more interesting than going along the coast but it is a rough ride. For more details, see the *Peru Handbook* and the *South American Handbook*.

Sleeping and eating   Zumba: All in the centre of the village within a block or two of each other. **E** *Oasis*, next to *Banco de Fomento*. With bath, modern. **F** *La Choza*. Shared bath, cold water, good restaurant. **F** *Chinchipe*. Shared bath, cold water. Also *Miraflores*. For eating, try *Las Cañitas* or *Rincón Zumbeño*.

A poor road continues south from Zumba 1½ hours to a border crossing at La Balsa. There are two daily *rancheras* (open-sided trucks with benches), at about 0800 and 1430, returning to Zumba at about 1230 and 1730, US$1.50; pick-ups may also be hired for this trip. The immigration post is at La Balsa, where a vehicle bridge was under construction in 2002. Until this is completed, an oil-drum raft crosses the river to the Peruvian border post, from where there is a minibus service to Namballe 15 minutes away (one cheap hotel) and San Ignacio, two hours south. From San Ignacio there is transport to Jaén, 2½ hours further south, along a good unpaved road.

Crossing to Peru
You can buy Soles from shopkeepers in Zumba

Loja to the Peruvian border

An established alternative to the Huaquillas border crossing is the more scenic route via Macará. The road is fully paved and Macará offers most facilities and services, see page 273. Other smaller border posts include **Zumba** (see above) as well as **Jimbura** and **Lalamor** (see below). Facilities are limited in these small towns and immigration officers may not always be available to stamp passports at the latter two crossings.

Leaving Loja on the main paved highway going west, the airport at **La Toma** (1,200 m) is reached after 35 km. If flying to or from La Toma, you can stay at Catamayo, nearby. (Note that the two names, La Toma and Catamayo, are used interchangeably.) There are a couple of weekend resorts around Catamayo where you can relax by the pool in a warmer climate than Loja. There are taxis to the airport (US$1) or it's a 20-minute walk from the town.

To the northwest of town is one of the largest *ingenios*, sugar-processing plants, in Ecuador. High up in the mountains, to the northwest of Catamayo off the paved road to Machala, is the small village and much venerated pilgrimage site of **El Cisne**. El Cisne is dominated by its incongruous French-style Gothic church. There is a small museum housing religious art pieces and all the sequinned and jewelled clothes which have been donated to dress the statue of the Virgin del Cisne for every conceivable occasion.

Catamayo
*Phone code: 07
Colour map 6,
grid B3
Population: 17,000
Altitude: 1,250 m*

Sleeping and eating C *Los Almendros*, on the main road west of town, T677293, F570393, private bath, hot water, pool, restaurant and bar, parking. **D** *Bella Vista*, on a side road off the main road west of town, T677255, F677842. Private bath, cold water, gardens and pool. Nice views but cramped layout and out of the way. **E-F** *Reina del Cisne*, Isidro Ayora on the plaza, T677414, cheaper with shared bath, cold water, fan, simple but OK. **E-F** *Rossana*, Isidro Ayora y 24 de Mayo, T677006, cheaper with shared bath, cold water, also cheaper annexe next door.

There are several very cheap comedores around the plaza

Beyond Catamayo is a network of secondary roads, mostly unpaved, running south and west to either the Peruvian border or the coast, through sparsely populated hot dry country. First, at Catamayo, the road divides into two branches. The rougher partly paved southern branch runs to **Gonazanamá**, **Cariamanga**, **Quilanga**, **Amaluza** and **Jimbura** on the Peruvian border (see below). The fully paved western branch climbs steeply to **San Pedro La Bendita** (the turn-off for **El Cisne**, see above). Ahead on the western branch, at **Las Chinchas**, an unpaved road branches north to **Portovelo**, **Zaruma** (see page 296) and **Piñas**, and, beyond, the paved road again divides into a northwestern branch to **Balsas** (continuing down to Machala) and a southwestern branch to **Catacocha**.

This is Ecuador far off the tourist trail, with grand views, friendly people and limited services

Southern Highlands

Catacocha
Phone code: 07
Colour map 6, grid B2
Population: 5,400
Altitude: 1,800 m

Catacocha is a spectacularly placed town perched on a hilltop overlooking the surrounding valleys. It is authentic and very friendly. The views from Shiriculapo, behind the hospital, are marvellous. This used to be a notorious 'lover's leap'. Ask to walk through the hospital grounds to see it. There are pre-Inca ruins around the town, which was once inhabited by the Palta Indians, a group which now only exists in history books. There is an archaeology museum in the high school, Colegio Marista.

Sleeping and eating D *Tambococha*, in front of the church, T683551. Private bath, shower, modern, comfortable, friendly. **D-E** *Buena Esperanza*, Vivanco y Celi, T683031. Cheaper with shared bath and cold water, older simple place but very friendly. There are a couple of other cheap places to stay. For eating try *Salón Macará* on Vivanco.

South to Macará

From Catacocha, the paved road runs west and then south to the border at Macará. A turn-off at the military checkpoint at **El Empalme**, 48 km from Catacocha, leads west to **Celica**, **Alamor** and on to the petrified forest at **Puyango** (see page 298) and Arenillas.

Celica
Phone code: 07
Population: 3,700
Altitude: 2,000 m

This charming town perched on a hill has a nice church and very friendly people. There are lovely views of the surrounding valleys. North of town is the Guachanamá Ridge, between 2,000 and 2,800 m, with many rare southwestern endemic birds.

Sleeping and eating **E-F** *Pucará*, C Manuela Cañizares half a block from the main park, T657159. Cheaper with shared bath, nice, comfortable and friendly. **E** *Central*, on the main park, T657120. Cheaper with shared bath, electric shower, comfortable. There are a couple of places around the plaza to eat.

Alamor
Phone code: 07
Population: 3,800
Altitude: 1,150 m

This warm market town, 26 km northwest of Celica, has a busy agricultural fair around the 15th of each month. It is a convenient place to stay in order to visit the Puyango petrified forest (see page 298), but Celica is more attractive. There are hourly rancheras from Alamor to Arenillas which take you to the turn-off for Puyango, 29 km north. Several buses bound for Machala or Huaquillas also go this way.

Sleeping and eating D *SICA*, C 10 de Agosto, 2 blocks from the park, T680230. Comfortable rooms with private bath and cold water, parking. **E** *Puyango*, 10 de Agosto 7-34 at the main park, T680137. Cheaper with shared bath, cold water, nice and friendly. Other basic hotels and eating places can be found by the main park.

South from Celica a road heads southwest to **Zapotillo** (population: 2,000, altitude: 325 m), a hot riverside town on the Peruvian border, also reached by a paved road from Macará. Nearby is the **Ceiba Grande nature reserve** which protects a 6,600-ha tract of Tumbesian forest, information at *Hotel Los Charanes* (see below). **D** *Los Charanes*, Quito y Roldós, across from the bus stop, T659249. Private bath, cold water, fan, modern, new in 2001. Next door is **E** *Misheel*, cheaper with shared bath, cold water, basic; and around the corner **F** *Los Angeles*, T659156, shared bath, cold water, basic. There are cheap *comedores* near the plaza.

Zapotillo feels like and is the end of the line. There is long-haul bus service to Loja (US$6.50, 7 hrs), and even Quito (US$15, 17 hrs). Southwest of Zapotillo, 21 km along a dirt road, is the hamlet of **Lalamor**, with a tiny border post (not always staffed). Hire a rowboat for US$0.20 or wade across the river.

On the Peruvian side you can get a vehicle to Lancones and on to Sullana, three hours away, US$3 per person or US$18 to have the car to yourself. There is hardly any traffic.

South from Catamayo

The road running south from Catamayo first reaches Gonzanamá, a pleasant, sleepy little town famed for the weaving of beautiful *alforjas* (multi-purpose saddlebags). Ask around and buy direct from the weavers as there are no handicraft shops. Gonzanamá also produces a good soft cheese. Travellers should note that the town has a somewhat unusual reputation in the south for the high incidence of deafness. So don't be paranoid if everyone seems to be ignoring you! **F** *Residencial Jiménez*, with bath, cold water.

Gonzanamá & villages to Macará

From Gonzanamá there is an old and poorly maintained road to **Malacatos** (near Vilcabamba), passing through the isolated village of **Purunuma**. There is almost no traffic but the views are great. It may be possible to get a ride in the morning up to the village, then it's a long hike down to the river and back up to Malacatos.

Cariamanga, about 27 km southwest from Gonzanamá, is an important regional centre with several hotels and reasonable services.

Beyond Cariamanga the roads are unpaved and poor. One heads southeast to **Lucero**, **Amaluza** and **Jimbura**, in the most southerly and least visited parts of the country. There are two basic hotels in Amaluza (best is **F** *El Rocío*, on the plaza), from where a daily bus runs to Quito, taking about 24 hours. At Jimbura is a small border post with connections to Ayabaca in Perú.

Another road twists its way westwards from Cariamanga to **Colaisaca** then follows a steep, rough descent through 2,000 m to **Utuana**. From there the road heads northwest to **Sozoranga**, 75 km from Gonzanamá. The town has one hotel (**F**, shared bath, cold shower). The road then continues south for 36 km to Macará on the border. North of Sozoranga, a road goes to **Nueva Fátima**, along this route are remnants of a wide variety of native forests between 1,300 and 2,600 m, rich in bird life. A total of 190 species of birds are known from this area, including many southwestern endemics.

Macará

This hot, noisy town with convoluted streets is on the border and in the centre of a rice-farming area. There are good road connections to Sullana north of Piura on the Peruvian coast. Macará is growing and sees increasing traffic but it remains a much more relaxed place to cross to Peru than Huaquillas.

Phone code: 07
Colour map 6, grid C2
Population: 11,500
Altitude: 500 m

D *El Conquistador*, Bolívar y Calderón, T694057. Includes breakfast, hot water, fan, parking, modern and comfortable, new in 2002. **D** *Espiga de Oro*, C Ante opposite the market, T695089. Cold water, fan, parking, OK. **D** *Gran Hotel Macará*, on bypass to border, T694162. Cold water, parking, modern, new in 2002. **D** *Parador Turístico*, on road from town to the border, T/F694099. Restaurant, disco on weekends, cold water, OK. **D** *Santigyn*, Bolívar y Rengel, T695035. Hot water, fan, some rooms with fridge, modern, comfortable. **E** *Bekalus*, Valdivieso entre 10 de Agosto y Rengel, T694043. Cheaper with shared bath, cold water, parking, simple but good value. **E** *Hostal del Sur*, on Veintimilla, T694189. Private bath, cold water, modern, small rooms, new in 2002. **E-F** *Paraíso*, Veintimilla 553, T694107. Cheaper with shared bath, cold water, simple. **G** *Amazonas*, Rengel 418, T694067. Shared bath, cold water until 1000, very basic.

Sleeping
■ *on map, page 274*

Eating   There is not a great deal to choose from. Cheap set meals and sometimes à la carte at *Colonial Macará*, Rengel y Bolívar; *Emperador*, on Carlos Veintimilla; *Chifa Internacional*, Sucre y Bolívar; and a few other small places.

Transport   *Coop Loja* and *Cariamanga* have frequent buses, daily, from Macará to **Loja**, US$5, 5-6 hrs. *Loja Internacional* buses which have direct service **Loja-Piura**, 3 daily, can also be boarded in Macará. They pass through at 0330, 1300 and 1830; US$3.40 to Piura, 3 hrs. *Coop Loja* also has service to **Quito**, US$14, 17 hrs, and **Guayaquil**, US$9, 9 hrs

Directory   **Communications**   There are *Pacifictel* offices by the main plaza for all phone calls, but no internet as yet in late 2002.

Macará-La   The international bridge over the Río Macará is 2½ km from town. There is a taxi
Tina border   and pick-up service from the small park near the market, US$0.25 shared taxi, US$1 private. On the Peruvian side, minivans and cars run La Tina-Sullana, US$3 per person or US$12 for a private car, 1½-2 hours. The road is fully paved. For more details see the *Peru Handbook* or *South American Handbook*.

Ecuadorean immigration   Open 24 hrs. Formalities are reported much easier here than at Huaquillas. When entering Ecuador, ask for 90 days if you need it.

Peruvian immigration   Open 24 hrs. Formalities are likewise easier than at Huaquillas–Aguas Verdes.

Exchange   During the day there are money changers dealing in Soles at the the international bridge, and in Macará at the park where taxis leave for the border. There is also a *Banco Financiero* on the Peruvian side of the bridge which changes Soles, Mon-Fri 0900-1300, 1430-1800, Sat 0900-1200. All transactions are cash only; there is nowhere to change TCs.

Macará

Sleeping
1 Amazonas
2 Bekalus
3 El Conquistador & Santigyn
4 Espiga de Oro
5 Gran Hostal Macará
6 Hostal del Sur
7 Parador Turístico
8 Residencial Paraíso

Eating
1 Chifa Internacional
2 Colonial Macará
3 Emperador

Southern Highlands

Guayaquil and Southern Pacific

Introducing Guayaquil and the Southern Pacific

The coastal plains are the agro-industrial heartland of Ecuador. Rice, sugar, coffee, African palm, mango, cacao, shrimp and especially bananas are produced in these hot and humid lowlands and processed or exported through Guayaquil. The largest and most dynamic commercial centre in the country, Guayaquil is also Ecuador's main port and the city's influence extends throughout the coast and beyond. This 'working Ecuador' is most frequently seen by business visitors rather than tourists, but Guayaquil is undergoing a cultural revival and has some attractions to offer. Trips to Galápagos can also be organized from here.

The coastline south to the Peruvian border gives the impression of being one giant banana plantation, while increasing numbers of shrimp farmers battle it out with conservation groups over the future of the mangroves that still line parts of the Gulf of Guayaquil.

The climate from May to December is dry with often overcast days but pleasantly cool nights, whereas the hot rainy season from January to April can be oppressively humid.

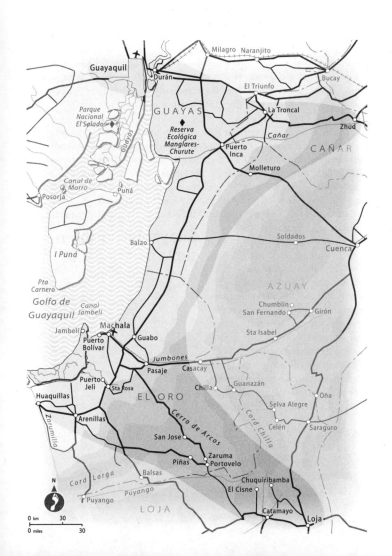

Things to do in Guayaquil and the Southern Pacific

- Stroll the **Malecón 2000** in Guayaquil, page 280.
- Catch the view and breeze from atop **Cerro Santa Ana** in Guayaquil, page 281.
- Visit **Guayaquil's Botanical Gardens**, page 282.
- Tour the **Cerro Blanco** nature reserve outside Guayaquil, page 282.
- Discover the seldom visited uplands of **El Oro**, page 295.

Guayaquil

Phone code: 04
Colour map 4, grid C3
Population: 2,000,000
Altitude: sea level

Ecuador's largest city and the country's chief sea port and industrial and commercial centre lies on the west bank of the chocolate-brown Río Guayas, some 56 km from its outflow into the Gulf of Guayaquil. Founded in 1534 by Diego de Almagro and moved to its current location, near the native settlement of Guayaquile, by Sebastián de Benalcázar in 1535, the city couldn't be more different from its highland counterpart and political rival, Quito. It is hot, sticky, fast-paced, bold and brash. It may lack the capital's colonial charm, but Guayaquileños are certainly more lively, colourful and open than Quiteños. Since 2000, Guayaquil has been working hard to attract more tourism.

The Puerto Marítimo, opened in 1964, handles three-quarters of the country's imports and almost half of its exports. It is a constant bone of contention between the *costeños* and the *serranos* that Guayaquil is not given better recognition of its economic importance in the form of more central government funds. Since the late 1990s there have been organized movements for autonomy of Ecuador's coastal provinces, spearheaded by Guayaquil.

Guayaquil's suburbs sprawl to the north and south of the centre, with middle-class neighbourhoods and some rather upscale areas in the north and poorer working class neighbourhoods and slums to the south. The city is a magnet for internal migration. A side effect of the population explosion is that the city's services have been stretched beyond the limit. The authorities struggle to control the chaotic transport system, garbage collection, as well as itinerant street vendors and the many informal markets which choke the main downtown traffic arteries and sidewalks.

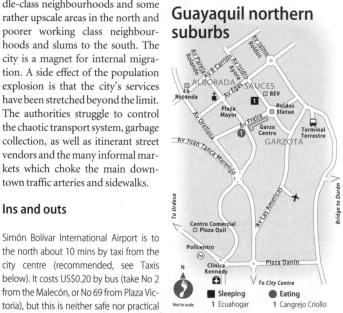

Guayaquil northern suburbs

Sleeping
1 Ecuahogar

Eating
1 Cangrejo Criollo

Not to scale

Ins and outs

Getting there
See also Transport, page 289

Related map Guayaquil, page 280

Simón Bolívar International Airport is to the north about 10 mins by taxi from the city centre (recommended, see Taxis below). It costs US$0.20 by bus (take No 2 from the Malecón, or No 69 from Plaza Victoria), but this is neither safe nor practical with luggage. If you are going straight on to another city, take a cab directly to the bus station, which is close by. If you are arriving in Guayaquil during the daytime and need a taxi from the airport, walk half a block from the terminal out to Av de las Américas, where taxis and camionetas wait for passengers. The fare will be about half of what you will be charged for the same trip by one of the drivers who belong to the airport taxi cooperative, but it is not safe to leave the terminal area at night. See below for taxi fares.

The Terminal Terrestre is just north of the airport, just off the road to the Guayas bridge. The company offices are on the ground floor, long-distance buses leave from the top floor and regional buses (for Playas, Salinas, etc) leave from the ground floor. When you purchase a ticket, ask where your bus leaves from. There is no left luggage depot, don't leave anything unattended. The terminal is busy at weekends and holidays. There are some restaurants, shops and a *Pacifictel* office for calls. Lots of local buses go from the bus station to the city centre, but this is not safe with luggage; take a taxi. Bus No 84 goes to Plaza Centenario and No 111 leaves you 2 blocks from Plaza Centenario.

A street numbering system is in place since 2001. According to this scheme, the city is divided into 4 quadrants separated by a north-south axis and an east-west axis. All north-south streets are called avenidas and the east-west streets are calles. Each has an alpha-numeric designation such as Av 12 south-east. The airport and bus terminal are in the northeastern quadrant, the commercial heartland in the southeastern quadrant. Although this system is officially in place, the old street names persist and the population uses only the old nomenclature. **Getting around**

Not surprisingly for a city of this size, you will need to get around by public transport. A number of hotels, however, are centrally located near the riverfront. City buses are often confusing and overcrowded at rush hour (watch out for pickpockets) and cost US$0.20. There are also minibuses (*furgonetas*), US$0.20, which post their routes in the windscreen. Buses are only permited in a few streets in the centre; northbound buses go along the Malecón and on Rumichaca, southbound along Boyacá. Bus No 15 will take you from the centre to Urdesa, 13 to Policentro, 14 to Albanborja, 74 to La Garzota and Sauces. Outside rush hour, buses are a good, cheap alternative to taxis, but you need to know where you're going. **Taxis** have no meters, so prices are very negotiable and overcharging is notorious. From the airport or bus terminal to the centre is US$3-4. From the centre to Urdesa, Policentro or Alborada is US$2-3. From the airport to the bus terminal and short trips costs US$2. It is often quicker to walk short distances in the centre, rather than take a bus or taxi, but on no account walk around after dark.

Ministerio de Turismo, P Ycaza 203 y Pichincha, 5th and 6th floors, T2568764. Friendly, Spanish only, open Mon-Fri 0900-1730. They sell a map of Ecuador. Maps also from **INOCAR**, in the planetarium building at the naval base near the port, who have a comprehensive stock of maps. A useful website dedicated to Guayaquil is **www.turismoguayas.com** **Tourist information**

People continue to migrate from the countryside to Guayaquil in search of jobs. The population is growing and there are many slums, shanty towns and *invasiones* (squatter settlements); poverty and crime are serious problems. Residential neighbourhoods hide behind bars and protect themselves with armed guards. Since 2000, the authorities have placed much emphasis on improving public safety. The Malecón, parts of Av 9 de Octubre and the Las Peñas neighbourhood are heavily patrolled and reported safe. The rest of the city carries the usual risks of a large seaport and metropolis. Don't walk around with valuables and always take taxis at night. **Safety**

Guayaquil & Southern Pacific

Sights

Malecón Simón Bolívar

The Malecón is patrolled and safe, a favourite place to stroll

A wide, tree-lined waterfront avenue, the Malecón Simón Bolívar runs alongside the Río Guayas from the exclusive **Club de la Unión**, by the Moorish clock tower, past the imposing **Palacio Municipal** and **Government Palace** and the old Yacht Club to Las Peñas. The riverfront along this avenue is an attractive promenade, known as **Malecón 2000**, where visitors and locals can enjoy the fresh river breeze and take in the views. There are gardens, fountains, monuments and walkways. You can dine at upmarket restaurants, cafés and food courts. Towards the south end are souvenir shops, a shopping mall and the old **Mercado Sur** (prefabricated by Eiffel 1905-07), now a gallery housing temporary exhibits. The **Museo Antropológico** is scheduled to relocate to the north end of the Malecón in 2003. Halfway along the Malecón,

Guayaquil

Sleeping ■
1 Alexander
2 Best Western Doral
3 Continental
4 Gran Guayaquil
5 Hampton Inn Boulevard
6 Palace
7 Plaza & Unipark
8 Rizzo
9 Sol de Oriente
10 Vélez

Eating ●
1 Casa Basca
2 Chifa Himalaya
3 Hare Krishna
4 Salud Solar

Related map
Guayaquil northern
suburbs, page 278

0 metres   100
0 yards   100

Guayaquil & Southern Pacific

Boulevard 9 de Octubre, the city's main street, starts in front of **La Rotonda**, a statue to mark the meeting between Simón Bolívar and José San Martín in 1822 (see box on page 283). Halfway up 9 Octubre is **Plaza Centenario** with its towering monument to the liberation of the city erected in 1920.

Guayaquil's second showpiece is the old district of Las Peñas, a vestige of old **Las Peñas** Guayaquil at the north end of the Malecón. This picturesque neighbourhood, built on the Cerro Santa Ana hill, at the edge of the river, is undergoing gentrification in 2002. Part of the renovation process has been completed and visitors now walk up its steep stairway amid the brightly painted wooden houses. There are cafés, bars and lovely views from the top. The area is heavily guarded and safe. The renovation process continues and will eventually cover the entire hill. For the time being, however, don't venture from the guarded area, it is not safe. During the *fiestas julianas* (24-25 July), young painters exhibit their art at Las Peñas. The main artery is a narrow cobbled street (Numa Pompilio Llona). The entrance is guarded by two cannon pointing riverward, a reminder of the days when pirates sailed up the Guayas to attack the city. Guayaquil was sacked and destroyed by fire a number of times, so almost none of its original wooden buildings remain. There are several important churches which were rebuilt on several occasions, otherwise, most of its colonial history is confined to the history books.

There are several noteworthy churches. **Santo Domingo**, founded by the **Churches** Dominicans in 1548, stands just by Las Peñas. It was sacked and burned by pirates in 1624. Its present form was built in 1938, replacing the wooden structure with concrete in classical style. Pirates also sacked the original church of **San Agustín**; the present building dates from 1931.

The original wooden structure of the **Cathedral**, built in 1695, survived both sackings and fire, but the years took their toll and a new building was completed in 1822. In 1924 construction on the present building was started, in the classical Gothic style, and it was inaugurated in the 1950s. The pleasant, shady **Parque Bolívar** in front of the Cathedral is filled with tame iguanas which scuttle out of the trees for scraps.

Other notable churches are **San Francisco**, with its restored colonial interior, off 9 de Octubre and Pedro Carbo, and the beautiful **La Merced**.

At the north end of the centre, below Cerro El Carmen, the huge, spreading **Cemetery**, with its dazzling, high-rise tombs and the ostentatious mausoleums of the rich, is worth a visit. A flower market over the road sells the best blooms in the city. Go on a Sunday when there are plenty of people about.

The **Museo Municipal** is housed in the Biblioteca Municipal, where there are **Museums** paintings, gold and archaeological collections, shrunken Shuar heads, a section on the history of Guayaquil and also a good newspaper library. ■ *Tue-Sat 0900-1700, guided tours available, free. Sucre y Chile.*

Museo Antropológico del Banco Central has excellent collections of ceramics, gold objects and paintings. It also houses the collection of religious art from the former Museo Nahim Isaías. There are English speaking guides. ■ *Closed for renovations and due to reopen at the Malecón 2000, in 2003.*

Museo del Banco del Pacífico is a beautiful small museum mainly of archaeological exhibits. ■ *Mon-Fri 0900-1700. Free. T2328333. Ycaza 200 y Pichincha, 3rd floor.*

Museo de la Casa de la Cultura has an impressive collection of prehistoric gold items in its archaeological museum (refurbished in 2002). Also at the Casa de la Cultura is the Pinacoteca Manuel Rendón Seminario, a photo collection of old Guayaquil. ■ *Tue-Fri 1000-1800, Sat 0900-1500. US$0.50. English guides available. 9 de Octubre 1200 y P Moncayo.*

Other attractions   The **Botanical Gardens** are in the Ciudadela Las Orquídeas to the northwest. There are over 3,000 plants, including 150 species of Ecuadorean and foreign orchids. The views are good and it is the ideal place for a pleasant stroll. Recommended. ■ *0800-1600 daily. US$5, guides available for US$10. T2417004. Av Francisco de Orellana, Las Orquídeas (bus line 63).*

There is a pier near the Terminal Terrestre, where *chivas acuáticas* can be hired for rides along the river, with fine views of the city. Guayaquil is also a city of shopping malls, where consumerism flourishes in air-conditioned comfort. Here you will find many banks, restaurants, bars, discos, cinemas, cyber cafés and of course shops. For a complete list see Shopping, below.

Residential areas   **Barrio Centenario** to the south of the centre is the original residential sector, now a peaceful, tree-shaded haven. Other residential areas are **Urdesa**, northwest of the centre, between two branches of the Estero Salado (about 15 minutes from downtown). Near the international airport and bus terminal, which are conveniently close to each other, are the districts of **La Garzota**, **Sauces** and **Alborada**. Cleaner, less congested and safer than the centre, but with all services, entertainment and shops, these areas are 10-15 minutes by taxi from downtown, and five minutes from the airport and Terminal Terrestre. The fanciest neighbourhoods are more peripheral, such as **La Puntilla** and **Isla Sol** on the road to Samborondón and **Los Ceibos**, **Los Olivos** and **Santa Cecilia**, on the road to the coast. Overpasses in the city's roads are decorated with murals, replicas of works by Ecuador's most renowned artists.

Excursions

Bosque Protector Cerro Blanco   This nature reserve is set in tropical dry forest along the Río Blanco with an impressive variety of birds (over 190 species listed), such as the Guayaquil Green-macaw (symbol of the reserve), Crane Hawk, Snail Kite and so on, and with sightings of Howler Monkeys, ocelot, puma, jaguar and peccaries, many reptiles, among others. The reserve is run by Fundación Pro-Bosque, edif Promocentro, local 16, Eloy Alfaro y Cuenca, T2417004. ■ *US$5, additional fee charged for each trail visited, US$4 for 1 trail, US$5 for 2, US$8 for 3, camping $7 per person. Guides can be hired. Reservations required during weekdays and for groups larger than 8 on the weekends, and for birders wishing to arrive before or stay after normal opening hours (0800-1530). On the Vía a la Costa, Km 16, the entrance is beyond the Club Rocafuerte. Taxi from Guayaquil US$10-20. The yellow and green 'Chongonera' buses leave every 30 mins from Parque Victoria and pass the park entrance on the way to Puerto Hondo.*

Manglares de Puerto Hondo   On the other side of the road from Cerro Blanco, at Km 17 on the Vía a la Costa, is **Puerto Hondo**. Canoe trips through the mangroves can be made from here, a good way to see many migratory birds. This is also a good place to try local seafood specialties. ■ *Boat rentals can be arranged on the spot at weekends from the Fundación Pro-Bosque kiosk for US$7 per person with guides, or during the week with their Guayaquil office (see above).*

Parque El Lago   Also along the road to the coast, at Km 26, is El Lago, a recreational park with a lake for boating, walking paths and picnic areas. ■ *0800-1700. US$0.40 per vehicle, boat rentals US$1.60, bicycle rentals US$0.80. T2872033.*

The Liberators of America

Guayaquil's most famous monument, La Rotonda, commemorates the meeting of the liberators of South America – Simón Bolívar of Venezuela and José San Martín of Argentina – in the city on 26 July 1822. One month later San Martín, who had played a vital role in the independence of Argentina, Chile and Peru, suddenly abandoned his participation in the South American revolutionary campaign.

What happened? The most irreverent commentators suggest that San Martín contracted so violent a case of dysentery as could only be acquired in tropical Guayaquil. Far more plausible however, is that the meeting of the two great heroes of independence was in fact the height of political intrigue, a monumental arm-wrestle on the shores of the Guayas.

Guayaquil was an independent city state and its strategic port was coveted by both of its large emerging neighbours: Colombia to the north and Peru to the south. On 21 June 1822, Bolívar wrote, "We cannot give up Guayaquil, it would make more sense to give up Quito." So both libertadores raced to Guayaquil to woo the city to their respective sides,

with diplomacy and troops. Bolívar got there first, on 11 July, while San Martín arrived from Lima two weeks later. Seeing that Colombian forces had already taken up positions at the mouth of the Río Guayas, San Martín ordered his ships to sail back to Peru, and proceeded to meet Bolívar with only a handful of aides.

At their meeting San Martín offered to serve as Bolívar's subordinate in order to conclude the campaign against royalist forces in Peru, but Bolívar (perhaps rightfully suspicious) refused the collaboration. On 29 August, San Martín wrote Bolívar that he was unconvinced by the latter's polite excuses and that if, as it seemed, Bolívar wanted all the glory for himself, then he could have it.

Guayaquil became part of Bolívar's Gran Colombia and later the main port of an independent Ecuador. During the many years of border conflict with Peru it was always on the front lines. That conflict was finally settled in 1998, yet political intrigue is alive and well on the shores of the Guayas, in the shadow of La Rotonda and the liberators of America.

About 45 minutes southeast of Guayaquil, preserving mangroves in the Gulf of Guayaquil and forests of the Cordillera Churute, is Reserva Ecológica Manglares Churute, part of the national park system. It is a rich natural area with five different ecosystems. There is a trail through the dry tropical forest (1½ hours' walk) and you can also walk (one hour) to Laguna Canclón or Churute, a large lake where ducks nest. Many waterbirds, animals and dolphins can be seen. ■ *US$10 per person. Guide fee US$4 for group up to 10. Boat tour (2 hrs), US$40 for group up to 15 passengers; arrange several days ahead through the Ministerio del Ambiente office in Guayaquil, Dept Forestal, Av Quito 402 y Padre Solano, p 10, T2397730; or Biólogo Fernando Cedeño, T09-9619815 (mob). Entrance to the reserve is along the road Guayaquil-Naranjal-Machala. Buses (CIFA, Ecuatoriano Pullman, 16 de Junio) leave the terminal terrestre every 30 mins, going to Naranjal or Machala. Ask to be let off at the Churute information centre. The reserve can also be reached by river. Tour operators also arrange tours to the reserve.*

Reserva Ecológica Manglares Churute
Canoe trips into the mangroves with guides should be arranged several days in advance

The Parque Histórico is north of the city, in Entrerríos, on the way to Samborondón. It recreates Guayaquil and its rural surroundings at the end of the 19th century. There is a natural area with native flora and fauna, a traditions section where you can learn about rural life and how crafts are made, an urban section with wooden architecture and an educational farm. A pleasant

Parque Histórico

place for a stroll. ■ *Tue-Sun 0900-1700. US$2, seniors US$0.50. T2833807, www.parquehistorico.com CISA buses to Samborondón leave from the terminal terrestre every 20 mins, US$0.25.*

Essentials

Sleeping
■ *on maps,
pages 278 and 280
Price codes:
see inside front cover*

Hotel prices, which are higher than in Quito, are usually posted by the front desk. It is common practice to have dual rates in the more upmarket establishments; one for nationals and a much higher one for foreigners. Always check the rate first; also whether 22% service and taxes are included in the given price (as they are in the following list). Rooms in the better hotels can be in demand and booking is advised.

Most hotels are downtown, so take a taxi from the airport or bus station. The cheapest hotels are pretty basic and many cater to short-stay customers. The area around Plaza Centenario is the best bet for budget travellers wishing to stay downtown. Note however that all of the downtown area is unsafe, especially at night. As an alternative, there are a few good places in residential neighbourhoods in our **B-C** range.

LL *Hampton Inn Boulevard*, 9 de Octubre 432 y Baquerizo Moreno, T2566700, F2566427, www.hampton.com.ec Buffet breakfast, restaurant, internet, central, very good facilities. **LL** *Hilton Colón*, Av Francisco de Orellana in Kennedy Norte (outside downtown), T2689000, F2689149. Largest luxury hotel in town, all facilities, 5 restaurants and bars, 2 pools. **L** *Continental*, Chile y 10 de Agosto, T2329270, F2325454. Includes breakfast, 24-hr restaurant and good coffee shop, a KLM Golden Tulip hotel, 5-star, central. **L** *Oro Verde*, 9 de Octubre y Gracía Moreno, T2327999, F2329350, www.ororverdehotels.com 4 restaurants (*El Patio* open 24 hrs), deli and bar, pool, gym, business centre, limo service, airport transfers, top class. **L** *Unipark*, Clemente Ballén 406 y Chile, T2327100, F2328352, uni_gye@ororverdehotels.com Good restaurants, café and bar, meeting and banquet facilities, gym, golf and tennis, 5-star luxury.

AL *Gran Hotel Guayaquil*, Boyacá 1600 y 10 de Agosto, T2329690, F2327251, www.grandhotelguayaquil.com Good restaurants, a/c, pool (US$6 for non-residents), traditional. **AL** *Palace*, Chile 214 y Luque, T2321080, F2322887. Includes breakfast, 24-hr cafeteria, a/c, modern, traffic noise on Av Chile side, good value for business travellers. Recommended. **AL** *Ramada*, Malecón 606 y Orellana, T2565555, F2563036. Incudes buffet breakfast, a/c, pool, internet, good location right on the Malecón. **A** *Sol de Oriente*, Aguirre 603 y Escobedo, T2325500, F2325904. Includes breakfast, restaurant, a/c, minibar, gym, excellent value. Recommended.

B *Best Western Doral*, Chile 402 y Aguirre, T2328002, F2327088, hdoral@gye.satnet.net Includes breakfast, restaurant, a/c, internet, good rooms and value, central. Recommended. **B** *Del Rey*, Aguirre y Marín, behind tennis club, T2452909. Includes breakfast, restaurant and bar, a/c, quiet and friendly. Recommended. **B** *Plaza*, Chile 414 y Clemente Ballén, T2324006, F2324195, jplamas@impsat.net.ec Includes breakfast, cafeteria, a/c, internet, international newspapers. Recommended. **B** *Rizzo*, Clemente Ballén 319 y Chile, T2325210, F2326209. Includes breakfast, *Café Jambelí* downstairs for seafood, a/c, central, some windowless rooms. **B** *Tangara Guest House*, Manuela Sáenz y O'Leary, Manzana F, Villa 1, Ciudadela Bolivariana (a residential area between the airport and downtown), T2284445, F2284039. A/c, fridge, nice and friendly. Recommended.

C *Alexander*, Luque 1107 y Pedro Moncayo, T2532000, F2514161. Cafeteria, a/c, comfortable, good value, some rooms without windows, can be noisy. **C** *Casa Alianza*, Av Segunda 318 y Calle 12, Los Ceibos, T2351261, F2350736, www.casaalianza.com Restaurant, a/c, cheaper with shared bath and fan, very far from centre, run by a Norwegian NGO. **C** *Ecuahogar*, Av Isidro Ayora, opposite *Banco Ecuatoriano de La Vivienda*, Sauces I, T2248357, F2248341, youthost@telconet.net Includes breakfast, restaurant, cheaper in dorm with shared bath, cooking and laundry facilities, discount for IYHF members. Overpriced and several negative reports. **C** *Hostal de Alborada*, Alborada IX, Manzana 935, Villa 8, near airport, T2237251. A/c, friendly. **C** *La Torre*, Chile 303 y Luque, T2531316, F2531354. Includes breakfast, cafeteria, central location. **C** *Ritz*, 9 de Octubre y Boyacá, T2324134, F2322151. A/c, OK.

D *Acuario*, Luque 1204 y Quito, T2533715. Fan, OK. **D** *Capri*, Luque y Machala, T2326341. Cafeteria, a/c, fridge, busy at weekends. **D-E** *Luque*, Luque 1214 y Quito, T2523900. A/c, cheaper with fan, OK. **E** *Sander*, Luque 1101 y Moncayo, T2320030. Private bath, a/c, cheaper with fan and no windows, OK. **E** *Vélez*, Vélez 1021 y Quito, T2530356. Private bath, a/c, cheaper with fan, best budget option downtown, often full. Very good value. Recommended. **F** *Libertador*, Santa Elena 803 y VM Rendón, T2304637. Private bath, fan, basic.

The main areas for restaurants are in the centre with many in the larger hotels, around Urdesa, or the newer residential and commercial centres of La Alborada and La Garzota, which have many good eating places. In the smarter places 22% service and tax is added to the bill.

Eating
● *on maps,*
pages 278 and 280

International **Expensive**: the fancier hotels such as *Hilton Colón*, *Unipark*, Sheraton, *Continental*, *Gran Hotel Guayaquil* and *Oro Verde* all have good restaurants with international menus. *La Balandra*, C 5a 504 entre Monjas y Dátiles, Urdesa. For good fish, French dishes and more, upmarket ambience, live music every night. Daily 1000-1500, 1900-0000. Also has a crab house at Circunvalación 506 y Ficus, Urdesa. *Juan Salvador Gaviota*, Kennedy Norte, Av Fco de Orellana. Good seafood and other international food. *Posada de las Garzas*, Urdesa Norte, Circunvalación Norte 536. Also French-style dishes. **Mid-range to expensive**: *El Parque*, top floor of Unicentro. For excellent popular buffet breakfast, lunch or dinner. Daily 0700-0000.

Italian **Very expensive**: *La Trattoria da Enrico*, Bálsamos 504 y las Monjas. The best in food and surroundings, good antipasto, very exclusive. Daily 1200-1500, 1900-0000, closed Sat lunch. **Expensive**: *La Casa di Carlo*, Ciudadela Guayaquil Norte, C Primera, Manzana 19, Villa 9. Good home made pasta, antipastos, Mediterranean ambiance. Mon-Sat 1230-1530, 2000-0000, Sun1230-1630. *Trattoria de Pasquale*, Estrada y Guayacanes, Urdesa and Av Francisco de Orellana. Good food and atmosphere. Daily 1000-0000. **Mid-range**: *Cozzoli's*, Av Miraflores 115. Pizza and other Italian dishes. Mon-Sat 1000-0000, Sun 1000-1300. Recommended. *El Hornero*, Av Estrada 906 e Higueras, Urdesa. Very good pizza and other dishes. Mon-Sat 1000-0000, Sun 1000-1300. *Riviera*, Estrada y Ficus, Urdesa and Mall del Sol. Good pasta, antipasto, salads, bright surroundings, good service. Open daily. **Mid-range to cheap**: *El Salinerito*, Av Estrada, Urdesa and Av Guillermo Pareja Rolando, La Garzota. Excellent pizza, pasta made on the spot, good value. Mon-Sat 1000-0000, Sun 1000-1300. *Pizzería Del Ñato*, Estrada 1219. Good value, sold by the metre.

Mexican **Expensive**: *Cielito Lindo*, Circunvalación 623 y Ficus. Good food and atmosphere, live mariachi music. Open daily for lunch and dinner. *Noches Tapatías*, Primera y Dátiles, Urdesa. Fun, good live music at weekends. Tue-Sun 1200-0000. *Red Peppers*, Torres del Norte, at Kennedy Norte. Tex mex menu, grill, bar. *Viva Mexico*, Dátiles y Estrada, in Urdesa. The best authentic dishes. Mon-Sat 1000-0000, Sun 1000-1300.

Also fast food taco chains in all parts of town

Chinese Large selection in the centre and up north, most do takeaway, are **cheap** and good value, and open daily except Sun evening. *Asia*, Sucre 321 y Chile. Good food, vegetarian dishes on request. *Chifa Himalaya*, Sucre 309 y P Carbo. Slow service but good for the price. *Gran Chifa*, P Carbo 1016. Wide variety, good value. *Cantonés*, Av G Pareja y C 43, La Garzota. Huge rather glaring emporium with authentic dishes and all-you-can-eat menu for US$9, karaoke. *Pagoda*, Circunvalación Sur 916 e Ilanes, in Urdesa. Great crab wantan.

Japanese   Japanese restaurants are not as common as Chinese and prices are in the **expensive** to very expensive range. *Tsuji*, Estrada 815, Urdesa and Guayacanes e Higueras. Wonderful, authentic dishes, Teppan Yaki. Very expensive. Tue-Sun 1200-1300, 1900-2300. *UniBar* in *Unipark Hotel* complex. Sushi. *Kioto* at *Hotel Hilton Colón*. *Sushi Bar* at Hotel Oro Verde.

Crab houses are almost an institution and great fun   **Seafood**   Prices at crab restaurants are quite uniform: a stuffed crab, *carapacho relleno* (delicious), costs about US$10, an *arroz con cangrejo* US$4-5. *Manny's*, Av Miraflores y Segunda and at Av Plaza Dañín. Good quality and value, try the excellent *arroz con cangrejo*. *Casa del Cangrejo*, Av Plaza Dañín, Kennedy. For crab dishes of every kind; several others along the same street. *Red Crab*, Estrada y Laureles, Urdesa. Interesting décor, wide variety of seafood. Expensive. *El Cangrejo Criollo*, Av Rolando Pareja, Villa 9, La Garzota. Excellent, varied seafood menu. Recommended. *Sandunga's*, Av Plaza Dañín frente al Asilo de Ancianos. Deliciuos seafood dishes. Tue-Fri 1200-1600, 1800-2330, Sat-Sun 1200-2330. *El Lechón*, Victor Manuel Rendón y Boyacá in the centre. Good seafood. Cheap to mid-range.

Spanish   Expensive: *Casa Baska*, Chile 406 y C Ballén. Wonderful hole-in-the-wall place, specializes in seafood and paellas, cash only, house wine good value, great atmosphere, gets very crowded. The same owner runs *Tasca Vaska*, Chimborazo between Clemente Ballén y Aguirre. Same selection. *Caracol Azul*, 9 de Octubre 1918 y Los Ríos. Very good. **Mid-range to expensive**: *Patio Andaluz*, V M Rendón y Bayacá. A variety of Spanish dishes.

Steak houses   There are many *parrilladas* and *asaderos*, usually open Mon-Fri 1200-1600, 1800-2330, Sat-Sun 0900-0000. **Expensive**: *Parillada Del Ñato*, Estrada 1219. Huge variety and portions. **Mid-range**: *La Selvita*, Av Olmos y Las Brisas, Las Lomas de Urdesa. Good atmosphere and fine panoramic views, also at Calle D y Rosa Borja, Centenario. *Columbus*, Las Lomas 206 off Estrada, Urdesa. Very good quality. *La Vaca Gaucha*, Urbanor Av Principal y Av Las Aguas. Excellent quality, open Tue-Sun until 2330.

Typical   Expensive: *Lo Nuestro*, Estrada 9-03 e Higueras, Urdesa. Colonial décor, great seafood platters. **Mid-range**: *Artur's Café*, Numa Pompilio Llona 127, Las Peñas. Wonderful atmosphere and view over the river, live music, local snacks and meals, popular. *El Manantial*, Estrada y Las Monjas, Urdesa. Seafood specialties, good. *La Pepa de Oro*, at *Grand Hotel Guayaquil*. Good variety and quality, pleasant atmosphere. Open 24 hrs. **Mid-range to cheap**: *Café Jambelí*, in *Rizzo Hotel* for coastal dishes and seafood. *La Canoa* in *Hotel Continental* (see above), mid-range, and in *Mall del Sol*, cheap. Open 24 hrs, for traditional dishes rarely found these days, with different specials during the week. *Salón Melba*, Córdova 720 y Junín. Old fashioned eating house/coffee shop. **Cheap**: *Mama Lu*, Av Francisco Orellana y Albeto Borges. Manabí specialties, set meals (seriously cheap) and à la carte, good value. Open 0900-2200. *Pique Y Pase*, Lascano 16-17 y Carchi. Popular with students, lively. Open daily, all day. *Rey del Pescado Frito*, Boyacá y Junín, Malecón 2000 and Av Pareja, Alborada. Good quality. Open daily, all day.

Vegetarian   You can usually get **seriously** cheap set lunches and **cheap** à la carte. *Maranatá I*, Chile y Cuenca, and *II*, Quisquis y Rumichaca. *Super Nutrión I*, Chimborazo y 10 de Agosto, and *II* Chimborazo y Letamendi. *Girasol*, Chile y Colón. *Renacer*, G Avilés y Sucre. *Hare Krishna*, 1 de Mayo y 6 de Marzo near Plaza Centenario. Good food, pleasant atmosphere. Mon-Sat 1200-1800. *Salud Solar*, Pedro Moncayo y Luque. *Ollantay*, Tungurahua 508 y 9 de Octubre. The best choice for vegetarian food.

Fast food   The shopping malls of *Riocentro Los Ceibos*, *Mall del Sol* and *Riocentro Entrerios* have the usual chains of *Kentucky Fried Chicken*, *Pollo Tropical*, *Burger King*, *Pizza Hut*, *Taco Bell*, *Miami Subs* and *Dunkin' Donuts*, plus other local chains serving typical Cajun, Chinese, sushi, sandwiches, yoghurt and pastries.

Snacks   There are many places selling all sorts of snacks. Try *pan de yuca*, *torta de choclo*, or *empanadas*, but beware of eating at street stalls. Excellent sandwiches at

Submarine, 9 Octubre y Chile. *Bopán*, Estrada y Las Monjas, Urdesa and Policentro and Etreríos shopping centres. Excellent sandwiches and local snacks, salads, coffee, breakfast starting 0700 at Urdesa. Cheap. *Uni Deli* downstairs in the Unicentro, Aguirre y Chimborazo. Good bakery, salami and cheese. Mid-range prices. Open 1000-1900. *Yogurt Persa*, P Carbo y 10 de Agosto and many other locations. Cheap breakfast, pan the yuca. *La Chivería*, Circunvalación y Ficus for good yoghurt and *pan de yuca*. *La Selecta*, Estrada y Laureles. Good sandwiches, coffee, baked goods. Cheap. *Pasteles & Compañía*, LKuque y Pichincha nad Policentro. A variety of sandwiches and baked goods. Mid-range prices. Open 0900-2000. **Coffee**: great coffee served hot, cold, frozen in milkshakes or ices in the foodhalls of *Riocentro Los Ceibos*, *Riocentro Samborondón*. **Ice-cream**: *Top Cream*, *Pingüino*, *Baskin Robins*. Many outlets throughout the city, open 0900-2000.

The **Kennedy Mall** is Guayaquil's main centre for upmarket nightlife, with an ample selection of bars and discos. Prices vary from mid-range to expensive.

Bars & nightclubs

Bars In Urdesa are: *Fuente Alemana Peña Bar*, Estrada y Jiguas; *International Pool*, Estrada y Las Monjas, with pool tables. *Café del Sol*, Av Estrada. Bar and restaurant, nice atmosphere, older crowd. Expensive.

Discos Most discos charge a cover of around US$5-9 and drinks are expensive. There are discos, bars and casinos in most of the major hotels such as *Oro Verde*, *Unipark, Boulevard*. *Achumachai*, in Albán Borja, bar and disco, older crowd, expensive. *Equs*, Av Estrada, Urdesa, disco and bar, mature crowd, expensive. *Jardín de la Salsa*, Av de la Américas, largest in the city, lively, popular, free Salsa classes. *La Creme*, Albán Borja, young crowd, expensive. *TV Bar*, Av Rolando Pareja in La Garzota, good drinks and music, young crowd, moderate prices. There are several others.

The **Centro Cívico**, heading south, provides an excellent theatre/concert facility and is home to the Guayaquil Symphony Orchestra which gives free concerts throughout the year. The **Teatro Centro de Arte** on the road out to the coast is another first class theatre complex, with a wide variety of presentations. The city is also well provided with museums, art galleries and cinemas, details of which are in *El Universo* or *El Telégrafo*. Cinemas are at the main shopping centres and cost around US$3.

Entertainment

The foundation of Guayaquil (actually its relocation from a previous site), known as *Fiestas julianas*, is celebrated on **24-25 Jul**, and the city's independence on **9-12 Oct**. Both holidays are lively and there are many public events; cultural happenings are prolonged throughout Oct. Other civic and religious holidays are the same as the rest of the country (see Festivals, page 445). During Easter there is an important procession of Cristo del Consuelo.

Festivals

There are lots of shopping malls. *Centro Comercial Malecón 2000* is the city's newest, at the south end of the Malecón. *Mall del Sol* is near the airport on Av Constitución y Juan Tanca Marengo and is the largest mall in the country. Other malls are: *Riocentro Los Ceibos*, on the coast road beyond Los Ceibos; *Unicentro*, Aguirre y Chile; *Policentro* and *Plaza Quil*, both on Av San Jorge, Kennedy Norte; *Albán Borja*, Av Arosemena Km 2.7; *Garzocentro 2000*, La Garzota, Av R Pareja; *La Rotonda*, entrance to La Garzota; *Plaza Mayor*, La Alborada, Av R Pareja and, nearby, *Albocentro*; *Riocentro*, Av Samborondón, across the river. There are several others.

Shopping

Throughout the city are very cheap, 'dump' stores selling below-market-price clothing. You can find great bargains, but you can also be badly cheated

The *Bahía*, a huge bazaar area on either side of Olmedo from Villamil to Chile, by the south end of el Malecón, is still the most popular place for electrical appliances, clothing and shoes. It was traditionally where contraband was sold from boats which put into the bay and is one of the city's oldest market places. It has been cleaned up a bit in recent years but you must still watch your valuables and be prepared to bargain.

Guayaquil & Southern Pacific

Books *Librería Científica*, Luque 223 y Chile and Plaza Triángulo on Av Estrada in Urdesa. English books, field guides to flora and fauna, travel in general. *El Librero*, in the Ríocentro, has English books. *Sagitario*, at Mall del Sol. Excellent bookstore, has English books. *Nuevos Horizontes*, 6 de Marzo 924, book exchange. *Selecciones*, at Av 9 de Octubre 830 and in *Albán Borja Mall*, expensive novels and lots of magazines in English.

Camping equipment Camping gas is available from *Casa Maspons*, Ballén 517 y Boyacá. *Marathon*, 9 de Octubre y Escobedo, or in many shopping centres, outdoor clothing and boots. *Kao Policentro*, fishing, camping and sports gear at good prices.

Handicrafts For the greatest variety try the *Mercado Artesanal* between Loja y Montalvo and Córdova y Chimborazo, almost a whole block of permanent stalls, with good prices. There's a good variety of *artesanías* in the *Albán Borja Mall* at *El Telar*, which is expensive but of superb quality, especially ceramics, jewellery and embroidery; and *Ramayana* for reasonably priced ceramics. Also several craft shops at the south end of the *Malecón 2000*. The *Mall del Sol* has more than 20 crafts shops in the Plaza de Integración section. *Cerámica Vega*, VE Estrada 1200 y Laureles, Urdesa, for brightly-painted Cuenca ceramics. *La Casa de Mimbre*, Eloy Alfaro 1018 y Brasil. A rough area but a fascinating collection of wicker baskets, furniture, hammocks and other bits and pieces at good prices. *Centro de Artesanías Montecristi*, Juan Tanca Marengo Km 0.5. For straw and wicker goods and furniture. *Manos* Cedros 305 y Primera, Urdesa. Closes until 1530 for lunch. Otavalo Indians sell their crafts along Chile between 9 Octubre y Vélez.

Photography Film deteriorates more quickly in the hot climate, always check the expiry date. Photos can be developed reliably at *Rapi-Color*, Boyacá 1418 y Luque, or *Photo Market*, VE Estrada 726 y Guayacanes, Urdesa, prints and slides. There are Kodak stands in most supermarkets which offer a reasonable service. Camera repairs at *Cinefoto*, Luque 314 y Chimborazo, English spoken. Cheap film and instant ID photos from *Discount New York* in *Albán Borja*.

Sport There are numerous sports clubs for golf, tennis, sailing and swimming (pool at Malecón Simón Bolívar 116). The horse racetrack of El Buijo is set in lovely surroundings some 5 km outside the city. There are 2 football stadiums and the enclosed Coliseo Cerrado for boxing, basketball and other sports. There is an ice-skating rink, *Zona Fría*, at Km 2.5 on the autopista La Puntilla-Samborondón.

Tour operators A 3-hr city tour costs about US$14 per person in a group or US$21 per person for a private tour. Many operators run regional tours to the beaches and whale-watching tours in season (Jun-Sep). A number of the agencies listed operate Galápagos cruises and also have offices in Quito. There are many travel agencies for airline bookings, at the Malecón 2000 and in the large shopping centres.

Canodros, Urb Santa Leonor, Mz 5, local 10, T2285711, F2287651, www.canodros.com Runs luxury Galápagos cruises and also operates the Kapawi Ecological Reserve in the southern Oriente (see page 384). *Cayo's Tour*, Gen Córdova 630 y Solano, p 1, T/F2301772, www.puertocayo.com Whale-watching tours in the Puerto Cayo area, tours to all regions of Ecuador. *Centro Viajero*, Baquerizo Moreno 1119 y 9 de Octubre, No 805, T2562565, F2565550, centrovi@telconet.net Custom-designed tours to all regions, travel information and bookings, car and driver service, well informed about good value options for Galápagos, English spoken, very friendly, open daily. Highly recommended. *Ecoventura*, Av Francisco de Orellana 222, Mz 12, Solar 22, Kennedy Norte, T2283182, F2283148, www.ecoventura.com Excellent high-end Galápagos tours. *Ecuadorian Tours*, 9 Octubre 1900 y Esmeraldas, T2286900, F2280851, www.ecuadoriantoursgye.com.ec Sells land tours in all regions and Galápagos cruises. Amex representative. *Galasam*, Edificio Gran Pasaje, 9 Octubre 424, No 1108, T2304488, F2311485, www.galapagos-islands.com Has a large fleet of boats in different categories for Galápagos cruises, city tours, tours to reserves near Guayaquil, diving trips, also run highland and jungle tours. *Kleintours*, Av Alcívar, Mz 410, Solar 11, Kennedy Norte, T2681700, F2681705, www.kleintours.com Runs land and Galápagos tours. *La Moneda*, Av de las Américas 809 y C 2, and P Icaza 115 y Pichincha, T2690900, F2690911, www.lamoneda.com.ec City and coastal tours, whale-watching, tours in other areas of Ecuador. *Macchiavello Tours*, Antepara 802-A y 9 Octubre, T2286079. Very good whale and dolphin watching tours, for more details, see Tour operators in Salinas. *Metropolitan Touring*, Antepara 915 y 9 de Octubre and at *Hotel Hilton Colón*, T2320300, F2323050, metrogye@ipse.net, www.metropolitan-touring.com High-end land tours and Galápagos cruises. *Pescatours*, T2443365, fishing tours, see Tour operators in Salinas.

Car hire There are several car hire firms in booths outside the national terminal of the airport. *Avis*, T2287906 (airport), T2692884 (at *Hotel Hilton Colón*). *Budget*, T2288510 (airport), T2328571 (by *Hotel Oro Verde*).*Expo*, T228246/ (airport). *Localiza* T2011462 (airport). For rental prices and procedures see Car hire, page 56.

Transport

Air Airport facilities: there's an information desk with erratic hours. *Wander Cambio* is open 7 days a week, 0900-1400; also several bank ATMs. There's a modern cafeteria (open 24 hrs) and a post office. Note that to get to the baggage claim area you must leave the airport and re-enter further down the building. Show your boarding pass to enter and baggage ticket to leave.

Air services: To **Quito**, US$60 one way, *TAME* has service throughout the day, *Icaro*, *Austro Aéreo* and *Aerogal* have fewer flights. *TAME* also fies to **Cuenca**, US$40, **Loja**, US$36, **Machala**, US$32 and **Galápagos** (see page 406). *Icaro* also flies to Loja and Cuenca and *Austro Aéreo* to Cuenca. There are commuter flights in small 5-17 seater planes from the Terminal de Avionetas on the city side of the international airport: *Cedta* to Machala, or *AECA* charters to Bahía de Caráquez, Manta, Portoviejo and Pedernales (reported unreliable). When passing through Guayaquil by air, do not put valuables into backpacks checked into the hold as things sometimes go missing.

Road There is a 3¼-km bridge (Puente de la Unidad Nacional) in 2 sections across the rivers Daule and Babahoyo to Durán. Several paved roads run from there, connecting Guayaquil with the rest of the county. The most direct route to the highlands goes via El Triunfo, Bucay (also known as Cumandá and as General Elizalde) and Pallatanga to connect with the Panamericana at Cajabamba, near Riobamba (see page 225). Also from Durán main roads go to Babahoyo, Quevedo and Santo Domingo (the most frequently used route to Quito), to Cuenca either via La Troncal and Zhud or via Puerto Inca, Cajas and Molleturo, and to the southern lowlands by Machala, connecting to Loja. An important road, the Vía a la Costa, goes southwest from Guayaquil to the Santa Elena Peninsula and, at the town of Santa Elena, connects with the coastal road running north all the way to Mataje on the Colombian border. Another important road goes north towards Daule, then northwest to Jipijapa and Portoviejo.

Bus Several companies to/from **Quito**, 8 hrs, around US$9, up to US$13 for *Rey Tours* non-stop, a/c service (office in *Gran Hotel*). To **Cuenca**, via Zhud, 5 hrs, via Molleturo and Cajas, 3½ hrs, US$7 either route. To **Riobamba**, 5 hrs, US$3.60. To **Santo Domingo de los Colorados**, 5 hrs, US$5. To **Manta**, 3 hrs, US$4.20 ejecutivo service, US$3 regular service. To **Esmeraldas**, 8 hrs, US$8. To **Atacames**, 8 hrs, US$8.50. To **Portoviejo**, 3½ hrs, US$3-4.20. To **Jipijapa**, 2½ hrs, US$2, change here for Puerto López. To **Bahía de Caráquez**, 6 hrs, US$6 ejecutivo, US$4.50 regular. To **Ambato**, 6½ hrs, US$4.80. Frequent buses to **Playas**, 2 hrs, US$1.90. To **Salinas**, 2½ hrs, US$2.70. To **Santa Elena** 2¼ hrs, US$2.70; change here for Puerto López. To **Olón**, also for Montañita, *CLP* at 0500, 1300, 1630, 3½ hrs, US$4.20. To **Machala** 3 hrs, US$3. For the **Peruvian border**, to **Huaquillas**, direct, US$4.40, 4½ hrs; via Machala, 6 hrs.

Directory **Airline offices** *TAME*, 9 de Octubre 424, edif Gran Pasaje, T2692500. *Icaro*, Av Francisco de Orellana, edif Wall Trade Centre, T2294265. *Aerogal*, at the airport, T2289313. *Austro Aéreo*, at the airport, T2284048. *Aerolitoral/Cedta*, at the airport, T2287481. *AECA*, Av de la Américas, T2286267. *Aero Continente*, Boyacá 1012 y P Icaza, T2302900 (for Guayaquil-Lima and flights within Perú). *American Airlines*, Gen Córdova y Av 9 de Octubre, edif San Francisco, 20th Floor, T2564111. *Continental*, 9 de Octubre 100 y Malecón, T2567241, F2567249. *Copa*, Circunvalación Sur 631 A y Ficus, Urdesa, T2888127 *Iberia*, Av 9 de Octubre 101 y Malecón, T2320664. *KLM*, at the airport, T2282713. *TACA*, 9 de Octubre y Malecón, edif Banco de la Previsora, T2562950.

Banks *Banco del Pacífico*, Icaza 200, p 4. TCs and ATM for MasterCard. *American Express*, *Ecuadorian Tours*, 9 de Octubre 1900 y Esmeraldas. Replaces lost Amex TCs and sells TCs to Amex card holders, but does not exchange TCs or sell them for cash. Open Mon-Fri 0900-1300, 1400-1800. *Banco de Guayaquil*, Pichincha y P Ycaza, Visa ATM. TCs and Mastercard advances at head office at P Carbo y 9 de Octubre, edif San Francisco 300, 7th Floor. There are few **Casas de Cambio** following dollarization: *Cambiosa*, 9 de Octubre y Pichincha; *Wander Cambios* at the airport (see Transport above). Try *Hotel Oro Verde* and similar places for TCs, but service may be only for guests.

Communications **Internet**: There are many cyber cafés in the centre and suburbs, many concentrated in shopping malls (see above). Also at the Youth hostel (see Sleeping above). Prices around US$0.50 per hr for internet access, U$0.50 per min for Net to Phone. **Post/Telephone**: *Pacifictel*, the telephone company, and the central post office are in the same block at Pedro Carbo y Aguirre. There are coin-operated phones and debit card cellular phones throughout the city. There are branch post offices in Urdesa, Estrada y Las Lomas; first floor of Policentro; at the airport and bus terminal. The major hotels also sell stamps. Many courier services for reliable delivery of papers and packages: *DHL*, one branch at Pichincha y Luque, T2287044, is recommended for international service; *Servientrega*, offices throughout the city, for deliveries within Ecuador.

Consulates *Argentina*, Aguirre 104 y Malecón, T2323574. *Austria*, 9 de Octubre 1312 y Quito, No 1, T2282303. *Belgium*, Lizardo García 301 y Vélez, T2364429. *Bolivia*, Cedros 400 y la 5ta, Urdesa, T2889955. *Brazil*, Av San Jorge 312 y Calle 3 Este, Nueva Kennedy, T2293046. *Canada*, Córdova 808 y VM Rendón, edif Torre de la Merced, p 21, T2563580. *Colombia*, 9 de Octubre y Córdova, edif San Francisco, p 2, T2568753. *Denmark*, Gen Córdova 604 y Mendiburo, p 3, T2308020. *France*, José Mascote 909 y Hurtado, T2294334. *Germany*, Av Carlos Julio Arosemena Km 2, Ed Berlín, T2200500. *Italy*, Baquerizo Moreno 1120, T2312523. *Netherlands*, P Ycaza 454 y Baquerizo Moreno, edif *ABN-AMRO Bank*, T2563857. *Panama*, Aguirre 509, T2512158. *Peru*, 9 de Octubre 411 y Chile, p 6, T2322738. *Spain*, Urdesa calle Circunvalación, Solar 118 y Calle Unica, T2881691. *Sweden*, Km 6.5 vía a Daule, T2254111. *Switzerland*, 9 de Octubre 2105, T2453607. *UK*, Gen Córdova 623 y Padre Solano, T2560400. *USA*, 9 de Octubre 1571 y García Moreno, T2323570. *Venezuela*, Chile 329 y Aguirre, T2326566.

Laundry *Sistematic*, F Segura y Av Quito, or C 6a y Las Lomas, Urdesa. *Martinizing*, Sucre 517 y Boyacá, and in CC La Gazota, for dry cleaning, many other outlets, but don't rely on their 1-hr service.

Medical services **Doctors**: *Dr Angel Serrano Sáenz*, Boyacá 821 y Junín, T2301373. English speaking. *Clínica Santa Marianita*, Boyacá 1915 entre Colón y Av Olmedo, T2322500. Some doctors speak English. *Dr James Peterson*, C Acacias 608 y Av Las Monjas, Urdesa, T2888718, T09-9770670 (mob). Homeopath and chiropractor, speaks English. **Hospitals:** the main hospital used by the foreign community is the *Clínica Kennedy*, Av San Jorge y la 9na, T2289666. Also has a branch in Ciudadela La Alborada XII Mz-1227. Consulting rooms of almost every kind of specialist doctor and diagnostic laboratory (Dr Roberto Morla speaks German, T2293470). Very competent

Cocoa

◀◀

In the late 18th century the Guayas basin, with its fertile soils, hot climate, abundant rainfall and easy river transport, became the most important area in the world for the production and export of cacao, a plant native to the Americas. At the time of independence cacao was the new Republic's only major export. The unhealthy coastal climate, especially notorious for yellow fever, and political instability hindered expansion of plantations until the 1870s. Meanwhile the demand for cacao was small until new processing techniques in Europe and the US in the mid-19th century made chocolate cheaper and more widely available. As it ceased to be an expensive luxury in Europe and the USA and world consumption multiplied eightfold between 1894 and 1924, cocoa plantations expanded rapidly around the Río Guayas estuary. Grown on large plantations, cocoa made fortunes for a new coastal élite, who backed the Radical Liberal Party which seized power in 1895. By 1900 over 60% of government income came from taxes on cocoa exports. Great development schemes were begun, building roads, ports and railway lines, the most important of

which, between Guayaquil and Quito, was completed in 1908.

Although Ecuador maintained its lead in cocoa production until the outbreak of the First World War, the planters were unprepared for a series of setbacks at the end of the war. Competition from African plantations in the British colonies hit the world cocoa price while witch broom disease swept through the plantations. Large areas of land were abandoned, most of the grand building projects were left incomplete and the Guayaquil élite was driven from power by a group of young army officers in the 1925 Revolution.

Today, cacao continues to be produced and exported on a more modest scale. The Ecuadorian variety is prized for its aroma and a small amount is a necessary ingredient in the world's finest chocolates. Meanwhile, the boom and bust cycle of Ecuadorean export agriculture continues. Shrimp were the great miracle of the 1980s and 90s, until mancha blanca (white spot disease) wiped out most producers. At the start of the 21st century the flower plantations around Cayambe in the northern highlands seem destined for endless growth, until.

emergency department. Also reliable are: *Clínica Alcívar*, Coronel 2301 y Azuay, T2580030; *Clínica Guayaquil*, Padre Aguirre 401 y General Córdova, T2563555 (Dr Roberto Gilbert speaks English and German).

Places of worship *Anglican-Episcopalian Church*, Calle D entre Bogotá y A Fuentes, T2443050. Centro Cristiano de Guayaquil, Pastor John Jerry Smith, Av Juan Tanca Marengo, Km 3, T2271423. *Baptist Church*, Ximena 421, T2302137. *Watch Tower Bible and Tract Society*, Capitán Zaera 319 y Bolívia, T2448764. Many other sects are represented. *Latter Day Saints*, C 9 y C H, Kennedy, T2289570.

Shipping agents Isaac Alvia, Elizalde # 119 y Pichincha, Oficina 2-4, T2517215, isaacalviao@andinanet.net Speaks English, helpful. Luis Arteaga, Aguirre 324 y Chile, T2533592/670, F2533445. Fast, variable prices, generally expensive. Fees for car entry services start at US$150.

Useful addresses Immigration: Av Río Daule, near the bus terminal, T2297010. For visa extensions.

Guayaquil & Southern Pacific

South to Peru

*The Guayaquil-
Machala road has
been among the worst
in the country for bus
holdups: never travel
this route at night*

From Durán, across the river from Guayaquil, one road heads south to Puerto Inca, Naranjal and on to Machala, centre of Ecuador's most important banana-producing region, and a useful stopover before heading on to Huaquillas at the Peruvian frontier. At Puerto Inca, one road goes inland to La Troncal, then climbs to Zhud and the Panamericana near El Tambo, a useful route to Ingapirca and on to Cuenca. Just south of Puerto Inca another road goes southeast and climbs to Molleturo, goes through Parque Nacional Cajas and on to Cuenca. This is the fastest route between Guayaquil and Cuenca. From Machala, roads also run through Pasaje and Girón to Cuenca (188 km), and via Arenillas to Loja (216 km).

Machala

*Phone code: 07
Colour map 6, grid B2
Population: 200,000*

The capital of the province of El Oro, this booming agricultural city is the centre of a major banana producing and exporting region with an annual international banana fair in September. It is also an important shrimp-producing area. The city is not particularly attractive, being somewhat dirty and oppressively hot, but it is prosperous and a good stopping point on the way to Peru.

The main square, Parque Juan Montalvo, is spacious and has an attractive church. Hotels are fairly central and the city centre is compact. There aren't many sights in Machala but excursions can be made to Puerto Bolívar and mangrove islands in the Archipiélago de Jambelí. Inland from Machala are the seldom visited but beautiful uplands of El Oro and along a road to Loja is the Puyango petrified forest. (See Around Machala below for all these sites.)

Tourist information **Ministerio de Turismo**, 9 de Octubre entre 9 de Mayo y Montalvo, p 1, T/F932106, infotour@telconet.net Spanish only, open Mon-Fri 0830-1700.

Sleeping
■ *on map*
*Price codes:
see inside front cover*

L *Oro Verde*, Circunvalación Norte in Urbanización Unioro, T933140, F933150, www.oroverdehotels.com Includes breakfast, 2 restaurants, nice pool (US$6 for non-residents), beautiful gardens, tennis, casino, full luxury. Best in town. **B** *Oro Hotel*, Sucre y Juan Montalvo, T930032, F933751, orohotel@oro.satnet.net Pricey restaurant and cheaper café downstairs, a/c, parking, refurbished and good, helpful, rooms to street are noisy. Recommended. **B** *Centro Hotel*, Sucre y Guayas, T931640, F935110.

Guayaquil & Southern Pacific

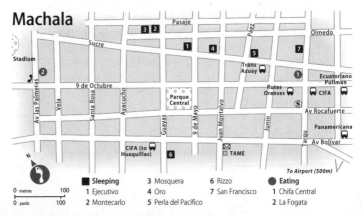

Machala

■ Sleeping	3 Mosquera	6 Rizzo	● Eating
1 Ejecutivo	4 Oro	7 San Francisco	1 Chifa Central
2 Montecarlo	5 Perla del Pacífico		2 La Fogata

Cafeteria, a/c, parking, modern, new in 2001. **B** *Montecarlo*, Guayas y Olmedo, T931901, F933104. Restaurant, a/c, modern. **C** *Ejecutivo*, Sucre y 9 de Mayo, T923162, F933992. Cafeteria, a/c, parking, modern and good. **C** *Perla del Pacífico*, Sucre 603 y Páez, T930915, F937358. Restaurant, a/c, parking, run down. **C** *Rizzo*, Guayas y Bolívar, T921906, F921502. Restaurant, a/c, pool, suites available, casino, noisy disco, poor beds and service. **C-D** *Mosquera*, Olmedo entre Guayas y Ayacucho, T931752, F930390. Restaurant, cold water, a/c, cheaper with fan, OK. **C-D** *San Francisco*, Tarqui entre Sucre y Olmedo, T922395. Restaurant, a/c, cheaper with fan, parking, OK. **D** *Araujo*, 9 de Mayo y Boyacá, T931464. A/c, parking, some rooms are small, good value but noisy disco next door. **D** *Julio César*, 9 de Mayo 1319 entre Pasaje y Boyacá, T937978, F923485. Fan, OK. **D** *San Miguel*, 9 de Mayo y Sucre, by market, T935488. Cold water, a/c, cheaper with fan, fridge, good value and quality. **F** *Pesántez*, 9 de Mayo y Pasaje, T920154, Private bath, cold water, fan, basic but clean.

Cafetería San Francisco, Sucre block 6. Good, filling breakfast. *200 Millas*, 9 de Octubre entre Santa Rosa y Vela. Seafood specialties. *Don Angelo*, 9 de Mayo just off the main plaza. Open 24 hrs, good elaborate set meals and à la carte, also good for breakfast, cheap. *Copa Cabana*, on the main plaza. Good clean snack bar. *Chifa Central*, Tarqui y 9 de Octubre. Good Chinese. *Chifa Gran Oriental*, 9 de Octubre entre Guayas y Ayacucho. Good food and service. *Mesón Hispano*, Av Las Palmeras y Sucre. Very good grill, attentive service. *Palacio Real*, 9 de Octubre y Ayacucho. Good set meal. *Aquí es Correita*, Av Arízaga y 9 de Mayo. Popular for seafood, closed Sun. *La Fogata*, Av Las Palmeras near the telephone office, for good chicken.

Eating
● *on map, page 292*
The best food is found in the better hotels

Ice-cream *Zanzibar*, Rocafuerte y Tarqui. *Pingüino*, Juan Montalvo y Rocafuerte. *Tocayo*, Juan Montalvo y Bolívar.

Cinema *Unioro*, Ubanización Unioro. A/c, cushioned seats and good sound, admission US$2. **Discos** Some of the better ones include: *La Contradition*, Av las Palmeras y Callejón 12, good atmosphere. *La Ego*, Tarqui y Rocafuerte, popular with local youth. *Twister Club*, Av Paquisha Km ½, good music and atmosphere, older crowd.

Entertainment & nightlife

Supermarkets *Frigocentro*, Olmedo y Ayacucho. *Mi Comisiarato*, Unioro Shopping Centre, Circunvalación Norte.

Shopping

Swimming A development just outside Machala on the Pasaje road has 2 large outdoor swimming pools.

Sport

Orotour, Bolívar 924 y Guayas, T931557. *Glendatur*, Bolívar 912 y Guayas, T937670.

Tour operators

Air The airport is at the south end of the city, less than 1 km from the centre of town. *TAME*, Juan Montalvo y Bolívar, T930139. To **Guayaquil**, US$42, and **Quito**, US$60, Mon and Fri. *CEDTA*, at the airport, T932802. To **Guayaquil**, Tue and Thu, US$42.

Transport

Bus Most of the bus company offices are also quite central, but there is no *terminal terrestre*. Do not take night buses into or out of Machala as they are not safe. Hold-ups are especially frequent on the route Guayaquil-Machala.
    To **Quito**, with *Occidental* (Buenavista entre Sucre y Olmedo), 10 hrs, US$7, 8 daily; and with *Panamericana* (Colón y Bolívar), 7 daily, luxury service, 10 hrs, US$9. To **Guayaquil**, 3 hrs, US$3, hourly with *Ecuatoriano Pullman* (Colón y 9 de Octubre), *CIFA* (9 de Octubre y Tarqui) and *Rutas Orenses* (9 de Octubre y Tarqui), see also Vans and taxis below. To **Loja**, 5 hrs, US$5. with *Transportes Loja* (Tarqui y Bolívar). There are 3 different routes from Machala to Loja, with bus service along all of them; ask for the one you need. They are, from north to south: via Piñas, and Zaruma (see below) partly

For the route Machala-Cuenca, see page 258 For Machala-Loja, see Uplands of El Oro below

unpaved and rough but very scenic; via Balsas, fully paved and also scenic; and via Arenillas and Alamor, for Puyango petrified forest. To **Cuenca**, every 30 mins with *Trans Azuay* (Sucre y Junín), 3½ hrs, US$3.60. To **Huaquillas**, with *CIFA* (Bolívar y Guayas) and *Ecuatoriano Pullman* (Colón y 9 de Octubre), direct, 1 hr, US$1.50, every 30 mins; via Arenillas and Santa Rosa, 2 hrs, every 10 mins. There are 2 passport checks on this route. To **Piura**, in Peru, with *Transportes Loja* (Tarqui y Bolívar), daily at 1230, US$6.30, 7 hrs; from Piura to Machala at 2230. **Vans and taxis**: to Guayaquil, *Orotaxis* run a scheduled taxi service between the *Hotel Rizzo*, Machala, and *Hotel Rizzo*, Guayaquil, every hr, 0600-2000, US$8 per person, T934332. A/c vans also run hourly to Guayaquil from Guayas y Pichincha, comfortable good service, US$8.

Directory **Banks** *Banco del Austro*, Rocafuerte y Guayas, for Visa. *Banco de Guayaquil*, Rocafuerte y Guayas, for Visa, Mastercard and TCs. *Banco del Pacífico*, Rocafuerte y Junín. TCs. *Banco de Machala*, Rocafuerte y 9 de Mayo, Visa ATM and cash advance, friendly and efficient. **Communications** Internet: US$0.80-1.20 per hr; a couple on 9 de Octubre, also on C Sucre. Post: Bolívar y Montalvo. **Telephone**: *Pacifictel*, Av las Palmeras near the stadium. **Consulates** *Peruvian Consulate*, northwest corner of Colón y Bolívar, 1st floor, T930680.

Around Machala

Puerto Bolívar Built on the Canal de Santa Rosa among mangroves, and 9 km west of Machala, this is a major export outlet for over two million tonnes of bananas annually, 85% of the country's total. There is a pleasant waterfront and from the old pier a motorized canoe service crosses to the beaches of **Jambelí** on the far side of the mangrove islands which shelter Puerto Bolívar from the Pacific. Three daily canoes make the return trip to Jambelí, US$2 per person. The beaches of Jambelí are safe and long with straw beach umbrellas for shade (the sun is fierce), but unfortunately dirty and the accommodation here is poor.

The Archipiélago de Jambelí is a maze of islands and channels just offshore, stretching south between Puerto Bolívar and the Peruvian border. These mangrove islands are rich in birdlife (and insects for them to feed on, take repellent), the water is very clear and you may also see fish and reefs. Boats can be rented for excursions here, to explore the narrow channels near Puerto Bolívar and go to Isla del Amor, a few minutes away, or further afield to Isla Santa Clara (1½ hours) or Costa Rica (two hours). Take your passport as a military post has to be crossed. Canoe hire to Costa Rica for the day is about US$70 for 15 people. It's cheaper to arrange a trip from Huaquillas.

Sleeping and eating Puerto Bolívar: B *Solar del Puerto*, Córdova y Rocafuerte, T928793, solarpto@ecua.net.ec Hot water, a/c, **C** with fan, restaurant, nice, best in town. **C** *Acosta*, Municipalidad y Córdova, T928443. Private bath, cold water, a/c, cheaper with fan, disco next door, overpriced. **E** *Pacífico*, Gen Páez 244 y Córdova, T09-9299628 (mob). Cheaper with shared bath, basic. Lots of seafood kiosks between the old and new piers. Food here is better and cheaper than in Machala. *Acuario*, Rocafuerte 120, half block from the Malecón. Good food, cheap, quieter than at the Malecón, English spoken, good source of information. Recommended. *Waikiki*, good food, pleasant atmosphere. *Pepe's*, good. *El Portezuela*, Rocafuerte y Córdova.

Jambelí: water supply poor and town dirty. **E** *Casa de la Luna*, north end of beach. Best of a poor lot. **E** *María Sol*, T937461. No mosquito nets, restaurant, not very clean.

Communications Internet: *Speed@net*, Córdova y Municipalidad, 1 block from the Malecón, Puerto Bolívar.

Some 30 km south on the main road to the Peruvian border lies Santa Rosa, an **Santa Rosa**
agricultural market town. Just by the airstrip at Santa Rosa is a turn-off for
Puerto Jelí, a tiny fishing village 4 km at the road's end, right in the mangroves
on a branch of the main *estero*. Good eating at *Riberas del Pacífico*, *El Chino*, *El
Pez Dorado* and others. Canoe trips can be arranged through the mangroves
with Segundo Oyola (ask for him opposite the dock) to the beach of Las
Casitas, for fishing or clam collecting. Price varies according to group size and
bargaining is recommended. At San José, 8 km from Santa Rosa is Laguna La
Tembladera, a popular lake among fishermen. There is an annual shrimp festival in Santa Rosa, 24-30 August, with a contest for the best *ceviche*.

Sleeping and eating D *Santa Rosa*, 1 block from plaza. Good with a/c, private bath.
Cheap *residencias* on Av Colón. Several *chifas* serve good food.

Uplands of El Oro

Inland from Machala is a tranquil corner of Ecuador overlooked by most travel- *A great area in which*
lers. A transition zone between the great coastal plain and the Andes, it has forests *to get off the beaten*
(live and petrified), waterfalls, charming colonial cities, gold mines that give the *path*
province its name, good walking, friendly people and a very pleasant climate.

A number of scenic roads cross this green hilly country connecting the lowlands and highlands. From Machala to Loja, the most direct road starts near
Santa Rosa and goes through Balsas. A second road branches off the Balsas
road, goes through Piñas and Zaruma from where an unpaved road rejoins
the Balsas route higher up in the highlands. Zaruma can also be reached
through a secondary unpaved road from Pasaje, on the Machala-Cuenca
road. A more southerly route starts by **Arenillas**, between Santa Rosa and
Huaquillas, goes near the Bosque Petrificado Puyango (see below), then
climbs to Alamor and Celica (see page 272), from where you can go to
Catacocha and Loja or to the Peruvian border at Macará.

The main Machala-Loja road starts 33 km south of Machala, just south of **Balsas**
Santa Rosa, on the road to Huaquillas. The winding road follows the Río *Phone code: 07*
Santa Rosa southeast, passing several river beaches and a couple of villages. At *Colour map 6,*
Saracay (also known as Zapote), 22 km from the turn-off, a paved road *grid B2*
branches east to Piñas (29 km) and Zaruma (48 km). The main road contin- *Population: 3,000*
ues to climb 13 km to **Balsas**. Just west of town is a lookout with lovely views. *Altitude: 700 m*

Balsas is at the centre of a coffee, cattle and poultry producing area. It is a
pleasant town, with a colourful tiled church, nestling amid green hills. A secondary road goes southwest from Balsas to Marcabelí (**E-F** *Residencial Alexander*, at the park, T956251, private or shared bath, and a couple of places to
eat). Nearby is the La Chorrera river bathing beach. A very poor road continues from Marcabelí to the Arenillas-Puyango road.

Sleeping and eating E-F *Express Hotel*, on the highway, T954211. Private bath, cold
water, clean and friendly. **F** *Café Hotel*, on the highway, T954 128. Private bath, cold
water, clean and friendly. There are several places to eat along the highway. *Don Pepe*,
2 km east of town has good cheap set meals.

After Balsas the road crosses into the province of Loja and climbs steeply to
Chaguarpamba, **Olmedo** (two *residenciales* and some *comedores*) and
Velacruz (78 km from Balsas) where a road goes southwest to Catacocha and
Macará (see page 272). About 16 km ahead is another turn-off, a dirt road

going northwest to Portovelo and Zaruma. From here the road continues 23 km to Catamayo and 34 km from there to Loja.

Zaruma
Phone code: 07
Colour map 6, grid B2
Population: 8,700
Altitude: 1,170 m

Some 100 km southeast from Machala is the lovely colonial town of Zaruma, perched on a hilltop at the heart of a pre-hispanic gold-mining area. It is reached from Machala by paved road via Piñas, by a scenic dirt road off the main Loja-Machala road, or via Pasaje and Paccha on another scenic, dirt road off the Machala-Cuenca road.

Founded in 1549 on the orders of Felipe II to try to control the gold extraction, Zaruma is characterized by steep, twisting streets and painted wooden buildings. The beautiful main plaza is marred by the cement municipality, facing one of Ecuador's loveliest wooden churches. A preservation order now protects the town centre from similar acts of architectural vandalism.

Many of the noticeably white-skinned inhabitants of direct Spanish stock still work as independent gold miners; there are a few industrial companies too. On the outskirts of town you can see large *chancadoras*, primitive rock-crushing operations, where independent miners take their gold-bearing rocks to be crushed then passed through sluices to wash off the mud. It is possible to visit some of the small roadside mining operations and watch the whole process. **Mina del Sexmo**, one of the oldest mines in the area (exploited by the Spanish since 1539 and the natives before that), is an easy walk from the centre (access at the end of Calle El Sexmo). At the entrance to town is **Compañía Bira**, a more technified mine, which can also be seen. Other mines are in Portovelo (see below).

Agricultural production in this area includes coffee (the best in the country according to some), citrus and cattle ranching. *El Cafetal* shop in Zaruma roasts its own for sale and sends weekly shipments to Quito.

The **Museo Municipal**, on the second floor of the Municipio, at the main square, has a small collection of artefacts of local history. ■ *Wed-Sat 0800-1200, 1400-1800, Sun 0800-1200. Free.* There is another museum at Colegio Nacional 26 de Noviembre. The Zaruma area has a number of prehispanic archaeological sites and petroglyphs are also found in this area.

On top of the small hill beyond the market (follow Calle Pichincha) is a public swimming pool, from where there are amazing views over the nearby valleys. For even grander views, walk up **Cerro del Calvario** (follow Calle San Francisco); go early in the morning as it gets very hot.

A worthwhile excursion is to **Orquideario Gálvez**, on the road north to Malvas, 4 km from Zaruma, T964063. They have a collection of orchids and also a tree house to rent (see Sleeping below). It's a pleasant relaxing place, with friendly people. Northeast of Zaruma is **Salvias**, one of the access points to Cerro de Arcos, along the 'Gold Rush Trail', see page 259.

Local festivals include: 12-20 July in honour of the Virgen del Carmen, in addition to the religious celebrations there is an agricultural fair; 10 November-10 December, Mes de la artes, Cultura y Civismo, in honour of the city's foundation and independence, when there are parades and cultural events. Carnival is also very lively.

Sleeping D *Cerro de Oro*, Sucre 40, T/F972505. Modern. Recommended. **D** *Roland*, at entrance to town on road from Portovelo, T972800. Comfortable, lovely views. **D-E** *Colombia*, on main plaza next to municipio, T972173. Cheaper with shared bath, cold water, very basic. **E** *Finca Gálvez*, Santa Marianita, vía a Paccha Km 3 (enquire at Bazar María Alejandra, Sucre 005), T964063. Includes breakfast, meals on request, tree house on a coffee plantation, orchid garden, family run, quiet and friendly, a lovely out-of-the-way spot.

Eating Zaruma specialties often include plantain. Try *tigrillo*, ground plantain fried with eggs, cheese and onions. *Barcelona*, Bolívar by the steps to the church. Varied à la carte and set luches. *Cafetería Uno*, C Sucre. Very good Zaruma specialties, cheap. *Chamizal*, Bolívar y San Francisco and on C Sucre. Variety of à la carte dishes, Chinese food, also set meals. *Mesón de Joselito*, at the entrance to town from Portovelo. Good for seafood. *200 Millas*, Av Honorato Márquez. Seafood. *Sabor Tropical*, C Colón. *Encebollados* (fish with onions and *yuca*). *Veros*, Colón y Pichincha. Local dishes, set meals, breakfast.

Transport Bus companies are along Av Honorato Márquez, some local service goes from C Pichincha near *Banco del Pichincha*. To **Machala**, with *TAC* or *Trans Piñas*, hourly, US$2.45, 3 hrs. To **Piñas**, take a Machala bound bus, US$0.80, 1 hr. To **Guayaquil**, with *TAC*, 5 daily, US$5.20, 6 hrs. To **Quito**, with *TAC*, 4 daily, US$9, 12 hrs. To **Loja**, with *TAC* or *Trans Piñas*, 7 daily, may have to change buses at Portovelo, US$4, 5 hrs. To **Cuenca**, with *TAC* at 0030, *Trans Piñas* at 0315 and *Azuay* at 0730, US$5.40, 6 hrs. Rancheras to **Portovelo**, with *24 de Julio*, every 30 min 0600-1830, US$0.30, 20 mins.

Banks *Banco del Pichincha*, Pichincha y Luis Crespo. *Banco de Machala*, at the main square, Visa ATM. **Communications** Internet: *Zarumanet*, Colón y 10 de Agosto, US$2 per hr, open 0800-2100 but closed at meal times and Sun after 1400. **Telephone**: *Pacifictel*, Pichincha y Luis A Crespo. . **Directory**

About 19 km west of Zaruma, along the road to Machala is Piñas, a pleasant town which conserves just a few of its colonial-era wooden buildings. There are buses along scenic secondary roads to **Paccha**, up in the hills to the north (**E** *Residencial Reina del Cisne*, clean, pleasant), and to **Ayapamba** and many other old gold mining villages. Northwest of Piñas, 20 minutes along the road to Saracay and Machala, is **Buenaventura**, to the north of which lies an important area for bird conservation. Many rare birds have been found in the few remaining tracts of forest, with over 310 bird species recorded in the area. The Jocotoco Foundation (www.jocotoco.org) protects a 300-ha forest in this region. The Piñas area is also rich in orchids. Along the road to Portovelo are several *complejos turísticos* with river beaches. **Museo Rubén Torres**, 8 de Noviembre 25-82, has a private collection of archaeological and historical artiefacts. The owner, a school teacher, is also knowledgeable about orchids. Local tour operator *Contac-tour*, García Moreno entre Loja y Rumiñahui, T/F913312, know the region well and are very helpful.

Piñas
Phone code: 07
Colour map 6,
grid B2
Population: 12,600

Sleeping and eating **D-E** *Dumari*, 8 de Noviembre y Loja, T976118. Cheaper with shared bath, hot water, simple. **F** *Las Orquídeas*, Abdón Calderón y Montalvo, T976355. *Punto del Sabor*, Sucre y Montalvo, by the main park. Good choice of set meals. There are several restaurants along C Angel Salvador Ochoa: *La Brasa*, at the entrance from Machala, good à la carte and set meals; *Parrilladas del Gallo*, grill; *Pizzería Chesco*.

South of Zaruma and in the lower valley of the Río Amarillo, Portovelo is the site of the largest gold mine in the area. It was exploited by French and British companies in the early 1800s, followed by American companies until 1949. The huge gold mine took many hundreds of tonnes of gold out of the country but allegedly never paid any taxes.

Portovelo
Phone code: 07
Colour map 6,
grid B2
Population: 6,600

Portovelo was deemed too hot and unhealthy so the miners' families were moved to the top of the neighbouring hill and the beautiful wooden town of Zaruma. There are numerous tiny chapels scattered across the surrounding hills and, in the times when the mines were functioning, it was fashionable to

Guayaquil & Southern Pacific

take a trip by horse and carriage to these outlying chapels for the Sunday services. In 2002, the mine was being exploited by 'Río Amarillo', once again a large company. Enquire locally about visits.

The **Museo Magner Turner**, run by the grandson of one of the early US geologists, is set inside a mine shaft. It has an interesting, eclectic collection of minerals, historical documents and paraphernalia. ■ *Open daily after 1300. No charge, but contributions are appreciated. T949345. At the old Campamento Americano, in the hills above town.*

There are hot thermal springs at **Aguas Calientes**, 6 km from Portovelo, but no facilities. From Portovelo, the very scenic road to Loja follows the Río Amarillo, then climbs steeply to join the Balsas road on the ridge top west of San Pedro de la Bendita and Catamayo. A nice walk is 5 km on this road to Río Pindo or Río Luís.

Sleeping and eating F *Residencial Mónica*, near the Iglesia de Fátima, Barrio Machala, basic. For eating try *Las Gaviotas* or *Costa Azul*, both in the centre of town.

Transport Rancheras to **Zaruma**, every 30 min 0600-1830, US$0.30, 20 mins. Frequent buses to Piñas and Machala, several daily departures to Loja.

Puyango
This petrified forest is supposedly the most extensive outside Arizona

The **Bosque Petrificado Puyango** is 110 km south of Machala, off the Arenillas-Alamor road. A great number of petrified trees, ferns, fruits and molluscs, 65 to 120 million years old, have been found in this 2,659 ha reserve in the valley of the Río Puyango. A deciduous dry tropical forest at elevations between 270 m and 750 m covers the area. Over 120 species of birds can be seen here, including several endemics. In 2002 the Reserve was administered by the regional municipality of Las Lajas, they have good Spanish-speaking guides who do an interesting tour of a small segment of the reserve. The village of Puyango is 5 km from the Arenillas road; the reserve's information centre and a small museum with interesting fossils is 250 m past the village; the *mirador*, a gazebo at the entrance to the trails, is 1 km beyond. There is no accommodation in the village, camping is permited by the *mirador*, where there are toilets and water, you can also ask around for floor space in town or at the information centre. If not, there is one basic residencial in Las Lajas, 30 minutes towards Arenillas, and several options in in Alamor. ■ *US$5 includes tour. Camping US$5 per person.* For further information, contact the Dirección Provincial de Turismo, Machala T932106.

There are several military checkpoints between Puyango and Machala

Transport Puyango is west of the highway, the turn-off is at the bridge over the Río Puyango, where there is a military control. There are hourly rancheras between Arenillas and Alamor. Buses from **Machala**, with *Transportes Loja* at 0930, 1315 and 2130, US$2.50, 2½ hrs. From **Loja**, with *Transportes Loja* at 0900, 1430 and 1930, US$5, 5 hrs. From **Huaquillas**, with *Transportes Loja* at 0730, US$1.50, 1½ hrs. Returning to **Machala**, buses pass the bridge about 1100, 1330 and 1700, their final destination may not be Machala, so ask. To **Huaquillas**, about 1000.

Huaquillas

Phone code: 07
Colour map 6, grid B1
Population: 40,000

The most commonly used route overland to Peru is via Machala. Many buses from there (see above) go to Huaquillas, the Ecuadorean border town, a commercial centre which is something of a shopping arcade for Peruvians. It has grown into a city with a number of hotels and other services. It is a very hot, bustling place.

Many of the cheaper hotels in Huaquillas are mostly for short-stay customers. **D** *Hernancor*, Primero de Mayo y Hualtaco, T906467. Cafeteria, a/c, best in town. **D** *Vanessa*, 1 de Mayo y Hualtaco, T/F907263. A/c, fridge, parking, OK. **D-E** *Rodey*, Tnte Córdovez y 10 de Agosto, T906581. A/c, cheaper with fan, basic. **E** *Alameda*, Tnte Córdovez y José Mendoza. Private bath, fan, mosquito net, basic. **E** *Internacional*, Machala y 19 de Octubre, T907963. Cheaper with shared bath, fan, small rooms, basic. **E** *San Martín*, Av la República opposite the church, T907083. Private bath, fan, mosquito net, refurbished in 2002. **F** *Guayaquil*, Remigio Gómez 125, T907303. Limited water supply, fan, mosquito net, noisy.

Sleeping
■ *on map*
Price codes:
see inside front cover

Chesito, Av la República y Costa Rica. Across from the police station, large portions, good. There are several other cheap and simple places to eat. *Chic*, behind *Hotel Guayaquil*. Very cheap set meal US$1. *Chifa China Norte*, Santa Rosa y Tnte Córdovez. Chinese. *Flamingo*, Tnte Córdovez y 10 de Agosto. *Mini*, opposite Transportes Loja. Good set lunch, cheap.

Eating

Bus To **Machala**, with *CIFA* (Santa Rosa y Machala) and *Ecuatoriano Pullman* (Av la República y 19 de Octubre), direct, 1 hr, US$1.50, every hr from 0400-2000; via Arenillas and Santa Rosa, 2 hrs, every 10 mins. To **Quito**, with *Occidental* (Remigio Gómez 129 y Portovelo), every 2 hrs, 12 hrs, US$9; with *Panamericana* (on Remigio Gómez), fancier service, 11½ hrs, 3 daily via Santo Domingo, US$10; 2 daily via **Riobamba** and **Ambato**, 12 hrs, US$9. To **Guayaquil**, frequent service with *CIFA* and *Ecuatoriano Pullman*, about 5 hrs, US$4.05. To **Cuenca**, with *Azuay* or *Sucre* (Cordovez y 10 de Agosto), 8 daily, US$5. If in a hurry to reach Quito or Guayaquil, it might be better to change buses in Machala. To **Cuenca**, several daily, with *Trans Azuay* or *Sucre* (Cordovez y 10 de Agosto), 5 hrs, US$5. To **Loja**, with *Transportes Loja* (Tnte Córdovez y Arenillas) 2 daily, 5 hrs, US$4. To **Tulcán**, for the Colombian border, with *Panamericana*, at 1830, 15 hrs, US$13. The main roads to Guayaquil, Quito, Cuenca and Loja are all paved. To **Piura**, Peru, at 1400 with *Transportes Loja*, 5 hrs, US$5.

Transport
There are checkpoints (transit police, customs and military) along the road north from Huaquillas, so keep your passport to hand

Banks Check on the rate of exchange with travellers leaving Peru. Fair rates are available for soles and dollars cash on both sides of the border, but you will always be offered a low rate when you first enquire. On the Ecuadorean side there is an *Asociación de Cambistas*, whose members wear ID tags, but be cautious nonetheless. Ask around before changing, do your own arithmetic and don't be rushed into any transaction. Especially avoid those changers who chase after you. Be sure to count your change carefully. The money changers (recognized by their black briefcases) are very clever, particularly with calculators, and sometimes dishonest. Watch out for counterfeit US bills and 20 Soles notes. It is difficult to change TCs but try the banks along the main street. **Communications** Internet: several on Av La República, US$1.50 per hr. Post: Av la República. **Telephone:** *Pacifictel* Av la República, opposite post office.

Directory

Guayaquil & Southern Pacific

Huaquillas

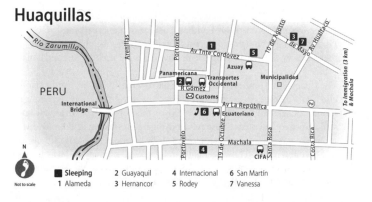

■ **Sleeping**
1 Alameda
2 Guayaquil
3 Hernancor
4 Internacional
5 Rodey
6 San Martín
7 Vanessa

Not to scale

Frontier with Peru

Leaving or arriving in Ecuador The border runs along the Río Zarumilla and is crossed by the international bridge at the western end of Avenida La República. It is a shortish walk from the bus terminals which are just off the main street. Tricycle taxis are available to help with luggage (keep an eye on your belongings). Right near the bridge is a tourist information office.

At the border **Ecuadorean immigration** Passports are stamped 3 km north of town along the road to Machala. There is no urban transport; inter-city buses charge US$0.15 from Huaquillas, taxis US$1. The border is open 24 hours. Allow up to one to two hours to complete formalities, although it can sometimes be much quicker. To cross to Peru, walk along the main street in Huaquillas and across the international bridge to Aguas Verdes. At the bridge, the police may check passports.

Crossing by private vehicle Both Ecuadorean and Peruvian customs are located on either side of the international bridge. If there is a problem entering with a car, contact Tulio Campoverde Armijos, Agente Afianzado de Aduanas, Gómez 123 y Portovelo.

Peruvian immigration The main Peruvian immigration and customs complex (open 24 hours) where passports are stamped is outside Zarumilla, about 3 km past the international bridge.

Into Peru *See Peru Handbook and South American Handbook for further details* Aguas Verdes is a small town with basic facilities, including a simple place to stay and a travel agency (Aguilar Manuel) which can book flights out of Tumbes. There are three forms of transport between the frontier and Tumbes in Peru. Some *colectivos* (shared taxis) leave from near the bridge. They charge higher prices, especially for foreigners, so beware of rip-offs. Other, cheaper ones leave two blocks down along the main street by a small plaza opposite the church; US$1 per person, or US$6 per car. *Colectivos* should stop and wait at the immigration complex on the Peruvian side, but they are not always willing to do so. Buses and minivans leave from an esplanade three blocks east from the *colectivo* stop and go to the market in Tumbes, US$0.60 (they don't wait at immigration). There are also mototaxis from the bridge to the Zarumilla immigration complex, US$0.90 for up to two people. Taxi to Tumbes, including the wait at immigration, US$6.

Coming from Peru into Ecuador: take a bus to Tumbes and a *colectivo* from there to immigration and on to the border. A ticket out of Ecuador is not usually asked for at this border.

Both the *Peru Handbook* and the *South American Handbook* give details on the services and excursions at **Tumbes**. There are national parks and beaches to visit, a fair range of hotels and places to eat and good transport links south down the coast as far as Lima, including flights five times per week to Piura and Lima.

Alternative crossings to Peru The Huaquillas-Tumbes crossing can be harrowing, made worse by the crowds and heat. You must always watch your gear carefully. In addition to cheating by money changers and cab drivers (see above), this border is known for its minor shakedowns of travellers. These are annoying but fortunately seldom serious. It is not uncommon to be asked for a small bribe by one of the many officials you will encounter here. Those seeking a more relaxed crossing to or from Peru should consider Macará (see page 273) or other more out-of-the-way crossings (see Zumba and Loja to the Peruvian Border, page 271).

Northern Pacific Lowlands

Introducing the Northern Pacific Lowlands

The coastal region covers a third of Ecuador's total area. Though popular with Quiteños and Guayaquileños, who come here in their droves for weekends and holidays, the Northern Pacific lowlands receive relatively few foreign visitors, which is surprising given the natural beauty, diversity and rich cultural heritage of the coast. You can surf, watch whales at play, visit ancient archaeological sites, or just relax and enjoy the best food that this country has to offer. The jewel in the coastal crown, Parque Nacional Machalilla, protects an important area of primary tropical dry forest, precolumbian ruins, coral reef and a wide variety of wildlife. Further north, in the province of Esmeraldas, there are not only well-known party beaches, but also opportunities to visit the remaining mangroves and experience two unique lifestyles: Afro-Ecuadorean on the coast and native Cayapa further inland.

Even if your time is limited, the coast is easily accessible from Quito, making it the ideal short break from the Andean chill. The water is warm for bathing and the beaches, many of them deserted, are generally attractive.

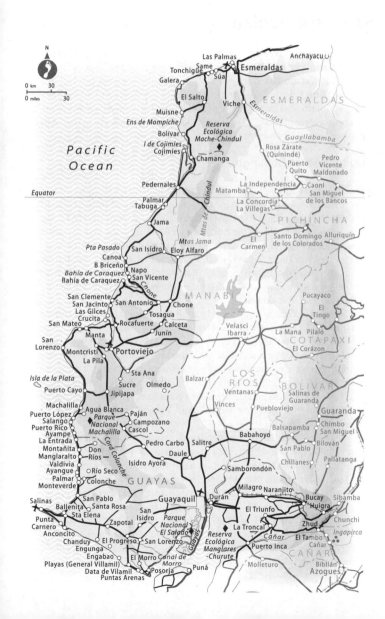

Things to do in the Northern Pacific Lowlands

- Go whale watching from **Puerto López** or other coastal towns, page 321.
- Visit **Isla de La Plata** and **Parque Nacional Machalilla**, page 324.
- Take an eco-tour from **Bahía de Caráquez**, page 333.
- Get beached at **Canoa**, page 338.
- Visit mangroves and Afro-Ecuador to the north of **Esmeraldas**, page 352.

Western Lowlands

Between the foothills of the Andes and the coast lie the western lowlands, a vast expanse of flat or rolling country, devoted to agriculture. This warm and lush land produces Ecuador's number one agricultural export product, the banana. Other crops include African palm for oil extraction, cocoa, rice, palm hearts, and tropical fruits. The region has a few nature reserves protecting remnants of tropical rainforest. It is a good area for taking a dip in one of its many rivers and for observing butterflies and tropical birds.

Quito to Santo Domingo

From **Alóag**, about one hour's drive south of Quito on the Panamericana, a paved road goes west to the lowlands. This is the most important link between Quito and Guayaquil and one of the busiest highways in the country. After the pass, it follows the valley of the ríos Naranjal/Pilatón/Blanco, and continues past **Tandapi** (the official name Manuel Cornejo Astorga is never used), 45 km from Alóag. There are two hotels, **F** (basic with shared bath), and many roadside restaurants. Then comes **Alluriquín**, with accommodation in **D** *Eco-hostería Ku Runa*, at Km 104, with bath, swimming pool, restaurant, horse riding, busy at weekends

The drive is scenic, sit on the right for the best views going down, but on the left side look for El Poder Brutal, a devil's face, complete with horns and fangs, carved in the rock face, 2½ km west of Tandapi. This road is very busy. It gets a lot of heavy truck traffic and it can be dangerous owing to careless drivers passing on the many curves, especially when foggy and at night. This is also the route used by rafting agencies in Quito for trips on the Toachi and Blanco rivers (see Rafting, page 76). Alternative routes from Quito are via Calacalí and La Independencia (see page 143) and a much smaller road through Chiriboga (see page 151).

The main road to Santo Domingo passes near some forest remnants with many birds, flowers and butterflies. About 17 km east of Santo Domingo, to the south of the road, is **Tinalandia**, a great introduction to the world of tropical birds, where more than 360 species have been seen. There are many colourful birds and they are easier to see here than at most other places. There is a pleasant lodge here, **AL** *Tinalandia*, poorly signposted, look for a large rock painted white, T09-9494727 (mob), T/F02-2449028 (Quito), www.tinalandia.net Chalets with bath, full board, excellent meals. There is an unused golf course overlooking the Toachi valley and many trails in the woods behind. Take repellent, there are biting insects in the evening. Lunch (with the right to use the facilities) costs US$10 for non-residents.

Santo Domingo de los Colorados

Santo Domingo de los Colorados is an important commercial centre 129 km from Quito. The city became Ecuador's main transport hub in the mid 1960s when the road from Quito through Alóag was completed. Since that time it has experienced very rapid growth and many immigrants from Colombia have settled here.

Phone code: 02
Colour map 2, grid C3
Population: 200,000
Altitude: 500 m

The name de los Colorados is a reference to the native Tsáchila men. The Tsáchila nation are known locally as the Indios Colorados because of their custom of coating their hair with red vegetable dye, although they do not approve of this name. There are less than 2,000 Tsáchilas left, living in eight communities off the roads leading from Santo Domingo to Quevedo, Chone and Quinindé. Their lands make up a reserve of some 8,000 ha. Today the Tsáchila only wear their native dress on special occasions and they can no longer be seen in traditional garb in the city, except for the Monumento al Colorado statue, at the west end of the city centre where the roads to Quevedo, Chone and Esmeraldas meet.

Background

Santo Domingo is a very important commercial centre for the surrounding palm oil and banana producing areas. The city itself is noisy, streets are prone to flooding after heavy rains and it has little to offer the tourist, except for access to nature reserves nearby. Sunday is market day and therefore many shops in town are only open from Tuesday to Sunday. The main plaza is Parque Joaquín Zaracay.

Santo Domingo is not safe at night. Take care at all times in the market areas, the walkway along 3 de Julio and in peripheral neighbourhoods

Santo Domingo de los Colorados

Northern Pacific Lowlands

0 metres 300
0 yards 300

N

■ **Sleeping**
1 Caleta
2 Diana Real
3 Génova
4 Sheraton
5 Tropical Inn
6 Zaracay

Excursions   There are several options for rafting, horse riding, fishing and bird/butterfly watching excursions in the Santo Domingo area (see Sleeping, Out of town, below). With an all-terrain vehicle, the old road to Quito, via Chiriboga and San Juan, offers access to a forested area on the east bank of the Río Toachi. The turn-off is just east of La Unión del Toachi, between Alluriquín and Tandapi. Tours can be arranged through tour operators, see below. See also Southwest of Quito, page 151, for details of the nature reserves in this area.

Sleeping   **NB** There are many hotels along Av 29 de Mayo, which is a busy noisy street, so ask for a
■ *on map, page 305*   room away from the road. Several of the cheaper establishments also cater to
Price codes: short-stay customers.
see inside front cover
   In town   C *Diana Real*, 29 de Mayo y Loja, T2751380, F2754091. Restaurant serves good set meals, hot water only at night, fan, fridge, comfortable and spacious rooms. **D** *Aracelly*, Vía a Quevedo esquina Galápagos, T2750334, F2754144. Restaurant, electric shower, parking, large rooms. **D** *El Colorado*, 29 de Mayo y Esmeraldas, by the Colorado monument and traffic circle, T2750226. Cold water, parking, a bit noisy and run down, but friendly and still OK. **D** *Puerta del Sol*, 29 de Mayo y Cuenca, T/F2750370. Small upscale restaurant, fan, nice rooms, refurbished in 2002, good value.
   E *Caleta*, Ibarra 141, T2750277. Restaurant, private bath, cold water, basic. **E** *El Ejecutivo*, 29 de Mayo entre Ambato y Cuenca, T2763305. Good restaurant, private bath, cold water, OK. **E** *Génova*, 29 de Mayo e Ibarra, T2759694. Private bath, electric shower, OK. **E** *Jennifer*, 29 de Mayo y Latacunga, T2750577. Restaurant, private bath, hot water, parking, rooms away from the street are quieter, good value. **E** *Las Brisas #2*, Av Quito y Cocaniguas, T2753283. Private bath, cold water, parking, modern. **E** *Sheraton*, on Av Abraham Calazacón opposite the bus terminal, T2751988. Private bath, cold water, parking, modern, good value. **E** *Unicornio*, 29 de Mayo y Ambato, T2760797. Restaurant, private bath, cold water, parking, OK. **F** *San Fernando*, 2 blocks from the bus terminal, T2753402. Private bath, cold water, parking, simple.

   Out of town   Along the road to Quito: **AL** *Zaracay*, Av Quito 1639, 1½ km from the centre, T2750316, F2754535. Includes breakfast, restaurant, gardens and swimming pool, parking, casino, noisy disco, good rooms and service. Advance booking advised, especially on weekends. **B-C** *Hostería Los Colorados*, Km 12, just west of the toll booth and police control, T/F2753449. Restaurants, pool, parking, nice cabins with fridge, artificial lake with fish, good cafeteria. **C** *Tropical Inn*, Km 1, just west of Zaracay, T2761771, F2761775. Fridge, parking, modern. **D** *Hotel del Toachi*, just west of Zaracay, T/F2754688. Pool, parking, spacious rooms.
   Along other roads out of Santo Domingo: **D** *Complejo Campestre Santa Rosa*, Vía Quevedo Km 16, T2754145, F2754144. Restaurant, cold water, parking, office in Santo Domingo at Hotel Aracelly, on the shores of the Río Baba, swimming, fishing, salsoteca.

Eating   There are a number of grills serving meat at mid-range prices: *Parrilladas Argentinas*, on Quevedo road Km 5, good. *Parrilladas Che Luis*, on the road to Quito. *D'Mario*, 1 block southwest of the roundabout for Quito. Good steaks and international food. Several others nearby. There are several *marisquerías* (seafood restaurants) along Av 29 de Mayo, including: *El Conchal Cavelita*, at the corner of C Latacunga. Good ceviches. There are several chicken places in the Cinco Esquinas area where Avs Quito and 29 de Mayo meet, including *Rico Pollo*, Quito y Río Pove. For good set meals, very cheap: *Mocambo*, Tulcán y Machala. *La Fuente*, Ibarra y 3 de Julio. There are several restaurants on Av Abraham Calazacón across from the bus terminal, including *Sheraton*, which is popular. Along the roads leading out of town are a number of *paradores* serving a choice of meals, where buses stop.
   Ice-cream   *Heladería* at Edificio San Francisco, Av Quito entre Río Blanco y Río Toachi. Good, made on the premises, also sell fresh cheese. Opposite is *Pingüino*.

Aruba's Disco, Av de los Tsáchilas y 29 de Mayo. *Fiber*, Cocaniguas at 5 esquinas, varied music, older crowd. *Sky*, Guayaquil y Av Calazacón, latin and other music. Discos in the peripheral neighbourhoods are not considered safe. **Entertainment**

Turismo Zaracay, 29 de Mayo y Cocaniguas, T2750546, F2750873. Runs tours to the Tsáchila commune for US$12 per person, minimum 5 persons. Fishing trips US$24 per person, 8 hrs, bird/butterfly watching tours. **Tour operators**

Road If passing through Santo Domingo, it is not necessary to drive through the congested centre of the city as there is a bypass road around it. **Transport**

Bus The bus terminal is on Av Abraham Calazacón, at the north end of town, along the city's bypass. Long-distance buses don't enter the city. A taxi downtown from the terminal costs US$0.80 and public bus is US$0.20.

As it is a very important transportation centre, you can get buses going everywhere in the country. To **Quito**, via Alóag, US$2, 3 hrs, via San Miguel de los Bancos, US$4, 5 hrs. To **Guayaquil**, US$5, 4 hrs. To **Machala**, US$4.55, 6 hrs. To **Huaquillas**, US$5.20, 7½ hrs. To **Esmeraldas**, US$3, 3 hrs. To **Ambato**, US$3.20, 4 hrs. To **Loja**, US$12, 12 hrs. To **Manta**, US$4.50, 6 hrs. To **Bahía de Caráquez**, US$4, 4 hrs. To **Pedernales**, US$3, 2½ hrs.

Banks *Banco de Guayaquil*, Av Quito y Calazacón. *Banco del Pichincha*, Av La Paz y Santa Rosa. *Produbanco*, Av Quito 1246 y Chorrera de Napa. **Communications** Internet, many in the centre, US$1.30 per hour.**Post**: Av de los Tsáchilas y Río Baba, 0800-1830. Fax 0800-1630. **Telephone**: *Andinatel*, Av Quito between Río Blanco y Río Toachi and at the bus terminal, 0800-2200 daily. **Directory**

Santo Domingo to the Coast

A busy paved highway connects Santo Domingo de los Colorados with Esmeraldas, 185 km to the northwest (see page 346). Some 26 km from Santo Domingo a secondary road branches off northeast to San Miguel de los Bancos (see page 149). Along this road in 2 km you reach the pleasant town of **Valle Hermoso**, surrounded by scenic country on the shores of the Río Blanco. Near town are: **L** *La Cascada*, 600 m from the park on the road to Los Bancos, T02-2773193, F02-2773194, lacascada@punto.net.ec Breakfast included, comfortable rooms, restaurant, pool, spa, horse riding, bike rentals, kayaking and rafting, excursions. In a lovely setting by a 15-m waterfall. **D** *Hostería Valle Hermoso*, 300 m east of the park, T02-2773208, in Santo Domingo T/F2759095. With hot shower, fan, restaurant, pool, sauna, horse riding, fishing. Set in 120 forested hectares on the shores of the Río Blanco, with lake and waterfalls. **To Esmeraldas**

Transport From the terminal in Santo Domingo, take any bus bound for La Concordia or Quinindé, get off at the turn-off (US$0.50) from where there are taxis to town (US$1.50). From the centre of Santo Domingo, by the Monumento al Colorado, you can get a bus that goes right through Valle Hermoso on its way to Los Bancos, these take longer.

Along the main road to Esmeraldas, 14 km northwest of the turn-off to Valle Hermoso, is the entrance to the private **La Perla Forest Reserve**, rich in birdlife and a nice place for a walk (US$3 entry, T2725344). Just north of the reserve and 40 km from Santo Domingo is **La Concordia** (phone code: 02), a commercial town sprawling along the sides of the highway. Here are: **B** *Hotel Atos*, at southeast end of town, T02-2725445, with a/c, fridge, nice restaurant, comfortable, very good. **D** *Los Pinos*, opposite the plaza, T02-2725118, cheaper with shared bath, cold water, fan, simple but clean. North of La Concordia by 5 km is the small town of **La Independencia** with a few fruit stalls, and just north of it the junction with the road from San Miguel de Los Bancos, Calacalí and Quito. Along the latter road are a number of reserves and lodges, see page 143.

Phone code: 06
Population: 23,000
Altitude: 350 m

Quinindé, the official name of which is **Rosa Zárate**, the second largest city in the province of Esmeraldas, is 40 km north of La Independencia.

Sleeping and eating D *Turista*, Km 1 Vía a Santo Domingo, at south end of town, T736784. **E** with shared bath, fan, parking, quieter than central hotels. **E** *Sanz*, on the main street, T736522. With bath, TV, clean, parking, very noisy. **F** *Residencial Paraíso*, 6 de Diciembre 669 in the centre, T736505. A few rooms with private bath, cold water, clean, quite good. Three blocks south of town on the main road is *Restaurant Jean*, T736831, which serves excellent steaks and seafood, huge portions, good salads, reasonable prices, probably the best restaurant for miles. The road deteriorates north of Quinindé.

Near Quinindé is the **Bilsa Reserve and Biological Station**, owned by the Jatun Sacha Foundation. It protects 3,000 ha of very unusual lowland and foothill forest at an altitude of 300-750 m. The forest here contains many bird species virtually impossible to see elsewhere, including the Long-Wattled Umbrellabird and Banded Ground-Cuckoo. From town take a truck to La Y de la Laguna; from there hike three hours to the reserve. Accessibility depends on weather conditions and is easiest July to August; at other times a much longer hike may be required. Accommodation in the **C** range. Contact Jatun Sacha Foundation for visits or volunteer opportunities (see page 82).

To Bahía, Manta or Pedernales Another paved road from Santo Domingo to the coast runs west to **El Carmen** (population 33,000), with a cattle market on the outskirts. There are several basic hotels on the noisy main street, and some quieter ones behind the central plaza, including: **E-F** *San Miguel*, next to the church, T05-660189, private bath, hot water, fan. **E-F** *Puerta de Oro*, 4 de Diciembre y Eloy Alfaro, T/F05-660274, cheaper with shared bath, hot water, fan, clean and good. From El Carmen a paved road goes to **Pedernales** on the coast (see page 340). Continuing southwest of El Carmen is **Chone** (see page 337 for further details) where the road to the coast divides, either to **Bahía de Caráquez** (207 km from Santo Domingo, 340 km from Quito, see page 333), or to **Portoviejo** and **Manta** (257 km from Santo Domingo, 390 km from Quito).

To Guayaquil South from Santo Domingo another highway goes southwest to Quevedo, 1½ hours by bus. At Km 47 (Km 54 from Quevedo) is the **Río alenque** scientific station, set in one of the last remaining islands of western lowland forest, at an altitude of 200 m. It is a very rich birding area, with 370 species. It has however begun to lose some species because of its isolation from other forests. Here is **B** *Río Palenque*, a lodge with capacity for 20, restaurant, US$5 for a day visit. Reservations required from Fundación Wong, Guayaquil, T04-2208680 (ext 1431), on site T09-9745790 (mob).

Phone code: 05
Population: 120,000

Quevedo is set et in fertile rice and banana lands and often flooded in the rainy season, Quevedo has a fair-sized Chinese colony. It is a hot, noisy, crowded and unsafe city which has grown exceptionally rapidly over the last 25 years.

Sleeping and eating A *Olímpico*, Bolívar y 19a. Near the stadium, T750455. A/c, *All hotels are noisy* huge pool (open to the public for US$2), best restaurant in town at mid-range prices. **C** *Quevedo*, C 12 y Av 7 de Octubre, T751876. Modern rooms with a/c, fridge. **D** *Ejecutivo Internacional*, 7 de Octubre y C Cuarta, T751780. Modern, large rooms, a/c, private bath, good value, the least noisy. **D** *Rancho Vinicio*, 1 km from the centre on the road to La Maná, T753674. Quiet rooms, private bath, a/c, cheaper with fan, pool.

For eating try, on 7 de Octubre: *Chifas* at Nos 806, 809 and 707. *Tungurahua*, No 711. Good breakfast. *Hong Kong*, C Ambato. Recommended.

Transport Bus: Quevedo is an important route centre. To **Quito**, US$4, 5 hrs. To **Latacunga**, via La Maná-Zumbahua, US$3, 5 hrs. To **Guayaquil**, via Babahoyo, US$1.65, 3 hrs. To **Portoviejo**, from 7 de Octubre and C 8, 5 hrs, US$4.50. Portoviejo, Tosagua and several coastal towns can be reached via Velasco Ibarra, Pichincha, Rocafuerte and Calceta.

Quevedo is connected with Guayaquil by two paved highways: one runs through Balzar and Daule; the other passes through the city of **Babahoyo**, capital of the province of Los Ríos, from where another scenic road goes to Guaranda in the highlands (see page 224).

Sleeping and eating C *Hotel Cachari*, Bolívar 120 y Gen Barona, T734443, F731317. *Phone code: 05* With bath, a/c, restaurant serving set meals (cheap) and à la carte, sauna. *Colour map 4, grid B4* **D** *Hotel Emperador*, Gen Barona, T730535. Bath, a/c, hot water, cheaper with fan and *Population: 76,000,* cold water, restaurant with set meals (very cheap) and à la carte. Eating places include *Chifa Sin Log*, 10 de Agosto y Sucre. Chinese food. *Münich*, Eloy Alfaro y 10 de Agosto. Local and international food.

The old highway which runs from Quevedo up to Latacunga in the highlands **Quevedo to** carries very little traffic. It is extremely twisty in parts but it is one of the most **Latacunga** beautiful of the routes connecting the highlands with the coast. Between **La Maná** (39 km from Quevedo) and Zumbahua (see page 203) are the pretty little towns of **Pilaló** (two restaurants and petrol pumps) and **El Tingo** (two restaurants and lodging at *Carmita's*). The road is paved from Quevedo to Pilaló. This is a great downhill bike route done from the highlands to the coast.

Sleeping D *Hostería Las Pirámides*, 2½ km west from La Maná on the way to Quevedo, T03-688003/281. Accommodation in cabins and pyramids, pool, restaurant, friendly. *La Herradura*, east of town on the road to Zumbahua. More basic hotels are in town.

The coast from Guayaquil to Puerto López

Southwest of Guayaquil is the beach resort of Playas and, west of it, the Santa Elena **Ruta del Sol** *Peninsula, with Salinas at its tip. North of Santa Elena, the coastal road stretches* See www.rutadelsol *for 737 km to Mataje on the Colombian border; along the way are countless beaches* .com.ec *and fishing villages, and a few cities. The coastal strip is known as 'Ruta del Sol'. Along it are several archaelogical sites and museums, scenic beaches like Ballenita and Olón, the popular surfing beach of Montañita, the forested hills of the Cordillera Chongón-Colonche, and Puerto López, the perfect base from which to explore the beautiful Parque Nacional Machalilla. Coastal resorts are busy and more expensive during the temporada de playa, December to April.*

Northern Pacific Lowlands

The beach resorts of Salinas and Playas near Guayaquil are very popular with vacationing Guayaquileños. Playas is the blue-collar beach and receives huge numbers of day visitors, yet retains something of its former fishing village atmosphere in the low season. Salinas is the seaside playground of highbrow Guayaquileños, the place to be seen during the *temporada*. Both resorts are reached along a paved toll highway from Guayaquil. The road divides after 63 km at El Progreso (Gómez Rendón).

Playas

Phone code: 04
Colour map 4, grid C2
Population: 25,000

One branch of the highway from Guayaquil leads to General Villamil, normally known as Playas, the nearest seaside resort to Guayaquil. Look out for the bottle-shaped ceibo (*kapok*) trees between Guayaquil and Playas as the landscape becomes drier, turning into tropical thorn scrub. Fishing is important in Playas and a few single-sailed balsa rafts can still be seen among the motor launches returning laden with fish. These rafts are unique, highly ingenious and very simple. Without sails, they are used to spread nets close to the shore, then two gangs of men take two to three hours to haul them in.

Tourist information

Av Pedro Menéndez Gilbert y 10 de Agosto opposite the church, T760758, helpful and friendly.

The beach
Beware of thieves when the beach is crowded and don't walk along it at night, it is not safe

As the closest resort to Guayaquil, Playas is popular with city dwellers and prone to severe crowding, especially during the high season, when there are frequent promotional beach parties. The beach shelves gently, is 200-400 m wide, lined with square canvas tents hired out for the day (US$3). It is very nice for bathing. There are cafés, showers, toilets and changing rooms along the beach, with fresh water, for a fee. Local authorities work at keeping the beach clean, but it is difficult when busy. Beware of thieves when it is crowded and don't walk along the beach at night, it is not safe. Out of season, when it is cloudier, or midweek the beaches are almost empty especially for anyone who walks north up the beach towards Punta Pelado (5 km). Playas is also a popular surfing resort with six good surf points.

Playas

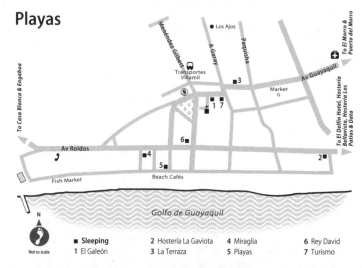

Sleeping
1 El Galeón

2 Hostería La Gaviota
3 La Terraza

4 Miraglia
5 Playas

6 Rey David
7 Turismo

Northern Pacific Lowlands

An interesting walk, or short drive, is to the village of **El Morro**, east of Playas. **Excursions**
It has a disproportionately large wooden church built in 1737, with an
impressive façade (under 'permanent' repair), and nearby there is the mysterious rock formation of the Virgen de la Roca, where there are a small shrine
and marble stations of the cross. There is regular pick-up service from the
crossroads of Av Guayaquil y Av Paquisha.

Some 3 km further down the road is **Puerto del Morro**, up a scenic mangrove estuary in the Gulf of Guayaquil, where there are several working
wooden trawlers and other traditional boats. It is possible to rent a canoe for
three hours to visit the mangroves and probably see dolphins (about US$25).
There's no accommodation, but a few basic eating places.

Following the coast southeast, a road goes to the quiet beaches of **Data de
Villamil** and **Data de Posorja**, then crosses the peninsula east to **Posorja**, an
important fishing port on the Gulf of Guayaquil. Guayaquil-Playas buses
continue to Posorja.

Northwest up the coast is **Engabao**, a small settlement where you can find
deserted beaches and wooden fishing boats along the coast. There's no food
or lodging here, but there are some surfing points. A pick-up goes here from
the crossroads, a 30-minute bumpy ride down sandy tracks. Along this road,
1 km from Playas, is the *Centro Ecológico de Playas*, where horses are rented.

A *Bellavista*, Km 2 on road to Data, T2760600. Restaurant, a/c, rooms or suites in com- **Sleeping**
fortable bungalows on the beach, Swiss-run, booking necessary. **C-D** *Las Redes*, 300 m ■ *on map*
on the road to Posorja, T2760222. A/c, cheaper with fan, some rooms with fridge, the *Price codes:*
more expensive rooms are nice, otherwise fair. **C-D** *Rey David*, Malecón y Calle 9a, *see inside front cover*
T2760024. A/c, cheaper with fan, centrally located, clean and functional. **D** *Dorado*, on *Most hotels are*
the Malecón, T2760402, doradoplayas@hotmail.com A/c, cheaper with fan, OK. *5 mins' walk from*
D-E *Jesús del Gran Poder*, Guayaquil y Garay, T2760589. Cheaper with shared bath, *either bus station*
small rooms, basic but clean. **D-E** *Playas*, On the Malecón, T2760121. Restaurant, private bath, a/c, cheaper with fan, parking, older place but clean and good value.
E *El Galeón*, Beside the church, T2760270. Cheaper with shared bath, OK.

Recommended beach cafés are *Cecilia's* at No 7 or *Barzola* at No 9. In town: **Eating**
Cabaña Típica, next to *Rey David*. Good food, mid-range prices, closed Mon. *Seafood and typical*
Rincón de Mery, Av Jaime Roldós, varied à la carte menu, Lebanese specialties on *dishes are available*
request, good, cheap to mid-range. Good set meals at *Hotel Playas*, cheap. *Mario's*, *from over 50 beach*
central plaza opposite Banco de Guayaquil, big hamburgers, good yoghurt. *Los Ajos*, at *cafés, but most are*
the end of the street leading from the plaza. Good soups, varied menu but variable *closed in low season*
quality. Giant oysters and 'mule foot' black conches are opened and served from stalls,
ask where to find them. Worth a look if nothing else.

Motivos, at the south end of the Malecón, high season only. *Patio Cervecero*, oppo- **Bars &**
site the church, young crowd. *Oh Sole Mio*, near *Hotel Rey David*, also serves meals, **nightclubs**
older crowd.

Bus *Transportes Posorja* and *Transportes Villamil* leave from stations along Av **Transport**
Menéndez Gílbert, a couple of blocks back from the beach. To **Guayaquil**, frequent, 2
hrs, US$1.90; taxi costs US$25.

Banks *Banco de Guayaquil*. **Communications** Internet: a couple of places in town, **Directory**
US$2 per hr. **Telephone**: *Pacifictel*, Av Jaime Roldós Aguilera, service good, open Sun.

Northern Pacific Lowlands

Santa Elena Peninsula

Phone code: 04
Colour map 4, grid C1
West of El Progreso (Gómez Rendón), a good quality road runs to Santa Elena where the road forks west for Salinas or north for the northern coastal towns. About halfway between these towns is Zapotal, west of which is the turn-off for **Chanduy**, a tiny, picturesque port with accommodation at the restaurant on the east side of the bay. About 12 km along is the **Museo Real Alto**, which offers a well laid-out explanation of the peoples, archaeology and customs of the area. ■ *Daily 1000-1700. US$1. T09-9772699 (mob).*

Santa Elena
Population: 27,000
In Santa Elena are a tourist information office (at the entrance to town, open daily 0800-1700), *Hostal El Cisne* on the plaza, restaurant *Echeverría*, and *Bambú Arte* (on Rocafuerte y Félix Sarmiento, regional crafts). Near Santa Elena is the **Museo de los Amantes de Sumpa**, which has a very interesting display on the Las Vegas culture, which lived in this area between 8,800 and 4,600 BC. A burial site with 200 skeletons was found in this spot, including an embracing couple, which is displayed *in-situ*, hence the name of the site. These are the oldest remains to have been discovered in Ecuador. The interesting museum also includes information about other ancient cultures of the Península de Santa Elena and the history of this region. There is also a native dwelling where the old-timer's way of life is demonstrated. ■ *Wed-Sun 0900-1230, 1330-1700. US$1. From Santa Elena follow the road to Salinas, past the Shell gas station on your left, take the first street left, follow it for 2 blocks and turn left again to the museum.*

Baños de San Vicente
About 7 km before Santa Elena, a well signed turn-off leads 8 km to Baños de San Vicente, Ministerio de Turismo-run hot thermal baths, which consist of a swimming pool and a big mudhole which claim to cure assorted ailments. It's best to go early or late to avoid the crowds. ■ *0600-1800. US$0.30, massages extra.* Accommodation next to the baths at **E** *Hotel Florida*, basic but clean.

La Libertad
Population: 76,000
To the west of Santa Elena the road passes a petroleum refinery and enters the busy port and regional market centre of La Libertad. It's not the most appealing of towns, and you'll be eager to jump on the first bus out. Thankfully, these are frequent, so there's no need to spend the night here. Puerto Lucía is the local yacht club. Car racing takes place at the Autódromo halfway between La Libertad and Santa Elena. **Warning** Muggings are frequent, take a taxi between terminals.

Sleeping and eating **C** *Las Gaviotas*, Av Solórzano y la Y, Vía a Salinas, T2784456, F2782841. A/c, hot water, cheaper with fan, cheap restaurant with set meals and à la carte. **D** *Costa Brava*, Av 12 de Octubre, Barrio 12 de Octubre, near the bus terminal for Montañita and points north, T2785860. With bath, fan, good. **D** *Seven Seas*, on Malecón, T2786858. With bath, fan, **E** with shared bath, very basic. **E** *Turis Palm*, Av 9 de Octubre, opposite *CLP* bus terminal, T2784546. Fan, with bath, **F** without, bit run down. Next door and similar is **F** *Reina del Pacífico*.

Transport Buses to **Guayaquil**, with *Coop Libertad Peninsular (CLP)*, on 9 de Octubre y C19, and *CICA* across the street, every 15 mins (the 2 companies alternate departures), US$2.70, 2½ hrs. Get off at Progreso for **Playas**, 1 hr, US$1.15. Buses leave every 30 mins until 1715 to **Manglaralto**, US$1.25, **Puerto López**, US$3.40, 2½ hrs, **Jipijapa**, US$4, and **Manta**, US$4.50, from the terminal on Dagoberto Montenegro y C 10, 1 km from town. To **Quito**, with *Trans Esmeraldas* (opposite *Coop Libertad Peninsular*), 2 nightly, US$9, 9½ hrs.

A few kilometres further on, surrounded by miles of salt flats, is Salinas, Ecuador's answer to Miami Beach. Upscale hotels, high-rise holiday flats, restaurants, bars, and shops line the attractive *malecón*, while a few more modest establishments are to be found in the back streets. There is safe swimming in the bay, though the beach is narrow, with coarse sand and not too clean. More appealing is the (still urban) beach of Chipipe, south of the well-equipped and very exclusive Salinas Yacht Club. There are waves for surfing at the east end of the bay, by an old shipwreck and also by Mar Bravo and near the Chocolatera (see Excursions below). Whale-watching, birdwatching and fishing trips can be arranged here (see Tour operators below).

During *temporada* (December to April) it can be overcrowded, overpriced, noisy, with traffic jams, rubbish-strewn beaches and water shortages. At this time the highway from Guayaquil becomes one-way, depending on the time of day, and is said to resemble a Grand Prix racetrack, especially on Sunday. During the off season it is cheaper, quieter, but still not for 'getting away from it all'.

The **Museo Salinas Siglo XXI** has well displayed collections of naval history and regional archaeology. ■ *Malecón corner Guayas y Quil. Wed-Fri 0800-1200, 1500-1800, Sat-Sun 1000-1300, 1500-1900. US$2.* There is another interesting museum in Ballenita, see North to Puerto López. At the entrance to town there is a crafts cooperative.

Salinas
Population: 30,000

Tourist office and information *Turismo Municipal*, Av Rafael Serrano, behind the Municipio, T/F2773931. Friendly.

Sleeping There are almost 50 hotels in Salinas, of which we list only a few. Quality varies but price is determined more by the season than by the facilities provided. Good places are expensive the year round and nothing is cheap during *temporada*.

High season prices are listed, lower rates may be available at other times

L-AL *Barceló Colón Miramar*, Malecón entre C 38 y C 40, T2771610, F2773476, www.barcelo.com Restaurant, pool and spa, high-rise by the sea, most luxurious in town. **AL** *Calypsso*, Malecón near Capitanía de Puerto, T2773605, F2773583, calypsso@gye.satnet.net Restaurant, a/c, pool and gym, casino, crafts shop, full facilities.

A *El Carruaje*, Malecón 517, T/F2774282. Includes breakfast, good restaurant, a/c, comfortable rooms with ocean view, all facilities. **A** *Francisco I*, Enríquez Gallo y Rumiñahui, T2774106. Restaurant, a/c, pool, comfortable and very nice. **A** *Francisco II*, Malecón y Las Palmeras, T2773471. A/c, pool, modern and comfortable. **B** *Suites Salinas*, Gral Henríquez Gallo y 27, T2772759, F2774267, hotelsalinas@porta.net Restaurant, a/c, pool, internet, fridge, parking, modern. **B-C** *Salinas*, Enríquez Gallo y Estrella, T/F2772993. A/c, cheaper with fan, small rooms.

C *Cocos*, on the Malecón, T2774349. Comfortable rooms, nice terrace overlooking the bay, may be noisy from restaurant/bar downstairs. **C** *Salinas Costa Azul*, C 27 y Enríquez Gallo, T2774268, F2774269, hotelsalinas@porta.net A/c, cheaper with fan, pool, plain but OK. **C-D** *Yulee*, downhill from church, near the baech, T2772028. Restaurant, a/c, cheaper with fan and shared bath, older place but well maintained. Cheaper rooms are simple and good value. **D** *Rachel*, C 17 y Av Quinta, T2772526. A/c, cheaper with fan and shared bath, clean and good value.

Eating **Expensive**: *La Bella Italia*, Malecón y C 17, near *Hotel El Carruaje*. Pizza and international food, good. **Expensive to mid-range**: *Mar y Tierra*, Malecón y Valverde. Excellent seafood and some meat dishes. **Mid-range**: *Cozzoli's* , Malecón y Valverde. Pizzeria. *Pescao Mojao*, Malecón y José de la Cuadra. Meals, bar, pool table. **Cheap**: *Nuevo Flipper*, Malecón y 24 de Mayo. Simple, clean and friendly. *El Colonial*, Malecón y Guayas y Quil. Live music at weekends in season. **Cheap to seriously cheap**: *Selva del Mar*, Enríquez Gallo y 24 de Mayo. Good *pescado con menestra*, cheap and

Northern Pacific Lowlands

seriously cheap set meals. There are several eateries near the Municipio serving seriously cheap set meals and cheap à la carte dishes: *La Ostra Nostra* and *Menú de Yiyín*, both on Eloy Alfaro y Los Almendros, are recommended. A couple of blocks in from the Malecón are some complexes with food stalls serving good ceviches and freshly cooked seafood, a ceviche costs US$3-4; *Cevichelandia* is on María González y Las Palmeras; *La Lojanita*, Enríquez Gallo y Leonardo Avilés, is popular and recommended; others are around the *Libertad Peninsular* bus station, María González y León Avilés. *Il Gelato*, Malecón y Fidón Tomalá. Good ice-cream.

Tour operators *Calypsso*, at the hotel, T2772425. Whale-watching tours with specialist guides, US$25 per person. Fernando Félix, a recommended guide, is a marine biologist who has studied whales in the area for many years, he is fluent in English. For information about the Humpback Whale, see box A whale of a time, page 322. *Centro Informativo Natural Peninsular*, T2778329, bhaase@ecua.net.ec Naturalist guide Ben Haase runs birdwatching tours at the Ecuasal ponds (see Around Salinas below), US$20 per group of up to 10 people. He is very knowledgeable about birds and also whales. *Pesca Tour*, Malecón y 24 de Mayo, T2772391, www.pescatours.com.ec Regional tours, fishing trips (US$350 per day for up to 6 passengers), sailboat and water-skis rental.

Transport City buses (US$0.20), minivans (US$0.20) and shared taxis (*taxi rutas*, US$0.40) run 1 and 2 streets back from the Malecón and continue to **La Libertad**. For the beaches along the Ruta del Sol including **Puerto López** and points north, transfer at La Libertad or Santa Elena. To **Guayaquil**, *Coop Libertad Peninsular*, María González y León Avilés, every 10 mins, US$2.70, 2½ hrs. For *Playas* transfer in El Progreso.

Directory **Banks**: *Banco de Guayaquil*, Malecón y 24 de Mayo, TCs, advances on Mastercard, VISA ATM. *Banco del Pacífico* Av Enríquez Gallo, TCs. *Banco del Pichincha*, Malecón y Armando Barreto, advances on VISA. **Communications**: Pacifictel C 17, 2 blocks from the Malecón. **Internet**: *Café Planet*, Av Enríquez Gallo y Rafael de la Cuadra, US$2 per hr. *Cybermar*, Av Sixto Durán y Fidón Tomalá, US$1.80 per hr.

Around Salinas Beyond Chipipe, the western end of the peninsula is occupied by a navy base. Within it, at the westernmost point of Ecuador, is **La Chocolatera**, a blow hole in the rocky cliffs. Although erosion has diminished the once very impressive jet stream, it is still a magnificent spot with wild surf stirring the turquoise waters. Ask for permission to enter at the gate on the naval base, it is 2.5 km from there.

On the southern shore of the Santa Elena peninsula, 8 km south of La Libertad, is **Punta Carnero**, built on headlands high above the sea. West of it stretches a magnificent 15-km beach with wild surf and heavy undertow (not suitable for swimming), which is virtually empty during the week. In July, August and September there is great whale-watching. Buses (US$0.40) and taxi rutas (US$0.70), between La Libertad and Anconcito, take you to within walking distance of Punta Carnero. Places to stay include **AL** *Punta Carnero*, T/F2948477, info@hotelpuntacarnero.com All rooms with lovely sea view, a/c, fridge, restaurant, swimming pool (day use US$2), **C** in low season. **A-B** *Hostería del Mar*, T2948370, F2948480. With or without a/c, restaurant, swimming pool, **C** in low season, family suites to let on a weekly basis.

Between Punta Carnero and **Mar Bravo**, just east of Salinas along the southern shore of the peninsula, are the **Ecuasal Ponds** (commercial salt pans), which offer the spectacle of thousands, at times tens of thousands, of shorebirds and water birds. More than 100 species have been identified here, sometimes there are even Chilean Flamingos, visiting from their breeding grounds near Piura, Peru. Birds can be seen from the road, but if you wish to get a closer look, you must go with Ben Haase, the naturalist guide who studies the birds (see Tour operators above). Independent visits are not permited by *Ecuasal*, the company which owns the 500-ha property.

A few kilometres to the east of Punta Carnero, along the coast, lies **Anconcito**, a scenic fishing port at the foot of steep cliffs. Pelicans and frigate birds gather round the colourful boats when the catch is brought in. There's nowhere in town to stay. Further on is **Ancón**, centre of the declining local oil-field, where a few houses built by the American oil company in the 1920s can still be seen.

Santa Elena to Puerto López

The coastal road north from Santa Elena to Puerto López is known as the 'Ruta del Sol', it parallels the coastline, provides access to some beautiful beaches and crosses the Chongón-Colonche coastal range. Note that not all beaches are suitable for bathing; the surf and undertow can be strong in some places. Between June and September whales may be seen in this area. *Phone code: 04*

The northern fork of the road at Santa Elena leads past **Ballenita**, which has a pleasant beach. At Lomas de Ballenita is **C** *Hostería Farallón Dillon*, T2785611, F2786643, www.farallondillon.com.ec Lovely setting high above the sea, a/c, hot water, good restaurant, nice views. Run by Douglas Dillon who is knowledgeable about the area. On the premises is **Galería Náutica**, an interesting, eclectic collection of nautical objects from many countries; antiques are restored and sold. **C** *Ballenita Inn*, at the fork for Ballenita, T2784485, large simple rooms, cheaper with fan.

North of Ballenita are a couple of luxury private beach-side developments, with exclusive yacht clubs at **Punta Centinela** and **Punta Blanca**. Further north is the village of **San Pablo**, just north of which is **C** *Hostería Las Olas*, Km 18 Vía Santa Elena, T2610513. Cabins with hot water, a/c, fridge, porch with hammocks, restaurant, pool.

The road hugs the coast, passing **Monteverde**, and then **Palmar**, with pop-ular beaches and beach cafés, but no accommodation.

Continuing north is **Ayangue**, in a beautiful horseshoe bay, 2.7 km from the main highway. There is snorkeling and diving by Islote El Pelado and Islote El Viejo off shore. It gets very crowded and dirty at peak weekends and holidays. You can stay at **AL** *Cumbres de Ayangue*, on the south point of the bay 2 km from town, T2916040, which has nice cabins, restaurant, pool and impressive views. In season you might see whales from here. **D** *Hostal Un Millón De Amigos*, is in town, T2916014, with fan and bath, very nice and friendly. **E** *Los 5 Hermanos*, T2916029, is very basic, overpriced.

San Pedro and Valdivia are two unattractive fishing villages which merge together. Just south of San Pedro, on a hill above the ocean, is **B** *Valdivia Ecolodge*, at Km 40, T2916128, valdiviaecolodge@hotmail.com Screened cabins without walls, with bath, hot water, breakfast included, restaurant, pool, access to a nice bathing beach. There are many fish stalls; *Cevichería Playa Linda* is reported as reliable. **Valdivia** *Phone code: 04*

This is the site of the 5,000 year-old Valdivia culture (see box page 317). Many houses offer 'genuine' artefacts and one resident at the north end of the village will show you the skeletons and burial urns dug up in his back garden. It is illegal to export precolumbian artefacts from Ecuador. The replicas are made in exactly the same manner as their predecessors and copied from genuine designs, so they may not be the real thing, but at least you're not breaking the law and at the same time you can provide some income for the locals. Ask for Juan Orrala, who makes excellent copies, and lives up the hill from the museum. Most of the genuine artefacts discovered at the site are in museums in Quito and Guayaquil. Some pieces remain in the small, local **Ecomuseo Valdivia**, which also has artefacts from other coastal cultures and *in-situ* remains. There is also a handicraft section, where artisans may be seen at work, and lots of local information. ■ *Daily, US$0.60.* At the museum there is also a restaurant and five rooms with bath to let, **G** per person.

There is a simple **aquarium** with three tanks and several huts with exhibits about marine life. ■ *Daily 0900-1800. US$1, local children will guide you and expect a tip. T2780375.* By the aquarium are also a restaurant, open in season, and space for camping. You can rent a boat here for excursions to **Islote El Pelado** or **Islote El Viejo**, small islands off shore. It is a good area for snorkeling (bring your own gear) and whales may be seen in season.

About 8 km northeast of Valdivia is **Reserva Comunal Loma Alta**, a reserve which protects a tract of *garúa* forest in the Cordillera Chongón-Colonche. Access is via a secondary road from Valdivia, through Sinchal, Barcelona and Loma Alta to El Suspiro, one hour by car. From there it is 3-4 hours on foot to the shelter. Guides are available at the Comunal Loma Alta.

North of Valdivia is the village of **Libertador Bolívar**, where hammocks and crafts made of wood, *paja toquilla* and banana fibres are produced. There is lodging at a *Hospedería Comunitaria*, see Manglaralto below.

Manglaralto
Phone code: 04

This is the main centre of the region north of Santa Elena, 180 km northwest of Guayaquil. There is a *tagua* nursery and you can ask to see examples of these 'vegetable ivory' nuts being turned into intricate works of art. It is a pleasant place, with a good, quiet beach and good surf. There's little shelter, so take plenty of sun screen.

Pro-pueblo is an organization working with local communities to foster family-run orchards and cottage craft industry, using *tagua* nuts, *paja toquilla* (used to make Panama hats) and other local products. They have a craft shop in town (opposite the park), an office in San Antonio south of Manglaralto, T2780230, and headquarters in Guayaquil, T2201630, propueb1@propueblo.org.ec *Programa de Manejo de Recursos Costeros (PMRC)* is an organization promoting ecoturism in the local communities. It encourages tourists to go on trips with locals and stay with families in the villages. The have a network of community lodgings, *Red de Hospederías Comunitarias*, **G** per person and many interesting routes into the interior have been set up. They have lodgings in Manglaralto, Libertador Bolívar, Olón and San José. Their office is near the park, T2901343, F2901118, pmrclib@gye.satnet.net Inland, 4 km northeast of Manglaralto, is **Dos Mangas**, in the Cordillera Chongón Colonche. Crafts are produced here and it is a good area for walking.

Sleeping and eating **D** *Marakaya*, 2 blocks south of the main plaza, 1 block from the beach, T2901294. With bath, hot water, a/c, mosquito net, clean, comfortable, good value. **D** *Manglaralto*, hald a block north of Plaza, T2901369. Private bath, fan, restaurant, clean and pleasant, new in 2001. **D** *Kamala*, north of town after crossing the river, T09-942 3754 (mob), cabins by the sea, diving courses. **F** *Alegre Calamar*, at the north end of town. Shared bath, mosquito nets, basic, water in morning only, restaurant. To stay with a family contact the *Red de Hospederías Comunitarias*, see above, Sr Manuel

The Valdivia culture

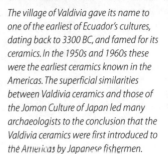

The village of Valdivia gave its name to one of the earliest of Ecuador's cultures, dating back to 3300 BC, and famed for its ceramics. In the 1950s and 1960s these were the earliest ceramics known in the Americas. The superficial similarities between Valdivia ceramics and those of the Jomon Culture of Japan led many archaeologists to the conclusion that the Valdivia ceramics were first introduced to the Americas by Japanese fishermen.

However, discoveries over the past 35 years show that ceramic manufacture in the Americas has its own long path of development and that the idea of a Japanese contribution to pre-European cultures in South America should be discarded.

A much more compelling notion is that ceramic production in Ecuador had its origins in the non-Ecuadorean eastern Amazon basin. New claims from Brazilian sites place early pottery there at between 6000-5000 BC. It is possible that ceramic technology was transmitted from the Amazon basin through commerce or movement of people. The third alternative is that the development of pottery occurred locally and may have

accompanied the development of a more sedentary lifestyle on the Colombian, Venezuelan and Ecuadorean coasts.

The impressive Valdivia figurines are, in general, female representations and are nude and display breasts and a prominent pubic area. Some show pregnancy and in the womb of these are placed one or more seeds or small stones. Others have infants in their hands and some have two heads.

These figurines fill museum cases throughout the country (notably the excellent museums of the Banco Central in Guayaquil, Quito and Cuenca). They are still being produced by artesans in the fishing village of Valdivia today and can be purchased here or at the site museum in Salango, further north near Puerto López. In fact, according to several Ecuadorean archaeologists, many of the figurines housed in the museum collections were made in the 1950s and 1960s because the archaeologists working at that time would pay for any figurines that were found. (Jonathan D Kent, PhD, Associate Professor, Metropolitan State College of Denver).

Northern Pacific Lowlands

Alfonso, *Hospedería Los Tulipanes*, T2901260, is one good option, friendly and well informed. Eating places include *La Calderada*, at the Plaza. Very good seafood, try their *calderada*, expensive, closed Tue. *Alegre Calamar*, at the hotel, good local fare, cheap. *Laurita*, home cooking, cheap.

Transport Bus: to **La Libertad**, US$2, 1½ hrs. **Santa Elena**, US$1.80, 1¼ hrs, change here for Guayaquil. To **Guayaquil** direct, see Olón schedule below. To **Jipijapa**, via Puerto López, US$2, 3½ hrs. To **Puerto López**, US$1.50, 1 hr.

A popular destination among travellers, with a good surfing beach, Montañita is 3 km north of Manglaralto. The main village has experienced haphazard growth and is crowded with small hotels. There are also restaurants, surf-board rentals, tatoo parlours, craft/jewellery vendors and sundry other services. At the north end of the bay, 1 km away, is another hotel area with more elbow-room, referred to as **Baja Montañita**, after one of the hotels. Between the two is a lovely beach where you'll find some of the best **surfing** in Ecuador. Various competitions are held during the year and at weekends, in season, the town is full of Guayaquileños.

Montañita
There are many street dogs in town, don't contribute to the problem by feeding them during your stay

Warning Drugs are a problem in Montañita. There are periodic police raids and several people, including foreigners, are serving long sentences in jail. Avoid getting involved – see Drugs, page 47.

Quieter places are found on the outskirts of the village

Sleeping **In Montañita**: **D** *Nativa Bambú*, on hill, across highway in back of town, T2901293, nativabambu@hotmail.com Shared bath, cold water, mosquito net, nice view and breeze. **D** *Tierra Prometida*, in town, T09-7149037 (mob), cecicortez2000@yahoo.es Cheaper with shared bath, fan, colourful and popular. **D-F** *Funky Monkey*, in town, T09-9353342 (mob), www.funkymonkeyhostal.com Popular restaurant and bar, cheaper with shared bath or in dorm, simple rooms with mosquito nets.

E *Camp Pely*, take road east after crossing bridge at north end of town, follow signs, T09-9414465 (mob), camppely@yahoo.de Shared bath, cold water, basic little huts or camp for US$2 per person. Very clean facilities, quiet, German run and very friendly. Recommended. **E** *Hotel Montañita*, on beach at north end of village, T2901296, F2901299, hmontani@telconet.net Restaurant, private bath, cold water, fan, pool, parking, mosquito net. Larger place, nice courtyard with plants, simple rooms. **E** *Pakaloro*, at north end of town, next to the river estuary, T2904366, pakaloro@hotmail.com Private bath, hot water, mosquito net, small garden, hammocks on porch, clean and pleasant, French-Ecuadorean run, friendly. Recommended. **E** *Paradise South*, just north of town across bridge, T2901185, paradise_south@hotmail.com Restaurant, cheaper with shared bath, pool, pleasant grounds, sports fields and ping-pong tables, quiet, good value. **E-F** *Casa Blanca*, C Guido Chiriboga, T2901340, lacasablan@hotmail.com Cheaper with shared bath, sporadic hot water. **E-F** *Centro del Mundo II*, on the beach. Cheaper with shared bath, mosquito net, older 4-story timber and thatch building. **F-G** *Rickie*, in town. Cheaper with shared bath, cold water, cooking facilities, mosquito net, basic, clean and friendly. There are many other places in town, all quite similar.

In Baja Montañita: **B** *Baja Montañita*, T2901218, F2901227. Includes breakfast, restaurant, a/c, pool, parking, comfortable rooms, a small resort off on its own. **B-D** *La Casa del Sol*, T/F2901302, www.casasol.com Restaurant, a/c, cheaper with fan and shared bath, large rooms available, surfing packages. **E** *Tres Palmas*, by the beach, T09-9426380 (mob). Tex-Mex restaurant, private bath, mosquito net, simple, US run.

Eating *Aura*, next to the park, good set meals, cheap. *La Cabañita*, at the beach, good and cheap. *Ebeneezer*, good set meals, very cheap. *Manuel*, pizzas, fruit juices and milkshakes. *Tiburón*, good pizza. *La Lojanita*, ceviches. *Zao*, good for breakfast, also serve meals. *Mahalo Bar* is upstairs from Zao. *Pelícano*, in Baja Montañita, good pizzas, disco, open till 2200, later in season. *Tres Palmas*, in Baja Montañita, grill and Tex-Mex, friendly. There are many other restaurants, food and prices quite uniform.

Tour operator *Rocatur*, at Casa del Sol in Baja Montañita, T09-9321210 (mob), offers regional tours.

Transport **Bus**: See Olón below: Montañita is a few minutes south of Olón.

Directory **Communications**: Internet: on street closest to the river, US$3 per hr. **Telephone**: there is no *Pacifitel* in town, only in Manglaralto or Olón; one shop rents a private phone. **Laundry**: *Lavandería Espumita*, near the church, charges by piece. **Surfboards**: *Hostal Papaya*, US$1 per hour. Next door is *Tatoo*, US$3-3.50 for half day, US$5-6 per day, also sells boards. *Balsa House*, opposite *Hotel Tierra Prometida*, US$4 half day, US$6 full day.

Olón   About 3 km further north, Olón has a spectacular long beach. Starting here and continuing to the north, the surroundings get greener. On the headland between Montañita and Olón, built atop a cliff by the sea, is the **Sanctuary of**

Santa María de Fíat. There is access from either side and the views are spectacular. Nearby, 1 km north of Olón, past the bridge is **El Cangrejal de Olón**, a 7-ha dry tropical forest, with mangroves, home of the blue crab (*Cardisoma crasum-smith*), a species in danger of extinction. To visit contact Eustacio Salinas, at the copy shop on the highway, T09-9320091 (mob). Horse-riding tours in the area are available from Dr Wilmer Cevallos, T09-9767981 (mob).

Sleeping and eating **F** *Hostería Olón Beach*, T2901191. Clean, basic, with public phone. **D** *Hostería N & J*, on the beach, T2780174. Simple rooms with bath, cold water, fan, parking. **F** *Hospedaje Rosa Mistía*, in family home, part of *Red de Hospederías Comunitarias*, see Manglaralto above, there are 2 others in town. Fanny Tomalá also rents rooms in the village. *Flor de Olón*, in the village, simple but good food. *María Verónica*, just off the beach. Scruffy, good seafood.

Transport **Bus**: *Transportes Manglaralto* to **La Libertad**, US$2.50, 2 hrs. *CLP* have daily direct buses starting in Olón going to **Guayaquil**, at 0500, 1300, 1630 (same schedule from Guayaquil), US$4.20, 3½ hrs. It is inconvenient, but cheaper to transfer in Santa Elena. To **Puerto López**, US$1.20, 45 mins.

A beautiful beach continues 10 km north by the villages of Curía, San José (lodging with a family) and La Núñez, to **La Entrada**, where the Cordillera Chongón Colonche comes out to the sea. This is the provincial boundary between Guayas and Manabí. There are good walking possibilities in this area. North of La Entrada, a road goes inland to Guale, 3½ km along it is the access to **D** *Cantalapiedra*, run by *Alandaluz* (see Puerto Rico below), cabins in a lovely forested setting by the Río Ayampe, with restaurant. Day-trips here can also be arranged at *Alandaluz*, it can also be reached by walking three hours along the river from Ayampe.

Located at the foot of the Cordillera Chongón Colonche, on the south shore of the river of the same name, Ayampe is a small, poor village, with friendly people, but no services. Just south of it are a group of hotels offering a good option for those seeking tranquillity. This is a good base for trips up to the Cordillera Chongón Colonche. The area produces crafts with banana fibres, known as *sapán*.

Ayampe
Phone code: 04

Northern Pacific Lowlands

Sleeping and eating **L-AL** *Hotel Atamari*, on the headland south of Ayampe, T2780430, T02-2228470 (Quito), F02-2234075, atamari@hoy.net Beautiful, cabins with rooms and suites, in spectacular surroundings on cliffs above the sea, restaurant with wonderful food, pool. Buses between Puerto López and Manglaralto go through, then a 15-min walk from the highway. **B** *Hotel Almare*, T2780611, F2780614, almare@porta.net Lovely wooden construction, comfortable rooms and suites with fan, hot water, balcony, restaurant. Fine views especially at sunset, English spoken, friendly. Recommended.
    C *Cabañas la Tortuga*, T2780613, tortuga@porta.net Cabins with hot water, fan, restaurant, nice grounds. **D** *Cabañas de la Iguana*, T2780605, ayampeiguana@ hotmail.com Cabins with room for 4, with bath, mosquito nets, meals with advance notice, cheap, clean, quiet, excursions, Swiss-Ecuadorian run, family atmosphere, very friendly, helpful and knowledgeable. Recommended. **D** *Finca Punta Ayampe*, on a hill south of the other hotels, T2780616, info@fincapuntaayampe.com Bamboo structure built high on a hill with great ocean views, rooms with bath, cold water, mosquito nets, meals available.

Las Tunas
Puerto Rico
& Río Chico
Phone code: 04

North of Ayampe are the villages of Las Tunas, Puerto Rico and Río Chico; there are places to stay all along this stretch of beach. In **Las Tunas** you can arrange for horse tours with *Kankagua*, opposite *Hotel La Barquita*. Just south of **Puerto Rico** is the **Alandaluz Ecological Centre**, an organization involved in promoting ecologically sound practices in nearby communities, including recycling of rubbish, water and organic agriculture. It is also a very good *hostería* (see below) and gives working demonstrations of its innovative practices. Near Río Chico, at Hostería Piqueros Patas Azules, there is a small private museum displaying ceramics, stone artefacts and funerary urns found at the site by archaeologist Presley Norton. These correspond to the Manteña, Valdivia, Machalilla and other prehistoric coastal cultures. A prize piece is the 2-cm high 'Venus de Valdivia' statue, the smallest of its kind.

Sleeping and eating **B-C** *Hostería Alandaluz*, T2780686, F2780690, T/F02-254 3042 (Quito), alandalu@interactive.net.ec Part of the ecological centre, has a variety of cabins ranging from bamboo with palm-leaf thatched roofs and compost toilets to more luxurious with flush toilets, all with private bath. It is a very peaceful place, with a clean beach and stunning organic vegetable and flower gardens in the middle of a desert. Camping with your own tent is **F** per person. There are student and IYHF discounts. Good homemade organic food, vegetarian or seafood, at mid-range prices, and there's a bar. Expensive tours in the area are also offered. Reservations are necessary as it is popular, friendly and recommended.

 C *Hostería La Barquita*, by Las Tunas, 4 km north of Ayampe and 1 km south of Alandaluz, T2780683, F2780051, barquita2000@yahoo.com Private bath, hot water, mosquito nets, **F** per person in room with bunk beds and shared bath. The restaurant (mid-range) and bar are in a boat on the beach with good ocean views, a unique concept. Discounts for longer stays and IYHF members, tours. Swiss-Ecuadorean run, French, English and German spoken, friendly. **B** *Piqueros Patas Azules*, A 10-min drive from Río Chico towards the beach, T2780279. Cabins overlooking the beach, with bath, fan. Price includes entry to the local museum and visit to cave along the beach. **E** *Albergue Río Chico*, a couple of blocks from the highway in Río Chico, T2780280. Cabins for 5 and some rooms with bath, fan, fridge, restaurant, a 15-min walk to the beach. There are a couple of basic cabins for rent by the beach in Puerto Rico, for about US$6 per person, enquire locally; Don Julio Mero, owns one of these.

Salango
Phone code: 04

Just north of Río Chico and 5 km south of Puerto López is Salango, a commercial fishing port with a fish meal plant. It is worth visiting for its excellent Presley Norton **archaeological museum** housing artefacts from the excavations in town. ■ *Daily 0900-1200, 1300-1700. US$1. Crafts shop. Towards the north end of town.* Just offshore is Isla Salango, a good place for snorkelling.

Sleeping and eating **E** *Cabaña Mar*, on the Malecón, T2780722. Bamboo cabin, with shared bath, simple, clean, friendly, good value. Owner offers snorkelling tours to Isla Salango, US$40 for 4. **E** *Cabañas Costamar*, near the museum, T2780306. Basic cabins, with mosquito nets, private bath, water problems. *El Delfín Mágico*, excellent food but chronically slow service, so it's best to order your meal before visiting the museum; try the *spondilus* (spiny oyster) in fresh coriander and peanut sauce with garlic coated *patacones*, mid-range prices. Also offering excellent seafood at slightly cheaper prices is *El Pelícano*, behind the church; caters for vegetarians.

Puerto López

This pleasant little fishing town is beautifully set on a turquoise horseshoe bay, with a broad sweep of beach enclosed by headlands to the north and south. The beach is cleanest at the far north and south ends, away from the fleet of small fishing boats moored offshore. The streets are either dusty or muddy, depending on the season. A lookout above the south end of the bay along the main road offers great views.

Phone code: 05
Colour map 4, grid B1
Population: 7,600
Altitude: sea level

Tourism is second only to fishing in Puerto López, with a wide array of hotels, restaurants and tour operators catering to the many foreign and Ecuadorean visitors who flock here every year during 'whale season' or *temporada de ballenas*, approximately mid-June to September (see box, A whale of a time, page 322). Whale watching is reasonably well organized, but things can get out of hand during the height of the season in July and August, when prices rise and touts await tourists arriving in town. During these peak months, fishermen may offer whale-watching trips for less than authorized tour operators. Such improvised excursions are seldom recommended, your safety may be compromised and the whales threatened by boatmen who have not been trained how to best approach them. You may wish to reserve accommodation and tours in advance during high season. Whales can also be seen from other points along the coast where tours are likewise available.

Whale watching
Puerto López is the whale-watching capital of Ecuador

A year-round attraction in the Puerto López area is **Parque Nacional Machalilla** (see below) with mainland sites and **Isla de la Plata** offshore, an island with bird colonies and good snokelling. Excursions here are combined with whale watching in season. This has been called a 'cheap alternative to Galápagos', which is overstating the case. Excursions to Isla de la Plata are definitely worthwhile and recommended, but your expectations should be reasonable. In town there is a national park information centre, Calle Eloy Alfaro y García Moreno, open daily.

Excursions

A *Manta Raya Lodge*, 3 km south of town, T/F604233, advantagetravel@andinanet.net Restaurant and bar, pool, comfortable rooms, nice view, colourful décor. Horse-riding, fishing and diving trips organized. **A-D** *Pacífico*, Malecón Y González Suárez, T604147, F604133, hpacific@manta.ecua.net.ec Includes breakfast, restaurant, a/c, much cheaper in old wing with fan and shared bath but full use of facilities, pool, parking. New rooms are comfortable, older ones are good value, nice grounds, run boat tours, friendly and helpful. Recommended.

Sleeping
Price codes:
see inside front cover
Puerto López has
many hotels, but
may nonetheless fill
up in July and August.
Reserve in advance
if you want to stay
in a particular
establishment

C *La Terraza*, on hill north of centre, behind the clinic, T604235. Meals available on request, great views over the bay, gardens, spacious, run by German Peter Bernhard, free car service to/from town if called in advance. Highly recommended. **C** *Mandala*, Malecón beyond fish market, at north end of the beach, T/F604181. Good but pricey restaurant, cabins with screened windows, lovely grounds, Swiss-Italian run, friendly and helpful. Recommended.

D *Los Islotes*, Malecón 532 y Gen Córdova, T604108. Fan, modern and clean. Good value. Recommended. **D** *Tuzco*, Gen Córdova y JL Mera, 3 blocks uphill from market, T604120. Meals on request, fan, large rooms available for families or groups, simple but OK. **D-E** *Villa Colombia*, on García Moreno behind market, T604105. Cheaper in dorm with shared bath, clean and very friendly. **E** *Cueva del Oso*, Lascano 116 y Juan Montalvo, T611671, F604124, fmachali@mnb.satnet.net Shared bath, hot water, cooking facilities, good dormitory accomodation. Recommended. **E** *Internacional Machalilla*, Lascano y Montalvo, T604155. Private bath, fan, parking,

Northern Pacific Lowlands

▶▶ **A whale of a time**

Whale watching has taken off as a major tourist attraction along the coast of Ecuador. One of the prime sites to see these massive mammals is around Isla de La Plata but whales travel the entire length of Ecuador's shores and well beyond.

Between June and September, each year, groups of up to 10 individuals of this gregarious species make the 8,000 km-long trip from their Antarctic feeding grounds to the equator. They head for these warmer waters to mate and calve. Inspired by love, we presume, the humpbacks become real acrobats. Watching them breach (jump almost completely out of the water) is the most exciting moment of any tour. Not far behind, though, is listening to them 'sing'. Chirrups, snores, purrs and haunting moans are all emitted by solitary males eager to use their chat-up techniques on a prospective mating partner. These vocal performances can last half an hour or more.

Adult humpbacks reach a length of over 15 m and can exceed 30 tonnes in weight. The gestation period is about one year and newborn calves are 5-6 m long. The ventral side of the tail has a distinctive

series of stripes which allows scientists to identify and track individual whales.

Humpbacks got their English name from their humped dorsal fins and the way they arch when diving. Their scientific name, Megaptera novaeangliae, which translates roughly as 'large-winged New Englanders', comes from the fact that they were first identified off the coast of New England, and form their very large wing-like pectoral fins. In Spanish they are called ballena jorobada or Yubarta.

These whales have blubber up to 20-cm thick. Combined with their slow swimming, this made them all too attractive for whalers during the 19th and 20th centuries. During that period their numbers are estimated to have fallen from 100,000 to 2,500 worldwide. Protected by international whaling treaties since 1966, the humpbacks are making a gradual recovery. Ironically, the same behaviour that once allowed them to be harpooned so easily makes the humpbacks particularly appealing to whale watchers today. The difference is that each sighting is now greeted with the shooting of film instead of lethal harpoons.

good value, new in 2001. **E** *Manteña*, On Malecón north of centre. Private bath, hot water, cooking facilities, simple cabins with mosquito nets, Hungarian-Ecuadorean run, German spoken, friendly. **E** *Máxima*, González Suárez y Machalilla, gmaxmill2@hotmail.com Private bath, hot water, parking, modern and comfortable, English spoken, good value. **E** *Yubarta*, on Malecón just north of river. Bar, private bath, cold water, mosquito net, simple, arranges tours.

E-F *Monte Líbano*, Southern extreme of Malecón, T604117. Cheaper with shared bath, hot water, basic, popular and friendly. **E-F** *Sol Inn*, Montalvo entre Eloy Alfaro y Lascano, hostal_solinn@hotmail.com Cheaper with shared bath, hot water, laundry and cooking facilities, parking, popular, nice atmosphere, English and French spoken, good value. **F** *Turismar*, Malecón y Sucre, at the south end, T604174. Private bath, cold water, sea view, family run, good value, basic.

Eating   There are many good places along the Malecón serving local fare, fish and seafood, all quite similar; they usually have a cheap set meal which isn´t necessarily listed (ask for it, if that is what you want) and à la carte for mid-range prices. These include: *Carmita*, *Myflower*, *Spondylus*, *Soda Bar Danny*. *Flipper*, on Gen Córdova next to Banco del Pichincha. Good set meals, very cheap, friendly. Recommended. *The Whale Café*, towards the south end of the Malecón. Good pizza, sandwiches and meals, good cakes and pies, nice breakfasts. US-run, owners Diana and Kevin are very helpful and provide travel information. Recommended. *Bellitalia*, Montalvo y Abdón Calderón, one block back from the Malecón and near the river. Excellent Italian food, try their spinach soup. Pleasant garden seatting, Italian run. Highly recommended. The *panadería* behind the church serves good banana bread and other sweets. *Magic Night Bar*, towards the south end of the Malecón. Small and informal, latin music, popular with locals.

The *Yaguarundi* handicrafts cooperative is run by local women and sells *tagua* (vegetable ivory), cactus fibre baskets and pottery. They can also arrange visits to homes to see handicrafts being made and to sample the local cuisine. For details, T2780184. They have outlets at *Alandaluz* (see above) and other hotels and restaurants. **Shopping**

There is a good fleet of small boats (16-20 passengers) running excursions, all have life jackets and a toilet. All agencies offer the same tours for the same price. In high season: US$30 per person for whale watching, Isla de la Plata and snorkelling, including a snack and drinks, US$25 for whale watching only. In low season tours to Isla de la Plata and snorkelling cost US$25 per person, US$20 for whale watching only. These rates don't include the National Park fee (see below). Trips start about 0800 and return around 1700. Agencies also offer tours to the mainland sites of the national park. A day tour combining Agua Blanca and Los Frailes costs US$25 per person. **Tour operators**
The whale-watching season runs from June to September/ October

Bosque Marino, on the highway, near the bus stop, T09-9173556 (mob). Experienced guides, some of whom speak English. They also offer hikes through the forest and birdwatching tours to Agua Blanca (see below) and Las Goteras for US$20 per day for groups of 2-3. *Ecuador Amazing*, Gen Córdova, T604239, T02-2542888 (Quito), www.ecuadoramazing.com Tours to Isla de la Plata and whale watching. *Excursiones Pacífico*, Malecón at *Hotel Pacífico*, T/F604133. Comfortable boat and good service. Also tours to San Sebastián, Agua Blanca, Los Frailes. *Exploratur*, on Malecón next to *Spondylus* restaurant, T604123. French-run outfit based in Quito. They have two 8-12 person boats and their own compressor to fill dive tanks. PADI divemaster accompanies qualified divers to various sites, but advance notice is required, US$85 per person for all-inclusive diving day tour (2 tanks). Also offer diving lessons. *Machalilla Tours*, on Malecón next to *Viña del Mar* restaurant, T604206. They also offer horse-riding, surfing and fishing tours; all cost US$25 per person for a day trip. *Manta Raya*, on Malecón Norte, T604233. They have a comfortable and spacious boat. They also have diving equipment and charge US$100.00 per person, all inclusive. *Sercapez*, Gen Córdova, T604173. All inclusive trips to San Sebastián, with camping, local guide and food run US$30 per person, per day. They also work with *Guacamayo Bahía Tours* and organize trips further north (see Bahía de Caráquez below). They also offer transfers to the airport in Manta or Portoviejo and to other cities. There are other legitimate agencies not listed here.

For **deep sea fishing**, contact Kevin at the *Whale Café*.

Bus To **Quito**, Carlos Aray at 0500, 0900, 1830, from Quito at 1010 and 1900, US$8, 11 hrs. To **Jipijapa**, frequent service, US$1, 1 hr. To **Portoviejo**, US$2, 2 hrs. To **Manta**, via Portoviejo, hourly, 2½ hrs, US$2.40. To **Manta**, direct via the coastal route, every 2 hrs with *CTMJ*, US$2.40, 2 hrs. To **Guayaquil**, via Jipijapa, 3 hrs, US$2.80. To **La Libertad**, every 30 mins, US$3.40, 2½ hrs. To **Manglaralto**, US$1.50, 1 hr. **Pick-ups** for hire to nearby sites are by the market, east of the highway. **Transport**

Banks *Banco del Pichincha*, Gen Córdova y Machalilla, TCs and VISA. **Bicycle rentals** Gen Córdova by the cyber café, US$1 per hr, US$6 per day. **Communications** Internet: Gen Córdova next to *Banco del Pichincha*, US$2 per hr. **Telephone**: *Pacifictel*, on Av Machalilla (the highway). **Language classes** *La Lengua*, Abdón Calderón y García Moreno, next to the Municipio, east of the highway, same school as in Quito, T2543521, www.la-lengua.com **Directory**

Northern Pacific Lowlands

Parque Nacional Machalilla

The park extends over 55,000 ha, including Isla de la Plata, Isla Salango offshore, and the magnificent beach of Los Frailes. It preserves marine ecosystems as well as the dry tropical forest and archaeological sites on shore. The park is recommended for birdwatching, especially in the cloud forest of Cerro San Sebastián, and there are also several species of mammals and reptiles. The continental portion of the park is divided into three sections which are separated by private land, including the town of Machalilla.

Ins & outs   Entrance fee for Isla de la Plata, US$15. For mainland part only, US$12. For both mainland and Isla de la Plata, US$20. Children under 11 and seniors pay half price. Fee is payable at the park office next to the market in Puerto López (open 0700-1800) or directly to the park rangers (insist on a receipt). The ticket is valid for several days so you can visit the different areas.

Los Frailes   This stunning beach, one of the nicest on the entire coast, is 11 km north of Puerto López and and 1 km south of the town of Machalilla. At the north end of the beach is a trail through the forest leading to a lookout with great views. You can continue along this trail to the town of Machalilla. Bathing at Los Frailes is best at the ends of the bay; in the centre there is a strong undertow. Note that there are poison wood trees (*manzanillo*) by the beach, take care not to take shelter from the sun under them. ■ *To get there, take a tour, a bus bound for Jipijapa (US$0.25) or a pick-up (US$7), the beach is a 30-min walk from the turn-off. Camping is only permitted by the ranger's house where you can get some water, US$5 per tent. The park gates close at 1700.*

Agua Blanca   About 5 km north of Puerto López, at Buena Vista, on the road to Machalilla, there is a dirt road to the east marked to Agua Blanca. Here, 5 km from the main road, in the national park, amid hot, arid scrub, is a small village and a fine, small archaeological museum containing some fascinating ceramics from the Manteño civilization found at the site. ■ *0800-1800. The commune charges US$2 for a 2-3 hr guided tour of the museum, ruins (a 45-min walk), funerary urns and sulphur lake. Horses can be hired for the visit. To get there, take tour, a pick-up (US$8) or a bus bound for Jipijapa (US$0.20); it is a hot walk of more than 1 hr from the turning to the village. Camping is possible and there's a cabin and 1 very basic room for rent above the museum for US$5 per person.*

San Sebastián   A recommended trip is to San Sebastián, 9 km from Agua Blanca up in tropical moist forest (altitude 800 m), for sightings of orchids and possibly howler monkeys. This is the best nature hike in the park, going through successively more humid forests until reaching true cloud forest at Cerro San Sebastián. Although part of the national park, this area is administered by the *Comuna* of Agua Blanca, which charges its own fees in addition to the park entrance (see Ins and outs above). You are not allowed to go without one of their guides. You can also make alternative excursions in the Cordillera Chongón Colonche further south, which might prove to be cheaper. ■ *It's 5 hrs on foot or by horse. A tour to the forest costs US$20 per day for the guide (fixed rate). You can camp (US$2), otherwise lodging is with a family at extra cost. Horses are also extra and you have to pay to get to Agua Blanca to start the excursion.*

On this island, about 24 km offshore, there are nesting colonies of waved alba- **Isla de la Plata**
tross, frigates and three different booby species. A small colony of sea lions
also makes its home here and whales can be seen from June to September. As
in Galápagos, it is easy to see the bird life, you will walk just by their nests. It is
also a precolumbian site with substantial pottery finds, and there is good diving and snorkelling (most agencies provide snorkelling equipment).

The island must be visited in a day trip, staying overnight is not permitted.
There are two walks, of three and five hours (take water), the national park controls access to these and you will probably be taken along only one of the two
loops. See Puerto López Tour operators, page 323, for details of tours and agencies. Take dry clothes, water, and precautions against sun and seasickness.

North of Puerto López

Machalilla is a small fishing village just north of Los Frailes beach. Neither the   **Machalilla**
town nor its beach are very attractive.

Sleeping and eating On the main road is **D** *Hotel Internacional Machalilla*,
T589107. A conspicuous cement building, clean with fans, talk to the manager about
cheaper rates for longer stays. **G** *La Canoa Camping*, by the beach at north end of the
village, lacanoac@hotmail.com   Very basic thached loft with room for 4, tents for hire
or use your own tent, no restaurant, kitchen facilities.

North from Machalilla is Puerto Cayo where the road forks, one branch turns   **Puerto Cayo**
inland for Jipijapa and the coastal road continues north to Manta. The beach is   *Phone code: 05*
dirty here, but improves a bit as you walk away from town. Puerto Cayo pro-   *High season:*
motes itself as a whale-watching destination, but it can be hard to organize a trip   *July-August*
from here outside July and August. Town is completely dead in the off season.

Sleeping and eating **B** *Luz de Luna*, 5 km north of town on the coastal road,
T616032, T02-2400562 (Quito). Comfortable spacious rooms with balcony, pool, restaurant, **D** in low season, nice clean beach. **C** *HostalLos Frailes*, T616014,
hostallosfrailes@latinmail.com   A/c, cheaper without a/c, clean, TV, fridge, restaurant,
tours. **C** *Puerto Cayo*, at the south end of the beach, T616019, cayos@puertocayo.com,
www.puertocayo.com   Comfortable rooms with terrace overlooking the sea and
hammocks, good restaurant at mid-range prices, try their *pescado al ajillo*. Friendly service. **C** *Las Palmeras*, 3 km north of town on coastal road, T09-7011900 (mob), in
Portoviejo, T930831. Fully equiped cabins with kitchen, bath, hot water, restaurant,
A cabin for 6, spacious and comfortable, clean beach, nice. **D** *Residencial Zavala*, on
the Malecón, T616020. Simple rooms with bath, cold water, fan, clean, ask for sea view,
cheap restaurant. **A** *Expedición Cayo*, at the north end of the beach, T922447. Large
cabins with kitchen, hot water, for up to 6, **C** cabin for 4, spacious but bare. *D'Carlos*,
next to *Zavala*. Good cheap seafood.

The paved road climbs over humid hills to descend to the dry scrub around   **Jipijapa**
Jipijapa, an unattractive town but an important centre for the region's trade in   *Phone code: 05*
cotton, cocoa, coffee and kapok. Try **D** *Hostal Jipijapa*, Santiesteban y Eloy   *Population: 36,000*
Alfaro, two blocks south of the cemetery, T601365. A/c, hot water, fridge, res-
taurant Monday-Friday, clean. **D** *Agua Blanca*, Km 1 via a Puerto Cayo,
T600759, private bath, a/c, hot water, **E** with fan and cold water. Buses to
Manglaralto, two hours, US$2. To Puerto López, US$1, one hour. To Manta,
US$1, one hour. To Quito, US$6.40, 10 hours. Buses leave from the plaza.

Northern Pacific Lowlands

At **La Pila**, due north of Jipijapa, the road turns east for Portoviejo. The village's main industry is fake precolumbian pottery, with a thriving by-line in erotic ceramics.

Montecristi
Phone code: 05
Population: 15,000

A few kilometres further west from La Pila is this quiet, dusty town, set on the lower slopes of an imposing hill, high enough to be watered by low cloud which gives the region its only source of drinking water. The town is one of the main centres of Panama hat production and is renowned for the high quality of its output (see Arts and Crafts, on page 442). Varied straw and basketware is also produced here (much cheaper than in Quito), and wooden barrels which are strapped to donkeys for carrying water. Ask for José Chávez Franco, Rocafuerte 203, T/F606343, where you can see Panama hats being made. He also sells wholesale and retail. Montecristi is also famous as the birthplace of the statesman Eloy Alfaro.

Coastal road

From Puerto Cayo a scenic paved coastal road goes northwest, travelling slightly inland through forested hills. In 17 km is a turn-off for the undeveloped beach of **San José**. Another 12 km further north, by the village of **Santa Rosa**, where there are food stalls serving seafood, the road takes to the coastline and follows a beautiful stetch of beach, 6 km to **San Lorenzo**, by the cape of the same name. Here are a lighthouse atop towering headlands (an easy 45-minute walk for lovely views, but beware of the cliffs below), a waterfall accessed from behind the church, several simple eateries in the centre of town and **B** *La Cueva*, towards the north end of the bay, T615902, in Manta T622772. Includes breakfast, cabins with a/c, hot water, **AL** for cabin for 5, reservations required. Excellent restaurant serving seafood and international food at mid-range prices, popular with Manteños on weekends, call ahead if midweek.

North of San Lorenzo the road goes inland to an area of forested hills, known as **Bosque de Pacoche**. Here, near the village of **El Aromo**, is *Hostería San Antonio*, T09-991 6201, in Manta contact Delgado Travel, T627925. A hacienda in the mountains with restaurant, horse riding, mountain bikes, a zoo. A good place to learn about the *montubio* (rural coastal people) culture. A lodge is under construction, due to open in 2003. Day trips including lunch US$25 per person. About 20 km from San Lorenzo is a turn-off for **San Mateo**, a fishing village with good surfing, especially December through April. It is 9 km from San Mateo to Manta.

Manta

Phone code: 05
Colour map 4, grid A1
Population: 183,000
Altitude: sea level

Manta is the quintessential maritime city. Ecuador's second port after Guayaquil and home to the county's largest fishing fleet, it has hundreds of boats of all sizes moored offshore. This busy lively city has grown and prospered over the past decade. The thriving port and a controversial US air force base (ostensibly for drug surveillance) give the city a cosmopolitan flavour and have driven up prices. Cruise ships call on Manta from time to time.

Tourist information

Ministerio de Turismo, Paseo José María Egas 1034 (Av 3) y Calle 11, T622944, very helpful, some English spoken. Mon-Fri 0830-1700. **Cámara de Turismo**, Centro Comercial Cocco Manta, Malecón y C 23, T620478. Helpful, map available, English spoken. Mon-Sat 0900-1300, 1500-1800, Sun 0900-1300. **Oficina de Información ULEAM**, Malecón Escénico, T624099. Staffed by tourism students from the Universidad Laica Eloy Alfaro. Wed-Sun 0900-1700.

A constant sea breeze tempers the intense sun and makes the city's *malecones* **Sights** (oceanfront avenues) pleasant places to stroll. The Malecón Escénico, at the gentrified west end of town has a cluster of bars and seafood restaurants. It is a lively place especially at weekends, when there is good music, free beach aerobics and lots of action. This promenade is built along Playa Murciélago, a popular beach with wild surf (enquire locally before bathing, flags are placed on the beach to indicate whether it is safe or not). It is also a good surfing beach

Manta

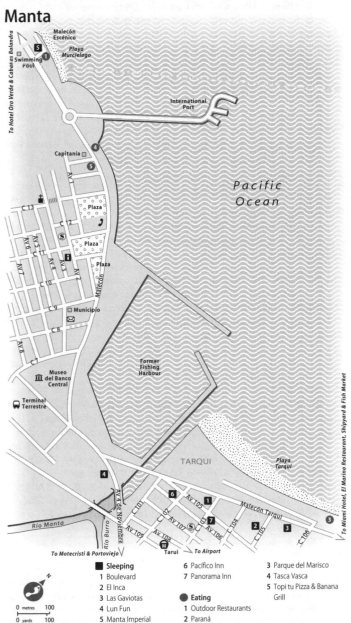

■ Sleeping
1 Boulevard
2 El Inca
3 Las Gaviotas
4 Lun Fun
5 Manta Imperial

6 Pacífico Inn
7 Panorama Inn

● Eating
1 Outdoor Restaurants
2 Paraná

3 Parque del Marisco
4 Tasca Vasca
5 Topi tu Pizza & Banana Grill

0 metres 100
0 yards 100

from December to April. Manta's growing number of upmarket hotels and restaurants are found in the neighbourhoods near Playa Murciélago. Further west is Playa Barbasquillo.

The centre of town, built on a hill, conserves some older wooden buildings and a bazaar-like atmosphere. Shops, banks, the terminal terrestre (due to be relocated in 2003), the Banco Central museum and a tourist information office are here, but no hotels and few restaurants.

The **Museo del Banco Central** has an excellent collection of archaeological pieces from seven different civilizations which flourished on the coast of Manabí between 3500 BC and AD 1530. It is well displayed, with Spanish explanations. ■ *Tue-Sat 1000-1800. US$1. Av 8 y Calle 7, behind the bus station.*

Tarqui
Tarqui beach is too polluted for swimming and east of Calle 110 it is unsafe at all hours

Two bridges join the main town with Tarqui on the east side of the Río Manta. Many hotels, including all the economy ones, are located near the ocean here. This is not a safe area at night (take a taxi to your hotel), but a stroll along the Tarqui Malecón can be interesting during the day (do not take valuables). Visit the fish market and *astillero* around Calle 110, where large wooden fishing boats are built. At the Malecón y Calle 106 is the Parque del Marisco, with many small seafood restaurants, but mind the hygiene here.

Sleeping
■ *on map*
Price codes:
see inside front cover
Manta hotels are more expensive than in other parts of coastal Ecuador

In Manta L *Oro Verde*, Malecón y C 23, T629200, F629210, www.oroverdehotels.com Includes buffet breakfast, restaurant, pool, all luxuries, best in town. **AL** *Cabañas Balandra*, Av 8 y C 20, Barrio Córdova, T620316, F620545. A/c, parking, comfortable cabins. **AL** *Costa del Sol*, Malecón y Av 25, T620025, F620019. Includes breakfast, a/c, pool, parking, modern, comfortable, ocean-side rooms with balconies are very nice, new in 2001. **AL** *Lun Fun*, Av 11 y C 2, near bridge to Tarqui, T622966, F610601. Includes breakfast, restaurant, a/c, parking, comfortable and nice but in unpleasant area. **A** *Aeropuerto*, Calle M3 y Av 24, Ciudadela el Murciélago (nowhere near the airport), T628040. Includes breakfast, a/c, in converted private home, quiet residential neighbourhood, out of the way. **A** *Barbasquillo*, at playa Barbasquillo, T620718, F628111. Includes breakfast, restaurant, a/c, pool and gym, fridge, parking, comfortable. **A** *María José*, Av Flavio Reyes y C 29 #110, Barrio Umiña, T628562. A/c, in private home with nice terrace, quiet residential neighbourhood, far from everything. **B** *Manta Imperial*, Malecón by Playa Murciélago, T621955, F623016. A/c, cheaper with fan, pool, parking, ageing and in need of renovation.

In Tarqui A *Las Gaviotas*, Malecón 1109 y C 106, T620140, F620940. Restaurant, a/c, the best in Tarqui. **C** *El Inca*, C 105 y Malecón, T610986, F622447. Cold water, a/c, cheaper with fan, parking, well maintained older place. **C-D** *Panorama Inn*, C 103 y Av 105, T622996, F611552. Restaurant, cold water, a/c, cheaper with fan, pool, parking, nice new section across the street, older rooms fair, friendly and helpful. **D** *Americana*, Av 106 y C 105, T623069. Cold water, basic. **D** *Boulevard*, Av 105 y C 103, T625333. Cold water, a/c, cheaper with fan, parking, sea view, OK. **D** *Pacífico Inn*, Av 106 y C 101, T623584, F622475. A/c, cheaper with fan, OK. **E** *Del Mar*, Av 105 y C 104, T920140. Private bath, cold water, basic. **E** *Miami*, C 108 y Malecón, T611743. Private bath, cold water, fan, very basic. There are several other cheap places on Tarqui beach but mind cleanliness and safety.

Eating
● *on map*
Most restaurants are on the Manta side

Expensive *Tasca Vasca*, Malecón y C 16. Fine Spanish food. Fine restaurants are found at *Hotel Oro Verde* and *Cabañas Balandra*.

Mid-range *Chavecito*, C 106 y Av 106, Tarqui. Ceviches, fish dishes. *Club Ejecutivo*, Av 2 y C 12, top of the Banco del Pichincha building. First class international food and service, great view. *El Marino*, Malecón y C 110, Tarqui. Classic fish and seafood restaurant, for ceviches, sopa marinera and other delicacies.

Recommended. *Palmeira's*, Circunvalación y Av 29. Grill and also Italian dishes. *Riviera*, C 20 y Av 12, first class Italian food. *Mamma Rosa*, Flavio Reyes y C26. Italian and also grill. *Soley*, at Hotel *Lun Fun*. Chinese.

Cheap *Beachcomber*, C 20 y Av Flavio Reyes, cheap set lunch and mid-range grill in the evening. *Chifa Macau*, Av 15 y C 13. Good Chinese. *Delfín*, C 8 y Av 24. Cheap seafood. *El Rincón de Fey*, Av Flavio Reyes y C 26, Colombian home cooking. *Flipper*, C 14 y Av 14. Varied seafood. *Juventud Italiana*, Av 24 y C 10. Ceviches. *La Barca*, Malecón y C 16. Cheap lunch or à la carte, also café serving local snacks. *Paraná*, Malecón y C 17, near the port. Excellent quality and value cheap set lunch, also mid-range grill in the evening. Highly recommended. *Rincón Criollo*, Av Flavio Reyes y C 20. Regional cooking, cheap set lunch, a/c.

The Malecón Escénico has 18 restaurants, most serve local seafood specialties. The Parque del Marisco, at the beach in Tarqui, has 20 *comedores* serving cheap seafood, keep an eye on hygiene.

Fast food *Ch'Farina*, at El Paseo Shopping and Centro Comercial Manicentro. Good pizza. *Maxi Pizza*, Malecón y C 20. Pizza. *Topi Tu Pizza & Banana Grill*, Malecón Y C15. Large menu, also ice-cream, mid-range prices. *Fruta del Tiempo*, Malecón y C 13. Fruit salads, sandwiches, snacks, cheap. *American Deli*, Centro Comercial Cocco Centro, sandwiches and meals at mid-range prices.

Bars *Grepy*, Av 3 y C 12. Bar and snacks, pleasant atmosphere, soft music. *Poco Loco Funny Bar*, Malecón y C 16. Nice atmosphere. | **Bars & nightclubs**

Discos *Madera Fina*, Av Flavio Reyes y Av 23. Latin music, shows, mature crowd. *Santa Fe*, Av 22 y Av Flavio Reyes. Varied music, occasioanl shows, mature crowd. *La Sal*, C 20 y Av Flavio Reyes. Techno, young crowd. *Madera Fina*, Av Flavio Reyes y Av 27. Modern, young crowd.

Cinema *Super Cines*, at El Paseo Shopping, starting 1400. | **Entertainment**

There are several shopping centres in town: *El Paseo Shopping*, on Av 4 de Noviembre, the main road entering town from Portoviejo (buses run there from the beach end of town), large mall where you can find some crafts shops, supermarket, restaurants and everything else. *Manicentro*, Av Flavio Reyes y C 23, has a supermarket, restaurant and other shops. *Centro Comercial Cocco Manta*, Malecón y C 23, small, has an information office, restaurants and a few shops. | **Shopping**

Delgado Travel, Av 2 y C 13, T627925, vtdelgad@manta.ecua.net.ec City and regional tours, visits to *Hostería San Antonio* (see Coastal road above), whale-watching trips, Parque Nacional Machalilla. *Metropolitan Touring*, Av 4 y C 13, T623090. Local, regional and nationwide tours (see Quito operators). | **Tour operators**

Local **Car hire**: *Avis*, Vía a Jaramijó, near the airport, T628512. *Budget*, Malecón y C 15, T629919. *Delgado Rent a Car*, C2 y Malecón, T629333. *Localiza*, Av Flavio Reyes y Av 21, T622434. | **Transport**

Long distance **Air**: Eloy Alfaro airport is east of Tarqui, along the route to Jaramijó, T622590. *TAME* flies to **Quito** daily.

Bus: the Terminal Terrestre is on C 7 y Av 8 in the centre, mind your belongings here. There are plans to relocate it to Av Circunvalación in 2003, enquire locally. A couple of companies have their own private terminals and run services to their own terminals in Quito. To **Quito**, 7 daily, US$6.50, 8½ hrs. *Ejecutivo* (slightly fancier service) to Quito costs US$8.50 with *Flota Imbabura*, Malecón y C 8, T610566, 3 daily, *Panamericana*, Av 4 y C 12,

T625898, 2 nightly and *Reina del Camino*, from the terminal, T620963, 4 daily. To **Guayaquil**, hourly, US$3, 3 hrs. Ejecutivo with *Reina del Camino*, hourly, US$4.50. To **Santo Domingo**, hourly, US$4.50, 6 hrs. To Ambato with *Reina del Camino*, 2 daily, US$6.80, 10 hrs. To **Portoviejo**, every 10 mins, US$0.50, 45 mins. To **Jipijapa**, every 20 mins, US$1, 1 hr. To **Bahía de Caráquez**, hourly, US$2.20, 3¼ hrs. To **Pedernales**, 6 daily, US$4.60, 6 hrs. To **Esmeraldas**, 3 daily, US$7, 10 hrs. To **Puerto López**, hourly, US$2.40, 2½ hrs via Jipijapa with *Manglaralto* or *CTMJ*, 2 hrs via the coastal route with *CTMJ*.

Directory **Airlines** *American Airlines*, Av 1 y C 12. **TAME**, Malecón y C El Vigía in the centre, T622006. **Banks** *Banco del Pichincha*, Av 2 y C 11, 2nd floor, TCs, VISA. *Banco del Pacífico*, Av 2 y C 13, TCs. *Mutualista Pichincha*, Av 4 y C 9, Mastercard. **Communications** Internet: service runs about US$0.80. *Coolweb.ec*, Paseo José María Egas (Av 3) y C 11, fast link, spacious. Recommended. *Patiño Cyber*, Av 106, Tarqui. **Post**: Av 4 y C 8. **Telephone**: *Pacifictel*, Malecón near C 11. **Language courses** *Academia Sur Pacífico*, Av 24 y C 15, 3rd floor. **Medical services** *Clínica Manta*, Av 4 de Noviembre, T921566, is a good private, pricey, hospital open 24 hrs. *Hospital Rodríguez Zambrano*, Vía a San Mateo, T611849, is a public hospital. **Shipping agents** The Ministerio de Turismo has a list of agents, see Tourist office above.

Portoviejo

Phone code: 05
Colour map 4, grid B2
Population: 170,000

Some 40 km inland from Manta and 65 km northeast from Jipijapa, Portoviejo is the capital of Manabí province and a major commercial centre. It was once a port on the Río Rocafuerte, but as a result of severe deforestation the river has silted and almost completely dried up. In the rainy season, however, it floods badly, often breaking its banks.

Sights
Portoviejo is not a safe city, take routine precautions here at all hours

The cathedral, overlooks Parque Eloy Alfaro, you can see sloths taking it easy in the plaza's trees and you may be tempted to do the same in this, Ecuador's hottest city. Portoviejo is one of the main places where kapok mattresses and pillows are made from the fluffy fibre of the seed capsule of the *ceibo*. In Calle Alajuela you can buy *montubio* hammocks, bags, hats etc made by the coastal farmers, or *montubios*, as they are known. The Jardín Botánico is along Av Universitaria in the north of the city. About 10 minutes from town, on the road that later branches to Bahía, is the village of **Sosote**; its main street is lined with workshops where figurines are carved out of *tagua* nuts (vegetable ivory) into innumerable shapes. The *Ministerio de Turismo* is at Pedro Gual y J Montalvo, T630877.

Sleeping
B *Hostería California*, Ciudadela California, T634415. A/c, very good. **B** *Máximo*, C Cumaná y 5 de Junio, T636521. With a/c, fridge, cheaper with fan, restaurant. **C** *Cabrera Internacional*, García Moreno y Pedro Gual, T633201. A/c, **D** with fan, restaurant, clean, noisy. **C** *Conquistador*, 18 de Octubre y 10 de Agosto, T633259, F631481. A/c, **D** with fan Friendly. **C** *New York*, Fco de P Moreira y Olmedo, T632044. A/c and fridge, **D** with fan, clean, nice, restaurant downstairs. **D** *El Gato*, Pedro Gual y 9 de Octubre, T632856. **E** *Pacheco*, 9 de Octubre 1512 y Morales, T631788. With or without bath, fan. **F** *París*, Plaza Central, T652727. One of the oldest hotels in town, classic, with bath, fan. **F** *San Marco*, Olmedo 706 y 9 de Octubre, T630651.

Eating
La Carreta, C Olmedo y Alajuela and at Andrés Vera near the terminal. Good food and service. *La Crema*, Central Park. Clean and cheap, serves lunch and dinner. *El Tomate*, on the road to Crucita and Bahía. Excellent traditional Manabí food. One of the best places to get typical food in the province. *La Fruta Prohibida*, C Chile. Fast food, Portoviejo's gringo hang out. *El Galpón*, C Quito, very good food and prices, local

music at night, very popular. *Zalita*, Primera Transversal entre Duarte y Alajuela. Lunch only, popular. There are several good *chifas* (chinese restaurants) in town including *Wing Wat*, Pacheco y Pedro Gual.

Viejoteca, for the oldies, good live music. *Discoteques Sótano*, *Pachanguero* and *Taguara*, all in the area of Av Manabí. **Bars & discos**

Ventura Travel, Alejo Lascano y Pedro Gual, T634122. International flight changes and confirmations. Very friendly and good service **Tour operators**

Air The Reales Tamarindos airport is northwest of the centre. Flights to Quito 3 times a week. **Bus** The bus station is 1 km south of the centre, on the opposite side of the Río Portoviejo. A taxi to/from town costs US$0.90. To **Quito**, US$6, 9 hrs. Routes are either east via Quevedo (147 km), or, at Calderón, branch northeast for Calceta, Chone and on to Santo Domingo de los Colorados. To **Guayaquil**, US$3.20, 3 hrs. To **Manta**, US$0.50, 45 mins. **Transport**

Communications Internet: Prices around US$1.75 per hr. *Café Royal*, C Chile y 10 de Agosto. *Habla por Menos*, C Cordova y Morales. . **Directory**

Crucita is an oceanside playground for folks from Portoviejo and Manta, less than an hour's ride from either city. It gets busy at weekends and holidays. The beach is long, with gentle surf, and small hotels and restaurants line the Malecón. What makes Crucita special however, are its ideal conditions for several aeronautical sports: paragliding, hang-gliding and kite-surfing. Tandem paragliding flights for novices (US$15), as well as lessons for all these sports can be arranged through *Hostal Los Voladores* at the south end of the beach. The best season for flights is July to December. For those who prefer to keep their feet on the ground, a walk north along the beach to the village of Arenales allows you to see how millions of sardines are brought ashore each day and are processed by hand, before being trucked to the cannery. There is an abundance of sea birds in the area, including brown pelicans, frigates, blue-footed boobies, gulls and sandpipers.

Crucita
Phone code: 05
Colour map 4, grid A2
Population: 8,300

Sleeping From south to north along the beach: **D** *Hostal Voladores*, south end of beach, away from town, T676200, www.geocities.com/hostalvoladores Private bath, cold water, small pool, simple but nice, very friendly and helpful. **D** *Hipocampo*, the oldest in town. Private bath, basic, friendly. **D** *Rosita*, small rooms with balcony, bath, fan, cold water, parking, clean. **C** *Barandhua*, T676159, comfortable with bath, hot water, fan, restaurant, pool, good service. **C** *Hostería Zucasa*, T676133. Fully equipped cabins for up to 6, with fan, hot water, cheaper with cold water, pool, very nice, friendly. **C** *Hostería Venecia*, T676301. Rooms with balcony and hammocks, hot water, small indoor pool, modern building, internet US$2.50 per hr. **E** *Las Cabañitas*, T652660 in Portoviejo. Cabins for 4-5 people, very basic, friendly. **E** *La Cabaña de Balboa*, 1 block back from the beach, T676302. Small rooms, private bath, cold water, bar. **D** *Sol Alondra*, 150 m back from the beach, T676246. Private bath, cold water, fan, some with fridge, parking, friendly. **D** *Rey David*, T676143. Private bath, cold water, a/c, cheaper with fan, pool, parking, nice. **E** *Euro Hostal*, T676336. Private bath, cold water, OK.

Eating There are many simple restaurants and kiosks serving mainly fish and seafood along the seafront. To the south along the beach, all serving set meals and à la carte, all good and cheap are: *Alas Delta 1 & 2*, try their *conchas asadas*, both have terrace eating with good ocean views; *El Gordito Parapente* and *Las Gaviotas*.

Northern Pacific Lowlands

Transport Buses run along the malecón, there is frequent service to **Portoviejo**, US$0.80, 45 mins and **Manta**, US$1.30, 1½ hrs (these do not take a direct route).

Communications Telephone: *Pacifictel*, for long-distance phone calls, 2 blocks back from the beach on the highway.

About 2 km north along a paved road running parallel to the beach is the fishing village of **Las Gilces**, with less tourism. Accommodation is available in the *Hotel Centro Turístico Las Amazonas*.

San Clemente & San Jacinto
Phone code: 05
Colour map 4, grid A2

About 60 km north of Portoviejo (60 km northeast of Manta, 30 km south of Bahía de Caráquez) are San Clemente and, 3 km south, San Jacinto, in an area known for its salt production. Both get crowded during the holiday season (July and August) but are deserted the rest of the year. The long beach and ocean are very nice, but be wary of the strong undertow.

Sleeping and eating San Clemente: **C** *Hostería San Clemente*. Modern clean cabins for 6-10 persons, pool, restaurant, book ahead in season, closed in low season. **D** *Las Acacias*, 150 m from the beach, 800 m north of San Clemente, T02-2541706 (Quito). Nice 3-storey wooden building with huge verandas, prices go up in high season, with bath, good seafood, clean. Recommended. **E** *Hostal El Edén*, 1 block from beach along the main street, T09-9866974 (mob). Some rooms have bath, some have sea views, clean, basic. **F** *Las Palmas*, on the main street, simp,e cabins with several rooms, with fan, restaurant, friendly. **F** *Cabañas Espuma del Mar*, on the beach south of town. Good restaurant, family-run. *San Estéban*, next to Espuma del Mar, new hotel in 2002. Two good, cheap restaurants near the beach are *Tiburón* and *Costa del Sol*.

San Jacinto: **D** *Hotel San Jacinto*, on the beach. Simple rooms with bath, hot water, pool. **D** *Cabañas del Pacífico*, 1 block back from the beach, T02-2523862 (Quito). Private bath, fan, fridge. **D** *Cabañas Rocío*, T615476. Nice cabins with well equiped kitchen, hot water, a bit cramped. **E** *Briggitte*, in the centre of town, T615505. Private bath, cold water, tiled floors. There are a couple of other very basic lodgings in town, as well as, several simple restaurants. *Laurita Chone*, has good food, cheap.

Between San Clemente and San Jacinto: **C** *Hostal Chediak*, T615499, F02-2464322 (Quito). Comfortable nicely furnished rooms, with hot water, fan, mosquito net, great views from upper floor balconies, restaurant, parking. **D** *Cabañas Tío Gerard*, T615517, F02-2258250 (Quito). With bath, cold water, kitchenette, small simple rooms, clean, fan.

Transport Bus: To **Portoviejo**, every 15 mins, US$0.90, 1¼ hrs. To **Bahía de Caráquez**, US$0.50, 30 mins, a few start in San Clemente in the morning or wait for a through bus at the highway.

Bahía de Caráquez

Set on the southern shore at the seaward end of the Chone estuary, Bahía is a friendly, relaxed resort town and a pleasant place in which to spend some time. The riverfront is attractively laid out with parks on the Malecón Alberto Santos, which becomes Circunvalación Dr Virgilio Ratti and goes right around the point. The road follows the beach around the point. The beaches right in Bahía are nothing special, but there excellent beaches nearby between San Vicente and Canoa as well as at Punta Bellaca, see Excursions below. High season for Bahía and surroundings is July and August.

Phone code: 05
Colour map 4, grid A2
Population: 20,000
Altitude: sea level

Getting there Buses coming into Bahía stop by the obelisk at the Malecón end of Ascázubi before returning to the bus office. Departing buses do not go to the centre

Ins & outs
See Transport, page 336, for further details

Getting around Bahía is small and very manageable. Not surprisingly a number of hotels are clustered around the ferry which links the town with San Vicente across the estuary, others are along the peninsula, closer to the beach.

Tourist information Ministerio de Turismo, Bolívar 700 y Mateus, T/F691124, mturlitoral@ec-gov.net Very helpful and informative. Mon-Fri 0830-1300, 1400-1700.

Bahía has declared itself an 'eco-city', where recycling projects, organic gardens and ecoclubs are common (information about the eco-city from Fundación Stuarium, T693490 or the Planet Drum Foundation, planetdrum@igc.org, www.planetdrum.org). The city is also a centre of the less than ecologically friendly shrimp farming industry, which has boosted the local economy but also destroyed much of the estuary's precious mangroves. With awareness of the damage done, there is now a drive for alternative methods. Bahía boasts the first and only certified organic shrimp farm in the world, and a paper recycling scheme, involving communities who previously lived from the mangrove forests.

Sights

The **Museo Bahía de Caráquez** of the Banco Central (refurbished in 2001) has an interesting collection of arcaheological artefacts from various prehispanic coastal cultures. The well organized display includes a very impressive life-size balsa raft. Another section of the museum is devoted to modern sculpture. ■ *Tue-Fri 1000-1700, Sat-Sun 1100-1500. US$1. Malecón Alberto Santos y Aguilera.* **Casa Velázquez** is a 1900 vintage residence with a museum open to the public. It is a fine sample of the old wooden coastal architecture which is now a rarety. ■ *Tue-Sun 0900-1200, 1500-1900. US$1. Mejía y Eloy Alfaro, up on the hill.* Another fine construction houses the **Casa de la Cultura**, with a library and temporary exhibits. ■ *Malecón y Peña.*

Excursions

The Rio Chone estuary has several islands with mangrove forest. The area is rich in birdlife, dolphins may also be seen, and conditions are ideal for photographers because you can get really close, even under the mangrove trees where birds nest. The male frigate birds can be seen displaying their inflated red sacks as part of the mating ritual; best from August to January.

Río Chone estuary
See also Chone, page 337

Northern Pacific Lowlands

Isla Fragatas is 15 minutes by boat from Bahía and various species of birds can be seen there. A visit to the island is included in some tours which make multiple stops.

Further up the estuary is **Isla Corazón**, where a boardwalk has been built through an area of protected mangrove forest. At the end of the island are some bird colonies which can only be accessed by boat.

The village of **Puerto Portovelo**, reached by bus from San Vicente, has an information centre for the area, including an interesting video. The community is involved in mangrove reforestation and runs an ecotourism project. ■ *US$5 pp for a tour with a native guide. You can visit independently, taking a Chone bound bus from San Vicente (allow enough time to get back to San Vicente before dark) or with an agency. Agency tours might do part of the trip by boat, which has the advantage of travelling through the estuary and seeing several islands. Visits here are tide sensitive, so even to go independently, it is best to check with the agencies when go. Bahía Dolphin tours is in radio contact with Puerto Portovelo, so they will advise the guides to expect you and sell you the entry ticket. Agency tours are US$12-17 pp.*

Bahía de Caráquez

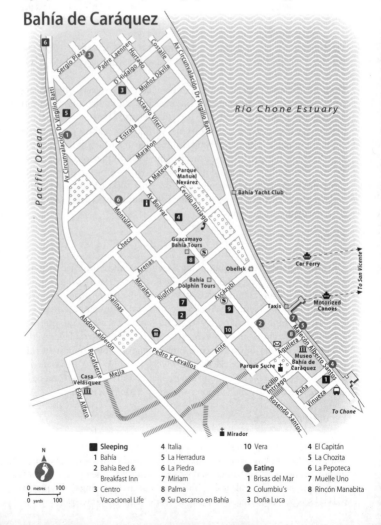

■ **Sleeping**	4 Italia	10 Vera	4 El Capitán
1 Bahía	5 La Herradura		5 La Chozita
2 Bahía Bed &	6 La Piedra	● **Eating**	6 La Pepoteca
Breakfast Inn	7 Miriam	1 Brisas del Mar	7 Muelle Uno
3 Centro	8 Palma	2 Columbiu's	8 Rincón Manabita
Vacacional Life	9 Su Descanso en Bahía	3 Doña Luca	

The Chirije archaeological site is a 45-minute ride south of Bahía. This site was a seaport of the Bahía culture (500 BC to AD 500), which traded as far north as Mexico and south to Chile. There is a museum on site. It is surrounded by dry tropical forest and good beaches. There are **B** cabins with ocean views and a mid-range restaurant. There are walking, horse-riding and birdwatching possibilities in the area. Tours from Bahía take you in an open-sided *chiva* along the beach (US$30 per person, includes lunch). On the way to Chirije is the scenic **Punta Bellaca**, near it is the **Cerro Viejo** or **Cerro de las Orquídeas** hill, with dry tropical forest, worth exploring. A walking tour through the forest to Punta Bellaca costs US$14.

Chirije

About 10 km north of Canoa (see below), the Río Muchacho organic farm promotes agro-ecology and reforestation in the area and runs an environmental primary school. A three-day visit to the farm is recommended in order to explore the area. Accommodation is rustic but comfortable, and the food is good, mainly vegetarian. It's an eye-opener to rural coastal (*montubio*) culture and to organic farming. Volunteer programmes can be set up for those wishing to contribute to the farm's projects. Highly recommended. ■ *Daily fee C per person full board, includes transport; there are group discounts. Reservations necessary, contact Guacamayo Bahía Tours or Arena Bar in Canoa.*

Río Muchacho organic farm

This private park owned by biologist Alfredo Harmsen is 5 km from Bahía along the bay. The waterfront setting is striking, as is the unusual combination of native and domestic animals and birds, many of which interact freely with each other and humans. There are sloths, coatimundi, deer, ostriches, rabbits, macaws, a donkey, a cow, peacocks and geese. There is also a Japanese bonsai garden, cactus collection, spiritual centre, accommodation and restaurant. The food is first class vegetarian. ■ *T398331, reached by taxi or any bus heading out of town, US$2. A visit here is included in some agency tours of the area.*

Saiananda

AL *La Piedra*, Circunvalación near Bolívar, T690780, F690154, apartec@uio.satnet.net Good expensive restaurant, a/c, pool, modern, good service, access to beach, lovely views. **B** *Italia*, Bolívar y Checa, T/F691137. Restaurant, a/c, older but comfortable. **C-D** *La Herradura*, Bolívar e Hidalgo, T690446, F690265. Restaurant, a/c, cheaper with fan and cold water, older but very well maintained, cheaper rooms are good value. **D** *Centro Vacacional Life*, Cecilio Intriago y Muñoz Dávila, T690496. Cooking facilities, parking, fully furnished cottages. Private facilities for company employees, but may rent to public if there is space available. **D** *Su Descanso en Bahía*, Bolívar y Azcázubi, T691213. Cold water, small simple rooms. **D-E** *Bahía Bed & Breakfast Inn*, Ascázubi 322 y Morales, T690146. Includes breakfast, cheaper with shared bath, cold water, older place with renovated common area, rooms are run down and basic, discount for Canadians. **D-E** *Bahía Hotel*, Malecón y Vinueza, T690509, F693833. Fan, parking, variety of different rooms, those in back are nicer and more quiet. Good value. Recommended. **E-F** *Palma*, Bolívar 914 y Riofrío, T690467. Cheaper but poor with shared bath, cold water, very basic. **F** *Miriam*, Montúfar entre Ascázubi y Riofrío. Shared bath, cold water, very basic but clean. **F** *Vera*, Ante 112 y Montúfar, T691581. Cheaper with shared bath, cold water, very basic but OK.

Sleeping
■ *on map*
Only hotels with their own supply do not suffer water shortages

Mid-range *Muelle Uno*, by the pier where canoes leave for San Vicente. Good grill and seafood in a lovely setting over the water. Recommended.

Cheap *Brisas del Mar*, Hidalgo y Circunvalación. Good ceviches and fish. *Chifa Lau*, Malecón y Ascázubi. Chinese. *Doña Luca*, Cecilio Intriago y Sergio Plaza, towards the

Eating
● *on map*

tip of the peninsula. Excellent local fare, ceviches, desayuno manabita (a wholesome breakfast), lunches. Recommended. *El Capitán*, Malecón opposite the *Hotel Bahía*. Chicken and seafood dishes. *La Chozita*, on the Malecón south of the pier where canoes leave for San Vicente. Barbecue-style food, good. *La Terraza*, on the Malecón. Varied menu including vegetarian, good. *Rincón Manabita*, Malecón y Aguilera. Good *comida criolla*, local home cooking, including menestra.

Seriously cheap *Columbius*, Av Bolívar y Ante. Good à la carte (cheap to mid-range) and set meals (seriously cheap), try the *corvina al pimentón* or the dishes *al ajillo*, good service and value. Recommended. *La Pepoteca*, Montúfar y Mateus. Good food and service, seriously cheap set meals and mid-range à la carte.

Bars & nightclubs *Palma Morena*, Morales y Ascázubi. Bar, good soft music and atmosphere. *Eclipse*, Malecón y Arenas. Disco, open weekends. *Salsoteca Alcatraz*, Malecón near San Vicente launches pier (small entrance). Latin music, pleasant atmosphere at the water's edge. *Insomnio*, Av Unidad Nacional y Riofrío, on the Pacific side. Disco, Latin music, open on long weekends.

Tour operators All companies listed here offer tours to the estuary islands, wetlands (see Chone below), to see environmental projects in the area including the Río Muchacho farm and the organic shrimp farm, to the Chirije archaeological site, Punta Bellaca dry forest, beaches, whale watching and to Machalilla. See Excursions above. For information about the Humpback Whales see box, A whale of a time, page 322. *Guacamayo Bahía Tours*, Av Bolívar y Arenas, T691107, F691412, ecopapel@ecuadorexplorer.com, www.riomuchacho.com Runs tours, rents bikes, sells crafts and is involved in environmental work including Río Muchacho. Part of the tour fees go to community environmental programmes. *Bahía Dolphin Tours*, Av Bolívar 1004 y Riofrío, T692086, F692088, archtour@ecua.net.ec, www.bahiadolphin.com Runs tours, helps with the Puerto Portovelo eco-tourism project and manages the Chirije site. *Santours*, at *Hotel Vacaciones* in San Vicente, T690774, F675192. Runs regional tours.

Transport **Air** The airport is at San Vicente across the estuary, no comercial flights operate here. For charters contact NICA, T690332 or AECA, T674198.

Boat Motorized canoes (*lanchas* or *pangas*) cross the estuary to San Vicente, from the dock by the Malecón opposite C Ante, by *Muelle 1 Restaurant*. Frequent service 0615-1800, US$0.24; from 1800-2300, larger and slower boats make the crossing when they fill, US$0.35. A car ferry runs from a ramp near the obelisk, next to the Repsol gasoline station, at the end of C Ascázubi. It crosses every 20 mins or so, 0630-2000, US$2 for small vehicles, US$0.50 for motorcycles, free for foot passengers. Depending on the tide, the very steep ramps may be difficult for low clearance cars.

Bus Two classes of bus service operate to/from Quito and Guayaquil: *ejecutivo* buses are more comfortable, have a/c, videos, and only stop to pick up passengers at terminals, thus they are safer if not nearly as colourful as the regular service. The *Coactur* and *Reina del Camino* offices are on the Malecón 1600 block.

To **Quito**, *ejecutivo*, at 0900 and 2200, US$8, 6 hrs; regular, 3 daily, US$6, 8 hrs. To **Santo Domingo de los Colorados**, *ejecutivo*, US$6, 3½ hrs; regular, US$4, 4½ hrs. To **Esmeraldas**, at 1515, US$7, 8 hrs. To **Chone**, *ejecutivo*, US$1.50, 1½ hrs; regular, US$1.10, 1½ hrs. To **Portoviejo**, US$1.50, 2 hrs, hourly. To **Puerto López**, go to Manta, Portoviejo or Jipijapa and change buses. To **Guayaquil**, *ejecutivo*, 3 daily, US$6, 5 hrs; regular service, hourly, US$4.50, 6 hrs. To **Manta**, via Portoviejo, hourly, US$2.20, 3 hrs.

Roads From Bahía de Caráquez to the highlands there are 3 main roads. The first one is via Chone and El Carmen to Santo Domingo. The road is paved. It climbs quickly over the coastal range, with views of the estuary, the remaining mangroves and the shrimp ponds that destroyed them. In the following wetlands, with more shrimp ponds, are also cattle *fincas* and bamboo houses on stilts. The second road is via San Clemente and Rocafuerte to Pichincha, Velasco Ibarra and on to Quevedo and Santo Domingo. Alternatively you can go via Calceta, then on an unpaved dry season road directly to Pichincha. This road is very scenic but rarely passable. There are 2 rivers without bridges, which are not deep. A 4WD is recommended. The third route is via Pedernales (see page 340) to El Carmen and Santo Domingo, which is quicker.

Banks *Banco de Guayaquil*, Av Bolívar and Riofrío. TCs up to $200 daily, Mastercard advances. *Banco del Pichincha*, Bolívar y Ascázubi, VISA advances only. **Communications** Internet: Rates about US$2 per hour. *Genesis Net*, Malecón opposite the ferry from San Vicente, also net2phone. *Systemcom*, Calle Riofrío y Av Bolívar. **Telephone:** *Pacifictel*, Malecón y Arenas. **Directory**

Around Bahía

Chone is 1½ hours east from Bahía. At the Santo Domingo exit is a strange sculpture of four people suspending a car on wires across a gorge. It represents the difficulty faced in the first ever trip to Quito by car. One of the figures is the famous explorer, Carlos Alberto Aray, who formed one of the first bus companies in Manabí, which still exists. There is a bus terminal just out of town. You can catch a bus there from the centre. The *Pacifictel* office is opposite the post office at Bolívar y Atahualpa.

Chone
Phone code: 05
Population: 45,000

About 20 minutes west of Chone, in the Parroquia San Antonio, is the **Ciénega de la Segua**, a Ramsar site, a huge marshland, home to 158 species of birds, including 250,000 waterbirds. Another wetland in this region is **Simbocal**. Tours to the wetlands are available from agencies in Bahía (US$25 per person) and local guides can be hired in the neighbouring towns of La Segua and La Sabana. More information from www.ramsar.org/w.n.ecuador_segua.htm

North of Chone, by an attractive stream, is **La Cueva Dibujada**, a cave with ancient drawings. Agencies in Bahía can take you there (US$30 per person); be prepared to walk or ride a horse uphill for 1½ hours. Northeast of town is Cascada **La Guabina**, a 17-m waterfall, by the town of the same name.

Sleeping and eating **C** *Atahualpa de Oro*, Av Atahualpa y Páez, T696627. With bath, TV, restaurant, garage, clean, very good. **D** *Chone*, Pichincha y Páez, T695014. A/c, private bath, garage. **D** *Chonanas*, T695236. Private bath, a/c, **E** with shared bath and fan. There are others, **F**, which are very basic. Restaurants include *Maikito*, Av Atahualpa. Cheap à la carte, very cheap set meals, typical food, clean. *Rico Pollo*, Bolívar y Colón. Friendly, fast food, clean, cheap.

Northern Pacific Lowlands

North to Esmeraldas

San Vicente
Phone code: 05
Colour map 4, grid A2
Population: 8,100

San Vicente, on the north side of the Río Chone, can be reached by taking the ferry from Bahía de Caráquez, or the road west from Chone. Its attractive waterfront and wide sandy beach were lost to El Niño in 1998. However it is still the access point for the impressive stretch of beach between San Vicente and Canoa. It has an airport; however no commercial flights operate from here (see Bahía Transport above for charters). There is a small market near the waterfront and a second one on the road to San Isidro. The Santa Rosa church, 100 m to the north of the wharf, is worth checking out for the excellent mosaic and glass work by José María Peli Romeratigui (better known as Peli). The views of Bahía from town, especially from the hill are excellent.

Sleeping and eating On the road to Canoa (all across the road from the beach): **C** *Cabañas Alcatraz*, T674566. Cabins for 5, a/c, cheaper in older cabins with fan, cold water, clean pool, older but still nice. **C** *Monte Mar*, T674197, F674357, montemar@interactive.net.ec Excellent food, pool, views, simple cabins for 5. **C** *El Velero*, T674387. Cabañas and suites, pool, restaurant, good. **D** *Toronto*, T6742443, F674450. Private bath, cold water, fan, modern, friendly. *Restaurant La Piedra*, beyond Alcatraz just over the bridge on the way to Canoa, T674451, also rents apartments.

In town: **D** *Vacaciones*, close to where the canoes arrive, near the small market, T674116, F674117. Bath, some rooms with a/c, dirty pool, tennis court, restaurant, disco for residents only, tour operator. **D** *Génesis*, at north end of town, T674688. Private bath, cold water, fan, comfortable, friendly. **E** *San Vicente*, Av Primera y C 1, opposite the small market, T674182. With bath, **F** without, basic, clean, mosquito nets. There are several simple eating places in town and one pizzeria.

Transport Bus All companies have offices along the Malecón, not far from the canoe dock to Bahía. There is frequent service to Guayaquil via Portoviejo, to Chone, and north to Pedernales. **Portoviejo**, US$1.50, 2½ hrs. To **Chone**, 7 daily, US$1, 1¼ hrs. To **Guayaquil**, US$5.25, 5 hrs. To **Quito**, at 0900 with *Reina del Camino*, US$6, 8½ hrs, more service from Bahía, or take a bus to Pedernales and transfer there. To **Pedernales**, US$3, 2½ hrs. For **Esmeraldas** and northern beaches, take a bus to **Chamanga**, at 0810, 1430 or 1700, US$4.50, 3¼ hrs, and transfer there.

Roads A road runs along the bay southeast to Chone. Another goes north to Pedernales and on to Chamanga, Atacames and Esmeraldas. A third road goes inland, northeast to San Isidro.

Boat Motorized canoes and a car ferry cross the estuary to Bahía. See Bahía transport for details.

Canoa
Phone code: 05
Colour map 4, grid A2
The widest beach in Ecuador, good surfing, great bathing

The beautiful 17-km beach between San Vicente and Canoa is a good walk or bike ride. Just north along the beach are several natural caves at the cliff base. You can walk there at low tide but allow time to return. **Canoa** is a quiet fishing and tourist town, with a 200-m wide, clean and relatively isolated beach, one of the nicest in Ecuador. Surfing is good, especially during the wet season, December to April. In the dry season there is good wind for windsurfing. It is also a good place for hang-gliding and paragliding, although there is nowhere to take lessons or rent equipment. Horses can be hired for riding along the beach. Tents for shade and chairs are rented at the beach for US$4 a day.

Sleeping A *Hostería Canoa*, 1 km south of town, T616380, ecocanoa@ mnb.satnet.net Comfortable cabins and rooms, includes breakfast, a/c, hot water, pool, sauna, whirlpool, good restaurant (mid-range) and bar. **C** *País Libre*, 3 blocks from the beach, T616387, www.paislibre.net Spacious rooms, cheaper with shared bath, upper floors have pleasant breeze and good views, pool, restaurant, parking, surf board rentals, new in 2001. **D** *Sol y Luna*, 2 km south of town, T616363. Large comfortable rooms private bath, restaurant, small pool. **D** *Bambú*, on the beach, T09-9753696 (mob). A variety of rooms and prices, cheaper with shared bath, hot water, restaurant with good food at mid-range prices, camping US$2 per person, pleasant atmosphere, very popular, English and Dutch spoken. Recommended. **D** *Posada de Daniel*, at the back of the village, T616373. An attractive renovated homestead, private bath, some with a/c and hot water, nice grounds, pool, internet (US$3 per hr), nice views, friendly. **D** *Pacific Fun Cabins*, 3 km south of town, T09-982 5526. Simple cabins with bath, cold water, friendly. Next door is **D** *Sundown Inn*, 3 km south of town, T616359, www.ecuadorbeach.com At the beach, nice rooms with private bath, hot water, fan, restaurant, Spanish lessons. **E** *Hostal ShelMar*, 1 block from the beach, T09-9842460 (mob), shelmar3@hotmail.com With bath, basic but clean, restaurant, small surf boards for rent. **F** *El Tronco*, 1 block from the beach, T616635. Cheaper with shared bath, very basic cramped cabins, restaurant.

Eating *Comedor Jixsy*, on main street near the beach. Set meals, fish dishes, cheap. *Costa Azul*, on main street. Tasty but reports of food poisoning, cheap. *El Torbellino*, 4 blocks from the beach along the main street. Good for typical dishes, cheap, huge servings, set meals and à la carte, popular with locals, lunch only. *Arena Bar* at the beach. Breakfast, fruit salads, great pizza, snacks, beer, T-shirts for sale, hammocks. Owner Santiago gives surfing lessons, also organizes horse-riding tours to **Guaché Forest**, a nice day-trip through farmland, bamboo and humid forest. Trips to **Lobster Bay**, an isolated beach where you can stay in a cabin and the **Río Muchacho** organic farm (see Bahía Excursions above) can also be arranged here.

Transport Buses to **San Vicente**, every 30 min, 0700-1730, US$0.50, 30 mins. Taxi to San Vicente US$5. To **Pedernales**, every 30 min, 0600-1800, US$2.50, 2 hrs.

North of Canoa along the shore is **Cabo Pasado**, where howler monkeys might be seen in the forest; it was a stopping point for whalers who used to resupply with water at a spring. From Canoa the road goes inland, through the more humid pasture-lands, north to the small market centre of **Jama**, 1½ hours from San Vicente. South of town is El Matal, a fishing village and beach (not clean), reached by pick-up from the park.

Sleeping and eating **E** *Cabañas Barbudo*, 5 blocks from the park, T05-672117. Bamboo cabins, with bath, hammocks, clean, good value and quality restaurant. Recommended. **F** *Hostal Río Jama*, at the main park, T05-672188. Simple rooms with shared bath, cold water, modern construction, OK. There are a couple other very basic places to stay.

North of Jama the road gets closer to the shore once again. About 10 km ahead is the village of **Don Juan**, by a nice beach. Right at the highway is **G** *Hostal Turista*, very basic accommodations with shared bath. Nearby is **Reserva Tito Santos**, a dry forest reserve run by the Jatun Sacha Foundation (see Volunteer opportunities, page 82). Another 4 km north is **Punta Prieta** and **B** *Punta Prieta Guest House*, about 40 km from Pedernales, T09-9837056 (mob), T/F02-2862986 (Quito), puntaprieta@yahoo.com A gorgeous setting on a headland high above the ocean with access to pristine beaches. Comfortable cabins with bath, hot water, fridge, balcony with hammocks, meals available, nice grounds. The perfect place to get away from it all, very relaxing. Another 3 km north, at the next headland and by the hamlet of **Punta Blanca** is C *Punta Blanca Tent Camp*, T09-9227559 (mob), T02-2342763 (Quito). Furnished tents, hot showers, mid-range restaurant, about 20 m above the beach with nice views. North of Punta Blanca the road goes by Tabuga and La Cabuya before crossing the equator and reaching Pedernales, 36 km from Punta Blanca.

Pedernales
Phone code: 05
Colour map 2, grid B1

Pedernales, a market town and crossroads, is the closest bathing beach to Quito and is doing its best to attract tourism. To the north are good undeveloped beaches, while those in town are less attractive, despite efforts to keep them clean. Pedernales feels more like a commercial lowland city than a beach resort. A mosaic mural on the church overlooking the plaza is one of the best pieces of work by Peli (see San Vicente above), and lovely examples of his stained glass can be seen inside the airy church. About 50 more examples of his work can be seen throughout the country.

Sleeping and eating C *Catedral del Mar*, Pereira y Malecon, T681136. Spacious rooms with private bath, hot water, a/c, fridge, restaurant, parking, near the beach. D *Cocosolo*, on a secluded beach 20 km north, see Cojimies below. D *Mr John*, Plaza Acosta y Malecón, 1 block from the beach, T681107. Nice rooms and views, private bath, cold water, balcony, fan, parking, modern, good value, new in 2002. D *Arena*, Eloy Alfaro y Gonzalez Suárez, T681170. A/c, cold water, cheaper with fan, modern. D *América*, García Moreno y 27 de Noviembre, across from Texaco station T681174. Private bath, cold water, a/c, balcony, parking, OK. D-E *Playas*, Juan Pereira y Manabí, near the airport, T681125. With bath, fan, mosquito nets, clean, comfortable.

E *Albelo*, Plaza Acosta y Malecón, near the beach, T681372. Private bath, cold water, fan, simple, friendly, new in 2001. E *La Ola*, Plaza Acosta y Malecón, 1 block from the beach, T681384. Simple cabins with bath, cold water, fan, mosquito nets, parking. E *Pedernales*, on Av Eloy Alfaro, 2 blocks from the plaza, T681092. With bath, fan, nets, rooms at front have windows, basic. There are several other cheap and basic places to stay and many good simple restaurants in town. *El Rocío*, on Eloy Alfaro. Good cheap food. *Habana Club*, next to *Hotel Playas*. Good seafood, cheap. *San Isidro*, on main street, cheap. There are several good soda bars on Eloy Alfaro.

Transport Air: There is a landing strip, but no commercial flights. **Bus**: to **Santo Domingo**, via El Carmen, every 15 mins, US$3, 2½ hrs , and transfer for Quito. Direct to **Quito**, at 1140, 1340, 1700 and 2300 US$5, 5½ hrs. To **Chamanga**, US$1.60, 1½ hrs, continuing to **El Salto**, where you can make a connection for **Muisne**, or continue to **Esmeraldas**, US2.50, 2 hrs from Chamanga. To **San Vicente**, US$3, 2½ hrs. To **Guayaquil**, US$7.20, 10 hrs. For **Cojimies**, pick-ups leave from the main park, US$1, 45 mins along the beach at low tide.

Roads An unpaved road goes north through cattle ranches to Cojimies. The main coastal highway goes south to San Vicente and north to Chamanga, El Salto and Esmeraldas. Another important road goes inland to El Carmen and on to Santo Domingo de los Colorados; this is the most direct route to Quito.

Directory Banks Several in town including *Banco del Pichincha* and Banco del Pacífico. **Communications** No cyber cafés in 2002.

This is a real friendly one-horse town, with unpaved streets. It is continually being eroded by the sea and has been moved about three times in as many decades. Because the coastal highway does not pass through town, it is a poor, forgotten corner of the coast. There is a road conecting Pedernales and Cojimíes, however, at low tide, all traffic goes along the beach (follow the locals, you cannot get off just anywhere). You can hire a canoe to visit the mangroves around town (US$10 per hour). Places to stay include **F** *Costa Azul*, with shared bath, very basic. Slightly better looking is **F** *El Descanso*, with bath. The best option is **E** *Paraíso del Atardecer*, cabins at the entrance to the beach. *Restaurant Flavio Alfaro*, by the beach, is friendly and cheap.

Cojimíes
Colour map 2, grid B1

Some 14 km south of Cojimíes on an undeveloped beach is **D** *Cocosolo*, a lovely hideaway set among palm trees. Cabins with bath and rooms without bath, clean, restaurant, French, English and Italian spoken, camping, horses for hire. T09-9215078.

Transport Bus: Pick-ups ply back and forth along the beach at low tide. It's an exhilarating 30-min ride, US$1, the last one leaves at around 1500. **Boat**: Motorized canoes to Daule, from where you can access the main coastal highway (a long walk on the beach). To hire a canoe costs US$10 per hr.

North of Pedernales the coastal highway veers northeast, going slightly inland, then crosses into the province of Esmeraldas near **Chamanga** (San José de Chamanga), a thriving little hub with houses built on stilts on the freshwater estuary. This is a good spot from which to explore the nearby mangroves, there is one basic *pensión* to stay at and frequent buses north and south. Town is 1 km from the highway. Inland, and spanning the provincial border is the **Reserva Ecológica Mache Chindul**, administered by the Jatun Sacha Foundation, see Volunteer opportunities page 82. North of Chamanga is **Portete**, with nice estuary and beach. Here is **D** *Caña Brava*, overpriced cabins. It is a long walk along an undisturbed beach to **Daule**, where a canoe crosses to Cojimíes. When there are no passengers, you can hire the canoe for a ride in the estuary (US$5 per hour). Beyond Portete and 7 km from the main road along a poor side road is **Mompiche**, one of Ecuador's best beaches for surfing. Once a few shacks at the end of the beach, this fishing village is undergoing rapid development.

Sleeping and eating **A** *Casa Blanca*, T02-2252077 (Quito). Spacious clean cabins, nice expensive dinning area by the beach (open to the public), beach bar. **C** *Iruna*, east along the beach, access only at low tide or by launch, T09-9472458 (mob). A lovely secluded hideaway, nice gardens, Spanish run. **D** *Gabeal*, 300 m east of town, T09-9969654 (mob). Includes breakfast, bamboo construction with nice ocean views, especially from the 2nd floor balconies, small rooms with private bath, good restaurant at mid-range prices, the owner has a private forest reserve good for birdwatching and can arrange visits there. Simpler places are **E** *Delfín Azul*, cabins, and **E** *Chao Pescao*, in town, popular with surfers. There are several good local *comedores* serving fish.

Transport Bus: From **Esmeraldas** at 0830, 1230 and 1530, US$3, 3½ hrs.

North of Mompiche and inland is **El Salto**, the turn-off for Muisne, with a few *comedores* and the place to wait for a bus connection. The road to Muisne leads to **El Relleno**, from where motorized canoes cross the river to Muisne (US$0.20). There are a few basic hotels here (in case you arrive too late to cross to Muisne) and boat service to other villages in the area.

Northern Pacific Lowlands

Muisne

Phone code: 06
Colour map 2, grid B1
Population: 6,200

The town, on an island across a narrow stretch of water, is a bit run-down but lively and friendly. About 15 minutes' walk from town (or a tricycle ride for US$0.50), is a long expanse of beach, which makes for a pleasant walk at low tide but practically disappears at high tide. The beach end of town is a great place in which to kick back and relax for a few days. The atmosphere is friendly and peaceful and there is some very good food on offer.

The main streets in town are Calle Manabí and Calle Isidro Ayora, which run about 500 m between the Río Muisne, the stretch of water separating it from El Relleno on the mainland, and the beach. Between them and one block from the Río Muisne is the Parque Central; the church is opposite it. Behind the church is a tourist information office, which also has information on mangrove preservation in the area, friendly and helpful. *Pacifictel* is on Ayora, half a block from the park towards the Río Muisne, and the post office is around the corner in a perpendicular street. There are no banks, ask for Marco Velasco's store, near the dock, he changes travellers' cheques. Buses stop on the mainland.

Being mainly pedestrian, the town has a very relaxed feeling. The beach is wide, with coconut palms and lots of driftwood. Walking into isolated areas away from the developed parts of the beach is not recommended, it is not safe. There are horses for rent on the beach (US$3 for a long ride). Also on the beach is a Spanish school, with some rooms to rent (see Sleeping below).

The region produces bananas and shrimp. Between 1987 and 2000, over 97% of the 20,000 ha of mangrove forest in the area was destroyed and replaced by shrimp ponds, despite 1994 legislation which prohibits cutting mangroves. There are reforestation efforts underway by the *Fundación de Defensa Ecológica* which works with local communities; this is a slow and difficult process. Marcelo Cotera and Nisvaldo Ortíz arrange boat trips to see the mangrove forests which are being replanted (donations welcome, contact them through the tourist office). Boat trips to the Reserva Ecológica Mache Chindul (see above) can also be organized here. On the Río Sucio, inland from Muisne and Cojimíes, is an isolated group of Cayapa Indians, some of whom visit the town on Sunday.

Sleeping   **C** *Hostal Mapara*, at the beach, T480147, mapara@accessinter.net Ample and well furnished rooms, restaurant. Modern wooden construction. Best in town. Recommended. **D** *Oasis*, C Manabí, about 150 m from the beach, T480186. Cabins with bath, fan, nets. Clean, friendly. **D** *Cabañas San Cristóbal*, on the beach to the right coming from town, T480264. Cabins with bath. **D** *Calade*, 150 m away at the south end of the beach, T480279. With bath, cheaper without, hot water. Clean, comfortable but overpriced, negotiable for longer stays, excellent meals including vegetarian, internet US$3.50 per hour. **D** *Galápagos*, 200 m from the beach, T480289. With bath, fan, mosquito nets, restaurant. Modern, clean. Recommended. **E** *Playa Paraíso*. Turn left as you face the sea, then 200 m, T480192. Clean, basic, mosquito nets, friendly. **E** *Marango Spanish School*, at the beach, 40 m to the left, T480301, www.marango.org Spanish lessons US$4-5, rooms for students with shared bath, kitchen facilities, German-Ecuadorian run. Will also rent to non students.

In town: **E** *Don José*, T480396, with bath. Good. **F** *Sarita*, very basic, and a couple other simple places. Insist on a mosquito net.

El Tiburón. Good, cheap. Recommended. *Las Palmeiras*. Excellent seafood, try **Eating**
camarones a la plancha. Near the beach is *Restaurante Suizo-Italiano*. Good pizza *Try encocado de*
and pasta, breakfast on request, good atmosphere. Book exchange. Swiss owner *cangrejo, crab*
Daniel is friendly and very knowledgeable about the area. Good Venezuelan-run café *in coconut*
on the beach. *Habana Club*. Good rum and reggae. There are many other excellent
kiosks on the beach.

Boat Canoes ply the narrow stretch of water between the island and mainland (El **Transport**
Relleno); US$0.20. Boats can be chartered to go to Chamanga and Cojimies. It is easier
to reach Cojimies going by bus towards Chamanga and getting off at Daule, north of
Chamanga, from where you walk and take a canoe to Cojimies.
  Bus All buses go from El Relleno. To **Esmeraldas**, every 30 mins, US$1.60, 2½ hrs.
To **Quito**, a direct bus once a night. For **Pedernales**, take a bus to **El Salto**, US$0.50, 30
mins, on the Esmeraldas road, from where there are buses going south to **Chamanga**,
US$1.50, 1½ hrs, where you change for Pedernales, US$1.60, 1½ hrs. At 0600 there is a
direct bus Muisne-Chamanga.

Tonchigüe is a quiet little fishing village with an OK beach, two hours north **Tonchigüe**
from Muisne and 1½ hours southwest of Esmeraldas. There are a couple sim- **Punta Galera &**
ple places to stay, good *comedores* and transportation to Atacames (US$0.70) **points south**
and to Esmeraldas (US$1.50).
  About 2 km south of Tonchigüe a road goes west and follows the shore to
Punta Galera, from where it continues south to **Quingüe**, **Estero del
Plátano, San Francisco** and **Bunche**. This area is off the beaten path and has
some natural wonders to offer. There are forests and waterfalls. Bunche has a
community hall where you can stay, **G** per person. Between June and September, whales are sometimes seen from the shore at Estero del Plátano. Boat
excursions to see the whales go from Súa and Atacames (see below).

Sleeping Punta Galera area: 2 hotels, both with private beaches. **A** *Cumilinche*, 11
km from Tonchigüe and 5 km from Punta Galera, T733256. Upscale cabins for 4, with
a/c, hot water, terrace with hammocks, expensive restaurant by the beach, popular
with family groups. **D** *Playa Escondida*, 10 km from Tonchigüe and 6 km from Punta
Galera, T733106, judithbarett@hotmail.com, www.intergate.ca/playaescondida A
charming beach hideaway, set in 100 ha stretching back to secondary tropical dry forest. It is run by Canadian Judith Barett on an ecologically sound basis. Volunteers are
welcome for a reforestation project in the area. Accommodation is in rustic but nice
cabins overlooking a lovely little bay, camping **G** per person. The food is excellent,
swimming is safe, and you can walk along the beach at low tide. The place is completely isolated and wonderfully relaxing.

Transport Take a *ranchera* or bus from Esmeraldas for Punta Galera. River Tavesao
departs at 0530, 0830 and 1200 and La Costeñita at 0730 and 1600, 2 hrs. From Quito
take a bus to Esmeraldas or Tonchigüe and transfer there. A taxi from Atacames is
US$12 and a pick-up from Tonchigüe US$5.

Northeast of Tonchigüe is Playa de Same, with a beautiful, long, clean, grey **Same**
sandy beach lined with palms, it's safe for swimming. There are very few eco- *Phone code: 06*
nomical accommodation options here; mostly high-rise apartment blocks for *Colour map 2, grid A2*
rich Quiteños. In season there are many *comedores* serving fish on the beach.

Sleeping and eating Booking is advisable at holiday times and weekends. In the low season good deals can be negotiated. **LL** *Club Casablanca*, T733159, T02-2252077 (Quito),

Northern Pacific Lowlands

F2253452, www.ccasablanca.com Full board, restaurants, tennis courts, swimming pools, luxurious, the place to be seen for rich Quiteños. **A** *El Rampiral*, at south end of the beach, T/F02-2264134 (Quito), rampiral@uio.satnet.net Good value cabins by the sea.

C *Seaflower*, near the beach, T733369. Nice rooms, excellent expensive restaurant with special menu and top ingredients and presentation. German-Chilean-run. **C** *El Acantilado*, on the hill by the sea, south of Same, T733466, T02-2453606 (Quito), elacantilado@ andinanet.net Rooms and cabins for up to 5 people, includes breakfast, excellent food, pool, popular, whale-watching tours in season. **C** *Cabañas Isla del Sol*, at south end of beach, T733470. Cabins with fan, kitchenette, pool, cafeteria serves breakfast. **D** *La Terraza*, on the beach, T733320. Nice cabins for 3-4, with bath, fan, hammocks, large terrace, includes breakfast, good restaurant, Spanish and Italian owners. **D** *La Posada*, a more economical option. **E** *Azuca*, on the road at the entrance to town, large rooms, clean, good restaurant. *Unicornio Azul* and *Moscú* are both reasonable eating places.

Transport Buses every 30 mins to and from **Atacames**; La Costeñita, 15 mins, 18 km, US$0.35. Make sure it drops you at Same and not at *Club Casablanca*. To **Muisne**, US$0.60.

Súa

Phone code: 06
Colour map 2, grid A2

This is another beach resort, a 15-minute bus ride southwest of Atacames. Except in the high season (July to September) it is a quiet and friendly little place, set in a beautiful bay with pelicans and frigate birds wheeling overhead when the fishing boats land their catches. Hotel prices are lower out of season. Between June and September there are whale-watching excursions from here. The sighting area is to the south of Punta Galera (see above), 40-60 minutes by boat. ■ *Boats depart 0800-1100, US$15-20, per person.*

Sleeping and eating **D** *Buganvillas*, on the beach, T731008. Very nice, room 10 has the best views. **D** *Chagra Ramos*, on the beach, T731006. Good restaurant, fan, noisy disco in season, good value. **D** *El Peñón de Súa*, T734036. Restaurant, pool, parking, OK. **D** *El Triángulo*, on the street going to the beach, T731286. Fan, pool, parking, OK. **D** *San Fernando*, near the road, T731085. Parking, basic cabins. **E** *Los Jardines*, 150 m from the beach, T731181. Private bath, cold water, fan, parking, very nice, good value. **E** *Malibu*, on the beach, T731380. Cheaper with shared bath, basic. **E** *Mar y Sol*, on the Malecón, T731293. Private bath, OK. **E** *Súa*, on the beach, T731004. Café-restaurant, fan, 6 rooms, comfortable. There are many other similar places to stay. *Restaurant Bahía* serves big portions. *Café-Bar*, on the beach past *Hotel Buganvillas*, reggae.

Atacames

Phone code: 06
Colour map 2, grid A2
Population: 9,900
Altitude: sea level

Some 25 km south of Esmeraldas, Atacames is one of the main resorts on the Ecuadorean coast. It's a real 24-hour party town during the high season (July-September) as well as at weekends and national holiday, and the beach is none too clean at these times. Those who enjoy peace and isolation or who like to sleep at night should avoid the place; there are more tranquil alternatives further south such as Punta Galera (see above). The **Museo del Mar** is an aquarium with an interesting collection of fish, gastropods and other sea creatures. ■ *At the east end of the Malecón, daily 1000-2200, US$0.50.*

The main park and services such as the post office, *Pacifictel* and the bus stops are to the south of the Río Atacames. Most hotels are in a peninsula between the river and the ocean. There are whale-watching tours from here in season (see Caída del Sol, Sleeping below). **NB** The sale of black coral jewellery has led to the destruction of much of the offshore reef. Consider the environmental implications before buying.

Safety Many assaults on campers and beach strollers have been reported in recent years. People walking along the beach from Atacames to Súa regularly get assaulted at knife point where there is a small tunnel. Gangs seem to work daily. Note also that the sea can be very dangerous, there is a powerful undertow and many people have been drowned.

Prices quoted are for the high season. Discounts are available in the low season and midweek. Hotels are, generally, expensive for Ecuador. It's best to bring a mosquito net as few hotels supply them.

A *Juan Sebastián*, towards the east end of the beach, T731049, hotelj.s@uio.satnet.net Includes breakfast, restaurant, a/c, pool, parking, luxurious, a little Disneyland. **A** *La Marimba*, T731321. A/c, pool, parking, quiet and comfortable. **A** *Lé Castell*, T731476, F731442. Restaurant, pool, parking, comfortable. **B** *Tahiti*, T731078. Includes breakfast, good restaurant, fan, pool, parking, mosquito nets, cheaper in cabins. **C** *Arco Iris*, east end, T731069, F731437, arcoiris@andinanet.net Fridge, charming, English, German and French spoken. Recommended. **C** *Caída del Sol*, Malecón del Río, 150 m from beach, T/F731479. Fan, fridge, parking, spacious, quiet, good value, Swiss-run, organize whale-watching tours.

D *Cabañas de Rogers*, west end of the beach, T731041, F731599. Restaurant and bar, constant water supply, nice and reasonably quiet. Very good value. Recommended. **D** *Chavelito*, along the river, T731113. Quiet. **D** *Jennifer*, ½ block from the beach on a perpendicular street, T731055. Cheaper with shared bath, some cabins with cooking facilities, OK. **D** *La Casa del Manglar*, 150 m from the beach beside the footbridge, T731464. Cheaper with shared bath and without fan. Recommended. **D** *Los Bohíos*, 1 block from the beach by the pedestrian bridge, T731089. Comfortable bungalows, good value.

Sleeping
■ *on map*
Price codes:
see inside front cover
There are well over
100 hotels in
Atacames, of which
we list but a few

Atacames

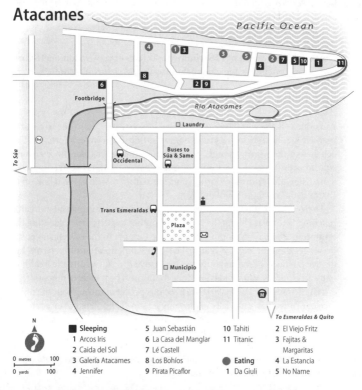

Sleeping	5 Juan Sebastián	10 Tahiti	2 El Viejo Fritz
1 Arcos Iris	6 La Casa del Manglar	11 Titanic	3 Fajitas &
2 Caida del Sol	7 Lé Castell		Margaritas
3 Galería Atacames	8 Los Bohíos	● **Eating**	4 La Estancia
4 Jennifer	9 Pirata Picaflor	1 Da Giuli	5 No Name

0 metres 100
0 yards 100

Recommended. **D** *Mi Nati*, at west end, T731271. Fan, large rooms for up to 8 available, quiet. **D** *Pirata Picaflor*, Malecón del Río, 1 block from beach, T09-9928084. Italian run. **D** *Rincón del Mar*, on the beach, T731064. Cosy, English, French and German spoken. Recommended. **D** *Titanic*, at east end, T731643. Restaurant, parking, german and English spoken. **E** *Galería Atacames*, on the beach, T731149. Restaurant, private bath, fan, simple.

Eating ● *on map* *Many restaurants on* *the beach rent rooms*	The beach is packed with bars and restaurants, too numerous to list. Most offer seafood at similar prices. The best and cheapest *ceviche* is found at the stands at the west end of the beach and at the market, but avoid *concha*. Ask for *almuerzo*, these set meals are usually good value. *Marco's*. Good steak and fish, popular. Recommended. *El Tiburón*, on the beach. Good seafood, cheap. *Paco Foco*. Great seafood, very popular. *Walfredos*, by the river. Always crowded. Along the Malecón are: *La Estancia*. Very good food, expensive. Recommended. *Da Giuli*. Spanish and Italian food. Good. *El Viejo Fritz*. German and International food, seafood, meat, good breakfasts, bar. *El Cubano*. Very popular. *No Name*, good pizza. *Fajitas & Margaritas*, Mexican food. *Cocada*, a sweet made from coconut, peanut and brown sugar, is sold in the main plaza.
Bars & **nightclubs**	*Scala*, on the Malecón, disco, admission US$1. Recommended. *Sambaye Club*, Malecón, by *Hotel Tahiti*, bar, disco, very popular.
Transport	**Tricycle taxi** A ride almost anywhere costs US$0.50, way west or east US$0.75, from the beach to the bus US$1.00. **Bus** To/from **Esmeraldas**, every 15 mins, US$0.60, 40 mins. To/from **Muisne**, every 30 mins. To **Guayaquil**, US$7, 8 hrs. To **Quito**, 3 daily, US$6.50, 6½ hrs. *Trans Esmeraldas* station is by the main park.
Directory	**Banks** *Pacífico*, by the main park, TCs. **Communications** Internet: by the main park, US$3.60 per hr. **Laundry** A couple of blocks east of the pedestrian bridge, on the south side of the river, US$1 per kg.

Northeast of Atacames are **Castelnuovo** and **Tonsupa**, two additional resorts with a variety of hotels and clubs behind walls and chain link fences.

Esmeraldas

Phone code: 06
Colour map 2, grid A2
Population: 96,000
Altitude: sea level

Esmeraldas is the capital of its province. The city itself has little to recommend it. It is hot, sticky, not too safe, and suffers from water shortages. The beaches to the north, though, are quieter and cleaner than those around Atacames and good for swimming. A new paved road has been completed from Esmeraldas north to Borbón and San Lorenzo, with a paved link up to Ibarra in the northern highlands.

There are gold mines in the area, tobacco and cacao are grown inland, cattle ranching takes place along the coast, and timber exports are decimating the rainforest. There is an oil pipeline from the Oriente to the oil refinery at the ocean terminal at nearby Balao. The development of shrimp farms has destroyed much of the surrounding mangrove forest. Despite the wealth in natural resources, Esmeraldas is among the poorest provinces in the country.

NB Mosquitoes and malaria are a serious problem throughout the province of Esmeraldas, especially in the rainy season. Take plenty of insect repellent. Most *residenciales* provide mosquito nets (*toldos* or *mosquiteros*). It's best to visit in the June-December dry season.

Tourist **information**	**Ministerio de Turismo**, Bolívar 221 entre Mejía y Salinas. Mon-Fri 0830-1700.

Northern Pacific Lowlands

The area is rich in culture. La Tolita, one of the earliest cultures in Ecuador, developed in this region, and the most important archaeological site is at **La Tolita** island to the north. This culture's ceramic legacy can be seen at the **Museo del Banco Central**, Espejo entre Olmedo y Colón.

Sights

Esmeraldas is also the heartland of Ecuador's Afro-Ecuadorean community. Its *marimba* music and dance is worth experiencing, as is the local cuisine which makes extensive use of coconut and plantain.

A *Apart Hotel Casino*, Libertad 407 y Ramón Tello, T728700, F728704. Good restaurant, a/c, fridge, parking, casino, excellent quality. **D** *El Cisne*, 10 de Agosto y Olmedo, T723411. Cold water, a/c, parking, friendly and good. **D** *Galeón*, Piedrahita 330 y Olmedo, T723820. Cold water, a/c, cheaper with fan, OK. **D** *Zulema 2*, Malecón y Rocafuerte, T726757. Cold water, fan, parking, modern. **E** *Diana*, Cañizares y Sucre, T724519. Private bath, cold water, fan, OK.

Sleeping
■ *on map*
Price codes:
see inside front cover
Generally, hotels on
the outskirts are better
than in the centre

Chifa Asiático, Cañizares y Bolívar. Chinese, excellent. *La Marimba Internacional*, Libertad y Lavallén. Recommended. *Las Redes*, main plaza. Good fish, cheap, friendly. *Budapest*, Cañizares 214 y Bolívar. Hungarian-run, clean, pleasant. *Balcón del Pacífico*, Bolívar y 10 de Agosto. Nice atmosphere, good view overlooking the city, cheap drinks. *Los Alamos*, 9 de Octubre, near the plaza. Good, popular. There are numerous typical restaurants and bars by the beach selling *ceviche*, fried fish and *patacones*.

Eating
● *on map*

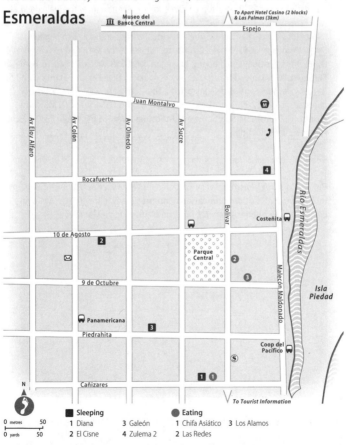

Esmeraldas

Entertainment   *El Portón*, Colón y Piedrahita, peña and disco. *El Guadal de Ña Mencha*, 6 de Diciembre y Quito, peña upstairs, marimba school at weekends. *Bar Asia* on Bolívar by Parque Central. Good.

Shopping   There is a Cayapa basket market across from the Post Office, behind the vegetables. Also 3 doors down, Tolita artefacts and basketry. The market near the bus station is good for buying mosquito nets. *Más por Menos* supermarket has a good selection of imported goods.

Transport   **Air**   General Rivadeneira Airport is near the town of **Tachina** (a couple of basic places to stay), on the coastal road north of Esmeraldas. A taxi to the city centre (30 km) is about US$5. Buses to the Terminal Terrestre from the road outside the airport pass about every 30 mins. Daily flights except Wed and Sat to **Quito** with *TAME*, 30 mins, US$37 one way. Check in early as planes may leave 30 mins before scheduled time. Buses to La Tola, Borbón, San Lorenzo or Ibarra pass near the airport so it is not necessary to go into town if northbound.

Bus   To Quito and Guayaquil there is *servicio directo* or *ejecutivo*, a better choice as they are fancier buses, faster and don't stop on the side of the road to take passengers. To **Quito**, US$5 regular, US$6 *directo*, 5-6 hrs, via Santo Domingo, frequent service on a good paved road, with *Trans-Esmeraldas* (10 de Agosto y Sucre, at main park, recommended), *Occidental* (9 de Octubre y Olmedo) and *Aerotaxi* (near the main park); also with *Panamericana* (Colón y Piedrahita) twice daily, slow but luxurious, US$8. Alternatively, it's 7 hrs via San Miguel de los Bancos and La Independencia. To **Santo Domingo**, US$3, 3 hrs. To **Ambato**, 5 times a day with *Coop Sudamericana*, US$6, 8 hrs. To **Guayaquil**, hourly, US$7 regular, US$8 *directo*, 8 hrs. To **Bahía de Caráquez**, via Santo Domingo de los Colorados, US$6.50. To **Manta**, US$7.50. *La Costeñita* (Malecón y 10 de Agosto) to **La Tola** 7 daily, US$2.80, 3 hrs. To **Borbón**, frequent service, US$2.80, 3 hrs. To **San Lorenzo**, 8 daily, US$4, 4 hrs. To **Muisne**, every 30 mins, US$2, 2 hrs. To **Súa, Same** and **Atacames**, every 15 mins from 0630-2030, to Atacames US$0.60, 1 hr.

Boat   You can take a bus to La Tola from where there are launches to points north.

Directory   **Banks**   *Banco del Austro*, Bolívar y Cañizares, for Visa. *Banco del Pichincha*, Bolívar y 9 de Octubre, for Visa. **Communications**   Internet: many in town. **Post**: Av Colón y 10 de Agosto. **Telephone**: *Andinatel*, Malecón Maldonado y J Montalvo.

North of Esmeraldas

There are good beaches for swimming north of Esmeraldas. The polluted water of the Río Esmeraldas reaches no further than **Camarones**, 20 km north of the city, where you can arrange to go out with the fishermen. Here is **E** *Hostería La Fragata*, T726175, cabins with bath, a bit run down, restaurant serving regional specialities, fishing and land tours. *Restaurant Sombrita*, has good food. **Río Verde**, at the outflow of the river of the same name, which was the setting for Moritz Thompson's books on Peace Corps life, *Living Poor* and *Farm on the River of Emeralds*, is a good place to spend a few relaxing days. It's two hours north of Esmeraldas. The beach gets little use and the water temperature is pleasant all year round.

Esmeraldas to Las Peñas
Colour map 2, grid A2/A3

Sleeping and eating   C *Hostería Pura Vida*, on a stretch of deserted beach just south of Palestina, which is just south of Río Verde, T744203. *Cabañas* with bath, a/c, balcony and hammocks, some simpler rooms, all rooms have nets and are very clean, pool, parking. Excellent restaurant and bar with a wide range of fruit juices. Recommended as beautiful and peaceful. **E** *Cabañas Manabitas*, in town 100 m from the beach, T744112. Cabins with bath, thached roof. **E** *Hostal Río Verde*, in town, 50 m from the beach, T744274. Rooms with private bath, fan. There are a couple other basic *residenciales* in **F** range.

Beyond Río Verde is **Rocafuerte**, a hot town with no hotels, recommended as having the best seafood in the province. About 25 km further east, and just 2 km from the paved coastal highway, is **Las Peñas**, a sleepy seaside village with a nice wide beach, just waiting to take off. With the completion of the paved highway from Ibarra (see Ibarra to the Coast, page 183), Las Peñas is only 4 hours from Ibarra, the closest beach from any highland capital. Development is starting and there are scheduled weekend buses from Ibarra (US$4, 4 hours).

Sleeping and eating   C *Cumbres Andinas*, at the beach, T786065. Private bath, fan, restaurant, has cheaper annexe (**E**) 2 blocks from the beach. **D** *Las Peñas*, at the beach. **D-E** *Cabañas D'Amor*, at the beach, T786044. Shared bath, basic. *Comedores* are set up on the beach selling fish and seafood dishes.

At the outflow of the Río Cayapas, 122 km north of Esmeraldas (8 km from Las Peñas) is **La Tola**, a hot town, dusty in the dry season, muddy in the wet, the access point for Limones and La Tolita (see below). Here the shoreline changes from sandy beaches to the south to mangrove swamp to the north. The wildlife is varied and spectacular, especially the birds. East of town is **El Majagual** forest with the tallest mangrove tree in the world (63.7 m): there is a walkway, good birdwatching and many mosquitos, take repellent. In this area, **Action for Mangrove Reforestation** (ACTMANG), a Japanese NGO, is working with the community of **Olmedo**, just northwest of La Tola, on environmental protection projects. The **Women's Union of Olmedo** runs an ecotourism project; they have accommodation, cheap meals and tours in the area.

La Tola
Colour map 2, grid A3

To the northeast of La Tola and on an island on the northern shore of the Río Cayapas is **La Tolita**, a small, poor village, where the culture of the same name thrived between 300 BC and AD 700. Many remains have been found here, several burial mounds remain to be explored and looters continue to take out artefacts to sell. Inmense quantities of gold where stolen and the streets are paved with broken pre-Colombian pot shards and lithics. A small site museum was also looted, so replicas have replaced some valuable pieces. Archaeologic studies continue, now at a site further inland.

Sleeping and eating La Tola in not a pleasant place to stay, women especially may be harassed. The best option in the area is in Olmedo, at **E** *Casa del Manglar*, a 20-min walk or short boat ride from La Tola, T780239 (Sra Carmen Mina in San Lorenzo for advance arrangements and pick-up at La Tola, or go directly). Shared bath, balcony with hammocks, clean, quiet and pleasant, meals, tours to El Majual and other spots. Part of the eco-tourism project (see above). **D** *Residencial Arist*, at La Tola. Shared bath, basic, overpriced. *Maurita*, good restaurant in La Tola. Next door is a bar, a good place to hear *marimba* music at weekends. *Bero*, opposite *Arist*, for meals.

Transport Bus: To Esmeraldas, 7 daily, US$2.80, 3 hrs. **Boat**: launches between La Tola and Limones connect with buses to/from Esmeraldas. There are launches between La Tola and Limones every 1½ hrs, US$2.50, 1 hr.

Limones
Colour map 2, grid A3

Officially called **Valdez**, but generally known as Limones, the town is the focus of traffic downriver from much of northern Esmeraldas Province, where bananas from the Río Santiago are sent to Esmeraldas for export. The Cayapa Indians live up the Río Cayapa and can sometimes be seen in Limones, especially during the crowded weekend market, but they are more frequently seen at Borbón.

Nancy Alexander, of Chicago, writes that about 75% of the population of Limones, Borbón and San Lorenzo has come from Colombia in the last 50 years. The people are mostly black and many are illegal immigrants. Smuggling between Limones and Tumaco in Colombia is big business (hammocks, manufactured goods, drugs) and there are occasional drug searches along the north coastal road.

Limones has two good shops selling the very attractive Cayapa basketry. It is also 'the mosquito and rat capital of Ecuador', a title disputed by Borbón which has the highest rate of malaria in the country.

Sleeping Accommodation is very basic, San Lorenzo has much better choices. **E** *Mauricio Real*, by the dock, T789219. With bath, **F** without. **F** *Puerto Libre* and **F** *Limones*, both shared bath, very basic.

Transport There are launches between La Tola and Limones every 1½ hrs, US$2.50, 1 hr, and 3 daily Limones-San Lorenzo, 1 hr US$2.50. From Limones you can also get a canoe or boat to Borbón. A hired launch provides a fascinating trip through mangrove islands, passing hundreds of hunting pelicans; US$10 per hr.

Borbón
Colour map 2, grid A3

On the Río Cayapas, upriver from La Tola and about 110 km along the coastal road from Esmeraldas, is Borbón, a lively, dirty, busy, somewhat dangerous place. It is a centre of the timber industry. Ask for Papá Roncón, the King of Marimba, who, for a beer or two, will put on a one-man show. Across from his house are the offices of *Subir*, the NGO working in the Cotacachi-Cayapas reserve; they have information on entering the reserve and guide services. *Ministerio del Ambiente* in Quito can also provide information. Chachi handicrafts are sold in town and at the road junction outside town. The local *fiestas* with *marimba* music and other traditional Afro-Ecuadorean traditions are held the first week of September.

Sleeping and eating **E** *Castillo*, Near Trans Esmeraldas bus office, T786613. Private bath, fan, parking. Best in town. **E** *Costa Norte*. Private bath, good. **E** *Tolita Pampa de Oro*, T Quito 256 6075. Bath, cheaper without, clean, mosquito nets, picturesque setting by the water, helpful, popular. **F** *Bahía Norte*, basic. **F** *Residencial Capri*, very basic. There are many *comedores*, serving fish and other regional dishes. The *panadería* across from the church is good for breakfast.

Transport Bus: To **Esmeraldas**, several companies, frequent service, US$2.80, 3 hrs. To **San Lorenzo**, US$1.20, 1 hr. **Boat**: See Upriver from Borbón below.

Upstream are Cayapa Indian villages and some Afro-Ecuadorean communities. From Borbón four passenger motor launches run to different communities upriver, leaving daily, 1030-1200. Check how far each one is going as only the first one to leave goes as far as San Miguel (see below). On the Río Cayapas, after the confluence with the Río Onzole is the community of **Santa María**, 2¼ hours by launch, US$5.

Upriver from Borbón

Sleeping B *Chocó Lodge*, a few minutes past the village. Full board in double rooms with private bath, tours available (about US$80 per day for a guide and launch), packages out of Borbón or Quito including transport and tours are also available. Run by the Chachi community of El Encanto, part of a tourism project sponsored by **Fundeal**, a Quito based NGO, T2507245, fundeal@andinanet.net **B** *Steve's Lodge*, at the confluence of the Cayapas and Onzole, 30 mins before Santa María. A fine lodge built by Hungarian Stephan Tarjany, full board, clean, warm showers. Jungle walk with guide and small canoes at no extra charge. Longer trips available. For advance bookings write to Stephan Tarjany, Casilla 187, Esmeraldas. Try to enquire about this lodge before going, there was talk of it closing in late 2002. **E** *Sra Pastora*, at the missionary station, basic, mosquito nets, meals US$3, unfriendly, her brother offers river trips. **F** *Residencial*, basic, will prepare food but fix the price beforehand, the owner offers 5-hr jungle trips to visit Cayapa villages.

Zapallo Grande, further upriver, is a friendly village with many gardens, where the American missionary Dr Meisenheimer has established a hospital, pharmacy, church and school. There is a ceremonial centre downriver from town, interesting during holidays. There is an expensive shop. You will see the Cayapa Indians passing in their canoes and in their open long houses on the shore. **San Miguel**, the access point to **Reserva Ecológica Cotacachi-Cayapas**, has a church, a shop (but supplies are cheaper in Borbón) and a few houses beautifully situated on a hill at the confluence of the San Miguel and Cayapas rivers. Borbón to San Miguel, US$10 per person, five hours, none too comfortable but an interesting jungle trip.

Trips from San Miguel into the **Reserva Ecológica Cotacachi-Cayapas** (entry US$5) cost US$100 for a group with a guide. One guide in this area is Don Cristóbal. You can sleep in the rangers' hut, **F** per person, basic, take mosquito nets (no running water, no electricity, shared dormitory, cooking facilities, rats), or camp alongside, but beware of chiggers in the grass; also **F** *residencial*.

From Borbón, the coastal road follows the Río Cayapas south, then crosses it and goes east to cross the Río Santiago. Just off the road on the south bank of the Río Santiago is the village of **Maldonado**. This is the access to the **Humedal de Yalare**, a wetland rich in birdlife, located to the north of the river, along the highway (more information on this site from the Care office in Borbón). A secondary road goes east of Maldonado, following the south bank of Río Santiago to **Selva Alegre** (a couple basic residenciales). This is the access to **Reserva Playa de Oro**, on the north bank of the Santiago, another good place for birdwatching. The reserve can also be reached by boat from Borbón, but it is much more expensive.

Borbón to San Lorenzo

From the Río Santiago the coastal road goes northeast through Yalare, crosses the railway line and, near the town of **Calderón,** meets the Ibarra-San Lorenzo road. The two roads run together northwest towards San Lorenzo for a few kilometres before the coastal road turns north to the Río and town of **Mataje,** the border with Colombia. The roads from Ibarra continues to San Lorenzo.

San Lorenzo

Phone code: 06
Colour map 2, grid A4
Population: 14,500
Altitude: sea level

The hot, humid town of San Lorenzo stands on the Bahía del Pailón, which is characterized by a maze of canals. The town was once notable as the disembarkation point on the thrilling train journey from Ibarra, high up in the sierra (see below). The train has now been replaced by the bus, but San Lorenzo is still interesting (note however safety below). There's a very different feel to the place, owing to a large number of Colombian immigrants, and the people are open and friendly. The culture is distinct and there are opportunities for trips into virgin rainforest, mangroves, wetlands and beaches. This is also a good place to hear *marimba* music, see the wonderfully sensual dances and learn more about the Afro-Ecuadorean culture.

The area around San Lorenzo is rich in timber and other plants, but unrestricted logging is putting the forests under threat. The prehistoric La Tolita culture thrived in the region. The local festival is held 6-10 August. When arriving in San Lorenzo, you may be hassled by children wanting a tip to show you to a hotel or restaurant. During the rainy season, insect repellent is a 'must'.

Excursions

San Lorenzo is close to the Colombian border. Enquire about public safety before visiting and enquire again in San Lorenzo before venturing outside town

San Lorenzo is in the Chocó bio-geographic region (see Vegetation and Wildlife, page 456). There are a number of nature reserves, including the **Reserva Ecológica Cayapas-Mataje,** which protects some of the islands in the estuary northwest of town; the lowland section of the **Reserva Ecológica Cotacachi-Cayapas,** inland and upriver along the Río Cayapas (see Upriver from Borbón above); **Reserva Playa de Oro,** upriver along the Río Santiago (see Upriver from Borbón above); **Bosque Protector La Chiquita,** north of the junction of the Mataje and Ibarra roads; **Bosque Humedal del Yalare,** a wetland on the road to Esmeraldas (see Upriver from Borbón above); and **El Majagual** (see La Tola above). There are also some reserves which protect the last indigenous groups of the Ecuadorean coast, the Awa and the Cayapas or Chachi.

Launches can be hired for excursions: *Coopseturi,* Calle Imbabura, T/F780161 and *Costeñita,* on the same street, offer transport and tours

San Lorenzo

Bahía del Pailón
Port
Boat Tickets
Malecón
Parque Central
10 de Agosto
Ayora
Imbabura
26 de Agosto
Eloy Alfaro
Tácito Ortiz
José Garcés

N
0 metres 100
0 yards 100

■ **Sleeping**
1 Carondelet
2 Continental
3 Imperial
4 Pampa de Oro
5 Puerto Azul
6 San Carlos

● **Eating**
1 La Conchita
2 La Red

in the region, price varies according to the size of the boat about US$10 per hour. To visit the **Reserva Playa de Oro**, enquire with Victor Grueso, who has a store in town and also works for the **Instituto de Permacultura Madre Selva**, on the outskirts of San Lorenzo, near the football field (T780257, you can also stay at the institute, **G** per person including breakfast, find out about permaculture and do various trips in the area). Basic accommodation is available on the trip to Playa de Oro, but bring your own food and water; meals are cooked on request. The truly adventurous can take a trip upriver from Playa de Oro into unspoiled rainforest, where you can see howler and spider monkeys and maybe even jaguars. Contact Mauro Caicedo in San Lorenzo. For information on how to contact Mauro, T02-252 9727 (Quito), or Jean Brown at *Safari Tours* in Quito (see page 130).

At the seaward end of the bay are several beaches which can be reached by canoe. There are no hotels or restaurants, but you can usually arrange for a meal or to stay with a family or in the community hall (**G** per person). On weekends canoes go to the beaches around 0700-0800 and 1400-1500. The cost is US$2-2.50 for the 1-2 hour ride. **San Pedro** is one hour from San Lorenzo, **Palma Real** is 1¾ hours away towards the border, there are others. Note that this area is close to the Colombian border and it may not be safe. Enquire locally before going.

Sleeping
■ *on map*
Price codes:
see inside front cover

D *Continental*, C Imbabura, T780125, F780127. A/c, parking, mosquito nets, family-run. **D** *Puerto Azul*, C 26 de Agosto near the train station, T780220. A/c, cheaper with fan, OK. **E** *Carondelet*, on the plaza, T780202. Some rooms with private bath, fan, mosquito nets, some rooms are small. **E** *Imperial*, T780221. Cheaper with shared bath, fan, mosquito nets. **E** *Pampa de Oro*, C 26 de Agosto, T780214. Private bath, a/c, cheaper with fan, OK. **E** *San Carlos*, C Imbabura near the train station, T780240, F780284. Cheaper with shared bath, fan, mosquito nets.

Eating
● *on map*

La Red, Imbabura y Ayora, good seafood, not too clean. *La Conchita*, 10 de Agosto. Excellent fish. Recommended. *Casablanca*, near the train station.

Entertainment

Marimba can be seen during the local fiestas in August. Groups practice Thu-Sat. One on C Eloy Alfaro, another near the train workshops. Ask the kids at the train station (for a price). There are 2 discos near the plaza.

Transport

The train station is in the south of town, some buses also arrive at the train station, others opposite the *Hotel San Carlos*. The pier is at the north of town, 1 block from the main park. **Bus** To Ibarra, 10 daily, US$4, 4 hrs, leave from the train station or near *Hotel San Carlos*. To **Esmeraldas** via Borbón and Camarones, 8 daily, US$4, 4 hrs. **Train** The spectacular train journey to Ibarra, up in the highlands, has been replaced by buses (see Ibarra, page 177). However, the train still runs twice a day for 1 hr to service inland communities which are not on the road. US$1 return. **Boat** Two companies offer launch service. To **Limones**, 3 daily, US$2.50, 1 hr. **Limones-La Tola**, every 1½ hrs US$2.50, 1 hr. For direct service to **La Tola**, you must hire the launch, US$90.

Frontier with Colombia
See Dangerous areas, page 47

The Río Mataje is the border with Colombia. From San Lorenzo, Colombia can be reached by boat, arriving eventually at the port of Tumaco in Colombia, or inland along the coastal road which ends on the Ecuadorean side at the village of Mataje. There are no facilities to get immigration entry or exit stamps at either of these locations. Given the poor public safety situation and the armed conflict in Colombia, travel in this area is not recommended.

Northern Pacific Lowlands

Oriente Jungle

Introducing the Oriente Jungle

East of the Andes the hills fall away to the vast green carpet of tropical lowlands. Much of this beautiful wilderness remains unspoiled, unexplored and sparsely populated with indigenous settlements along the tributaries of the Amazon. The Ecuadorean jungle has the added advantage of being relatively accessible and the tourist infrastructure is well developed, with emphasis on environmental and cultural awareness and conservation.

Most tourists love the exotic feeling of the Oriente, and El Oriente needs tourists. A large proportion of the northern jungle – in the provinces of Sucumbíos, Orellana, Napo and Pastaza – is taken up by the protected areas of Yasuní National Park, the Cuyabeno Wildlife Reserve and the Cayambe-Coca Ecological Reserve, but is nevertheless under threat. Colonists have cleared parts of the forest for agriculture, while other areas are the site of petroleum exploration and production. The region's irreplaceable biodiversity and traditional ways of life can only be protected if sustainable eco-tourism offers a viable economic alternative.

The southern Oriente, made up of the provinces of Morona-Santiago and Zamora-Chinchipe, is less developed, for tourism as well as other activities. Precisely for this reason, it offers unique opportunities and demands extraordinary respect.

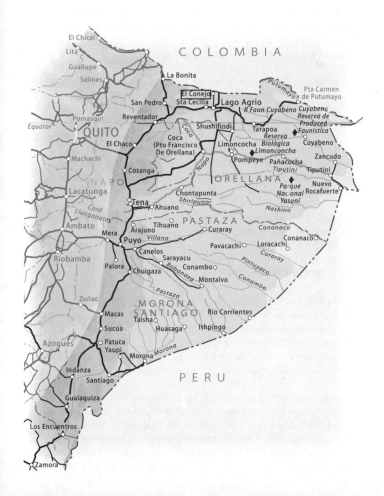

> **Things to do in the Oriente Jungle**
>
> · Splurge on a visit to a **jungle lodge**, see below.
> · Visit stunning **San Rafael Falls** northeast of Baeza, page 364.
> · Go white water rafting from **Tena**, page 374.
> · See the **'near oriente'** from Misahuallí, page 377.
> · Explore the undeveloped **southern Oriente** from Macas or Zamora, page 382.
> · Sail the lower **Río Napo** from Coca to Peru, page 367.

Ins and outs

Getting there   Ecuador's Eastern tropical lowlands can be reached by 4 different road routes: from Quito, Ambato, Cuenca or Loja. These roads are narrow and tortuous and subject to landslides in the rainy season, but all have regular, if poor, bus services and all can be attempted in a jeep or in an ordinary car with good ground clearance. Their construction has led to considerable colonization by highlanders in the lowland areas. Several of the towns and villages on the roads can be reached by air services from Quito and places further into the immense Amazonian forests are generally accessible by river canoe or small aircraft from Shell or Macas. A 5th road route, from Guamote (south of Riobamba) to Macas is nearing completion, but remains controversial due to its impact on Parque Nacional Sangay (see page 384). Transport details are given under the relevant destination; see also Getting around (page 51).

Public safety   There are frequent military checks in the Oriente, so always have your passport handy.
Enquire before visiting   The Oriente, especially the northern Oriente, has also been affected by conflict in
remote areas in   neighbouring Colombia. Always enquire about public safety before visiting remote
northern Oriente   sites, particularly north of the Río Napo, and avoid all areas immediately adjacent to the Colombian border. (Also see Dangerous areas, page 47.) At the same time, you should remember that the Ecuadorean Amazon has traditionally been safe and tranquil, and the very few incidents which have taken place mostly involved foreign oil workers rather than tourists. Baeza, Tena, Misahuallí, Puyo and their surroundings, as well as jungle areas to the south, have experienced no difficulties.

Health   Anti-malaria tablets are recommended and be sure to take an effective insect repellent. A mosquito net may be helpful if you are travelling independently. A yellow fever vaccination is also required.

Ecotourism in the Oriente

The Northern Oriente offers an extensive variety of ecotourism services and programmes, which can be divided into three basic types: lodges; guided tours; and indigenous ecotourism. A fourth option is independent travel without a guide, not advisable for reasons given below. The Southern Oriente, comprising the province of Morona-Santiago and Zamora-Chinchipe, is less developed and lacks the same level of tourist infrastructure.

Jungle lodges   These cabaña complexes are normally located in natural settings away from towns and villages and are in most cases built to blend into the environment through the use of local materials and elements of indigenous design. They are generally owned by urban-based nationals or foreigners, have offices in Quito and often deal with national or international travel agencies. When staying at a jungle lodge, you will need to take a torch, insect repellent, protection

Orellana and the Amazon

The legends of the Incas only served to fuel the greed and ambition of the Spanish invaders, who dreamed of untold riches buried deep in the Amazon jungle. The most famous and enduring of these was the legend of El Dorado which inspired a spate of ill-fated expeditions deep into this mysterious and inhospitable world.

Francisco Pizarro, conqueror of the Incas, sent his younger brother, Gonzalo, to seek out this fantastic empire of gold. An expedition under the command of Gonzalo Pizarro left Quito with 220 Spanish soldiers, 4,000 Indian slaves, 150 horses and 900 dogs, as well as a great many llamas and livestock. They headed across the Andes and down through the cloud forest until they reached the Río Coca. In 1541 Pizarro's expedition was joined by Francisco de Orellana, the founder of Guayaquil, accompanied by 23 more conquistadores.

After following the Coca for some distance, the expedition began to run out of food. Rumours that they would find food once they reached the Río Napo led Orellana to set out with his men to look for this river and bring back provisions. But the jungle natives fled their small farms as soon as they saw the Spanish approach and Orellana and his party found nothing.

Without food and not being able to return up river against the current, Orellana sent three messengers on foot to inform Gonzalo Pizarro of their decision to continue downstream. On February 12, 1542, Orellana reached the confluence of the Napo and the Amazon – so called by him because he claimed to have been attacked by the legendary women warriors of the same name.

On August 26, 1542, 559 days after he had left Guayaquil, Orellana and his men arrived at the mouth of the Amazon, having become the first Europeans to cross the breadth of South America and follow the world's greatest river from the Andes to the Atlantic. Totally lost, they followed the coastline north and managed to reach the port of Cubagua in Venezuela. In the meantime, Gonzalo Pizarro had suffered enormous losses and limped back to Quito with only 80 starving survivors.

Orellana returned to Spain and organized a second expedition which sailed up the Amazon in 1544, only to meet with disaster. Three of his four vessels were shipwrecked and many of the survivors, including Orellana himself, died of fever (most likely yellow fever). The 'discoverer' of the Amazon was buried near the present site of Monte Alegre, Brazil.

against the sun and a rain poncho that will keep you dry when walking and when sitting in a canoe. Rubber boots can be hired.

Experiencing the jungle in this way usually involves the purchase of an all-inclusive package in Quito or abroad, quick and convenient transport to the lodge, a comfortable stay at the lodge and a leisurely programme of activities suited to special interests. Getting to the lodge may involve a long canoe ride, with a longer return journey upstream to the airport, perhaps with a pre-dawn start. Standards of services are generally high and most lodges show a relatively high degree of environmental awareness, have standardized arrangements with neighbouring indigenous communities and rely on well-qualified personnel. Their contribution to local employment and the local economy varies.

Guided tours of varying length are offered by tour operators, river cruise companies and independent guides. These should, in principle, be licensed by the Ministerio de Turismo. Tour companies and guides are mainly concentrated in Quito, Baños, Puyo, Tena, Misahuallí, Coca and Lago Agrio – and to a lesser extent in Macas and Zamora – where travellers tend to congregate to form or join groups and arrange a jungle tour, usually of between one

Guided tours

and seven days. In these towns there is always a sufficient number of guides offering a range of tours to suit most needs, but there may be a shortage of tourists for group travel outside the months of July and August.

Since the cost of a tour largely depends on group size, the more budget-conscious travellers may find that in the off-season it will take several days to assemble a reasonably sized group. In order to avoid such delays, it may be easier to form a group in Quito or Baños, before heading for the Oriente. Conversely, the lack of tourists in the off-season can give you more bargaining power in negotiating a price.

When shopping around for a guided tour ensure that the guide or agency specifies the details of the programme, the services to be provided and whether park fees and payments to indigenous communities are involved. Serious breaches of contract can be reported to the Ministerio de Turismo, but you should be reasonable about minor details. Most guided tours involve sleeping in simple cabañas or camping shelters (open-sided with raised platforms) which the guides own or rent. On trips to more remote areas, camping in tents or sleeping under plastic sheets is common.

Indigenous ecotourism In recent years a number of indigenous communities and families have started to offer ecotourism programmes on their properties. These are either community-controlled and operated, or organized as joint ventures between the indigenous community or family and a non-indigenous partner. These programmes usually involve guides who are licensed as *guías natívos* with the right to guide within their communities.

Accommodation typically is in simple cabañas of varying, but generally adequate, quality, and safe food. A growing number of independent indigenous guides are working out of Puyo, Tena, Coca and Misahuallí, offering tours to their home communities.

Wrap everything in several layers of plastic bags Essential items for a trip of any length are: rubber boots (or, if you prefer, two pairs of suitable light shoes – keep one pair dry); sleeping bag; rain jacket; trousers (not shorts); binoculars; insect repellent; sunscreen; mosquito net; water-purifying tablets; sticking plasters.

Tours without a guide Though attractive from a financial point of view, this is not to be encouraged, for several reasons. From a responsible travel perspective, it does not contribute adequately to the local economy and to intercultural understanding and it may be environmentally damaging. Furthermore, it involves a greater risk of accident or injury.

While unguided trekking is possible in some settled areas, such as around Baeza, and in cleared areas, particularly in the Tena region, travellers should definitely avoid unguided river travel, unguided hiking in remote forested areas and unguided entry into indigenous community lands.

Choosing a rainforest A tropical rainforest is one of the most exciting things to see in Ecuador, but it isn't easy to find a good one. The key is to have realistic expectations and choose accordingly. Think carefully about your interests. If you simply want to relax in nature and see some interesting plants, insects, small birds and mammals, you have many choices, including some that are quite economical and/or easily accessible. If you want to experience something of the cultures of rainforest people, you must go farther. If you want the full experience, with large mammals and birds, you will have to go farther still and spend more, because large creatures have been hunted out around settled areas.

A visit to a rainforest is not like a visit to the Galápagos. The diversity of life in a good rainforest far exceeds that of the Galapagos, but creatures don't sit around and let themselves be seen. You will need to work to find them but the more nearly virgin the forest, the less you will have to work. In forests where people hunt, the few animals that remain will do their best to avoid you. In a truly untouched forest, on the other hand, even the larger animals and birds do not fear people, and it is possible to have intimate encounters with them instead of mere glimpses. Nevertheless, even in the best forests, your experiences will be unpredictable – none of this 'today is Wednesday, time to see sea lions'. A rainforest trip is a real adventure; the only guarantee is that the surprises will be genuine, and hence all the more unforgettable.

There are things that can increase the odds of really special surprises. One of the most important is the presence of a canopy tower. Even the most colourful rainforest birds are mere specks up in the branches against a glaring sky, unless you are above them looking down. Towers add an important dimension to bird and mammal watching. A good guide is another necessity. Because the life of the rainforest is subtle, you will depend on your guide's eyes and ears to find things. If you are a bird watcher, look for a guide who knows bird calls, since most birds are initially detected by ear. Point out a few birds in your field guide (Rusty-belted Tapaculo or Black-faced Antthrush would be good choices) and ask him to imitate them. If he can't, go elsewhere. Avoid guides (and lodges) that emphasize medicinal plants over everything else. This usually means that there isn't anything else around to show. If you are interested in exploring indigenous cultures, give preference to a guide from the same ethnic group as the village you will visit.

If you want to see real wilderness, with big birds and mammals, don't go to any lodges you can drive to. Expect to travel at least a couple of hours in a motorized canoe. Don't stay near villages even if they are in the middle of nowhere. In remote villages people hunt a lot, and animals will be scarce. Indigenous villages are no different in this regard; most indigenous groups (except for a very few, such as certain Cofán villages that now specialize in eco-tourism) are ruthlessly efficient hunters.

If economy is important, the newest and least well established lodges offer the best values. An economic alternative to a lodge is a canoe camping trip on a remote river like the Cononaco. These trips are also a good way to experience real jungle cultures. Just make sure there are whole days spent in the forest; some guides turn these trips into canoe marathons and forget that the forest is the reason for your visit. Another economic alternative to the fancy jungle lodges are the community-based lodges run by local people. An added advantage of these lodges is that your money goes straight to the community, providing an economic incentive for conservation.

Responsible jungle tourism

Some guides or their boatmen will try to hunt meat for your dinner – don't let them, and report such practices to other tourists and to guidebooks. Don't buy anything made with animal or bird parts. Avoid making a pest of yourself in indigenous villages; don't take photographs or videos without permission, and don't insist. Many native people believe that photographs can steal one's soul. In short, try to minimize your impact on the forest and its people. Also remember when choosing a guide that the cheapest is **not** the best. What happens is that guides undercut each other and offer services that are unsafe or harm local communities and the environment. Do not encourage this practice.

Oriente Jungle

Northern Oriente

Quito to Lago Agrio

The most northerly route into the Oriente is from Quito via Baeza to Lago Agrio. The road crosses the Eastern Cordillera at a pass, just north of the volcano **Antisana** (5,705 m), and then descends via the small villages of **Papallacta** (excellent thermal baths, see page 154) and **Cuyuja** to the old mission settlements of **Baeza** and **Borja**. The road is paved and in very good condition until 5 km before Papallacta, and road construction was taking place in 2002 with plans to pave the route all the way from Quito to Tena. The trip between the pass and Baeza has beautiful views of the heavily glaciated slopes of **Antisana** (clouds permitting), high waterfalls, *páramo* and a lake contained by an old lava flow.

This is a colonist dairy-farming region with little indigenous presence, surrounded by the Cayambe-Coca, Antisana and Sumaco-Galeras Biological Reserves. The mountainous landscape and high rainfall have created many spectacular waterfalls, pristine rivers and dense vegetation. Because of the climate, *ceja de montaña* (cloud forest), orchids and bromeliads abound. The numerous hiking trails make this ideal territory for trekking, and for fishing enthusiasts, the lakes and rivers have trout.

Baeza
Colour map 3, grid B1

At the heart of this region is this small town, in the beautiful setting of the Quijos pass. The town is about 1 km from the main junction of the Lago Agrio and Tena roads. You need to get off the Lago Agrio bus at the police checkpoint and walk up the hill, but the Tena bus goes through the town. The town of Baeza is divided in two: **Baeza Colonial** (Old Baeza) and **Andalucía** (New Baeza). The old settlement, however, is dying as people have moved to the new town, 1 km down the road towards Tena, where the post office and Andinatel are located. Regular buses to Tena can be caught outside the *Hostal San Rafael*; two hours. Buses to Quito stop at the bus stop just below the *Hotel Jumandí* in the old town.

Sleeping and eating D *Casa Bambú*, in the new town. Cheaper with shared bath, hot water, OK, new in 2002. E *Hostal San Rafael*, in the new town. Shared bath, clean, friendly, spacious, cheaper cabins at rear, parking. E *Mesón de Baeza*, on the plaza in the old town. Shared bath, electric shower, popular with kayakers. E-F *Samay*, in the new town. Shared bath, basic and friendly. E-F *Jumandí*, in the old town. Basic, full of character, very friendly. F *Oro Negro*, at the highway junction. Trucker's stop, basic. The best restaurant is *Gina*, cheap, friendly, great trout. Also good is *El Viejo*, next to *Hostal San Rafael*.

Hikes around Baeza

There are many hiking trails in this region which generally can be done without a guide. A recommended source for maps and route descriptions is *The Ecotourist's Guide to the Ecuadorian Amazon*, by Rolf Wesche, which is available in Quito, or in the *Hostal San Rafael*.

　　Camino de la Antena This is a three to four hour round trip, with a moderate climb and beautiful views along a mountain road which passes through pasture and, at the top, dense cloud forest. The trail is straightforward and easily accessible, with lots of birdlife to be seen. In the rainy season parts can be difficult due to deep mud.

The climb starts in Old Baeza, beside the church. Pass the cemetery and head up the antenna maintenance road. After about 500 m, you cross a wooden bridge and turn left. Then there's a steep uphill climb to the top (accessible with four-wheel drive vehicles), but on a clear day the views of the Quijos Valley are fantastic.

Baeza to Tena

At Baeza the road divides. One branch heads south to Tena, with a branch road going directly via Loreto to Coca (seven hours). The route from Baeza to Tena passes near several important lodges, reserves and national parks. About 12 km from Baeza is **C** *The Magic Roundabout*, includes breakfast and supper, cabins or cheaper in dorm, shared bath, hot water, horseback riding available, British-Ecuadorean run, friendly. Under construction in 2002, contact magicroundabout@hotmail.com

Near **Cosanga**, approximately 30 minutes from Baeza, is **LL** *Cabañas San Isidro*, including three excellent meals. This is a 1,200-ha private reserve with rich bird life, comfortable accommodation with private bath, hot water and warm hospitality. Recommended. There is a small easily accessible Cock-of-the Rock lek on the reserve, and feeders make the local humming-birds easy to see. Reservations are necessary: T02-2547403 (Quito), F2228902, birdecua@hoy.net, www.ecuadorexplorer.com/sanisidro

Higher up in the same area is **L** *SierrAzul*, including three meals. This is an ecotourism development with a slightly different set of birds than San Isidro. Cabins are very nice, private bath, hot water; access is via a 1-km walk starting at the end of the road 12 km beyond San Isidro. Mountain Tapir tracks are sometimes seen. Quito office: Pinto 439 y Amazonas, T02-2564915, F2909482, www.sierrazul.com

Between San Isidro and SierrAzul is a biological station, **Yanayacu**, run by Harold Greeney. This is intended as a base for students studying the cloud forest. Contact Harold at yanayacu@hotmail.com

About 20 minutes towards Tena from Cosanga is the **Guacamayos Ridge**, part of the Reserva Ecológica Antisana. There is a good stone path at the antennae (just before the shrine on the right side of the road), which enters one of the wettest and most interesting cloud forests in the area. Many rare birds and plants are found here, including several orchids found nowhere else in the world. On a clear day there is a view of the vast Oriente spread out below.

The Guacamayos trail is described in Trekking in Ecuador (see page 464)

The Guacamayos trail is described in Trekking in Ecuador (see page 464)

Much of the Baeza-Tena road southeast of the Guacamayos antennas is flanked by very good forest, making this stretch ideal for birdwatching or 'botanizing'. Another excellent forested road nearby is the Hollín-Loreto road which branches off the Baeza-Tena road near Narupa and goes on to Coca. The upper half of this road is famous for exciting and colourful birds, butterflies and plants. Even such rare birds as Military Macaws can sometimes be seen from there. It is worth going at least as far as the beautiful gorge of the Río Hollín. A car is necessary, as buses are scarce.

Baeza to Lago Agrio

The other branch of the road from Baeza goes northeast to Lago Agrio, following the Río Quijos past the villages of **Borja**, a few kilometres from Baeza, and **El Chaco** (cabins on the edge of town and excellent food at the restaurant on the road) to the slopes of **Volcán Reventador**. At the village there is *Pensión de los Andes*. Basic, clean, and a restaurant. Also *Hotel Amazonas*.

Oriente Jungle

Reventador Trek

Colour map 3, grid B2

Warning, it is currently dangerous to climb or trek near El Reventador

Volcán Reventador (3,560 m) is an active volcano which lies on the edge of the Reserve Ecológica Cayambe-Coca, poking up from the Oriente rainforests. Until recently, It consisted of a blown-out crater opening to the south. In the centre was an active cone with a small crater and fumaroles venting steam and volcanic gases. Eruptions of lava occurred in the mid-1970s to leave the upper part of the mountain covered only with moss and shrubs. There was no indication that another eruption was imminent when, in November 2002, the volcano suddenly reentered activity. The spectacular eruption produced a 20-km high ash cloud and there was significant ash fall in Quito. It is currently dangerous to climb or trek near El Reventador. The situation continued to unfold as this book went to press and with regret we have withdrawn the popular Reventador Trek from this edition.

San Rafael Falls

These are an impressive 145 m, believed to be the highest in Ecuador

The road to Lago Agrio winds along the north side of the Río Quijos, past these falls. To get to them take a Quito-Baeza-Lago Agrio bus. About two to three hours past Baeza (500 m before the bridge crossing the Río Reventador), look for a covered bus stop and an INECEL sign on the right-hand side of the road. **NB** In 2002 this area was a road construction camp and visitors to the falls were sometimes turned back by guards. You can to insist politely or offer to pay a small 'entry fee'.

The path to the falls begins behind the INECEL complex. It's an easy 1½-hour round trip through cloud forest. After about five minutes, you will come to an intersection; take the right-hand path, then cross the river and it's a further 30-minute walk to falls. At the ridge overlooking the falls is a small cross commemorating the death of a Canadian photographer who got too close to the edge. Camping is possible, take all equipment and food. An extremely steep and slippery trail leads down to the bottom of the falls but enquire locally before attempting it.

Many birds can be spotted along the trail, including Cock-of-the-Rock, and there are swimming holes and waterfalls near the INECEL complex, making this a worthwhile stopover on the way to or from Coca or Lago Agrio.

From San Rafael the road crosses the watershed between the Coca and Aguarico rivers and runs along the north bank of the river to the developing oil towns of Santa Cecilia and Lago Agrio.

Lago Agrio

Phone code: 06
Colour map 3, grid B3
Population: 35,000

Despite its importance for tourists as the access for Cuyabeno Wildlife Reserve, Lago Agrio is first and foremost an oil town. It is also has close connections with neighbouring Colombia. Lago Agrio has grown in recent years and the infrastructure has improved, but it remains very much on the frontier. It is the capital of the province of Sucumbíos. Avenida Quito is the main street.

Safety

Lago Agrio is among the places in Ecuador that has been most affected by the armed conflict in neighbouring Colombia (see Dangerous areas, page 47). Enquire about public safety before travelling here and enquire again in Lago Agrio before visiting outlying regions of the province of Sucumbíos. On no account venture into areas directly along the Colombian border.

History

The town's official name is Nueva Loja, owing to the fact that the majority of the first colonizers were from the province of Loja. The name Lago Agrio comes from Sour Lake, the US headquarters of Texaco, the first oil company to exploit the crude reserves beneath Ecuador's rainforest. They were in effect

Oriente Jungle

the new *conquistadores* and turned the Ecuadorean Amazon into a place where barrels of oil meant more than human rights. Hundreds of thousands of barrels of oil flow out of Lago Agrio every day along a pipeline that snakes over the Andes and down to the coast for export. A second oil pipeline was under construction in 2002. Wells and pipelines criss-cross the devastated terrain. The natural habitat around Lago Agrio is destroyed and the rivers poisoned. The way of life of the native Cofán, Siona and Secoya people has been permanently altered and this tragic history threatens to be repeated elsewhere in Oriente. See *Amazon Crude*, by Judith Kimerling (Natural Resource Defense Council, 1991).

Cattle were subsequently introduced to the region, however these are unsuitable animals for grazing on the poor or non-existent soils of the rainforest. Now there are desert-like areas where only useless grasses cover the land. The latest assault on the area's natural environment has taken the form of broad spectrum herbicides sprayed from aircraft to destroy coca plantations across the border, under the auspices of the US-sponsored 'Plan Colombia'. Local agriculture and the health of the population of Sucumbíos are also being affected.

Sleeping
■ *on map*
Price codes:
see inside front cover

A *Arazá*, Quito 610 y Narváez, T830223. Includes breakfast, restaurant, a/c, best in town. Recommended. **A** *Gran Hotel de Lago*, Km 1½ Vía Quito, T832415. Includes breakfast, restaurant, a/c, pool, internet, parking, cabins, nice gardens, quiet. Recommended.

B *El Cofán*, 12 de Febrero y Av Quito, T830526. Includes breakfast, restaurant, a/c, fridge, parking, OK. **B-D** *Gran Colombia*, Quito y Pasaje Gonzanamá, T831032. Restaurant, a/c, cheaper with fan and cold water, parking, clean, convenient location. **C** *Cuyabeno*, 18 de Noviembre y Colombia, T832479. Includes breakfast, restaurant, a/c, fridge, looks good. **C** *D'Mario*, Quito 171, T880989. Restaurant, a/c, cheaper with fan, fridge, central, a meeting place. Recommended. **C** *San Carlos*, 9 de Octubre y Colombia, T830122. A/c, fridge, OK.

D *La Cabaña*, Quito y Amazonas, T831471. Fan, clean, convenient location. **D** *La Posada*, Quito y Orellana, T830302. Restaurant, fan, parking, good value. **D** *Lago Imperial*, Colombia y Quito, T830453. Fan, convenient location, good value. **D** *Machala 2*, Colombia y Quito, T830037. Restaurant, sometimes has water shortages, fan, parking, OK. **D** *Sayonara*, Quito y Colombia, T830193. A/c, cheaper with fan, parking, OK.

Oriente Jungle

Lago Agrio

To Colombia

To Terminal Terrestre

9 de Octubre

Progreso · Vilcabamba · 24 de Mayo · Narváez · Guayaquil · Orellana · TAME · La Ronda · Plaza

Av Colombia

To Gran Hotel de Lago

18 de Noviembre

Eloy Alfaro

12 de Febrero

Añasco

Manabí · Pasaje Gonzanamá

To Airport (5 km)

Av Quito

N

0 metres 100
0 yards 100

■ **Sleeping**	4 D'Mario	7 La Posada	11 San Carlos
1 Arazá	& Gran Colombia	8 Lago Imperial	12 Sayonara
2 Chimborazo	5 El Cofán	9 Machala 2	
3 Cuyabeno	6 La Cabaña	10 Oro Negro	

F *Chimborazo*, Manabí y Quito, T830502. Private bath, fan, adequate. **E** *Oro Negro*, Quito y Pasaje Gonzanamá, T830174. Shared bath, fan, basic. **E-F** *Cumandá*, In front of bus terminal, T830381. Cheaper with shared bath, fan, basic.

Eating There are restaurants at the better hotels (see above) and various cheap *comedores*. *Mi Cuchita*, beside *El Cofán*, serves roast chicken.

Transport **Air** The airport is 5 km southeast of the centre. *TAME* and *Icaro* fly to **Quito**, daily except Sun, US$55 one way. It's best to book 1-2 days in advance, and reconfirm often. **Bus** To **Quito**, US$10, 10-11 hrs. To **Baeza**, US$7, 7 hrs. To **Coca**, US$2.50, 3 hrs. To **Tena**, US$8.30, 9 hrs. **NB** There are 2 routes from Lago Agrio to Quito, both with bus service. The northern road via Lumbaquí is more prone to hold-ups, better to take the southern route via Coca and Loreto.

Directory **Exchange** TCs are very difficult to negotiate in Lago Agrio and credit cards can only be used in the best hotels; no cash advances.

Frontier with A road to the north connects Lago Agrio with Colombia, but goes through
Colombia an area with very serious public safety problems due to armed conflict in the neighbouring country. Do not travel this route unless the situation has greatly improved.

Cuyabeno Wildlife Reserve

See advice about safety under Lago Agrio and on page 358 Some 30 years ago Lago Agrio was set deep in the jungle and a favourite of entomologists who came here to collect the vast array of insects attracted by the night light of the oil camps. Today, there is no virgin jungle anywhere close. It is, however, the best access for the Cuyabeno Wildlife Reserve, a huge tract of pristine rainforest covering 602,000 ha.

Down the Aguarico from Lago Agrio, Cuyabeno is an extensive jungle river area on the Río Cuyabeno, which drains eventually into the Aguarico 150 km to the east. In the Reserve there are many lagoons and a great variety of wildlife, including river dolphins, tapirs, capybaras, five species of caiman, ocelots, 15 species of monkey and over 500 species of birds. In order to see as many animals as possible and minimally impact their habitat, look for a small tour group (eight people or less) which scrupulously adheres to responsible tourism practices. ■ *Foreigners US$20. Transport is mainly by canoe and motorboat, except for one road to Río Cuyabeno, 3 hrs by truck from Lago Agrio.*

Cuyabeno Lodge
Ecolodge in the Cuyabeno National Park

- Naturalist Bilingual and Natives Guides
- Richest wildlife in the Amazon
- Located in the Laguna Grande
- Pioneer Lodge in the Cuyabeno Reserve
- Operation with minimum impact to the environment
- Independent cabins with private bathrooms.
- Solar energy

Neotropic Turis. Avda. Amazonas N24-03 y Wilson, Quito
Tel: (00 593) (2) 2521212 Fax: (00 593) (2) 2554902
Mobile: (00 593) (9) 9803395 (24 hrs.)
Email: info@neotropicturis.com www.neotropicturis.com

Most Cuyabeno tours are booked through agencies in Quito or other popular tourist destinations. The following all have offices in Quito (phone code 02). *Neotropic Turis*, Amazonas N24-03 y Wilson, T2521212, F2554902, T09-9803395 (mob) www.neotropicturis.com Operates the *Cuyabeno Lodge*, cabins with private or shared baths, US$250 per person for 4 days/3 nights, including all meals and bilingual guides, but excluding transport to and from Lago Agrio (see above) and the park entry fee. *Native Life*, Foch E4-167 y Amazonas, Quito, T/F2229077, natlife1@natlife.com.ec Lincoln Reyes runs tours to their *Nativo Lodge* in Cuyabeno Reserve. 5 days/4 nights for US$210. All of the following have been recommended for jungle trips to Cuyabeno: *Dracaena*, Pinto 446 y Amazonas, Quito, T2546590, www.amazondracaena.com; *Green Planet*, JL Mera N23-84 y Wilson, T2520570, greenpla@interactive.net.ec; and *Kapok Expeditions*, Pinto E4-225, T/F2556348, www.kapokexpeditions.com

Jungle lodges & tour operators

At Lago Agrio, a temporary ferry crosses the Río Aguarico (bridge washed away), then the road heads south to Coca. The route from Tena via Loreto also involves a ferry crossing a few kilometres before Coca.

South to Coca

Coca

Officially named Puerto Francisco de Orellana, Coca is a hot, sprawling oil town at the junction of the Ríos Coca and Napo. It is the capital of the province of Orellana. The view over the water is nice, and the riverfront can be a pleasant place to spend time around sunset. As a tourist centre, however, Coca offers few attractions other than being closer to undisturbed primary rainforest than the main jungle towns further west.

Phone code: 06
Colour map 3, grid B3
Population: 19,000

Hotel and restaurant provision is adequate and there are plenty of bars and discos. Considering its relative isolation, food and supplies are not that much more expensive than other, more accessible parts of the country.

Coca is a small town and easy to walk around. The road from Lago Agrio enters from the northeast. There is also a rougher but scenic road from Baeza or Tena, through Loreto (safer than travelling via Lago Agrio). Coca is the starting point for the adventurous river journey east to Peru and Brazil (see Boats below).

Although further from the Colombian border, and generally more *tranquilo* than Lago Agrio, the same general precautions apply to Coca and surroundings (see Lago Agrio above).

A-D *El Auca*, Napo entre Rocafuerte y García Moreno, T880600. Restaurant and disco, a/c, cheaper with fan, parking, comfortable, big garden with hammocks, manager speaks English, good meeting place to make up a tour party. Recommended. **C** *La Misión*, by riverfront, T880260, F880263. Restaurant and disco, a/c, pool, internet, parking, elegant, English spoken, arranges tours. Recommended.

Sleeping
■ *on map, page 368*
Price codes:
see inside front cover

D *Amazonas*, 12 de Febrero y Espejo, T880444. Restaurant, fan, parking, away from the centre, quiet. Recommended. **D** *Coca*, Cuenca y Rocafuerte, T881841. Modern and nice, new in 2002. **D** *Florida*, on main road from the airport, T880177. Cheaper with shared bath, cold water, with fan, dark rooms, basic. **D** *San Fermín*, Quito y Bolívar, T880802. Parking, very nice, modern and comfortable, new in 2001.

D-F *Cotopaxi*, Espejo y Amazonas. Cheaper with shared bath, mediocre. **E** *Lojanita*, Cuenca y Napo, T880032. Private bath, cold water, simple and noisy. **E** *Oasis*, near the bridge at the E end of town, T880206. Private bath, fan, parking, simple.

There are good restaurants at the larger hotels (see above). Two expensive grills are *Parrilladas Argentinas*, Cuenca y Amazonas, and *El Portón*, Bolívar y Quito. *Ocaso*, Eloy Alfaro between Napo and Amazonas, serves mid range set meals and à la carte.

Eating
● *on map, page 368*

Oriente Jungle

Media Noche, Napo, in front of *Hotel El Auca*. Cheap chicken dishes. *Mama Carmen*. Very cheap and simple, good for early breakfast. There are many other cheap comedores.

Bars Two friendly bars are *Pappa John's*, Napo y Chimborazo by the river, open from 1600 hrs, and *Maito's*, Napo y Eloy Alfaro.

Transport **Air** The airport is in the north of the town, on the same road as the bus terminal. To/from **Quito**, 2-3 flights daily with *Icaro* Mon-Sat US$56 one way; reserve as far in advance as possible and always reconfirm. Flights in and out of Coca are heavily booked, military and oil workers have priority. Planes are small and flights can be very bumpy. *Icaro* office is in *Hotel La Misión*. *TAME* office is at Napo y Rocafuerte, T/F881078; *TAME* flights have been suspended since 2000, but may be resumed.

Bus Long distance buses depart from company offices in town (see map); local destinations, including Lago Agrio, are served from the terminal. To **Quito**, US$8, 8 hrs, several daily. To **Lago Agrio**, US$2.50, 3 hrs. To **Tena**, US$6, 6 hrs. To **Baeza**, US$6, 8 hrs. To **Baños**, US$10, 11 hrs.

Boats To **Nuevo Rocafuerte** on the Peruvian border, motorized canoes depart Mon and Thu early morning, US$26 for foreigners, a full day's ride (take water, hat, sunscreen, etc), stopping on route at **Pompeya**, US$10, and **Limoncocha/Pañacocha**, US$16. There are plans to inaugurate a new tourist riverboat to sail **Coca – Iquitos (Peru)** starting 2003; enquire with *Kempery Tours* in Quito (page 129). See also Coca to Nuevo Rocafuerte, below. There is no regular boat service from Coca upriver to Misahuallí. For a price, however, the willing traveller can hire a canoe with owner and outboard motor to take them anywhere along the Napo; ask around at the Capitanía.

Coca

Sleeping
1 Amazonas
2 Coca
3 Cotopaxi
4 El Auca
5 Florida
6 Lojanita
7 Oasis
8 San Fermin

● Eating
1 Dragón Dorado
2 El Portón
3 Media Noche
4 Ocaso
5 Pappa John's
6 Parrilladas Argentinas

The Huaorani people

South of Coca is the homeland of the Huaorani, a forest people who traditionally lived a simple, nomadic life in the jungle as hunters and subsistence farmers. They refer to anyone living outside their communities as cohuode, meaning either 'those that cut everything to pieces' or 'people from other places/not living in the territory', and, until recently, lived in complete isolation. There are presently 18 Huaorani communities spread over a large area reaching south into Pastaza province.

Since the 1970s the Huaorani have been greatly affected by the activities of the petroleum industry and have suffered at the hands of an uncontrolled tourist trade. Both have dramatically changed their culture and disturbed their traditional village life. The Huaorani have responded to the tourist invasion by imposing tolls for the use of their rivers and entrance fees to their communities as well as demanding gifts. This latter practice has been encouraged by oil companies who have used it to their advantage when bargaining with Huaorani communities. There has even been some conflict between the indigenous people and tour guides, with violent confrontation in the past. Overall, though, tourism has had a negative effect on the Huaorani people.

Randy Smith, author of Crisis Under the Canopy, who has worked with the indigenous peoples of Ecuador on the development of ecotourism projects, states that tourism has taken a major toll in the deculturation process of the Huaorani as the guides offer gifts or cash for the use of their lands or services. He continues that the tourist dollar offers the Huaorani a chance to join the cash economy. The Huaorani visit the various centres outside their territory for food, staples and clothes and therefore require money to sustain this new way of life that many of them have chosen.

For some time, ONHAE (the Huaorani Indigenous organization) opposed tourism, but revised its position in 1992, allowing a number of ONHAE-approved guides to operate in their territory. Lately a number of communities have shown greater interest in getting involved in ecotourism, as the Huaorani have become more integrated into the money economy and are now aware of the amount of money that outside guides receive for taking tourists through their land. They would like to have more control over the tourism that comes through their area and derive more benefits from it. If you wish to visit the Huaorani then, for your own safety as well as for the sake of their critically endangered culture, do so only with an ONHAE-approved guide.

Banks Casa de Cambio, Napo y García Moreno, 4% commission for TCs. Banco de Pichincha, Bolívar y 9 de Octubre, VISA cash advances only. **Communications** Internet: prices around US$2 per hr. **Telephone**: Andinatel, Eloy Alfaro y 6 de Diciembre. 0800-1100, 1300-1700. **Immigration** Rocafuerte y Napo, Edificio Amazonas, 3er piso, 0730-1230, 1500-1800. Directory

Jungle tours from Coca

Most of the Coca region is taken up by the **Yasuní National Park** and **Huaorani Reserve**. This uninterrupted lowland rainforest offers excellent opportunities for a true jungle experience, but wildlife in this area is under threat and visitors should insist that guides and all members of their party take all litter back and ban all hunting and shooting; it really can make a difference.

This area is unsuited to tours of less than three days owing to the remoteness of its main attractions. Most tours, including visits to lodges, require extended periods of canoe travel there and back. Shorter visits of three to four

Allow a minimum of 4-5 days for tours to the Huaorani Reserve and Yasuní Park**S**

Oriente Jungle

days are worthwhile in the Coca-Yuturi segment of the Río Napo, where the lodges are concentrated.

Guides   If a guide offers a tour to visit the Huaorani, ask to see his/her permission to do so. The only guides permitted to take tourists into Huaorani territory are those who have made agreements with the Huaorani organization ONHAE. See box, The Huaorani people.

All guides out of Coca charge about US$40-60 per person per day, but you may have to bargain down to this. At popular times it may be difficult to find a choice of worthwhile tours or English-speaking guides. You are strongly advised to check what precisely is being offered, and that the price includes equipment such as rubber boots, tents, mosquito nets, cooking equipment and food, and transport.

Jungle lodges   Note that all Napo area lodges count travel days as part of their package, which means
& floating   that often a '3-day tour' spends only 1 day actually in the forest. Also, keep in mind that
hotels   the return trip must start before dawn if it is to connect to that day's Coca-Quito flight; if it starts later it will be necessary to spend the night in Coca. Most lodges have fixed departure days from Coca (eg Mon and Fri) and it is very expensive to get a special departure on another day. Ask the lodges for up-to-date departure day information before planning your trip. The following lodges, sites and riverboats are listed in order of their distance down river from Coca, the closest first.

Yarina is the closest lodge to Coca, about 1 hr downstream along the Río Napo. It has accomodation in thatched roof cabins and a 40-ft canopy tower. 4 days/3 nights cost US$220. Itineraries can combine visits here and to *Yuturi* (their contact information is also the same), see below.

Sacha is an upmarket lodge 2½ hrs downstream from Coca. Cabins are very comfortable, with private bath and hot water, and meals are excellent. The bird list is outstanding, and they have a local bird expert, Oscar Tapuy (T06-881486), who can be requested in advance by birders. Guides are generally knowledgeable. Boardwalks through swamp habitats allow access to some species that are difficult to see at other lodges, and nearby river islands provide another distinct habitat. They also have a butterfly farm and an exciting canopy tower. Several species of monkey are commonly seen. A 5-day package costs US$720 per person, excluding flight from Quito. Quito office: Julio Zaldumbide 375 y Toledo, Quito, T02-2566090, F2236521, www.sachalodge.com

La Selva is also an upmarket lodge, 2½ hrs downstream from Coca and close to Sacha. It is professionally run and situated on a picturesque lake surrounded by excellent forest, especially on the far side of Mandicocha. Bird and animal life is exceptionally diverse.

Many species of monkey are seen regularly. A total of 580 bird species can be found here, one of the highest totals in the world for a site at a single elevation, and some of the local guides (eg José) are very good at finding them. There is a biological station on the grounds (the Neotropical Field Biology Institute) as well as a butterfly farm. Cabins have private bath and hot water. Meals are excellent. Usually the guides are biologists, and in general the guiding is of very high quality. A new canopy tower was built in 2001. Four-night packages from Quito including all transport, lodging, and food, cost US$684 per person. Quito office: 6 de Diciembre 2816, T02-2550995, F2567297, www.laselvajunglelodge.com, or book through most tour agencies in Quito.

Añangucocha is operated by and for the local Añangu community, across the Río Napo from La Selva, 2½ hrs downstream from Coca. This area of hilly forest is rather different from the low flat forest of some other sites, and the diversity is slightly higher. There are big caimans, good mammals, including Giant Otters, and the birding is excellent. The local guide, Giovanny Rivadeneyra, is one of the most knowledgeable birders in the Oriente. Facilities are basic at present, palm-thatch huts and an outhouse, but the price is very low compared to the big-name lodges (US$40 per person per day) and most of the money goes directly to the community. More elaborate facilities and a canopy tower are planned. For more information contact Norby López, Quito T02-2894525, ecotours@uio.satnet.net, www.ecoecuador.org

Sani, www.sanilodge.com, is another lodge near La Selva. All proceeds go to the Sani Isla community, who run the lodge with the help of outside experts. It is located on a remote lagoon which contains the nearly extinct Amazonian Manatee and also has 4-5 m long Black Caiman. This area is rich in wildlife and birds, including many species such as the Scarlet Macaw which have disappeared from most other Napo area lodges. There is good accommodation and a canopy tower. An effort has been made to make the lodge accessible to people who have difficulty walking; the lodge can be reached by canoe (total 4 hrs from Coca) without a walk. 5 days/4 nights costs US$380, which is very good value.

Pañacocha is located halfway between Coca and Nuevo Rocafuerte, nearby is the magnificent lagoon of Pañacocha on the Río Panayacu. This has been declared a protected forest region. Several agencies and guides (see below) run tours from Coca. Accommodation is available at an **F** *Pensión*, in Pañacocha. Friendly, but watch out for chiggers in the mattresses.

Yuturi is 4 hrs downstream from Coca. Birdwatching is excellent, and there are some species (eg Black-necked Red Cotinga) that are difficult to find at other lodges. There is a wide variety of habitats here, and wildlife is good. The guides are usually local people accompanied by translators. Four nights cost US$350, exclusive of airfare. Itineraries can combine visits here and to *Yarina*, see above. Quito office: Amazonas 1324 y Colón, T/F02-2504037, www.yuturilodge.com In Coca contact through Hotel *Oasis*.

Bataburo, a lodge in Parque Nacional Yasuní, is on the Río Tigüino, a 3-6 hr canoe ride from the end of the Vía Auca out of Coca. Two cabins have private baths, while the others share baths. There are shared shower facilities. Guides are mostly local people. The birds here have been little studied but macaws and other large species are present. The mammal population also appears to be quite good. Prices are US$265 for 5 days/4 nights; cabin with private bath US$20 additional. Quito office: *Kempery Tours*, Pinto 539 y Amazonas, T02-2226583, F2226715, www.kempery.com

Tiputini Biodiversity Station is far from any settlement and has experienced very little hunting, not even by native people. The result is the best site in Ecuador for observing the full range of Amazonian wildlife and birds. Facilities are extremely well designed and merge into the forest; the canopy tower and canopy walkway are exceptional. Food is good. It is a scientific station, not a tourist facility, and potential visitors must form or join an educational group and receive approval in advance; services are oriented towards scientists. Spider monkeys, curassows, large macaws, large raptors

Oriente Jungle

and other threatened wildlife are more common and more confiding here than at most other sites, and this is the best place in Ecuador for jaguar (but you still have to be lucky to see one). If you would like to join an educational workshop contact Carol Walton, USA T1-512-2630830, F2632721, tiputini@aol.com Scientists wishing to do research should contact tbs@mail.usfq.edu.ec

Manatee floating Hotel. This luxury 30 passenger vessel began service in 2002 on the Río Napo. 5 day/4 night packages cost US$505, not including transport to Coca. Quito office: *Advantage Travel*, El Telégafo E10-63 y Juan de Alcántara, T02-2462871, F2437645, www.advantageecuador.com

Tour operators & guides
A common misconception is that it is always easy to find a cheap tour in Coca. For people travelling alone in the low season (especially Feb to May) it is difficult to find a big enough group to get a bargain rate. Most jungle tours out of Coca cost US$40-60 per person per day. Furthermore, you should beware of cut-rate operators who may compromise on safety, quality or responsible practices. The following operators and guides have been recommended, and there are many others.

In Coca: *River Dolphin Expeditions*, García Moreno y Napo, T/F881563, rde4amazon@yahoo.com Work with *Hotel El Auca*. *Witoto*, on riverfront near the bridge. Small local outfit, run personal tours to their own villages, Spanish only. *Wymper Torres*, T880336, ronoboa@latinmail.com He specializes in the Río Shiripuno and Pañacocha areas, Spanish only.

In Quito: Almost all Quito agencies offer tours out of Coca, only the most frequently recommended are listed below along with their Coca offices, if any. See page 127 for Quito contact information. *Emerald Forest Expeditions*, Napo y Espejo in Coca. Guide Luis Alberto García has many years experience, speaks English, and runs tours to the Pañacocha area. *Kempery* offers good 4 to 15-day tours to Huaorani villages. *Safari* offers 4-day all-inclusive trips with the Huaorani; responsible practices, contributions made to the community. *Tropic Ecological Adventures* runs ecologically-sound tours with local and bilingual naturalist guides, and work closely with Cofan, Secoya and Huaorani communities.

Coca to Nuevo Rocafuerte

Twice weekly motorized canoe service from Coca (see Boats, page 368) goes to **Limoncocha**, the Capuchin mission at **Pompeya** with a school and museum of Napo culture, **Pañacocha** (see Jungle lodges, above) and on to **Nuevo Rocafuerte**, on the border with Peru. Canoes from Nuevo Rocafuerte return to Coca.

The Laguna de Limoncocha is an excellent spot for birding. The area was once used by *Metropolitan Touring*, until 1991, but they moved on and left the cabaña complex to the local villagers, who have created a Biological Reserve. The facilities are beautifully situated, overlooking the lagoon.

Nearby is the **Pompeya Capuchin mission**, on the left bank of the river, about two hours downriver from Coca. Upriver from Pompeya is **Monkey Island**. You can rent a canoe to visit the small island with free-roaming monkeys.

Nuevo Rocafuerte
Colour map 3, grid C6
The end of the line is Nuevo Rocafuerte, with simple *comedores* and one F *Hostal*, erratic water and electricity, basic but OK for where it is. If travelling to Peru, hire a motorized canoe in Nuevo Rocafuerte to take you to Pantoja on the other side of the frontier, 1-2 hours downstream, US$10 per person, negotiable. There are several military posts along the way, so have your passport at hand. Get your Ecuadorean exit stamp in Nuevo Rocafuerte and your Peruvian entry stamp in Pantoja, a tiny village with very basic facilities. From

Pantoja, in 2002, there was irregular boat service downriver to Iquitos, 4-5 days, US$20, primitive conditions and severe crowding toward the end of the journey. A 'real adventure'. **NB** This is a new border crossing, opened in 2002, and the details are likely to change. Confirm formalities with immigration office in Coca before you head down river.

Archidona

Roads from both Baeza and Coca go south to Archidona, 65 km from Baeza. Founded in 1560, at the same time as Tena, 10 km to the south, this was an important mission and trading centre. The small painted church is striking and said to be a replica of one in Italy (possibly in Sienna).

Phone code: 06
Colour map 3, grid C1
Population: 4,300

The road leaving Archidona's plaza to the east goes to the village of San Pablo, and beyond to the Río Hollín. Along this road, 7 km from Archidona, is the **Reserva Ecológica Monteverde**, a 25-ha reserve with primary and secondary forest, and medicinal plants. There are walking trails, river bathing, fishing, cultural presentations for groups, and 5 cabins with bath and cold water (**C per person with full board**). **Entry for day visits US$1. Reservations necessary, contact** *Residencial Regina* (see Sleeping below) or Quito T02-2891041. Pick-up from Archidona US$5.

Excursions

Along the same road, 15 km from Archidona, is **Reserva El Para**, an 80-ha forest reserve with many rare birds like the Reddish-winged Bare-eye, various flatbills, and the Striated Antbird (known in Ecuador only from this site). It is owned by *Orchid Paradise* (see Sleeping below), who run tours to the reserve, US$40 plus transport for a group of up to 10.

Tours can be arranged to the **Izu Mangallpa Urcu (IMU) Foundation**, 3 km east of Archidona off a side turning down the road to San Pablo, set up by the Mamallacta family to protect territory on Galeras mountain. They charge US$35 per day for accommodation and day trips, taking groups of 8-10; US$65 per day for groups of two. It is tough going but the forest is wonderful. Ask around or book through *Safari* in Quito, T02-2552505.

Just outside Archidona, to the south, a small turning leads to the river. About 200 m along there is a large rock with many **petroglyphs** carved on its surface. There are quite a few others within a 30-km radius of Archidona, but most are very difficult to find. These precolumbian petroglyphs are unique to this area. The symbols are no longer understood by the local Quichua people.

AL *Orchid Paradise*, 2 km north of town, T889232, T02-526223 (Quito). Cabins in nice secondary forest with lots of birds. Meals not included, restaurant on site. **A** *Hakuna Matata*, via Chaupi Shungo, 4 km south of Archidona, F889617, www.hakunamat.com Includes all meals, comfortable cabins in a spectacular setting by the Río Inchillaqui. Dutch/Belgian run, good food, horse riding. Recommended. **D** *Res Regina*, Rocafuerte 446, T889144. Modern, cheaper without bath, pleasant. Recommended. *Hostal Archidona*, hidden down a back street, 5 blocks south of the plaza. There are few decent places to eat, though *Restaurant Los Pinos*, near *Res Regina*, is good.

Sleeping & eating

Oriente Jungle

Tena

Phone code: 06
Colour map 3, grid C1
Population: 17,000

Some 75 km south of Baeza, and 10 km south of Archidona, is Tena, the capital of Napo Province. Once one of the important early colonial missionary and trading posts of the Amazon, it is now a commercial centre with a plaza overlooking the confluence of the Ríos Tena and Pano. Along the rivers are several popular sand and pebble beaches. There is a beautiful riverside walk starting down the steps behind town.

The road from the north passes the airstrip and market and heads through the town centre as Avenida 15 de Noviembre on its way to the bus station, nearly 1 km south of the river. Tena is quite spread out. There is a pedestrian

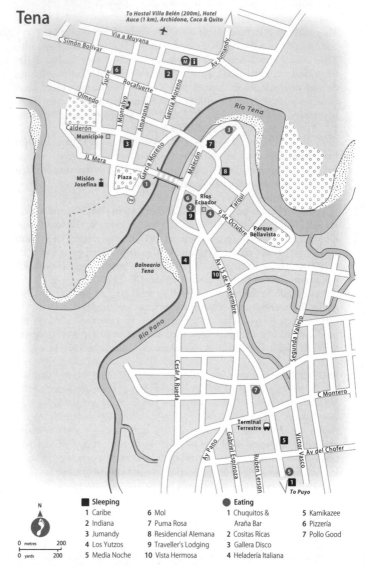

Tena

To Hostal Villa Belén (200m), Hotel
Auca (1 km), Archidona, Coca & Quito

Río Tena

Río Pano

■ Sleeping
1 Caribe
2 Indiana
3 Jumandy
4 Los Yutzos
5 Media Noche
6 Mol
7 Puma Rosa
8 Residencial Alemana
9 Traveller's Lodging
10 Vista Hermosa

● Eating
1 Chuquitos &
  Araña Bar
2 Cositas Ricas
3 Gallera Disco
4 Heladería Italiana
5 Kamikazee
6 Pizzería
7 Pollo Good

bridge which links the two halves of the town. The tourist office is located at Bolívar y García Moreno, near the market at the north end of town.

Tena has a large lowland Quichua Indian population living in the vicinity, some of whom are panning for gold in the rivers. These Indians are unlike the groups further into the Oriente forests, they are Quijos, of Chibcha stock. Despite external pressure from the ever-encroaching modern world, many of these communities have maintained their distinct ethnicity, mythologies and customs. The Tena area, which lacks the pristine jungle found deeper in the Oriente, has instead developed interesting and worthwhile opportunities for ethno-tourism.

The **Jumnadí caves** are located 15 km north of Tena, 5 km north of Archidona. The main cave has electric lights (take a torch anyway), and a recreation complex with pools and waterslides has been built at the entrance. It gets crowded at weekends. ■ *US$2.*

Trips are organized to **Amarongachi** by *Amarongachi Tours/Traveler's Lodgings*, see below. Accommodation in simple wooden cabins, visits with local communities.

Comunidad Capirona is one hour by bus, then three hours on foot from Tena. Visits can be arranged here or to nine other communities in the area. This is part of a highly regarded project which combines eco/ethno-tourism and community development. There are also opportunities for volunteers. Contact the *Red Indígena de las Comunidades del Alto Napo para la Convivencia Intercultural y El Ecoturismo (Ricancie)*, 15 de Noviembre 722, T/F887072, ricancie@ecuanex.net.ec

The **Cerda family** provide tours of various lengths, camping or staying in *cabañas*. Tours focus on local indigenous life. They also offer rafting trips on the Río Jatunyacu and one day motorized canoe tours from Misahuallí to Ahuano. German spoken. Contact through *Hotel Jumandy* in Tena, see above.

Sr Delfín Pauchi, Tena T886434/886088, has built *Cabañas Pimpilala*, 45 minutes by taxi from Tena, where for 2-4 days you can live with a Quichua family. Trails for hiking have been made on his 30 ha of undeveloped land, but emphasis is on culture rather than wildlife. Delfín speaks only Quichua and Spanish.

Also, *Hacienda Jatún Yacu*, a family farm in the rainforest, is excellent. Contact through *Ríos Ecuador* (see below) or *Safari Tours* in Quito.

Excursions & jungle tours

Tena is an increasingly popular base for white water rafting and kayaking excursions. See Tour operators, below

Sleeping

■ *on map*
Price codes: see inside front cover
The water supply in most cheaper hotels is poor

B *Los Yutzos*, at the south end of town overlooking the Río Pano, T886717, F886769, www.geocities.com/losyutzos A/c, cheaper with fan, swimming in river, parking, comfortable rooms, beautiful grounds, quiet, family-run. Recommended. **B-C** *Mol*, Sucre 432, T886215. Meals available on request, a/c, cheaper with fan, laundry and cooking facilities, parking.

D *Establo de Tomás*, in Muyuna village, 5 km from Tena on the road to San Antonio, T/F886318, paorivade@hotmail.com Meals available on request, swimming in river, parking, cabins in a pleasant setting, sports fields, nice but can get noisy on weekends. **D** *Indiana*, Bolívar entre Amazonas y García Moreno, T886334. Restaurant for breakfast only, parking, has tour agency for jungle trips. **D** *Puma Rosa*, on Malecón near vehicle bridge, T/F886320. A/c, parking, nice grounds. Recommended. **D** *Villa Belén*, on Baeza road (Av Jumandy) north of town, T886228, F888091. Meals available on request, fan, laundry and cooking facilities, parking, excellent rooms, quiet. Recommended. **D** *Vista Hermosa*, 15 de Noviembre 622, T886521. Restaurant, a/c, parking, nice views over river, friendly.

Oriente Jungle

D-E *Caribe*, 15 de Noviembre y Eloy Alfaro, T886518, F886522, voyagefantastic@latinmail.com Restaurant, parking, OK. **D-E** *Traveler's Lodging*, 15 de Noviembre 422, T888204. A/c, simple, helpful, many different kinds of rooms, more expensive ones have view, may be noisy. **D-F** *Media Noche*, 15 de Noviembre 1125, near bus station, T886490, F888373. Restaurant, cheaper with shared bath, cold water, fan, parking, good. **E** *Limoncocha*, Sangay 533, Sector Corazón de Jesús, on the hill 300 m from the bus terminal, T887583, limoncocha@andinanet.net Cafeteria, shared bath, hot water, internet, laundry and cooking facilities, parking, terrace with hammocks, German-Ecuadorean run, enthusiastic owners organize tours, pleasant atmosphere but noisy neighbours. **E** *Resiscencial Alemana*, Díaz de Pineda 210 y Av 15 de Noviembre, T886409. Private bath, electric shower, fan, parking, clean and OK. **F** *Jumandy*, Amazonas y Abdón Calderón, T886329. Shared bath, cold water, with balcony, basic, run by the Cerda family who also arrange jungle tours.

Eating
● *on map, page 374*

Baños, half a block from the bus terminal, for cheap set meals. *Chuquitos*, García Moreno by Plaza. Popular. *Cositas Ricas*, 15 de Noviembre, next to *Hostal Traveler's Lodging*. Tasty meals, vegetarian available, good fruit juices. *Heladería Italiana*, 9 de Octubre y Tarqui. Excellent ice-cream. Open 0930-2130 daily. Recommended. *Kamikazee*, 1½ blocks south of bus terminal. Good pancakes and shrimp. Open 0800-1500. *Pizzería*, Malecón y 9 de Octubre, by the river. Expensive and really nice. Open from 1700 onwards. *Pollo Good*, 15 de Noviembre 1 block north of bus terminal. Tasty chicken. *Toro Asado*, on the left arriving from Archidona. Good *almuerzo*. There are also *chifas* in town. Bars include *Araña Bar*, García Moreno by the Plaza. Nice, on the riverfront, open from 1700. *Gallera*, on the Malecón. Large disco, open Sat and Sun.

Tour operators

Most operators offer cultural and jungle tours as well as rafting and kayaking. Be mindful of safety standards for the latter two activities. *Amarongachi Tours* (see *Hostal Traveler's Lodging* above for address and phone; see also Jungle tours above). *Ríos Ecuador*, 15 de Noviembre y 9 de Octubre, T886346, F886727, www.riosecuador.com Founded by Gynner Coronel, highly recommended white-water rafting and kayak trips and a 4-day kayak school. See also Rafting, page 25. *Voyage Fantastic*, Av 15 de Noviembre, opposite the bus terminal, T888424, F886490, voyagefantastic@latinmail.com *Kanoa Tours*, 15 de Noviembre, opposite Cositas Ricas. *Ecoindiana*, inside *Hostal Indiana* (see above). *Limoncocha*, at *Hostal Limoncocha*. Rafting US$35 and jungle trips US$25 per person per day, German spoken. *Runa Ñambi*, on the Malecón, T886318, runanambi@yahoo.com

Transport

Bus To **Quito**, US$5, 5 hrs. To **Baeza**, US$2, 2 hrs. To **Ambato**, via Baños, US$5, 5 hrs. To **Baños**, 4-5 hrs, US$4. To **Riobamba**, via Puyo and Baños, 5-6 hrs, US$6. To **Archidona** every 20 mins, US$0.20, 15 mins. To **Misahuallí**, hourly, US$1, 45 mins, buses leave from the local bus station not the long distance terminal. To **Coca**, US$6, 6 hrs. To **Lago Agrio**, US$9, 9 hrs. To **Puyo**, US$3.50, 3-4 hrs.

Directory

Communications **Internet**: several cyber cafés in town. **Telephone**: *Andinatel*, Olmedo y Juan Motalvo.

Tena to Misahuallí

From Tena the main highway runs south towards Puyo (curiously, only the northbound lane is paved). **Puerto Napo**, a few kilometres south of Tena, has a bridge across the Río Napo. Pato García, a guide, has a **F** room to rent here.

On the north bank a road runs east to Misahuallí, about 17 km downstream. From Puerto Napo you can catch a local bus from Tena to Misahuallí. If you're travelling north from Puyo, avoid going into Tena by getting off the bus here.

Misahuallí

This small port at the junction of the Napo and Misahuallí rivers was once the westernmost access for navigation on the Río Napo and very important because of the lack of roads. Its decline as a port began with the opening of the Loreto road to Coca. Fortunately for Misahuallí the tourist trade was already established, and as commerce declined, tourism replaced it. Now, the town is almost totally devoted to tourism.

Phone code: 06
Colour map 3, grid C2
Population: 2,000

Misahuallí is perhaps the best place in Ecuador from which to visit the **'near Oriente'**, but your expectations should be realistic. The area has been colonized for many years and there is no extensive virgin forest nearby (except at Jatun Sacha, see below). Access is very easy however, prices are reasonable, and while you will not encounter large animals in the wild, you can still see birds, butterflies and exuberant vegetation – enough to get a taste for the jungle. There is a fine, sandy beach on the Río Misahuallí, but don't camp on it as the river can rise unexpectedly.

See Jungle tours from Misahualli, below, for further details

There is a *mariposario* (butterfly farm) in Misahuallí, two blocks from the plaza. Several colourful species can be observed and photographed close up. Interesting and worthwhile. Make arrangements through *Ecoselva* (see Tour operators below).

Sights

A good walk is along the **Río Latas**, 7 km west of Misahuallí, where there are some small waterfalls. You walk through dense vegetation for about 1½ hours, often muddy, to get to the largest fall where you can bathe. To get there catch the bus towards Tena and ask to get off by the river at the metal bridge, the third one out of Misahuallí. On the west shore of the river a short path leads to a commercial bathing area, popular with locals. On the east shore, the longer and more difficult trail described above leads to the falls.

Excursions
Always wear rubber boots when walking in this area

A strenuous day trip can be made to **Palmeras**. Take the road north and cross the bridge over the Río Misahuallí, a muddy road goes through fields skirting the jungle. There are many birds in this area. Palmeras, a friendly village with no services (take food and water), is reached after about three hours. Continue to a patch of primary forest where there are side trails. If you are lucky, and quiet, you may see monkeys.

Oriente Jungle

A *Jardín Alemán*, on the shores of the Río Misahuallí, several km from town, access along a road north before you reach Misahuallí, T890122, www.eljardinaleman.com Restaurant, fan, parking, comfortable rooms, pleasant garden setting, offers tours and spanish classes. **B** *Misahuallí Jungle Hotel*, across the river from town, T890063, F890064, www.misahuallijungle.com Includes breakfast, restaurant, electric shower, fan, pool, cabins for up to 6, nice setting.

Sleeping

C *France Amazonia*, on road from Tena across from high school. Includes very good breakfast, parking, small rooms (not for tall people), French run, helpful. **D** *El Albergue Español*, on Arteaga, T890127, F890004, www.alberguespanol.com Upscale restaurant, fan, screened rooms with balconies overlooking the river, nice place but not the friendliest. **D** *Marena Inn*, Arteaga y Santander, T890002, F890085. Fan, fridge, parking, nice and comfortable. **D-E** *La Posada*, Napo opposite the plaza, T890113, F890035. Restaurant, simple, offers tours.

E *El Paisano*, Rivadeneyra y Tandalia, T890027. Private bath, hot water, simple rooms, pleasant atmosphere, good value. **E** *Granilandia*, on Santander at entrance to town, T890062. Private bath, cold water, fan, basic but clean. **E-F** *Sacha*, by river beach, T890065. Cheaper with shared bath, cold water, basic but nice location. **E-F** *Shaw*,

Santander on Plaza, T890019, ecoselva@yahoo.es Cheaper with shared bath, cold water, simple clean rooms, operate their own tours, English spoken, very friendly and knowledgeable. Good value.

Eating
There are a handful of general stores well stocked with basic supplies

Doña Gloria, Arteaga y Rivadeneyra by corner of plaza. Open 0730-2030 daily. Very good cheap set meals. Recommended. Slightly upmarket is the restaurant at *Albergue Español* (see above). *Bar Atarraya*, at the end of Santander. Good atmosphere, drinks and snacks. *Peco's Café*, on the plaza, tacos and other fast food. *La Posada*, at the Plaza. Varied à la carte menu, good food, nice porch setting, slow service.

Transport
Bus Local buses run from the plaza. To **Tena**, every 45 mins 0745-1800, US$1, 45 min. Make long distance connections in Tena, or get off at Puerto Napo to catch south-bound buses although you may not get a seat. To **Quito**, 2 buses a day, US$5.50, 6 hrs.

Boat With the increase in roads, river traffic is diminishing along the upper Napo. All scheduled passenger service from Misahuallí has been discontinued. Motorized canoes wait at the beach and can be hired for touring (but better to go with a guide) or transport to the location of your choice.

Jungle tours from Misahuallí

There are many guides available to take parties into the jungle for trips of one to 10 days, all involving canoeing and varying amounts of hiking. Try to pay part of the cost on completion of the trip. The going rate is between US$15 and US$40 per person per day, depending on the season, size of group and length of trip. This should include food and rubber boots, which are absolutely essential. Quality varies, so try to get a personal recommendation from travellers who have just returned from a trip.

Tour operators
The following have been recommended to us, but there are many others. *Ecoselva*, Santander on the plaza, T890019, ecoselva@yahoo.es Recommended guide Pepe Tapia speaks English and has a biology background. Trips from 1-6 days. Well organized and reliable. *Viajes y Aventuras Amazónicas*, on the plaza. Friendly, good food.

Guides
Most hotels can arrange guides. The following have all been recommended, but there are others. *Pepe Tapia González* speaks English and is recommended as honest and knowledgeable (see *Ecoselva* above). *Héctor Fiallos*, contact via *Sacha Hotel* on the beach (see above). *Marcos Estrada* is knowledgeable, honest and offers tours of different lengths. Contact *France Amazonia* office on plaza or enquire at the hotel (see above).

A *Anaconda*, on Anaconda Island in the Río Napo, about 1 hr down river by canoe from Misahuallí. It consists of 10 bungalows of bamboo and thatch, with space for about 48 guests, no electric lights, but flush toilets and cold showers. The meals are good. Canoe and hiking trips arranged, guides only speak Spanish.

Jungle lodges on the upper Napo

Opposite, on the north bank at **Ahuano**, is **L** *Casa del Suizo*. Swiss/Ecuadorean-owned, price includes all meals and tour, buffet meals only which cater for vegetarians, every room has a private bath, 24-hr electricity, pool, animal sanctuary, trips arranged. Highly recommended for hospitality and location. For further information contact their office at Julio Zaldumbide 375 y Toledo, Quito, T02-2566090, F2236521, sachalod@pi.pro.ec, www.casadelsuizo.com

The south shore of the Napo has road access from Tena, with frequent bus service. Along this road are several hotels, including **A** *Isla Amazonica*, near **Venecia**, includes breakfast and dinner, reservations required, call Baños T03-740609. Rustic cabins on riverfront, with private bath, hot water. Meals available.

A *Hotel Jaguar*, 1½ hrs downstream from Misahuallí, includes meals, vegetarian available. Tours arranged. Operated by *El Albergue Español*, see Misahuallí hotels above. **LL** *Yachana Lodge*, is based in the indigenous village of Mondaña, 2 hrs downstream from Misahuallí. All proceeds from the lodge go towards supporting community development projects. The lodge is comfortable, has 10 double rooms and family cabins and solar power. *Yachana* offers highly recommended packages which include transport from Ahuano or Coca, all meals, lodging and guides; US$225 for 4 days. Quito office: Baquedano 385 y JL Mera, T/F02-2523777, www.yachana.com

About 8 km downriver from Misahuallí, reached by road or river, is the **Jatun Sacha Biological Station** ('big forest' in Quichua), a reserve set aside for environmental education, field research, community extension and ecotourism. The biological station and the adjacent Aliñahui project together conserve 1,300 ha of tropical wet forest. So far, 507 birds, 2,500 plants and 765 butterfly species have been identified at Jatun Sacha. They offer excursions with good views and walking on a well-developed trail system.

Jatun Sacha

Lodging is at **L** *Cabañas Aliñahui*. 8 cabins with 2 bedrooms and bath, lush tropical garden, rainforest and nature trails. Includes 3 delicious meals in the dining hall. US$6 for entrance only. Profits contribute to conservation of the area's rainforest. Quito office: *Fundación Jatun Sacha*, Pasaje Eugenio de Santillán N34-248 y Maurian, T432246, F453583, www.jatunsacha.org

Puyo

The capital of the province of Pastaza is the largest urban centre in the whole Oriente. It feels more like a small lowland city anywhere, rather than a typical jungle town. Visits can nonetheless be made to nearby forest reserves and tours deeper into the jungle can also be arranged from Puyo. It is the junction for road travel into the northern and southern Oriente, and for traffic heading to or from Ambato via Baños. The road from Macas enters from the southeast, the road to Tena leaves to the north. The Sangay and Altar volcanoes can occasionally be seen from town.

Phone code: 03
Colour map 5, grid A2
Population: 25,000

Ministerio de Turismo, Ceslao Marín y Atahualpa, 2nd floor. Mon-Fri 0900-1700. Tourist information is also available from the *Consejo Provincial*, Orellana 145 y 27 de Febrero, ground floor.

Tourist information

Oriente Jungle

Sights & excursions   The **Museo Etno-Arqueológico**, Atahualpa y 9 de Octubre, third floor, has displays of the traditional dwellings of various cultures of the province of Pastaza.

Omaere is a 15.6-ha ethnobotanical reserve located 2 km north of Puyo on the road to Tena. It was changing ownership and not functioning in 2002. There are other small private reserves of varying quality in the Puyo area and visits are arranged by local tour operators (see below). You cannot however expect to see large tracts of undisturbed primary jungle here nor many wild animals. Sites include: **Criadero de Vida Silvestre Fátima**, 9 km north on the road to Tena, which attempts to 'rehabilitate' captive jungle animals, entry US$2; **Jadín Botánico La Orquideas**, 3 km south on the road to Macas, with orchids and other tropical plants, entry US$4; **Fundación Ecologica Hola Vida**, 27 km from Puyo near **Porvenir**, which offers rustic accommodation in the forest, and a 30-minute canoe trip.

Sleeping
■ *on map*
Price codes:
see inside front cover

B *Hostería Safari*, outside town at Km 5 on the road to Tena, T885465. Includes breakfast and supper, pool, parking, ample grounds, peaceful and out of the way. **B** *Turingia*, Ceslao Marín 294, T886344, F885384, turingia@andinanet.net Restaurant, fan, small pool, parking, comfortable rooms, nice garden. **C-D** *El Araucano*, Ceslao Marín 576, T885686, F883834. Restaurant, fan, many different types of rooms at various prices, ranging from simple to basic. **D** *El Colibrí*, C Manabí entre Bolívar y Galápagos, T883054. Parking, away from centre, modern, friendly, good value. Recommended. **D** *Gran Hotel Amazónico*, Ceslao Marín y Atahualpa, T883094, F884753, turisvejar@andinanet.net Restaurant, fan, small rooms. **D** *Los Cofanes*, 27 de Febrero 6-29 y Ceslao Marín, T885560, F884791. With fan, a bit run down. **D** *Majestic Inn*, Ceslao Marín y Vaillamil, T885417, F885238. Cafeteria, fan, clean and simple. **D-E** *Cristhian's*, Atahualpa entre 9 de Octubre y 27 de Febrero, T883081, F885874. Fan, fridge, large modern carpeted rooms, but could be cleaner. **E** *Chasi*, 9 de Octubre y Orellana, T883059. Private bath, cold water, basic.

Eating
● *on map*
Price codes:
see inside front cover

Mid-range *El Jardín*, on the Paseo Turístico in Barrio Obrero. International food. *La Carihuela*, Mons Alberto Zambrano, near the bus station. Upmarket dining including good set meals. The restaurants in *Turingia* and *Gran Hotel Amazónico* are reliable.

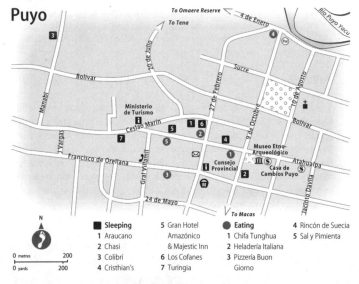

Sleeping	5 Gran Hotel	Eating	4 Rincón de Suecia
1 Araucano	Amazónico	1 Chifa Tunghua	5 Sal y Pimienta
2 Chasi	& Majestic Inn	2 Heladería Italiana	
3 Colibrí	6 Los Cofanes	3 Pizzería Buon	
4 Cristhian's	7 Turingia	Giorno	

0 metres 200
0 yards 200

Pizzería Buon Giorno, Orellana entre Villamil y 27 de Febrero. Good pizza and salads. Pleasant atmosphere, very popular and recommended.

Cheap *Rincón de Suecia*, at the end of 9 de Octubre. Pizza. *Chifa Tunghua*, Atahualpa entre 27 de Febrero y 9 de Octubre. Good Chinese, large portions. There is another *chifa* across the street and *Chifa China*, 9 de Octubre y 24 de Mayo. *Sal y Pimienta*, Atahualpa y 27 de Febrero. Grilled meats. Very cheap and popular. *Cafetería Panadería Susanita*, Ceslao Marín y Villamil. Bakery, also serves breakfast and very cheap lunch. *Heladería Italiana*, 27 de Febrero y Atahualpa. Good ice-cream. Recommended.

At Barrio Obrero, along the river on the road north to Tena, are several bars and discos in a pleasant setting.

Bars & nightclubs

There are many well stocked shops for supplies. *Amazonía Touring*, Atahualpa y 9 de Octubre, has a good selection of local crafts.

Shopping

All of the following offer jungle tours of varying lengths. Prices range from US$25-50 per person per day. *Amazonía Touring*, Atahualpa y 9 de Octubre, T883219. The *Organización de Pueblos Indígenas de Pastaza (OPIP)* operates *Papangu Tours*, 9 de Octubre y Orellana, T883875. *Entsa Tours*, Mentor Marino is helpful and knowledge-able. Call in the evening at T885500.

Tour operators

Air There are military flights from Shell to Quito and villages deep in the Oriente. These are generally not open to foreigners. Also 2 commercial flights a week to Quito (see Shell, below).

Transport

Bus The terminal terrestre is on the outskirts of town, on the Shell and Baños road in the southwest, a 10-15 min walk from the centre. To **Baños**, US$1.50, 2 hrs. To **Ambato**, US$2, 3 hrs. To **Quito**, US$4, 6 hrs via Ambato (9 hrs via Baeza). To **Tena**, US$2, 3 hrs. To **Macas**, US$4.50, 4½ hrs. To **Riobamba**, US$3, 4 hrs.

Banks *Casa de Cambios Puyo*, Atahualpa y 9 de Octubre, T/F883064. 3% commission for US$ TCs. Also Euros, cash only. Helpful and friendly. Recommended. *Banco del Austro*, Atahualpa entre 10 de Agosto y Dávila, cash advances on Visa. **Communications** Internet: US$2-3 per hr. Post: 27 de Febrero between Atahualpa and Orellana. Telephone: *Andinatel*, Villamil y Orellana. Long lineups.

Directory

The road from Puyo to Baños is a spectacular journey with superb views of the Pastaza valley and a plethora of waterfalls. **Shell** is 13 km west of Puyo, 50 km from Baños (1½ hours). It has an airfield (watch out for aircraft crossing the road!) and an army checkpoint where foreigners must sometimes register; passport required.

Puyo to Baños

Sleeping and eating D *Los Copales*, west of Shell on the road to Baños, T795290. Comfortable cabins with private bath and electric shower. Restaurant on site, quiet set-ting. Friendly. **D** *Germany Hostal*, down a side street (not easy to find), T795134. Pri-vate bath, hot water on request, restaurant. Nice quiet setting. Family-run, very friendly. **E-F** *Hostal Cordillera*, on main street. Cheaper with shared bath. Restaurant. Basic, friendly. There are several cheap and simple *comedores* on the main street; *El Portón*, near the west end, is good.

Transport Military flights from Shell are generally not open to foreigners. *Servicio Aereo Regional*, T02-2592032 (Quito), T795175 (Shell), flies to Quito Mon and Fri, US$45. Also charters a light aircraft for 7 passengers.

Southern Oriente

Stretching south of the Río Pastaza, the southern Oriente is made up of the provinces of Morona-Santiago and part of Zamora-Chinchipe. This is a less developed region and tourism is only just getting started. The area has maintained its natural and cultural integrity in part because of the traditionally determined – at times hostile – attitude of the Shuar and Achuar people who live here. Also because there has been relatively little petroleum development to date, although mining poses a hazard. The signing of a peace treaty in 1998 between Ecuador and Peru over their disputed border is helping to introduce tourism to the region. A new development in 2002 was the introduction of a river trip from Morona (Ecuador) to Iquitos (Peru), operated by Neotropic Turis *of Quito (see under Cuyabeno tour operators, page 367). There is a great deal to explore here, but all visitors to virgin territory should remember that they have an especially important obligation to be responsible tourists (see page 44).*

Puyo to Macas The first leg of the Puyo-Macas bus journey goes for three hours as far as the Río Pastaza. Here is an impressive and hair-raising suspension bridge suitable only for small cars. Bus passengers disembark and walk across. On the opposite shore, another bus takes you the rest of the way (2½ hours) to Macas. It stops often at small settlements, mostly inhabited by Shuar. The ride is slow and rough, the road hard packed dirt, full of potholes. The jungle which once bordered this road has mostly become farmland.

Macas

Phone code: 07
Colour map 5, grid B1
Population: 14,000
Altitude: 1,000 m

See www.macas-ecuador.com

Capital of Morona-Santiago province, situated high above the broad Río Upano valley, Macas is a pleasant tranquil town. The climate is not too hot and the nights are even cool. It was established by missionaries in 1563. The immense snow-capped Sangay volcano can be seen on rare clear mornings from the plaza, creating an amazing backdrop to the tropical jungle surrounding the town. Puffs of smoke may sometimes be seen and, even more infrequently, a red glow at night from the crater of this still very active volcano – an unforgettable sight!

Sights The town is small enough to walk around. Hotels are dotted around a bit but easy to get to. The modern cathedral, completed in 1992, with beautiful stained-glass windows, houses the much venerated image of La Purísima de Macas. It overlooks a neat central plaza. Five blocks north of the cathedral, along Don Bosco, is the shady Parque Recreational which affords great views of the Upano Valley. It has a small orchid collection.

Excursions The Salesian **Sevilla-Don Bosco mission** is east of town. The modern archaeological museum, Don Bosco y Montalba, is a good place to rest and see views of the Río Upano, and there is a recreation area nearby. About 3 km north is **La Cascada**, beside the Río Copueno, with a picnic area, with swimming, slide, football and volleyball.

Complejo Hombre Jaguar is an archaeological site with many *tolas*. It is north of town near Santa Rosa and Guapula on the way to Sangay National Park (see below). Allow two days to see everything; ask for directions if you're using public transport. Day tours can be arranged with *Winia Sunka* (see Tour Operators below)

In clear weather the surrounding hills give excellent views of the active volcano **Sangay**, within **Parque Nacional Sangay**. The lowland area of the park has interesting walking with many rivers and waterfalls, and can be reached by taking a bus to the little village of 9 de Octubre (no services), daily at 0700 and 1600, US$1.50, 1½ hours. Local residents may be able to guide you from there (take all gear and provisions) or arrange a tour from Macas, see Tour operators below.

AL *Cabañas Ecológicas Yuquipa*, a 1½ hr walk from Km 12 on the road to Puyo. Package includes accommodation, 3 meals, guide and transport. Contact *Panesa* bakery at Soasti y Tarqui, T700071 or 700768. **C** *Manzana Real*, at southern entrance to town, T700191. Includes breakfast, restaurant, pool, parking, suite available. Upmarket for where it is but double rooms are small.

Sleeping
■ *on map*
*Price codes:
see inside front cover*

D *Casa Blanca*, Soasti 14-29 y Sucre, T700195, F701584. Includes breakfast, clean and comfortable, very friendly and helpful. Recommended. **D** *Esmeralda*, Cuenca 6-12 y Soasti, T700130. Family run, clean and friendly but some rooms are a bit small. **D** *La Orquídea*, 9 de Octubre 13-05 y Sucre, T700970. OK. **D** *Peñón del Oriente*, Domingo Comín 8-37 y Amazonas, near market and bus terminal, T700124, F700450. Cheaper with cold water, in multi-storey building, noisy, rooms vary but overall a bit run down. **D** *Safari*, Soasti y Tarqui, T700113. Cold water, OK. **D-E** *California*, 29 de Mayo at south end of town, T/F701237. Cheaper shared bath, electric shower, parking, modern, new in 2001. **D-F** *Esplendit*, Soasti 15-18 y Domingo Comin, T700120. Cheaper with sahred bath, parking, new section is nice and comfortable, older rooms cheap and basic. **E-F** *Residencial Macas*, 24 de Mayo 14-35 y Sucre, T700254. Above *Restaurante Carmita*, cheaper with shared bath, cold water, old wooden building, simple but clean, good value. **F** *Sangay*, Tarqui 605, T700457. Shared bath, cold water, very basic but friendly. There are several other cheap and very basic places on C Tarqui.

Macas

Oriente Jungle

■ Sleeping		● Eating
1 Casa Blanca	6 Residencial Macas	1 Café El Jardín
2 Esmeralda	7 Safari	2 Carmita
3 Esplendit	8 Sangay	3 Chifa Welcome
4 La Orquídea		4 Chonta Cafetería
5 Peñon del Oriente		5 Pagoda China

0 metres 50
0 yards 50

Eating
● *on map,*
page 383

Mid-range *Chifa Pagoda China*, Amazonas y Domingo Comín. Very good Chinese food. Recommended. **Cheap** *Carmita*, 24 de Mayo y Sucre. Good set meals. *Chonta Cafetería*, 24 de Mayo y 10 de Agosto. Breakfast, juices, snacks and lasagna. Cheap and good. *El Jardín*, Amazonas y Domingo Comín, across from the market. Cheap set meals. **Seriously cheap** *Chifa Welcome*, Soasti 14-34. Very cheap set lunch.

Several small *comedores* along Domingo Comín serve local specialties such as *aymapacos*, spiced chicken or palm hearts wrapped in *bijao* leaves and roasted over the coals. They are tasty but keep an eye on cleanliness.

Bars &
nightclubs

Discos *Acuario*, Soasti y Sucre, good music. *Cachorros*, 24 de Mayo y Bolívar, starting 2100 daily except Sun. Varied music.

Tour operators

Winia Sunka, Domingo Comín y Amazonas, the kiosk in front of *Chifa Pagoda China*, T/F700088. Runs cabins and tours in the Santa Rosa area north of Macas, as well as tours east of the Cordillera de Cutucú, near the Peruvian border. The owner, Pablo Velín, is a recommended guide. *Kujáncham*, 24 de Mayo 16-22 y 10 de Agosto, T700299, erikacoronadoec@yahoo.com Erika Coronado at the craft shop organizes tours to Sangay National Park and Shuar communities.

Transport

Air The airport is within walking distance, at Cuenca y Amazonas. Flights to/from **Quito** with *TAME* on Mon and Thu, US$56 for foreigners (schedule subject to change, sit on the left for the best views of Sangay). The *TAME* office is at the airport, T701162. In 2002 *Austro Aereo* was flying to Cuenca on Mon and Fri, US$45, but check schedule in advance. No office, local contact T701992. *Servicio Aereo Misional*, at the airport, T700142, serves small communities in the jungle. No scheduled routes but they can charter light aircraft for US$250 per hour.

Bus To **Puyo**, US$4.50, 4½ hrs. To **Quito**, via Puyo, Baños and Ambato, US$8, 9 hrs. To **Cuenca**, US$7, 8-10 hrs, the views are spectacular but roads are subject to landslides after heavy rain. To **Gualaquiza**, where you can get a bus to Zamora and on to Loja, US$6.50, 9 hrs, a long rough ride. To **Sucúa**, every 30 min, US$0.75, 1 hr.

A controversial new road runs from **Macas to Guamote** in the central highlands near Riobamba, cutting through Parque Nacional Sangay (see page 383). It had been almost completed in late 2002 and deforestation and colonization of the area had begun. It will, however, make a spectacular ride once it is open to traffic; enquire locally.

Directory

Banks Nowhere to change TCs. *Banco del Austro*, 24 de Mayo y 10 de Agosto. Visa. *Banco del Pichincha*, Soasti y 10 de Agosto, Visa cash advances through ATM only. **Communications** Post Office: 9 de Octubre y Domingo Comín, next to the park. Andinatel: 24 de Mayo y Sucre. Internet: US$1.40 per hr. **Shopping** Shops are well stocked with most supplies but prices are a little higher because of the remote location. Kujáncham, 24 de Mayo 16-22 y 10 de Agosto, sells local crafts.

East of Macas

Kapawi
jungle lodge
Colour map 5, grid B4

Kapawi is a top-of-the-line jungle lodge located on the Río Pastaza in the heart of Achuar territory not far from the Peruvian border. It is accessible only by small aircraft and motor canoe. The lodge was built in partnership with the indigenous organization **OINAE** and offers flexible programmes adapting to the interests and conditions of the eco-tourist. It is also built according to the Achuar concept of architecture, using typical materials, and emphasizes environmentally friendly methods such as solar energy, biodegradable soaps and rubbish recycling. It is in a zone rich in biodiversity, with many opportunities for seeing the forest and its inhabitants. Four nights in a double cabin costs US$700, plus US$150 for transport to and from Quito. The location, quality of service, cabin accommodation and food have all been highly recommended. Operated by Canodros, Quito office: Portugal 448 y Catalina Aldaz, T02-2256759, vgarcia@canodros.com, www.canodros.com Or book through agencies in Quito or abroad.

Sucúa

About 23 km from Macas, Sucúa is of particular interest as the centre of a branch of the ex-head-hunting Shuar (Jívaro) Indians. Their crafts can be seen and bought but it is tactless to ask them about head-hunting and shrinking (a practice designed to punish those who bewitched others and to deter anyone wishing to cause sickness or disaster in future).

Phone code: 07
Colour map, grid B1
Population: 6,300

You can contact the **Shuar Federation** at Domingo Comín 17-38, T/F740108, for information about visiting traditional villages, but the federation is officious and generally uninterested in tourists. There is a small craft shop across the street from the Shuar Federation.

Nearby is the Río Upano, a 1½-hour walk, with plenty of Morpho butterflies. Also close by is the Río Tutanangoza, a 15-minute walk, with rapids and good swimming, but be careful of the current after rain.

D-E *Don Guimo*, Domingo Comín y Kiruba, T/F740483, Includes breakfast, cheaper with shared bath, hot water, parking, modern and comfortable, new in 2001. Recommended. **E** *Hostal Karina*, on the southwest corner of the plaza, T740153. Cheaper with shared bath, hot water, clean and bright. **F** *Hostería Orellana*, at the south end of town, T740193. One room with bath, others without. **F** *Hostal Alborada*, Domingo Comín. T740149. Shared bath, cold water. There are several other cheap and basic places in town. *La Fuente*, Domingo Comín near the plaza. Bar/restaurant, good cheap set meals and à la carte. *La Orquidea*, 8 de Diciembre y Domingo Comín, very cheap set meals, good.

Sleeping & eating

Kapawi
Amazon Rain Forest at a very low price

Contact your travel agency.
www.kapawi.com
Canodros S.A. Ecuador-South America

Sucúa to Morona and Limón

From Sucúa, the road heads south for one hour to **Logroño**. A short walk out of town are extensive limestone caves; take a torch, rope, etc. They are subject to flash floods during rainstorms. There is a gate; get the key before walking out of the village. A guide is useful. Another one hour south is (Santiago de) **Méndez**, a nice town with a modern church.

Sleeping and eating E *Hostal Los Ceibos*, C Cuenca just off plaza, T760133.

Oriente Jungle

▶▶ The family of Achuar

The Achuar is one of the four groups of the linguistic family Jívaro: Achuar, Shuar (or Shiwiar), Aguaruna and Huambisa. This is by far the most important remaining indigenous culture in the Amazon Basin, with a population of around 80,000, and occupying huge tracts of Ecuador and Peru's rainforest. They get their name from the Shuar word achu meaning morete, a kind of palm that grows in flooded areas, and shuar, meaning people.

Though known in the past for their internal wars, the Achuar live today in peace, mostly in small villages. They hunt, fish and forage in the forests and also tend small plots (chacras) where they practise slash-and-burn cultivation. This is a necessary practice given that the rainforest soils are particularly infertile. Each chacra covers an area of roughly 4,000 sq m, generally near a river, and is used for an average of three years before being left in favour of a new plot of land.

The Achuar believe in multiple spirits that give them guidance for a harmonious relationship with the rainforest and its wildlife. Magic and healing powers are used by the shaman (uwishin), who gets his force by means of hallucinogenic plants like natem. They maintain a very intimate relationship with nature and its processes. Primarily based in astronomical calculations and biological cycles, the Achuar have created a model of representation of annual cycles in the rainforest much more precise than any developed by modern biologists or meteorologists. Since they did not have a written language before the arrival of missionaries, the use of myths has been very important in keeping the traditions alive.

Until the end of the 18th century, the region occupied by the Achuar was only occasionally visited by the most determined of missionaries. The region was not affected by the rubber boom, which converted thousands of Zápara Indians into slaves during the 19th century. Although from the end of the 19th century to the 1950s this area was visited by some explorers and naturalists, it was, for the most part, considered terra incognita until the late 1960s. Between 1968 and 1970 Catholics and Evangelists established the first contacts with the group in order to convert them to Christianity, a process that drastically altered their way of living. Since 1991 the majority of the Achuar belong to OINAE (Organization of Ecuadorean Achuar Nationalities). Today OINAE is divided into three groups, each one with its own centre.

Private bath, hot water. Impeccably clean and friendly. Recommended. **F** *Hostal Los Sauces*, T760165. Places to eat include *El Reportero*, Domingo Comín y Cuenca; and *16 de Agosto*, Cuenca y Guayaquil.

South of Méndez, passports are checked at a checkpoint at **Patuca**, the first village after the bridge over the Río Upano. This road is subject to landslides in the rainy season.

Near Méndez a road goes east into the jungle to **Morona**. Along the road is the junction of the Zamora-Coangos rivers. East of the confluence, at the village of **Santiago**, a canoe can be hired to a point from where you can walk in 2½ hours to the **Cueva de Los Tayos**, a huge cave, 85 m in depth. The trail is obscure, and a guide is necessary.

It is 10 hours by bus from Macas (three a day) to the village of (San José de) **Morona**, located on the Río Morona near the Peruvian border. There is no accommodation but camping is possible, and there is a house where you can get meals and drinks.

Two hours, 50 km south of Méndez is Limón, official name General Leónidas Plaza, a mission town founded in 1935, now a busy, friendly place, surrounded by high jungle. Buses, all from Calle Quito, go to Cuenca, Macas and Gualaquiza.

Limón
Phone code: 07
Colour map 6, grid A5
Population: 3,500

Sleeping and eating E *Dream House*, C Quito. Friendly. **E** *Residencial Limón*, T770114. Shared bath, cold water, basic, clean and friendly, front rooms noisy. **F** *Residencial Dianita*, T770122. Shared bath, cold water, basic. There are several basic *chifas* in town and the *El Viajero* restaurant at bus the terminal.

From Limón, a road to Cuenca (132 km) passes through Gualaceo, via Jadán. From Limón the road rises steeply with many breathtaking turns and the vegetation changes frequently, partly through cloud forest and then, at 4,000 m, through the *páramo*, before dropping very fast down to the valley of Gualaceo. There is a police checkpoint at Plan de Milagro, where foreigners have to register. There is nowhere to stay along the Limón-Gualaceo road.

Limón to Cuenca
This is one of the best roads in Ecuador for birdwatching

South to Zamora

Continuing south from Limón the road passes **Indanza** (very basic *residencial* and *comedor*), before reaching **Gualaquiza**, a pioneer town off the tourist track. It is surrounded by densely forested mountains, in which many interesting side trips can be made. If you intend to explore the area, bring a tent and sleeping bag.

Gualaquiza
Phone code: 07
Colour map 6, grid B5
Population: 6,500

Among the excursions from Gualaquiza are the caves near **Nuevo Tarqui** and the Salesian mission at *Bomboiza*, which has a small museum. The **Tutusa Gorge** is three hours' walk, then two hours by boat; take a guide, such as Sr José Castillo.

It's a six-hour walk to **Aguacate**, near where are pre-Columbian ruins (food and bed at Sr Jorge Guillermo Vázquez). **Yumaza** is a 40-minute walk, for more pre-Columbian ruins (two sites).

Sleeping and eating E *Amazonas No 2*, Domingo Comín 08-65 y Gonzalo Pesantes. Basic, friendly. **E** *Guakiz*, Orellana 08-52, T780138. With private bath, friendly, the best in town. The best restaurant is *Oro Verde*, near the *Hotel Guakiz*. Excellent food and service. Also *Cabaña*, and *Los Helechos*, opposite the bus station.

Transport Bus: To Cuenca, US$5, 6 hrs. To Zamora, US$2.80, 4 hrs. To Loja, US$4.80, 7 hrs. To Macas, US$6.50, 9 hrs.

Directory Communications: Telephone: *Pacifictel*, García Moreno y Ciudad de Cuenca.

Here, we change the direction of our description, which had been proceeding from north south along the western edge of Oriente. Instead we now follow the route from Loja, east to Zamora and then north to Gualaquiza.

From Loja (see page 262) the road to the Oriente crosses a low pass and descends rapidly to Zamora. It was paved and in reasonably good condition in 2002, but is subject to frequent landslides and deteriorates rapidly during heavy rains. The road is beautiful as it wanders from *páramo* down to high jungle, crossing mountain ranges of spectacular cloud forest, weaving high above narrow gorges as it runs alongside the Río Zamora.

Oriente Jungle

Zamora

Phone code: 07
Colour map 6, grid B4
Population: 10,500
Altitude: 1,000 m

The southernmost city in Oriente and capital of the province of Zamora-Chinchipe, Zamora is an old mission settlement at the confluence of the Ríos Zamora and Bombuscara. It has traditionally been far off the beaten path but is now gradually opening up to tourism following the peace treaty with Peru. Mining is an important part of the province's economy and also a threat to its natural environment.

Sights   The **Orquideario Tzanka**, one block from the plaza, features an interesting collection of almost 1,000 plants including rare specimens (not for sale). ■ *On Calle José Luis Tamayo, US$2, daily. Contact Mario González, T605692.* There is also **Orquideario Paphinia**, 5 km from town.

Excursions   Zamora's most important attraction is the easy access it provides to the sub-tropical part of **Podocarpus National Park**, via the **Bombuscara** entrance.

Information from the Ministerio del Ambiente office at the entrance to town from Loja   The entrance trail along the Bombuscara River is very pleasant and full of subtropical birds hard to find elsewhere in Ecuador (such as Coppery-chested Jacamar, White-breasted Parakeet, several rare Fruiteaters, and many more). Take the road east out of Zamora and turn right when you reach the Rio Bombuscara. Do not cross the river; take the road that follows the river upstream. The road ends in a car park, where the trail begins. About 30 minutes' walk takes you to the visitors' centre and more trails, including a river trail and a 30-minute loop trail. It is highly recommended for nature lovers, especially those who might have difficulty walking on steep trails. The trail to the visitors' centre is virtually flat, unlike almost all other trails at this elevation in Ecuador.

Sleeping   **D** *Maguna*, Diego de Vaca, T605113. Electric shower, parking, fridge, quiet and friendly. **E** *Seyma*, 24 de Mayo y Amazonas, T605583. Shared bath, parking, OK. **F** *Gimyfa*, Diego de Vaca, 1 block from Plaza, T605104. Private bath, quiet and nice. **F** *Venecia*, Sevilla de Oro, T605289. Shared bath, basic. **F** *Zamora*, Sevilla de Oro y Pío Jaramillo, T605253. Shared bath, parking, OK, basic.

Eating   The restaurant in *Hotel Maguna* is good. **Comedor Don Pepe**, set meals and à la carte. *Esmeraldas*, in the market area opposite the bus terminal. Good.

Transport   **Bus**: leave from the Terminal Terrestre. To **Loja**, frequent service, US$2, 2 hrs. To **Gualquiza**, US$4.80, 7 hrs, where you can catch a bus for the long haul north to Macas.

The road north from Zamora passes through **Yantzaza** (four hotels, including the F *Inca*, and several cheap *comedores*) and **El Pangui** (F *Hotel Estrella del Oriente*) on its way to Gualaquiza, allowing for connections to Cuenca, Macas and Puyo (see above).

Galápagos Islands

Introducing the Galápagos Islands

A trip to the Galápagos is a unique and unforgettable experience. As Charles Darwin put it, 'the Natural History of this archipelago is very remarkable: it seems to be a little world within itself'. The islands are world-renowned for their fearless wildlife but no amount of hype can prepare the visitor for such a close encounter with nature. Here, you can snorkel with penguins and sea-lions, watch giant 200 kg tortoises lumbering through cactus forest and enjoy the courtship display of the

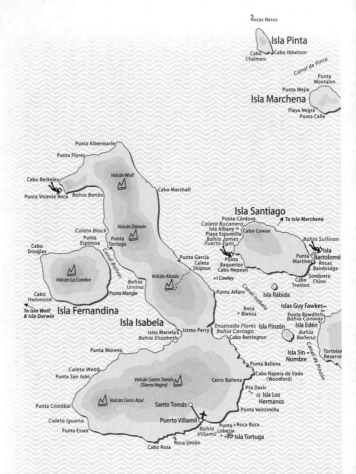

Galápagos Islands

N

0 km   10
0 miles   10

blue-footed booby and frigatebird, all in startling close-up.

A visit to the islands doesn't come cheap. The return flight from Quito and national park fee add up to almost US$500; plus a bare minimum of US$60 per person per day for sailing on the most basic boat, when you can find space at this price. Luxury vessels cost up to five times as much: there is at present simply no way to enjoy Galápagos on a shoestring. For those with the money and interest however, the experience is well worth the cost. At the same time, these high prices are one way of keeping the number of visitors within reasonable levels in order to limit impact on the islands and their wildlife.

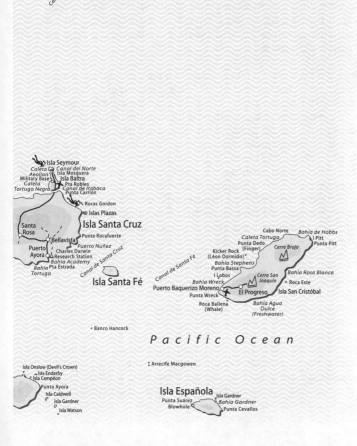

Facts about the islands

See also the colour
wildlife section in
the middle of the
book and the box
on Charles Darwin,
page 396
Lying on the Equator, 970 km west of the Ecuadorean coast, the Galápagos consist of six main islands: San Cristóbal, Santa Cruz, Isabela, Floreana, Santiago and Fernandina (the last two are uninhabited). There are also 12 smaller islands – Baltra and the uninhabited islands of Santa Fe, Pinzón, Española, Rábida, Daphne, Seymour, Genovesa, Marchena, Pinta, Darwin and Wolf – as well as over 40 small islets.

The Galápagos have never been connected with the continent. Gradually, over many hundreds of thousands of years, animals and plants from over the sea somehow migrated there and as time went by they adapted themselves to Galápagos conditions and came to differ more and more from their continental ancestors. Thus many of them are unique: a quarter of the species of shore fish, half of the plants and almost all the reptiles are found nowhere else. In many cases different forms have evolved on the different islands. Charles Darwin recognized this speciation within the archipelago when he visited the Galápagos on the *Beagle* in 1835 and his observations played a substantial part in his formulation of the theory of evolution. Since no large land mammals reached the islands (until they were recently introduced by man), reptiles were dominant just as they had been all over the world in the very distant past. Another of the extraordinary features of the islands is the tameness of the animals. The islands were uninhabited when they were discovered in 1535 and the animals still have little instinctive fear of man.

Classification
Plant and animal species in the Galápagos are grouped into the following three categories. These are terms which you will hear often during your visit to the islands. **Endemic species** are those which occur only in the Galápagos and nowhere else on the planet. Examples are the Marine and Land Iguana, Galápagos Fur Seal, Flightless Cormorant and the 'Daisy tree' (*Scalesia pedunculata*). **Native species** make their homes in the Galápagos as well as other parts of the world. Examples include all three species of boobies, Frigate birds and the various types of mangroves. Although not unique to the islands, these native species have been an integral part of the Galápagos ecosystems for a very long time. **Introduced species** on the other hand are very recent arrivals, brought by man, and inevitably the cause of much damage. They include cattle, goats, donkeys, pigs, dogs, cats, rats and over 500 species of plants such as elephant grass (for grazing cattle), and fruit trees such as the raspberry and guava. The unchecked expansion of these introduced species has upset the natural balance and seriously threatens the unique endemic species for which Galápagos is so famous.

Geology
See also Geology,
page 454
The islands are the peaks of gigantic undersea volcanoes, composed almost exclusively of basalt. Most of them rise about 2,000 to 3,500 m above the surrounding seabed, but over 7,000 m above the deepest parts of the adjacent ocean floor to the west of Fernandina. The highest summit is Volcán Wolf on Isabela island, 1,660 m above sea level. Eruptions have taken place in historical times on Fernandina, Isabela, Pinta, Marchena and Santiago. The most active today are Fernandina, Isabela, Pinta and Marchena, and fumarolic activity may be seen intermittently on each of these islands. The islands are also very gradually drifting eastward, due to the movement of the tectonic plate on which they rest. Hence the oldest islands lie to the east,

including San Cristóbal and Española which are approximately three to 3½ million years old. The youngest islands, such as Fernandina and Isabela are in the west of the archipelago, and have been in existence for some 700,000 to 800,000 years.

The Galápagos climate can be divided into a hot season (January through **Climate** April), when the sea temperature rises and there is a possibility of brief heavy showers, and the cool or *garúa* season (May through December), when the ocean is cooler and days generally are more cloudy with some mist or light drizzle. During July and August the southeast trade winds can be very strong. At night, temperatures can fall below 15°C, particularly at sea. The underwater visibility is best from January to March. Ocean temperatures are usually higher to the east and lower at the western end of the archipelago. Despite all these variations, conditions are generally favourable for visiting Galápagos throughout the year.

The islands' climate and hence their wildlife are also affected by the phenomenon known as El Niño (see page 457). This cyclical increase in ocean temperature alters the food chain upon which depend the Galápagos marine fauna. The result is high levels of mortality especially among sea lions, penguins and other seabirds. This is, however, part of the natural life cycle. When the phenomenon subsides, food supplies are replenished and the different species recover. An El Niño year is also when you can see the islands at their greenest.

The islands were discovered accidentally by Tomás de Berlanga, the Bishop of **History of** Panama, in 1535. He was on his way to Peru when his ship was becalmed and **human** swept 800 km off course by the currents. Like most of the early arrivals, Bishop **settlement** Tomás and his crew arrived thirsty and disappointed at the dryness of the place. He did not even give the islands a name, although he did dub the giant tortoises 'Galápagos'.

The islands first appeared on a map in 1574, as 'Islands of Galápagos', which has remained in common use ever since. The individual islands, though, have had several names, both Spanish and English. The latter names come from a visit in 1680 by English buccaneers who, with the blessing of the English king, attacked Spanish ships carrying gold and relieved them of their heavy load. The pirates used the Galápagos as a hide-out, in particular a spot North of James Bay on Santiago island, still known as Buccaneers' Cove. The pirates were the first to visit many of the islands and they named them after English kings and aristocracy or famous captains of the day.

The Spanish also called the islands *Las Encantadas*, 'enchanted' or 'bewitched', owing to the fact that for much of the year they are surrounded by mists giving the impression that they appear and disappear as if by magic. Also, the tides and currents were so confusing that they thought the islands were floating and not real islands.

Between 1780 and 1860, the waters of the Galápagos became a favourite place for British and American whaling ships. At the beginning of the whaling era, in 1793, a British naval captain erected a barrel on Floreana island, to facilitate communication between boats and the land. It is still in place today, at Post Office bay.

The first island to be inhabited was Floreana, in 1807, by a lone Irishman named Patrick Watkins, who stayed for two years. After his departure they were more or less uninhabited, until 1832, when Ecuadorean General José Villamil founded a colony on Floreana, mainly composed of convicts and political prisoners, who traded meat and vegetables with whalers. In February 1832, following the creation of the young republic, Colonel Ignacio Hernández took official possession of the archipelago in the name of Ecuador. Spanish names were given to the islands, in addition to the existing English ones.

The Galápagos Affair One of the more bizarre and notorious periods began in 1929 with the arrival of German doctor, Friedrich Ritter, and his mistress, Dore Strauch. Three years later, the Wittmer family also decided to settle on the island, and Floreana soon became so fashionable that luxury yachts used to call in. One of these visitors was Baroness von Wagner de Bosquet, an Austrian woman who settled on the island with her two lovers and grandiose plans to build a hotel for millionaires. (Such ambitions were eventually realized in 2002 with the opening of the *Royal Palm* hotel on Santa Cruz Island, see Puerto Ayora Sleeping, page 417.) Soon after landing in 1932 the Baroness proclaimed herself Empress of Floreana, which was not to the liking of Dr Ritter or the Wittmer family, and tensions rose. There followed several years of mysterious and unsavoury goings-on, during which everyone died or disappeared, except Dore Strauch and the Wittmer family. The longest survivor of this still unexplained drama was Margret Wittmer, who lived at Black Beach on Floreana until her death in 2000, at age 95. Her account of life there, entitled *Floreana, Poste Restante*, was published in 1961 and became a bestseller. Also see *The Galápagos Affair*, by John Treherne, under Books, page 464.

Current settlements Human settlement on the Galápagos is currently limited to about 3% of the islands' land area of 7,882 sq km, but nevertheless, the resident population of the islands has grown very rapidly in recent years. The 2001 census counted 18,555 people but this may not include a floating population (people 'temporarily' living on the islands, sometimes for many years) of about 3,000. The population is concentrated in eight settlements. Two are on San Cristóbal (Chatham), at Puerto Baquerizo Moreno and a small village inland called El Progreso. San Cristóbal has a population of around 7,000, and Puerto Baquerizo Moreno is the administrative capital of the province of Galápagos and Ecuador's second naval base. There are three settlements on Santa Cruz (Indefatigable) – Puerto Ayora, the largest town and the main tourist centre, Bellavista and Santa Rosa, two small farming communities inland. Santa Cruz is the most populated island, with around 10,000 inhabitants. On Floreana, the longest inhabited island, there are 90 souls, most of which are at Black Beach and on Isabela (Albemarle), the largest island, there is a thriving community of 1,600 mostly at Puerto Villamil and a village inland at Tomás de Berlanga. Residents of the Islands, now into their third and fourth generation, call themselves *colonos*, *Galapagueños* or *carapachudos*. The latter literally means 'those with a shell', a tongue-in-cheek reference to the giant tortoises.

There is a navy base on Baltra (South Seymour) at the site of an old US Airforce camp. Flights from the mainland arrive either at Baltra, which has a good road to Puerto Ayora, or on San Cristóbal. There is also an airstrip for light aircraft at Puerto Villamil on Isabela. All the other islands are accessible only by sea.

Evolution and conservation

The continuing volcanic formation of the islands in the west of the archipelago has not only created a unique marine environment, but the drift eastwards of the whole island group at the nexus of several major marine currents has created laboratory-type conditions where only certain species have been allowed access. Others have been excluded; most significantly, practically the whole of the terrestrial kingdom of mammals. The resulting ecology has evolved in a unique direction, with many of the ecological niches being filled from some unexpected angles. A highly-evolved sunflower, for instance, has in some areas taken over the niche left vacant by the absence of trees.

Within the islands, evolutionary pressures are so intense that there is a very high level of endemism (species confined to a particular area). For example, not only have the tortoises evolved differently from those in the rest of the world, but each of the five main volcanoes on Isabela has evolved its own subspecies of giant tortoise. This natural experiment has been under threat ever since the arrival of the first whaling ships and even more so since the first permanent human settlement. New species such as horses, cattle, donkeys, goats, pigs, dogs, cats and rats, as well as over 500 species of plants, were introduced and spread very rapidly. The unique endemic species that had gradually evolved to fill the ecological niches in the Galápagos are now at risk of being evicted and destroyed by the more recent introductions. More recently still, quarantine programs have been implemented by the authorities in an attempt to prevent the introduction of even more species. There have also been campaigns to eradicate some introduced species on some islands, but this is inevitably a very slow, expensive and difficult process.

The human effect

The most devastating of the newly introduced species are human beings, both visitors and settlers. To a large degree, the two groups are connected, one supporting the other economically, but there is also a sizeable proportion, over half of the islands' permanent residents, who make an income independent of tourism from working the land or at sea.

While no great wealth has accumulated to those who farm, fortunes have been made by fishermen in a series of particularly destructive fisheries: black coral, lobster, shark fin and sea cucumber. Sharks were caught by setting gill nets across a bay. These nets took a wide range of marine animals and birds as a by-catch, including pelicans, boobies, seals, turtles and dolphins. As none have any commercial value, they were dumped. Each successive fishery was encouraged by foreign demand involving large amounts of money.

It is, however, farmers who are responsible for the largest number of introduced species. Recent introductions (since the formation of the National Park) include elephant grass to provide pastures, the ani to eat parasites living on cattle (although in the Galápagos it prefers baby finches when it can get them) and walnut trees planted on Isabela.

Neither are tourists nor the industry which they support blameless. In 2001 a small tanker which supplied fuel for tour boats and locals ran aground in the entrance to Puerto Baquerizo Moreno harbour. Thanks to favourable currents most of the resulting oil spill was carried out to sea and relatively little damage was inflicted on any of the Galápagos Islands or their animals. It was, however, a very close call and stringent regulatory measures are required if such accidents are to be prevented in the future.

Galápagos Islands

▶▶ Charles Darwin and the Galápagos

Without doubt, the most famous visitor to the islands is Charles Darwin. His short stay in the archipelago proved hugely significant for science and for the study of evolution.

In September 1835, Darwin sailed into Galápagos waters on board the HMS Beagle, captained by the aristocratic Robert FitzRoy whose job was to chart lesser known parts of the world. FitzRoy had wanted on board a companion of his own social status and a naturalist, to study the strange new animals and plants they would find en route. He chose Charles Darwin to fill both roles.

Darwin was only 22 years old when he set sail from England in 1831 and it would be five years before he saw home again. They were to sail around the world, but most of the voyage was devoted to surveying the shores of South America, giving Darwin the chance to explore a great deal of the continent. The visit to the Galápagos had been planned as a short stop on the return journey, by which time Darwin had become an experienced observer. It was indeed a stroke of luck that he had been picked for this unique cruise.

During the five weeks that the Beagle spent in the Galápagos Darwin went ashore to collect plants, rocks, insects and birds. The unusual life forms and their adaptations to the harsh surroundings made a deep impression on him and eventually inspired his revolutionary theory on the evolution of species. The Galápagos provided a kind of model of the world in miniature. Darwin realized that these recently created volcanoes were young in comparison with the age of the Earth, and that life on the islands showed special adaptations. Yet the plants and animals also showed similarities to those from the South American mainland, where he guessed they had originally come from.

Darwin concluded that the life on the islands had probably arrived there by chance drifting, swimming or flying from the mainland and had not been created on the spot. Once the plants and animals had arrived, they evolved into forms better suited to the strange environment in which they found themselves. Darwin also noted that the animals were extremely tame, because of the lack of predatory mammals. The islands' isolation also meant that the giant tortoises did not face competition from agile mammals and could survive.

On his return to England, Darwin in effect spent the rest of his life publishing the findings of his voyage and developing the ideas it inspired. It was however only when another scientist, named Alfred Russell Wallace, arrived at a similar conclusion to his own that he dared to publish a paper on his theory of evolution. Then followed his all-embracing The Origin of the Species by means of Natural Selection, in 1859. It was to cause a major storm of controversy and to earn Darwin recognition as the man who "provided a foundation for the entire structure of modern biology".

Conflicting interests Each of the colonizing groups on the islands – scientists, the tourist industry, settlers, farmers and fishermen – have all become powerful pressure groups. Each has its own agenda, with different expectations of the islands. The most sophisticated pressure groups are probably those involved in tourism, divided between boat owners and guides. Being mostly Ecuadorean, the boat owners are easily identified and, as they are looking for long-term stability and profit, they can be monitored through a system of licences and permits issued by both the Ministerio del Ambiente and the Navy. Of all the commercial groups, the boat owners are the most likely to support attempts by the Park authorities to conserve the islands. Among the guides, there has been some rivalry between foreigners (such as multilingual and specialist guides) on the one hand, and Galapagueño or Ecuadorean guides on the other. Needless to say, the *'colonos'*, colonist farmers and especially fishermen, have a completely different set of priorities which have at times led to overt conflict with the National Park.

The number of tourists to the island is controlled by the authorities to protect the environment but critics claim that the ecology is seriously threatened by current levels. Limits were increased from 25,000 in 1981, reaching a record number of 60,000 visitors in 1997, and roughly maintained ever since. There were almost 100 tourist boats operating in Galápagos in 2002, ranging in capacity from 10 to 100 passengers, as well as growing land-based tourism; but no new permits are supposed to be issued in the near future. Even by international standards, tourism in Galápagos is quite well organized and regulated; by Latin American standards or those of mainland Ecuador, it is remarkably so.

At least five different authorities have a say in running Galápagos – the islands **The** and surrounding marine reserve. These include: 1) **Instituto Nacional** **authorities** **Galápagos** (INGALA), under control of the president of Ecuador, which was once responsible for most of the islands' infrastructure and today decides who is entitled to the status of *'colono'* (colonist, or Galápagos resident); 2) the **National Park Service**, under the authority of the Ministerio del Ambiente, which regulates tourism and manages the 97% of the archipelago which is parkland; 3) the **Charles Darwin Research Station**, part of an international non-profit organization devoted to supporting scientific research and channelling international funds for conservation; 4) the **Ecuadorean Navy**, which patrols the waters of the archipelago and attempts to enforce regulations regarding both tourism and fishing; 5) local **elected authorities** including municipalities and the provincial council, which – in principle – advocate the interests of all the islands' residents. All of the above must work together but since they represent different sets of interests, this is not always an easy task.

Those planning to carry out scientific research, commercial or documentary filming and any other special activities which are not part of usual tourism may require permits. It is best to enquire and make all arrangements well in advance. A useful contact is Roslyn Cameron at the **Charles Darwin Research Station** in Puerto Ayora, T05-526146 (ext 120), cdrs@ fcdarwin.org.ec, www.darwinfoundation.org For the **National Park Service** in Puerto Ayora contact Alexandra Bajamonde, T05-526189, F05-526190, alexb@spng.org.ec

Because tourism is so easily controlled and involves relatively large amounts **The impact** of money, it is this area which has been debated more than any other. Tourists **of tourism** and their guides form the vast majority of the visitors to the 97% land area that is Park, but it is equally true that, from the point of view of the islands as a whole, it is settlers who are responsible for the largest amount of damage. The remains of abandoned habitations can be seen on Floreana, at Post Office Bay, at Puerto Egas (an abandoned salt works on Santiago Island), near Puerto Villamil and most extensively on Baltra. There is no will to remove them.

The impact of tourism in the Park can best be seen at places like the Plaza islands on the east side of Santa Cruz and a photostudy by the Darwin Station shows many of the changes. Tourists are limited to some 56 landing sites throughout the entire island group. Each has a clearly defined trail from which visitors are not allowed to deviate. The impact that a farmer can have, importing just one species, or one family of settlers, is therefore far greater than that of tourism, which has been largely successfully controlled.

The impact of immigration Among the other pressing problems that have accumulated over the past two decades, top of the list was uncontrolled immigration. For some Ecuadoreans, the Galápagos Islands are an El Dorado, with strong economic growth, plenty of work opportunities and salaries about 50% higher than on the mainland. Population growth has been astronomic and land prices have soared. Legislation passed in 1998 and finally implemented two years later restricts migration from mainland Ecuador and attempts to better regulate tourism, fishing and agriculture. At the same time, it enshrines the rights of those residents who were established in Galápagos prior to 1996. The current population of the islands is young and, even without further immigration, is likely to grow steadily in coming years. The human threat to Galápagos is therefore far from under control.

But Ecuador is a poor country and it has many pressing social problems. The economy needs the foreign currency generated in the Galápagos Islands, by tourism as well as other activities. Having gained international support for its efforts to conserve the land-based ecology of the Galápagos, Ecuador also needs international support for marine conservation. It therefore faces a difficult task in balancing domestic political opinion, the nation's urgent needs and international credibility when drawing up policies for the benefit of the islands.

Visitor sites

The Galápagos have been declared a World Heritage Site by UNESCO and 97% of the land area and 100% of the surrounding ocean are now part of the Galápagos National Park and Marine Reserve. Within the area of the park there are some 56 landing sites, each with defined trails, so the impact of visitors to this fragile environment is minimized and the park preserved for future generations.

Each of the landing sites has been carefully chosen to show the different flora and fauna, and with the high level of endemism nearly every trail has flora and fauna that can be seen nowhere else in the world. The itineraries of tourist boats are strictly regulated in order to avoid crowding at the visitor sites and some sites are periodically closed by the park authorities in order to allow them to recover from the impact of tourism. Certain sites are only open to smaller boats, and additionally limited to a maximum number of visits per month.

The total lack of fear exhibited by the birds and reptiles that inhabit the islands enables visitors and scientists a unique opportunity to see and study nature. Never miss the opportunity to go snorkelling when visiting. There is plenty of underwater life to see, including rays, turtles, sharks, sea lions, penguins and many spectacular fish and invertebrates. The other islands not mentioned below are closed to tourists.

Never touch any of the animals, birds or plants. Do not transfer sand or soil from one island to another. Do not leave litter anywhere – it is highly undesirable in a National Park and is a safety and health hazard for wildlife – and do not take food on to the islands.

Galápagos Islands

Santa Cruz

Most of the inhabitants live in and around **Puerto Ayora**, but there are farming settlements inland at **Bellavista** and **Santa Rosa**. Puerto Ayora is the economic centre of the Galápagos and every cruise visits it for one day anchoring at Academy Bay. The main visit is to **Charles Darwin Research Station** and there is free time to do some shopping, make phone calls and so on.

This island is the principal inhabited island with a population of about 10,000

In 1959, the centenary of the publication of Darwin's *Origin of Species*, the Government of Ecuador and the International Charles Darwin Foundation established, with the support of UNESCO, the Charles Darwin Research Station at Academy Bay, a 20-minute walk from Puerto Ayora. A visit to the station is a good introduction to the islands as it provides a lot of information. Collections of several of the rare sub-species of giant tortoise are maintained on the station as breeding nuclei, though, sadly, no mating partner has yet been found for Lonesome George, the sole remaining member of the Isla Pinta sub-species. There is also a tortoise-rearing area where the young can be seen. The Darwin Foundation staff will help bona fide students of the fauna to plan an itinerary, if they stay some time, and hire a boat. There are several beaches by the Darwin Station, which get crowded at weekends (see Puerto Ayora). ■ *Station offices Mon-Fri 0700-1600, visitor areas 0600-1800 daily.*

Some itineraries include a guided visit to the interior of the island. The highlands and settlement area of Santa Cruz are worth seeing for the contrast of the vegetation with the arid coastal zones. There are five main vegetation zones while going inland from Puerto Ayora on the southern side of the island. The highest point is at 864 m. You can hike to the higher parts of the island called **Media Luna**, **Puntudo** and **Cerro Crocker**. The trail starts at Bellavista, 7 km from Puerto Ayora. A round trip from Bellavista is four to eight hours, depending on the distance hiked (10-18 km). A permit and guide are not required, but a guide is advisable. Also take water, sun block and long-sleeved shirt and long trousers to protect against razor grass.

There are a number of sites worth visiting in the interior, including **Los Gemelos**, a pair of twin sinkholes, formed by a collapse of the ground above a fault. The sinkholes straddle the road to Baltra, beyond Santa Rosa. If you're lucky, you can take a *camioneta* all the way, otherwise take a bus to Santa Rosa (see below), then walk. It's a good place to see the Galápagos hawk and barn owl.

There are several **lava tubes** (natural tunnels) on the island. There are some 3 km from Puerto Ayora on the road to Bellavista. They are unsigned, but look on the left for the black-and-white posts. Barn owls can be seen here. Two more lava tubes are 1 km from Bellavista. They are on private land, and therefore can be visited without an official guide. It costs US$1.50 to enter the tunnels (bring a torch) and it takes about 30 minutes to walk through the tunnels. Tours to the lava tubes can be arranged in Puerto Ayora.

Another worthwhile trip is to the **El Chato Tortoise Reserve**, which is a 7-km hike. The trail starts at Santa Rosa, 22 km from Puerto Ayora. Horses can be hired at Santa Rosa for US$6 each, and a guide is compulsory. A round trip takes one day. The Puerto Ayora-Bellavista bus (see below) stops at the turn off for the track for the reserve. It's a hot walk, so take food and drink. To walk to the Reserve from Santa Rosa, turn left past the school, follow the track at the edge of fields for 40 minutes, turn right at the memorial to the Israeli, 20 minutes later turn left down a track to Chato Trucha.

Next to the reserve is the Butterfly Ranch (Hacienda Mariposa), where you can also see giant tortoises in the wild, but only in the dry season. In the wet

Galápagos Islands

season the tortoises are breeding down in the arid zone. Vermillion flycatchers can be seen here also. The ranch is beyond Bellavista on the road to Santa Rosa (the bus passes the turn-off). Entry US$3, including a cup of hierba luisa tea, or juice.

Transport **Santa Rosa** and **Bellavista** From San Francisco school in Puerto Ayora, 3 daily buses leave for Santa Rosa and Bellavista. It's a 30-min trip, and buses return immediately. The fare for all destinations is US$0.40. There are also trucks, which are cheaper. On roads to the main sites hitching is easy but expect to pay a small fee.

Other sites on Santa Cruz include **Caleta Tortuga Negra**, on the northern part of the island (restricted to small groups). Here you can drift by dinghy through the mangrove swamps which are home to marine turtles, white-tipped sharks, spotted eagle rays and yellow cow-nosed rays. Nearby is **Las Bachas**, a swimming beach, also on the north shore. **Conway Bay** is a rarely visited landing site on the northwest coast, inhabited by a large colony of sea lions. **Whaler Bay** is the site of one of the oldest whaling camps on Santa Cruz. It was to here and the other similar camps that the giant tortoises were brought before being loaded on board the whalers. **Cerro Dragón** is located on the north shore of Santa Cruz, where land iguanas may be seen as well as the occasional flamingo.

Baltra Once a US Airforce base, Baltra is now a small military base for Ecuador and also the main airport into the islands. The island is quite arid and that, along with the rubble left by the USAF, gives it the appearance of a junk yard. Also known as South Seymour, this is the island most affected by human habitation. **Mosquera** is a small sandy bank just north of Baltra, home to a large colony of sea lions.

Seymour Norte Just north of Baltra, Seymour Norte is home to sea lions, marine iguanas, swallow-tailed gulls, magnificent frigatebirds and blue-footed boobies. The tourist trail leads through mangroves in one of the main nesting sites for blue-footed boobies and frigates in this part of the archipelago.

Daphne Major West of Baltra, Daphne island has a very rich birdlife, in particular the nesting boobies. Because of the possible problems of erosion, only small boats may land here and are limited to one visit each month.

Plaza Sur One of the closest islands to Puerto Ayora is Plaza Sur. It's an example of a geological uplift and the southern part of the island has formed cliffs with spectacular views. It has a combination of both dry and coastal vegetation zones. Walking along the sea cliffs is a pleasant experience as the swallowtail gull, shearwaters and red billed tropic birds nest here. This is the home of the Men's Club, a rather sad looking colony of bachelor sea lions who are too old to mate and who get together to console each other. There are also lots of blue-footed boobies and a large population of land iguanas.

Santa Fe This island is located on the southeastern part of Galápagos, between Santa Cruz and San Cristóbal, and was formed by volcanic uplift. The lagoon is home to a large colony of sea lions who are happy to join you for a swim. From the beach the trail goes inland, through a semi-arid landscape of cactus. This little island has its own sub-species of land iguana.

San Cristóbal is the easternmost island of Galápagos and one of the oldest. The principal town is **Puerto Baquerizo Moreno** which is the capital of the province of Galápagos.

There are four buses a day inland from Puerto Baquerizo Moreno to **El Progreso** (6 km, 15 minutes, US$0.15), then it's a 2½ hour walk to El Junco lake, the largest body of fresh water in Galápagos. There are also frequent pick-up trucks to El Progreso (US$1), or you can hire a pick-up in Puerto Baquerizo Moreno for touring: US$15 to El Junco, US$35 continuing to the beaches at Puerto Chino on the other side of the island, past a planned tortoise reserve. Prices are return and include waiting. At El Junco there is a path to walk around the lake in 20 minutes. The views are lovely in clear weather but it is cool and wet in the *garúa* season, so take adequate clothing. In El Progreso is *La Casa del Ceibo*, a tree house, for rent, and there are some eating places. Another road from El Progreso continues to **La Soledad**, a school above which is a shrine, a deserted restaurant and a *mirador* overlooking the different types of vegetation stretching to the coast. There are two buses to La Soledad, on Sundays only, when the restaurant is open. From El Progreso a trail also crosses the highlands to **Cerro Brujo** and **Hobbs Bay**, and also to **Stephens Bay**, past some lakes.

It's a three-hour hike to **Galapaguera** in the northeast, which allows you to see tortoises in the wild. Isla Lobos is a large sea lion colony and nesting site for sea birds northeast of Puerto Baquerizo Moreno.

NB Always take food and plenty of water when hiking on your own on San Cristóbal. There are many crisscrossing animal trails and it is easy to get lost. Also watch out for the large-spined opuntia cactus and the poisonwood tree (*manzanillo*), which is a relative of poison ivy and can cause severe skin reactions.

Kicker Rock (León Dormido), the basalt remains of a crater, is not strictly speaking a landing site, but the rock is split by a narrow channel and is navigable to the smaller yachts. It is home to a large colony of many seabirds, including masked and blue-footed boobies, nesting in the cliffs rising vertically from the channel. This is also a diving site. **Punta Pitt**, in the far northeast of the island, is a tuff formation which serves as a nesting site for many sea birds, including all three boobies. Up the coast is **Cerro Brujo** beach with sea lions, birds and crabs, though not in any abundance.

This is the southernmost island of the Galápagos and, following a successful programme to remove all the feral species, is now the most pristine of the islands with many migrant, resident and endemic sea birds. **Gardner Bay**, on the northeastern coast, is a beautiful white sand beach with excellent swimming and snorkelling. **Punta Suárez**, on the western tip of the island, has a trail through a rookery. As well as a wide range of sea birds (including blue-footed and masked boobies) there is a great selection of wildlife including sea lions, the largest and most colourful marine iguanas of the Galápagos and the original home of the waved albatrosses.

This is the longest inhabited of the islands and the site of the mysterious 'Galápagos Affair' in the 1930s (see page 394). There are opportunities for accommodation or camping with some of the 70 residents here, but you should be as self-sufficient as possible (see page 426).

Devil's Crown, a dramatic snorkelling site to the north of Punta Cormorant, is an almost completely submerged volcano. Erosion has transformed the cone into a series of jagged peaks with the resulting look of a crown.

There is usually a wide selection of fish, sharks and turtles easily visible in about 6 m of water.

Punta Cormorant is on the northern part of Floreana. The landing is on a beach of green sand coloured by olivine crystals, volcanic-derived silicates of magnesium and iron. The trail leads to a lake normally inhabited by flamingos and other shore birds and continues to a beach of fine white sand particles known as Flour Beach, an important nesting site for turtles.

Post Office Bay is west of Punta Cormorant. The Post Office barrel was placed and used in the late 18th century by English whaling vessels and later by the American whalers. It is the custom for visitors to place unstamped letters and cards in the barrel, and deliver, free of charge, any addressed to their own destinations. There is a short walk to look at the remains of a Norwegian commercial fish drying and canning operation that was started in 1926 and abandoned after a couple of years. A lava tube that extends to the sea is also visited. **Black Beach** is a small settlement on the western side of the island (see History of human settlement above).

Isabela   This is the largest island in the archipelago. The extensive lava flows from the six volcanoes – Alcedo, Cerro Azul, Darwin, Ecuador, Sierra Negra and Wolf – joined together and formed Isabela. Five of the six volcanoes are active and each have (or had) their own separate sub-species of giant tortoise.

Puerto Villamil on the south coast, the main settlement, was founded in 1897 by Antonio Gil as the centre of a lime producing operation. It is today inhabited by some 3,000 people. Nearby are several lagoons, nesting sites of flamingos and common stilts. A visit to **Punta Moreno**, on the southwest part of Isabela, starts with a dinghy ride along the beautiful rocky shores where penguins and shore birds are usually seen. After a dry landing there is a hike through sharp lava rocks.

Elizabeth Bay, on the west coast, is home to a small colony of penguins living on a series of small rocky islets and visited by dinghy. **Sierra Negra Volcano** is reached from Villamil. The crater, some three miles across, is the biggest volcanic crater in the world. It takes at least a full day to climb up the volcano to see the tortoises. It can be climbed on foot, horseback or by pick-up.

Punta García, across the Isabela Channel from Santiago Island, is the only landing site on the eastern side of Isabela. From here it is possible to hike up to **Alcedo volcano** with its own sub-species of giant tortoise. You can see flightless cormorants here and there are also several active fumaroles.

Urbina Bay, at the base of Alcedo Volcano on the west coast, was the site of a major uplift in 1954, when the land rose up about 5 m. This event was associated with an eruption of Alcedo volcano. The coastline rose as far as 1 km out to the sea and exposed giant coral heads. The uplift was so sudden that lobster and fish were stranded on what is now the shore. **Tagus Cove**, located on the west coast across the narrow channel from Fernandina island, is an anchorage that has been used by visiting ships going back to the 1800s, and the ships' names can still be seen painted on the cliffs. A trail leads inland from Tagus Cove past **Laguna Darwin**, a large salt water lake, and then further uphill to a ridge with lovely views. **Punta Tortuga**, on the north of Tagus Cove on the west coast of Isabela, is a bathing beach surrounded by mangroves. **Punta Albermarle**, on the northern part of Isabela, was used as a radar base by the US during the Second World War.

This is the youngest of the islands, about 700,000 years old. **Punta Espinosa** is on the northeast coast of Fernandina. The trail from the landing site goes up through a sandy nesting site for huge colonies of marine iguanas. The nests appear as small hollows in the sand. You can also see flightless cormorants drying their atrophied wings in the sun and go snorkelling in the bay.

Fernandina
The most volcanically active of the islands, with eruptions every few years

This large island, also known as James, is northwest of Santa Cruz. It has a volcanic landscape full of cliffs and pinnacles, home to several species of marine birds. This island has a large population of goats, one of the four species of animals introduced in the early 1800s.

Santiago

James Bay is on the western side of the island, where there is a wet landing on the dark sands of **Puerto Egas**. The trail leads to the remains of an unsuccessful salt mining operation. Fur seals are seen nearby. **Espumilla Beach** is another famous visitor site. After landing on a large beach, walk through a mangrove forest that leads to a lake usually inhabited by flamingos, pintail ducks and stilts. There are nesting and feeding sites for flamingos. Sea turtles dig their nests at the edge of the mangroves. **Buccaneer Cove**, on the northwest part of the island, was a haven for pirates during the 1600s and 1700s. **Sullivan Bay** is on the eastern coast of Santiago, opposite Bartolomé Island. The visitor trail leads across an impressive lunar landscape of lava fields formed in eruptions in 1890.

This is probably the most easily recognized – the most visited and most photographed – of the islands in the Galápagos with its distinctive **Pinnacle Rock**. It is a small island located in Sullivan Bay off the eastern shore of Santiago. The trail leads steeply up to the summit, taking 30-40 minutes, from where there are panoramic views. At the second landing site on the island there is a lovely beach from which you can snorkel or swim and see the penguins.

Bartolomé
One of the most popular and impressive sites

This island is just to the south of Santiago. The trail leads to a salt water lagoon, occasionally home to flamingos. There is an area of mangroves near the lagoon where brown pelicans nest. This island is said to have the most diversified volcanic rocks of all the islands. You can snorkel and swim from the beach.

Rábida

This is just off the southeastern tip of Santiago, or James, and its name refers to its shape. It is most noted for the volcanic landscape including sharp outcroppings, cracked lava formations, lava tubes and volcanic rubble. This site is only available to yachts of less than 12 passengers capacity.

Sombrero Chino

Located at the northeast part of the archipelago, this is an outpost for many sea birds. It is not an easy trip for the captain and crew since it takes an 8-10 hour all-night sail from Puerto Ayora. Genovesa and Fernandina are best visited on longer cruises or ships with larger range.

Genovesa

One of the most famous sites is **Prince Phillip's Steps**, an amazing walk through a seabird rookery that is full of life. You will see tropic birds, all three boobies, frigates, petrels, swallow-tailed and lava gulls, and many others. There is also good snorkelling at the foot of the steps, with lots of marine iguanas. The entrance to **Darwin Bay**, on the eastern side of the island, is very narrow and shallow and the anchorage in the lagoon is surrounded by mangroves, home to a large breeding colony of frigates and other seabirds.

Galápagos Islands

Scuba diving

The Galápagos Islands are among the most desirable scuba diving destinations. At first look you might wonder why. During much of the year the water is cold enough to require thick wetsuits with hood and boots. Strong currents make many sites into drift dives, and can sometimes turn threatening if the unpredictable moving water becomes a downward flow at walls or steep reefs. There is no convenient place where you can just start your dive from the shore. Thirty metres of visibility here is considered great, but usually it's 15 m or less. So what is the attraction?

Marine life There are animals here in such profusion and variety that you won't find in any other place, and so close up that you won't mind the low visibility. Not just reef fish and schooling fish and pelagic fish, also sea lions, turtles, whale sharks, schools of hammerheads, flocks of several species of rays, diving birds, whales and dolphins; an exuberant diversity including many unique endemic species, and representing every kind of environment, from parrot fish to penguins. You could be with a Galápagos marine iguana, the world's only lizard that dives and feeds in the sea, or perhaps meet a glittering man-size sailfish. Make no mistake, this is no tame theme park, nor like some other well-travelled dive destinations where a predictable fish is given a pet name by the locals. Galápagos is adventure diving where any moment could surprise you.

Dive options
See Puerto Ayora, page 420, and Puerto Baquerizo Moreno, page 421, for details of companies offering day-trips, live-aboard diving tours or equipment rental

There are basically two options for diving in the Galápagos: live-aboard cruises and hotel-based day-trips. Live-aboard operations usually expect the divers to bring their own equipment, and supply only lead and tanks. The day-trip dive operators supply everything. At the time of writing, day trip diving is mostly offered by boats operating out of Puerto Ayora on Santa Cruz, and one small operator in Puerto Baquerizo Moreno on San Cristobal (but service is not always available here).

Live-aboard cruises usually are reserved many months in advance. This is the only way to travel all around the archipelago, combining shore visits to the National Park and up to three dives per day and occasional night dives, on an itinerary of a week or more. The live-aboards take passengers to some of the National Park's most outstanding wildlife colonies, using a system of assigned itineraries, naturalist guides, and marked trails to protect these natural treasures. A few of the live-aboard cruises voyage to the isolated northern islands of Wolf and Darwin. Shore visits are forbidden there, but the extraordinary diving makes the long trip worthwhile.

Day-trip diving is more economical and spontaneous, often arranged at the dive shop the evening before. The distances between islands limit the range of the day-trip boats to the central islands. Nevertheless, day boats can offer reliable service and superb dive locations including Gordon Rocks, world famous for schooling hammerheads. The day-trip dive boats do not take passengers ashore at the more frequently visited marked trail sites, but can offer special trips to isolated landings for travellers who want a less structured experience of this teeming ecology. Non-diving day tour boats also go to the National Park trail sites.

A third option is a combination of the first two. Through your agent or by email, make prior arrangements to combine the day-trip dive services with one of the non-diving live-aboard cruise yachts. Before or after the live-aboard cruise, visitors based at a hotel can make day-trip dives. Another way is a rendezvous of cruise yacht and dive boat at some other island.

Visitors should be aware of some of the special conditions in Galápagos. The National Park includes practically all of the land and the surrounding waters. The National Park prohibits collecting samples or souvenirs, spear-fishing, touching animals, or other environmental disruptions. Guides apply the National Park rules, and they can stop your participation if you do not co-operate. The experienced dive guides can help visitors have the most spectacular opportunities to enjoy the wildlife.

Nonetheless, diving requires self reliance and divers are encouraged to refresh their skills and have equipment serviced before the trip. Though the day trip operators can offer introductory dives and complete certification training, this is not a place where a complete novice should come for a diving vacation. On many dives you could meet any combination of current, surge, cold water, poor visibility, deep bottom and big animals. Like many exotic dive destinations, medical care is limited, as are communications and transportation. The nearest recompression chamber is 1,000 km away on the mainland (and not always functioning). To avoid the risk of decompression sickness, divers are advised to stay an extra day on the islands after their last dive before flying to the mainland, especially Quito at 2,840 m above sea level.

General advice

Santa Fe This site offers wall dives, rock reefs, shallow caves, fantastic scenery and usually has clear calm water. You can dive with sea lions, schooling fish, pelagic fish, moray eels, rays, Galápagos sharks. Like everywhere in Galápagos, you can expect the unexpected.

Dive sites
These are some of the better known dive sites in the central islands

Seymour Norte You can see sea lions, reef fish, hammerhead sharks, giant manta rays, white tip reef sharks, invertebrates. Occasionally whale sharks, humpback whale and porpoises.

Floreana Island The dive sites are offshore islets, each with its own character and scenery. **Devil's Crown** is a fractured ring of spiked lava around coral reefs. **Champion** is a little crater with a nesting colony of boobies, sea lion beaches and underwater rocky shelves of coral and reef fish. **Enderby** is an eroded tuff cone where you often meet large pelagics; rays, turtles, tunas and sharks. **Gardner** has a huge natural arch like a cathedral's flying buttress. These and other islets offer diving with reef fish, schooling fish, sea lions, invertebrates, rays, moray eels, white tip reef sharks, turtles, big fish including amberjack, red snapper, and grouper. Sometimes you can see giant mantas, hammerheads, Galápagos sharks, whales, seahorses, and the bizarre red lipped batfish.

Gordon Rocks This is a wall dive, with a deep bottom. Usually there is strong current, making this a drift dive along the wall. It is not recommended for novices. Gordon Rocks is world famous for diving with schools of hammerhead sharks, but there are also reef fish, amberjacks, snappers, barracudas, white tip reef sharks, turtles, invertebrates, rays, octopi and morays. Big pelagic fish could include wahoo, tuna, and even sailfish. Sometimes there are mantas, porpoise, whales and Galápagos sharks.

Galápagos Islands

Ins and outs

Airports There are two airports which receive flights from mainland Ecuador, but no international flights to Galápagos. The most frequently used airport is at Baltra (South Seymour), across a narrow strait from Santa Cruz, the other at Puerto Baquerizo Moreno, on San Cristóbal. The two islands are 96 km apart and on most days there are local flights in light aircraft between them, as well as to Puerto Villamil on Isabela island. There is also irregular boat service between Puerto Ayora, Puerto Baquerizo Moreno, Puerto Villamil and Floreana island. See Getting around, below.

All flights originate in Quito At the close of this edition only *TAME* was operating flights to Galápagos, although other domestic airlines keep promising to introduce service. *TAME* has 2 flights daily to Baltra and operates Mon, Wed and Sat to San Cristóbal. The return fare in high season (1 Nov-30 Apr and 15 Jun-14 Sep) is US$390 from Quito, US$345 from Guayaquil. The low season fare costs US$334 from Quito, and US$300 from Guayaquil. The same prices apply regardless of whether you fly to San Cristóbal or Baltra; you can arrive at one and return from the other. You can also depart from Quito and return to Guayaquil or vice versa. The ticket is valid for 21 days from the date of departure. Independent travellers must get their boarding pass (*pre-chequeo*) for outward and return flights 2 days before departure. This is especially critical during high season and from San Cristóbal at all times.

The prices indicated above are subject to change without notice. Discount fares for Ecuadorean nationals and residents of Galápagos are not available to foreigners and these rules are strictly enforced. A 15% discount off the high season fare may be available to students with an ISIC card; details from *TAME* office at edif Pichincha, 4th Floor, Amazonas y Colón, Quito.

Boat owners make block bookings with the airlines in the hope of filling their boat. Visitors may buy tickets where they like, but in the busy season will have to take the ticket to the tour operator for the reservation. Tickets are the same price everywhere, except for student discounts with *TAME* as above.

To and from the airport Two buses meet flights from the mainland at Baltra: one runs to the port or *muelle* (10 mins, no charge) where the cruise boats wait; the other goes to Canal de Itabaca, the narrow channel which separates Baltra from Santa Cruz. It is 15 mins to the Canal, free, then you cross on a small ferry for US$0.70, another bus waits on the Santa Cruz side to take you to Puerto Ayora in 45 mins, US$1.50. If you arrive at Baltra on one of the local inter-island flights (see below) then you have to wait until the next flight from the mainland for bus service, or you might be able to hire a taxi. For the return trip to the airport, *CITTEG* buses leave from opposite the company's office/café near the pier (see map, page 418) to meet flights at Baltra (enquire locally for current schedules). It's best to buy a ticket the night before, though this is not possible for the Saturday bus. Hotels may make prior arrangements.

The pleasant airport in **Puerto Baquerizo Moreno** is within walking distance of town, but those on prearranged tours will be met by transport. Pick-up trucks can be hired if you are on your own and have have lots of gear.

Sea In 2002, the small cargo vessels which sail from Guayaquil to Galápagos were not permitted to carry passengers and the rules were strictly enforced. Based on experience from previous years, this was never a good option to visit Galápagos anyway, nor did it save much money. Those who insist on trying can enquire in person where the ships dock in Guayaquil, at the Muelle del Retén Naval, just south of Mercado Caraguay. This is an unsafe area so take a taxi.

Every foreign visitor has to pay a National Park Tax of US$100 on arrival, cash only. Be **Entry tax**
sure to have your passport to hand. Do not lose your park tax receipt; boat captains
need to record it. A 50% reduction on the national park fee is available to children
under 12, but only those foreigners who are enrolled in an Ecuadorean university are
entitled to the reduced fee for students.

Emetebe Avionetas offers inter-island flights in 2 light twin-engine aircraft (a 5-seater **Getting around**
and a 9-seater). There is no firm schedule but flights usually operate Mon-Sat in the
morning between Puerto Baquerizo Moreno (San Cristóbal), Baltra and Puerto Villamil
(Isabela), depending on passenger demand. Baggage allowance 30 lbs, strictly
enforced. Fares range from US$90-120 one way, including taxes; charter rates from
US$400-500 per hour. *Emetebe* offices in Puerto Baquerizo Moreno, Puerto Ayora and
Puerto Villamil are given in the corresponding sections below. In Guayaquil T2292492,
emetebe@ecua.net.ec

Fibras (fiberglass motor launches) operate most days between Pto Ayora (Santa
Cruz), Pto Villamil (Isabela), and Pto Baquerizo Moreno (San Cirstóbal), US$25-30 one
way, check at the Capitanía de Puerto. There is also an irregular boat service from
Puerto Ayora to Floreana; check at the Capitanía de Puerto. You must be flexible in your
itinerary and allow plenty of time if you wish to travel between islands in this way.

Island cruises

*There are two ways to travel around the islands: a 'tour navegable', where you
sleep on the boat, or less expensive tours where you sleep ashore at night and travel
during the day. On the former you travel at night, arriving at a new landing site
each day, with more time ashore. On the latter you spend less time ashore and the
boats are smaller with a tendency to overcrowding in high season. All tours begin
with a morning flight from the mainland on the first day and end on the last day
with an afternoon flight back to the mainland. Prices are no longer significantly
cheaper in the low season, but you will have more options available. .*

It is not possible to generalize about exactly what you will find on the boat in
which you cruise around the Galápagos Islands. The standard of facilities varies from one craft to another and you basically get what you pay for. Once on
shore at the visitor sites, no matter what price you have paid, each visitor is
shown the same things because of the strict park rules on limited access. Note
however that smaller and cheaper boats may not visit as many or as distant
sites. On the other hand, larger vessels may not be allowed to take passengers
to some of the more fragile landings (Daphne Major, for example).

*The islands get very
busy in July and
August (high season),
when it is impossible
to make last minute
arrangements*

Each day starts early and schedules are usually full (if they aren't you're not
getting your money's worth). If you are sailing overnight, your boat will probably have reached its destination before breakfast. After eating, you disembark for a morning on the island. The usual time for snorkelling is between the
morning excursion and lunch. The midday meal is taken on board because no
food is allowed on the islands. If the island requires two visits (for example
Genovesa/Tower, or Española/Hood), you will return to shore after lunch,
otherwise part of the afternoon may be taken up with a sea voyage. After the
day's activities, there is time to clean up, have a drink and relax before the
briefing for the next day and supper.

Itineraries are controlled by the National Park to distribute tourism evenly
throughout the islands. Boats are expected to be on certain islands on certain
days. They can cut landings, but have to get special permission to add to a

Galápagos Islands

planned itinerary. All boats must re-provision and this is done in Puerto Ayora once a week. On the day the boats are in port the passengers visit the Darwin Station and either the highlands or lava tubes or Tortuga Bay. Boats do not put into port just to take off or put on passengers, however some boats do take advantage of the day they are in Puerto Ayora anyway, to change some or all of their passengers.

Choosing a tour

The less expensive boats are normally smaller and less powerful so you see less and spend more time travelling; also the guiding is likely to be in Spanish only (with the odd exception). The more expensive boats will probably have 110 volts, air conditioning, hot water and private baths, all of which add to the comfort factor but are not critically important. All boats have to conform to certain minimum safety standards and have VHF radio; more expensive boats are better equipped. A water maker can make quite a difference as the town water from Puerto Ayora or Puerto Baquerizo Moreno should not be drunk. Note that boats with over 18 passengers take quite a time to disembark and re-embark people, while the smaller boats have a more lively motion, which is important if you are prone to seasickness. Note also that there may be severe limitations for vegetarians on the cheaper boats, enquire in advance.

The least expensive boats (called economy class) cost about US$60-80 per person per day; they are usually small and slow. For around US$80-100 per day (tourist class) you will be on a faster small boat which can travel more quickly between visitor sites, leaving more time to spend ashore. US$100-200 per day (tourist superior and first class) is the price of the majority of better boats, most with English guiding. Over US$200 per day is entering the luxury bracket, with English guiding the norm, far more comfortable cabins and a superior level of service and cuisine. No boat may sail without a park-trained guide.

Booking a cruise

You can book a Galápagos cruise in several different ways: 1) over the the internet (see box, Galápagos on the web); 2) from either a travel agency or directly though a Galápagos wholesaler in your home country; 3) from one of the very many agencies found throughout Ecuador, especially in Quito but also in Guayaquil; or 4) from agencies in Puerto Ayora but not Puerto Baquerizo Moreno. The trade-off is always between time and money:

booking from home is most efficient and expensive, Puerto Ayora cheapest and most time-consuming, while Quito and Guayaquil are intermediate. Prices for a given category of boat do not vary all that much however, and it is not possible to obtain discounts or make last-minute arrangements in high season. Those who attempt to do so in July, August or over Christmas/New Year often spend several very frustrating weeks in Puerto Ayora without ever seeing the islands. The following section lists recommended agencies and operators abroad and in Puerto Ayora. Agencies in Quito and Guayaquil are listed on pages 127 and 288, respectively.

UK In Britain, contact David Horwell, who arranges tailor-made tours to Ecuador and the Galápagos Islands. For further details contact *Galapagos Adventure Tours*, 79 Maltings Place, 169 Tower Bridge Rd, London SE1 3LJ, T020-7407 1478, F020-7407 0397, www.galapagos .co.uk Penelope Kellie also comes recommended, pkellie@yachtors.u-net.com T01962-779317, F779458, www.quasar nautica.com She is the UK agent for *Quasar Nautica* (see Quito Tour operators, page 127). *Galapagos Classic Cruises*, 6 Keyes Rd, London NW2 3XA, T020-8933 0613, F8452 5248, www.GalapagosCruises.co.uk, specializes in tailor-made cruises and diving holidays to the islands with additional land tours to Ecuador and Peru available on request.

North America *Galapagos Holidays*, 14 Prince Arthur Av, Suite 109, Toronto, Ontario M5R 1A9, T416-4139090, T1-800-6612512, www. galapagosholidays.com *Galápagos Network*, 6303 Blue Lagoon Drive, Suite 140, Miami, FL 33126, T305-2626264, T800-6337972 (toll free), F305-2629609, info@galapagosnetwork.com, www.eco ventura.com *International Expeditions*, One Environs Park, Helena, Alabama, 35080, T205-4281700, T1-800-6334734 (toll free), www.international expeditions.com *Sol International*, 13780 S. W.,

Galápagos Islands

Galápagos Islands

56 St, Suite 107, Miami, FL 33175, T305-3826575, T1-800-7655657 (toll free), F305-3829284. *TAMBO TOURS*, PO Box 60541, Houston, Texas, T1-281-5289448, F5287378, www.2GOPERU.com *Wilderness Travel* (801 Allston Way, Berkeley, CA 94710, T1-800-3682704) and *Inca Floats*, (Bill Robertson, 1311 63rd Street, Emeryville, CA 94608) have also been recommended.

Shopping around the many agencies in Quito is a good way of securing a value-for-money cruise, if you have the time. It is worth asking if the vessel has 1-3 spaces to fill on a cruise, you can try to get them at a discount. There are of course a great many other agencies throughout Ecuador which sell Galápagos tours, the key is to shop around carefully and not let yourself be rushed into a decision.

Quito & Guayaquil
See Tour operators in Quito, page 127, and Guayaquil, page 288, for further details

Galápagos Islands

Puerto Ayora
In the high season, purchase your cruise before arriving in Galápagos

If you wish to wait until you reach the islands, Puerto Ayora is the only practical place for arranging a cruise; this cannot be done in Puerto Baquerizo Moreno. In Puerto Ayora you may find slightly better prices than the mainland, especially off-season at the last minute, but bear in mind that you could be faced with a long wait. In the high season (July, August, and mid-December to mid-January) there is no space available on a last-minute basis.

To arrange last-minute tours, a recommended contact is the *Moonrise* travel agency. There are also several other agencies, including *Galaptour*, in Puerto Ayora who offer this service (see Puerto Ayora Tour operators, below). Especially for cheaper boats, try to get a personal recommendation from someone who has recently taken a tour and check carefully about what is and is not included (for example drinking water, snorkelling equipment and

Galápagos Islands

▶▶ Galápagos on the web

The following table lists various categories of boats operating in Galápagos with their respective websites where you can see photos and obtain additional information. The list is not exhaustive and lack of inclusion does not imply poor quality; there are many other good boats. The categories and prices shown are approximate and subject to change. The names, owners, operators, agents or websites of boats may likewise change. Remember also that captains, crews and guides regularly change on all boats. These factors, as well as the sea, weather and your fellow passengers will all influence the quality of your experience.

Name	Capacity (Passengers)	Website
Luxury Class (over US$200 per person per day)		
Ambasador I	86	www.ambasadorcruises.com
Coral II	22	www.kleintours.com
Coral I	20	www.kleintours.com
First Class (US$150-200 per person per day)		
Galápagos Explorer II	100	www.canodros.com
Galapagos Legend	90	www.kleintours.com
Santa Cruz	90	www.metropolitan-touring.com
Isabela II	38	www.metropolitan-touring.com
Delfin II	36	www.metropolitan-touring.com
Eric	20	www.ecoventura.com
Flamingo	20	www.ecoventura.com
Letty	20	www.ecoventura.com
Edén	18	www.galapagostours.net
Lammar Law	18	www.quasarnautica.com
Reina Silvia	16	www.reinasilvia.com
Sagitta	16	www.angermeyercruises.com
Parranda	14	www.quasarnautica.com
Alta	12	www.quasarnautica.com
Andando	12	www.angermeyercruises.com
Mistral	12	www.quasarnautica.com
Cachalote	10	www.enchantedexpeditions.com
Nortada	10	www.quasarnautica.com
Resting Cloud	10	www.quasarnautica.com
Diamant	8	www.quasarnautica.com
Rachel III	8	www.quasarnautica.com
Tourist Superior Class (US$100-150 per person per day)		
Angelito	16	www.enchantedexpeditions.com
Beluga	16	www.enchantedexpeditions.com
Dorado	16	www.galasam.com
Estrella Del Mar	16	www.galasam.com
New Daphne	16	www.gotogalapagos.com
Seaman	16	www.galapagosseaman.com.ec
Tip Top II	16	www.rwittmer.com
Tip Top III	16	www.rwittmer.com
Samba	12	www.angermeyercruises.com
Encantada	10	www.scubagalapagos.com

Name	Capacity (Passengers)	Website

Tourist Class *(US$80-100 per person per day)*

Aida Maria	16	www.galapagostours.net
Cruz Del Sur	16	www.galasam.com
Pelikano	16	www.galapagos-tours.com
Angelique	12	www.kempery.com
Sulidae	12	www.enchantedexpeditions.com
Antartida	10	www.galasam.com
Rumba	10	www.galapagostours.net

Economy Class *(US$60-80 per person per day)*

Pulsar	10	www.galapagostours.com

so on). **NB** Among the cheaper boats we have received serious complaints in 2002 about the *Free Enterprise* (reportedly sometimes also called *Discovery*).

General advice

Tipping A ship's crew and guides are usually tipped separately. The amount is a very personal matter; you may be guided by suggestions made onboard or in the agency's brochures, but the key factors should always be the quality of service received and – of course – your own resources.

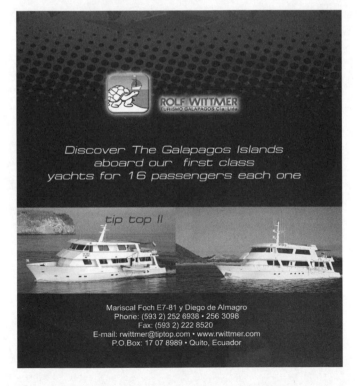

Galápagos Islands

Problems   **Legitimate complaints** may be made to any or all of the following: the **Jefe de Turismo** at the national park office in Puerto Ayora, the **Ministerio de Turismo** office or the **Capitanía de Puerto**. Any 'tour navegable' will include the days of arrival and departure as full days. Insist on a written itinerary or contract prior to departure as any effort not to provide this probably indicates problems later.

If a crew member comes on strong with a woman passenger, the matter should first be raised with the guide or captain. If this does not yield results, a formal complaint, in Spanish, giving the crew member's full name, the boat's name and the date of the cruise, should be sent to Sr Capitán del Puerto, Base Militar de Armada Ecuatoriana, Puerto Ayora, Santa Cruz, Galápagos. Failure to report such behaviour will mean it will continue. To avoid pilfering, never leave belongings unattended on a beach when another boat is in the bay.

What to take   Daytime clothing should be lightweight and even on 'luxury cruises' should be casual
See Books, page 464,   and comfortable. At night, particularly at sea and at higher altitudes, **warm clothing** is
for recommended   required. Note that boots and shoes soon wear out on the lava terrain. A remedy for
reading   **seasickness** is recommended; the waters south of Santa Cruz are particularly rough. A good supply of **sun block** and skin cream to prevent windburn and chapped lips is essential, as are a **hat** and **sunglasses**. You should be prepared for dry and wet landings. The latter involves wading ashore.

Take plenty of **film** with you. The animals are so tame that you will use far more than you expected. Two 36-exposure rolls a day will barely be enough for the least enthusiastic of photographers. A telephoto lens is not essential, but bring it if you have one. Take filters suitable for strong sunlight. An underwater camera is also an excellent idea.

Snorkelling equipment is particularly useful as much of the sea-life is only visible under water. Few of the cheaper boats provide equipment and those that do may not have good snorkelling gear. If in doubt, bring your own, rent in Puerto Ayora, or buy it in Quito. It may be possible to sell it afterwards either on the islands or back in Quito.

A recommended **map** is *The Galápagos Islands*, 1:500,000 map by Kevin Healey and Hilary Bradt (Bradt Publications, 1985). Also recommended is the *Galápagos Pocket Guide* (and map) by Nelson Gómez, available in most Quito bookshops.

Puerto Ayora

Phone code: 05   *Puerto Ayora on Isla Santa Cruz is the largest town of the Galápagos archipelago*
Population: 8,200   *and the main tourist centre, with a wide range of hotels, restaurants and shops. If*
Colour map 1   *you choose to arrange a tour from here, instead of from the mainland, it's a pleasant place to spend a few quiet days waiting.*

The cost of living in Puerto Ayora, and throughout the Galápagos, is higher than in the mainland, particularly in the peak season (December, January, July and August). Most food has to be imported although certain meats, fish, vegetables and fruit are locally produced.

Tourist   **Ministerio de Turismo/CAPTURGAL**, Av Charles Darwin by south end of Pelican Bay,
information   T526174, cptg@pa.ga.pro.ec, open Mon-Fri 0800-1200, 1500-1600. Information also available at the boat owners' cooperative office nearby.

Excursions

One of the most beautiful beaches in the Galápagos Islands is at **Tortuga Bay**, an hour's walk (5 km) west from Puerto Ayora on a marked and cobbled path. Start at the west end of Calle Charles Binford; further on there is a gate where you must register, open 0600-1830 daily. The sunsets here are excellent. Take drinking water and do not go alone (occasional incidents have been reported). Also take care of the very strong undertow, the surf is calmer on the next cove to the west. Camping is not permitted.

See Visitor sites, page 398, for a description of the sites around Santa Cruz

Las Grietas is a beautiful gorge with a pool at the bottom which is ideal for bathing. It is to the southwest of town, a 20-minute walk from *Hotel Delfín* (see Sleeping below). Follow the signs to the lagoon, then walk round the left side of the lagoon (follow the green and white posts) and head uphill at the far end of the lagoon on a clear path. Strong shoes or boots are advised. It can also be accessed by boat.

There are some areas of interest at and near the grounds of the Darwin Station. A small rocky beach is halfway between the interpretation centre and the entrance and is popular with local families at weekends. Past the interpretation centre on the paved road, and to the right of the Tomas Fischer Science building, a trail leads to a rocky beach where marine iguanas and crabs can be observed. Following a small trail between the gift shop at the entrance and the *Hotel Galápagos*, you can see the stone house built by the Norwegian pioneer Sigurd Graffer in 1933.

Tour operators in Puerto Ayora (see below) run excursions to the highland sites for about US$20-30 per person, depending on the number of sites visited and the size of the group. These may include visits to ranches such as Rancho Mariposa (enquire at *Moonrise Travel*).

Bay excursions in glass-bottom boats (*Aqua Video*, best visibility, and *Mainao*, small glass window) visit sites near Puerto Ayora such as Isla Caamaño, Punta Estrada, Las Grietas, Franklin Bay and Playa de los Perros. It involves some walking and you are likely to see sea lions, birds, marine iguanas and marine life including sharks. Snorkelling can be part of the tour. Half-day tours (at 0900 and 1400) are US$25 per person and can be arranged at the pier or through travel agencies.

Essentials

Hotel space at the upper end of the market is limited and reservations are strongly recommended in the high season. There is a choice of budget hotels and a room shouldn't be difficult to find, except at the busiest times. Some hotels charge national and foreign rates; try to ask for national rates in the low season.

Sleeping
■ *on map, 418*
Price codes: see inside front cover

LL *Delfín*, On a small bay south of Puerto Ayora, accessible only by boat, T526297, F526283. Includes breakfast, restaurant, pool, lovely beach, bar, good service, comfortable rooms. Book through *Metropolitan Touring* in Quito. Scheduled to close for renovations in late 2002. **LL** *Royal Palm*, in the highlands of Santa Cruz, T527409, F527408, www.millenniumhotels.com Includes breakfast, spa, villas and suites with all luxuries, private lounge at airport, part of *Millennium international* chain, new in 2002. At up to US$950 per night (6 months' local wages) this is the most expensive hotel in Ecuador. **LL-L** *Red Mangrove Inn*, Darwin y las Fragatas, on the way to the research station, T527011, F526564, www.redmangrove.com Includes breakfast, restaurant, jacuzzi, deck bar. Owner Polo Navaro offers day tours and diving. Warmly recommended. **L** *Galápagos*, Av Darwin at the entrance to the scientific station, T526292, F526330, jack@hotelgalapagos.com Includes breakfast, restaurant serving set meals, fruit and meat from hotel farm, ocean-view, day excursions, also diving with *Scuba Iguana*.

L *Silberstein* (formerly *Hotel Angermeyer*), Darwin y Piqueros, T526277, F526066. Includes breakfast, pool, meals available, tours, diving.

AL *Fernandina*, 12 de Noviembre y Los Piqueros, T526499, F526122. Includes breakfast, restaurant, a/c, pool (open weekends to non guests), jacuzzi. **A** *Las Ninfas*, Los Colonos y Berlanga, T526127, F526128. Includes breakfast, good restaurant, a/c,

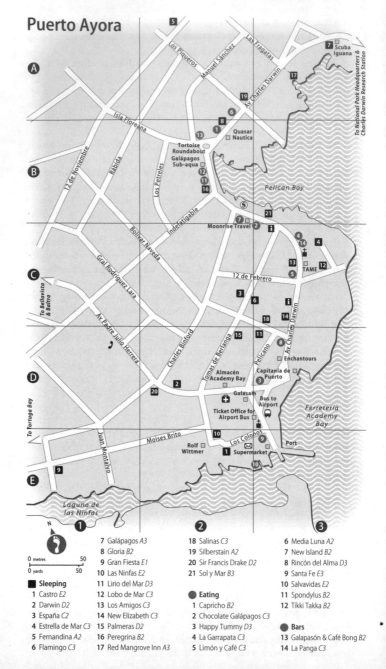

Puerto Ayora

To National Park Headquarters & Charles Darwin Research Station

Galápagos Islands

Sleeping	7 Galápagos *A3*	18 Salinas *C3*	6 Media Luna *A2*
1 Castro *E2*	8 Gloria *B2*	19 Silberstain *A2*	7 New Island *B2*
2 Darwin *D2*	9 Gran Fiesta *E1*	20 Sir Francis Drake *D2*	8 Rincón del Alma *D3*
3 España *C2*	10 Las Ninfas *E2*	21 Sol y Mar *B3*	9 Santa Fe *E3*
4 Estrella de Mar *C3*	11 Lirio del Mar *D3*		10 Salvavidas *E2*
5 Fernandina *A2*	12 Lobo de Mar *C3*	**Eating**	11 Spondylus *B2*
6 Flamingo *C3*	13 Los Amigos *C3*	1 Capricho *B2*	12 Tikki Takka *B2*
	14 New Elizabeth *C3*	2 Chocolate Galápagos *B2*	
	15 Palmeras *D2*	3 Happy Tummy *D3*	**Bars**
	16 Peregrina *B2*	4 La Garrapata *C3*	13 Galapasón & Café Bong *B2*
	17 Red Mangrove Inn *A3*	5 Limón y Café *C3*	14 La Panga *C3*

full range of services, has its own boat at reasonable price for day trips and Fernando Ortiz is helpful with arrangements. **B** *Castro*, Los Colonos y Malecón, T526113, F526508. Restaurant, cold water, a/c $10 extra, fan, owner Miguel Castro arranges tours, he is an authority on wildlife. Recommended. **B** *Palmeras*, Berlanga y Naveda, T526139, F526373. Restaurant, a/c, pool, good value. **B** *Sol y Mar*, Darwin y Binford, T526281, F527015. Fan, variety of rooms in different categories.

C *Estrella de Mar*, Darwin y 12 de Febrero, T526427, F526080. Fan, spacious rooms (more expensive with sea view), communal sitting area. **C** *Gran Hotel Fiesta*, Brito y Las Ninfas, T/F526440, fiestur@pi.pro.ec Restaurant, a/c, cheaper with fan, a 5-min walk inland from the seafront, hammocks, quiet, reasonable value but a bit remote.

D *Flamingo*, Berlanga y Naveda, T/F526556. With fan, decent but hot. **D** *Lirio del Mar*, Naveda y Berlanga, T526212. Laundry facilities, cafetería, pleasant, good value. **D** *Lobo de Mar*, 12 de Febrero y Darwin, T526188, F526569. Modern. **D** *Los Amigos*, Darwin y 12 de Febrero, T526265. Shared bath, laundry facilities, cool and airy rooms (upstairs best). Recommended. **D** *New Elizabeth*, Darwin y Berlanga, T/F526178. Reasonable, owner very helpful. **D** *Salinas*, Naveda y Berlanga, T526107, F526072. Restaurant, with bath and fan, good value. **D** *Sir Francis Drake*, Herrera y Binford, T526221. With fan, good.

D-E *Peregrina*, Darwin e Indefatigable, T526323. Includes good breakfast, a/c, cheaper with fan, good. **E** *Darwin*, Herrera y Binford, T526193. Private bath, good but don't leave valuables in your room. **E** *España*, Berlanga y Naveda, T520108. OK. **E** *Gloria*, Darwin y Piqueros, T527033. Private bath, simple.

Salvavidas, right on the seafront overlooking the activity at the pier. Good set lunch, good breakfast, seafood, hamburgers. *Santa Fe*, overlooking the bay. Bar and grill, popular. *Cucuve*. Traditional snacks like *humitas* and *tamales*. *Sabrosón*, above Hotel Palmeras, open air grill. OK food, nice decor. *Happy Tummy*, opposite the Capitanía de Puerto. Varied menu, good, open late even Sun. *Rincón del Alma*, north of the harbour. Good food, reasonable prices. *Limón y Café*, corner 12 de Febrero. Good snacks and drinks, lots of music, pool table, open evenings only, popular. *La Garrapata*, north of *TAME*, next to *La Panga* disco. The best food in town, attractive setting and good music, open morning and evening but not Sun, drinks expensive. *New Island*, by Charles Binford, near *Moonrise Travel*. Breakfast, fruit juices, seafood, ceviches. *Chocolate Galápagos*, opposite *Banco del Pacífico*. Good snacks, burgers, raclette. *Spondylus*, north of Indefatigable. Regional, Italian and international. Recommended. *Tikki Takka*, for breakfast, good bread, expensive. *Capricho*, by the tortoise roundabout. Good vegetarian food, salads and juices, breakfast. Recommended. *Media Luna*, near corner Los Piqueros. Good, pizza, also sandwiches, excellent brownies, evenings only. *Viña del Mar*. Padre J Herrera. Popular with locals. Along Charles Binford, near Padre J Herrera are kiosks selling traditional food at economic prices; *Tía Juanita* cooks well, seafood.

Bakeries The most popular one is almost opposite the telephone office – it opens early and serves hot bread and drinking yoghurt before the early bus leaves for the airport. The restaurant at the bus company office also does a cheap breakfast.

Outside Puerto Ayora There are some expensive to very expensive restaurants in ranches in the highlands serving lunch. Arrangements have to be made in advance, agencies or hotels with a VHF radio can help you make a reservation. *Narwhal*, at Km 14 on the way to Santa Rosa. Set meals, food is OK. *Rancho Mariposa*, also near Santa Rosa. For groups only, reserve through *Moonrise Travel*. *Rancho Altair*, in the Cascajo area, near the lava tunnels. Ask for Tim Gray and Anita Salcedo at *Garrapata* restaurant.

La Panga, Av Charles Darwin y Berlanga and *Five Fingers*, Av Charles Darwin opposite the Capitanía de Puerto, are popular bar/discos. *Galapasón* is a popular salsa bar at the tortoise roundabout. *Salsa 10*, on Naveda, good latin music. *Café Bong*, above *La Panga*, popular rooftop hangout.

Eating
● *on map*
These restaurants are on the main street unless mentioned otherwise, starting at the dock and moving north towards the Darwin Station

Bars & nightclubs

Galápagos Islands

Shopping

Most basic foodstuffs generally can be purchased on the islands, but cost more than on the mainland. The *Proinsular* supermarket opposite the pier is the best place (try their delicious locally-made yoghurt drink). The *mercado municipal* is on Padre J Herrera, beyond the telephone office, on the way out of town to Santa Rosa. Medicines, sun lotions, mosquito coils, film, and other useful items all cost more than on the mainland and at times might not be available. *Galapaguito* can meet most tourists' needs, the owners are very helpful. There is a wide variety of T-shirt and souvenir shops along the length of Av Charles Darwin.

Sport

Bicycling Mountain bikes can be hired from travel agencies in town, US$8-16 per day; or at the *Red Mangrove Inn*, US$5 per hour. *Galápagos Tour Center*, T526245, runs cycling tours in the highlands, US$16 per day.

Diving There are several diving agencies in Puerto Ayora offering courses, equipment rental, dives within Academy Bay (2 dives for US$75-85), dives to other central islands (2 dives, US$110-120), daily tours for 1 week in the central islands (12 dives, US$1,260) and several day live-aboard tours (1 week tour of central islands US$1,960). Two agencies that offer all services and have been repeatedly recommended are: *Galápagos Sub-Aqua*, Av Charles Darwin by Pelican Bay (Quito: Pinto 439 y Amazonas, office 101, T565294, F569956; Guayaquil: Dátiles 506 y Sexta, T304132, F314510), sub_aqua@accessinter.net Instructor Fernando Zambrano offers full certificate courses up to divemaster level (PADI or NAUI). Open 0800-1200, 1430-1830. *Scuba Iguana*, at the *Hotel Galápagos*, T526292, F526330, www.scuba-iguana.com (Quito: *Scala Tours*, Foch 746 y Amazonas, T545856, F258655). Run by Jack Nelson and Mathias Espinosa, who are both experienced and knowledgeable about different sites, Mathias offers full certificate courses up to instructor level. Open 0730-1900. Divers must have their certificates and log books and can expect to be asked to do a test dive in the bay before going to more advanced sites. You can arrange to be met by a divemaster during a regular Galápagos cruise and dive while your companions do a land visit.

Horse riding For horse riding at highland ranches, enquire with *Moonrise Travel*.

Kayaking and windsurfing Equipment rental and tours available from the *Red Mangrove Inn*, US$10 per hr.

Snorkelling Masks, snorkels and fins can be rented from travel agencies and dive shops, US$4-5 a day, US$60 deposit. Some bay tours include snorkelling. A full day snorkelling tour with *Scuba Iguana* is US$35 including equipment, wet suit and lunch. The closest place to snorkel is by the beaches near the Darwin Station.

Surfing There is surfing at Tortuga Bay (see Excursions, above) and at other more distant beaches accessed by boat. Note that there is better surfing near Puerto Baquerizo Moreno on San Cristóbal. *Galápagos Tour Center* rents surfboards US$10 per day and organizes surfing tours, US$55 and up. Vladimir Palma is a local surfer who can sometimes be found at the *Galapasón* bar.

Tour operators

Moonrise Travel Agency, Av Charles Darwin, opposite *Banco del Pacífico*, T526348, T/F526403, sdivine@pa.ga.pro.ec Last-minute cruise bookings, day-tours to different islands, bay tours, highland tours, airline reservations. Knowledgeable, helpful and reliable. Recommended. *Galaptour*, Rodríguez Lara y Genovesa, T526088, F527021. Last-minute cruise bookings. *Sr Victor López*, at Ferretería Academy Bay, Padre J Herrera, opposite the hospital. Runs day-tours on the *Elizabeth*. *Galápagos Tour Center*, Padre J Herrera, opposite the hospital, T526245. Bicycle rentals and tours, surf boards, snorkelling gear, motorcycle rentals. Run by Victor Vaca who also arranges last-minute tours. They work with several different boats including the *Free Enterprise*; we have received serious negative reports about the latter. *DHL* courier and *Western Union* agents are located in front of the *Hotel Silberstein*.

Bus To **Bellavista** and **Santa Rosa** in the highlands, 3 daily, US$0.40. **Taxi** To Santa Rosa US$4.

Boat Water taxis from the pier to nearby beaches such as **Las Grietas**, US$0.50. *Fibras* (fiberglass motor launches) operate most days to Pto Baquerizo Moreno (San Cirstóbal) and to Pto Villamil (Isabela), US$25-30 one way, check at the Capitanía de Puerto.

Transport
See also Getting there, page 406 and Getting around, page 407 for buses to the airport, flights and boats between islands, etc

Airline offices *TAME*, Av Charles Darwin north of 12 de Febrero, T526165. Open Mon-Sat 0830-1230, Mon-Fri 1400-1730. *Emetebe*, Av Charles Darwin opposite the port, 3rd floor of post office building, T526177. **Banks** *Banco del Pacífico*, Av Charles Darwin by Pelican Bay. Open 0800-1500, US$5 commission per transaction to change TCs, maximum US$200. Cirrus ATM and cash advance on Mastercard only. Note that there is nowhere in the islands to get cash advances on Visa or other credit cards and no other ATM networks. Mastercard is the most commonly accepted card on the islands, although the more upmarket businesses may take others. A hefty surcharge may be applied to credit card purchases, and many places do not accept any credit cards at all. Most boats accept Tcs. **Communications** **Internet**: US$2 per hr. **Post**: by the port. It often runs out of stamps (never leave money and letters), ask in the 'red boat' (*Galería Johanna*) or *Artesanías Bambú*. Many postcards never reach their destination, so it's probably best to take them home with you. **Telesphone**: *Pacifictel*, Padre J Herrera, 4 blocks from Av Charles Darwin. No collect or country-direct calls can be made from here. International calls can also be made from public cellular card phones (both *Bell South* and *Porta*), you can also receive calls at these phones. **Embassies and consulates** British Consul, David Balfour, c/o *Etica*, Barrio Estrada, Puerto Ayora. **Laundry** *Lavagal*, by the football stadium, machine wash and dry US$1.50 per kilo, good, reliable, US$1 taxi ride from town. **Medical facilities** Hospitals: there is a hospital on Padre J Herrera. Consultations cost about US$10, medicines reasonably priced, but they cannot perform operations. **Useful addresses** **Immigration**: Only the immigration police in Puerto Baquerizo Moreno (San Cristóbal) are authorized to extend tourist visas. **Lost property**: information and retrieval of lost property, you can try *Radio Santa Cruz*, next to the Catholic Church.

Directory

Puerto Baquerizo Moreno

On San Cristóbal island to the east, this is the capital of the province of Galápagos. The island is being developed as a second tourist centre. It is a pleasant place to spend a few days, with interesting excursions in the area.

Phone code: 05
Population: 6,500

The provincial chamber of tourism, **CAPTURGAL**, on Malecón Charles Darwin y Española, has a list of services in town. **Asociación de Guías**, Malecón Charles Darwin y Wolf, is helpful with general information and has a book exchange. In the same office is the **Fundación Ecológica Albatros**, a local environmental group.

Tourist information

In town, the **cathedral**, on Avenida Northía, two blocks up from the post office, has interesting mixed-media relief pictures on the walls and altar. ■ *0900-1200, 1600-1800*. Next door is the small **Franciscan museum** of natural history. It has stuffed exhibits, old photos, and a tortoise called Pepe. ■ *Mon-Fri 0800-1200, 1500-1730. US$1.*

To the north of town, opposite Playa Mann, is the Galápagos National Park visitors' centre or **Centro de Interpretación**. It has an excellent display of the natural and human history of the islands. Highly recommended. ■ *Mon-Fri 0700-1200, 1300-1700, Sat 0730-1300, 1330-1730, Sun 0730-1200, 1300-1700. Free. T520138.*

Sights

Galápagos Islands

Excursions

See Visitor sites, page 398, for a detailed description of the sites around San Cristóbal

A good trail goes from the Centro de Interpretación to the northeast through scrub forest to **Cerro Tijeretas**, a hill overlooking town and the ocean, 30 minutes away (take water). Side trails branch off to some lookouts on cliffs over the sea. Frigate birds nest in this area and can be observed gliding about, there are sea lions on the beaches below. To go back, if you take the trail which follows the coast, you will end up at **Playa Punta Carola,** a popular surfing beach, too rough for swimming. Closer to town is the small **Playa Mann** (follow Avenida Northía to the north), more suited for swimming and in town is **Playa de Oro**, where some hotels are located. Right in the centre of town, along the sand by the tidal pool, sea lions can be seen, be careful with the male who 'owns' the beach. Further afield to the northeast, and reached by boat (15 minutes) is **Puerto Ochoa**, another beach popular with locals.

To the south of town, 20 minutes' walk past the airport, is **La Lobería,** a rocky bay with shore birds, sea lions and marine iguanas. You can continue along the cliff to see tortoises and rays, but do not leave the trail.

Sleeping

■ *on map*
Price codes:
see inside front cover

B *Islas Galápagos*, Esmeraldas y Colón, T520203, F520162. A/c, a bit run down. **B** *Northía*, Northía y 12 de Febrero, T/F520041. Includes breakfast, a/c, pleasant but pricey. **B** *Hostal Galápagos*, at Playa de Oro, T520157. A/c, fridge, nice cabins. **B** *Orca*, Playa de Oro, T/F520233. A/c, fridge, often filled with groups, has its own boat for cruises.

C *Cabañas Don Jorge*, above Playa Mann, T520208. Fan, simple cabins in a quiet setting overlooking the ocean, meals available. **C** *Chatham*, Northía y Av de la Armada Nacional, on the road to the airport, T520137. Includes breakfast, fan, meals on request. **C** *Mar Azul*, Northía y Esmeraldas, T520139, F520384. With fan, on the road to the airport, nice gardens, good value. Highly recommended.

D *Flamingo*, Hernández y Av Quito, T520204. Cold water, basic. **D** *Los Cactus*, Juan José Flores y Av Quito, near Pacifictel, T520078. Simple and family run. **D** *San Francisco*, Malecón Charles Darwin y Villamil, T520304. Cold water, fan, rooms in front are nicer, simple, good.

Out of town In El Progreso in the highlands is **D** *La Casa del Ceibo*, T520248. A cane treehouse atop a kapoc, equipped for short or long stays.

Eating

● *on map*

There are several restaurants by the intersection of Ignacio de Hernández y General Villamil, including: *Rosita*. Set meals and varied à la carte menu, very good. *Barracuda*. Grilled meat, fish, and *menestras*, cheap. *Pizzería Bambú*. Good cheap set meals and mid-range pizza as well as à la carte dishes. *Sabor Latino*, Hernández y Manuel J Cobos. Good set meals, busy at lunch. *La Playa*, Av de la Armada Nacional, by the navy base. Nice location, popular. *Miconia*, Darwin e Isabela, Varied menu, meat, fish, pizza, Italian. *Albacora*, Av Northía y Española. Good set meals, cheap. *Casa Blanca*, Malecón by the whale statue. Breakfast, ceviches, snacks, grill at weekends, closed Mon. *Genoa*, Malecón Charles Darwin by Post office. A la carte, evenings only, music, good atmosphere, popular with surfers. *Galapaluz*, Malecón Charles Darwin y Manuel J Cobos. Snacks, coffee, drinks. *Panadería Fragata*, Northía y Rocafuerte. Excellent bread and pastries, good selection.

Out of town In El Progreso in the highlands are *La Casa del Ceibo* and *Quinta de Christi* open at weekends only and serving Ecuadorean dishes and parrilladas.

El Barquero, Hernández y Manuel J Cobos. Bar and *peña*. Open daily. *Blue Bay* and *Neptuno*, both at Malecón Charles Darwin y Herman Melville, opposite the whale and opposite each other. Discos, young crowd, open Tue-Sat 2030-0300. *La Terraza*, at bottom of Manuel J Cobos, by the waterfront. Disco, large dance floor. There are other bars along Av de la Armada Nacional towards the waterfront. **Bars & nightclubs**

There are a few souvenir shops along the Malecón selling T-shirts and a some crafts. Do not buy black coral. Paintings with Galápagos motifs can be bought from the following artists: *Arni Creaciones*, Av Quito y Juan José Flores, near Pacifictel. Humberto Muñoz, very nice work. Recommended. *Fabo Galería de Arte*, Malecón Charles Darwin, opposite the whale statue. Paintings by the owner Fabián, silk screened T-shirts. He also directs the *Mar de Lava* theatre group which has periodic presentations at the Centro de Interpretación. There is small produce market in town. **Shopping**

Puerto Baquerizo Moreno

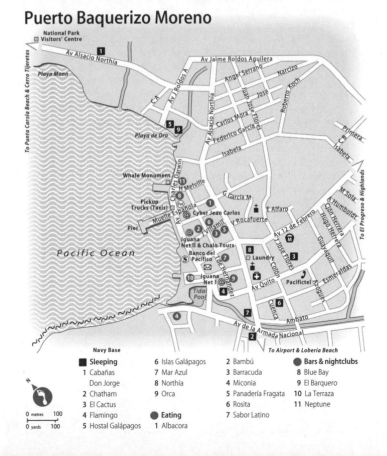

■ Sleeping	6 Islas Galápagos	2 Bambú	**● Bars & nightclubs**
1 Cabañas Don Jorge	7 Mar Azul	3 Barracuda	8 Blue Bay
2 Chatham	8 Northía	4 Miconia	9 El Barquero
3 El Cactus	9 Orca	5 Panadería Fragata	10 La Terraza
4 Flamingo		6 Rosita	11 Neptuno
5 Hostal Galápagos	**● Eating**	7 Sabor Latino	
	1 Albacora		

Navy Base   To Airport & Lobería Beach

0 metres 100
0 yards 100

Galápagos Islands

Sport   **Cycling** Mountain bikes can be hired from travel agencies in town, US$0.80 per hr.
Diving There are several diving sites around San Cristóbal, most popular being Kicker Rock, Roca Ballena and Punta Pitt (at the northeastern side). Gonzalo Quiroga of *Chalo Tours* is a divemaster offering tours to these sites, however he is not always available.

Surfing There is good surfing in San Cristóbal, the best season is Dec-Mar. **Punta Carola** near town is the closest surfing beach; popular among locals. There is a championship during the local *fiestas*, the 2nd week of Feb.

Tour operators   *Chalo Tours*, Malecón Charles Darwin y Villamil, T520953. Bay tours US$35 per person (minimum 5 people) to Kicker Rock, Isla de los Lobos, boat tours to the north end of the island US$65 per person, highland tours to El Junco and Puerto Chino beach, US$20 per person, diving tours US$75-90 per person, bike rentals, snorkelling gear, surf boards, book exchange.

Transport   **Bus** To **El Progreso** in the highlands, see Visitor sites, page 398.
See also Getting there, **Boat** *Fibras* (fiberglass motor launches) operate most days to **Pto Ayora** (Santa
page 406, and Getting Cruz), US$25-30 one way, check at the Capitanía de Puerto.
around, page 407

Directory   **Airline offices** *TAME*, at the airport, entrance around the side of main building, T521089. Reconfirm here and pick up your boarding pass 2 days in advance, there is a shortage of space on all flights. Open Mon-Fri 0900-1230, 1400-1600, Sat 0900-1230. *Emetebe*, at the airport terminal, T520036. Open Mon-Fri 0700-1300, 1500-1730, Sat 0700-1300. **Banks** *Banco del Pacífico*, Malecón Charles Darwin y 12 de Febrero, by the waterfront. Same services as in Puerto Ayora. Open Mon-Fri 0800-1530, Sat 1000-1200. **Book exchange** At the *Asociación de guías* and *Chalo Tours*. **Communications** Internet: US$2-3 per hr. Post: Malecón Charles Darwin y 12 de Febrero. **Telephone**: *Pacifictel*, Av Quito, 3 blocks from the Malecón, same services as in Puerto Ayora, there are also card-operated public cellular phones. **Laundry** *Lavandería Limpio y Seco*, Av Northía y 12 de Febrero. Wash and dry for US$2. Open daily 0900-2100. **Medical facilities** There is a hospital providing only basic medical services. Dr David Basantes, opposite *Hotel Mar Azul*, is a helpful general practitioner. *Farmacia San Cristóbal*, Villamil y Hernández, is the best stocked pharmacy in town. **Useful addresses** Immigration: at Police Station, Malecón Charles Darwin y Española, T/F520129.

Isabela Island

Isabela is not highly developed for tourism but if you have a few days to spare it is worthwhile spending time there. It looks like most people's image of a Pacific island: coconut palms, azure ocean, white sand beaches, rocky inlets, mangroves, laid back lifestyle, funky little seafood restaurants offering lobster all the year round – and very few tourists. Just the place for some to pursue hardcore relaxation while the more energetic tramp round the island. Most residents live in Puerto Villamil.

Puerto Villamil
Phone code: 05
Population: 1,400

Horses can be rented for US$5 to US$10 a day, depending on the destination. Book one day in advance. Contact Sr Modesto Tupiza T529217 (he also has a truck for hire), or Sr Tenelema T529102 or T529057. Antonio Gil is a guide.

It is 2½ hours each way to **Muro de las Lágrimas**, built by convict labour; horses available for part of route. The **Centro de Crianza** is 30 minutes' walk west of town, a breeding centre for seven species of giant tortoise. There are several good **beaches**; west of town for surfing, east of town for mangroves and rocky inlets for snorkelling, in front of town for swimming. Fishermen can take you to see the white-tipped sharks at **Las Grietas,** US$8 per boat. In the **agricultural zone** you can visit small farms and harvest citrus fruit.

Day-trips can be arranged through *Isabela Tours*, on the plaza, T529207, F529201, expensive. Dora at *Ballena Azul* will help arrange trips, for example volcano tours for about US$20 per person, minimum two people. Tours are also arranged by *La Casa de Marita* and *Hotel San Vicente* (see below).

Excursions from Puerto Villamil
See also Visitor sites, page 398
There is a Pacifictel office four blocks from the plaza. There are no bank

A *La Casa de Marita*, at east end of village, T529238, F529201, hcmarita@ga.pro.ec Includes breakfast, set menu for other meals, order in advance. Rooms with kitchenette, beautiful place. Has tour agency. **C** *Ballena Azul* and *Isabela del Mar*, T529220, F529125. Good meals on request, Swiss run. Recommended. **D** *San Vicente*, Cormoran y Las Escalacias, T529140. Cold water, fan, meals on request, good value, popular. **D** *Tero Real*, Tero Real y Opuntia, T529195. Cabins with private bath, cold water, fan, meals on request. **E** *Antonio Gil* rents 2 rooms with shower. Helpful, guides tours.

Sleeping
All in Puerto Villamil

El Encanto de la Pepa, east of the plaza. Lots of character, good food, attractive setting, friendly. Best and most expensive in town. *Casa de Marita*, at hotel. Elegant, family-style, 1 set meal per day, order in advance. *Ballena Azul*, at hotel. Very pleasant, good food, many choices, but order in advance. *Costa Azul*, facing the Capitanía. Clean, modern, good daily specials. *La Ruta*, on the plaza. Simple, small, set meals and à la carte. *Caracol*, kiosk next to police station. One set meal per day, good and cheap, but arrive early or they sell out. *Campo Duro*, in the highlands at Merceditas. Parrilladas, weekends only, popular. Comedores: *Jacqueline* and *Perla del Pacifico*, both good and cheap but limited menu.

Eating

Air/boat There is regular service from Baltra and Puerto Ayora by light aircraft and boat, respectively. See Getting around, page 407, for details.

Transport

Bus Two daily to the highlands, 48-km round trip: 1st departs 0700 by the market, returns 0845; 2nd departs 1200, returns around 1400. The bus passes villages of Santo Tomás, Marianitas, La Esperanza and La Cura. From La Cura it is a 20-min walk to where one can take horses up to the Sierra Negra volcano. Trucks can be rented to various destinations around the village or in the agricultural zone.

Galápagos Islands

Floreana Island

Phone code: 05 Floreana, the island with the richest human history, has 90 inhabitants, most in Puerto Velasco Ibarra, the rest in the highlands. There is one school in town and one telephone at the Wittmers. There are about 14 people who were born on the island, they now include a director of the National Park, a boat owner, several naturalist guides and captains.

Unless you visit with one of the few boats which land at black beach for a few hours, it is difficult to get onto and off the inhabited part of the island. This is an ideal place for someone who wants peace and quiet, to write or escape the world. Services are limited however; don't go unless you can be self-sufficient and very flexible about travel times. Staying with the Wittmers is delightful, the pace of life is gentle and locally produced food is good, but you will not be entertained. Margret Wittmer died in 2000 at age 95, however you can meet her daughter, granddaughters and great grandsons.

The climate in the highlands is fresh and comfortable, good for birdwatching – of special note is the Floreana finch. Some 200 species of ants have also been described here. Visit the natural water source for the island at Asilo de la Paz. A three-hour hike goes to flamingo lagoons and a marine turtle nesting site, but be careful wandering off on your own as people have become seriously lost.

Sleeping & eating **A** *Pensión Wittmer*, T520150 (only evenings when the generator is on). Includes 3 good meals. Rooms with private bath, hot water and fan (when there is electricity), also 2 family bungalows. Or, with the Wittmers' permission, camp near the caves where the island's first inhabitant, Patrick Watkins, lived in the early 1800s.

Transport **Boat** There is an irregular service from Puerto Ayora (Santa Cruz), and occasionally other islands. No fixed schedule. **Bus** Mixto bus/truck 0600 to highlands Mon-Sat returns 0730 for school, 1500 to highlands returns 1700; Sun up 0700 returns 1000. The bus journey takes 30 mins, walking down takes 2½ hrs, 8 km from Asilo de la Paz.

Background

History and politics

Pre-conquest history

Earliest civilizations The oldest archaeological artefacts which have been uncovered in Ecuador date back to approximately 10000 BC. They include obsidian spear tips and belong to a pre-ceramic period during which the region's inhabitants are thought to have been nomadic hunters, fishers and gatherers. A subsequent formative period (4000-500 BC) saw the development of pottery, presumably alongside agriculture and fixed settlements. One of these settlements, known as **Valdivia**, existed along the coast of Ecuador and remains of buildings and earthenware figures have been found dating from 3500-1500 BC (see box, page 317).

Between 500 BC and AD 500, many different cultures evolved in all the geographic regions of what is today Ecuador. Among these were the Bahía, Guangalá, Jambelí and Duale-Tejar of the coast; Narrío, Tuncahuán and Panzaleo in the highlands; and Upano, Cosanga and Yasuní in Oriente. The period AD 500-1480 was an era of integration, during which dominant or amalgamated groups emerged. These included, from north to south in the Sierra, the Imbayas, Shyris, Quitus, Puruhaes and Cañaris; and the Caras, Manteños and Huancavilcas along the coast.

This rich and varied mosaic of ancient cultures is today considered the bedrock of Ecuador's national identity. It was confronted, in the mid-15th century, with the relentless northward expansion of the most powerful pre-Hispanic empire on the continent: the Incas.

The Inca Empire The Inca kingdom already existed in southern Peru from the 11th century. It was not until the mid-15th century however that they began to expand their empire northwards. Pachacuti Yupanqui became ruler of the Incas in 1428 and, along with his son Túpac Yupanqui, led the conquest of the Andean highlands north into present-day Ecuador. The Cañaris resisted for a few years but were defeated around 1470. Their northern counterparts fought on for several more decades, defeating various Inca armies.

Huayna Capac, Túpac Yupanqui's son, was born in **Tomebamba**, site of present-day Cuenca, which became one of the most important centres of the Inca Empire. Quito was finally captured in 1492 (a rather significant year) and became the base from which the Incas extended their territory even further north.

A great road was built between Cusco and Quito, but the empire was eventually divided; ruled after the death of Huayna Capac by his two sons, Huáscar at Cusco and Atahualpa at Quito.

Conquest and colonial rule

Civil war broke out between the two halves of the empire, and in 1532 **Atahualpa** secured victory over Huáscar and established his capital in Cajamarca, in northern Peru. In the same year, Pizarro's main Peruvian expedition set out from Tumbes, on the Peru-Ecuador border, finally reaching Cajamarca. There, **Pizarro** captured the Inca leader and put him to death in 1533. This effectively ended Inca resistance and their empire collapsed.

Pizarro claimed the northern kingdom of Quito, and his lieutenants Sebastián de Benalcázar and Diego de Almagro took the city in 1534. Pizarro founded Lima in 1535 as capital of the whole region, and four years later replaced Benalcázar at Quito with Gonzalo, his brother. **Gonzalo Pizarro** later set out on the exploration of the Oriente. He moved down the Napo River, and sent **Francisco de Orellana** ahead to prospect. Orellana did not return. He drifted down the river finally to reach the mouth of the

Cursed treasure

◀◀

When Francisco Pizarro, at the head of only 63 conquistadores, managed to take Atahualpa prisoner at Cajamarca, he probably knew little or nothing about the proportions of the empire – larger than all of Spain – whose sovereign he had just captured. What Pizarro and his men did know was that the Incas had gold and that they, the Spaniards, wanted it.

Legend-cum-history tells us that Atahualpa offered, in exchange for his freedom, to fill a room nearly 7 m long by 5 m wide with gold and silver to the height of his fully raised arm. Chasquis (messengers) were sent forth at once to the four suyos (cardinal points) of the great empire, and caravans of llamas and porters eventually began to return with the coveted treasure. Cajamarca however is located almost 800 km south of Quito and over 1,000 km northwest of Cuzco, as the condor flies, and delivering the ransom took time.

As the weeks dragged into months something even more powerful than greed began to grip the conquistadores: fear. The natives fanned the flames of the white men's paranoia with rumours of a great army commanded by a general from Quito named Rumiñahui (literally 'stone-face'), who was allegedly marching on Cajamarca with over 200,000 warriors. After eight months they could stand it no longer, and Pizarro and his men put Atahualpa to death on 29 August, 1533, well before the ransom could be completed.

Once again word spread throughout the provinces that the Inca was dead. Rumiñahui apparently took the reins of the crumbling empire, razed Quito before the Spanish could capture it, and hid all the treasure that was still on route to Cajamarca, by far the greater part of the promised ransom. The lesser part, that which was delivered to the Spaniards, came to over six tons of 22½ carat gold and almost 12 tons of fine silver.

Where is the hiding place of so fabulous a fortune? Five hundred years of history and generations of treasure hunters, many of whom perished or went mad in their quest, have yet to provide a definitive answer. Most trails seem to lead to the Llanganates, a particularly inaccessible chain of mountains situated roughly between the Cotopaxi and Tungurahua volcanoes. Rumiñahui, who remains a national hero in Ecuador, was a nobleman of the Puruhá nation which lived near the Llanganates. Further legend has it that he not only hid the treasure but also cursed it. Or was it the greed of the conquerors which cursed the treasures of the New World?

Amazon, thus becoming the first white man to cross the continent in this way; an event which is still considered significant in the history of Ecuador (see box, page 359).

Conquest & colonial rule

Quito became a *real audiencia* under the Viceroyalty of Peru. For the next 280 years Ecuador reluctantly accepted the new ways brought by the conqueror. Gonzalo Pizarro had already introduced pigs and cattle; wheat was now added. The Indians were Christianized, and colonial laws, customs and ideas introduced. The marriage of the arts of Spain to those of the Incas led to a remarkable efflorescence of painting, sculpting and building at Quito, one of the very few positive effects of conquest.

The Spanish introduced the *encomienda* into the Audiencia. This feudal system assigned the Indians to a Spanish landowner. They lived on his land and were forced to work for him, in exchange for a tiny piece of land, a few crumbs of food and religious guidance. Of course, the Indians were permanently in debt to their landowner and their children inherited this debt.

So the indigenous people effectively became slaves, with the size of the population greatly reduced by death and disease as a result. Following economic recession at the beginning of the 18th century the Spanish began to take over the remaining areas of land in Indian hands and turn them into huge private estates, called *haciendas*. Those

Indians whose land had been confiscated had little choice but to work for the Spanish landlords under the same conditions as had existed during the *encomienda* system. In Quichua, this new form of serfdom was known as *huasipungo*, which means 'at the door of the house', referring to the tiny plot of infertile land on which they lived. This system actually survived until the 1964 land reforms (see below). In the 18th century the production and export of cocoa began and black slave labour was brought in to work cocoa and sugar plantations near the coast.

Independence and after

Ecuadorean independence came about in several stages. In 1809, taking advantage of the chaos produced in Spain by Napoleon's invasion and the forced abdication of the Spanish king, some members of the Quito élite formed a junta and declared independence. This lasted only three months before being put down by royalist troops. Fearing further trouble, the royalists executed the leaders of the junta the following year, provoking an uprising and the establishment of another junta which governed in Quito until it was crushed by a royalist army two years later. The defeat of these early moves for independence discouraged any further opposition to Spanish rule in Quito, though members of the coastal élites led an uprising in 1820. Independence therefore had to wait until royalist forces were defeated by **Antonio José de Sucre** in the Battle of Pichincha in 1822. For the next eight years Ecuador was a province of Gran Colombia under the leadership of **Simón Bolívar**. As Gran Colombia collapsed in 1830 Ecuador became an independent state.

After independence Ecuadorean politics were dominated by the small élite, divided between a coastal faction, based in Guayaquil, and a faction from the Sierra, based in Quito. Separated by different landholding systems, distinct economic patterns and interests and widely divergent social attitudes, these two factions struggled for control of Ecuador through the 19th century and beyond. Although there were several presidents from the coast, all governments until 1895 represented the interests of the conservative landowners of the Sierra against the commercial interests of the agro-exporting landowners and traders of Guayaquil and the coast whom they disdainfully called *monos* (monkeys), an epithet which persists to the present day.

After 1830 Ecuador became a chronic example of the political chaos and instability which affected much of Spanish America in the 19th century. Of the 21 individuals and juntas who occupied the presidency for a total of 34 times between 1830 and 1895, only six completed their constitutional terms of office. Four men stand out as the most notorious of the *caudillos* (political strongmen) who dominated politics, either as presidents or from behind the scene: **General Juan José Flores** (president 1830-34, 1839-45), a Venezuelan who led the struggle for independence from Gran Colombia; **José María Urbina** (1851-56) who abolished slavery but imposed stern military rule; **Gabriel García Moreno** (1860-65 and 1869-75) who built roads linking the coast and highlands but was most renowned for his attempts to force Catholicism on the population and for eventually being hacked to death by machete at the entrance of the presidential palace; and **Ignacio Veintimilla** (1876-83), who was so unpopular that he united all the factions in the country against his dictatorship.

The 20th century

The seizure of power in 1895 by the coastal élite, led by the Radical Liberal *caudillo* **Eloy Alfaro** (president 1895-1901 and 1906-11), was followed by important changes as the Radical Liberals began to implement a programme which they saw as bringing Ecuador into the modern world. A key part of this was reducing the power of the church. Secular education, civil marriage and divorce were introduced and church lands were

Constitutions and revolutions ◀◀

Two prominent features of Ecuador's turbulent history are its numerous constitutions and its frequent revolutions. Since the creation of the republic in 1830 Ecuador has had 18 constitutions although few of the changes in these have made much difference to the lives of most of the population. One of the most notable was the so-called 'Black Charter' of 1869 decreed by Gabriel García Moreno, which enhanced the power of the Catholic church giving it complete control over education and denying citizenship to non-Catholics. The 1906 Constitution introduced by the Radical Liberal Eloy Alfaro separated church and state. Women gained the vote in the 1929 Charter but illiterates had to wait until the Constitution of 1979. The latest contitution, passed in 1998, enshrined a number of additional civil rights.

Although there have been many violent and unconstitutional changes of government, it is hard to accept Ecuador's image as a country of revolutions: few of these uprisings have led to anything more than a change of the faces in power. Only the Revolutions of 1895 and 1925 deserve the title: the first brought the coastal Radical Liberal Party to power and led to important social, political and economic changes; the second ended the rule of the Radical Liberals and brought the Conservatives of the sierra back into office.

The most recent governments to be overthrown were those of Abdalá Bucaram in 1997 and Jamil Mahuad in 2000, both – it should be pointed out – almost without violence. When the dust settled however most Ecuadoreans realized that, yet again, very little had changed. Irreverent comments, like "We have a new mascot but on the same old leash" reveal an insight into how little room for maneuvering most Ecuadorean presidents actually have.

---

confiscated. Ambitious plans were drawn up for construction of a railroad deep into the Oriente and capital punishment was abolished.

The overthrow of the Radical Liberals by a group of military officers (Alfaro, his two brothers and closest allies were killed and their bodies dragged through the streets of Quito before being publicly burned), led to the restoration to power of the Quito élite. Between 1925 and 1931 the military-backed government of **Isidro Ayora** carried out some of the reforms suggested by a team of economic advisors from the US, including the establishment of a Central Bank. The onset of the Great Depression, however, led to severe economic problems as demand for Ecuador's exports collapsed and prices fell. In the following years the country experienced its worst period of political instability. Between 1931 and 1948 there were 21 governments, none of which succeeded in completing its term of office. "There were ministers who lasted hours, presidents who lasted for days, and dictators who lasted for weeks." (G Abad, *El proceso de lucha por el poder en el Ecuador*, Mexico 1970.)

Political stability was only restored after 1948 when Ecuador entered another period of economic expansion, this time based on the production of bananas on coastal plantations. Banana exports grew from 18,000 tons in 1945 to 900,000 tons in 1960, by which time they accounted for two-thirds of exports. With cocoa and coffee prices also improving, there was a shift in population from the Sierra to the coast, where Guayaquil grew rapidly.

Between 1948 and 1960 three successive presidents managed to complete their terms of office. However, conflict between **Velasco Ibarra** and Congress in 1961 brought a return to instability. Velasco was succeeded by his vice-president, **Carlos Julio Arosemena**, a *costeño* who was attacked by the Quito elite who saw him as favourable to the Cuban Revolution. Arosemena scandalized *quiteños* and the military with his indecorous behaviour. He was incapably drunk at a formal reception for the

Background

Chilean President, once received a visiting mission dressed in his bathrobe and enjoyed visiting sleazy bars and shooting at the waiters. Insulting the US ambassador at a banquet provided the military with an excuse to overthrow him.

Between 1963 and 1979 Ecuador experienced two periods of military rule. The first, from 1963 to 1966, took strong measures against what it saw as a threat of Communism. An Agrarian Reform Law introduced in 1964, though inadequate to challenge many of the country's outdated landholding practices, was enough to upset the élite and the *junta* was forced from office. During the brief interlude of civilian rule which followed, new elections in 1968 led to the return of Velasco Ibarra (in all, he was elected president on four different occasions). His overthrow by the armed forces in 1972 coincided with the increase in oil revenues from the Oriente and was followed by seven years of military rule.

Between 1972 and 1976 **General Rodríguez Lara** led a 'revolutionary and nationalist' government, of which the aim was to use the oil revenues to build up the country's infrastructure and to finance agricultural, industrial and social projects. In fact, the Rodríguez Lara government lacked clear objectives, while disagreements within the armed forces and the opposition of many of the powerful sections of Ecuadorean society eventually led to the president's replacement by a junta which promised to return the country to civilian rule.

Return to democracy Since 1979 Ecuador has enjoyed its longest period of civilian constitutional government since independence. In 1978 a young and charismatic **Jaime Roldós** was elected president on a platform of using oil revenues to build up the country's infrastructure. By the time of Roldós' death in a plane crash in 1981 his plans had been frustrated by a decline in oil prices and the opposition of Congress. Roldós' successor, his vice-president **Oswaldo Hurtado** of the Democracia Popular (DP) party, was threatened by a series of political and economic crises which might have led to military intervention. He managed to hold out however and eventually became one of the very few respected elder statesmen in Ecuadorean politics.

In 1984 elections, **León Febres Cordero** of the right-wing Partido Social Cristiano (PSC) obtained a narrow victory. His attempt to introduce a neoliberal economic programme failed to control inflation or end recession, but sparked an upsurge in political violence and confrontation including coup attempts and clashes with students and workers. Febres Cordero was subsequently elected to two consecutive terms as mayor of Guayaquil and, although in failing health, he retains a very strong following among *guayaquileños* and the country's political right as well as considerable influence in all circles of power.

When **Rodrigo Borja** of the centre-left Izquierda Democrática (ID) won the 1988 election, his inheritance from Febres Cordero was difficult: high inflation, high unemployment and a large public spending deficit. The latter half of Borja's presidency was marked by conflict with Congress and labour unrest.

The elections of 1992 were won by **Sixto Durán Ballén** of the centre-right Partido de Unidad Republicana in coalition with **Alberto Dahik** of the Partido Conservador (who became vice-president). The popularity of Durán Ballén's government declined steadily with his attempts to implement an economic modernization programme. The resulting strikes and protests were temporarily interrupted when Ecuadoreans responded to the 1995 border conflict with Peru (see below) with a massive display of national unity, backing their government and armed forces to an extent not seen before. This backing was short-lived however and followed by a major corruption scandal which culminated with vice-president Dahik fleeing the country in 1996 at the controls of his private aircraft. He became the first of many contemporary national figures to seek asylum and self-imposed exile.

Durán Ballén's government limped to the end of its term in 1996, but disenchantment with the political establishment as a whole was so great that a flamboyant populist named **Abdalá Bucaram** of the Partido Roldosista Ecuatoriano (PRE) was swept to power in the next elections. Bucaram's erratic government lasted barely six months and by February 1997 all manner of scandal had implicated his entire government and family. A 48-hour national strike and mass demonstrations were followed by a congressional vote to remove Bucaram from office on the grounds of 'mental incapacity'. There followed a period of political chaos during which Ecuador had three simultaneous presidents: Bucaram, Vice-president **Rosalía Arteaga**, who claimed the office, and **Fabián Alarcón**, chosen by Congress, of which he was president. The military sided with Alarcón and Bucaram fled to Panama from where he remains closely involved with Ecuadorean politics by remote control, as his PRE party holds an important following especially among poor *costeños*.

After the departure of Bucaram, Alcorón was overwhelmingly elected president by Congress until new general elections were held in 1998. His interim government was marred by further accusations of corruption and continuing economic decline. A number of his closest collaborators eventually fled the country and Alarcón himself was imprisoned for several months on corruption charges after the end of his presidency, but later released. A constituent assembly was convened during the interim government and drew up the country's 18th constitution. It was in many ways a noble and progressive document but contributed little or nothing to solving the country's problems (see box, page 431).

Jamil Mahuad of the DP, a former mayor of Quito, was narrowly elected president in 1998, amid renewed border tensions with Peru. He immediately diffused this explosive situation and in less than three months had signed a definitive peace treaty, putting an end to decades – even centuries – of conflict (see below). This early success was Mahuad's last, as a series of bank failures (many fraudulent and perpetrated by bankers who had helped finance the president's election campaign) sent the country into an economic and political tailspin (also see Economy, page 438). In 1999 Mahuad decreed an austerity package including a freeze on bank accounts, effectively confiscating all assets on deposit in excess of US$200. (In late 2002 not quite all of these deposits had yet been reimbursed.) Even such a drastic measure did not prevent additional banks from collapsing however, and the mortally wounded economy embarked on a process of hyperinflation, previously unknown in Ecuador.

By the end of 1999 the country's social, political and economic situation was completely out of control and Mahuad decreed the adoption of the US dollar as the national currency in a desperate bid for monetary stability. Less than a month later, on 21 January 2000, he was forced out of office by Ecuador's indigenous people led by the Confederación de Nacionalidades Indígenas del Ecuador (CONAIE) and disgruntled members of the armed forces. This was the first overt military *coup* in South America in more than two decades, but it lasted barely three hours before a combination of local intrigue and international pressure handed power to vice-president **Gustavo Noboa**. Mahuad soon joined the ranks of other Ecuadorean politicians in exile. The colonels involved in the *coup* were subsequently pardoned but dismissed from the military. **Colonel Lucio Gutiérrez**, the leader of the *coup*, went on to found his own political party and was elected president in 2002. Most significantly, all of the foregoing years of social unrest were never accompanied by serious bloodshed.

The 21st century

Noboa, a political outsider and academic, stepped into Mahuad's shoes with remarkable aplomb. With assistance from the US and the International Monetary Fund (IMF), his government managed to flesh out and implement the dollarization scheme. This achieved a measure of economic stability but significantly increased the cost of living, imposing further hardship on the majority of the population. Noboa also continued the previous administration's drive for better tax collection, albeit in an arbitrary and heavy-handed fashion, and improved the country's road system. Social unrest diminished, mainly out of weariness, as Ecuadoreans resigned themselves to sit out another interim administration. Presidential elections were held in October 2002, with a field of 11 contenders including the first ever woman and the first ever indigenous candidate. In a second round run-off one month later, Colonel Lucio Gutiérrez, leader of the 2000 *coup*, was elected president by a comfortable majority.

Ecuador's neighbours

Peru   After the dissolution of Gran Colombia in 1830 (largely present-day Venezuela, Colombia and Ecuador), repeated attempts to determine the extent of Ecuador's eastern jungle territory failed. While Ecuador claimed that its territory has been reduced from that of the old Real Audiencia de Quito by gradual Colombian and especially Peruvian infiltration, Peru insisted that its Amazonian territory was established in law and in fact before the foundation of Ecuador as an independent state.

The dispute reached an acute phase in 1941 when war broke out between the two countries. The war ended with military defeat for Ecuador and the signing of the Rio de Janeiro Protocol of 1942 which allotted most of the disputed territory to Peru. Since 1960 Ecuador denounced the Protocol as unjust (because it was imposed by force of arms) and as technically flawed (because it refers to certain non-existent geographic features). According to Peru, the Protocol adequately demarcated the entire boundary.

Sporadic border skirmishes continued throughout subsequent decades. In January 1995 these escalated into an undeclared war over control of the headwaters of the Río Cenepa. Argentina, Brazil, Chile and the USA (guarantors of the Rio de Janeiro Protocol) intervened diplomatically and a ceasefire took effect. Negotiations followed and a definitive peace treaty was signed on 26 October 1998, finally ending the seemingly interminable dispute.

Under the terms of the agreement Ecuador gained access to two Peruvian ports on the Amazon, Ecuador's navigation rights on the river were confirmed and, in the area of the most recent conflict, it was given a symbolic square kilometre of Peruvian territory as private property. Although there is some lingering discontent among hardliners on both sides, relations have improved rapidly between the two former adversaries. New border crossings have opened and more international bus routes are being established. Adventurous travellers can now sail from the Ecuadorean Amazon to Peru (and Brazil), and tour operators are beginning to offer interesting packages involving both countries. Peruvian visitors are coming to Cuenca and Guayaquil, while some Ecuadoreans are – for the first time – enjoying the beaches of northern Peru.

Colombia   Ecuador and Colombia have traditionally enjoyed excellent relations. Their bigger, more progressive, neighbour to the north was for many decades regarded as a role model by some Ecuadoreans. With escalating crime and violence in Colombia, however, that admiration has gradually turned to fear. At the same time, commercial ties remain very strong.

Colombia's long-standing internal armed conflict continues to escalate, fuelled in part by the election in 2002 of a hard-line administration in Bogotá and by ongoing US support for the Colombian military. Hundreds of thousands of Colombians live in Ecuador, either as refugees or as ordinary migrants, and are unfairly blamed for the rising crime rate throughout this country. They have on occasion been singled out for strict measures by the Ecuadorean authorities.

The northern border provinces of Ecuador, however, can rightfully claim to have been adversely affected by the conflict next door. Esmeraldas, Carchi, and especially Sucumbíos receive the highest number of Colombian refugees. Small armed groups from Colombia have occasionally entered Ecuadorean territory and carried out kidnappings or confronted the local armed forces. Drug producers and drug runners have likewise begun to operate in Ecuador, as an alternative to Colombia. Broad spectrum herbicides sprayed from aircraft near the border, to eradicate coca plantations in Colombia, have affected agriculture and the health of people in Sucumbíos.

To date, the Ecuadorean government has always maintained an officially neutral policy, stressing that the Colombian armed conflict is internal to that country. It is becoming increasingly evident, however, that such a policy alone cannot shield Ecuador from the consequences of strife along its northern frontier.

Although not a geographic neighbour, the United States is certainly Ecuador's 'big brother'. The US is by far Ecuador's most important trading partner, it has a very important say in Ecuador's economy both directly and through multilateral institutions such as the International Monetary Fund (IMF), and it can exert unusually powerful leverage since the dollarization of the Ecuadorean economy. **United States**

US influence is not only economic. Going back as far as the Second World War, when a US air force base was built on the Galápagos Islands to guard the Panama Canal, there has at times been a small but locally significant US military presence here. In 1999 the Ecuadorean government hastily approved a 10-year accord authorizing the use of a base at Manta by the US air force, ostensibly for drug surveillance flights. It has been a bone of contention ever since, with many Ecuadoreans opposed to the foreign military presence and concerned about possible retaliation by Colombian insurgents.

With large numbers of Ecuadorean migrants going legally and otherwise to the USA (see Population, poverty & migration, below), and American businessmen and tourists coming to Ecuador, there has also been cultural projection from the north. This is most noticeable in large urban centres, but exists to a lesser degree throughout the country.

Over the years, this complex and often lopsided relationship has been remarkably harmonious. During the Noboa government, however, strains emerged over the base in Manta, over US sponsored activities in Colombia (see above), and over US pressures for unpopular economic reforms in Ecuador. In late 2002, a spat between the government and US oil companies working in Ecuador, resulted in the elimination preferential tariffs for Ecuadorean exports to the USA and put a hold on economic support from the IMF.

Government

There are 22 provinces, including the Galápagos Islands. Provinces are divided into *cantones* which are subdivided into *parroquias* for administration.

Under the 1998 constitution, all citizens over the age of 18 are both entitled and required to vote. The president and vice-president are elected for a four-year term and may be re-elected. The president appoints cabinet ministers and provincial governors. The parliament, or Congress (Congreso Nacional), has 123 members who are elected for a four-year term at the same time as the president.

Background

Modern Ecuador

Society: opportunities & challenges

Despite its troubled history and current economic woes, Ecuador is a land of outstanding opportunities. This is the case not only because of the country's extraordinary diversity in a very small area, but also because of the resilience and adaptability of its people. From the Inca invasion in the 1400s to Colombian insurgency in the 21st century, Ecuadoreans have had a knack for getting by despite adversity. They gleaned new manual skills from the *encomienda* (forced labour) system of early colonial times no less than they are acquiring new cosmopolitan competence from today's mass migrations to Europe and North America. At present, the country faces many important challenges and perceives the need to overhaul its infrastructure and institutions. This is indeed asking a lot, but it is also worth remembering that for the past 600 years, or more, the common people of Ecuador have gone about their daily lives without paying much heed to national infrastructure or institutions.

Population, poverty & migration
See the website of the Instituto Nacional de Estadística y Censos (INEC) at www.inec.gov.ec

The 2001 census counted 12.2 million Ecuadoreans, an 18% increase since 1990. Population pressure is strong on Ecuador's most elemental resources – land and water, and an important threat to the country's outstanding biodiversity. Migration and a slowly declining birth rate have eased this pressure only slightly in recent years and the country's future depends, more than anything else, on achieving a sustainable balance between its population and renewable resources. This is true worldwide of course, but all the more so in Ecuador because of its small geographic size. Family planning programs exist but are not widely accepted, and such efforts must contend with the great power and influence of the Roman Catholic Church.

As in other Andean countries with large indigenous populations, wealth is distributed along ethnic lines, with indigenous people and blacks suffering the greatest poverty. (An exception which proves this rule is the economic dominance of native people in Otavalo.) At the same time there is a tiny – mostly white – élite, who are spectrally wealthy. Estimates are that more than 70% of the population live in poverty. Many of those who are fortunate enough to be formally employed (the minority) must survive on a monthly take-home pay of barely US$140. The basic cost of living for an Ecuadorean family is estimated at US$340 per month, the minimum subsistence level is US$260 per month. As well as poverty, some Ecuadorean women also suffer domestic violence from drunken husbands, but in this macho culture such abuse often goes unreported and may even be tolerated, although attitudes have gradually begun to change.

In an attempt to escape rural poverty, many have migrated from the coast and the highlands to the towns and cities, particularly Guayaquil and Quito, where they are usually even worse off. In the countryside those with even a tiny plot of land or a fishing net can usually manage to eat, whereas in the city one must either earn or steal money in order to survive. This can be seen by the increase in crime as well as the many people trying to scrape together an honest living as *ambulantes*: by selling various goods or offering services on the streets of the major cities, particularly Quito. Rather worryingly, a high percentage are young children.

The most recent economic crises forced many Ecuadoreans to seek even more distant opportunities, in North America and Europe, especially Spain. Approximately 380,000 people (3% of the population, although this is likely an under-estimate) emigrated from Ecuador between 1995 and 2001. So many Ecuadoreans wanted to leave that passports at times became scarce and, once they managed to get one, people queued for days outside the Spanish embassy in Quito in hopes of obtaining a visa. Families were often split up as one spouse migrated in search of work, while the other remained behind with the children, and tearful farewells were an everyday sight at Quito and Guayaquil airports. Illegal emigrants faced much greater hardship; they paid

US$10,000 or more to a *coyote* who offered to smuggle them overland through Central America, or in small vessels by sea, to the USA. Since few people have this sort of cash, the migrants usually signed over the family home or farm to *chulqueros* (loan sharks) who work together with the *coyotes*. Some were defrauded of their property without ever reaching the 'promised land' while others perished on route. Once in Spain, Italy, Germany, the USA or Canada, many of the illegal migrants were mistreated and under-paid, but there was sufficient demand for cheap labour in these countries that Ecuadoreans continued to emigrate. Some, especially those who eventually legalized their status, did well economically and began to send funds back to their relatives in Ecuador. In 2001 this income (locally known as *remesas*) added up to US$1,400 mn, almost as much as petroleum exports for the same period, and accounted for 30% of Ecuador's total foreign revenue.

Health

See the website of the Pan American Health Organization (PAHO) at www.paho.org

The gulf between rich and poor in Ecuador is exacerbated by the two-tier healthcare system. This division works on two levels – rural and urban and state and private. Two thirds of doctors and hospitals are concentrated in Quito and Guayaquil, and private hospitals thrive at the expense of a badly under-funded and crumbling state health service.

Despite this, things have improved in recent decades. Infant mortality has decreased to 30 per 1,000 and life expectancy has increased to an average of 70.3 years (PAHO 1999-2000). The main causes of death are no longer those associated with a typical developing country but those of the developed world: cancer, heart and lung disease. A large number of people are also killed in traffic accidents. Although abortion is illegal, it is commonly carried out in unsanitary conditions and many admissions to gynaecological departments are related to the termination of pregnancies.

Education

See also www.unesco.org

Children are entitled to nine years of compulsory education by law, but in practice this is not always the case. In rural areas most complete elementary school, but not all go on to secondary education. This is mainly because the rural population is greatly dispersed and the cost of travelling such large distances is prohibitive. Other factors are that many families cannot afford the costs of uniforms and materials and schools lack teaching resources.

Illiteracy is no longer the problem it was a generation or two ago. The literacy rate is almost 92% (UNESCO 1999, INEC 2001), and bilingual (Spanish and Quichua) education is available in some highland Indian communities. Overall standards for public education are extremely variable however, with a handful of highly regarded state schools in Quito and provincial capitals, while more remote classrooms and teachers can be severely deficient. Funds are always scarce and education, especially much needed investment in teacher training, has not been a priority for recent governments.

Corruption

See the website of Transparency International (TI) at www.transparency.org

In its 2002 Corruption Perceptions Index, Transparency International classified Ecuador as the second most corrupt country in South America. This unenviable distinction is felt at various levels. Vast quantities of public resources can end up in the pockets of senior officials. In a late 2002 scandal, for example, several under-secretaries of finance were implicated in demanding bribes before releasing national funds to municipalities. The minister of finance was subsequently sacked and fled the country hours before a warrant was issued for his arrest.

While cases like the above make headlines, the real impact of widespread corruption is far more subtle and pervasive. Most minor official business, anything from registration of a motor vehicle to repair of a broken phone line, can be an agonizingly slow and complicated process. If, however, you have 'connections' or can pay for the services of a 'facilitator' then all is expedited. The Ecuadorean judicial system has likewise come in for its share of criticism, with corrupt practices being blamed for both the extended detention of the innocent as well as the prompt release of criminals.

Background

All this is not to say that most Ecuadoreans are dishonest people. Quite to the contrary, they have strong sense of reciprocity, of always giving something in return for a favour received. Ironically perhaps, this attitude encourages rather than precludes the giving and receiving of favours in the situations described above.

Economy

In the 1970s, Ecuador underwent a transformation from an essentially agricultural economy to a predominantly petroleum economy. Substantial oil output began in 1972, from when economic growth has largely followed the fortunes of the international oil market and the country as a whole – economically, politically and socially – has been extremely vulnerable to these fluctuations.

Farming & fishing The contribution of agriculture and fishing to gdp has dwindled since the start of petroleum exports, but many jobs are still in farming and agro-exports still generate important foreign earnings. Ecuador is the world's largest exporter of bananas. Efforts have been made to expand markets following the introduction of EU import restrictions, to introduce a variety of banana resistant to black sigatoka disease and to reduce costs and increase efficiency; all with limited success. In 2002 Ecuador faced international criticism over the use of child labour on some of its banana plantations. Coffee is the most extensive of Ecuador's cash crops, accounting for over 20% of total agricultural land, but it is very low yielding. Cocoa yields have also fallen and a programme for better maintenance and replacement of old trees is under way. Several non-traditional crops are expanding rapidly, especially roses and other flowers in the Sierra within reach of Quito airport; also mangoes, strawberries, palm hearts, asparagus and other fruits and vegetables, many of which are processed before export.

The fishing industry is a major export earner, partly from the catch offshore of tuna, sardines and white fish, but mostly from shrimp farming along the coast. Shrimp farms offer employment in underdeveloped areas where other jobs are scarce, but their development is controversial and a large portion of Ecuador's mangroves has been destroyed. Most of the forest around Bahía and Muisne is gone and that which remains is threatened. In the Gulf of Guayaquil, the shrimp have suffered from high mortality in recent years, allegedly because of pollution from agrochemicals used intensively by banana growers. Since 1999, the shrimp industry as a whole has been hard hit by an epidemic disease known as *mancha blanca* (white spot) which caused mortality rates up to 100% on some farms.

Oil production Although Ecuador's share of total world oil production is small (about 1%), foreign exchange earnings from oil exports are crucial, accounting for almost one half of total exports and government revenues alike. In 2001 Ecuador exported approximately US$1,600 mn worth of petroleum. The main producing area is in the northern Oriente, and a 495-km trans-Andean pipeline carries the oil to Esmeraldas on the coast, where it is refined and/or exported. A second smaller pipeline takes oil to Colombia, from where it is exported through that country's pipeline system, but neither has the capacity required for planned development of new wells. A controversial new pipeline for heavy crude was under construction in 2002, through the heart of important nature reserves. Over the years, millions of hectares of Amazon forest have been opened to exploration, totally disregarding Indian reserves and national parks. The oil industry has had a considerable adverse affect on the Oriente's unique biodiversity as well as on indigenous communities, who have seen their lands polluted and deforested, and their way of life irreparably altered.

Tourism is a rapidly growing sector of the Ecuadorean economy, and the country's **Tourism**
third or fourth most important source of foreign revenue. Ecuador has received over
600,000 visitors a year since 2000, generating about US$350 mn in annual revenue.
Beach vacationers from Colombia have traditionally been the most numerous tourists in Ecuador but, following the signing of the peace treaty with Peru in 1998 there
has been a modest influx of Peruvians, contributing to the development of tourism
in the south. The Galápagos islands remain a particularly important destination for
visitors from Europe and North America, but there is an increasing trend toward eco-
and ethno-tourism in both the highlands and Oriente jungle. At the same time, tourism remains highly focused on certain well-known centres in Ecuador, with the
economies of places like Galápagos, Otavalo, Baños and Vilcabamba very heavily
dependent on foreign visitors.

Mining is not an important sector nationwide, but the discovery of about 700 tonnes of **Mining**
gold reserves around Nambija (Zamora Chinchipe) in the southeast created intense
interest in the late 1980s, and over 12,000 independent miners rushed to prospect
there. Over nine tonnes of gold are produced a year by prospectors along the Andean
slopes, polluting the waters with cyanide and mercury. Legislation has been designed
to encourage investors in large projects with better technology which would – in principle – be less harmful and could be more strictly controlled. Foreign companies are
interested in deposits of gold, silver, lead, zinc and copper in the south.

Despite the abundance of oil, over two-thirds of electricity generation comes from **Hydropower**
hydropower. Hydroelectric projects on the Paute, Pastaza and Coca rivers could raise
capacity from 2,300MW to 12,000MW. However, in the mid-1990s drought revealed
the dangers of overdependence on hydro and power shortages were widespread. Several thermal plants subsequently came into operation and the Government eased
restrictions on diesel imports. Privatization, especially in the electric energy sector, has
long been resisted by the labour movement. Recent governments have none-the-less
managed to break up the nationwide public electric company (INECEL) into a number
of smaller regional operators.

In 1999 the government of Ecuador defaulted on all its debts, national and foreign. **Recent trends**
The sucre – which had been the nation's currency for the previous 116 years –
reached 25,000 to US$1 (75% devaluation in one year) and President Mahuad
announced the adoption of the US dollar as the national currency in a desperate bid
for monetary stability. He was deposed shortly thereafter and the government of his
successor, Gustavo Noboa, was left to implement the dollarization scheme. The following year saw 100% real annual inflation (mostly at the outset as prices adjusted to
the new US dollar economy), which hit hard at the already battered population. In
2001 inflation was 25% and by 2002 it was down to approximately 10% (according
to disputed government figures, the real value is probably higher) but wages still
lagged far behind prices and poverty continued to grow. In late 2002, debt negotiations with the IMF stalled pending the outcome of presidential elections and
because of pressure by US and other international oil companies who were involved
in a tax dispute with the Ecuadorean government.

Background

Culture

People

About half of Ecuador's 12 million people are *mestizo*, descendants of Indians and Spaniards. *Cholo* is another (mildly derogatory) term for this group, infrequently used in Ecuador. Rural coastal dwellers are referred to as *montubios*. Roughly a quarter of all Ecuadoreans today belong to one of 14 different indigenous peoples.

Andean peoples The largest indigenous group are the **Andean Quichuas**, who number around three million. The common language, Quichua, was introduced by the Incas and is closely related to the Quechua spoken in parts of Peru and Bolivia. (Another theory suggests that Quichua/Quechua may have had its roots, centuries earlier, among trading peoples of Ecuador who carried the language south.) Though they speak a common language, indigenous dress differs from region to region. In the north, Otavaleño women are very distinctive with their blue skirts and embroidered blouses, while in the south the Saraguros traditionally wear black. A very important part of indigenous dress is the hat, which also varies from region to region.

Rainforest peoples The largest native groups in the Oriente are the Quichuas, in the north, and the **Shuar**, in the south. They number about 70,000 each. The **Amazonian Quichuas** speak a

Indigenous cultures

Cultural groups	
A Awa	**Q** Quichua of the Oriente
Ac Achuar	**Qs** Quichua of the Sierra
Ch Chachi	**S** Salasaca
C Cofán	**Sa** Saraguro
E Epera	**Se** Secoya
H Huaorani	**Sh** Shuar
N Negro-afroecuatoriano	**Si** Siona
O Otavaleño	**T** Tschila
	Z Zápara

different dialect than their highland counterparts, and their way of life is very different. Other Amazonian peoples of Ecuador include the **Achuar** (3,000 people) and **Huaorani** (2,000) as well as the **Cofán, Secoya, Shiwiar, Siona** and **Zápara**, all of whom have less than a 1,000 members and are clearly in danger of disappearing.

Those jungle peoples who maintain a traditional lifestyle, hunt and practise a form of itinerant farming which requires large areas of land, in order to allow the jungle to recover. Their way of life is under threat and many Amazonian Indian communities are fighting for land rights in the face of oil exploration and colonization from the highlands.

There are also small groups of Indians on the coastal plain. In Esmeraldas and Carchi provinces live around 1,000 **Awas**; nearer the coast and a little further south live around 4,000 **Chachis** and 250 **Eperas**; in the lowlands of Pichincha around Santo Domingo are some 2,000 **Tsáchilas**, also known as **Colorados**. These coastal Indians are also under threat from colonization.

Despite the many pressures they have faced throughout history and still today, the various indigenous groups of the Sierra, the coast and the Amazon rainforest have managed, to some degree, to survive and preserve their cultural identity. The interests of these different groups vary widely. Whereas in the Sierra and on the coast the main issues are obtaining infrastructure for native communities and access to water for irrigation, in the Amazon it is resistance to colonization and the ever-encroaching oil and mining industries. The single biggest threat to the Amazonian rainforest is the oil industry and its irresponsible methods.

Native organizations

Today, Ecuador's native people are among the best organized and politically savvy of any in Latin America. They have grouped themselves into various regional bodies as well as some other entities set up along religious lines (ie Catholic or Protestant). The national body which brings together many, but not all, of these regional organizations is the Confederación de Nacionalidades Indigenas del Ecuador (CONAIE). In addition to their political activities, these groups work with foreign NGOs and at times with the government, to foster native interests.

CONAIE in particular has played a key role in national political events, such as the overthrow of former president Jamil Mahuad. The organization's leadership has at times been criticized for pursuing its own political agenda rather than lobbying for the most immediate needs of its rank and file communities. The matter is controversial. Whatever the case, there can be little doubt that the *Indígenas* of Ecuador have made their voices heard in recent years and will certainly continue to do so in the future. In 2002, **Antonio Vargas** (originally from the Oriente and a former president of CONAIE) became the first indigenous candidate for the presidency of Ecuador. **Auki Tituaña**, the mayor of Cotacachi, is another indigenous leader who has achieved national and international prominence and has good potential as a future presidential candidate.

Afro-Ecuadoreans

Ecuador's black population is estimated at about 500,000. They live mostly in the coastal province of Esmeraldas and in neighbouring Imbabura, and are descended from slaves who were brought from Africa in the 18th century to work on coastal plantations. Although the slave trade was abolished in 1821, slavery itself continued until 1852. Even then, freedom was not guaranteed until the system of debt tenancy was ended in 1881, and slaves could at last leave the plantations. However, the social status of Ecuador's blacks remains low and most of them still work on banana plantations or in other types of agriculture. Furthermore, they suffer from poor education and the racism endemic in all levels of society.

Racism in Ecuador is not solely aimed at black people, but Indians in general. Its roots run deep and some whites and *mestizos* still view Indians as second-class citizens, but attitudes are gradually changing.

Background

Religion

According to official statistics, 93% of the population belongs to the Roman Catholic faith and the church remains a formidable force in society. In recent decades a variety of Evangelical Protestant groups from the US, Seventh-Day Adventists, Mormons and Jehovah's Witnesses, have increased their influence. Freedom of worship is guaranteed by the Ecuadorean constitution.

Arts and crafts

Ecuador is a shopper's paradise. Everywhere you turn there's some particularly seductive piece of *artesanía* being offered. This word loosely translates as handicrafts, but that doesn't really do them justice. The indigenous peoples make no distinction between fine arts and crafts, so *artesanía* are valued as much for their practical use as their beauty.

Panama hats   Most people don't even know that the Panama hat, Ecuador's most famous export, comes from Ecuador. The confusion over the origin of this natty piece of headwear dates back over 100 years.

Until the 20th century, the Isthmus of Panama was the quickest and safest seafaring route to Europe and North America and the major trading post for South American goods, including the straw hats from Ecuador. In the mid 19th century, at the height of the California gold rush, would-be prospectors heading west to seek their fortune picked up the straw hats. Half a century later, when work on the Panama Canal was in full swing, labourers found the hats ideal protection against the fierce tropical sun and, like the golddiggers before them, named them after the place they were sold rather than where they originated. The name stuck and, much to Ecuador's eternal chagrin, the name of the Panama Hat was born.

The plant from which these stylish titfers is made – *Carludovica Palmata* – grows best in the low hills north and west of Guayaquil. The hats are woven from the very fine fronds of the plant, which are boiled, then dried in the sun before being taken to the various weaving centres – Montecristi and Jipijapa in Manabí, and Azogues, Biblián and Sigsíg in Azuay. Montecristi, though, enjoys the reputation of producing the best *superfinos*. These are Panama hats of the highest quality, requiring up to three months work. They are tightly woven, using the thinnest, lightest straw. When turned upside down they should hold water as surely as a glass, and when rolled up, should be able to pass through a wedding ring.

From the weaver, the hat passes to a middleman, who then sells it on to the factory. The loose ends are trimmed, the hat is bleached and the brim ironed into shape and then softened with a mallet. The hat is then rolled into a cone and wrapped in paper in a balsawood box ready for exporting. The main export centre, and site of most of the factories, is Cuenca, where countless shops also sell the *sombreros de paja toquilla*, as they are known locally, direct to tourists.

Weavers of   During Inca times, textiles held pride of place, and things are no different today.
Otavalo   Throughout the highlands beautiful woven textiles are still produced, often using techniques unchanged for centuries. One of the main weaving centres is Otavalo, which is a nucleus of trade for more than 75 scattered Otavaleño communities, and home of the famous handicrafts market which attracts tourists in their thousands.

The history of weaving in Otavalo goes back to the time of conquest when the Spanish instead exploited the country's human resources through the feudal system of *encomiendas* (see History, page 428). A textile workshop (*obraje*) was soon established in Otavalo using forced indigenous labour. *Obrajes* were also set up elsewhere in the region, for example in Peguche and Cotacachi, using technology exported from Europe: the spinning wheel and treadle loom. These are still in use today.

Though the *encomiendas* were eventually abolished, they were replaced by the equally infamous *huasipungo* system, which rendered the indigenous people virtual serfs on the large *haciendas* that were created. Many of these estates continued to operate weaving workshops, producing cloth in huge quantities for commercial purposes.

The textile industry as it is known today was started in 1917 when weaving techniques and styles from Scotland were introduced to the native workers on the Hacienda Cusín. These proved successful in the national market and soon spread to other families and villages in the surrounding area. The development of the industry received a further boost with the ending of the *huasipungo* system in 1964. The *indígenas* were granted title to their plots of land, allowing them to weave at home.

Today, weaving in Otavalo is almost exclusively for the tourist and export trades by which it is quite naturally influenced. Alongside traditional local motifs, are found many designs from as far afield as Argentina and Guatemala. The Otavaleños are not only renowned for their skilled weaving, but also for their considerable success as traders. They travel extensively, to Colombia, Venezuela, North America and as far afield as Europe, in search of new markets for their products. As these begin to saturate, Otavaleños are now beginning to peddle their wares in Asia.

Woodcarving

During the colonial era, uses of woodcarving were extended to provide the church with carved pieces to adorn the interiors of its many fine edifices. Wealthy families also commissioned work such as benches and chairs, mirrors and huge *barqueños* (chests) to decorate their salons.

In the 16th and 17th centuries woodcarvers from Spain settled north of Quito, where San Antonio de Ibarra has become the largest and most important woodcarving centre in South America.

Initially the *mudéjar*, or Spanish-Moorish styles, were imported to the New World, but as the workshops of San Antonio spread north to Colombia and south to Chile and Argentina, they evolved their own styles. Today, everyone in San Antonio is involved with woodcarving and almost every shop sells carved wooden figures, or will make items to order.

Bags

Plant fibre is used not only for weaving but is also sewn into fabric for bags and other articles. *Mochilas* (bags) are used throughout the continent as everyday holdalls.

In Cotopaxi province, *shigras*, which are bags made from sisal, were originally used to store dry foodstuffs around the home. It is said that very finely woven ones were even used to carry water from the wells, the fibres swelling when wet to make the bags impermeable. These bags almost died out with the arrival of plastic containers, until Western demands ensured that the art survived. *Shigras* can be found at the market in Salcedo (early in the mourning) and are also re-sold at tourist shops throughout the country.

Like the small backstrap looms and drop spindles of the Andes, the bags are portable and can be sewn while women are herding animals in the fields. Today, women's production is often organized by suppliers who provide dyed fibres for sewing and later buy the bags to sell. A large, blunt needle is used to sew the strong fibres and the finished article is likely to last a lot longer than the user.

Bread figures

The inhabitants of the town of Calderón, northeast of Quito, know how to make dough. The main street is lined with shops selling the vibrantly-coloured figures made of flour and water which have become hugely popular in recent years.

The origins of this practice are traced back to the small dolls made of bread for the annual celebrations of All Soul's Day. The original edible figures, made in wooden moulds in the village bakery, were decorated with a simple cross over the chest in red, green and black, and were placed in cemeteries as offerings to the hungry souls of the dead. Gradually, different types of figures appeared and people started giving them as gifts for children and friends. Special pieces are still made for All Soul's Day, such as donkeys and men and women in traditional costume.

Primitivist paintings
In the province of Cotopaxi, near Zumbahua and the Quilotoa crater, a regional craft has developed specifically in response to tourist demand. It is the production of 'primitivist' paintings on leather, now carried out by many of the area's residents, depicting typical rural or village scenes and even current events. Following the volcanic eruptions of 1999, these began to figure prominently in the Tigua paintings – named after the town where the work originated. The paintings vary in price and quality and are now also widely available in Quito, Otavalo and other tourist destinations.

Andean dress pins
The dress of pre-Hispanic women in the Andean region consisted basically of the *urku*, the *lliclla* and the *chumpi*, or belt. The *urku*, the principal vestment, was a large rectangular cloak which covered the woman from her shoulders to her feet in the manner of a tunic. It was fastened at shoulder level with a pair of metal *tupu* and at the waist with a belt.

This garb was widely used in rural areas up until about 100 years ago, and survives today in a shortened and modified form. The *lliclla* was the outermost shawl, which covered the shoulders and was fastened at the chest with a single pin or a smaller clasp called a *ttipqui*. This garment is still worn today in the rural Andean world, although it is slowly being replaced by other western-style items of clothing.

Tupu and *ttipqui* are the ancient Quechua names for the two types of dress pins, but today all metal pins used by Indian women to fasten their clothing are known as *topos*, which is a Castellanization of the Quechua word *tupu*.

The use of the *tupu* and *ttipqui* is thought to have spread North from the Huari-Tiahuanuco empire throughout the entire Andean region. The first dress pins were simply cactus spines or carved from thin pieces of wood and of a strictly functional nature. However, the development of metallurgy allowed artesans to make the pins from metal, at first hammering gold and silver, and later through the smelting and moulding of copper.

Music and dance

Culturally, ethnically and geographically, Ecuador is very much two countries – the Andean highlands with their centre at Quito and the northern Pacific lowlands behind Guayaquil. In spite of this, the music is relatively homogeneous and it is the Andean music that would be regarded as 'typically Ecuadorean'.

The principal highland rhythms are the Sanjuanito, Cachullapi, Albaza, Yumbo and Danzante, danced by Indian and mestizo alike. These may be played by brass bands, guitar trios or groups of wind instruments, but it is the *rondador*, a small panpipe, that provides the classic Ecuadorean sound, although of late the Peruvian *quena* has been making heavy inroads via pan-Andean groups and has become a threat to the local instrument.

The coastal region has its own song form, the Amorfino, but the most genuinely 'national' song and dance genres, both of European origin, are the Pasillo (shared with Colombia) in waltz time and the Pasacalle, similar to the Spanish Pasodoble. Of Ecuador's three best loved songs, 'El Chulla Quiteño', 'Romántico Quito' and 'Vasija de Barro', the first two are both Pasacalles. Even the Ecuadorean mestizo music has a melancholy quality not found in Peruvian 'Música Criolla', perhaps due to Quito being in the mountains, while Lima is on the coast.

Music of the highland Indian communities is, as elsewhere in the region, related to religious feasts and ceremonies and geared to wind instruments such as the *rondador*, the *pinkullo* and *pifano* flutes and the great long *guarumo* horn with its mournful note.

The guitar is also usually present and brass bands with well worn instruments can be found in even the smallest villages. Among the best known musical groups who have recorded are Los Embajadores (whose 'Tormentos' is superb), and the duo Benítez-Valencia for guitar-accompanied vocal harmony, Ñanda-Mañachi and the Conjunto Peguche (both from Otavalo) for highland Indian music and Jatari and Huayanay for pan-Andean music.

There is one totally different cultural area, that of the black inhabitants of the Province of Esmeraldas and the highland valley of the Río Chota in Imbabura. The former is a southern extension of the Colombian Pacific coast negro culture, centred round the marimba, a huge wooden xylophone. The musical genres are also shared with black Colombians, including the Bunde, Bambuco, Caderona, Torbellino and Currulao dances and this music is some of the most African sounding in the whole of South America. The Chota Valley is an inverted oasis of desert in the Andes and here the black people dance the Bomba. It is also home to the unique Bandas Muchas, whose primitive instruments include leaves that are doubled over and blown through.

Festivals

Festivals are an intrinsic part of Ecuadorean life. In pre-Hispanic times they were organized around the solar cycle and agricultural calendar. After the conquest, the church integrated the indigenous festivals with their own feast days and so today's festivals are a mix of Roman Catholicism and indigenous traditions. Every community in every part of the country celebrates their own particular festival in honour of their patron saint and there are many more that are celebrated in common up and down the country, particularly in the Sierra.

Carnival Carnival is held in February or March during the week before Lent and ends on Ash Wednesday. While the Ecuadorean version can't rival that of Brazil for fame or colour, Ecuador has its own carnival speciality: throwing balloons filled with water or, less frequently, bags of flour and any other missile guaranteed to cause a mess. Water pistols are sold on every street corner at this time of year and even the odd bucket gets put to use. It can take visitors aback at first, but if you can keep your composure or – better yet – join in the mayhem, it can all be good fun. For the more sensitive tourist, there is the option of heading to Ambato, one hour south of Quito, where water-throwing is banned and flour is replaced by flowers at the city's *Fiesta de las Frutas y las Flores*.

Holy week The next major event of the festival calendar is Holy Week, or *Semana Santa*, which is held the week before Easter and begins on Palm Sunday (*Domingo de Ramos*). This is celebrated throughout the country, but is especially dramatic in Quito, where there is a spectacularly solemn procession through the streets on Good Friday. A particularly important part of Holy Week is the tradition of eating *fanesca* with family and friends. *Fanesca* is a soup made with salt fish and many different grains, and a good example of the syncretism of Catholic and earlier beliefs. In this case the Catholic component is the lack of meat, which was not consumed during Lent, while the many grains came from native traditions to celebrate the beginning of the harvest at this time of year.

Summer & autumn *Corpus Cristi* is a feast held on Thursday after Trinity Sunday, usually in mid-June. This is a major event in the central highlands, especially in the provinces of Cotopaxi and Tungurahua, but also in Chimborazo province and in Saraguro and Loja. In Salasaca (Tungurahua) the festival is celebrated with music, dance and elaborate costumes, while in Pujilí (Cotopaxi) groups of masked *danzantes* make their way through the streets and the valiant climb *palos encebados*, 10 m-high greased poles, in order to obtain prizes.

San Juan Bautista takes place on 24 June and is the main festival of the Otavalo valley. For an entire week, the local men dress up in a variety of costumes and dance constantly, moving from house to house. At one point, they head to the chapel of San Juan and start throwing rocks at each other, so keep your distance. This ritual spilling of blood is apparently a sacrifice to *Pachamama*, or Mother Earth.

Another major fiesta in Imbabura province is *San Pedro y San Pablo* (Saints Peter and Paul). This is held on 29 June, but the night before bonfires are lit in the streets and young women who want to have children are supposed to jump over the fires. This festival is particularly important in Cotacachi and Cayambe, and is also celebrated in southern Chimborazo, in Alausi and Achupallas.

Other important festivals include *Virgen del Carmen*, on 16 July, with the biggest celebrations going on in Cuenca and in Chambo, just outside Riobamba. *La Virgen de la Merced*, on 24 September, is a big festival in Latacunga, where a man dressed as *La Mama Negra*, the black mother, dances through the streets.

Day of the Dead One of the most important dates in the indigenous people's calendar is 2 November, Day of the Dead (*Día de los Difuntos* or *Finados*). This tradition has been practised since time immemorial. In the Incaic calendar, November was the eighth month and meant *Ayamarca*, or land of the dead. The celebration is another example of religious adaptation in which the ancient beliefs of ethnic cultures are mixed with the rites of the Catholic Church.

According to ancient belief, the spirit visits its relatives at this time of the year and is fed in order to continue its journey before its reincarnation. The relatives of the dead prepare for the arrival of the spirit days in advance. Among the many items necessary for these meticulous preparations are little bread dolls, each one of which has a particular significance. Horse-shaped breads are prepared that will serve as a means of transport for the soul in order to avoid fatigue.

Inside the home, the relatives construct a tomb supported by boxes over which is laid a black cloth. Here they put the bread, along with various other items important in the ritual. The tomb is also adorned with the dead relative's favourite food and drink. Most households also share a glass of *colada morada*, a syrupy, purple-coloured drink made from various fruits and purple corn. Once the spirit has arrived and feasted with their living relatives, the entire ceremony is then transported to the graveside in the local cemetery, where it is carried out again, along with the many other mourning families.

This meeting of the living and their dead relatives is re-enacted the following year, though less ostentatiously, and again for the final time in the third year, the year of the farewell. It does not continue after this, which is just as well as the costs can be crippling for the family concerned. Today, such elaborate celebrations are rare and most Ecuadoreans commemorate *Día de los Difuntos* in more prosaic fashion; by visiting the cemetery and placing flowers at the graveside of their deceased relatives.

Christmas Among the local Christmas (*Navidad*) celebrations is the *Pase del Niño* (procession of the child). On Christmas Eve all families which possess a statue of the baby Jesus carry them in procession to the local church, where they are blessed during a special Mass. The most famous *Pase del Niño* is in Cuenca on the morning of 24 December. Other notable celebrations take place in Saraguro, in Loja province, in Pujilí and Tanicuchí in Cotopaxi province and throughout the province of Cañar.

New Year A typically Ecuadorean aspect of New Year's celebrations are the *años viejos* (literally 'old years'), life-size effigies or puppets which are constructed and displayed throughout the country on 31 December. They usually depict politicians or other prominent local, national or international personalities and important events of the year gone by.

Children dressed in black are the old year's widows, and beg for alms: candy or coins. Just before midnight the *años viejo's* will is read, full of satire, and at the stroke of midnight the effigies are doused with gasoline and burned, wiping out the old year and all that it had brought with it. In addition to sawdust, the *años viejos* usually contain a few firecrackers making for an exciting finale; best keep your distance.

Outsiders are usually welcome at all but the most intimate and spiritual of celebrations and, as a *gringo*, you might even be a guest of honour. Ecuadoreans can be very sensitive however and you should make every effort not to offend (for example by not taking a ceremony seriously or by refusing food, drink or an invitation to dance). At the same time, you should keep in mind that most *fiestas* are accompanied by heavy drinking and the resulting disinhibition is not always pleasant. It is best to enjoy the usually solemn beginning of most celebrations as well as the liveliness which follows, but politely depart before things get totally out of control.

Appropriate behaviour

Literature

Much Ecuadorean literature has reflected political issues such as the rivalry between Liberals and Conservatives and between Costa and Sierra, and the position of the Indian and the marginalized in society, and many of the country's writers have adopted a strongly political line. Among the earliest were Francisco Eugenio de Santa Cruz y Espejo, who led a rebellion against Spain in 1795, José Joaquín de Olmedo, Federico González Suárez (archbishop of Quito) and Juan Montalvo.

José Joaquín de Olmedo (born Guayaquil 1780, died 1847) was a disciple of Espejo and was heavily involved first in the independence movement and then the formative years of the young republic. In 1825 he published *La Victoria de Junín, Canto a Bolívar*, a heroic poem glorifying the Liberator. His second famous poem was the *Canto al General Flores, Al Vencedor de Miñarica* (Juan José Flores was the Venezuelan appointed by Bolívar to govern Ecuador). In addition to poetry, Olmedo wrote political works such as *Discurso sobre las mitas* and *Manifiesto político sobre la Revolución del Seis de Marzo*.

The 19th century

Juan **Montalvo** (born Ambato 1832, died 1889) was an essayist who was influenced by French Romantics such as Victor Hugo and Lamartine, also by Lord Byron and by Cervantes. One of his main objectives as a writer was to attack what he saw as the failings of Ecuador's rulers, but his position as a liberal, in opposition to conservatism such as García Moreno's, encompassed a passionate opposition to all injustice. 'Ojeada sobre América', for instance (in *El cosmopólita*, 1866-68), is a diatribe against the 'natural law' of man, namely war and killing. Other collections of essays included *Los siete tratados* (1881-82) and *El espectador* (1886), in which he wrote, "If my pen had the gift of tears, I would write a book called *The Indian*, which would make the whole world weep." He never wrote that book. His *Capítulos que se le olvidaron a Cervantes* (1895) was an attempt to imitate the creator of Don Quijote, translating him into an Ecuadorean setting.

Montalvo's contemporary and enemy, **Juan León Mera** (born Ambato 1832, died 1894), did write a book about the Indian, *Cumandá* (1979). But this dealt not so much with the humiliated Sierra Indians as the unsubjugated Amazonian Indians, 'los errantes y salvajes hijos de las selvas' (the wandering and savage sons of the jungles). The book has provoked much debate, which has revolved around the concepts of civilization and barbarism, how colonialism leads to exploitation, but also the value of using nature and the 'savage' solely for ideological ends so that characters are reduced to nothing more than symbols.

Background

The 20th century In 1904, **Luis A Martínez** (1869-1909) published *A la costa*, which attempts to present two very different sides of the country (the coast and the highlands) and the different customs and problems in each. *Plata y bronce* (1927) and *La embrujada* (1923), both by **Fernando Chávez**, portray the gulf between the white and the Indian communities. In their distinct ways, the two writers moved beyond León Mera's use of an Ecuadorean setting for a Christian Romantic theme (shared, for example, by Chateaubriand in France – *René*) to books which are just Ecuadorean.

For the next 15-20 years, novelists in Ecuador produced a realist literature heavily influenced by French writers like Emile Zola and Maupassant, Russians like Gorki and the North Americans Sinclair Lewis, Dos Passos, John Steinbeck and Ernest Hemingway. This was realism at the expense of beauty. They wrote politically committed stories about marginalized people in crude language and stripped-down prose.

The first indication of this radically different prose was *Los que se van*, a collection of stories by **Joaquín Gallegos Lara** (1911-47), **Enrique Gil Gilbert** (1912-75) and **Demetrio Aguilera Malta** (1909-81). These stories created a scandal. They describe incidents in the lives of poor people whose own violence and sexual passions bring about their tragedy. Their dialect is transcribed faithfully, adding to the realism. Interestingly, *Los que se van* initiated a movement of protest literature without actually denouncing anyone or anything. The stories deal with social injustice, but in isolated, extreme cases.

Along with two other writers, **José de la Cuadra** (1903-41) and **Alfredo Pareja Diezcanseco** (1908-93), they formed the Grupo de Guayaquil. A sixth member, **Adalberto Ortiz** (born 1914), joined later. Among the books of these writers are: Gallegos Lara, *Las cruces sobre el agua* (novel, 1946); Gil Gilbert, *Yunga* (stories, 1933), *Nuestro pan* (novel, 1941); Aguilera Malta, the novels *Don Goyo* (1933), *Canal zone* (1935), *La isla virgen* (1942), *La caballeresa del sol* (1964), *Siete lunas y siete serpientes* (1970) and *El secuestro del General* (1973); de la Cuadra, many short stories, *Repisas* (1931), *Horno* (1934), and the novels *Los sangurimas* (1934), *Guasinto* (1938) and *Los monos enloquecidos* (1951). Pareja Diezcanseco's novels are concerned more with urban themes than the stories of his colleagues, for example *El muelle* (1933, set in Guayaquil and New York), *Baldomera* (1938), *Hombres sin tiempo* (1941), *Las tres ratas* (1944). He also wrote a group of books under the general title of *Los años nuevos* (including *La advertencia*, 1956, *El aire y los recuerdos*, 1959, *Los poderes omnímodos*, 1964) which show him breaking away from the Guayaquil Group, taking as his starting point the political events of 9 July 1925 and the founding of the Socialist Party. With *Las pequeñas estaturas* (1970) and *La mantíncora* (1974) he became more experimental with narrative forms, while introducing more imaginative material into the same historical lines. Adalberto Ortiz was born in Esmeraldas: his novel *Juyungo* (1943) relates the life of a black/Indian of that region. He also wrote *El espejo y la ventana* (1967), *La envoltura del sueño* (1981) and is a poet.

A slightly later Guayaquileño writer is **Pedro Jorge Vera** (1914-99), author of poetry in the 1930s and 1940s and novels such as *Los animales puros* (1946), *La semilla estéril* (1962), *Tiempo de muñecos* (1971) and *El pueblo soy yo* (1976), about Velasco Ibarra.

Of the writers of the 1930s and 1940s, outside Guayaquil, **Pablo Palacio** (1906-47) described himself as an observer. Besides the stories of *Un hombre muerto a puntapies* and *Débora* (1927), his best known book is *Vida del ahorcado* (1932), which is described as one of the rare cries of existential anguish in Ecuadorean literature.

A contemporary group, from Cuenca and Loja, included **Angel F Rojas** (born 1910), a poet and novelist closely associated with the Grupo de Guayaquil (*Banca*, 1940, *Un idiolo bobo* – short stories, 1946, *El éxodo de Yangana*, 1949), **G Humberto Mata** (1904-88), writer of the indigenist novels *Sal* (1963), *Sumac-Allpa* and *Sanagüín*, and **Alfonso Cuesta y Cuesta** (1912-1991), another writer concerned with indigenist themes and social comment (*Los hijos*, 1962).

The writing on the wall

One of Ecuador's great writers, Jorge Enrique Adoum, once wrote: "Here the only way to get read is by writing on the walls and door of the toilet". The people of Quito have certainly taken that opinion to heart. Graffiti now seems to pervade almost every part of Quito and the city's cultural élite are proud of this phenomenon. The Institute of Culture even published a book with hundreds of examples recorded for posterity.

The sentiments expressed vary from outrage and bitterness to irony and humour and cover everything from existential philosophy to environmental issues. One example warns: 'Forget your dreams, your dreams were sold'. *Another offers the rather pertinent advice:* 'Help the police - torture yourself'. *Disenchantment with the government's economic policies wrought:* 'Country with ocean view for sale, inquire at the Presidential Palace'. *On a more humorous note is:* 'Blessed are the alcoholics, for they shall see God twice'.

Quito's many graffiti poets belong to permanent groups, each with its own 'signature', and most of them are students from wealthy or middle-class families, venting their frustrations at the country's social injustices.

Another group of famous writers, from Quito, were **Fernando Chávez** (born 1902; see above), **Humberto Salvador** (1909-82 – *Camarada*, 1933; *Trabajadores*, 1935; *Noviembre*, 1939) and **Jorge Icaza** (1906-78). Icaza's novel of 1934, *Huasipungo*, has been described as "the most controversial novel in the history of Latin American narrative". Unlike some indigenist fiction (basically, writing about the Latin American Indian, especially in Peru and Bolivia), there is absolutely no attempt to portray the life of the Sierra Indians as anything other than brutal, inhuman, violent and hopeless. Even the landscape – cold, muddy, drenched in rain – has none of the beauty that is frequently the background to indigenist writing. The book has aroused much anger, either at the Indians' plight, or at Icaza's motives as a novelist. He wrote many other novels, among them *En las calles* (1935), *Cholos* (1938), *Media vida deslumbrados* (1942) and *Huairapamuchcas* (1948), but none achieved the fame of *Huasipungo*.

The 1960s ushered in the so-called Boom, with writers such as Gabriel García Márquez, Mario Vargas Llosa, Carlos Fuentes and Julio Cortázar gaining international recognition for the Latin American novel. At the same time, the Ecuadorean poet, essayist and novelist, **Jorge Enrique Adoum** (born 1923), wrote *Entre Marx y una mujer desnuda* (1976). This extraordinary novel is a dense investigation of itself, of novel-writing, of Marxism and politics, sex, love and Ecuador, loosely based around the story of the writer and his friends in a writing group, their loves and theorizing. Adoum has also written *Ciudad sin angel* (1995), plays (eg *El sol bajo las patas de los caballos* – 1972) and several collections of poetry, which is also intense and inventive (see, for example, *No son todos los que están, 1949-79*).

Of note among contemporary novelists are: **Nelson Estupiñán Bass** (1912-2002) who, in many of his works, has concentrated on *negritude* (black people, their culture and lack of rights): *Cuando los guayacanes florecían* (1954), *Al norte de Dios* (1994); Abdón Ubidia (born 1944, *Ciudad de invierno*, 1984; *Sueño de lobos*, 1986; and short story collections *Divertinventos*, 1989, and *El palacio de los espejos*, 1996); **Eliécer Cárdenas Espinosa** (born 1950), who has written many novels, including *Polvo y ceniza* (1978) and *Diario de un idolatra* (1991), short stories such as *Siempre se mira al cielo* (1988) and *La incompleta hermosura* (1997) and the play *Morir en Vilcabamba* (1990); **Miguel Donoso Pareja**, whose novels include *Henry Black* (1969) and *Hoy empiezo a acordarme* (1994), also short stories, *El hombre que mataba a sus hijos* (1968) and *Todo lo que inventamos es cierto* (1990), poetry and essays. **Alicia Yáñez Cossío** (born 1929) is one of Ecuador's best known writers. She has written nine novels, such as *Bruna Soroche y los tíos* (1972), *La casa del sano placer* (1989, described as a satire of traditional sexual norms) and, most recently *Y amarle pude...* (2000) and *Sé que vienen a matarme* (2001). She also writes short stories, plays and children's stories. Lucrecia Maldonado (born 1962) is a short story writer with a growing reputation: *No es el amor quien muere* (1994) and *Mi sombra te ha de hacer falta* (1998).

20th-century poetry   In *Lírica ecuatoriana contemporánea* (two volumes, Quito 1979), Hernán Rodríguez Castelo says that a generation of powerful lyric poets was born between 1890 and 1905. This included modernists like **Ernesto Noboa y Caamaño** and **José María Egas**, and many post-modernists. Among this second group were **Miguel Angel Zambrano** (1898-1969, *Diálogo de los seres profundos*, 1956), **Gonzalo Escudero** (1903-71, *Estatua del aire, Materia de ángel, Autorretrato, Introducción a la muerte*, written in the 1950s and 1960s), **Alfredo Gangotena** (1904-44, *Poesía*, 1956) and **Aurora Estrada y Ayala** (born 1901-67, *Como el incienso*, 1925).

The major figure, perhaps of all Ecuadorean poetry, was **Jorge Carrera Andrade** (1903-78). Son of a liberal lawyer, Carrera Andrade was involved in socialist politics in the 1920s before going to Europe. In the 1930s and 1940s, Carrera Andrade moved beyond the socialist realist, revolutionary stance of his contemporaries and of his own earlier views, seeking instead to explore universal themes. His first goal was to write beautiful poetry. He published many volumes, including the haiku-like *Microgramas*; see *Registro del mundo: antología poética* (1922-39), *El alba llama a la puerta* (1965-66), *Misterios naturales* and others. See also *Selected Poems*, translated by H R Hayes, Albany, New York, 1972, and *Winds of Exile* by Peter R Beardsell, Oxford, 1977.

From the 1940s onwards, many groups were writing in different parts of the country. A poet who was a major link between Carrera Andrade's generation and the new writers was **César Dávila Andrade** (1919-67: *Oda al arquitecto*, 1946; *Catedral salvaje*, 1951; *Arco de instantes*, 1959; *En un lugar no identificado*, 1963; *Materia real*, 1970). He was a member of the Madrugada group, as were **Enrique Noboa Arízaga** (*Orbita de la púpila iluminada*, 1947; *Biografía atlántida*, 1967) and **Jorge Crespo Toral**. There were two groups called Elan, in Cuenca and Quito. Other Quito groups were Presencia (eg **Francisco Granizo Ribadeneira** – born 1928, *Muerte y caza de la madre*, 1978; **Gonzalo Pesántez Reinoso**, *Palabras*, 1951), Umbral (1952, including **Alicia Yáñez Cossió**) and Caminos, whose stated concern was for the Ecuadorean people, denouncing social disorder. In Guayaquil in the 1950s the Club 7 de Poesía included **David Ledesma**, **Gastón Hidalgo Ortega**, **Sergio Román Armendáriz** and **Alvaro San Félix** (1931-99), both also playwrights, and **Ileana Espinel** (1933-2001), whose introspective, bitter poems confronted the meaninglessness of the 20th century human condition (see *Poemas escogidas*, 1978).

In the heat of the Cuban Revolution, Los Tzántzicos formed in Quito in 1961. They used shock tactics with direct, anti-bourgeois poetry, inciting people to revolution. A chief enemy was the conformist Caminos group. Some of the Quito Tzántzicos were **Abdón Ubidia** (see above), **Iván Egüez** (poet and novelist, born 1944 – see the novels *Los Linares* – 1975, *Pájara la memoria* and *El poder del gran señor* – both 1985, and poetry *Calibre catapulta* – 1969, *Libre amor* – 1999), **Rafael Larrea** (born 1943) and **Raúl Arias** (born 1944). In Guayaquil several writers followed the same line, notably **Sonia Manzano** (born 1947). As well as poems (from *El nudo y el trino*, 1972, to *Patente de corza*, 1997) she has written the novel *Y no abras la ventana todavía* (1994) and short stories. Many schools and workshops continue to promote poetry in Ecuador, notably the Centro Internacional de Estudios Poéticos del Ecuador (CIEPE), which has published collections like *Poemas de luz y ternura* (Quito 1993).

Bibliographical note   Many sources have been used in the preparation of this brief survey. Apart from books quoted in the text above, mention should be made of: Jorge

Enrique Adoum, *La gran literatura ecuatoriana del 30* (Quito: El Conejo, 1984); Benjamín Carrión, *El pensamiento vivo de Montalvo* (Buenos Aires: Losada, 1961); Jean Franco, *Spanish American Literature since Independence* (London, New York: Benn, 1973); Karl H Heise, *El Grupo de Guayaquil* (Madrid: Nova Scholar, 1975); Gerald Martin, *Journeys through the Labyrinth* (London, New York: Verso, 1989); Antonio Sacoto, *Catorce novelas claves de la literatura ecuatoriana* (Cuenca: 1990) and *The Indian in the Ecuadorean Novel* (New York: Las Americas, 1967); Darío Villanueva y José María Viña Liste, *Trayectoria de la novela hispanoamericana actual* (Madrid: Austral, 1991); Jason Wilson, *Traveller's Literary Companion: South and Central America* (Brighton: In Print, 1993). See also *Diez cuentistas ecuatorianos*, Libri Mundi, 1993, and the websites www.literaturaecuatoriana.com and www.wabash.edu/depart/lang/ecuador/literatura.html

Fine art and sculpture

Colonial Quito was a flourishing centre of artistic production, exporting works to many other regions of Spanish South America. The origins of this trade date back to the year of the Spanish foundation of Quito, 1534, when the Franciscans established a college to train Indians in European arts and crafts. Two Flemish friars, **Jodoco Ricke** and **Pedro Gosseal**, are credited with teaching a generation of Indians how to paint the pictures and carve the sculptures and altarpieces that were so urgently needed by the many newly-founded churches and monasteries in the region.

16th & 17th centuries

The college's success, based on the Franciscans' liberal attitude towards the Indians, became a political issue and in 1581 control was transferred to the Augustinians. By that time, however, Quito had an established population of indigenous craftsmen, and the legacy of the first Franciscan college is confirmed in the interior of San Francisco itself, lavishly furnished with 16th and early 17th century altarpieces, paintings and decorative carving. The influence of the ideology of the 16th century Franciscan missionary friars, their taste for images of ascetic penitent saints and badly wounded Christs, their fondness for theological allegory, and their devotion to the Virgin of the Immaculate Conception, can be discerned in religious art until the 19th century and beyond.

As well as the initial Flemish bias of the first Franciscans, stylistic influences on the Quito school came from Spain, particularly from the strong Andalucian sculptural tradition. Quito churches preserve several works imported from Seville in the later 16th and early 17th century which served as models for local craftsmen, and there are records of Quiteñan craftsmen going to Spain to broaden their experience, but few Spanish craftsmen emigrated to Ecuador. The Toledan **Diego de Robles** (died 1594), who worked in Madrid and Seville before arriving in Quito in 1584, is an exception, important not so much for the quality of his few surviving works but because the workshop he ran together with the painter **Luis de Ribera** provided the expertise in the techniques of painted and gilded statuary for which Quito was to become so famous.

Colonial painting was as much influenced by Italy as by Spain. An important early figure in this was the Quito-born mestizo **Pedro Bedón** (1556-1621). Educated in Lima where he probably had contact with the Italian painter Bernardo Bitti, Bedón returned home to combine the duties of Dominican priest with work as a painter. He is best-known for his illuminated manuscripts, where his decorated initials include all manner of grotesque heads, but he also established a religious brotherhood attached to the church of Santo Domingo whose membership included many of the painters trained by the Franciscans, where the influence of his slightly archaic Italian manner was considerable.

Indigenous influence is not immediately apparent in painting or sculpture despite the fact that so much of it was produced by Indians. The features of Christ, the Virgin and saints are European, but in sculpture the proportions of the bodies are often distinctly Andean: broad-chested and short-legged. This is especially true of figures of

Background

Christ, such as the anonymous late 17th-century *Ecce homo* in the San Francisco museum. In both painting and sculpture the taste – so characteristic of colonial art in the Andes – for patterns in gold applied over the surface of garments may perhaps be related to the high value accorded to textiles in pre-conquest times.

Important names in the field of 17th-century colonial sculpture include the shadowy **Padre Carlos**, active between 1620 and 1680, to whom is attributed the bleeding and emaciated San Pedro de Alcántara in the Franciscan chapel of the Cantuña. **José Olmos**, known as **Pampite**, also very poorly documented but perhaps a pupil of Padre Carlos, produced gory crucifixions, including one in the church of San Francisco and one now in the Museo del Banco Central where Christ's wounds are more like suppurating sores, contrasting starkly with the pale shiny flesh.

In painting the mestizo, **Miguel de Santiago** (died 1706) represents a break from the Italian mannerist style of Bedón. In 1656 he produced a monumental series of canvases on the Life of St Augustine for the Augustinian cloister based on engravings by the Flemish Schelte de Bolswert, but with local settings. He later devised a set of eight ingeniously complex allegories on the theme of Christian Doctrine for the Franciscans, which can be seen in the Museo de San Francisco. Santiago's daughter **Isabel** and nephew **Nicolás de Goríbar** (active 1685-1736) were also painters, influenced by the chiaroscuro of earlier Spanish artists – particularly Zurbarán and Murillo.

18th century Representations of the Virgin are very common, especially that of the Virgin Immaculate, patron of the Franciscans and of the city of Quito. This curious local version of the Immaculate Conception represents the Virgin standing on a serpent and crescent moon as tradition dictates, but unconventionally supplied with a pair of wings. It was popularized by Miguel de Santiago in the mid-17th century (Museo del Banco Central) perhaps with earlier roots, and is best known from the modern monument on the Panecillo hill, while 18th-century carved versions survive in churches throughout Ecuador.

The prolific **Bernardo de Legarda** (died 1773) was responsible for many of these including that on the high altar of San Francisco (1734), a lively, dancing figure with swirling robes. The theatricality of 18th-century Quiteñan sculpture is evident in Legarda's tableau in the old Carmelite convent (Carmen Alto) depicting the death of the Virgin, where 16 life-size free-standing figures of saints and angels mourn at the bedside.

In the later 18th century the sculptor **Manuel Chili**, known to his contemporaries as Caspicara 'the pockmarked', continued the tradition of polychrome images with powerful emotional appeal ranging from the dead Christ (examples in the Museo del Banco Central) to sweet-faced Virgins and chubby infant Christs (Museo de San Francisco). Outside Quito the best-known sculptor was **Gaspar Sangurima** of Cuenca who was still producing vividly realistic polychrome crucifixions in the early 19th century (example in the Carmen de la Asunción, Cuenca). After the declaration of Independence in 1822 Bolívar appointed him Director of the first School of Fine Arts, so confirming Cuenca's importance as a centre of artistic activity, an importance the city retains to this day.

Painting in the later 18th century is dominated by the much lighter, brighter palette of **Manuel Samaniego** (died 1824), author of a treatise on painting which includes instructions on the correct human proportions and Christian iconography, as well as details of technical procedures and recipes for paint.

Independence & after As elsewhere in Latin America, the struggle for Independence created a demand for subjects of local and national significance and portraits of local heroes. **Antonio Salas** (1795-1860) became the unofficial portrait painter of the Independence movement. His paintings of heroes, military leaders and notable churchmen can be seen in Quito's Museo Jijón y Caamaño. Antonio's son, **Rafael Salas** (1828-1906), was among those to make the Ecuadorean landscape a subject of nationalist pride, as in his famous birds-eye view of Quito sheltering below its distinctive family of mountain peaks (private collection).

Rafael Salas and other promising young artists of the later 19th century, including **Luis Cadena** (1830-89) and **Juan Manosalvas** (1840-1906), studied in Europe, returning to develop a style of portraiture which brings together both the European rediscovery of 17th-century Dutch and Spanish art and Ecuador's own conservative artistic tradition where the tenebrism of Zurbarán and his contemporaries had never been forgotten. They also brought back from their travels a new appreciation of the customs and costumes of their own country. The best-known exponent of this new range of subject matter was **Joaquín Pinto** (1842-1906). Although he did not travel to Europe and received little formal training, his affectionate, often humorous paintings and sketches present an unrivalled panorama of Ecuadorean landscape and peoples.

Pinto's documentation of the plight of the Indian, particularly the urban Indian, presaged the 20th-century indigenist tendency in painting whose exponents include **Camilo Egas** (1899-1962), **Eduardo Kingman** (1913-97) and most famously **Oswaldo Guayasamin** (1919-99). Their brand of social realism, while influenced by the Mexican muralists, has a peculiarly bitter hopelessness of its own. Guayasamin's home also includes a museum which is well worth a visit and Kingman's work can be seen at the Posada de las Artes Kingman. **The 20th century**

Their contemporary, **Manuel Rendón** (1894-1982), seems superficially more modern but his subject matter is traditional and often religious, the curvaceous patchwork designs reminiscent of stained glass windows. Several interesting artists of the subsequent generation have rejected social realism and explored aspects of precolumbian and popular art. **Aníbal Villacís** (born 1927) and **Enrique Tábara** (born 1930) use textures and glyphic motifs to evoke ancient pottery and textiles, while **Osvaldo Viteri** (born 1931) incorporates brightly-clad dolls into his compositions, contrasting the tiny popular figures with large areas of paint and canvas.

The civic authorities in Ecuador, particularly during the middle years of the 20th century, have been energetic in peopling their public spaces with monuments to commemorate local and national heroes and events. Inevitably such sculpture is representational and often conservative in style, but within these constraints there are powerful examples in most major town plazas and public buildings are generously adorned with sculptural friezes, such as in the work of **Jaime Andrade** (1913-89) on the Central University and Social Security buildings in Quito. **Estuardo Maldonado** (born 1930) works in an abstract mode using coloured stainless steel to create dramatic works for public and private spaces.

In recent years there have been lots of interesting artistic experiments which can be appreciated in museums and especially the galleries of the Casa de Cultura across the country: the lively expressionism of **Ramiro Jácome** (born 1948), the hyperrealism of **Julio Montesinos** (born 1947) or the complex dramas of **Nicolás Svistoonoff** (born 1945), for example, or the spare engravings of **María Salazar** and **Clara Hidalgo**. **Jorge Chalco** (born 1950) makes inventive use of popular motifs while **Gonzalo Endara Crow**'s (1936-98) success has led to numerous imitators of his picturesque formula combining faux-naif landscapes with elements of surrealism. His giant mosaic-tiled hummingbird has become a landmark in the Valle de los Chillos east of Quito.

Cuenca hosts an important Biennial and Ecuador is unusual among the smaller Latin American countries for its lively international art scene.

Background

Land and environment

Ecuador, named for its position on the equator, is the smallest country of South America (256,370 sq km) after Uruguay and the Guianas. It is bounded by Colombia in the north, by Peru to the east and south, and by the Pacific Ocean to the west. Its population of 12.2 million (in Nov 2001) is also small, but is larger than Bolivia and Paraguay as well as Uruguay and the Guianas. It has the highest population density of any of the South American republics, at 47.4 inhabitants per sq km.

The border had been a source of conflict with its neighbours, and Ecuador lost a significant part of its former territory towards the Amazon to Peru in 1941-42 (see Ecuador's neighbours, page 434).

The Galápagos Islands were annexed by Ecuador in 1832. They lie in the Pacific, 970 km west of the mainland, on the equator, and consist of six principal islands and numerous smaller islands and rocks totalling about 8,000 sq km and scattered over 60,000 sq km of ocean. They are the most significant island group in the eastern Pacific Ocean.

Geology

Geologically, Ecuador is the creation of the Andean mountain-building process, caused in turn by the South American Plate moving west, meeting the Nasca plate which is moving east and sinking beneath the continent. This process began in the late Cretaceous Period around 80 million years ago and has continued to the present day. Before this, and until as late as perhaps 25 million years ago, the Amazon basin tilted west and the river drained into the Pacific through what is now southern Ecuador.

The Andes between Peru and Colombia are at their narrowest (apart from their extremities in Venezuela and southern Chile), ranging from 100-200 km in width. Nevertheless, they are comparatively high with one point, Chimborazo, over 6,000 m and several others not much lower. Unlike Peru to the south, most of the peaks in Ecuador are volcanoes, and Cotopaxi is one of the highest active volcanoes in the world, at 5,897 m. The 55 volcanic craters which dot the landscape of the northern highlands suggest a fractured and unstable area beneath the surface. A dramatic example of volcanic activity was an eruption of Cotopaxi in 1877 which was followed by a pyroclastic flow or *nuée ardente* (literally, a burning cloud) which flowed down the side of the volcano engulfing many settlements. Snow and ice at the summit melted to create another volcanic phenomenon called a *lahar*, or mud flow, which reached Esmeraldas (150 km away) in 18 hours! The most recently volcanic episodes began in 1999, with the eruptions of Guagua Pichincha and Tungurahua. In 2002 Tugurahua remained visibly active as did Sangay (see below).

The eastern third of the country is part of the Amazon basin filled with sedimentary deposits from the mountains to the west. The coastlands rise up to 1,000 m and are mainly remnants of Tertiary basalts, similar to the base rocks of the Amazon basin on the other side of the Andes.

The Galápagos are not structurally connected to the mainland and, so far as is known, were never part of the South American Plate. They lie near the boundary between the Nasca Plate and the Cocos Plate to the north. A line of weakness, evidenced by a ridge of undersea lava flows, stretches southwest from the coast of Panama. This meets another undersea ridge running along the equator from Ecuador but separated from the continental shelf by a deep trench. At this conjuncture appear the Galápagos. Volcanic activity here has been particularly intense and the islands are the peaks of structures that rise over 7,000 m from the deepest parts of the adjacent ocean floor. The oldest islands are San Cristóbal and Española in the east of the archipelago: three to 3.5 million years old. The youngest ones, Fernandina and Isabela, lie to the west, and are between 700,000 and 800,000 years old. In geological terms, therefore, these islands have only recently appeared from the ocean and volcanic activity continues on at least five of them.

The Andes

The Andes form the backbone of the country. In Colombia to the north, three distinct ranges come together near Pasto, with three volcanoes overlooking the border near Tulcán. Although it is essentially one range through Ecuador, there is a trough of between 1,800 m and 3,000 m above sea level running south for over 400 km with volcanoes, many active on either side. The snowline is at about 5,000 m, and with 10 peaks over that height, this makes for a dramatic landscape.

Overlooking Quito to the west is Pichincha which was climbed by Charles-Marie de La Condamine in 1742, and in 1802 by Alexander Von Humboldt. Humboldt climbed many other Ecuadorean volcanoes, including Chimborazo, where he reached over 6,000 m (though not the top), the first recorded climb to this height. He christened the road through the central Andes the 'Avenue of the Volcanoes'.

Further south, near Riobamba, is Volcán Sangay, 5,230 m, which today is the most continuously active of Ecuador's volcanoes. There are fewer volcanoes towards the Peruvian border and the scenery is less dramatic. The mountains rarely exceed 4,000 m and the passes are as low as 2,200 m. Although active volcanoes are concentrated in the northern half of the country, there are many places where there are sulphur baths or hot springs and the whole Andean area is seismically active with severe earthquakes from time to time.

The central trough is crossed by several transversal ranges called *nudos*, made up of extruded volcanic material, creating separate basins or *hoyas*. South of Quito, the basins are lower, the climate hotter and drier with semi-desert stretches. The lack of surface water is aggravated by large quantities of volcanic dust which is easily eroded by wind and water and can produce dry 'badland' topography. Landslides in this unstable and precipitous terrain are common. A serious example was in the Paute valley near Cuenca in 1993 when a hillside which had been intensively cultivated gave way in unusually heavy rains. An earth dam was formed which later collapsed, causing further damage downstream.

The coast

West of the Andes, there are 100-200 km of lowlands with some hilly ground up to 1,000 m. The greater part is drained by the Daule, Vinces and Babahoyo rivers that run north to south to form the Guayas, the largest river on the Pacific coast of South America, which meets the sea at Guayaquil. There are several shorter rivers in the north including the Esmeraldas, whose headwaters include the Río Machángara which unfortunately is the open sewer of Quito. Another system reaches the ocean at La Tola. All of these rivers have created fertile lowlands which are used for banana, cacao and rice production, and there are good cattle lands in the Guayas basin. This is one of the best agricultural areas of South America.

Mangrove swamps thrived on coastal mudflats in tropical rainforest zones and were typical of parts of Esmeraldas, Manabí and Guayas provinces. These are now having to compete with shrimp fisheries, an important export product. Attempts are being made to restrict the destruction of mangroves in the Guayas estuary. South of Guayaquil, the mangroves disappear, and by the border with Peru, it is semi-arid.

Amazonia

The eastern foothills of the Andes are mainly older granite (Mezozoic) rocks, more typical of Brazil than the Pacific coast countries. As with most of the western Amazon basin, it has a heavy rainfall coming in from the east and much is covered with tropical forest along a dozen or so significant tributaries of the Amazon. Partly as a result of the territory being opened up by oil field exploitation, land is being cleared for crops at a high rate. However, certain areas are being developed for eco-tourism and it remains to be seen if this will help to arrest the destruction of the environment.

Background

With good water flow and easy gradients, many of the rivers of this region are navigable at least to small craft. The Napo in particular is a significant communications route to Iquitos in Peru and the Brazilian Amazon beyond. Following the end of the border conflict with Peru in 1998, an international navigation route has been opened downstream from Coca.

Climate

In spite of its small size, the range of tropical climates in Ecuador is large. The meeting of the north-flowing Humboldt current with the warm Pacific equatorial water takes place normally off Ecuador, giving the contrast between high rainfall to the north and desert conditions further south in Peru. Changes in the balance between these huge bodies of water, known as the *El Niño* phenomenon, can lead to heavy rains to the south, and this anomaly affects the region and the world in an irregular 5 to 10 year cycle (see box, page 457).

Coast   The climate along the Pacific coast is a transition area between the heavy tropical rainfall of Colombia and the deserts of Peru. The rainfall is progressively less south of Guayaquil. This change of climate is due to the offshore Humboldt current which flows north along the South American Pacific coast from Chile to Ecuador. This relatively cold water inhibits rain-producing clouds from 27° south northwards, but just south of the equator, the current is turned west and the climate is dramatically changed.

Andes &   Inland, the size of the Andean peaks and volcanoes create many different micro-cli-
Oriente   mates, from the permanent snows over 5,000 m to the semi-desert hollows in the central trough. Most of the basins and the adjoining slopes have a moderate climate, though at altitude daily temperature fluctuations can be considerable. In the north, the basins are higher and temperatures are warm by day and cool at night. It rains mostly between October and May; Quito has an average of 1,300 mm per year. Near the border with Peru, the mountain climate can be very pleasant. Vilcabamba in Loja province is reputed to have a most favourable climate for a long and healthy life. In the Oriente the climate is indistinguishable from the hot, very humid lands of the western Amazon basin. There is heavy rainfall all year round, particularly May to December.

Galápagos   Although lying on the equator, there is considerable variation in the weather of the Galápagos Islands. The islands are affected by the cool water from the southeast Pacific which turns west near the equator. Surface water temperatures can fall to 20°C in July-September, causing low cloud and cool air conditions. Temperatures are highest from January to May and brief tropical downpours occur frequently at this time.

Wildlife and vegetation

For the Galápagos   No country in the world has as much biological diversity in as little space as Ecuador. The
islands, see the colour   geologically recent uplift of the Andes has caused this diversity by dividing the country
wildlife section in the   into two parts, west and east, and by creating a complex topography that fosters the
middle of the book   evolution of new species. It is an exciting thing to experience this diversity firsthand, and Ecuador's extensive road system makes it easy. Our brief survey of this diversity, from west to east, gives an idea of the enormous range of Ecuador's life forms.

Northwestern   The westernmost part of mainland Ecuador is a broad rolling plain covered in the north
lowlands   by some of the wettest rainforest in the world. (There are some low coastal mountains but they do not reach significant elevations.) The biological centre of this region is the Chocó forest of neighbouring Colombia, so Ecuador's northwest shares many species

El Niño

What is El Niño and how can it so dramatically alter the world's climate? Aboriginal peoples of Ecuador appear to have been aware of these cyclical changes in weather, attributing them to the position of the earth relative to other heavenly bodies.

Among the early European scientists to visit South America, the German Alexander von Humboldt observed that a powerful ocean current flows from south to north along the coast of Peru; it was later given his name. Under normal conditions, this cold Humboldt current follows South America's Pacific coastline northward as far as the equator, causing very low precipitation (because of low evaporation from its cool waters) and creating deserts in northern Chile, Peru and southern Ecuador. At the equator the Humboldt current turns due west, sweeping past the Galápagos islands into the central Pacific.

Situated north of the equator, a warm countercurrent flows in the opposite direction, eastward towards Panama and then south along the Pacific coast (where it is called the Panama current) until it meets the Humboldt current at the equator. This warm current brings warm moist air and high precipitation to the Pacific coasts of Panama, Colombia and northern Ecuador.

The relative strength of these two currents, warm and cold, varies with the time of year. The warm Panama current can be stronger around Christmas and hence was dubbed the Corriente del Niño, the current of the (Christ) child. Under certain circumstances, which tend to recur in an irregular 5-10 year cycle, this warm current can be exceptionally strong and sweep as far south as Chile, causing very heavy rains and associated calamities in these normally desert areas.

More recently, scientists have looked beyond the explanations offered by these regional Pacific currents. They now regard the El Niño phenomenon, its causes and effects, as truly global; bringing a combination of floods and droughts to the entire planet. They note that under normal conditions the trade winds, which blow westward across the tropical Pacific Ocean pile up warm sea surface water in the west. Consequently, the sea level by Indonesia is normally about 50 cm higher than it is by Ecuador. This movement of warm water to the west causes an upwelling of deeper cold water in the east (the Humboldt current) resulting in a temperature difference of about 8°C at the same latitude, between the water by the coast of South America and that by Southeast Asia.

When the trade winds diminish in intensity, there is a gradual eastward-moving warming of surface water in the Pacific. Heavy rainfall follows the warmer water east to the Pacific coast of South America (the El Niño phenomenon) and is accompanied by simultaneous drought in Southeast Asia and Australia. The level of the ocean rises along the west coast of South America causing marejadas, exceptionally high tides which can destroy beaches and seaside property. The earth's entire atmospheric circulation is altered and important weather changes result in areas far removed from the equatorial Pacific. The two most recent El Niños took place in 1992-93 and 1997-98, and both were devastating for the Ecuadorean coast as well as many other parts of the world. Another El Niño has been forecast for 2002-03 but is expected to be weaker than its two predecessors.

Despite some of the simplified explanations presented here, El Niño remains a mystery to even the most sophisticated scientific theories. Why do the trade winds ease off in the first place, apparently initiating the phenomenon? Could it have something to do with the gravitational forces of other planets? Could the ancient inhabitants of El Niño's realm have understood something about these complex relationships which we still do not?

Adapted from the Latin American Travel Advisor, Issue 14, July 1997. For more information see www.elnino.noaa.gov

with that area. Among the so-called Chocó endemics that reach Ecuador are some very fancy birds like the **Long-wattled Umbrellabird, Banded Ground-Cuckoo** and **Scarlet-breasted Dacnis**. Many other birds, mammals and plants of this region are found all along the wet Pacific lowlands from northwest Ecuador to Central America. Visitors familiar with Central American wildlife will feel at home here amongst the **Mantled Howler Monkeys, Chestnut-mandibled Toucans** and **Red-capped Manakins**. Unfortunately this forest is severely endangered by commercial logging, cattle ranching and farming, and good examples of it are now hard to find.

Southwestern lowlands
The cold Humboldt ocean current creates a completely different environment in the southwestern lowlands. Here the forest is deciduous (driest in July and August), and the southernmost parts of this area are desert-like. The birds and plants of this region are very different from those of the wet northwest; they belong to the Tumbesian bioregion and many are restricted to this small corner of Ecuador and adjacent northwest Peru. Some of the Tumbesian endemic birds are the recently-discovered **El Oro Parakeet, Rufous-headed Chachalaca** and **Elegant Crescent-chest**. This is a densely populated region however, and many of the species endemic to it are threatened with extinction.

Western slopes
Rising suddenly from these flat lowlands are the western Andes, very steep and irregular. Here the constant mists keep the forest wet all the way from north to south. In southern Ecuador it is therefore possible to go from desert to cloud forest in the space of a few hundred metres of elevation. This cloud forest is thick, tall and dark, and every branch is loaded with bromeliads, orchids and mosses. Orchids reach their maximum diversity in Ecuadorean cloud forests, and many spectacular varieties are found in the west, especially the weird Draculas. Many of the birds in these mountains are restricted to western Ecuador and western Colombia, including spectacular species like the gaudy **Plate-billed Mountain-Toucan**. At higher elevations there are more similarities with the eastern slope of the Andes. Among the highlights of these forests are the mixed foraging flocks of colourful **tanagers**, with exotic names like Glistening-green, Beryl-spangled and Flame-faced Tanagers. Mammals are scarce; lower elevations have **capuchin**, **spider** and **howler monkeys**, while high elevations have the elusive **Spectacled Bear**. Insects too diminish as elevation increases and their role as flower pollinators is taken over by myriads of **hummingbirds**, including the Violet-tailed Sylph, Velvet-purple Coronet and Gorgeted Sunangel, to name but a few.

Western páramo
The cloud forest becomes low and stunted above about 3,300 m, and at higher elevations the forest is replaced by the grassland environment called *páramo*. Here, in contrast to the lower forests, the plants are largely from familiar temperate-zone families like the daisy and blueberry. They take on increasingly bizarre forms as the altitude increases, and the species of the highest elevations look like cushions of moss. Mammals are scarce but include **Spectacled Bear**, which feeds on the terrestrial bromeliads called Puyas or *achupallas* (which look a lot like pineapple plants); and rabbits, which can be so numerous that they make broad trails in the vegetation. Also preying on the rabbits are a form of **Great Horned Owl** and the **Andean Fox**. The birds and insects of these elevations are mostly drab, and many of the families represented here have their origins in North America or temperate southern South America. Forming islands of high forest in the *páramos* are the Polylepis trees, in the rose family; their distinctive flaky reddish bark is the favorite foraging substrate for the **Giant Conebill**.

Inter-Andean basins
Between the western and the eastern Andes lies the Inter-Andean Basin, really a series of basins formed by various river valleys. This region is in the rain shadows of both the western and eastern Andes, so it is relatively dry all year. Much of the original vegetation was destroyed centuries ago, replaced with grasses and more recently with

introduced pine and eucalyptus trees. Only on high mountains like Chimborazo or Cotopaxi do relatively undisturbed habitats remain. Here a desolate zone of volcanic ash and bare rock marks the upper end of the *páramo*. There is little vegetation beyond, apart from the valiant colonization attempts of lichens, which grow well even up to 5,000 m.

To the east of the Inter-Andean Basins are the high eastern *páramos*, very much like the western ones but wetter. Here **Mountain Tapirs** are the largest animal, but they, like all big chunks of meat in Ecuador, survive only in remote regions. **Spectacled Bears** are here too, along with **White-tailed Deer** and its faithful predator the **Mountain Lion**. A miniature deer, the **pudu**, also lives here but is rarely seen. **Andean Condors**, one of the largest flying birds in the world, can be seen soaring majestically overhead. Condors are scavengers and clean up the larger animals after they die. **Eastern páramo**

The eastern slope of the Andes is clothed in cloud forest like the western slope, but this cloud forest is much less seasonal, and has a higher diversity. Many west slope species of plants and birds have east slope sister species; the Plate-billed Mountain-Toucan, for example, is here replaced by the **Black-billed Mountain-Toucan**. The lower elevations have some Amazonian species like **Woolly Monkey**, and there are a few birds that have no western or Amazonian counterparts, like the strange **White-capped Tanager**. Plant diversity is very high here; **orchids** are especially diverse, even more so than in the west. The eastern cloud forests are much less damaged by man than the western ones, and there are still large wildernesses that are virtually unknown biologically. **Eastern slopes**

The eastern Amazonian lowland rainforest is the most diverse habitat in Ecuador for birds and mammals, with up to 14 primate species and 550 bird species at a single site. This is as diverse as life gets on this planet. Here is the home of the biggest snake in the world, the semiaquatic **Anaconda**, and various species of alligator-like **caimans**. The birds are very impressive, like the multicoloured **macaws**, the monkey-eating **Harpy Eagle**, the comical **Hoatzin** and the elusive **Nocturnal Curassow**. Mammals include five species of **cats**, three **anteaters**, a couple of **sloths**, two **dolphins** and an endless variety of **bats** – bats that troll for fish, bats that suck nectar, bats that catch sleeping birds by smelling them, bats that eat fruit, bats that catch insects, and even vampire bats that really drink blood. The variety of **fish** is even greater than the variety of birds and bats, and include piranhas, stingrays, giant catfish and electric eels. There are fewer epiphytes here than in cloud forests, but many more species of trees; 1 ha can have over 300 species of trees! Insect life reflects the diversity of plants; for example, there can be over 700 species of **butterflies** at a single site, including several species of huge shining blue **Morphos**. If one wants to see spectacular birds and animals and has only one opportunity to visit one mainland region of Ecuador, then this should be it. But you must choose the site carefully if you really want to see these things, see Choosing a rainforest, page 360. **Eastern lowlands**

Background

National parks

Reserva Ecológica Antisana, 120,000 ha in Pichincha and Napo provinces. Features varied altitude, Antisana volcano and Andean condors. ■ *US$5*. **Highland parks**
Parque Nacional Sangay, 517,725 ha, in Chimborazo, Tungurahua and Morona-Santiago provinces. Covers an area from 800 m up to 5,319 m. Features Altar, Sangay and Tungurahua volcanoes, rainforest, and contains several threatened mammals, eg spectacled bear, tigrillo, mountain tapir. ■ *US$10*.
Parque Nacional Cotopaxi, 33,939 ha, in Cotopaxi, Pichincha and Napo provinces, centred around the Cotopaxi Volcano. ■ *US$10*.

National parks & reserves

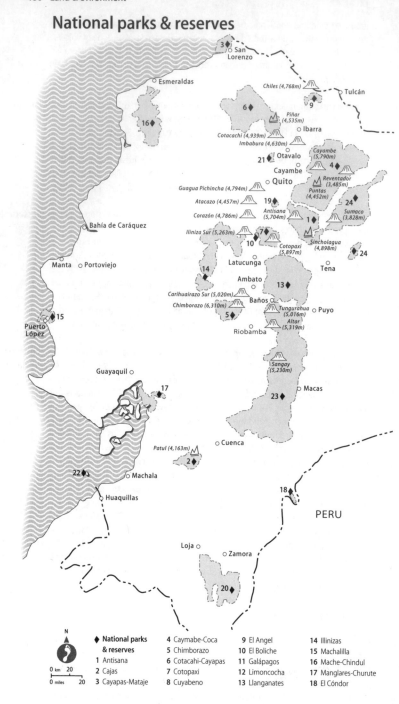

San
Lorenzo
3 ◆

Chiles (4,768m)   Tulcán

9 ◆

Esmeraldas ○   6 ◆

Piñar
(4,535m)

16 ◆   Cotacachi (4,939m)   ○ Ibarra

Imbabura (4,630m)

Cayambe
(5,790m)

21 ◆ ○ Otavalo   4 ◆

Cayambe

Reventador
(3,485m)

Guagua Pichincha (4,794m)   ○ Quito   Puntas
(4,452m)

Atacazo (4,457m)   19 ◆   24 ◆

Antisana   Sumaco
Corazón (4,786m)   (5,704m)   (3,828m)

Iliniza Sur (5,263m)   1 ◆

○ Bahía de Caráquez   10 ◆   Sincholagua
(4,898m)

7 ◆   Cotopaxi
(5,897m)   24 ◆

Manta ○   ○ Portoviejo   Latucunga

14 ◆   Tena ○

Ambato ○

Carihuairazo Sur (5,020m)   13 ◆

Chimborazo (6,310m)   Baños ○   Puyo ○

◆ 15   5 ◆   Tungurahua
(5,016m)

Puerto   Altar
López   Riobamba ○   (5,319m)

Guayaquil ○

Sangay
(5,230m)

17 ◆

23 ◆   ○ Macas

Patul (4,163m)

2 ◆

○ Cuenca

22 ◆◆   ○ Machala   18 ◆

Huaquillas   PERU

Loja ○

○ Zamora

20 ◆

N

◆ **National parks**
& reserves

0 km   20
0 miles   20

1 Antisana	4 Caymabe-Coca	9 El Angel	14 Illinizas
2 Cajas	5 Chimborazo	10 El Boliche	15 Machalilla
3 Cayapas-Mataje	6 Cotacahi-Cayapas	11 Galápagos	16 Mache-Chindul
	7 Cotopaxi	12 Limoncocha	17 Manglares-Churute
	8 Cuyabeno	13 Llanganates	18 El Cóndor

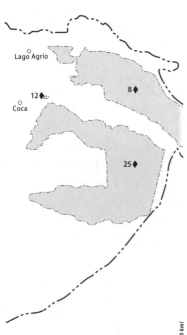

COLOMBIA

Lago Agrio

12◆

Coca

8◆

25◆

Galápagos

To Ecuador coast (1,000 km)

N

Not to scale

Pinta
(Abingdon)

Marchena
(Bindloe)

Santiago (San
Salvador/James)

Santa Cruz
(Indefatigable)

Fernandina
(Narborough)

11◆

Isabela

San Cristóbal
(Chatham)

Floreana
(Charles, Santa María)

19 Pasochoa
20 Podocarpus
21 Pululahua
22 Isla Santa Clara
23 Sangay

24 Sumaco
25 Yasuní

Reserva Ecológica Cayambe-Coca, 403,103 ha, in Imbabura, Pichincha and Sucumbíos provinces. Features a varied altitude with a diversity of flora and fauna, Cayambe volcano (dormant), lakes and waterfalls. ■ *US$10.*

Reserva de Producción Faunística Chimborazo, 58,560 ha, in Chimborazo, Bolívar and Tungurahua provinces. A centre for the preservation of llama, alpaca and vicuña, also features Chimborazo and Carihuairazo mountains. ■ *US$10.*

Reserva Ecológica Los Ilinizas, 150,000 ha, in Pichincha and Cotopaxi provinces. Features remnants of western slope forest and *páramo*; includes El Corazón, Los Ilinizas and Quilotoa. ■ *US$5.*

Reserva Geobotánica Pululahua, 3,383 ha, located 13 km northwest of Quito near the Mitad del Mundo monument. Features the extinct crater of Pululahua volcano. ■ *US$5.*

Parque Nacional Cajas, 28,800 ha, located 30 km from Cuenca. Features lakes and good trekking. ■ *US$10.*

Area de Recreación El Boliche, 1,077 ha, adjacent to Cotopaxi National Park. ■ *US$10.*

Reserva Ecológica El Angel, 15,715 ha, in Carchi province. Features *frailejon* plants, Chiles volcano, lakes and rivers. ■ *US$10.*

Parque Nacional Llanganates, 219,707 ha in the provinces of Cotopaxi and Tungurahua, Napo and Pastaza. Features Andean lakes and forest; access is difficult. ■ *US$5.*

Mixed habitats

Reserva Ecológica Cotacachi-Cayapas, 204,420 ha, in Imbabura and Esmeraldas provinces. Runs from the western slopes of the Andes to the coast. Features tropical forests, lakes (including Cuicocha) and rivers. ■ *US$5; no fee charged to visit only Cuicocha.*

Parque Nacional Podocarpus, 146,200 ha, in Loja and Zamora provinces. Features cloud forest, rivers and birdlife. ■ *US$10.*

Parque Nacional Sumaco, 205,249 ha, in Napo province. Features Andean and sub-tropical forests, rivers, and much fauna, including river otters, jaguar and spectacled bear. ■ *US$5.*

Background

Amazonian parks   **Parque Nacional Yasuní**, 982,006 ha, in Napo province. Amazonian rainforest with lakes, animals and birdlife. ■ *US$10.*

Reserva de Producción Faunística Cuyabeno, 655,781 ha, in Sucumbíos province. Rainforest, with lakes and abundant wildlife. ■ *US$20.*

Reserva Biológica Limoncocha, 4,613 ha, in Sucumbíos province. Features Limoncocha lake, with black caiman and good birdlife. ■ *US$5.*

Coastal parks   **Parque Nacional Machalilla**, 55,000 ha, in Manabí province. Features dry coastal forest, beaches, archaeology and Isla de la Plata. ■ *For Isla de la Plata and mainland portion: US$20. For Isla de la Plata only: US$15. For mainland portion only: US$12.*

Reserva Ecológica Manglares-Churute, 49,383 ha, in Guayas province. Features mangroves and dry tropical forest. ■ *US$10.*

Reserva Ecológica Mache-Chindul, in the province of Esmeraldas. Administered by the Jatun Sacha Foundation, see Volunteer opportunities, page 82.

Reserva Ecológica Cayapas-Mataje, 51,300 ha, in Esmeraldas province. Features islands rich in mangroves and bird life.■ *US$5.*

Galápagos   **The Galápagos Islands**, 693,700 ha. A description of the archipelago's unique wildlife is given in the colour section in the middle of the book. Entry fees for Galápagos are given on page 407.

Entry fees & offices   The entry fees given above are those officially established by the Ministerio del Ambiente in 2002. They are subject to change without notice. In the more remote areas there may not be any park infrastructure nor anyone to collect fees.

The offices of the Ministerio del Abiente are located in Quito, in the Ministerio de Agricultura y Ganadería building, 8th floor, Amazonas y Eloy Alfaro, T252 9845. They can provide some limited tourist information but it is best to contact the office in the city nearest the park you wish to visit, for example the Cuenca office for Cajas, Loja for Podocarpus and so on. Ecuador's national parks were previously administered by a government agency called INEFAN. Although this no longer exists some people still use the name when referring to the national park authorities.

Books

General   Collier, Simon, Skidmore, Thomas E, and Blakemore, Harold (editors) *The Cambridge Encyclopedia of Latin America and the Caribbean* (2nd edn 1992). Hemming, John *The Conquest of the Incas* (1983). Excellent read for anyone interested in the Spanish conquest. Hurtado, Osvaldo *El poder político en el Ecuador* (1981) Ariel, Barcelona. Medina, José Toribio (ed), Lee, Bertram T (trans), Heaton, HC (ed) *The Discovery of the Amazon* (1988) Dover, New York. Norton, Presley and García, Marco Vinicio (eds) *5000 años de ocupación: Parque Nacional Machalilla* (1992) Centro cultural Artes and Ediciones Abya-Yala, Quito. Especially 'Las culturas cerámicas prehispánicas del Sur de Manabí', by Presley Norton, pages 9-40. Parry, J H *The Discovery of South America* (1979). Wearne, Phillip *Return of the Indian: Conquest and Revival in the Americas* (1996) Cassell/LAB. Williamson, Edwin *The Penguin History of Latin America* (1992).

Also *Ecuador In Focus* (1997) Latin American Bureau. An excellent overall guide to politics, society and culture. Also good are: *Ecuador* Ediciones Libri Mundi; Kling, Kevin and Christianson, Nadia *Ecuador: Island of the Andes* (1988) Thames & Hudson; and Wesch, Rolf *The Ecotourist's Guide to the Ecuadorean Amazon* (1995).

Travelogues   More personal accounts given in the travelogues of early gringo visitors to Ecuador include: Darwin, Charles *Voyage of the Beagle* (see Galápagos below for details).

Whymper, Edward *Travels Amongst the Great Andes of the Equator* (1891); (1987) Gibbs M Smith, Salt Lake City. **Condamine, Charles-Marie de la** *Diario del viaje al Ecuador* (1745); N Gómez ed (1994) Ediguias, Quito. **Lara, Dario** *Viajeros Franceses al Ecuador en el Siglo XIX* (1972) Casa de la Cultura Ecuatoriana, Quito, 1972 and *Gabriel Lafond de Lurcy: Viajero y testigo de la historia ecuatoriana* (1988) Banco Central del Ecuador, Quito. Other recommended personal accounts are (see also Galápagos below): **Izaca, Jorge** *Huasipungo* (1962) London. **Michaux, Henri** *Ecuador* (1929, 1952) OUP. **Miller, Tom** *The Panama Hat Trail* (1986) Abacus. **Thomsen, Moritz** Living Poor Eland – also *The Saddest Pleasure* and *Farm on the River of Emeralds*.

A very useful book, highly recommended, aimed specifically at the budget traveller, is **Travel guides** *The Tropical Traveller*, by **John Hatt** (1993, 3rd edn) Penguin Books. Along similar lines is *The Practical Nomad*, by **Edward Hasbrouck** (1998) Moon Publications, Chico CA, USA. Of general interest is *South American Explorer*, published quarterly by South American Explorers (see page 25).

Recommended works of fiction based in Ecuador are: **Burroughs, William** *Queer* (1985) **Fiction** and **Vonnegut, Kurt** *Galápagos* (1986). The country is presented through the eyes of an *See also Literature,* orphaned Ecuadorean child in *El País de Manuelito*, by **Alfonso Barrera Valverde** (1981) *page 447, for* Editorial El Conejo, Quito. Its title at least has become a contemporary classic. *Ecuadorian writers*

Ridgely, R and Greenfield, P *Birds of Ecuador* (2001) Cornell University Press, Ithaca, **Birdwatching** NY. The definitive guide. **Hility, S** and **Brown, W** *A Guide to the Birds of Colombia* (1986) Princeton University Press, USA. Also very good. Virtually all northern Ecuadorean birds are treated here. In the south, however, this guide is less useful. **Fjeldsa, J** and **Krabbe, N** *Birds of the High Andes* (1990) Apollo Books, Svendborg, Denmark. Covers some additional species to *A Guide to the Birds of Colombia*. **Williams, R, Best, B** and **Heijnen, T** *A Guide to Birdwatching in Ecuador and the Galápagos* Biosphere Publications, UK. Much detailed site information is contained in this excellent book and some information presented here comes from that book. **Ridgley, R, Greenfield, P** and **Guerrero, M** *An Annotated List of the Birds of Mainland Ecuador* (1998) CECIA, Quito. An unillustrated but useful distributional checklist, with English and Spanish common names. **Hilty, S** *Birds of Tropical America: A Watcher's Guide to Behavior, Breeding and Diversity* Chapters Publishing, Shelburne, VT, USA. An excellent book on the natural history of tropical birds. **Canaday, C** and **Jost, L** *Common birds of Amazonian Ecuador: a guide for the wide-eyed ecotourist* (1997) by Ediciones Libri-Mundi, Quito. A nice beginner's guide with excellent illustrations. Finally **John V Moore**'s tapes and CDs of Ecuadorean birds are highly recommended and are available in Quito at Libri Mundi (Juan Leon Mera y Pinto) or directly from John V Moore Nature Recordings, 333 West Santa Clara Street #1212, San Jose, CA 95125 USA.

Brain, Yossi *Ecuador: A Climbing Guide* (2000), The Mountaineers, Seattle. The most **Climbing** up-to-date reference and covers routes on all the 'big 10' plus 10 additional mountains. **Cruz, Marco** *Montañas del Ecuador* (1993) Dinediciones, Quito. A beautiful coffee-table book packed full of colour photographs, taken by Ecuador's leading guide of the last 20 years. In Spanish. **Koerner, Michael** *The Fool's Climbing Guide to Ecuador and Peru* (1976) Buzzard Mountaineering. Concise and funny more than practical due to its age, but a very enjoyable read. **Kunstaetter, Robert and Daisy** *Climbing and Hiking in Ecuador* (see below under Trekking). overs a number of treks and sub-5,000 m peaks suitable for acclimatizing as well as general descriptions of routes on the 'big 10'. **Landazuri, Freddy** *Cotopaxi: Mountain of Light* (1994) Campo Abierto. A thorough history of the mountain in Spanish and English. **Landazuri, Freddy, Rojas, Ivan** and **Serrano, Marcos** *Montañas del Sol* (1994) Campo Abierto, Quito. A good climbing guidebook but it lacks top diagrams and public transport information. In Spanish. **Whymper, Edward** *Travels Amongst the Great Andes of the Equator* (details above). An absolute classic, one of the best books written about climbing anything anywhere (especially if you ignore any paragraph discussing the differences between the mercurial and aneroid barometers). Two excellent German climbing books are *Bergfürer Ecuador* by **Günter Schmudlach** (2001) Panico Alpinverlag, and *Die Schneeberge Ecuador*, by **Marco Cruz** (translated from Spanish).

Mountaineering journals include: *Campo Abierto* (not produced by the Travel Agency of the same name), an annual magazine on expeditions, access to mountains etc, US$1. *Montaña*, annual magazine of the *Colegio San Gabriel* mountaineering club, US$1.50.

Trekking   **Kunstaetter, Robert and Daisy** *Trekking in Ecuador* (2002) The Mountaineers, Seattle. The most up-to-date reference, covering 29 treks throughout Ecuador, mostly new routes; see www.trekkinginecuador.com   **Rachoweicki, Thurber** and **Wagenhauser** *Climbing and Hiking in Ecuador* (1997 4th edn) Bradt. An older comprehensive hiking guide.

Galápagos Islands

Many of these books are available at Libri Mundi and other bookshops in Quito, see page 122

General   Darwin, Charles *Journal of the Voyage of HMS Beagle*, first published in 1845. Penguin Books (UK) have published Darwin's account of the Galápagos in their Penguin 60s Classics series. Another interesting historical work is **Melville, Herman** *The Encantadas* [1854], published in *Billy Bud, Sailor and Other Stories* (1971) Penguin Books. **Treherne, John** *The Galápagos Affair* (1983) Jonathan Cape. Describes the bizarre events on Floreana in the 1930s. More personal is **Margret Wittmer**'s autobiography *Floreana* (1961) Michael Joseph. The story of another Galápagos pioneer family is beautifully told in *My Father's Island* by **Johanna Angermeyer** (1998) Anthony Nelson.

Field guides   Jackson, Michael H *Galápagos: A Natural History Guide* (1985) University of Calgary Press. Considered the Bible by all guides and the staff at the Charles Darwin Research Station. **Castro, Isabel** and **Phillips, Antonia** *A Guide to the Birds of the Galápagos Islands* (1996) Christopher Helm. **Constant, Pierre** *The Galápagos Islands* (2000) Odyssey. **De Roy, Tui** *Galapagos: Islands Born of Fire* (2001) Swan Hill Press. A highly acclaimed collection of photos and essays about the islands and the need to conserve them. **Horwell, David** *Galápagos: the Enchanted Isles* (1988) Dryad Press. Available through author's UK agency (see Galápagos chapter, Booking a cruise). **Hickman, John** *The Enchanted Isles. The Galápagos Discovered* (1985) Anthony Nelson. **Humann, Paul** *Reef Fish Identification* (1993) Libri Mundi. **Merlen, Godfrey** *A Field Guide to the Fishes of Galápagos* (1988) Libri Mundi. **Schofield, Eileen** *Plants of the Galápagos Islands* (1984) Universe Books, New York. **White, Alan and Epler, Bruce White, with photographs by Gilbert, Charles** *Galápagos Guide*. Published in several languages.

The **Galápagos Conservation Trust** (18 Curzon St, London W1Y 7AD, T020-7629 5049, F020-7629 4149) publishes a quarterly Newsletter for its members. *Noticias de Galápagos* is a twice-yearly publication about science and conservation in the islands. It is the official publication of the **Charles Darwin Foundation**. 'Friends of the Galápagos' (US$25 per year membership) receive the journal as a part of their membership.

Footnotes

Spanish words and phrases

No amount of dictionaries, phrase books or word lists will provide the same enjoyment as being able to communicate directly with the people of the country you are visiting. Learning Spanish is a useful part of the preparation for a trip to Ecuador and you are encouraged to make an effort to grasp the basics before you go. The following section is designed to be a simple point of departure.

Whether you have been taught the 'Castillian' pronunciation (all z's, and c's followed by *i* or *e*, are pronounced as the 'th' in 'think') or the 'American' pronunciation (they are pronounced as s), you will encounter little difficulty in understanding either; Spanish pronunciation varies geographically much less than English. There are, of course, regional accents and usages; but the basic language is essentially the same everywhere.

General pronunciation

The stress in a Spanish word conforms to one of three rules: 1) if the word ends in a vowel, or in n or s, the accent falls on the penultimate syllable *(ventana, ventanas)*; 2) if the word ends in a consonant other than n or s, the accent falls on the last syllable *(hablar)*; 3) if the word is to be stressed on a syllable contrary to either of the above rules, the acute accent on the relevant vowel indicates where the stress is to be placed *(pantalón, sábana)*. Note that adverbs such as *cuando* (when), take an accent when used interrogatively; *¿cuándo?* (when?).

Vowels

a	not quite as short as in English 'cat'
e	as in English 'pay', but shorter in a syllable ending in a consonant
i	as in English 'seek'
o	as in English 'shop', but more like 'pope' when the vowel ends a syllable
u	as in English 'food', after 'q' and in 'gue', 'gui' u is unpronounced; in 'güe'and 'güi' it is pronounced
y	when a vowel, pronounced like 'I'; when a semiconsonant or consonant, it is pronounced like English 'yes'
ai, ay	as in English 'ride'
ei, ey	as in English 'they'
oi, oy	as in English 'toy'

Consonants

Unless listed below consonants can be pronounced in Spanish as they are in English.

b, v	their sound is interchangeable and is a cross between the English **b** and **v**, except at the beginning of a word or after **m** or **n** when it is like English **b**
C	like English **k**, except before **e** or **i** when it is the **s** in English 'sip'
G	before **e** and **i** it is the same as **j**
H	when on its own, never pronounced
J	as the **ch** in the Scottish 'loch'
Ll	as the **g** in English 'beige'; sometimes as the 'lli' in 'million'

Ñ	as the 'ni' in English 'onion'
Rr	trilled much more strongly than in English
X	depending on its location, pronounced as in English 'fox', or 'sip', or like 'gs'
Z	as the **s** in English 'sip'

Pronouns

In the Americas, the plural, familiar pronoun *vosotros* (with the verb endings – *áis*, – *éis*), though much used in Spain, is never heard. Two or more people, including small children, are always addressed as *ustedes* (*uds*).

Inappropriate use of the familiar forms (*tú*, *vos*) can sound imperious, condescending, infantile, or imply a presumption of intimacy that could annoy officials, one's elders, or, if coming from a man, women. To avoid cultural complications if your Spanish is limited, stick to the polite forms: *usted* (*ud*) in the singular, *ustedes* in the plural, and you will never give offence. Remember also that a person who addresses you as *tú* does not necessarily expect to be *tuteada* (so addressed) in return. You should, however, violate this rule when dealing with a small child, who might be intimidated by *usted*; he/she is, after all, normally so addressed only in admonitions such as *¡No, Señor, ud no tomará un helado antes del almuerzo!* 'No, Sir, you will not have ice cream before lunch!'

Greetings, courtesies

In Ecuador the response to *¡Gracias!* is either *¡A la órden!* ('Yours to command!') or *¡De nada!* ('It's nothing!').

excuse me/I beg your pardon	*permiso/con permiso*
Go away!	*¡váyase!*
good afternoon/evening/night	*buenas tardes/noches*
good morning	*buenos días*
goodbye	*hasta luego/adiós/chao*
hello	*hola* (familiar only, otherwise use *buenos días*, etc)
How are you?	*¿cómo está?/¿cómo estás?*
I do not understand	*no entiendo*
leave me alone	*déjame en paz/no me moleste*
no	*no*
please	*por favor*
pleased to meet you	*mucho gusto/encantado/encantada*
see you later	*hasta luego/hasta pronto/nos vemos*
thank you (very much)	*(muchas) gracias/Dios le pague/ Dios se lo pague*
What is your name?	*¿Cómo se llama?*
yes	*sí*
I speak ...	*Hablo ...*
I speak Spanish	*Hablo español*
I don't speak Spanish	*No hablo español*
Do you speak English?	*¿Habla usted inglés?*
We speak German	*Hablamos alemán*
Please speak slowly	*hable despacio por favor*
I am very sorry	*lo siento mucho/disculpe*
I'm fine	*muy bien gracias*
I'm called_	*me llamo_*
What do you want?	*¿Qué quiere?*

I want	quiero
I don't want it	No lo quiero
good	bueno
bad	malo

Basic questions

Have you got a room for two people?	¿Tiene una habitación para dos personas?
How do I get to_?	¿Cómo llego a_?
How much does it cost?	¿Cuánto vale?/¿Cuánto cuesta?
How much is it?	¿Cuánto es?
When does the bus leave?/arrive?	¿A qué hora sale/llega el bus?
When?	¿cuándo?
Where is_?	¿Dónde está_?/¿Dónde queda_?
Where is the nearest petrol station?	¿Dónde está la gasolinera más cercana?
Why?	¿Por qué?

Basics

bank	el banco	change	el vuelto
bathroom/toilet	el baño	cheap	barato
bill	la factura/la cuenta	church/cathedral	La iglesia/catedral
cash	efectivo	exchange house	la casa de cambio
exchange rate	la tasa de cambio	post office	el correo
expensive	caro	supermarket	el supermercado
market	el mercado	telephone office	el centro de llamadas
notes/coins	los billetes/ las monedas	travellers' cheques	los travelers/los cheques de viajero
police (policeman)	la policía (el policía)		

Getting around

aeroplane/airplane	el avión	straight on	derecho/recto
airport	el aeropuerto	ticket office	la boletería
bus station	la terminal (terrestre)	ticket	el boleto/tiquet
bus stop	la parada	to walk	caminar
bus	el bus/el autobus	Where can I buy	¿Dónde puedo
bus route	el recorrido/la ruta	tickets?	comprar los boletos?
first/second class	primera/segunda clase	Where can I park?	¿Dónde puedo
on the left/right	a la izquierdo/derecha		parquear/estacionar?
second street on the left	la segunda calle a la izquierda	straight on	derecho/recto/ rectito

Orientation and motoring

arrival	la llegada	north	el norte
avenue	la avenida	oil	el aceite
block	la cuadra	passport	el pasaporte
border	la frontera	petrol/gasoline	la gasolina
corner	la esquina	puncture	el pinchazo
customs	la aduana	south	el sur
departure	la salida	street	la calle

east	*el este, el oriente*	that way	*por allí/por allá*
empty	*vacío*	this way	*por aquí/por acá*
full	*lleno*	tourist card	*la tarjeta de turista*
immigration	*la inmigración*	tyre	*la llanta*
insurance	*el seguro*	tyre repair shop	*vulcanizadora*
the insured	*el asegurado/*	unleaded	*sin plomo*

Accommodation

air conditioning	*el aire acondicionado*	Is service included?	*¿Está incluído el*
all-inclusive	*todo incluido*		*servicio?*
blankets	*las cobijas/las mantas*	Is tax included?	*¿Están incluidos los*
clean/dirty towels	*las toallas*		*impuestos?*
	limpias/sucias	noisy	*ruidoso*
dining room	*el comedor*	pillows	*las almohadas*
double bed	*la cama matrimonial*	restaurant	*el restaurante*
guest house	*la casa de huéspedes*	room	*el cuarto/*
hot/cold water	*el agua caliente/fría*		*la habitación*
hotel	*el hotel*	sheets	*las sábanas*
shower	*la ducha*	toilet paper	*el papel higiénico*
single/double	*sencillo/a/doble*	with private	*con baño privado*
soap	*el jabón*	bathroom	
to make up/clean	*limpiar*	with two beds	*con dos camas*
toilet	*el sanitario/baño*		

Health

aspirin	*la aspirina*	doctor	*el médico*
blood	*la sangre*	fever/sweat	*la fiebre/el sudor*
chemist/pharmacy	*la farmacia/la botica*	(for) pain	*(para) el dolor*
condoms	*los preservativos*	head	*la cabeza*
contact lenses	*los lentes de contacto*	period/towels	*la regla*
contraceptive (pill)	*el anticonceptivo (la*		*las toallas sanitarias*
	píldora anticonceptiva)	pregnant	*embarazada/en cinta*
diarrhoea	*la diarrea*	stomach	*el estómago*

Time

At one o'clock	*a la una*	It's five to nine	*son cinco para las*
At half past two/	*a las dos y media*		*nueve/son las nueve*
two thirty			*menos cinco*
At a quarter to three	*cuarto para las tres*	In ten minutes	*en diez minutos*
	or *a las tres menos*	five hours	*cinco horas*
	quince	Does it take long?	*¿Tarda mucho?/*
It's one o'clock	*es la una*		*¿Demora mucho?*
It's seven o'clock	*son las siete*	We will be back at …	*Regresamos a las …*
It's twenty past six/	*son las seis y veinte*	What time is it?	*¿Qué hora es?*

Days and months

Monday	*lunes*	April	*abril*
Tuesday	*martes*	May	*mayo*

Wednesday	*miércoles*	June	*junio*
Thursday	*jueves*	July	*julio*
Friday	*viernes*	August	*agosto*
Saturday	*sábado*	September	*septiembre*
Sunday	*domingo*	October	*octubre*
January	*enero*	November	*noviembre*
February	*febrero*	December	*diciembre*
March	*marzo*		

Numbers

one	*uno/una*	seven	*siete*
two	*dos*	eight	*ocho*
three	*tres*	nine	*nuevo*
four	*cuatro*	ten	*diez*
five	*cinco*	eleven	*once*
six	*seis*	twelve	*doce*
thirteen	*trece*	thirty	*treinta*
fourteen	*catorce*	forty	*cuarenta*
fifteen	*quince*	fifty	*cincuenta*
sixteen	*dieciseis*	sixty	*sesenta*
seventeen	*diecisiete*	seventy	*setenta*
eighteen	*dieciocho*	eighty	*ochenta*
nineteen	*diecinueve*	ninety	*noventa*
twenty	*veinte*	hundred	*cien or ciento*
twenty one, two	*veintiuno, veintidos etc*	thousand	*mil*

Key verbs

To go	*ir*	*Hay* means 'there is' and is used in	
I go	*voy*	questions such as *¿Hay cuartos?* 'are there	
you go	*vas*	any rooms?'; perhaps more common is	
(familiar singular)		*No hay* meaning 'there isn't any'	
he, she, it goes, you	*va*	To be (in a	*ser*
we go	*vamos*	I am (a teacher)	*soy (profesor)*
they, you (plural) go	*van*	You are	*eres*
To have (possess)	*tener*	He, she, it is, you are	*es*
I have	*tengo*	We are	*somos*
You have	*tienes*	They, you are	*son*
He she, it have, you have	*tiene*	To be (positional or temporary state)	*estar*
We have	*tenemos*	I am (in London)	*estoy (en Londres)*
They, you have	*tienen*	You are	*estás*
(Also used as 'To be', as in 'I am hungry'	*tengo hambre)*	He, she, it is, you are (happy)	*está (contento/a)*
(NB *Haber* also means		We are	*estamos*
'to have', but is used		They, you are	*están*
with other verbs, as in		To do/make	*Hacer*
'he has gone'	*ha ido)*	I do	*hago*
I have gone	*he ido*	You do	*haces*
You have said	*has dicho*	He, she, it does, you do	*hace*
He, she, it has,	*ha hecho*	We do	*hacemos*

you have done		They, you do	hacen
We have eaten	hemos comido		

The above section was compiled on the basis of glossaries by André de Mendonça and David Gilmour of *South American Experience*, London, and the *Latin American Travel Advisor*, No 9, March 1996

Useful Ecuadorean words and phrases

how are you?	¿qué tal? ¿qué fue?	pastry filled with	empanada
what's up?	¿qué más?	meat or cheese	
go ahead	siga no más	corner	esquina
right now (but it	ahorita	bus company	flota
usually means you've		ranch	hacienda/finca
got a long wait		ice cream parlour	heladería
ahead of you)		small bus or minibus	furgoneta/buseta
lodging, basic	alojamiento	office	oficina
accommodation		treeless plains	pampas
high Andean plain	páramo	mixed grill	parrillada
mountain pass	paso/abras	floor	piso
suburb or district	barrio	town or village	pueblo
of city		fruit drink	refresco
cabin	cabaña	small change (and	sueltos
person from the	campesino/	very difficult to find)	
countryside		small shop	tienda
shared taxi	taxi rutas	shop/store	almacén
restaurant specializing	churrasquería	barrier across road at	rompe velocidades
in meat dishes		beginning of village	

Food

avocado	el aguacate	fritters	las frituras
baked	al horno	garlic	el ajo
bakery	la panadería	goat	el chivo
banana chips	los chifles	grapefruit	la toronja
banana (sweet)	el guineo	grill	la parrilla
bean	el fréjol	grilled/griddled	a la plancha
beef	la carne de res	guava	la guayaba
beef steak	el bistec	guinea foul	la guinea
boiled rice	el arroz blanco	ham	el jamón
bread	el pan	hamburger	la hamburguesa
breakfast	el desayuno	hot, spicy	picante
butter	la mantequilla	ice cream	el helado
cassava, yucca	la yuca	jam	la mermelada
casserole	la cazuela	knife	el cuchillo
chewing gum	el chicle	lard	la manteca
chicken	el pollo	lime	el limón
chilli pepper	el ají	lobster	la langosta
clear soup, stock	el caldo	lunch	el almuerzo
conch	la concha	margarine, fat	la margarina
cooked	cocido/cocinado	meal, supper, dinner	la comida/la cena
dining room	el comedor	meat	la carne

egg	el huevo	minced meat	la carne molida
fish	el pescado	mixed salad	la ensalada mixta
fork	el tenedor	onion	la cebolla
fried	frito	orange	la naranja
pepper (green/black)	el pimiento/ la pimienta	small sandwich, filled roll	el bocadito
plantain, green banana	el plátano/el verde	soup	la sopa
		spoon	la cuchara
pasty, turnover	la empanada/ el pastelito	squash	el zapallo/la calabaza/el zambo
pork	el cerdo	squid	los calamares
potato	la papa	supper	la cena/la merienda
prawns/shrimp/	los camarones/	sweet	dulce
king prawns	los langostinos	sweet potato	el camote
raw	crudo	to eat	comer
restaurant	el restaurante/el salón	toasted	tostado (also
roast	el asado		specific for toasted
salad	la ensalada		maize)
salt	la sal		
sandwich	el sánduche	turkey	el pavo
sauce	la salsa	turtle	la tortuga
sausage	la longaniza/el chorizo	vegetables	las legumbres/los vegetales
scrambled eggs	los huevos revueltos	without meat	sin carne
seafood	los mariscos		

Drink

aged rum	el ron añejo	ice	el hielo
beer	la cerveza	juice	el jugo
boiled	hervido	lemonade	la limonada
bottled	en botella	milk	la leche
camomile tea	la manzanilla	mint	la menta
canned	en lata	orange juice	el jugo de naranja
cocktail	el coctel	pineapple milkshake	el batido de piña con leche
coconut milk	la leche de coco	rough rum, firewater	el aguardiente/
coffee	el café		el trago
coffee, strong	café bien cargado	rum	el ron
coffee, white	el café con leche/ café en leche	fruitdrink	el refresco
		soft fizzy drink	lacola
cold	frío/a	sugar	el azúcar
condensed milk	la leche condensada	sugar cane juice	el guarapo
cup	la taza	tea	el té
drink	la bebida	thick drink	colada
drunk	borracho	to drink	beber/tomar
fruit milk shake	el batido	water	el agua
fruit punch (non-alcoholic)	el ponche de frutas	water, carbonated	el agua mineral con gas
glass	el vaso	water, still mineral	el agua mineral natural/sin gas
glass of liqueur	la copa de licor		
herbal tea	agua aromática/ agüita	wine, red	el vino tinto
		wine, white	el vino blanco
hot	caliente		

Index

Map index

Advertisers' index

Credits

Footprint credits
Text editor: Tim Jollands
Map editor: Sarah Sorensen

Publishers: James Dawson and
Patrick Dawson
Editorial Director: Rachel Fielding
Editorial: Stephanie Lambe,
Sarah Thorowgood, Claire Boobbyer,
Felicity Laughton, Caroline Lascom,
Alan Murphy
Production: Jo Morgan, Mark Thomas,
Emma Bryers, Davina Rungasamy
Cartography: Claire Benison,
Kevin Feeney, Robert Lunn
Design: Mytton Williams
Marketing and publicity:
Rosemary Dawson, La-Ree Miners
Sales: Ed Aves
Advertising: Debbie Wylde,
Lorraine Horler
Finance and administration:
Sharon Hughes, Elizabeth Taylor,
Leona Bailey
Distribution: Pam Cobb, Mike Noel

Photography credits
Front cover: Imagestate/Alamy: woven
tapestries at El Ejido market, Quito
Back cover: Nature Picture Library
Inside colour section: Howard
Folsom/Alamy, Art Directors and TRIP,
Robert Harding Picture Library,
Harryhaussen/Alamy, David Horwell,
Impact Photo Library, Robert Kunstaetter,
Jamie Marshall, Edward Paine, José Luis
Rodriguez, South American Pictures,
Alois Speck.

Print
Manufactured in Italy by LegoPrint

Publishing information
Footprint Ecuador & Galápagos Handbook
4th edition
© Footprint Handbooks Ltd
February 2003

ISBN 1 903471 52 4
CIP DATA: A catalogue record for this
book is available from the British Library

® Footprint Handbooks and the Footprint
mark are a registered trademark of
Footprint Handbooks Ltd

Published by Footprint Handbooks
6 Riverside Court
Lower Bristol Road
Bath BA2 3DZ, UK
T +44 (0)1225 469141
F +44 (0)1225 469461
E discover@footprintbooks.com
W www.footprintbooks.com

Distributed in the USA by
Publishers Group West

Every effort has been made to ensure that
the facts in the Handbook are accurate.
However, travellers should still obtain
advice from consulates, airlines etc about
travel and visa requirements before
travelling. The authors and publishers
cannot accept responsibility for
any loss, injury or inconvenience
however caused.

Acknowledgements

The authors offer their warmest thanks to the following contributors:
Guido and **Jeaneth Abad** (Cuenca) are language teachers who run the *Sí Centro de Español* in Cuenca, as well as the *Goura* restaurant. **Jean Brown** (Quito, the Quilotoa circuit, Galápagos, and Esmeraldas), originally from England, is a founding member of *South American Explorers* in Quito, a partner in *Safari Tours* and a long-standing contributor to the *South American Handbook*. **Lou Jost** (bird watching, nature lodges, flora and fauna) hails from Milwaukee, USA, and now lives in Baños. A former naturalist guide and a specialist on miniature orchids, he is illustrator of *Common Birds of Amazonian Ecuador*. **Xavier and Beatrice Malo** (route from Cuenca to Machala and Huaquillas) own *Montaruna Tours* in Cuenca, specializing in horse-riding tours. **Grace Naranjo** (Quito) is a Quiteña who also provided much useful general assistance. **Michael Resch** (Baños, Ambato and Coca), an Austrian, lives near Baños where he translates texts, tends his garden, and watches eruptions of Tungurahua. **William Reyes** and **Popkje van der Ploeg** (Riobamba, Puyo, Misahuallí and Tena) own and operate the *Julio Verne* tour agency in Riobamba. **Delia María Torres** (Guayaquil and surroundings) is a native Guayaquileña who works for the historical archives of the Central Bank.
The authors would like to acknowledge the auspices of the **Ministerio de Turismo** of the government of Ecuador, as well as that of the **Centro Internacional de Estudios de los Espacios y Sociedades Andinas** and its president, **Dr Nelson Gómez**. We would also like to thank the following, all of whom provided valuable assistance: **Susana** and **Fenando Bermeo**, **Carolyn (Caz) Bointon**, the late **Yossi Brain**, **David Brown**, **Santiago Cabascango**, **Pablo Carvajal**, **Enrique Castro**, **Rosa Dalia Cevallos**, **Marco Cruz**, **Franco DeAntoni**, **Denis** (in Montañita), **Capitán Alberto and Yolanda Dillon**, **Douglas and Roxana Dillon**, **Miguel and Evelyn Falk**, **Fernando Félix**, **David Gómez**, **Pablo Gómez**, **Graciela Guadamud**, **Kevin and Dianne Gulash**, **Minard (Pete) Hall**, **Ben Haase**, **Soledad Kingman**, **Craig Kolthoff**, **Joanna May**, **Patricia Mothes**, **Marcelo Muñoz**, **Nory Carbo de Navas**, **Jack Nelson**, **Francisca Oleas**, **Victor Román**, **Sacha** (from Switzerland), **Steve Nomchong**, **Iván Suárez**, **Delia Tello**, **Mark Thurber**, and **Mayra Vera**.
This fourth edition of the *Ecuador & Galápagos Handbook* is built on the first and second editions, written by **Alan Murphy**, as well as on many previous editions of the South American Handbook, by **John Brooks** and **Ben Box**.
Thanks to the specialist contributors. **Dr Charlie Easmon** wrote the health section. His aid and development work has included: Raleigh International (Medical Officer in Botswana), MERLIN (in Rwanda his team set up a refugee camp for 12,000 people), Save the Children (as a consultant in Rwanda), ECHO (The European Community Humanitarian Office review of Red Cross work in Armenia, Georgia and Azerbaijan), board member of International Care and Relief and previously International Health Exchange. In addition to his time as a hospital physician, he has worked as a medical adviser to the Foreign and Commonwealth Office and as a locum consultant at the hospital for tropical diseases travel clinic, as well as being a specialist registrar in Public Health. He now also runs *Travel Screening* services (www.travelscreening.co.uk) based at 1 Harley Street. The Arts and Craft section was used courtesy of **Lucy Davies** and **Mo Fini** of *Tumi*. Another source of information for this section was *The Panama Hat* by Tom Miller. **Ben Box** wrote the Ecuadorean literature section. Also a big thank you to the entire Footprint editorial and production team, and in particular Tim Jollands. Finally our special thanks go to those 200-plus readers, too numerous to mention by name, who contributed their experiences and insights to the current edition and who make this book a living, evolving thing.

Keep in touch

Footprint feedback

We try as hard as we can to make each Footprint Handbook as up-to-date and accurate as possible but, of course, things always change. Many people write to us - with corrections, new information, or simply comments.

If you want to let us know about an experience or adventure - hair-raising or mundane, good or bad, exciting or boring or simply something rather special - we would be delighted to hear from you. Please give us as precise information as possible, quoting the edition number (you'll find it on the front cover) and page number of the Handbook you are using.

Your help will be greatly appreciated, especially by other travellers. In return we will send you details about our special guidebook offer. Email Footprint at:
ecu4_online@footprintbooks.com

or write to:
Elizabeth Taylor
Footprint Handbooks
6 Riverside Court, Lower Bristol Road
Bath BA2 3DZ UK

www.footprintbooks.com

Dip in and keep on the pulse with what Footprint are up to online.

- Latest Footprint releases
- Entertaining travel articles and news updates
- Extensive destination information for inspiration and trip planning
- Monthly competitions
- Easy ways to buy Footprint guides

Footnotes

Administration
- International border
- State border
- □ Capital city
- ○ Other city/town

Roads and travel
- —— Main road (National Highway)
- —— Other road
- ---- 4WD road, track
- ...... Footpath
- Railway with station

Water features
- River
- Lake
- Seasonal marshland
- Beach, dry river bed
- Ocean
- Waterfall
- Ferry

Cities and towns
- Sight
- Sleeping
- Eating
- Building
- Main street
- Minor street
- Pedestrianized street
- Tunnel
- → One way street
- Bridge

- Park, garden, stadium
- Steps
- Airport
- Trole stop
- Bank
- Bus station
- Hospital
- Market
- Museum
- Police
- Post office
- Tourist office
- Cathedral, church
- Petrol
- @ Internet
- Telephone office
- A Detail map
- A Related map

Topographical features
- Contours (approx), rock outcrop
- Mountain
- Volcano
- Mountain pass
- Escarpment
- Gorge

Other symbols
- Archaeological site
- National park/wildlife reserve
- Viewing point
- Campsite
- Dive site

photographies: P. Vallejo, MOT archives

Ecuador
¡Vívelo ahora!

Ministerio de Turismo
Ecuador

www.vivecuador.com

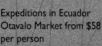

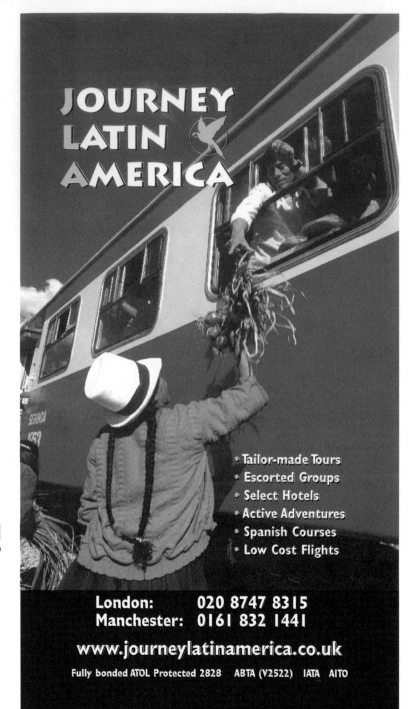
Footnotes

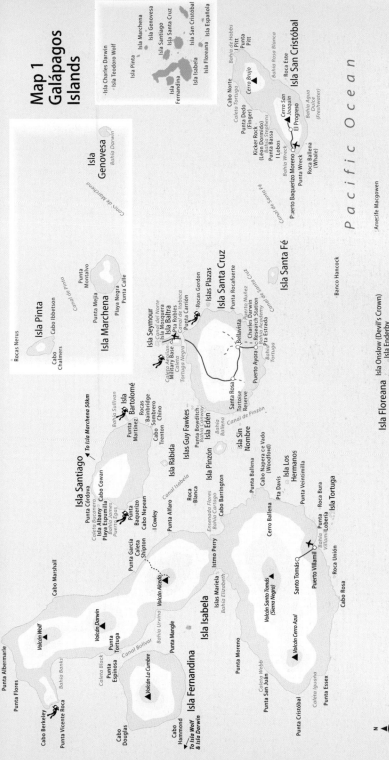

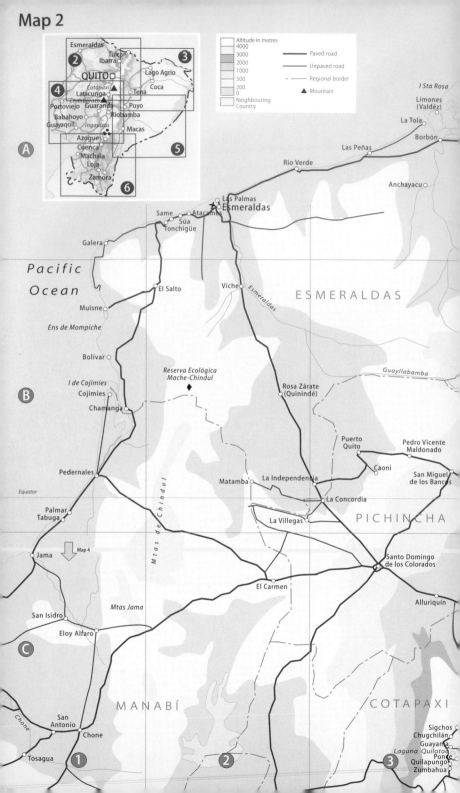

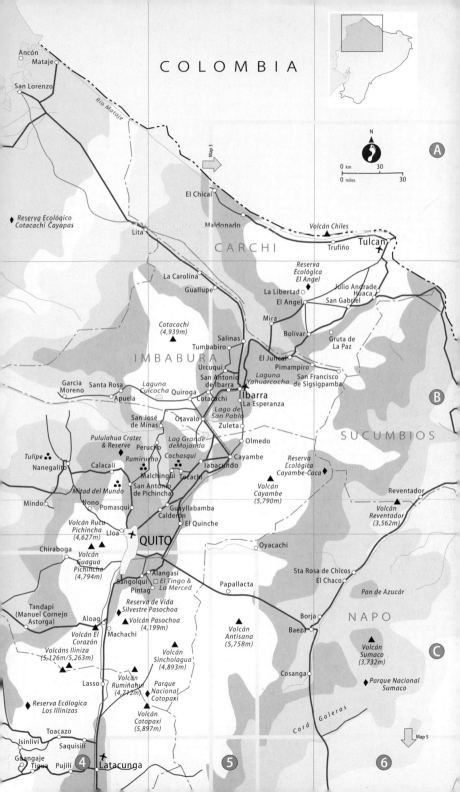

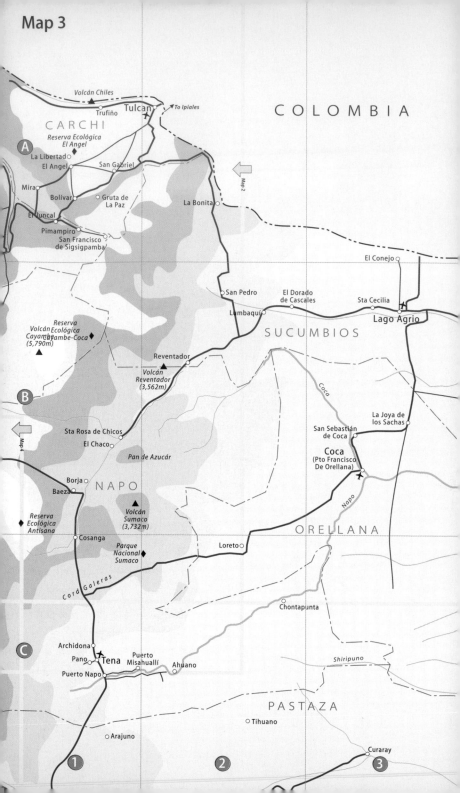

Map 3

COLOMBIA

Volcán Chiles

Trufiño

Tulcán

To Ipiales

CARCHI

Reserva Ecológica
El Angel

A

La Libertad

El Angel

San Gabriel

Mira

Bolívar

Gruta de
La Paz

El Juncal

La Bonita

Map 2

Pimampiro

San Francisco
de Sigsigpamba

El Conejo

San Pedro

El Dorado
de Cascales

Sta Cecilia

Lumbaquí

Lago Agrio

Reserva
Ecológica
Cayambe-Coca

Volcán
Cayambe
(5,790m)

SUCUMBIOS

Reventador

Volcán
Reventador
(3,562m)

Coca

B

La Joya de
los Sachas

San Sebastián
de Coca

Map 4

Sta Rosa de Chicos

El Chaco

Pan de Azúcar

Coca
(Pto Francisco
De Orellana)

Borja

Baeza

NAPO

Reserva
Ecológica
Antisana

Volcán
Sumaco
(3,732m)

Napo

Cosanga

ORELLANA

Parque
Nacional
Sumaco

Loreto

Cord Galeras

Chontapunta

C

Archidona

Pano

Tena

Puerto
Misahuallí

Ahuano

Shiripuno

Puerto Napo

PASTAZA

Arajuno

Tihuano

Curaray

1

2

3

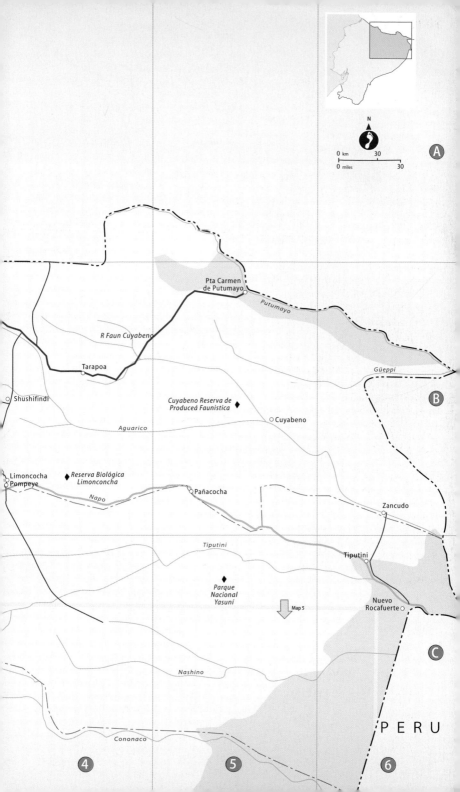

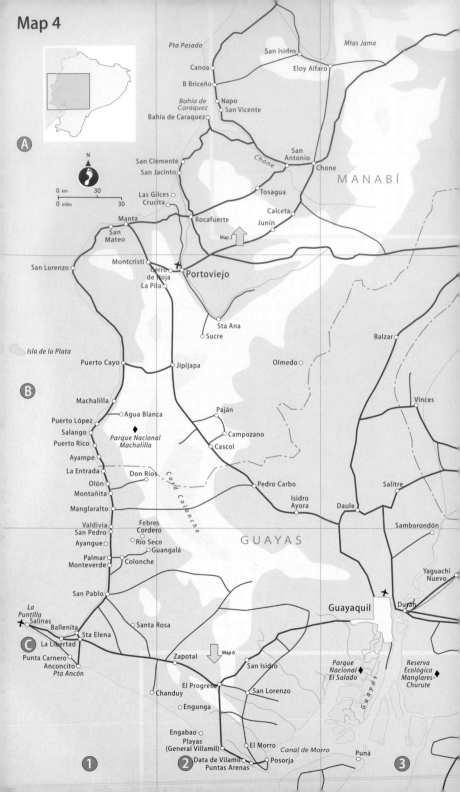

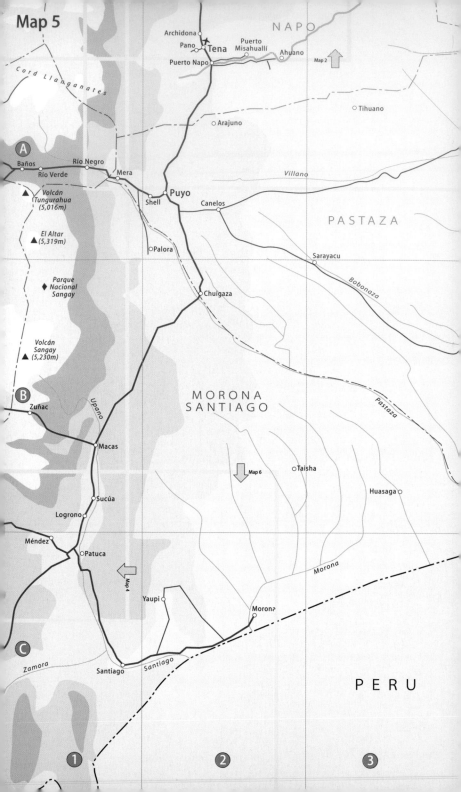

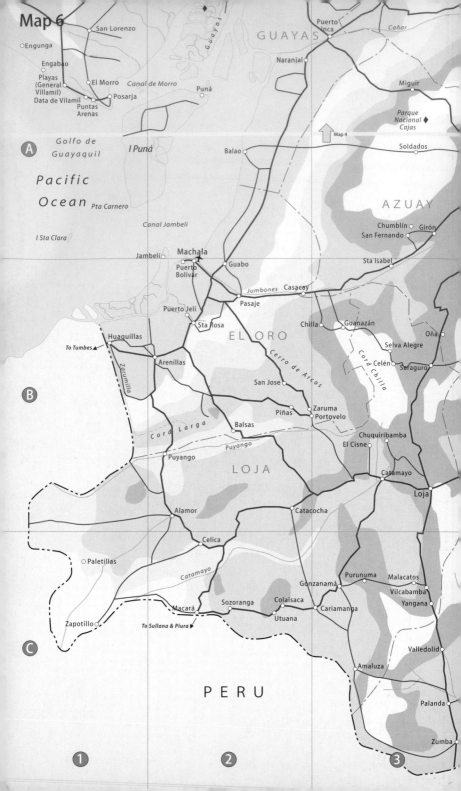

For a different view of Europe, take a Footprint